RESEARCH GUIDE TO AMERICAN HISTORICAL BIOGRAPHY

Volume V
Appendices I, II

Cumulative Contents
Volumes I-V
Cumulative Index
Volumes I-V

Beacham Publishing

RESEARCH GUIDE TO AMERICAN HISTORICAL BIOGRAPHY

Editors
Walton Beacham
Katharine D. McLucas
Charles J. Moseley

Editorial Assistant
Stephanie A. Fox

Library of Congress
Cataloging-in-Publication Data

Research Guide to American Historical Biography: Volume 5 / edited by
Walton Beacham, et al.—Washington, D.C.: Beacham Publishing, Inc.

Bibliography
Cumulative index

1. United States—Biography—Handbooks, manuals, etc. 2. United
States—Bio-bibliography. I. Beacham, Walton, 1943.

CT214.R47   1991   920'.073—dc19   88-19316

Description and evaluation of the most important secondary and primary
sources for 452 American historical figures in all five volumes.

Library of Congress Card Number: 88-19316
ISBN: 0-933833-24-5
Printed in the United States of America
First printing, September 1991

PREFACE

Volume V of the *Research Guide to American Historical Biography* contains bibliographical and other reference aids that allow the reader to explore more fully the lives of eighty-one prominent men and women who have helped to shape the contours of United States history. This volume of the *Research Guide* continues to add women, Native Americans, and minorities, which was the focus of Volume IV, plus explorers, artists and entertainers, colonial, Civil War and frontier figures, religious leaders and theologians. We have also included George III, Louis XVI, and Amerigo Vespucci. Although they were never on American soil, their stories offer an important perspective to the discovery and founding of America.

The *Research Guide* is designed to facilitate the research process for college and secondary school term papers, to assist graduate students and professors in areas outside their fields of expertise, and to provide librarians with an acquisitions tool, information to expedite interlibrary loans, and a ready reference. Our contributors, most of whom are affiliated with universities or special collections, have sifted through the available sources to direct the reader to those that are most useful.

Each entry is divided into several sections for quick reference: the *Chronology* provides a synopsis of major events in the subject's life; *Activities of Historical Significance* interprets the subject's accomplishments and places them in context; *Overview of Biographical Sources* notes any difficulties that the subject's biographers have encountered and comments on changes in scholarly opinion that have occurred over the years; *Evaluation of Principal Biographical Sources* is an annotated bibliography that evaluates the most important secondary sources for content, readability, and accuracy; *Evaluation of Biographies for Young People,* which appears in articles whose subjects have inspired at least three works in this genre, is a separate listing of biographies written for a young audience; *Overview and Evaluation of Primary Sources* cites autobiographical works by the subject, memoirs by the subject's family and acquaintances, pertinent government documents, and manuscript collections that contain an abundance of unpublished material; *Fiction and Adaptations* describes novels, films, plays, or other creative interpretations of the subject's activities; *Museums, Historical Landmarks, Societies* provides the name, location, and a brief description of relevant organizations or points of interest; and *Other Sources* is a bibliography of journal and encyclopedia articles, monographs, and works on the subject's era that put his or her role in historical context. The works that are cited in *Evaluation of Principal Biographical Sources* and in *Overview and Evaluation of Primary Sources* have A, G, or Y designations appended to the bibliographical information to indicate whether the work is most appropriate for an academic, general, or young audience.

As a further aid to students not well versed in all areas of American history, we have designed an appendix that groups the contents by the era in which each subject made his or her greatest contributions. Also included is an appendix that groups by state the most popular sites described in the *Museums, Historical Landmarks, Societies* section of the articles. If the figure to whom the site pertains is not self-evident, his or her name follows in parentheses.

Because this reference work is a basic research tool, the contents are largely a reflection of the availability of biographical and primary sources that are appropriate for our intended audience rather than a reflection of an editorial judgment about a given individual's historical significance. We have endeavored to include every woman or minority figure who is the subject of at least two book-length biographical or autobiographical works. Numerous important individuals have been excluded simply because of the paucity of published sources. Literary figures are generally excluded because they are covered in Beacham Publishing's *Research Guide to Biography and Criticism,* though a few writers are covered here because of their social contributions over and above their literary achievement.

Because of the critical and popular success of the research guide format in the *Research Guide to Biography and Criticism* (*Choice* magazine's "Outstanding Reference" 1985) and the *Research Guide to American Historical Biography* (*Choice* magazine's "Outstanding Reference" 1990), we are continuing the concept with the *Research Guide to European Historical Biography,* which covers about four hundred Europeans from all countries and across all areas of historical significance from 1400 to the present.

The *Research Guide to American Historical Biography* owes its existence to the labor of many individuals who have given generously of their time and talent, especially Robert Muccigrosso, the editor of the original three volumes of the *Research Guide.* Although Professor Muccigrosso was not involved in the publication of volumes 4 and 5, the supplements incorporate the format and the editorial standards that he helped to establish. The entire series is also indebted to Suzanne Niemeyer, whose high editorial standards are stamped like watermarks throughout the series.

Beacham Publishing is continually interested in producing books devoted to improving the research capabilities of students, and welcomes any suggestions for revising this title or ideas for other types of books. Write to: Beacham Publishing, Inc., 2100 "S" Street, NW, Washington, D.C. 20008.

Walton Beacham

CONTRIBUTORS

Steven Agoratus

Jim Baird
University of North Texas

Douglas Clark Baxter
Ohio University

Kirk H. Beetz
National University
Sacramento

Jean V. Berlin
Correspondence of
William T. Sherman
Arizona State University

John Braeman
University of Nebraska
Lincoln

Alan S. Brown
Western Michigan University

Paolo E. Coletta
U.S. Naval Academy (Ret.)

Frank Day
Clemson University

Justus D. Doenecke
New College of the
University of South Florida

William Ryland Drennan

University of Wisconsin
Baraboo/Sauk Campus

Margaret L. Dwight
University of North Carolina
Charlotte

Clara Estow
University of Massachusetts
Boston

Laura Gabel Hartman
Virginia Commonwealth University

Donald E. Heidenreich, Jr.
Kemper College

John T. Hiers
Valdosta State College

Diane Long Hoeveler
Marquette University

J. David Hoeveler, Jr.
University of Wisconsin
Milwaukee

Gerald Horne
University of California
Santa Barbara

Evelyn E. Hunt
Cleveland State University

Veda Jones

Robert S. La Forte
University of North Texas

Roger D. Launius
National Aeronautics and
Space Administration

William M. Leary
University of Georgia

Joseph M. McCarthy
Suffolk University

Pellegrino Nazzaro
Rochester Institute of Technology

Beverly Wilson Palmer
Pomona College

Keith Ian Polakoff
California State University
Long Beach

Clifton W. Potter, Jr.
Lynchburg College

Dorothy Potter
Lynchburg College

Howard L. Preston

Donald J. Richards
Manhattanville College

Kathleen Rout

Daniel Dean Roland

Edward L. Schapsmeier
Illinois State University

Frederick H. Schapsmeier
University of Wisconsin

Jack Shreve
Allegany Community College

Brooks Donohue Simpson
Arizona State University

Gretchen R. Sutherland
Cornell College

Welford Dunaway Taylor
University of Richmond

William T. Walker
Philadelphia College of
Pharmacy and Science

Peter Wallenstein
Virginia Polytechnic Institute
and State University

R. William Weisberger
Butler County Community College

Carol Wilson
Washington College

Charles E. Wynes
University of Georgia

VOLUME V CONTENTS

CUMULATIVE CONTENTS
VOLUMES I-V

RESEARCH GUIDE
TO AMERICAN
HISTORICAL BIOGRAPHY

LOUISA MAY ALCOTT
1832-1888

Chronology

Born Louisa May Alcott on November 29, 1832, in Germantown, Pennsylvania, to Amos Bronson Alcott and Abigail May Alcott; *1834* family returns to Boston; *1843* family joins a communal farm, Fruitlands, in Harvard, Massachusetts, with Charles Lane and Henry Wright; *1844* Fruitlands experiment fails; *1848* writes her first story, "The Rival Painters: A Tale of Rome"; *1851* goes into service to a family in Dedham, Massachusetts, but returns home after seven weeks; *1852* publishes "The Rival Painters" in the *Olive Branch*; *1853-1856* moves around New England, teaching school and publishing short stories and poems; *1857* the Alcotts move to Concord, Massachusetts; *1858* sister Elizabeth Sewall Alcott dies in March and the family moves into their new home, Orchard House, in July; *1859-1860* writes various books and sketches while accepting a variety of teaching and tutoring positions; *1862* wins a hundred-dollar prize from *Frank Leslie's Illustrated Newspaper* for the pseudonymous thriller, "Pauline's Passion and Punishment"; accepted as a nurse for the Union army at the Union Hotel Hospital in Georgetown, D.C.; *1863* falls ill with typhoid fever at the hospital and returns to Concord; writes about her experiences in *Hospital Sketches*, which are serialized that same year; *1864* publishes *Moods*, her first novel; *1865* publishes another thriller under the name A. M. Barnard; travels to Europe as the companion of Anna Weld; *1868 Little Women* (Part I) is published to great acclaim; *1869 Little Women* (Part II) duplicates the success of its predecessor; publishes *Hospital Sketches* and *Camp and Fireside Stories*; *1870* publishes *An Old Fashioned Girl*; returns to Europe; *1871* publishes *Little Men*; *1875* publishes *Eight Cousins;* moves to New York; *1876* publishes *Rose in Bloom*; *1877* returns to Concord to live with her widowed sister Anna in the Thoreau House; mother dies shortly thereafter; *1878* publishes *Under the Lilacs*; *1879* sister Abby May Alcott Nieriker dies in Paris after giving birth to a daughter, Louisa May; *1880* publishes *Jack and Jill; 1884* sells Orchard House and buys a cottage in Nonquitt, Massachusetts; *1887* publishes *Jo's Boys* after recovering from exhaustion; *1888* dies on March 6 and is buried in the Sleepy Hollow Cemetery in Concord, Massachusetts.

Activities of Historical Significance

Louisa May Alcott is one of America's best-known and best-loved authors. Her books for children, beginning with *Little Women*, were best sellers that differed from their contemporaries in their superior prose, more vivid characterization, and more realistic plots. Alcott's children's books reflect the challenges and difficulties facing children, especially girls, in mid-nineteenth-century America. Her works also served to disseminate her transcendentalist ideas about women, equality, society, and nature to a popular audience that seldom read philosophical tracts. Perhaps the greatest measure of her success is the continuing popularity of her feminist heroine, Jo March, in the 1990s.

Much of the story of Alcott's earlier years can be read in *Little Women*. She grew up in genteel but grinding poverty with a father who seemed to care more for ideas and abstractions than the concrete problems of his family. Following her rise to fame and fortune, she never forgot her family; she cared for her parents in their old age and provided generously for her sisters, nieces, and nephews.

In recent years feminist historians have begun to examine Alcott's life and works. They have interpreted the sympathetic character of Jo in *Little Women* as the forerunner of the modern woman who is trying to reconcile the conflicting demands of a career and a home. Jo eventually gets what she wants, but only after struggle and sacrifice. Alcott is clear, however, that Jo would be happier single and with her career than married to the wrong man. Alcott was one of the first Americans to tell women that domesticity was not everything, that a woman can reconcile the desires for both a career and a home. It is probably this message that accounts for the popularity of her works today.

Overview of Biographical Sources

There is not yet a first-rate scholarly reassessment of Alcott's life and work that makes use of the tremendous volume of recent research on nineteenth-century women. The most satisfying biography is Martha Saxton's *Louisa May: A Modern Biography of Louisa May Alcott* (1977). Other biographies tend to be semi-fictional accounts or written for juveniles. However, one biography for young people, *Invincible Louisa* (1933) by Cornelia Meigs, is excellent. Anyone who seeks to know Alcott and understand her work should rely on *Little Women*, *Hospital Sketches*, and her other writings.

Evaluation of Principal Biographical Sources

Anthony, Katharine Susan. *Louisa May Alcott*. New York: Knopf, 1938. (G) One of the many semi-fictional biographies.

Cheney, Ednah Dow. *Louisa May Alcott*. 1889. Reprint. Boston: Little, Brown, 1928. (A, G) This memoir and compilation of letters by one of Alcott's friends is still an invaluable aid, especially for the texts of manuscripts that have since disappeared.

Meigs, Cornelia. *Invincible Louisa.* Boston: Little, Brown, 1933. (**Y**) This Newbery Award-winning children's biography is an excellent introduction for young people and by far the best of the many juvenile biographies.

Saxton, Martha. *Louisa May: A Modern Biography of Louisa May Alcott.* Boston: Houghton Mifflin, 1977. (**A, G**) This scholarly and readable biography is the best one available.

Stern, Madeline. *Louisa May Alcott.* Norman: University of Oklahoma Press, 1950. (**G**) The first of the serious works on Alcott, Stern's book remains a standard in spite of its dramatic overwriting.

Worthington, Marjorie. *Miss Alcott of Concord: A Biography.* Garden City, NY: Doubleday, 1958. (**G**) Another over-written, semi-fictional account.

Overview and Evaluation of Primary Sources

While Alcott wrote a great many letters, very few of them survive. The editors of a recent compilation of her correspondence found only 649 of her letters in manuscript. A complete list of those items and their locations was published in "A Calendar of the Letters of Louisa May Alcott," *Studies in the American Renaissance 1988* (Charlottesville: University Press of Virginia, 1989; A). The editors chose to print approximately 350 of the most significant and interesting in Joel Myerson, et al., eds., *The Selected Letters of Louisa May Alcott* (Boston: Little, Brown, 1987; **A, G**). The largest collection of manuscripts can be found in the Alcott-Whitman Papers in the Houghton Library at Harvard University. Most of her journals were lost after Ednah Dow Cheney printed portions of them in 1889. The remaining journals are scattered throughout the country. Joel Myerson and his associates have also edited *The Journals of Louisa May Alcott* (Boston: Little, Brown, 1989; **A, G**), which reprints virtually all extant journals. It is an invaluable resource for those interested in Alcott.

All of Alcott's works are still widely available in libraries and bookstores. Her children's books, especially *Little Women* and *Little Men*, are perennial best sellers in spite of their dated tone. Alcott had a knack for creating lively young men and women who engage the attention and affection of the reader. She used her books and characters to try to show Americans that there was an alternative, healthier, way to raise children. *Little Women* showed that women could have careers as well as homes, and *Eight Cousins* took a stand against the unhealthy fashions worn by women in the late nineteenth century and the standards they represented.

Her book *Hospital Sketches* about her experience as a nurse during the Civil War is a touching and thoughtful meditation on the meaning of a war to the soldiers and their loved ones. She vividly describes the horrific conditions in the hospital, and her emotional and physical weariness comes through on every page.

Alcott's adult fiction is disappointing. She loses the natural quality of her prose when she reaches for the adult reader. Of more interest to scholars and readers are her collections of anonymous or pseudonymous thrillers, identified by the manuscript dealers Leona Rostenberg and Madeleine Stern. The stories were collected and published under the titles *Behind a Mask: The Unknown Thrillers of Louisa May Alcott* (New York: William Morrow, 1975; **A, G**), *Plots and Counterplots: More Unknown Thrillers of Louisa May Alcott* (New York: William Morrow, 1976; **A, G**), and *A Double Life: Newly Discovered Thrillers of Louisa May Alcott* (Boston: Little, Brown, 1988; **A, G**). Generally, the stories seek to understand and redeem fallen women, and Madeleine Stern's lengthy introductions are useful in understanding their significance.

Almost all of Alcott's work, especially her juvenile books, are available in multiple editions. Literary scholars have yet to turn their attention to her works.

Museums, Historical Landmarks, Societies

Fruitlands (Cambridge, MA). The site of the short-lived utopian community where Alcott lived as a child. The property is a privately-run museum.

Louisa May Alcott House (Concord, MA). This nineteenth-century, two-and-one-half story frame house where Alcott began *Little Women* is privately-run and open to the public.

Thoreau-Alcott House (Concord, MA). This two-story Greek Revival house was Thoreau's home for many years and was purchased by Alcott and her sister Anna in 1877 for their parents. The house remains in private hands and is not open to the public.

Other Sources

Elbert, Sarah. *A Hunger for Home: Louisa May Alcott and Little Women.* Philadelphia: Temple University Press, 1984. This slim study is perhaps the finest work available on the enduring appeal of Alcott and her classic novel. Elbert argues that Alcott defined the problems women face when they try to have both a career and a home long before most women realized that they could have both. She maintains that Alcott's own answers, presented in the relationship between Jo and her professor, still provide an example for many young women.

Gulliver, Lucile. *Louisa May Alcott: A Bibliography.* New York: Benjamin Franklin, 1973. Although dated, this bibliography is still useful.

MacDonald, Ruth K. *Louisa May Alcott.* Boston: Twayne, 1983. This critical study is a good introduction to Alcott.

Showalter, Elaine. *Alternative Alcott.* New Brunswick, NJ: Rutgers University Press, 1988. A good collection of Alcott's work which reflects the meaning which feminist scholars find in it.

Jean V. Berlin
Correspondence of William T. Sherman
Arizona State University

NANCY LANGHORNE ASTOR
1879-1964

Chronology

Born Nancy Witcher Langhorne on May 19, 1879, in Danville, Virginia, the eighth of eleven children of Nancy Witcher Keene and Chiswell "Chillie" Dabney Langhorne, former soldier in the Confederate army, salesman, auctioneer, and gentleman farmer; *1885* moves with family to Richmond, Virginia, where Chillie (pronounced Shillie) after several setbacks makes a fortune in tobacco and railroads; *1892* moves to Mirador, a country estate in Albemarle County; attends various schools in Richmond, but is primarily self-educated, with an emphasis on hunting, horsemanship, and the relaxed social life of the Virginia gentry; *1896* is sent to finishing school in New York City, where she is homesick and miserable; *1897* marries Robert Gould Shaw II of Boston; marriage is not a happy one, due to Shaw's alcoholism, and a series of separations follow; *1903* divorces Shaw for adultery and visits Europe with her mother and a friend; mother dies that summer; *1905* meets Waldorf Astor while on a return trip to England with her father; *1906* marries Waldorf Astor; the couple is given the great English country house Cliveden as a wedding present by William Waldorf Astor; *1909* Waldorf buys a house in Plymouth, runs for a seat in Parliament, and is elected Conservative member in December 1910; Nancy becomes a fashionable political hostess and with Waldorf becomes involved in the imperialist and nationalist group "Milner's Kindergarten" (named for mentor Lord Milner), whose aims are the preservation of the British Empire and the unity of English-speaking peoples; *1914* after a serious illness, accepts Christian Science and thereafter attempts to convert others to her views; *1914-1918* becomes heavily involved in hospital work in Plymouth and at Cliveden, which is converted into a military hospital for Canadian troops during World War I; *1919* Chillie Langhorne dies in February; William Waldorf Astor, now Viscount Astor, dies in October, obliging Waldorf to leave the House of Commons for the House of Lords; runs to fill his seat in the House of Commons and is elected over two male candidates with a majority of about five thousand votes, becoming the first elected woman to sit in Parliament (women were first able to vote in Great Britain in 1918; a female Sinn Fein candidate was elected to the House of Commons but declined to sit because, as an Irish nationalist, she would not pledge loyalty to the Crown); represents Plymouth for twenty-five years; *1931* the Astors, along with George Bernard Shaw and others, visit the Soviet Union and meet Stalin, later creating unfavorable publicity for both Nancy and Shaw;

1937-1939 accused by certain circles of the British press of forming an elite group, the so-called "Cliveden Set," to support pro-Nazi efforts in Great Britain; *1939-1944* Waldorf serves as lord mayor of Plymouth; the Astors spend much of their time in the city, despite parliamentary duties and German air raids in 1941; *1944* reluctantly does not attempt re-election, after being advised by her family of her increasing unpopularity; Waldorf becomes ill and does not seek re-election as lord mayor; *1946* visits America and offends a number of people by tactless remarks about Anglo-American relations; drifts apart from Waldorf, but they become closer as his health declines; *1951* attempts to write an autobiography but eventually abandons it; *1952* Waldorf dies; *1959* appointed a Freeman of Plymouth over the objections of some Labour party members; *1960-1964* health and memory increasingly diminish; dies of complications following a stroke on May 2 at Grimsthorpe, Lincolnshire (home of her daughter and son-in-law Wissie and James Ancaster) and is buried at Cliveden.

Activities of Historical Significance

Born only fourteen years after the end of the Civil War, Nancy Astor was unconventional, independent, and something of a proto-feminist. Growing up in an era when women's roles were both decorative and circumscribed, she did not hesitate to use boldness and determination to achieve success both in her political campaigns and in Parliament. An American who was proud of her origins, she was also the first woman to sit in the British House of Commons.

Two strong threads in the fabric of Astor's life were her religious feelings and an instinctive concern for the poor and dispossessed. As a young girl growing up at Mirador in the 1890s, she was strongly influenced by Frederick Neve, an archdeacon in the Episcopal church and a missionary to the poor farmers living in the Blue Ridge Mountains of Virginia. So attracted was Astor to his work that she briefly thought of pursuing that career herself, an idea that would not have found favor with her father had she decided to pursue it. That religion was very important to her is evident from the enthusiasm with which she embraced and maintained the Christian Science faith. During her parliamentary career she supported and often took the lead in legislation or debates related to slum clearances, unemployment, the increasing of widows' pensions, nursery school improvements, equal pay for women in the civil service, and suppression of prostitution.

Despite her concern for the less fortunate, Astor's love of humanity had its defined limits. Partially due to her unfortunate first marriage, she had no patience with drunkenness and was concerned about the effects of alcohol on those least able to deal with it. Her maiden speech in the House of Commons on February 24,

1920, was on controlling the sale of alcohol by putting the liquor industry under the management of a state-run board. Her most successful piece of legislation was enacted in 1923 when she was able to put through a bill that limited the sale of alcohol to minors. This stand, supported by her husband, took political as well as moral courage. The social strata in which the Astors moved were not teetotallers, nor was the British electorate at large in favor of limiting what was considered to be one of the few pleasures of the working people. In drawing attention to this issue, Astor was ahead of the sentiments of her time.

Astor was not tactful and was sometimes cruelly frank or even rude. Frequently she spoke without thinking, and she was aware of this flaw but could not or would not develop the circumspection essential to a professional politician. This habit of speaking her mind, inherited from her flamboyant father, made her "good copy" for the press, but often led to unfortunate misunderstandings. Her verbal exchanges with Winston Churchill, who did not approve of a woman in the House of Commons, became famous; on some occasions they even appeared to enjoy the interplay. As World War II approached and Churchill became increasingly critical of Neville Chamberlain, the elements of frivolity disappeared, for the Astors were friends of Chamberlain and loyalty rated high on Astor's list of virtues.

Despite her public image, it is still difficult to define Astor's historical significance. A wealthy world of social exclusiveness became hers after she married Waldorf. She presided over a glittering circle of politicians, intellectuals, and literary lights. George Bernard Shaw, Hilaire Belloc, the Asquiths, Alice Roosevelt Longworth, Ramsay MacDonald, and T. E. Lawrence were among her many friends.

But in contrast to the image of the brilliant court, there is also a dark side—the so-called "Cliveden set," whose membership and sinister purposes are still disputed. Although they may have been little more than a naive and rather foolish group who thought that certain provisions of the Versailles treaty (1919) were excessive and that Hitler was not beyond reason, they managed to provoke the press. The image of a pro-Nazi shadow government did Astor much harm and would ultimately force her abrupt and reluctant retreat from public life in 1944. The Astors were no more Nazis than they were converts to Communism after visiting Russia in 1931, but with the onset of World War II they became convenient scapegoats. Yet in underestimating and even tolerating such dictatorships as Stalin's or Hitler's, she was misled or naive. On a personal basis, however, Astor could charm almost anyone with her ready wit, and most of the people who knew her well remained devoted to her.

Her accomplishments remain elusive. Much of her interest lies in the fact that she was a beautiful and successful political hostess, in correspondence with such diverse persons as Margot Asquith and Bernard Shaw. She remains a popular heroine in Virginia, but such sentiments are part of local pride. That she, an American, became the first woman to sit in the House of Commons ensured her a place in history, but it was not without irony, as she herself admitted. Women members were inevitable after 1918, and if the Irish nationalist Countess Markievicz had overcome her scruples and taken both the oath of loyalty to the Crown and her place in Parliament, Astor might not have been viewed as such a unique phenomenon. She was not a great politician; she formed no lasting political legacy. It is more to her credit that she survived twenty-five years of electoral challenges, thus proving that a woman in Parliament was not an aberration but the coming order of things. Unfortunately after she left the House of Commons she found no second vocation, and relations with members of her family were at times difficult. She was the focus of world attention, but appeared to leave little trace after her career ended. However, her work for social changes, particularly those beneficial to women and children, and her desire for world peace would prove significant legacies.

Overview of Biographical Sources

After her retirement in 1944, Astor began to write her memoirs but eventually gave up on the project, leaving only a draft. This body of information, opinions, and anecdotes is sometimes contradictory or inaccurate, but its lively personal tone provided a starting point for her various biographers.

Maurice Collis, *Nancy Astor: An Informal Biography* (1960), was written during Lady Astor's lifetime, with her collaboration and approval. Astor could be both charming and formidable, and one can sense in this work the author's fondness for his subject as well as his desire to please. Three years later, son Michael Astor published *Tribal Feeling* (1963), a work which another Astor scholar, Christopher Sykes, describes in the preface to his own book as "the most interesting study of Lady Astor to appear so far."

In the 1970s a flood of family histories with Astor as the central figure appeared. Elizabeth Langhorne's *Nancy Astor and Her Friends* (1974), Rosina Harrison's *Rose: My Life in Service* (1975) and Alice Winn's *Always a Virginian* (1975) provide additional insights on Astor's complex personality, her family, and her contemporaries. Each concentrated on specific facets of her life, however, and thus are limited in scope.

It was also during this decade that Sykes published *Nancy: The Life of Lady Astor* (1972). Sykes's scholarly and comprehensive study is generally acknowledged to be the standard biography.

Both John Grigg, *Nancy Astor: A Lady Unashamed* (1981), and Anthony Master, *Nancy Astor, A Biography* (1981), continued to draw from existing materials and broke no new ground, but Grigg's study is more generous to his subject. In death as in life Astor continues to fascinate and perplex both students and the public, and a definitive treatment is yet to be written.

Evaluation of Principal Biographical Sources

Collis, Maurice. *Nancy Astor: An Informal Biography.* New York: E. P. Dutton, 1960. (G) Written with the approval and help of Lady Astor, this biography is one of the major starting points in any study of Astor, but is no substitute for the memoir she was never able to finish. Compared to later works it is less objective and lacks an overview.

Grigg, John. *Nancy Astor: A Lady Unashamed.* Boston: Little, Brown, 1981. (G) Popular biography directed to the general reader. Includes numerous photographs and a bibliography.

Masters, Anthony. *Nancy Astor, a Biography.* London: Weidenfeld and Nicolson, 1981. (G) This popular biography puts Astor in a less favorable light; contains a selected bibliography but lacks documentation.

Sykes, Christopher. *Nancy: The Life of Lady Astor.* New York: Harper and Row, 1972. (A, G) Sykes's lengthy study is readable, yet scholarly, with footnotes and documentation at the end of each chapter. His affection is clear throughout, for he knew Lady Astor and other members of the family well, but it does not appear to cloud his judgment. Sykes's focus is comprehensive; clearly this is the principal biography of Astor.

Overview and Evaluation of Primary Sources

The most immediate primary source concerning Astor is the draft of her autobiography, begun in the early 1950s. An American publisher who was a friend of the family suggested the project, and because she had retired from politics she made the attempt, but failed for various reasons to complete it. The main focus was from her early childhood through World War I. There is also a large body of materials related to the Astors at Reading University in the Astor Archive. Michael Astor, her fourth son, expanded a series of essays on his mother into *Tribal Feeling* (London: John Murray, 1963; A, G), an insightful personal study. Elizabeth Langhorne (who married into the Astor family), *Nancy Astor and Her Friends* (New York: Praeger, 1974; A, G), emphasizes British politics and family ties. The volume contains detailed notes and a bibliography. Another member of the family, Alice Winn, Astor's niece, provides an episodic, detailed, and sometimes confusing account of the Langhornes in *Always a Virginian* (Lynchburg, VA: J. P. Bell, 1975; G), which is lively and readable but lacks documentation. Rosina Harrison, who was lady's maid to Astor for thirty-five years, offers a unique though limited view of the Astors in *Rose: My Life in Service* (New York: Viking Press, 1975; G). Hansard, *Parliamentary Debates,* should be consulted for a record of the Astors' careers in the House of Commons and House of Lords. A number of letters and papers are also in private hands.

Fiction and Adaptations

In April-June 1984, a BBC television production entitled "Nancy Astor" was aired as part of the *Masterpiece Theatre* series. Created by screenwriter Derek Marlowe, the eight-week miniseries was shot at a number of historic locations and chronicled Astor's remarkable career from her childhood in Danville and Richmond, through her two marriages and six children, her life as a great English social figure, her war work, her parliamentary career, and reluctant retirement. The title role was played by Lisa Harrow who, in a strong performance with a fine supporting cast, convincingly portrayed Astor from young adulthood to an elderly woman. The series was generally favorable in tone, but certain fictitious scenes included for dramatic effect were objected to by members of the Astor family. Despite its mainly sympathetic portrait of Astor and her circle, the series did not ignore some of the more erratic and less attractive aspects of Lady Astor's personality.

Museums, Historical Landmarks, Societies

Astor Birthplace (Danville, VA). A marker indicates the site of the house, now demolished. Nearby is a street named "Lady Astor Street."

Mirador (Greenwood, VA). A plaque indicates the house's importance to the Astor family.

Cliveden (Buckinghamshire, England). The family seat of the Astors is now open to the public. Nancy and Waldorf Astor are buried here. In the woods near the house is a cemetery containing the graves of Canadian soldiers who died in the military hospital in World War I. Nancy modeled for the head of the statue symbolizing Canada.

House of Commons (London, England). The well-known portrait of Lady Astor being introduced in the House of Commons by Arthur Balfour and David Lloyd George created so much controversy (supposedly because the three subjects were still alive) when it was given by Waldorf to the Palace of Westminster it was soon taken down and eventually loaned to the University of Virginia, in Charlottesville. The present painting at Westminster is a copy.

Other Sources

Kavaler, Lucy. *The Astors: An American Legend.* New York: Dodd, Mead, 1966. A popular work, lacking documentation.

O'Connor, Harvey. *The Astors.* New York: Knopf, 1941. A general history of the Astor family. Devotes a chapter to Waldorf and Nancy. Readable but dated. Contains genealogical tables and a bibliography.

Sinclair, David. *Dynasty: The Astors and Their Times.* New York: Beaufort Books, 1984. An unflattering series of portraits of most of the Astor clan, including Nancy, who is dismissed as ridiculous. An entertaining but superficial account, this study lacks balance.

Dorothy Potter
Lynchburg College

JOHN JAMES AUDUBON
1785-1851

Chronology

Born John James Audubon on April 26, 1785, at Les Cayes plantation, Santo Domingo, the illegitimate son of French naval officer and trader; *1789* brought to France by his father; *1803* sent by father to America to avoid conscription in Napoleon's army; settled at father's estate at Mill Grove, near Philadelphia, Pennsylvania; *1808* marries Lucy Blackwell; the couple have nine children, seven of whom lived to maturity; *1808-1819* lives in Kentucky as a whiskey and dry goods trader; serves a short time in a Louisville prison for debt; *1819* works as taxidermist at the Western Museum, Cincinnati; develops a lifelong interest in drawing of birds; *1820-1826* travels to Natchez, New Orleans, and St. Francisville, Louisiana, to study and draw native birds; *1826-1829* travels to England to find engraver for bird drawings; *1827* first publication of *Birds of America* appears; *1829* returns to United States and spends time studying and drawing birds near Camden and Great Egg, New Jersey, and in the Poconos Mountains of Pennsylvania; *1830* begins work on *Ornithological Biography*; acclaim for his work results in his election as fellow of the American Academy; *1831-1837* travels to Charleston, Florida, Dry Tortugas, Labrador, Canada, Texas, and the Gulf Coast studying and drawing birds; *1837-1843* travels extensively selling subscriptions to *Birds of America*; *1843* makes last expedition up the Missouri River to draw quadrupeds; *1843-1851* works with son John in New York City completing *Viviparous Quadrupeds of North America* and selling subscriptions; *1851* dies on January 27 in New York City.

Activities of Historical Significance

John James Audubon was one of America's first and foremost naturalists, artists, and ornithologists. Over his lifetime he completed over four hundred drawings of birds and wildlife and purportedly discovered three new species of birds. His greatest achievement was *Birds of America,* which brought him international fame, displaying to the world the wonders of American fauna and flora.

Overview of Biographical Sources

Audubon has been the subject of a large number of biographies, monographs, and articles. Most major biographies have focused on his accomplishments as a naturalist and pioneer in bird studies. Important biographies have ranged from Francis Herrick's 1938 two-volume *Audubon the Naturalist: A History of His Life and Time,* to a more recent and interesting 1980 study, *On the Road with John James Audubon* by Mary Durant and Michael Harwood. Despite the number of studies concerning various aspects of his life and career, many of Audubon's feelings and views about his life and work remain hidden. This is a result of the loss of most of his journals and personal papers through destruction or neglect by family members.

Evaluation of Principal Biographical Sources

Adams, Alexander. *John James Audubon.* New York: Putnam's Sons, 1964. (A, G) A well-documented biography which both praises Audubon's achievement and exposes a number of his faults and foibles.

Arthur, Stanley C. *Audubon: An Intimate Life of the American Woodsman.* New Orleans: Harmanson, 1937. (G) An early biography particularly worthwhile on Audubon's years in Louisiana.

Durant, Mary, and Michael Harwood. *On the Road with John James Audubon.* New York: Dodd, Mead, 1980. (A, G) Though not technically a biography, this interesting and informative study chronicles Audubon's life and discoveries throughout North America from his first-hand accounts.

Ford, Alice. *John James Audubon.* Norman: University of Oklahoma Press, 1964. (A, G) An important and balanced biography which brings to light previously unused records, documents, and letters.

Herrick, Francis. *Audubon The Naturalist: A History of His Life and Time.* 2 vols. 2d ed. New York: D. Appleton-Century, 1938. (A, G) For many years an important and standard work on Audubon. This uncritical biography praises Audubon's many contributions as a premier naturalist, ornithologist, and artist.

Rourke, Constance. *Audubon.* New York: Harcourt, Brace, 1906. (G) An uncritical biography of Audubon written in a novelistic style.

Overview and Evaluation of Primary Sources

Audubon's works were all published in various editions before his death in 1851. Many subsequent editions have been published. His major works include:

Birds of America, Ornithological Biography, and *Viviparous Quadrupeds of North America.* Due to unstable family finances following his death, many of his original paintings for *Birds of America* were sold to the New York Historical Society where they were held in storage for over 100 years. Most of the copperplates used for this edition were subsequently melted down. In addition, an 1835 warehouse fire in New York City destroyed an undetermined number of Audubon's books, copperplates, equipment, papers, and drawings. Other original works were either sold to private individuals and organizations or have been lost. His wife Lucy's possessions were lost in a house fire in 1875.

Most of Audubon's private correspondence and journals have disappeared or were destroyed. His daughter Maria Audubon burned all of his unnumbered correspondence. His journal for the years 1822-1824 vanished. Maria edited and published some portions of his Labrador and European journals, though she probably destroyed the originals. One original journal of his 1820-1821 excursions in New Orleans is preserved at the Houghton Library, Harvard University. There are miscellaneous collections of Audubon papers at the Cincinnati Historical Society, the Missouri Historical Society, the Library of the National Audubon Society, and the Charleston Museum.

A number of Audubon's writings and other works have been edited and published. These include: John James Audubon, *Audubon Reader; The Best Writings of John James Audubon* (Bloomington: Indiana University Press, 1986; **A, G**); Howard Corning, ed., *Journal of John James Audubon Made During His Trip to New Orleans in 1820-1821* (Boston: The Club of Odd Volumes, 1929; **A, G**); Alice Ford, ed., *The 1826 Journal of John James Audubon* (Norman: University of Oklahoma Press, 1967; **A, G**); Alice Ford, ed., *Butterflies, Moths and Other Studies* (New York: Thomas Crowell, 1952; **A, G**); and Maria Audubon, ed., *Audubon and His Journals,* 2 vols. (New York: Scribner's, 1897; **A, G**).

Museums, Historical Landmarks, Societies

Audubon House (Key West, FL). The nineteenth-century house is believed by some to be Audubon's dwelling place during his 1831-1832 stay. The house is open to the public, has a reconstructed studio, and displays a complete set of the valuable *Birds of America.*

Audubon Museum (Henderson, KY). The memorial museum contains family letters, ledgers, deeds, photographs, a life-mask, and other memorabilia.

Mill Grove (Mill Grove, PA). Built in 1762, this home was acquired by Captain Jean Audubon in 1789. Young Audubon lived here from 1804 to 1806. The house is restored to include a display of Audubon memorabilia and works as well as an attic studio and taxidermy room where he worked. The house is open to the public and is registered as a national historic site.

National Audubon Society (New York, NY). The society contains a library and some of Audubon's works. It publishes a national magazine, and helps coordinate the efforts of chapter organizations throughout the United States.

New York Historical Society (New York, NY). The Society's Audubon Gallery displays many of Audubon's original paintings of *Birds of America.*

Trinity Churchyard (New York, NY). A monument placed in 1893 marks Audubon's final resting place near West 155th Street. His residence near Riverside Drive was demolished in 1932.

Some of Audubon's engravings and personal effects are located at the Museum of Natural History in New York City, the Library of Congress in Washington, D.C., and in scattered repositories and private collections.

There are numerous place names throughout the United States which bear Audubon's name. These include streets, lakes, parks, libraries, and museums. In 1899 a town in Pennsylvania near Mill Grove was renamed Audubon.

Other Sources

Ayars, James. *John James Audubon: Bird Artist.* Champaign, IL: Garrard, 1966. A short, well-illustrated book on Audubon designed for children.

DeLatte, Carolyn. *Lucy Audubon: A Biography.* Baton Rouge: Louisiana State University Press, 1982. The only biography of Audubon's wife explores the important and difficult role Lucy had in supporting her husband's many endeavors.

Lindsey, Alton. *The Bicentennial of John James Audubon.* Bloomington: Indiana University Press, 1985. Essays highlighting Audubon's achievements and legacy.

Peterson, Roger Tory, and Virginia Peterson, eds. *Birds of America.* New York: Abbeville, 1981. 435 reproductions of Audubon's original double elephant folio.

Donald J. Richards
Manhattanville College

JOAN BAEZ
b. 1941

Chronology

Born Joan Chandos Baez on January 9, 1941, in Staten Island, New York, the second of three daughters of Dr. Albert Vinicio Baez, a Mexican-American pacifistic physicist and professor, and Joan Bridge Baez, a Scottish-American dramatics teacher, herself the daughter of an Episcopal priest; *1941-1951* lives a nomadic childhood, following the worldwide itinerary of her father's various academic and business appointments, including stints in Iraq, Turkey, and Switzerland; childhood marked by bouts with what she calls her "demons," undiagnosed instances of panic, nausea, and chills; *1951-1958* attends junior and senior high school in Redlands and Palo Alto, California, where she is targeted for ethnic prejudice because of her relatively dark skin; responds by learning to play the ukelele and becoming the class entertainer; *1958-1959* moves with her family to a suburb of Boston, where her father has accepted teaching positions at M.I.T. and Harvard; very briefly attends drama school at Boston University; begins singing folk songs in Harvard Square coffee houses, attracting a loyal following; *1959* invited by folksinger Bob Gibson to the Newport Folk Festival, where her unannounced appearance causes a sensation; *1959-1962* records her first albums, which become immediate best-sellers for the Vanguard label; *1962-1966* forges a close relationship with singer/songwriter Bob Dylan, but strikes out on her own road of political protest; political songs increasingly dominate her concert repertoire; travels the country (and the globe) to demonstrate and perform for peace and resistance to the draft; marches with Martin Luther King, Jr., in the South to protest segregation; refuses for several successive years to pay sixty percent of her income taxes in protest against the Vietnam War; co-founds, with her mentor Ira Sandperl, the Institute for the Study of Nonviolence (now the Resource Center for Nonviolence) in Carmel, California; *1967* arrested and jailed following an antiwar demonstration at the Oakland, California, military induction center; savagely lampooned as "Joanie Phoanie" in Al Capp's "Li'l Abner" comic strip; *1968* publishes *Daybreak,* a collection of autobiographical sketches and a defense of nonviolence; marries Stanford political activist David Harris; *1969* Harris imprisoned for draft resistance; performs at the Woodstock Festival at Bethel, New York, while pregnant with her only child; *1971* records her only hit single, "The Night They Drove Old Dixie Down"; *1972* becomes involved in London-based Amnesty International; helps organize "Ring Around Congress" to protest Vietnam War;

sings Christmas carols in Hanoi during eleven days of U.S. bombing; *1973* divorces Harris; *1975* records "Diamonds and Rust," a song about her early relationship with Dylan; travels with Dylan on the "Rolling Thunder Revue" concert tour; *1977* sparks controversy by singing Spanish Republican anthem "No nos moveran" while on concert tour in Spain; *1979* withdraws from concert work for three years to found pacifist group Humanitas International; *1985* opens "Live Aid" rock concert in Philadelphia, telling the young audience, "This is your Woodstock, and it's long overdue!"; serenades Lech Walesa in Gdansk, Poland; *1987* publishes her detailed autobiography, *And a Voice to Sing With.*

Activities of Historical Significance

Baez's voice, early characterized as an "achingly pure soprano," was a dominant one during the socially aware 1960s. Whether singing ancient British ballads, songs written by Bob Dylan, or her own compositions, Baez exerted a compelling influence on popular music throughout the decade. Further, because folk music at the time was linked to progressive, left-leaning political views, Baez's singing and activism literally gave voice to a generation of like-minded young people, anxious for peace and social change. In Vietnam and in the American South, Baez stood resolutely for peace and freedom, and her association with world leaders gave her considerable influence. Millions of people worldwide identified her political positions with the protest songs that she sang—including "Blowing in the Wind," "If I Had a Hammer," and "We Shall Overcome"—and some social historians consider her one of the major voices that led America's young people to protest the Vietnam War so vigorously.

As American culture altered its views and priorities in the 1970s and 1980s, Baez's record sales and influence waned. Nevertheless, she remains enormously popular on American and European concert stages. She also remains a highly visible activist, a resolute and much-publicized advocate of Gandhian nonviolent resistance, political freedom, and world peace.

Overview of Biographical Sources

Biographical material on Baez arises from three principal sources: the artist's own published accounts of her life; brief, anecdotal biographical reviews in a great number of journals, popular magazines, and encyclopedias of music; and the interviews she has given to journalists from time to time throughout her career. Notably missing from this list is a full-length, objective, English-language biography. This fact is somewhat surprising, given the prominence and influence Baez enjoyed throughout the 1960s and beyond, both in the fields of popular culture and politics. (Biographies of her contemporary Bob Dylan, for example, are by no means lacking.) In a sense, however, Baez herself has pre-empted the field by writing two memoirs, *Daybreak* (1968) and *And a Voice to Sing With* (1987) which, between them, serve to chronicle both the early and more recent stages of her life and career.

But any autobiography, however candid, involves the possibility of unreliability. Further, the biographical material on Baez that does exist, while copious and wide-ranging, tends to be sketchy and incomplete; the singer has occasionally been a somewhat prickly interviewee, often deflecting questions about her personal life. For these reasons, a detailed, objective, and accessible biography would provide a real service to those interested in an accurate account of Baez and her times.

Evaluation of Principal Biographical Sources

Goldsmith, Barbara. "Life on Struggle Mountain." *New York Times Book Review* (July 20, 1987): 30. (**A, G**) In the course of her substantial review of *And a Voice to Sing With,* Goldsmith provides a clear and coherent account of Baez's life. While greatly admiring Baez's commitment to political activism, Goldsmith questions the accuracy and depth of the singer's self-appraisal.

Logan, Nick, and Bob Woffinden, comps. *The Illustrated Encyclopedia of Rock.* New York: Harmony Books, 1977. (**A, G, Y**) This upbeat, gossipy entry sees Baez as the "most important, and most controversial, female performer" of the 1960s.

Moritz, Charles, ed. *Current Biography Yearbook 1963.* New York: H. W. Wilson, 1964. (**A, G, Y**) A good overview of Baez's early career. The emphasis is on her music rather than on the political activism that came later. Accordingly, an updated entry for Baez in this standard series is needed.

Rodnitzky, Jerome L. *Minstrels of the Dawn: The Folk-Protest Singer as a Cultural Hero.* Chicago: Nelson-Hall, 1976. (**A, G, Y**) Purports that folk performers, operating in the long tradition of the protest song, gave both expression and impetus to the social turbulence of the 1960s. A long chapter on Baez ("A Pacifist St. Joan") traces her growing commitment to and involvement in the protest movement. Also discusses Woody Guthrie, Phil Ochs, and Bob Dylan.

"Sibyl with Guitar." *Time* (November 23, 1962): 54-56. (**A, G, Y**) This biographical article, contained in the issue featuring the famous portrait of Baez on the cover, is of considerable interest in terms of the history of popular culture, since it serves both to document and validate the burgeoning "folk revolution" of the time. In retrospect, however, perhaps the most conspicuous aspect of the article is its consistently arch and condescending tone toward the whole folk-based social protest movement. Baez is called "palpably nubile;" indeed, much space is spent on the artist's physical appearance and eccentric dress, perhaps because the author does not understand, or wish to admit, the significance of the emerging musical and political trends which Baez represents.

Sloman, Larry. *On the Road with Bob Dylan: Rolling with the Thunder*. Toronto: Bantam Books, 1978. (**A, G**) *Rolling Stone* magazine writer Sloman provides candid glimpses, including a brief interview, of Baez on Dylan's epochal concert tour.

Swanekamp, Joan. *Diamonds and Rust: A Bibliography and Discography on Joan Baez*. Ann Arbor, MI: Pierian Press, 1980. (**A, G**) A brief biographical sketch—one which draws heavily upon the *Current Biography* material—is followed by a selected bibliography (arranged chronologically, not by subject), a discography, and song and album indexes, covering the years 1961-1977. The bibliography seeks to provide a sampling of biographical and newsworthy material on Baez; it does not pretend to be exhaustive. Nor is the discography perfectly complete: it omits, for example, the seminal album "Folksingers 'Round Harvard Square," recorded in 1959 and released on the Veritas label in 1960. Still, this book, long in print and readily available, provides a useful entry into materials relating to Baez's early life and work.

Overview and Evaluation of Primary Sources

Most of what is known about Baez's life has been provided by the singer herself in countless interviews and in her two autobiographies. *Daybreak* (1968. Reprint. New York: Avon, 1969; **A, G, Y**) provides sharp portraits of Baez's parents, Ira Sandperl, and the late author Richard Fariña, who had been her brother-in-law. It unstintingly portrays Baez's inner turmoil throughout her youth, and issues a statement of her loyalty to the principles of nonviolence. Various critics have either praised the book for its lyricism or condemned it as treacly and simplistic. *And a Voice to Sing With* (New York: Summit Books, 1987; **A, G, Y**) offers a less fragmented, more coherent, and more revealing autobiographical review. Baez looks back on thirty years in the public eye and deals candidly with such matters as her relationship with Bob Dylan, her prominent role in a variety of protest movements, the break-up of her marriage, her many love affairs, her devotion to her son Gabriel, and the vagaries of stardom. Baez touches on many of these same issues in the course of her interviews; among the most important of them are those with James Finn in *Protest: Pacifism and Politics* (New York: Vintage, 1967; **A, G**); with David A. DeTurk and A. Poulin in *The American Folkscene: Dimensions of the Folk Song Revival* (New York: Dell, 1967; **A, G, Y**); with Kurt Loder in the rock journal *Rolling Stone* (April 14, 1983); with Anthony Scaduto in *Bob Dylan: An Intimate Biography* (New York: Grosset & Dunlap, 1971; **A, G, Y**); and, most definitively, with Nat Hentoff in *Playboy Interview: Joan Baez* (Chicago: Playboy Press, 1971; **A, G, Y**).

Fiction and Adaptations

Baez has appeared in half a dozen films, at least two of which are of significant biographical interest. Released in 1967, the much-praised *Don't Look Back,* directed by D. A. Pennebaker, is a grittily realistic documentary of Bob Dylan's 1965 concert tour of England, a tour which marked a break in one stage of Baez's relationship with him. Indeed, one memorable scene records Baez's walking out on Dylan. An apparently weary Baez sings two songs and engages in conversations with tour members. Another documentary, *Carry It On* (1970), directed and produced by Christopher Knight, Robert Jones, and James Coyne, involves the political activities of Baez and her husband David Harris. The film also depicts Baez's concert tour following Harris's imprisonment for draft resistance, recording her candid conversations with concert-goers on a variety of personal and political topics.

Additionally, most of Baez's self-penned songs harbor autobiographical allusions. For example, "Gulf Winds," from the 1976 A&M album of the same name, provides a lyrical treatment of Baez's childhood and her relationship with her sisters and father. In this light, Baez's book of her own musical compositions, *And Then I Wrote . . .* (New York: Big 3 Music Corp., 1979), may be viewed as a potentially valuable biographical resource.

Other Sources

DuBois, Fletcher Ranney. *A Troubadour as Teacher, the Concert as Class-room?; Joan Baez, Advocate of Nonviolence and Motivator of the Young: A Study in the Biographical Method.* Frankfurt: Haag and Herchen, 1985. A quirky, hard-to-find, but nonetheless fascinating addition to the canon on Baez. DuBois, for whom this work served as a doctoral dissertation at a German university, uses

Baez's autobiographical materials to argue that a folk singer performing in front of an audience serves the function of a teacher in front of students. Much emphasis is placed on Baez's experiences with and criticism of formal education. DuBois draws upon an enormously wide range of sources, including the notes of John L. Wasserman, music critic for the *San Francisco Chronicle,* whose untimely death cut short plans for a full-length Baez biography. A valuable, nearly exhaustive (to 1985) bibliography is appended to the volume. Grammatical, mechanical, and typographical errors abound on every page.

Harris, David. *Dreams Die Hard.* New York: St. Martin's Press, 1982. In the course of this book on the murder of former Congressman Allard Lowenstein by deranged activist Dennis Sweeney, Harris, Baez's ex-husband, touches upon his own relationship with Baez, tracing its dissolution to the disparity between their respective fame and fortunes. He sees their marriage as grounded more in shared political commitments than in romantic love.

Hitchcock, H. Wiley, and Stanley Sadie, eds. "Joan Baez." In *The New Grove Dictionary of American Music.* New York: Macmillan, 1986. A brief biographical overview with a selected bibliography.

Hood, Phil, ed. *Artists of American Folk Music.* New York: Quill, 1986. A concise biographical sketch.

Ligney, Nicole, and Pierre Grundmann. *Joan Baez.* Paris: Brea Editions, 1981. The only full-length biography of Baez seems to be this French-language work, which unfortunately has been adopted by very few North American libraries.

Swan, Peter. *Joan Baez: A Bio-Disco-Bibliography: Being a Selected Guide to Material in Print, on Record, on Cassette and on Film, with a Biographical Introduction.* Brighton: Noyce, 1977.

William Ryland Drennan
University of Wisconsin Center
Baraboo/Sauk County

P. T. BARNUM
1810-1891

Chronology

Born Phineas Taylor Barnum on July 5, 1810, in Bethel, Connecticut, the second of six children of Philo Barnum, a tailor and a tavern and express company proprietor, and Irena Taylor, a member of an old New England family; *1810-1816* grows up in the semi-public atmosphere of a tavern clientele; *1816-1823* attends Bethel Community School, where the "three R's" constitute the curriculum; *1823* forms a partnership with Hiram Weed to operate a general store; *1825* father dies; assumes support of mother and siblings as a trader for Keeler and Whitlock Traders in Grassy Plain near Bethel; *1826* moves to Brooklyn, New York, to learn merchandising, wholesaling, and auction buying; *1828* returns to Bethel to open a fruit and confectionery business featuring a lottery as a promotional device; *1829* marries Charity ("Chairy") Hallett and subsequently has four daughters; *1831-1834* becomes owner and editor of the *Herald of Freedom*, a Jacksonian Democrat weekly newspaper in Danbury, Connecticut, and achieves his first notoriety through three libel suits; *1835* purchases a boarding house in Brooklyn, New York, where he meets showman Coley Bartram and acquires the contract of "Joice Heth," a woman alleged to be George Washington's 161-year-old slave nurse; *1836* becomes an itinerant showman exhibiting "Joice Heth" on the theater circuit throughout the East; *1837-1840* joins Aaron Turner's Circus as a ticket-seller (i.e., promotional work), treasurer, and secretary, and then he purchases the circus converting it into "Barnum's Grand Scientific and Musical Theater"; *1841* begins to write advertising copy for Bowery Amphitheatre; purchases the American Museum on Broadway in New York City and presents freak shows, stage reviews, dramas, and lectures; *1842* gains international fame with the exhibit of General Tom Thumb (Charles Stratton), a midget only twenty-five inches tall; *1847* presents a series of popular concerts featuring Jenny Lind, the "Swedish Nightingale"; *1853* becomes part owner of the *Illustrated News*, a weekly New York City newspaper; *1857* takes his museum cast on first European tour; *1865* American Museum is destroyed by fire at a loss of $400,000, and is subsequently rebuilt as the New American Museum, which is also destroyed by a fire; serves in the Connecticut legislature to help ratify the Thirteenth Amendment to the Constitution; *1866* lectures on the Lyceum and YMCA circuit, espousing temperance; *1871* with W. C. Coup and Dan Constello, begins "Barnum's Great Museum, Menagerie, Circus and Travelling World's Fair"; *1872* builds "Hippotheatron" in

New York City; *1874* first wife dies; *1875* serves as mayor of Bridgeport, Connecticut; *1878* serves on board of trustees for Universalist Church; changes the name of museum to "P. T. Barnum's New and Greatest Show on Earth," which becomes the largest circus in America and a national institution in the late nineteenth century; *1881* hires James A. Bailey to manage his circus; *1882* marries second wife, Nancy Fish, an Englishwoman; creates sensation in circus world with Jumbo, the giant elephant he purchases from a London zoo; *1890* changes name of circus to "Barnum and Bailey Circus" and makes a triumphal tour of Europe; *1891* establishes endowment for Barnum Museum in Bridgeport; dies on April 7 at his home in Bridgeport, Connecticut, and is buried at nearby Mountain Grove Cemetery.

Activities of Historical Significance

Barnum's innovative showmanship revolutionized the mass entertainment business in America by aggressively promoting the public museum, popular musical concerts, carnival side shows, Broadway reviews, and the three-ring circus. His sensational advertising and publicity, based on outrageous stunts, exaggeration, and repetition, are the prototype for the modern advertising and public relations industry. The "Ringling Brothers, Barnum and Bailey Circus" still performs today with its parades, calliope (steam organ), acrobats, bareback riding, fire-eaters, and animal tamers. The saying "There's a sucker born every minute" is attributed to Barnum, although he disclaimed it. Jumbo, the name of Barnum's famous elephant has become a standard word describing anything huge in size. Barnum became friends with such historical personages as Queen Victoria, Abraham Lincoln, Mark Twain, Horace Greeley, Gideon Welles, William Gladstone, William M. Thackeray, and Grover Cleveland. Barnum epitomized nineteenth-century romanticism, with its emphasis upon the emotional and colorful rather than the rational and sedate.

Overview of Biographical Sources

Joel Benton wrote the first biography of Barnum, *Life of Hon. Phineas T. Barnum, Comprising His Boyhood, Youth, Vicissitudes of Early Years, His Genius, Wit, Generosity, Eloquence, Christianity* (1891), a work that draws heavily from Barnum's autobiography. Harvey W. Root's *The Unknown Barnum* (1927) presents a cursory review of his career but focuses upon his personal life, friends, and political beliefs. The novelist Irving Wallace wrote a highly readable, albeit nonscholarly biography entitled *The Life and Times of P. T. Barnum* (1959). Neil

Harris wrote a scholarly critique of Barnum's life in *Humbug: The Art of P. T. Barnum* (1973). He took a dim view of Barnum's exploitation of an unsophisticated public. Other biographies that shed light upon Barnum's career are Joan Bulman, *Jenny Lind: A Biography* (1956); George Conklin, *The Ways of the Circus, Being Memoirs and Adventures of George Conklin, Tamer of Lions* (1921); Richard E. Conover, *The Affairs of James A. Bailey: New Revelations on the Career of the World's Most Successful Showman* (1957); Alice Curtis Desmond, *Barnum Presents General Tom Thumb* (1954); and George Slaight, *A History of the Circus* (1980).

Evaluation of Biographical Sources

Durant, John, and Alice Durant. *Pictorial History of the American Circus.* New York: A. S. Barnes, 1957. **(Y)** A beautifully illustrated history of the circus with a well written narrative for youthful readers. Chapter three, "The Great Barnum," is an excellent primer on the subject. The authors incorporate highly interesting and excellent archival sources.

Saxon, A. H. *P. T. Barnum: The Legend and The Man.* New York: Columbia University Press, 1989. **(A, G)** This is the most comprehensive and scholarly of all Barnum biographies. The author holds a doctorate in the history of theatre and dramatic criticism from Yale University and is a fellow of the John Simon Guggenheim Foundation, which provided a grant for the many years of research involved. Having written scores of books and articles on the history of the theater, Saxon used his expertise to research all facets of Barnum's life and career. He has published corollary works in *The Autobiography of Mrs. Tom Thumb* (1979) and *Selected Letters of P. T. Barnum* (1983). A consultant to the Barnum Museum Foundation, he received the medal of the Barnum Festival Society of Bridgeport, Connecticut, for his contributions. His work is the definitive biography of Barnum.

Overview and Evaluation of Primary Sources

As a great showman, Barnum was quite aware of the value of self-publicity; hence he wrote his autobiography in three stages over a thirty-one-year period. *The Life of P. T. Barnum, Written by Himself* (1855) was the first chronicle of his life. This was followed fourteen years later with an updated version, *Struggles and Triumphs, or Forty Years' Recollections of P. T. Barnum, Written by Himself* (1869. Reprint. Salem, NH: Ayer, 1970; **A, G**), which included a chapter, "Art of Money-Getting," that offended many readers because it came close to advocating swindling. The chapter was modified in subsequent autobiographies. Seven years before his death, he published the final version of his autobiography, *Struggles and Triumphs, or Sixty Years' Recollections of P. T. Barnum, Written by Himself* (1884). His wife, Nancy Barnum, completed it posthumously with *The Last Chapter: In Memoriam, P. T. Barnum* (1893). These three autobiographies, plus the addendum by his wife, have been edited and condensed into two volumes by George S. Bryan and published as *Struggles and Triumphs, or the Life of P. T. Barnum, Written by Himself* (1927). More recently, Carl Bode produced an edition of the autobiography, *Struggles and Triumphs* (New York: Penguin, 1981; A, G).

Barnum also wrote books on other topics that interested him, such as *The Liquor Business: Its Effect Upon the Minds, Morals, and Pockets of Our People* (1854) and *The Humbugs of the World: An Account of Humbugs, Delusions, Impositions, Quackeries, Deceits, and Deceivers Generally in All Ages* (1865), an exposé that received much criticism at the time because many thought he advocated such behavior with his own fraudulent showmanship. Barnum humorously referred to himself as "The Prince of Humbugs" but tried to defend himself by maintaining that "the author of harmless mirth is a public benefactor." *Why I Am a Universalist* reveals Barnum's Unitarian-based religious beliefs, and *Funny Stories Told by Phineas T. Barnum* (1890) relates the many humorous jokes and anecdotes he collected over the years in show business.

A sampling of Barnum's correspondence has been edited by his foremost biographer, A. H. Saxon, and published as *Selected Letters of P. T. Barnum* (New York: Columbia University Press, 1983; A, G). The New York Public Library's rare books division holds some of Barnum's original manuscripts and private papers.

Fiction and Adaptations

Barnum's showmanship has been fictionalized in Roderick Thorp's novel *Jenny and Barnum* (1981), which was advertised as the "greatest love story on earth." Though the accolade may have pleased Barnum, it is completely apocryphal. His relationship with Jenny Lind was monetarily lucrative but the aristocratic Lind thought Americans crude plebeians. Twentieth Century-Fox produced a movie, *The Mighty Barnum* (1934), with the screenplay by Bess Meredyth and Bene Fowler. Full of myths, the role of Barnum was played in a stereotyped manner by Wallace Beery. A television movie called *Barnum*, produced by the Columbia Broadcasting System in 1972, was not much better, with Burt Lancaster playing a lackluster Barnum. The best circus movie of all time, *The Greatest Show on Earth*, was directed by Cecil B. DeMille in 1952. While not using Barnum's name, the film

was based on his circus and was named best picture of the year at the first tele-
vised Academy Awards ceremony. A Broadway musical show entitled *Barnum*
was a hit at the St. James Theater in New York City in 1980 with lyrics by
Michael Stewart and music by Cy Coleman. The extravaganza quality of Barnum's
showmanship lent itself well to a stage production.

Museums, Historical Landmarks, Societies

Barnum Avenue and *Barnum School* (Bridgeport, CT). Named after Barnum in
his hometown after he became famous.

Barnum Historical Collection (Bridgeport Public Library, Bridgeport, CT).
Contains a variety of manuscripts, papers, photographs, and letters.

Barnum Festival Society (Bridgeport, CT). An organization dedicated to commemorating Barnum.

Barnum Museum (Bridgeport, CT). Endowed by Barnum before his death, it
houses his memorabilia, photographs, scrapbooks, and personal belongings.

Bronze Statue of Barnum (Bridgeport, CT). Sculpted by Thomas Ball in Seaside
Park.

The Circus World Museum of Wisconsin (Baraboo, WI). Houses a huge collection of restored tents, wagons, cages, and equipment from all the famous circuses,
including Barnum's. Every July 4 a parade on Wisconsin Avenue in Milwaukee
uses all of the original circus paraphernalia.

Lindencraft (Fairfield, CT). The Barnum mansion is now a museum containing
all of the household furnishings.

Milner Library Circus Collection (Illinois State University, Normal, IL). Has a
very large collection of circus photographs and posters, including some from the
Barnum and Bailey Circus.

Miscellaneous Barnum Collection (Sterling Library, Yale University, New
Haven, CT). Has many theatrical items, such as scripts, stage equipment, photographs, costumes, and artifacts from the Hippotheatron.

Smithsonian Institution (Washington, DC). Holds a collection of circus items, posters, photographs, and Barnum memorabilia.

Special Barnum Collection (Tufts University, Medford, MA). Barnum helped found the university in 1852, and before his death he donated materials for a special exhibit and documents for the library archives.

Theatre Collection (Firestone Library, Princeton, NJ). Costumes, stage equipment, scripts, and artifacts from the American Museum.

Other Sources

Barnum, P. T. "I Thus Address the World." A cylinder recording of Barnum's voice made in London in winter 1889-1890. For a transcription and note on reissues in the present century, see A. H. Saxon, ed., *Selected Letters*. The voice, as well as the legacy of P. T. Barnum, remains a quintessential part of Americana.

Betts, John Richards. "P. T. Barnum and the Popularization of Natural History." *Journal of the History of Ideas* 20 (1959): 353-368. Discusses the exhibition of wild and strange animals.

Conover, Richard E. *The Circus: Wisconsin's Unique Heritage.* Baraboo, WI: State Historical Society of Wisconsin and The Circus World Museum, 1967. Baraboo, Wisconsin, was the winter quarters where equipment was repaired for many circuses, and it was used as a staging area for the summer season in the North.

Dahlinger, Fred, Jr. "The Development of the Railroad Circus." *Bandwagon* 27, 6 (1983): 6-11; *Bandwagon* 28, 1 (1984): 16-27; *Bandwagon* 28, 2 (1984): 28-36; *Bandwagon* 28, 3 (1984): 36-39. Barnum was the first to switch from horse-drawn wagons to railroads for transporting his circus. He required over two hundred railroad cars to ship the "Greatest Show on Earth."

Larrabee, Eric. "The Old Showman's Last Triumph." *American Heritage* (December 1961): 1890-1899. A description of Barnum's last London tour that is profusely illustrated from his scrapbooks.

Neafie, Nelle. *A P. T. Barnum Bibliography.* Published privately as a project for a compiler's degree in library science. Available in the Bridgeport Public Library, this work, although incomplete, is a useful guide to the Bridgeport Library's manuscript collection.

Palquist, David W. *Bridgeport: A Pictorial History*. Norfolk, VA: Donning Publishers, 1985. Photographs and pictures of the Barnum school, statue, and residence, as well as a discussion of his mayoralty.

Saxon, A. H. "Barnumiana: A Select Annotated Bibliography of Works by or Relating to P. T. Barnum." Forthcoming. This book-length manuscript is to be published in the near future and can be anticipated to be the definitive bibliography to match the author's biography.

―――――. "Barnum, Nineteenth-Century Science and Some 'Unnatural' History." *Discovery* 21, 1 (1988): 25-30. Barnum's chief biographer writes about his subject's exhibits for Yale University's Peabody Museum of Natural History magazine.

―――――. "P. T. Barnum: Universalism's Surprising 'Prince of Humbugs.'" *World* 2, 3 (1988): 407, 427-433. Saxon addresses Barnum's religious beliefs for the journal of the Unitarian Universalist Association.

―――――. "P. T. Barnum's American Museum." *Seaport* 20, 3 (Winter 1986-1987): 27-33.

―――――. "There's a Sucker Born Every Minute" *Bandwagon* 31, 2 (1987): 34-35.

Toole-Stott, R. *"Circus and Allied Art: A World Bibliography."* An unpublished manuscript by the English bibliographer who died in 1982. With a separate section on Barnum, he has annotated two hundred worldwide articles. The five-volume manuscript is housed at the University of California at Santa Barbara.

Wilmeth, Don B. *Variety Entertainment and Outdoor Amusements: A Reference Guide*. Westport, CT: Greenwood Press, 1982. The "Historical Summary" and "Survey of Sources" are excellent, and the essay "The Dime Museum and P. T. Barnum" is useful.

Frederick H. Schapsmeier
University of Wisconsin

JOHN WILKES BOOTH
1838-1865

Chronology

Born John Wilkes Booth on May 10, 1838, at Tudor Hall, the family farm in Belair, Harford County, Maryland, the ninth of ten children of Junius Brutus Booth, a celebrated actor, and Mary Ann Holmes (his parents do not marry until 1851); *1842-1854* lives with his family for part of the year in Baltimore (at various locations) but spends vacations on the farm; attends various schools in the Baltimore area, including a Quaker school in Cockeysville and St. Timothy's Hall in Catonsville; enjoys learning and reciting dramatic texts, and with his elder brother Edwin organizes private theatrical performances at home; *1855* makes his stage debut at St. Charles Theatre, Baltimore, playing Richmond in Shakespeare's *Richard III*; *1857-1858* plays minor roles at Arch Street Theatre, Philadelphia, under the name "Mr. J. B. Wilks"; *1858-1859* plays various roles with the Marshall (or Richmond) Theatre stock company in Richmond, Virginia; *1859-1860* is again a member of the Richmond company (of which his boyhood friend John T. Ford is co-manager); in late November 1859, convinces an officer in the "Richmond Grays" to allow him to accompany the military unit to Charlestown, Virginia, to guard the abolitionist John Brown and his party who are incarcerated there; witnesses Brown's hanging on December 2; *1860-1861* celebrated as a rising star, playing in Montgomery, Alabama, and Columbus, Georgia, in the autumn and then touring widely; plays the role of Pescara in Sheil's *The Apostate* in Albany, New York, and is stabbed by a jealous actress; *1861-1862* plays engagements in Cincinnati, Louisville, Pittsburgh, Chicago, and Baltimore (where he plays the lead in *Richard III*—an "incomparable impersonation"—in John Ford's Holliday Street theatre); *March 1862* celebrates the opening of Mary Provost's Broadway Theatre by performing *Richard III* to enthusiastic reviews; *May 1862* plays the Boston Museum; *1862-1863* plays in New York and Boston; *April 1863* acts for the first time in Washington, D. C. (at Grover's Theatre, with President Lincoln in the audience); *November 1863* plays a highly touted two-week engagement at the newly constructed Ford's Theatre in Washington, D. C. (Lincoln attends one performance); *1864* plays an unusually demanding schedule in New Orleans in March and April and is forced to abandon his engagements because of a bronchial illness; appears at the Boston Museum in late April; gives one of his most heralded performances in New York City on November 25, 1864, in a benefit performance of *Julius Caesar* (his last performance on the New York stage), playing with his two actor-brothers, Edwin and Junius Brutus Booth II; plots with several others to kidnap President Lincoln, spirit him to Richmond, and use him as a Confederate hostage; *1865* lives in Washington, D.C.; plays Romeo on January 20 and Pescara on March 18; on March 20 his plot to kidnap Lincoln fails when the president does not appear at the anticipated place; with three accomplices, decides to assassinate Lincoln and other government officials; on April 14 mortally wounds Lincoln during an evening performance of Tom Taylor's *Our American Cousin* at Ford's Theatre (Lincoln dies the following morning); escapes through southern Maryland; apprehended and fatally wounded near Port Royal, Caroline County, Virginia, on April 26; his final words are "Tell my mother—I died—for my country"; is subsequently buried secretly in the prison yard of the federal arsenal; *1867-1869* Arsenal Prison is torn down; his exhumed body is stored for two years in a warehouse and is reinterred in Greenmount Cemetery in Baltimore on February 20, 1869.

Activities of Historical Significance

That John Wilkes Booth is remembered primarily for assassinating perhaps the most revered and greatest American president is both inevitable and understandable. However, it should be borne in mind that this mad act cut short not only the life of the chief executive but that of a brilliant, if erratic, scion of the American stage. Booth died a few days shy of his twenty-seventh birthday, at a point in his professional development which indicated not only an extraordinary native talent, but a growing following among the American theatre-going public. Therefore, any historical assessment of Booth must address his achievement as an actor and the significance of a professional career that lasted less than a decade.

Booth grew up in an atmosphere defined by the theatre and theatrical literature; his father, Junius Brutus Booth, and his older brothers, Edwin and Junius ("June") Brutus Booth II, were all celebrated actors. His sister, Asia, wrote of assisting in his youthful oral recitations of poetry and Shakespearean tragedies (especially *Julius Caesar*). Also, he and Edwin were known to present their own amateur productions in their Baltimore home. These factors, plus his self-education in the areas of acting and elocution, seem to have constituted his only formal education in acting. A family anecdote has him riding out to the farm from Baltimore, after playing his first role (Richmond in *Richard III*) and announcing, "Guess what I've done! I've made my first appearance on any stage!" Indeed, much of his preparation seems to have been empirical, the minor roles he played at the Arch Street Theatre in Philadelphia at the beginning of his career serving as a brief, if effective, apprenticeship.

Knowledge of his personality tends to be anecdotal, and the various accounts are often contradictory. However, both negative and positive commentators agree on his natural dramatic flair and a desire to express himself forcefully by both word and gesture. Two of his strongest roles were those of the overpowering villains Richard III and Pescara in Sheil's long-forgotten *The Apostate*. His stage performances were often described as containing more fire and physical bravado than intellectual verve. Kate Reignolds, an actress with whom he occasionally played, summarized Booth the actor as having been "ever spoiled and petted, and left to his unrestrained will . . . He succeeded in gaining position by flashes of genius, and the necessity of ordinary study had not been borne in upon him. No life could have been worse for such a character than that of an actor."

Still, owing in part to the fact that he was a Booth, and that he "[was] full of the true grit," as his brother Edwin remarked, his rise was meteoric. Although his initial ambition, according to his sister Asia, was to be a "Southern" actor (he did gain early recognition in such provincial theatres as that of Richmond), when he opened in New York in the spring of 1862 it was as a star. However, comparing his acting career with those of Joseph Jefferson or Laura Keene is to acknowledge a somewhat erratic pattern. Once his reputation began its ascent he traveled widely, often for engagements that were short but which afforded him roles with a high profile. In the much celebrated production of *Julius Caesar* at the Winter Garden Theatre in New York in November 1864, his performance as Mark Anthony was ranked by many above those of his brothers Edwin (as Brutus) and Junius (as Cassius). However, what seems obviously lacking from his stage career is a dedication to a steady pattern of performing which might have given his career—and his life—a greater stability. There is reason to believe that had he lived longer he would have gained greater maturity and his performances would have reflected more intellect and less emotion.

So, it was fitting that Booth select a stage to carry out his drama of political revenge, and it is because of his familiarity with the personnel at Ford's Theater, and with the play, *Our American Cousin*, that he could make arrangements for the assassination without arousing suspicion.

Booth, a popular actor and a congenial colleague, frequented both Ford's and Grover's theaters, as each gave him freedom of the house. He routinely received his mail at Ford's and he could, and frequently did, walk into either establishment at any time he pleased. Everyone from managers, to actors, to stage hands knew him, and his visits to Ford's were often followed by drinks at Peter Taltavul's Star Saloon, which adjoined the theatre building.

At about 3:00 p.m. on April 14, as rehearsals were completed and as stage carpenters were storing scenery, Booth arrived at the theater, having learned from

John Ford at noon that President Lincoln would attend the performance that evening. But Booth's appearance on this Good Friday afternoon was no ordinary social call, nor was it his first that day—or his last. It was, however, a crucial visit for, although brief, it enabled him to complete the final details in a long and erratic scheme.

The success of Booth's plan lay, in part, with the design of the theater. Ford's Theatre was a relatively new building, having opened on August 27, 1863. Since that time Booth had come to know it well—as an actor on its boards, as a friend to its various personnel, and as a frequenter of its interior. It was a small building, measuring only 72 by 110 feet, but it contained various levels, which denoted several categories of seats. The President would occupy the state box on the second tier, near the dress circle. A small staircase ascended from the left of the downstairs lobby to the second tier. Here an outside door led into an alcove from which one gained access to the boxes. In addition to knowing the interior configuration of Ford's, Booth knew the play which would be presented there in a few hours.

Perhaps the key to the success of Booth's scheme was its simplicity. It called for no alteration in the normal course of life, and it aroused no suspicions. No one at the theatre would be surprised to see him during a performance. There was nothing unusual about leaving a horse in the public alley at the rear. Moreover, he had determined that the play itself afforded an ideal moment for making his move. There was a point in Act III, Scene 2 when a single actor would be on the stage, at far left. This is the scene in which the "American Cousin," Asa Trenchard, exposes the hypocrisy of Mrs. Mountchessington and her daughter. They exit, and he calls after them. This moment, one of the funniest in the play, always drew prolonged laughter. Tonight it would be his moment. Still, he would have to act quickly and decisively and, to some extent, trust luck. What of the guard usually posted outside the alcove door? Would he be in place tonight? Booth must wait. Meantime, he would let events evolve naturally.

And so they seemed to do. Between 5:00 and 6:00 p.m., Booth brought the lively mare from Pumphrey's and left her in a stable he rented behind the theatre, according to plan. A little past 7:30, following several last-minute delays, the Lincoln carriage left the White House. About 9:00 p.m. Booth appeared at the rear door of the theatre, leading the mare he had rented. He asked Ned Spangler, a stage hand, to hold the horse for him. Spangler could not leave his post; instead he had J. L. DeBonay, another stage-hand, summon "Peanuts" Burroughs (a youth who ran errands at the theatre) to hold the reins. Booth then asked DeBonay if he could pass across the stage. This was during the "dairy scene," which is set deep, leaving no room to cross behind the scenery. DeBonay crossed under the stage with Booth on the basement level. Then Booth exited the theater and, through a passageway alongside, went out to 10th Street. He entered the Star Saloon and had a shot of whiskey.

About 10:00 p.m., after having looked into the lobby several times, he entered the theater through one of the front doors. James E. Buckingham, the doorman, automatically extended his hand for a ticket. "You don't need a ticket, Buck," Booth replied. He then proceeded up the stairs to the dress circle (Buckingham remembered that he was humming a tune), well aware that the third act—his act—was under way. Booth's luck continued there. The guard who normally occupied the chair outside the alcove back of the boxes was not in place. Now he needed only to pass unnoticed through the outer door, secure it behind him with a bar, slip into Box 7, and wait.

Booth's moment was approaching. Asa was now alone on the stage. The audience responded predictably to the comeuppance given the two fortune hunters; even Mrs. Lincoln's laughter was observed—at the very instant that a sharp, pistol-like report was heard. Dropping the single shot derringer, Booth hissed in measured tones to the occupants of the box: "sic semper tyrannis" ("thus always to tyrants"). Major Rathbone, Lincoln's guest for the evening, was the first to grasp what had happened. He lunged for Booth, who deflected the attack with a long Bowie knife, stabbing Rathbone twice.

Still taking advantage of the surprise and bewilderment, Booth jumped the eleven feet from the box to the stage—his almost perfect escape foiled when he caught his spur in one of the Treasury Flags, which caused him to land unevenly and fracture the tibia of his right leg. Before crossing the stage to the right exit, he uttered the final words he would proclaim from the stage: "Revenge for the South!" He now crossed the stage—a distance of about forty feet—swept past Laura Keene, who was standing beside the prompter's box, and rushed down the broad right passageway to the rear door. On his way he passed orchestra leader William Withers who, annoyed over Miss Keene's decision to postpone "Honor to Our Soldiers" until the end of the performance, was standing in the passage on stage right. Booth slashed Withers twice. He then bolted out the door, kicked aside "Peanuts" Burroughs, mounted, and rode off into the night.

The sequel to these events is well known. Panic reigned in the theatre as frantic efforts were made to save the president. Once the building was cleared, Lincoln was moved directly across 10th Street to the Petersen house, where he died the following morning at 7:22 a.m.

Booth, of course, fled immediately. His path carried him across the Navy Yard Bridge and into southern Maryland. Before being apprehended and shot on the morning of April 26 on the Garrett farm in Caroline County, Virginia (near Port

Royal) he had crossed two broad rivers and spent many days hiding in the Maryland swamps.

Overview of Biographical Sources

As might be expected, interest in Booth was intense in the wake of his assassination of Lincoln. It was satisfied initially by biographical material that was inaccurate and some that was calculated to achieve a sensational effect. An example of these early treatments is a series of articles by George Alfred Townsend (who used the pseudonym "Gath"), a correspondent for the New York *World*. These were subsequently issued in pamphlet form and, although offered as "Sketches of a Correspondent," they contained much incorrect information on Booth and the assassination—information which numerous biographers subsequently took at face value. Also, all manner of rumor found its way into print. For instance, the May 25, 1865, issue of *Frank Leslie's Illustrated Newspaper* carried on its cover an artist's rendering—entitled "Assassin's End"—which showed the body of Booth, covered and weighted, being lowered into the Potomac River.

Such false notions were subsequently corrected as time began to calm the hysteria surrounding the assassination and the events immediately following; however, in the aftermath passion frequently clouded reason. The three conspirators directly involved in the assassination plot were executed on July 7, 1865; but so was Mary Surratt, whose connection was speculative at best and for whom clemency was recommended. (Her innocence is staunchly defended to this day.) Therefore, the most reliable biographical studies have attempted to de-mythologize and to correct past errors with solid fact and rigorous deliberation. While no definitive biography exists, there are numerous sources that treat Booth's life in whole or in part. Not surprisingly, Booth as an individual is often depicted at the foreground of studies treating the sweeping tragedy of the assassination. Others, some of them first-hand accounts, treat individual aspects of his life.

However, two areas of debate persisted and have been emphasized in varying degrees by later nineteenth- and twentieth-century biographers: whether the man killed at Garrett's farm on April 26, 1865, was really John Wilkes Booth, and the exact nature of the assassination conspiracy—its size, its motives, and its sponsorship. The first, which received much attention around the turn of the century, is of less interest by far. Based upon the positive identification of Booth's body at numerous times following the Garrett episode by a host of reliable witnesses, and upon the highly suspect nature of the claimants who later said they were Booth, serious biographers attach virtually no credibility to the notion that Booth escaped and lived for decades following the assassination. However, the conspiracy of which Booth was a part is still debated, and additional facts continue to be uncovered. The essential question is whether the assassination plot was confined to Booth and three close collaborators or whether he—and in turn the other three—were acting for a larger and more powerful agent, such as the Confederate government. For, despite efforts to depict him as a rabid Southern sympathizer, Booth's political motivations and activities represent perhaps the most shadowy area of his life.

Evaluation of Principal Biographical Sources

Bates, Finis. *The Escape and Suicide of John Wilkes Booth*. Memphis: Historical Publishing, 1907. (**A, G**) Though discredited by serious historians, this account of a Booth pretender—one John St. Helen—suggests the kind of fantasizing that has clouded Booth biography.

Bryan, George S. *The Great American Myth*. New York: Carrick & Evans, 1940. (**A, G**) Methodically demythologizes many aspects of the assassination, its immediate aftermath, and Booth himself. While not attempting a full-scale biography, Bryan devotes two detailed chapters to Booth's life up to the week of the assassination, often correcting former errors and explaining why they were made.

Clarke, Asia Booth. *The Unlocked Book: A Memoir of John Wilkes Booth*. New York: Putnam, 1938. (**A, G**) This invaluable resource for all biographers includes the brief but indispensable memoir written in 1874, plus some ancillary documents written by others close to Booth.

Hanchett, William. *The Lincoln Murder Conspiracies*. Urbanna and Chicago: University of Illinois Press, 1983. (**A, G**) This ground-breaking study explores the larger social perspectives, as opposed to the personal motives, which prompted Booth to assassinate Lincoln.

Jones, Thomas A. *J. Wilkes Booth*. Chicago: Laird & Lee, 1893. (**A, G**) An account of Booth's escape from Maryland to Virginia written by the Confederate sympathizer who facilitated it. One of many brief first-hand accounts of key segments in Booth's life.

Kimmel, Stanley. *The Mad Booths of Maryland*. Indianapolis and New York: Bobbs-Merrill, 1940. (**A, G**) The best informed and the most comprehensive treatment of the Booth family.

Lewis, Lloyd. *Myths After Lincoln*. New York: Harcourt, Brace, 1929. (**A, G**) Discusses evolution of the demon-like image often assigned to Booth.

Mahoney, Ella V. *Sketches of Tudor Hall and the Booth Family*. Belair, MD: Tudor Hall, 1925. (**A, G**) An intimate sketch of the Booths and their country seat by a subsequent owner of the estate, who had known various family members. Though occasionally anecdotal, this work corrects many distortions.

Samples, Gordon. *Lust for Fame: The Stage Career of John Wilkes Booth*. Jefferson, NC: McFarland, 1982. (**A, G**) An exhaustive study of Booth's theatrical career, thoroughly researched and developed.

Tidwell, William A., et al. *Come Retribution: The Confederate Secret Service and the Assassination of Lincoln*. Jackson and London: University Press of Mississippi, 1988. (**A, G**) The most modern and thoroughly researched study of the conspiracy. Prepared over some ten years, this volume convincingly asserts that Booth was indeed an instrument of the Confederate secret service.

Weissman, Philip, M. D. "Why Booth Killed Lincoln, A Psychoanalytic Study of a Historical Tragedy." In *Psychological Studies of Famous Americans,* edited by Norman Kiell. New York: Twayne, 1964. (**A, G**) Though technical in method, Weissman develops a credible psychological theory comprehensible to the layman.

Wilson, Frances. *John Wilkes Booth—Fact and Fiction of Lincoln's Assassination*. New York: Houghton Mifflin, 1929. (**A, G**) Though not as thorough as Bryan, Wilson accomplishes many of the same corrective results.

Museums, Historical Landmarks, Societies

Dr. Samuel Mudd Museum (Waldorf, MD). The home of the doctor who set Booth's broken leg hours after the assassination.

Ford's Theatre Museum (Washington, DC). This building has been restored to its appearance on the night of the assassination. Displays many artifacts relating to the assassination.

Petersen House (Washington, DC). Directly across the street from Ford's Theatre. The room where Lincoln died is authentically appointed and open to the public.

Surratt House and Tavern (Clinton, MD). A museum in the house occupied by the Surratt family prior to their moving to Washington, D.C.; contains a visitor center and research library.

Tudor Hall (Belair, MD). The country house of the Booth family. Though currently a private residence, efforts are underway for conversion into a museum.

Fiction and Adaptations

Booth, of course, figures in almost every account, fictional or cinematic, about Lincoln, but there is one novel in which he is the central character, Philip Van Doren Stern's *The Man Who Killed Lincoln* (1939). One of the earliest films that recreates the assassination in D. W. Griffith's *Birth of a Nation* (1915); one of the most recent is Kenneth Burns's PBS documentary, *The Civil War* (1990).

Other Sources

Gutman, Richard J. S., and Kellie O. Gutman. *John Wilkes Booth Himself*. Dover, MA: Hired Hand Press, 1979. The first book to treat all the known photographs of Booth, all of which (some four dozen) are reproduced.

Kunhardt, Dorothy Meserve, and Philip B. Kunhardt, Jr. *Twenty Days: A Narrative in Text and Pictures of the Assassination of Abraham Lincoln and the Twenty Days and Nights that Followed*. New York: Castle Books, 1965. A rich collection of period photographs of people and events from the assassination through Lincoln's entombment. Accompanied by a detailed and evocative text.

Taylor, Welford Dunaway, ed. *Our American Cousin: The Play That Changed History*. Washington, DC: Beacham Publishing, 1990. The extensive introduction to the play being performed when Lincoln was assassinated traces Booth's actions on the day of the assassination and explains how Booth's affiliation with Ford's Theater facilitated his plot.

Welford Dunaway Taylor
University of Richmond

JIM BRIDGER
1804-1881

Chronology

Born Felix James Bridger on March 17, 1804, in Richmond, Virginia, the oldest of three children of James Felix, an innkeeper and surveyor, and Chloe Bridger; *1812* moves with his family to an Illinois farm outside St. Louis; *1817* orphaned and left to care for his sister and maiden aunt; works on a ferryboat; *1817-1822* works as an apprentice blacksmith in St. Louis; *1822* becomes the youngest member of William H. Ashley's fur trapping brigade; *1824* is one of the first white men to go over South Pass; discovers the Great Salt Lake; *1825* attends first rendezvous on Green River to trade furs for supplies; tells incredulous trappers of his discovery of the Yellowstone region; *1826-1829* continues to trap for furs; *1830* with partners buys out trapping company and forms the Rocky Mountain Fur Company; *1832* wounded in battle with Blackfeet, but recovers; *1834* dissolves Rocky Mountain Fur Company; *c. 1835* marries Flathead woman (who dies in 1845 after bearing three children); *1839* returns briefly to St. Louis; *1840* attends last rendezvous; trade shifts to buffalo hides; *1843* with partner Louis Vasquez builds Fort Bridger to supply pioneers on their passage west; *c. 1847* marries Ute woman (who dies in 1849 giving birth to a daughter); *1850* marries Shoshoni woman (dies c. 1858) and moves family to farm near Santa Fe, Missouri (present day Kansas City); *1851* attends Treaty Council at Ft. Laramie; *1853* flees Ft. Bridger before Mormons have him arrested for illicit trade with the Indians; returns to Missouri; *1854* disputes the Mormons' claim that they have bought Ft. Bridger; *1855* guides Sir George Gore's big game safari out West; *1857-1858* guides the U.S. Army during the Utah War; *1859-1860* guides army exploration of headwaters of the Yellowstone and Missouri rivers; *1861* leads engineers in their search for a shorter route for stagecoach lines and the Pony Express; *1862-1863* works as a guide for the army; *1864* guides miners to Montana; *1865* guides army in the Powder River area and plots line for the Union Pacific Railroad; *1866-1867* scouts for Colonel Henry B. Carrington while Ft. Phil Kearney is built; *1868* retires to Missouri and lives with daughter; *1875* goes totally blind; *1881* dies at the age of seventy-seven on July 17; is buried on his farm, but in 1904 his body is transported to Mount Washington Cemetery in Kansas City where a monument is erected in his memory.

Activities of Historical Significance

Jim Bridger, fur trapper, explorer, guide, and army scout, was a legend in the early West. A true frontiersman, he lived by his own wits in the dangerous wilderness. Known for his geographical genius, he could draw a map of a region that he had passed through years earlier complete with every valley, creek, and hill. His memory of detailed reconnaissance coupled with his honesty and integrity earned him the respect of both Native American and white contemporaries.

Bridger was one of the first white men to journey through South Pass and he discovered the Great Salt Lake. He was foremost in describing the wonders of the Yellowstone Park area, although his tales of geysers and hot springs were not believed for many years. His expertise in the geography of the Rocky Mountains helped him find a shorter route for the Union Pacific Railroad.

Married to three Native-American women, Bridger knew the traditions of various tribes and could speak almost twelve different Indian languages. Although sympathetic to the Native-American way of life, he foresaw the end of their tribal nomadic existence, as he did the end of his own fur trapping days, resulting from the westward expansion of settlers. He interpreted for the Native Americans at the Ft. Laramie Peace Council and later scouted for the U.S. Army.

Overview of Biographical Sources

The first account of Bridger's life, *Biographical Sketch of James Bridger* (1905), was written by his friend and employer, Major General Grenville M. Dodge, who paid for the seven-foot monument erected at the frontiersman's burial site. Dodge recounts events that Bridger had told him in addition to his own recollections of his friend's life.

J. Cecil Alter's compilation and interpretation of sources concerning Bridger's career was first published as *James Bridger, Trapper, Frontiersman, Scout and Guide* (1950), and was the definitive biography for years. In 1962 he updated the volume, which still remains the premier biography.

Noted historian Stanley Vestal researched primary sources for his biography, *Jim Bridger, Mountain Man* (1946), yet he relies heavily on the original Alter volume. The two historians differ on their accounts of the popular story of Hugh Glass and the grizzly bear. The account has Bridger finally leaving the badly wounded Glass to die after staying with him for days in hostile Indian country. While Alter can not definitely place Bridger at the scene, Vestal does.

Gene Caesar's *King of the Mountain Man; The Life of Jim Bridger* (1961) is a general narrative that includes detailed descriptions. Vestal's volume falls into the popular category because his style of writing includes the use of dialect.

Evaluation of Principal Biographical Sources

Alter, J. Cecil. *Jim Bridger*. Rev. ed. Norman: University of Oklahoma Press, 1979. (A, G) This definitive biography of the frontiersman is written in an easy-to-read style, yet it maintains a scholarly approach. A careful bibliography and footnotes are included.

Caesar, Gene. *King of the Mountain Men; The Life of Jim Bridger*. New York: Dutton, 1961. (G) Uses source material for a popular narrative of Bridger's life. Describes the West in realistic detail and provides a bibliography.

Dahlquist, Laura. *Meet Jim Bridger*. Torrington, WY: n.p., 1948. (G) This thirty-eight-page pamphlet gives a brief history of Bridger and his trading post on the Green River's Black's Fork.

Dodge, Grenville M. *Biographical Sketch of James Bridger: Mountaineer, Trapper and Guide*. New York: Unz, 1905. (A, G) Dodge, chief engineer for the Union Pacific Railroad who hired Bridger to chart a railroad route through the Black Hills, chronicles Bridger's life in a twenty-seven-page book. Based on Bridger's accounts of events and on his own time spent with the mountain man.

Honig, Louis O. *James Bridger, the Pathfinder of the West*. Kansas City, MO: Brown-White-Lowell Press, 1951. (G) Part of the It Happened in America Series; includes a bibliography.

Vestal, Stanley. *Jim Bridger, Mountain Man*. 1946. Reprint. Lincoln: University of Nebraska Press, 1970. (A, G) Presents a well-documented appraisal of the famous mountain man. Especially well rendered is the section on Bridger's guiding and advising the U.S. Army. Provides notes and bibliography.

Wheeler, Keith. *The Scouts*. Alexandria, VA: Time-Life Books, 1978. (G) Contains a brief biography of Bridger and calls him one of the most trusted and respected of scouts. Frontispiece is a photo of Bridger taken in his later years.

Evaluation of Biographies for Young People

Allen, Merrit Parmalee. *Western Star: A Story of Jim Bridger*. New York: Longmans, Green, 1941. Interweaves geography and adventure in relating the Bridger story for ages ten to thirteen.

Anderson, Anita Melva. *Fur Trappers of the Old West*. Chicago: Wheeler, 1946. Bridger's story is told with dialogue sprinkled throughout. Illustrated by Jack Merryweather and told on a fourth-grade reading level.

Garst, Shannon. *Jim Bridger*. Boston: Houghton Mifflin, 1952. Written for the fifth- through seventh-grade reader, this account contains fictionalized conversation. An excellent map and illustrations by William Moyers supplement the narrative.

Grant, Matthew G. *Jim Bridger, The Mountain Man*. Mankato, MN: Creative Education, 1974. Illustrated by Nancy Inderieden, this volume on the second-grade level is part of the Frontiersmen of America Series.

Fleischman, Sid. *Jim Bridger's Alarm Clock and Other Tall Tales*. New York: Dutton, 1978. Tells three tall tales about Bridger and several of his unbelievable discoveries in the West.

Jones, Evan. *Trappers and Mountain Men*. New York: American Heritage Publishing, 1961. Part of the American Heritage Junior Library, this volume presents a comprehensive overview of life in the Rockies. A brief biography of Bridger is included. Pictures, drawings, and maps complement this book for junior high and high school students.

Kelsey, Vera. *Young Men So Daring; Fur Traders Who Carried the Frontier West*. Indianapolis: Bobbs-Merrill, 1956. Contains four biographies (Peter Pond, Manuel Liza, John Jacob Astor, and Jim Bridger) for the junior high reader.

Kherdian, David. *Bridger: The Story of a Mountain Man*. New York: Greenwillow Books, 1987. Like most juvenile biographies, this work contains dialogue to heighten its interest for children. Written for grades seven through nine, the book is well researched and gives a sense of the hardship and adventure in the West.

Luce, Willard, and Celia Luce. *Jim Bridger, Man of the Mountains*. 1966. Reprint. New York: Chelsea House, 1991. A Discovery Book for the second and third grades, illustrated by George I. Parrish.

Tousey, Sanford. *Jim Bridger, American Frontiersman*. Chicago: Albert Whitman, 1952. An incisive book for ages nine to twelve.

Winders, Gertrude Hecker. *Jim Bridger, Mountain Boy*. Indianapolis: Bobbs-Merrill, 1962. Part of the Childhood of Famous Americans Series, this volume is written on the third- to fifth-grade reading level. Illustrated by Robert Doremus.

Overview and Evaluation of Primary Sources

Jim Bridger could neither read nor write, but he made such an impression, that his role in western expansion is highlighted in the memoirs and journals of his contemporaries.

James Clyman, *James Clyman, American Frontiersman* (1928. Reprint. Portland, OR: Champoeg Press, 1960; **A, G**), accompanied Bridger on his first trip West. Nathaniel J. Wyeth, *Correspondence and Journals of Nathaniel J. Wyeth* (Eugene, OR: University Press, 1899; **A, G**), contains an account of the Battle of Pierre's Hole, which he witnessed. Rev. Samuel Parker, *Journal of an Exploring Tour Beyond the Rocky Mountains in 1835* (Ithaca, NY: Andrus, Woodruff & Gauntlett, 1844; **A, G**), attended the Green River rendezvous and briefly joined Bridger's expeditions. Kit Carson, *Carson's Own Story of His Life* (Taos: [n.p.], 1926; **A, G**), recounts many episodes with his good friend Jim Bridger. John C. Fremont, *Report of the Exploring Expedition to the Rocky Mountains . . . 1842 and to Oregon . . . 1843-44* (Washington: Gales and Seaton, 1845; **A, G**), relates events in Bridger's life as they crossed his own.

Washington Irving recounts the journals of Captain Benjamin L. E. Bonneville in *The Adventures of Captain Bonneville* (1835. Reprint. Norman: University of Oklahoma Press, 1986; **A, G**). Bonneville respected Bridger as a giant among mountain men. Father Pierre Jean De Smet, *Life, Letters, and Travels of Pierre Jean De Smet* (New York: F. P. Harper, 1905; **A, G**), recorded his indebtedness to Bridger for reliable information about routes.

Although the Mormon Papers are not available to the public, William Clayton's *Journal, 1846-1847* (Salt Lake City: Clayton Family Association, 1921; **A, G**), chronicles Bridger's encounters with the Mormons.

Bridger's role in establishing Ft. Kearny has been recounted by both Henry B. Carrington, *History of Indian Operations on the Plains: Hearings Before Special Commission* (Fort McPherson, NE: [n.p.], 1867; **A, G**), and his wife Margaret Carrington, *Ab-Sa-Ra-Ka (Home of the Crows): The Land of Massacre* (Philadelphia: J. B. Lippincott, 1869; **A, G**).

Major General Grenville M. Dodge's biography is based on conversations with Bridger and his own knowledge of the explorer. Although there are a few gaps in the narrative of Bridger's life, these contemporaries and others corroborate each others' stories, thus separating fact from legend.

Fiction and Adaptations

The history of the West lends itself to larger-than-life heroes who explored the untamed land. Through written and oral reports of those who knew Bridger, his fame spread, and novelist Ned Buntline exaggerated Bridger's adventures in the dime novels that were so popular in the nineteenth century.

Movies about westward expansion that feature Bridger include: *Jim Bridger's Indian Bride* (1910), *The Covered Wagon* (1923), *Kit Carson* (1928), *Kit Carson* (1940), *Tomahawk* (1950), *The Pony Express* (1952), and *The Gun That Won the West* (1955).

Television has not neglected the great mountain man. *Bridger* (1976) stars James Wainwright as Bridger; *The Incredible Rocky Mountain Race* (1977) features Jack Kruschen as Bridger; and *Centennial* (1978), a seven-part miniseries, includes Bridger in its account of the settlement of the West.

Museums, Historical Landmarks, Societies

Bridger, Montana and *Bridger, South Dakota*. Both of these towns were named for the explorer, as were the *Bridger Mountains* (central WY) and the *Bridger Range* (north of Bozeman, MT).

The Bridger Wilderness (near Pinedale, WY). Administered by the U.S. Forest Service, the Bridger Wilderness was designated by Congress as part of the National Wilderness preservation system in 1964. The area is approximately seventy-five miles long (on the west slope of the Wind River Range) and fifteen miles wide.

Bridger's Pass (southwestern WY). The pass is lined on both sides by 2,000 foot cliffs. The Pony Express and regular mail stages used the pass beginning in 1862.

Bridger's Peak (the Gallatin Range in Gallatin County, MT). The peak stands 9,000 feet above sea level.

Fort Bridger State Museum (Fort Bridger, WY). The museum is housed in the former enlisted men's barracks and contains Native-American and U.S. army artifacts, and the fort's history.

Jefferson National Expansion Memorial (St. Louis, MO). A 1,600 volume library on westward expansion is housed in the Old Courthouse (1839-1864). A portrait of Bridger and a drawing of his fort hang in the museum.

South Pass City State Historical Site (South Pass City, WY). Twenty-two authentic buildings and a museum feature the history of the Oregon Trail.

Other Sources

Cleland, Robert G. *This Reckless Breed of Men; The Trappers and Fur Traders of the Southwest.* 1950. Reprint. Albuquerque: University of New Mexico Press, 1976. This volume offers a vivid picture of the hardships that Bridger and other mountain men endured in their quest for better trapping grounds. Based on contemporary sources, the book contains a bibliography and an adequate index.

De Voto, Bernard A. *Across the Wide Missouri.* 1947. Reprint. New York: AMS Press, 1983. This carefully researched volume, which covers the years 1832 to 1838, is invaluable in understanding the passion behind the mountain men involved in the fur trade. Illustrations by artist Alfred Jacob Miller capture the flavor of the West. Notes and a bibliography document the book.

Driggs, Howard R. *The Old West Speaks.* Englewood Cliffs, NJ: Prentice-Hall, 1956. An accurate history, often told in the words of the settlers who crossed the plains, this volume deserves a place in any library about the old West. Paintings by William Henry Jackson record the history of the country.

————. *Westward America.* New York: G. P. Putnam, 1942. This volume features a chapter on Fort Bridger, combining its history with firsthand observations from pioneers who stopped there. Reproductions of forty watercolors by William Henry Jackson complement the text.

Phillips, Paul Christler. *The Fur Trade.* Norman: University of Oklahoma Press, 1961. Phillips died before completing the two volumes, therefore, concluding chapters were written by his associate J. W. Smurr. Nearly every major trading company and brigade of trappers are detailed according to operations, successes, and failures.

Rawling, Gerald. *The Pathfinders.* New York: Macmillan, 1964. This general history details the lives of the men who explored the West. The author calls Bridger "the senior professor of wilderness technique."

Russell, Carl P. *Firearms, Traps, & Tools of the Mountain Men.* New York: Knopf, 1967. This comprehensive study of the ironworks of the mountain men helps the reader understand the hardships these men endured. Drawings of several of Bridger's traps and tools are featured. The bibliography is extensive.

Ruth, Kent. *Great Day in the West: Forts, Posts and Rendezvous Beyond the Mississippi.* Norman: University of Oklahoma Press, 1963. This book gives a brief history of Fort Bridger. Pictures and photographs enhance the volume.

Sandoz, Mari. *The Beaver Men, Spearheads of Empire.* New York: Hastings House, 1964. For background on the beaver trade, this panoramic account is authoritative and complete, covering two-and-a-half centuries of trade and exploration.

Vestal, Stanley. *Mountain Men.* 1937. Reprint. Freeport, NY: Books for Libraries Press, 1969. The summer auction of furs at the rendezvous is described with vivid realism. Vestal gives accounts of episodes in the lives of Bridger, Hugh Glass, Jedediah Smith, John Colter, and Old Bill Williams.

Wishart, David J. *The Fur Trade of the American West, 1807-1840: A Geographical Synthesis.* Lincoln: University of Nebraska Press, 1979. Geographer Wishart presents the biological, geological, and cultural impact of the fur trade in the United States.

Veda Jones

GWENDOLYN BROOKS
b. 1917

Chronology

Born on June 7, 1917, in Topeka, Kansas, to David and Keziah Brooks; moves to Chicago with her family at the age of five weeks; educated in the Chicago public schools, attending three different high schools; *1936* graduates from Wilson Junior College; *1939* marries Henry Blakely, a fellow black Chicago poet; *1940* her son, Henry, Jr., is born on October 10; *1941* attends poetry workshop sponsored by Inez Stark in Chicago, where she develops her technical skills; *1943* wins the Midwestern Writers' Conference Poetry Award in Chicago; *1945* publishes *A Street in Bronzeville* to great public acclaim; *1948* writes reviews of poetry and novels for Chicago newspapers; *1949* publishes her second volume of poetry, *Annie Allen,* her most experimental verse; *1946-1950* awarded grants from the American Academy of Arts and Letters and the National Academy of Arts and Letters, two Guggenheim fellowships, and the Pulitzer Prize for Poetry; *1951* her daughter, Nora, is born on September 8; *1953* publishes her only novel, *Maud Martha,* a study of a young black girl coming of age in a racist atmosphere; *1956* publishes *Bronzeville Boys and Girls*; *1960* publishes *The Bean Eaters,* an examination of contemporary socio-political issues; *1963* accepts her first teaching position at Chicago's Columbia College; *1964-1971* receives honorary doctorate degrees from over fourteen universities and colleges; *1967* attends the Black Writers' Conference at Fisk University and is politically awakened to the black protest movement; *1968* publishes *In the Mecca* and *Riot*; *1968* named poet-laureate of Illinois; *1969* receives a "stirring tribute" from black artists of Chicago, later published as *To Gwen, With Love*; *1970* publishes *Family Pictures*; *1971* publishes *A Broadside Treasury: 1965-1970*; visits East Africa; publishes *Aloneness*; suffers a mild heart attack and retires from teaching; *1972* publishes autobiography *Report from Part One*; *1974* publishes *The Tiger Who Wore White Gloves*; *1975* publishes *Beckonings*; *1980* publishes *Primer for Blacks* and *Young Poet's Primer*; *1981* publishes *To Disembark*; *1983* publishes *Mayor Harold Washington and Chicago, the I Will City*; *1985* appointed poetry consultant to the Library of Congress; *1986* publishes *The Near-Johannesburg Boy and Other Poems,* dedicated to the students of the Gwendolyn Brooks Junior High School; *1987* represents the Chicago black community at "A Tribute to the Bicentennial of the Constitution" at the Supreme Court of Illinois; speaks at the Third World Press's "Twentieth Anniversary Conference on Literature and Society" at Chicago

State University; elected an honorary fellow of the Modern Language Association; *1988* publishes *Gottschalk and the Grande Tarantelle* and *Winnie,* a poem about Winnie Mandela and apartheid.

Activities of Historical Significance

Gwendolyn Brooks's substantial literary achievements reflect a growing social concern for the voices of otherwise suppressed and silent minorities—particularly those of African-American women. In her position as poet-laureate of Illinois, Brooks articulated the miseries of African-American citizens caused by urban poverty and institutionalized discrimination. Further, she instituted poetry workshops and contests for black high school students in order to encourage young talent. By editing collections of African-American poetry, such as *Jump Bad: A New Chicago Anthology* (1971), Brooks has provided exposure to an entire generation of young black poets.

Brooks's achievements have been recognized and appreciated by a remarkably diversified group of critics and readers. Most critics approach her work as an amalgamation of the concerns and techniques of three great twentieth-century poets: Langston Hughes, Carl Sandburg, and Robert Frost. She learned how to express the rhythms of black speech from Hughes; she learned the poetic response to complex social problems from Sandburg; and she mastered intricate poetic forms practiced by Frost. But she is in no way an imitator of anyone's work, and critics who compare her to her predecessors do so in admiration. Her Pulitzer Prize, awarded in 1950 for *Annie Allen,* and the dozens of honorary doctorate degrees awarded to her attest to the widespread appreciation of her work and her importance in American literature.

Although Brooks has always written about the plight of minorities, her mastery of high poetic form has caused her to be identified more with the literary establishment than with minority voices. During the 1960s, when "street poetry" emerged as the voice of black expression, Brooks continued to write in traditional forms. In 1967, however, after attending the Black Writer's Conference at Fisk University, she realized the political importance of identifying herself with the black caucus. She switched publishers, from the prestigious Harper & Row, who had published her first five books, including her Pulitzer Prize collection, to black-owned, small Detroit presses. She began to work for the recognition of young black poets, and to assure that predominantly white critics would take their work seriously. While other established black poets focused on the social and political power of black art, Brooks focused on the acceptance of poets as artists, as well as voices for minority causes. As a result of her aesthetic objectivity combined with her profound insights into human experience, Brooks's artistic reputation is assured.

Overview of Biographical Sources

The first book-length biographical and critical portrait of Brooks was Harry B. Shaw's brief study *Gwendolyn Brooks* (1980). Although this work is serviceable, it has been vastly surpassed by George Kent, *A Life of Gwendolyn Brooks* (1990), a full-scale biography, and D. H. Melhelm, *Gwendolyn Brooks: Poetry and the Heroic Voice* (1987). Maria Mootry and Gary Smith's volume, *A Life Distilled: Gwendolyn Brooks, Her Poetry and Fiction* (1987), contains a valuable biographical essay.

Evaluation of Principal Biographical Sources

Kent, George. *A Life of Gwendolyn Brooks*. Lexington: University Press of Kentucky, 1990. (A, G) Actually completed in 1982, this biography was written with Brooks's cooperation and assistance. It is more in the genre of appreciation, and less informed by literary concerns than Melham's work. It covers Brooks's life through 1978.

Melhelm, D. H. *Gwendolyn Brooks: Poetry and the Heroic Voice*. Lexington: University Press of Kentucky, 1987. (A) Contains a biographical treatment, as well as discussions of her poetry and prose. Melhelm claims that Brooks's stature is based on her identity as a "heroic epic poet" of the American black experience.

Mootry, Maria, and Gary Smith, eds. *A Life Distilled: Gwendolyn Brooks, Her Poetry and Fiction*. Urbana: University of Illinois Press, 1987. (A) A collection of contemporary essays on the life, poetry, and prose of Brooks. Contains an extensive bibliography of primary and secondary sources and a biographical overview.

Shaw, Harry B. *Gwendolyn Brooks*. Boston: Twayne, 1980. (A, G) Presents a short biography and discusses Brooks's works as they conform to a pattern found throughout her work: death, the fall from glory, the labyrinth, and survival.

Overview and Evaluation of Primary Sources

Brooks has published sixteen volumes of poetry from *A Street in Bronzeville* (New York: Harper & Brothers, 1945) to *Winnie* (Chicago: David, 1988). She has collected much of her early verse in *The World of Gwendolyn Brooks* (New York:

Harper & Row, 1971; **G**), *Blacks* (Chicago: David, 1987; **G**), and *Selected Poems* (New York: Harper & Row, 1963; **G**). Her early volumes—the *Bronzeville* poems, *Annie Allen* (New York: Harper & Brothers, 1949) and *Bean Eaters* (New York: Harper & Brothers, 1960)—are generally considered to be assimilationist, advocating integration as the solution for the black condition in urban America. The works written after Brooks's 1967 political awakening—*In the Mecca* (New York: Harper & Row, 1968), *Riot* (Detroit: Broadside, 1969), *Aloneness* (Detroit: Broadside, 1971), and *Beckonings* (Detroit: Broadside, 1975)—express anger and advocate militancy. Her latest work, *Winnie*, attacks the international nature of racism, as institutionalized by apartheid in South Africa.

Maud Martha (New York: Harper & Brothers, 1953), Brooks's one attempt at a novel, is generally considered to be only of mild interest or literary value. More recently Brooks has attempted to share her teaching interest in three volumes, *A Capsule Course in Black Poetry Writing* (Detroit: Broadside, 1975; **G**), *Young Poet's Primer* (Chicago: Brooks, 1980; **G**), and *Very Young Poets* (Chicago: Brooks, 1983; **G**). Brooks's autobiography, *Report from Part One* (Detroit: Broadside, 1972), is a valuable source of information for her early, formative years.

Fiction and Adaptations

Giovanni's "To Gwen Brooks from Nikki Giovanni" can be found in *Essence* (1 [April 1971]: 26). Michael S. Harper's "Madimba; Gwendolyn Brooks" is a poem written in honor of Brooks's contributions to black culture (used as frontispiece to *A Life Distilled*, above). Haki Madhubuti (Don L. Lee) edited an anthology in tribute to Brooks's seventieth birthday, *Say That the River Turns: The Impact of Gwendolyn Brooks*. The volume contains numerous poems, prose pieces, and reminiscences by black writer-colleagues and members of Brooks's family. The volume *To Gwen, With Love: An Anthology Dedicated to Gwendolyn Brooks*, (1971) edited by Patricia Brown, Don L. Lee, and Francis Ward contains a number of personal tributes to the poet.

Museums, Historical Landmarks, Societies

National Women's Hall of Fame (Seneca Falls, NY). The exhibit on Brooks includes a recording of the poetry reading she gave at her induction into the Hall of Fame.

Other Sources

Christian, Barbara. *Black Feminist Criticism: Perspectives on Black Women Writers*. Elmsford, NY: Pergamon, 1985.

Evans, Mari, ed. *Black Women Writers: A Critical Evaluation, 1950-1980.* New York: Anchor, 1984.

Furman, Marva R. "Gwendolyn Brooks: The 'Unconditioned' Poet." *College Language Arts Journal* 17 (September 1973): 1-10.

Gilbert, Sandra M., and Susan Gubar, eds. *Shakespeare's Sisters: Feminist Essays on Women Poets.* Bloomington: Indiana University Press, 1979.

Hansell, William H. "The Poet-Militant and Foreshadowings of a Black Mystique: Poems in the Second Period of Brooks." *Concerning Poetry* 10 (1977): 37-45.

Harris, Victoria. "The Voice of Gwendolyn Brooks." *Interpretations* 11 (1979): 55-66.

Hudson, Clenora. "Racial Themes in the Poetry of Brooks." *College Language Association Journal* 17 (1973): 16-20.

Lattin, P. H., and V. E. Lattin. "Dual Vision in Brooks' *Maud Martha.*" *Critique* 25 (1984): 180-188.

Miller, R. Baxter, ed. *Langston Hughes and Gwendolyn Brooks: A Reference Guide.* Boston: G. K. Hall, 1978.

Smith, Gary. "Brooks' *A Street in Bronzeville,* the Harlem Renaissance, and the Mythologies of Black Women." *Meleus* 9 (1983): 33-46.

Wade-Gayles, Gloria. *No Crystal Stair: Visions of Race and Sex in Black Women's Fiction.* New York: Pilgrim, 1984.

Washington, Mary Helen. " 'Taming All That Anger Down': Rage and Silence in Brooks' *Maud Martha.*" *Massachusetts Review* 24 (1983): 453-466.

Williams, Gladys M. "Brooks' Way with the Sonnet." *College Language Association Journal* 26 (1982): 215-240.

Diane Long Hoeveler
Marquette University

BUFFALO BILL
1846-1917

Chronology

Born William Frederick Cody on February 26, 1846, on a farm near Le Claire in Scott County, Iowa, the third of seven children of Mary Ann Bonsell Laycock Cody, a housewife and former teacher, and Isaac Cody, a Canadian-born pioneer, itinerant businessman, and unsuccessful farmer, who traced his lineage to colonial Massachusetts and claimed one child by an earlier marriage; *1853-1854* moves with his family first to Weston, Missouri, and then to Salt Creek Valley, near Leavenworth, Kansas Territory; *1857* works for Majors and Russell—later Majors, Russell, and Waddell—in Leavenworth following the death of his father, who had been wounded three years earlier while espousing anti-slavery views; *1857-1864* continues as an employee of the firm, first as a messenger boy and later as driver and wagon-master of freight expeditions west; *1862* serves temporarily with the Ninth Kansas Volunteer Cavalry Regiment as guide and scout in a campaign against the Kiowa and Comanche; *1864* after·a drinking spree joins the Seventh Kansas Volunteer Cavalry Regiment (the notorious "Jennison's Jay-hawkers") and fights in Tennessee, Mississippi, and Missouri; *1866* marries Louisa Frederici of St. Louis, and returns to Salt Creek Valley where he briefly runs a hotel; *1867-1868* serves as a hunter for Goddard Brothers, which supplies food for the Kansas Pacific Railroad; claims to have killed 4,280 buffalo and earns the sobriquet, "Buffalo Bill"; *1868-1872* acts as a scout, guide, and dispatch rider for the U.S. Army, engaging in battles with Native Americans and winning the Congressional Medal of Honor; leads hunting expeditions, including that of Grand Duke Alexis of Russia; *1869* meets Ned Buntline (Edward Zane Carroll Judson) who writes *Buffalo Bill, King of the Border Men*, the first of many dime novels about him; *1872* journeys to Chicago with Buntline and begins his stage career portraying himself in *Scouts of the Prairie*; *1873-1883* divides his time between the East, scouting for the military, and guiding celebrities in the West; becomes involved in the Great Sioux War, killing the Cheyenne subchief, Yellow Hand (actually Yellow Hair), in 1876; *1883* with Dr. William F. Carver and Major John M. Burke organizes Buffalo Bill's Wild West, a show that proves phenomenally popular but a weak financial undertaking; *1884-1907* continues the show with Nate Salsbury as his partner and plays several times in Europe, appearing before several monarchs and at Queen Victoria's Diamond Jubilee; *1907-1909* operates the show without a partner after Salsbury's death; *1909-1912* merges his show with Pawnee

Bill's show, forming a troupe that becomes popularly known as the "Two Bills Show"; *1912-1915* following a brief retirement enters into what becomes a financial debacle with the Sells-Floto Circus proprietors; *1916* works on salary and commission for the Miller & Arlington 101 Ranch Wild West; *1917* dies in Denver, Colorado, on January 10 and is interred on Lookout Mountain, near Golden, on June 3.

Activities of Historical Significance

Most legends are created by others after a person's death, but Buffalo Bill played a major role in inventing his own. He was a man of many accomplishments, and, as an admiring relative put it, "the last of the great scouts." He was at times an Indian fighter, cowboy, Union soldier, hunter, horseman, covered wagon and stagecoach driver, dime novelist, actor, showman, and entrepreneur. The sum of these activities, when coupled with reams of publicity, made him a living legend.

Left to his own care as a youth, Cody received only a spotty formal education, but quickly demonstrated frontier individualism and wanderlust. After trying a number of jobs, including military service during the Civil War, he gained fame by killing buffalo to feed hungry construction workers on the Kansas Pacific Railroad. The number of animals that he killed is disputed, but it was far fewer than the number slaughtered by buffalo hunters who decimated the herds for their pelts. Nevertheless, he became "Buffalo Bill," or at least the one that most people remembered. A jingle of the time expressed it best:

> Buffalo Bill, Buffalo Bill,
> Never missed and never will;
> Always aims and shoots to kill
> And the company pays his buffalo bill.

Despite his nickname, the most important job Cody had on the frontier was as an army scout. Military officers who served with him regularly noted his unerring judgment of distance, location, and direction; his memory of topography; and his remarkable ability to track. His most famous involvement as a scout was in the Great Sioux War of the mid-1870s, the uprising that witnessed "Custer's Last Stand." In July 1876, about one month after the Custer disaster, Cody, having just returned from the East, was scouting for the Fifth U.S. Cavalry when he and a few members of the troop happened upon a small band of Cheyenne braves led by Yellow Hand (Yellow Hair). No one is certain why Buffalo Bill and Yellow Hand charged each other, but they did, and Cody killed the sub-chief. This episode soon became a centerpiece of the Buffalo Bill legend.

Other than Cody himself, Ned Buntline is the person most responsible for the Buffalo Bill legend. He met Cody in 1869 and that same year published the first dime novel about him. Many more were to follow. Buntline co-wrote, with Cody, the first play in which he appeared, an incongruous drama entitled *The Scouts of the Prairie; or Red Deviltry As It Is*, which premiered at the Nixon Amphitheater in Chicago in December 1872.

Buffalo Bill, however, provided a dimension to his myth that other legends lacked—the wild west show, which he launched in the 1880s. He organized an "Old Glory Blow Out" for the 1882 Fourth of July celebration in North Platte, Nebraska, an event that initiated the modern rodeo and influenced his western show. In 1883 he started Buffalo Bill's Wild West, a romanticized, dramatic version of frontier days in the trans-Mississippi West. Naturally, stories of Cody's exploits—such as the killing of Yellow Hand and the 1869 Battle of Summit Springs, Colorado—were given prominence, but also included were episodes not drawn from Cody's experience, such as riding for the Pony Express.

Buffalo Bill's Wild West show and his early dramas are often considered as the beginning of the "western" as it evolved in movies, radio shows, and television productions. As the prototype of the western hero, Cody greatly influenced standard western characterizations and plots (in which courageous cowboys regularly chased badmen and engaged them in shootouts and hand-to-hand combat). Even his hairstyle, dress, and size (he was tall and lean) became standard in early movies. In recognition of Cody's seminal importance, Wayne Michael Sarf entitled his fine study of western movies, *God Bless You, Buffalo Bill: A Layman's Guide to History and the Western Film*. By the end of the first quarter of the twentieth century, William F. Cody embodied the essence of the "westerner" for the majority of the American people.

Overview of Biographical Sources

Buffalo Bill was probably the most discussed western frontiersman in American history. There exist countless biographies, and he is mentioned in an overwhelming number of magazine and newspaper articles, collected biographies, and monographs concerning the West.

Frank E. Bliss's *William F. Cody, Known as Buffalo Bill* (1879) is considered the first authentic biography, but until the publication of Richard J. Walsh's *The Making of Buffalo Bill* (1928), all biographies of Cody were suspect, depending as they did on either promotional hype or the 557 dime novels written about Buffalo

Bill. Only in the last three decades have reliable biographies appeared. The best and perhaps the definitive work is Don Russell's *The Lives and Legends of Buffalo Bill* (1960), but Nellie Yost's *Buffalo Bill, His Family, Friends, Fame, Failures, and Fortunes* (1979) and Joseph G. Rosa and Robin May's *Buffalo Bill and His Wild West, A Pictorial Biography* (1989) are excellent treatments.

In recent years, a great many articles in scholarly journals have added significantly to the body of knowledge on Buffalo Bill. Although some debunking literature exists, it has never been particularly significant.

Evaluation of Principal Biographical Sources

Blackstone, Sarah J. *Buckskins, Bullets and Business: A History of Buffalo Bill's Wild West*. Westport, CT: Greenwood, 1986. (A) This short, clear discussion contends that the Wild West show—along with dime novels and movies—must be understood if one is to form an accurate picture of the Buffalo Bill legend and the American West.

Bliss, Frank E. *William F. Cody, Known as Buffalo Bill, the Famous Hunter, Scout, and Guide*. Hartford, CT: F. E. Bliss, 1879. (A) Earliest authentic biography of Cody, based on interviews and newspaper stories.

[Brooklyn Museum; Museum of Art, Carnegie Institute; and Buffalo Bill Historical Center]. *Buffalo Bill and the Wild West*. Pittsburgh: University of Pittsburgh Press, 1981. (G) Contains pictures and essays about the West and Buffalo Bill based on artifacts at participating museums. Also includes a good chronology.

Buntline, Ned [E. Z. C. Judson]. *Buffalo Bill and His Adventures in the West*. 1883. Reprint. New York: Arno Press, 1974. (A, G) Sometimes considered juvenile fiction, this book supposedly introduced Buffalo Bill to the circus world. Even Cody was shocked by Buntline's exaggerations and lies. Originally titled *Buffalo Bill*.

Burke, John [Richard O'Connor]. *Buffalo Bill: The Noblest Whiteskin*. New York: George Putnam's Sons, 1973. (G) Chronicles Cody's story interestingly but without analysis.

Burke, John M. *"Buffalo Bill" from Prairie to Palace*. Chicago: Rand McNally, 1893. (A) Burke was Cody's press agent and, although very knowledgeable about his client, was of necessity interested in exaggeration. Designed to promote Cody, this book covers the period prior to Cody's tour of England.

Croft-Cook, Rupert, and W. S. Meadmore. *Buffalo Bill: The Legend, the Man of Action, the Showman*. London: Sidgwick and Jackson, 1952. (G) An example of a non-American biography published about this distinctly American legend. An objective and prosaic account, containing some errors.

Leonard, Elizabeth Jane, and Julia Cody Goodman. *Buffalo Bill: King of the Old West*. New York: Library Publishers, 1955. (A, G) Co-written by Cody's older sister, this work includes a genealogy of the Cody and Frederici families and provides new information on his youth. Especially useful on his days near Leavenworth, Kansas.

Nebraska, Ned. *Buffalo Bill and His Thrilling Adventures in the Wild West*. Baltimore: I. and M. Ottenheimer, 1915. (A) Famed western bibliographer Ramon Adams believed that this volume, replete with errors, was perhaps the worst book ever written about Cody.

Rosa, Joseph G., and Robin May. *Buffalo Bill and His Wild West, A Pictorial Biography*. Lawrence: University Press of Kansas, 1989. (G) Provides more discussion than photographs, and is helped by the fact that the authors are accomplished students of the American West. Relies a great deal on Russell's and Yost's biographies, but provides some new information. Cody did not have the Medal of Honor taken from him in 1916 as is sometimes reported.

Russell, Don. *The Lives and Legends of Buffalo Bill*. Norman: University of Oklahoma Press, 1960. (A, G) This premier biography of Cody captures the strengths and weaknesses, foibles and peccadilloes of Buffalo Bill, while disentangling fact from fiction. Includes a list of all known dime novels concerning Cody.

Shackleford, William Yancy. *Buffalo Bill: Scout and Showman*. Girard, KS: Haldemann-Julius Publisher, 1944. (A) One of the many "Little Blue Books" that made this socialist publishing house famous.

Sell, Henry Blackman, and Victor Weybright. *Buffalo Bill and the Wild West*. New York: Oxford University Press, 1955. (G) A useful overview that unfortunately misrepresents the Cody-Wild Bill Hickok relationship. The authors depended too much on Buffalo Bill's own autobiography. Includes many photographs.

Walsh, Richard John. *The Making of Buffalo Bill: A Study in Heroics*. Indianapolis: Bobbs-Merrill, 1928. (**A, G**) This work was started by Milton Salsbury, the son of Cody's long-time partner. After his death it was continued by Walsh, who based a great deal of the information on Nate Salsbury's scrapbooks. This is the first attempt at dispelling the myth and presenting serious biography. Johnny Baker, Cody's adopted son, also influenced the author.

Williams, Henry Llewellyn. *Buffalo Bill: Rifle and Revolver Shot; Pony Express Rider; Teamster; Buffalo Hunter; Guide and Scout*. London: George Routledge and Son, 1887. (**A**) Said to be the rarest of all biographies, but not especially useful otherwise.

Yost, Nellie Irene Snyder. *Buffalo Bill, His Family, Friends, Fame, Failures, and Fortunes*. Chicago: Swallow Press, 1979. (**A, G**) Presents a laboriously researched, authentic account that disproves debunkers. Includes extensive information about Cody's family life in North Platte, Nebraska.

Evaluation of Biographies for Young People

D'Aulaire, Ingri, and Edgar Parin. *Buffalo Bill*. Garden City, NY: Doubleday, 1952. Written for elementary school children, this book outlines Cody's life with emphasis on his supposed Pony Express days and relations with Native Americans.

Davidson, Mary R. *Buffalo Bill: Wild West Showman*. Scarsdale, NY: Garrard, 1962. Another overview with emphasis on his showmanship. Considered appropriate for second- through fifth-grade students.

Garst, Doris Shannon. *Story of Buffalo Bill*. Indianapolis: Bobbs-Merrill, 1938. In a slightly different form, it was published as Shannon Garst, *Buffalo Bill* (New York: Julian Messner, 1948). Contains a useful chronology. For junior and senior high school students.

Gowdy, George [James H. Gage]. *Young Buffalo Bill*. New York: Lothrop, Lee and Shepard Company, 1955. Fanciful description of Bill's imaginary youth for elementary students.

Grant, Matthew G. *Buffalo Bill*. Mankato, MN: Creative Education, 1974. This volume is typical of Grant's work in a series of short biographies about American heroes.

Havinghurst, Walter. *Buffalo Bill's Wild West Show*. New York: Random House, 1957. For fourth- through sixth-grade students. Unfortunately, the author does not distinguish between the acts in the show and the reality of the Old West. Annie Oakley and Sitting Bull get more attention than Cody.

Miers, Earl Schenck. *Wild and Wooly West*. Chicago: Rand McNally, 1964. Miers wrote popular adult history as well. Here, he presents stories of well-known western legends, including Buffalo Bill, for junior high school students.

Sabin, Edwin Legrand. *Buffalo Bill and the Overland Trail*. Philadelphia: Lippincott, 1914. An old, but thrilling, exaggerated account of trailblazing by Buffalo Bill. Sabin wrote several children's biographies on famous westerners.

Stevenson, Augusta. *Buffalo Bill: Boy of the Plains*. Indianapolis: Bobbs-Merrill, 1948. For third- through seventh-grade students. Part of the Childhood of Famous Americans Series. This book recounts Cody's early life, education, supposed Pony Express days, and the time he and his family spent around Weston, Missouri.

Overview and Evaluation of Primary Sources
Primary material concerning Buffalo Bill abounds. Clippings, photographs, scrapbooks, documents, letters, and programs may be found in the following collections and repositories: William F. Cody Collections at Arizona Pioneer Historical Society, Tucson; University of Arizona Library, Tucson; Buffalo Bill Memorial Museum, Lookout Mountain, Colorado; Buffalo Bill Museum, Cody, Wyoming; State Historical Society of Colorado, Denver; Denver Public Library, Denver; Kansas State Historical Society, Topeka; Nebraska State Historical Society, Lincoln; Newberry Library, Chicago; and Wyoming State Historical Society, Cheyenne.

The *National Union Catalog of Manuscript Collections* lists nine other collections that include material related to Cody, the most important being the Wyoming Collection at the University of California, Bancroft Library, Berkeley, which has one of Cody's pocket notebooks. Published editions of his letters include those he wrote to his sister, Julia Cody Goodman, *Letters From Buffalo Bill*, edited by Stella Adelyne Foote (Billings, MN: Foote Publishing, 1954; **A, G**). and *The Business of Being Buffalo Bill: Selected Letters of William F. Cody, 1879-1917*, edited by Sarah J. Blackstone (New York: Praeger, 1988; **A, G**).

During Cody's lifetime, several autobiographies bearing his name appeared. Undoubtedly he influenced the writing of all of them and may have written parts of some. They are *The Life of Hon. William F. Cody, Known as Buffalo Bill, the Famous Hunter, Scout and Guide: An Autobiography* (1879. Reprint. Lincoln: University of Nebraska Press, 1978; **A, G, Y**); *Buffalo Bill's Own Story of His Life and Deeds . . . Including a Full Account of His Death and Funeral . . . by William Lightfoot Visscher* (Chicago: John R. Stanton, 1917; **A, G, Y**), which was republished as *Life and Adventures of "Buffalo Bill"* (1927. Reprint. Golden, CO: Buffalo Bill Memorial Museum, 1939); and *Buffalo Bill's Life Story, An Autobiography of Buffalo Bill (Colonel W. F. Cody)* (New York: Rinehart, 1920; **A, G, Y**). The last of these is illustrated by N. C. Wyeth and contains the best-known stories about Cody. It was first serialized as "The Great West That Was, 'Buffalo Bill's' Life Story," in *Hearst's Magazine* from August 1916 to July 1917.

Twenty-four dime novels signed by Buffalo Bill were printed in the late nineteenth and early twentieth centuries. He also published three short stories. Some of the stories were repetitious and most were not his work. Factual magazine articles by him appeared in *Cosmopolitan* (June 1894), *Harper's Round Table* (January 1899), *Metropolitan* (August 1900), *Murray's Magazine* (June 1887), and *Sunday Magazine* (May 1907). Two other books, undoubtedly ghost written, were also published under his name: *Story of the Wild West and Camp-fire Chats* (Richmond, VA: B. F. Johnson, 1888; several reprint editions exist; **A, G, Y**), and *True Tales of the Plains* (New York: Empire, 1908; **A, G, Y**). For a more detailed discussion of Cody as an author see "Buffalo Bill, Author," in Don Russell, *The Lives and Legends of Buffalo Bill* (1960).

Reminiscences and memoirs by others also exist in great number, including Louisa Frederici Cody's, *Memories of Buffalo Bill* (New York: D. Appleton and Company, 1919; **A, G**), the work of his wife, with whom he had a troubled marriage; Helen Cody Wetmore, *Last of the Great Scouts: The Life Story of Col. William F. Cody, (Buffalo Bill) as Told by His Sister* (Duluth: Duluth Press, 1899; **A, G**), a sentimental recounting that was reprinted in 1918 with comments by Zane Grey; D. H. Winget, *Anecdotes of Buffalo Bill . . . by His Boyhood Friend and "Pard"* (Clinton, IA: n. p., 1912. Reprint. Chicago: Historical Publishing, 1927; **A, G**); and Dan Muller, *My Life With Buffalo Bill* (Chicago: Reilly and Lee, 1948; **A, G**), both written by friends of Cody's.

Fiction and Adaptations

On December 23, 1869, the first installment of Ned Buntline's serial story, *Buffalo Bill, the King of Border Men*, began appearing in the *New York Weekly*. This was the first of 557 dime novels about Buffalo Bill. If reprints are included, Don Russell fixes the aggregate number of dime novels at 1,700. Buntline wrote only four, but Colonel Prentiss Ingraham, who receives the most credit for creating this genre's Buffalo Bill, penned 121. Rarely mentioned, but as prolific in writing about Cody were W. Bert Foster (136 titles), William Wallace Cook (119 titles), and John Harvey Whitson (59 titles).

The titles employed by these writers suggest the contents of their fanciful melodramas: *Buffalo Bill's Leap for Life; or, The White Death of Beaver Wash*; *Buffalo Billy, the Boy Bullwhacker; or, The Doomed Thirteen*; and *Buffalo Bill's Spy Shadower; or, The Masked Man of Grand Canyon*. In the very earliest books he was treated much like his predecessors, the backwoodsmen. Soon, however, he emerged as a different type—the plainsman, who was a smooth-talking, hard-drinking gambler; a flamboyant romantic hero, who swept maidens off their feet; and a man of flawless social bearing with a keen sense of justice.

The stories were the epitome of simplicity. When used as the basis for Cody's stage plays, they were further graced with considerable bombast, as Cody and his fellow actors—Buntline, "Wild Bill" Hickok, or Captain Jack Crawford—ad-libbed and delivered harangues on such topics as temperance or law and order. By the 1870s Cody was also being portrayed by others in plays such as Fred G. Maeder's *Buffalo Bill*. In the twentieth century fewer novels and plays have involved Buffalo Bill, but the quality of those that do is markedly better than the earlier works.

Both Courtney R. Cooper, *The Last Frontier* (1923), and Hal G. Evarts, *Shaggy Legion* (1930), place Cody in episodes that figured prominently in his life: the building of the Kansas Pacific Railroad and the passing of the bison. Recent books that might have included a Buffalo Bill character but do not are Milton Lott, *Dance Back the Buffalo* (1958), concerned with the Ghost Dance War era, the 1890s, and William W. Haines, *The Winter War* (1961), about the Sioux War of the 1870s. Perhaps Cody is losing his fictional appeal.

The best modern drama is Arthur Kopit's *Indians*, published by Hill and Wang in 1969. Stacy Keach portrayed Buffalo Bill on the New York stage, and Robert Altman and Alan Rudolph partly based their movie *Buffalo Bill and the Indians; or, Sitting Bull's History Lesson* (1976) on the play. The most famous stage presentation involving a Buffalo Bill character is Irving Berlin's musical comedy *Annie Get Your Gun*, which opened at the Imperial Theater in New York on May 6, 1946. Herbert and Dorothy Fields wrote the play on which the musical was based, and Louis Calhern was a noble but slippery Buffalo Bill in the 1950 MGM movie version written by Sidney Sheldon.

There have been songs written about Buffalo Bill, such as Ray Henry and his orchestra's "Dance With Me" recording in the 1970s. There have been poems about him, such as e.e. cummings' "Buffalo Bill's" or "Buffalo Bill's Defunct" and Carl Sandburg's "Buffalo Bill." And there was a "Buffalo Bill Quartet" in *The Music Man* which premiered at the Majestic Theater in New York on December 18, 1957. But the legend of Buffalo Bill has survived into the modern period through movies and television.

William F. Cody played himself in nine silent movies from 1897 through 1917. Since then forty-five movies have been made with characters based either directly or indirectly on him. They range from substantial portrayals by Joel McCrea in *Buffalo Bill* (1944) and Charlton Heston in *Pony Express* (1953), to Clayton Moore's rendition in *Buffalo Bill in Tomahawk Territory* (1952), to Buffalo Bill in *Willy McBean and His Magic Machine* (1965), a delightful and technically superb puppet film, where Willy uses his time machine to visit the frontiersman. A rare silent film serial, *Fighting With Buffalo Bill* (1926) and three talkie serials, *Battling With Buffalo Bill* (1931), *Cody of the Pony Express,* (1950), and *Riding with Buffalo Bill* (1954), have been made. Most of the movies are no better as serious drama than these serials.

A television presentation, "Buffalo Bill, Jr." went through forty episodes in syndication in 1955 and CBS-TV produced "The Buffalo Billy Show," a puppet adventure series, in 1950. "The Legend of Buffalo Bill" was an ABC-TV program on "Colt-45" in 1958-1959. Four made-for-television movies have appeared since 1974; "Calamity Jane," the most recent, aired on CBS-TV on March 6, 1984.

Museums, Historical Landmarks, Societies

Buffalo Bill Dam (Cody, WY). Erected in 1910 as Shoshone Dam, 328 feet, and renamed in 1948.

Buffalo Bill Historical Center, Buffalo Bill Museum (Cody, WY). Founded in 1927 and operated by the Buffalo Bill Memorial Association. Contains considerable materials related to the Wild West Show. Also includes the Cody Firearms Museum, Plains Indian Museum, McCracken Research Library, and the Whitney Gallery, founded in 1959, which contains Gertrude Vanderbilt Whitney's equestrian bronze statue of Buffalo Bill and a number of fine paintings. The statue was originally to have been located at Lookout Mountain, Colorado.

Buffalo Bill Memorial Museum (Lookout Mountain, CO). Founded by Johnny Baker, Cody's adopted son, at the burial site. Although the bronze plate on the stone marker at his grave says, "At rest here by his request," he had wanted to be buried in Cody, Wyoming.

Buffalo Bill Statue (Oklahoma City, OK). Statue of Cody is located at the National Cowboy Hall of Fame and Western Heritage Center.

Cody Family Association. Composed of descendants of Philip and Martha Cody of Beverly, Massachusetts, there are several chapters in the United States and Canada. It has published several family directories, such as *The Cody Family in America 1698* (Kissimmee, FL: Cody Publications, 1954).

Cody, Wyoming. Founded on land given Buffalo Bill by the state, it was originally named Shoshone, but in 1896 the "Cody" post office was established, and in 1901 the town was officially known by its present name. Cody's famed TE Ranch was nearby.

Other Sources

Fredriksson, Kristine. *American Rodeo: From Buffalo Bill to Big Business.* College Station: Texas A&M Press, 1985. Starting with Cody, the author discusses groups and businesses involved in the growth of the modern rodeo. A doctoral dissertation at the University of California, Santa Barbara, in 1982.

Gray, John S. "Fact Versus Fiction in the Kansas Boyhood of Buffalo Bill." *Kansas History* 8 (Spring 1985): 2-20. Corrects, or debunks, stories about Cody's boyhood in the late 1850s, noting that Buffalo Bill never rode for the Pony Express.

Monaghan, Jay. *The Great Rascal Ned Buntline.* Boston: Little, Brown, 1952. Discusses the Cody-Buntline relationship and Buffalo Bill's early years as a performer.

Nieuwenhuyse, Craig F. "Six Guns on the Stage: Buffalo Bill Cody's First Celebration of the Conquest of the American Frontier." A doctoral dissertation at the University of California, Berkeley, in 1981. Nieuwenhuyse states that Cody's drama, while reflecting the reality of the West, also began the mythologization process.

Russell, Don. "Cody, Kings, and Coronets: A Sprightly Account of Buffalo Bill's Wild West Show at Home and Abroad." *American West* 7 (July 1970): 4-10. Cody was imitated by competitors but never equaled as a western showman, according to his major biographer.

Sayers, Isabelle S. *Annie Oakley and Buffalo Bill's Wild West.* New York: Dover, 1981. Annie joined the show as "Little Sure Shot" in 1884 and stayed until it folded several decades later, except for 1888 when she appeared with Pawnee Bill's Far East Show.

Vestal, Stanley [Walter S. Campbell]. "The Duel with Yellow Hand." *Southwest Review* 26 (Autumn, 1940): 65-77. There is no doubt that Buffalo Bill killed Yellow Hand and scalped him.

White, John I. "Red Carpet for a Romanoff: 1872 Hunting Party—Western Style in Honor of Russia's Grand Duke Alexis." *American West* 9 (January 1972): 4-9. Generals Sheridan and Custer, Chief Spotted Tail, and Cody took part in history's most celebrated hunt with Czar Alexander II's son.

Robert S. La Forte
University of North Texas

GEORGE BUSH
b. 1924

Chronology

Born George Herbert Walker Bush on June 12, 1924, in Milton, Massachusetts, the son of Dorothy B. Bush and Prescott Bush, a prominent banker (Brown Brothers, Harriman and Company) and U.S. senator from Connecticut (1952-1963); *1924-1942* grows up in Greenwich, Connecticut; attends Greenwich Country Day School and then the Phillips Academy in Andover, Massachusetts; *1942-1945* serves as pilot in the U.S. Navy during World War II; flies fifty-eight combat missions, and is shot down and rescued; *1945* marries Barbara Pierce, the daughter of a publisher, on January 6; enrolls at Yale University; *1948* graduates Phi Beta Kappa from Yale with a bachelor degree in economics; *1948-1953* works for Dresser Industries in Texas and California; *1953* cofounds the Zapata Petroleum Corporation; *1954-1966* serves as chairman of the board of Zapata; *1964* runs for the U.S. Senate and is defeated; *1967-1971* serves in the U.S. House of Representatives as a Republican representing Houston; *1970* again loses bid for U.S. Senate seat; *1971-1973* serves as permanent representative of the U.S. to the United Nations; *1973-1974* serves as chairman of the Republican National Committee; *1974-1975* heads the U.S. Liaison Office in Beijing, China; *1975-1977* serves as director of the Central Intelligence Agency; *1977-1980* returns to business and serves as adjunct professor at Rice University; *1980* seeks the presidential nomination of the Republican party; accepts vice-presidential nomination on ticket headed by Ronald Reagan; elected vice president of the U.S.; *1981-1989* serves two terms as vice president; *1988* elected president of the U.S.; *1989* initiates invasion of Panama and installation of pro-American regime; *1990* appoints David H. Souter to the Supreme Court after the resignation of William Brennan; condemns Iraq's August 2 invasion of Kuwait; orders military to Saudi Arabia on August 6-7; on November 29 a United Nations Security Council resolution authorizes the use of force against Iraq if it fails to withdraw from Kuwait by January 15; congressional support of the president is down from 62.6 percent in 1989 to 46.8 percent; unemployment hits a three-year high of 6.1 percent; the United States formally enters a recession in the fourth quarter of the year; *1991* as the deadline for Iraqi withdrawal nears, Secretary of State James Baker meets with Iraqi foreign minister Teriq Aziz, and the six-and-a half-hour meeting ends in a stalemate when Aziz refuses to deliver Bush's personal letter to Saddam Hussein; *January 10* urges Israeli non-involvement; *January 15* signs war order; the next day informs allies of his intentions and launches an air war on strategic targets in Kuwait and Iraq; the initial reportage of the bombing of Bagdad and Bush's television announcement of the air war on January 16 to the American public draws a record television audience; *February 15* initiates the ground war; *February 23* proclaims victory and sets a date for a cease-fire on February 27; his approval rating hits an all-time high, despite domestic economic problems.

Activities of Historical Significance

George Bush's election to the presidency in 1988 was the realization of a diligent, decade-long effort. Earlier in his career Bush gained valuable governmental experience while serving in the U.S. House of Representatives, as the U.S. ambassador to the United Nations during a turbulent period in the U.N.'s history, as the first official representative of the U.S. to the People's Republic of China, as the director of the Central Intelligence Agency while the agency struggled to regain public confidence in the wake of the Watergate scandal, and as the chairman of the Republican National Committee.

Despite his unsuccessful attempts for a U.S. Senate seat, Bush emerged during the 1980 presidential primaries as a forceful personality who could win elections; his victory in the Iowa primary shook the Reagan campaign and won Bush the respect of national Republican leaders. Bush enhanced his national credibility and support by accepting the vice-presidential nomination. During his tenure as vice president, Bush consistently demonstrated his loyalty to President Reagan. He coordinated the Reagan administration's effort to eliminate terrorism. In 1988 Reagan supported Bush's successful campaign for the Republican presidential nomination. Through much of his campaign against the Democratic nominee, Governor Michael Dukakis of Massachusetts, Bush was considered the underdog, but he defeated Dukakis by a wide margin.

After his first year as president, Bush achieved a level of popularity and credibility among the American people that, according to several indicators, exceeded the levels attained by any of his predecessors. The Bush administration has been confronted with slowing economic growth, the savings and loan debacle, the political transformation of Eastern Europe, the crisis that occurred in June 1989 when the Chinese government cracked down on student demonstrators in Beijing, the continuation of nuclear disarmament negotiations with the Soviet Union, the unfolding of Mikhail Gorbachev's reforms in the Soviet Union, and the crisis in the Persian Gulf triggered by Iraq's invasion of Kuwait.

On August 2, 1990, Iraq invaded Kuwait after promising its Arab neighbors that it had no intentions of doing so. Critics charged that the administration had ignored many danger signals and, in fact, entered into complicity with Iraqi President Saddam Hussein a week before his invasion of Kuwait by not making clear the consequences if Hussein moved his troops into attack position. Bush advisors interpreted Iraqi troop movements as Hussein's intimidation tactics, not as a prelude to war. On August 3, 1990, Secretary of Defense Richard B. Cheney and other top-level administration and military leaders began negotiations with Saudi Arabia to plan the defense of that country, which included establishing U.S. military defense lines. Over the course of the next few weeks, Bush aides were able to make advances on several fronts. In an unprecedented liaison, the Soviet Union agreed to join a consortium of twenty-eight other nations in a United Nations- sponsored resolution that required Iraq to withdraw from Kuwait by January 15, 1991 or face a combined military action to oust them. Bush issued the ultimatum, and negotiations, often through the news media, continued almost to the moment of the U.S. invasion of Iraq and Kuwait on January 16th.

The Persian Gulf War stands as one of the most unusual and gripping wars in U.S. history because, from the moment of the first attack on Bagdad, it was reported live on television. The American public saw the conflict unfold, and witnessed what it was like to endure relentless bombings and Scud missile attacks. At the literal, symbolic, and moralistic head of it all was Bush, who seemed to accept the war as his mission and destiny. His critics argued that he never intended to avert this war; that he saw Saddam Hussein as a threat to freedom and a merciless tyrant who was responsible for hundreds of thousands of deaths during the war with Iran. The United States had received a mandate from the free world to drive Iraq from Kuwait; the only question for Bush was how far should he go to destroy Saddam Hussein's government, which had announced that it would attack Israel as a first-strike target.

Without waiting for the consent of Congress, which was eventually granted, Bush doubled the number of U.S. military troops deployed to Saudi Arabia, bringing the total to 550,000 Americans. The full might of the marines, navy, and air force was put in place, along with significant fighting forces from Britain, France, and Egypt. The deadliest military coalition in history was aligned against a Third World dictatorship that boasted the fourth largest army but which, in fact, had been depleted and demoralized during the eight-year war with Iran (1980-1988). For Commander in Chief Bush, there was no question of necessity or victory; the only consideration was how to reduce allied casualties. Some analysts predicted that as many as 30,000 allied lives would be lost if they engaged in ground combat with Iraq's elite Republican Guard.

Bush accepted the military strategy drawn up by field commander General Norman Schwartzkopf and joint chief of staff chairman General Colin L. Powell that would destroy the Iraqi infrastructure, command centers, and ground forces through air attacks, then lure the enemy into thinking that the allied invasion would come from the sea along the Kuwati coast while secretly deploying massive troop strength for a ground attack. When the ground attack finally began on February 15th, U.S., French, and British forces swept across the desert and cut off lines of retreat to Bagdad, while Arab and U.S. marine forces attacked dug-in Iraqi troops head-on. Virtually trapped between Kuwait City and the border, Iraqi armored divisions were destroyed. Conservative estimates put Iraqi troop deaths during the first month of the war at 70,000.

After only one hundred hours of ground combat, Bush gave orders to cease fire, which permitted two Iraqi divisions to escape. Saddam Hussein used these troops to quell the uprising of Iraqi citizens in both the southern and northern provinces. When hundreds of thousands of Kurdish Iraquis fled to Turkey and Iran to escape persecution, the wisdom of Bush's decision to stop the war before the enemy was crushed became a national issue.

The manner in which Bush conducted the war may affect the use of presidential power. Given the opportunity to assert U.S. military superiority by the abdication of the Soviet Union to protect her Third World allies, Bush correctly saw that the U.S. could alter the balance of power in the Middle East and set up relations with Arab nations that would permit a strong U.S. military presence for years to come. Having shed a pro-Israeli image, Bush had placed himself in a unique position to represent both sides, with world opinion strongly behind him. Unlike most other U.S. military occupations since World War II, the American public understood and believed that their cause was just. The week after the air war started, a *New York Times*/CBS poll showed Bush's approval rating at eighty-two percent. At the conclusion of the war, with only 179 American casualties (most caused by freak accidents) and with American pride restored, Bush's approval rating reached ninety percent, the highest approval rating of any president since John F. Kennedy. Bush also circumvented the War Powers Act and congressional consent to conduct war, and has raised the constitutional question of who holds the *de facto* power to initiate war. Throughout the war, Bush gave the appearance that he single-handedly guided the ship of state as his cabinet and generals established the coalition of world leaders, skillfully negotiated United Nations politics and world opinion, insisted on Israeli neutrality, opened communications with hostile Arab nations, and conducted the most successful military operation in modern warfare.

Overview of Biographical Sources

No definitive biography of Bush is available, and most of the literature about him has been politically or commercially motivated. Two biographical works that are somewhat helpful are Nicholas King's *George Bush: A Biography* (1980) and Mark Sufrin's *George Bush: The Story of the Forty-First President of the United States* (1989). These two studies provide information about Bush's life, but they are not scholarly works. Both lack essential information on Bush's career at the CIA and the United Nations. J. Hyams's *Flight of the Avenger, George Bush at War* (1991) covers Bush's life during World War II and its formulative role in his current political philosophy. Bob Woodward's *The Commanders* (1991) reveals the motivation behind Bush's decision to send troops to the Middle East and examines the important figures participating in that crisis. To date, Bush has not commanded the interest of academic biographers or historians.

Evaluation of Principal Biographical Sources

Honegger, Barbara. *October Surprise*. New York: Tudor, 1989. (G) This controversial book presents Bush in an unfavorable light by maintaining that his involvement in the Iranian hostage scandal was broader than has been publicly acknowledged and by drawing connections between his family and the Texas savings and loan debacle.

Hyams, J. *Flight of the Avenger, George Bush at War*. New York: Harcourt Brace Jovanovich, 1991. (G) A provocative attempt to examine Bush's exploits during the Second World War and their impact on Bush's view of the world and America's place in it. Regrettably, the thesis is underdeveloped and presented in a rather pedantic style.

King, Nicholas. *George Bush: A Biography*. New York: Dodd, Mead, 1980. (G, Y) An adequate and sympathetic campaign biography of Bush that was published in the year of his first election to the vice presidency.

Sufrin, Mark. *George Bush: The Story of the Forty-First President of the United States*. New York: Dell, 1989. (G, Y) This biography of Bush provides an uncritical portrait; it is useful as a source for profile information.

Overview and Evaluation of Primary Sources

Most of the primary source material on Bush consists of the records associated with his positions as a member of Congress, permanent representative of the U.S. to the United Nations, liaison of the U.S. to the People's Republic of China, director of the Central Intelligence Agency, and vice president and president of the

U.S. Since much of this information is not readily available, researchers may have difficulty in gathering essential data.

Bush has produced two campaign-motivated autobiographies, *Looking Forward*, written with Victor Gold (Garden City, NY: Doubleday, 1987; G, Y), and *Man of Integrity*, written with Doug Wead (Eugene, OR: Harvest House, 1988; G, Y).

Other Sources

Halliday, Fred. *From Kabul to Managua: Soviet-American Relations in the 1980s*. New York: Pantheon, 1989. (A, G) Primarily a work on U.S. foreign policy, contains biographical information on Bush and covers his vice-presidential career in the context of foreign relations.

Radcliffe, Donnie. *Simply Barbara Bush: A Portrait of America's First-Lady*. New York: Warner, 1989. (G, Y) This uncritical account of Barbara Bush's life provides insights into her relationship with her husband and into the impact of politics upon their personal lives.

Woodward, Bob. *The Commanders*. New York: Simon and Schuster, 1991. One of the most renowned reporters in modern journalism, Woodward set out in early 1989 to investigate how senior military leaders make policy decisions. His concept for a book was changed irrevocably in December 1989 when the U.S. invaded Panama to kidnap Manuel Noriega, and again in August 1990 when Iraq invaded Kuwait. Based on four hundred interviews conducted over twenty-seven months, Woodward recreates the process by which the Bush administration and the military decided on political and military strategy in Panama and Kuwait. President Bush, of course, figures prominently, though not always in a flattering light. Woodward quotes extensively, almost as if he had been present during the conversation, and although he does not identify the sources of his information, he was given access to documents, handwritten notes taken during the meetings, schedules, and chronologies. Given Woodward's reputation for accurately probing the deepest secrets of government, the revelations contained here present a startling portrait of the administration, and especially Bush.

William T. Walker
Philadelphia College of Pharmacy and Science

SAINT FRANCES XAVIER CABRINI
1850-1917

Chronology

Born Maria Francesca Cabrini on July 15, 1850, in Sant'Angelo Lodigiano in Lombardy, Italy, the thirteenth child of Agostino Cabrini, a farmer, and Stella Oldini, a housewife; *1859-1868* attends the private school of the Daughters of the Sacred Heart at Arluno; granted a teacher's diploma and a teacher's certificate; applies for admission into the order but is refused by the mother superior, who considers her too weak for such a life; *1870* between February and December both parents die; *1871* attends the Pedagogical Training Courses at Lodi; *1872* contracts smallpox and is nursed back to health by her sister, Rosa; begins teaching at Vidardo, and decides to become a missionary; applies again for admission to the Daughters of the Sacred Heart and is rejected; applies to the Canossian Sisters in Crema and is refused; *1874-1876* appointed to head an orphanage in need of reform; *1877* takes vocational vows and is appointed superior of the House of Providence; *1880-1886* advised by Bishop of Lodi to found a missionary order; *1880* opens a convent with seven other sisters in the town of Codogno; acknowledged as "Mother Cabrini" by members of the Institute of the Missionary Sisters of the Sacred Heart of Jesus (M.S.C.); draws up the rules of the institute, establishing November 14 as its founding date; *1882-1885* opens four houses in Italy; *1887* leaves Milan for Rome to obtain papal approval of her institute and seek permission to open a house in the city; meets Giovanni Battista Scalabrini, bishop of Piacenza, who has just published *L'emigrazione italiana in America* ("The Italian Emigration to America"); *1888* returns to Rome and reports to Pope Leo XIII; desires to work in China, but the pope advises her: "You must not go to the East but to the West. Your mission will be in America"; *1889* embarks for New York, where within four months she founds the Asylum of the Holy Angel to house four hundred destitute children; *1890* takes possession of a former Jesuit property, Manresa, at West Park-on-the-Hudson, for her orphanage; *1891* establishes the novitiate; returns to Italy and opens a training college in Rome; plans to expand her missionary work into Central America; embarks with twenty-nine sisters for Nicaragua, where she opens a school in December; *1892* leaves Nicaragua for New Orleans, where she establishes a mission to assist Italian immigrants; asked to manage the Italian hospital in New York; the hospital experiences serious economic difficulties which lead to foreclosure; founds Columbus Hospital; returns to Rome and meets several times with Pope Leo XIII; *1893* the sisters are expelled from Grenada by a revolutionary government and move to Panama; *1894* returns to New York with fifteen sisters; to ease crowding at Columbus Hospital, purchases the old Post Graduate Hospital; *1895* tours New Orleans, Panama City, and Buenos Aires; journeys by mule across Cordillera of the Andes from Chile to Argentina; arrives in Buenos Aires and establishes a home on Christmas Day; *1896* opens the Academy of St. Rose in Buenos Aires with fifty students; institutes training for Spanish- and Portuguese-speaking Catholic sisters; sails for Spain where she opens a house to "help in the work in Spanish America"; returns to Italy; *1898* visits the pope, who calls her a "saint"; visits Paris, where she opens a boarding-house for women; the first paying guest of the boarding-house, Countess Spottiswood Makin, is influential in securing an invitation for the missionary sisters to come to Spain under the patronage of Queen Maria Cristina; visits England to establish an orphanage for Italian children; *1899* returns to New York to establish various schools and missions for Italian children; opens schools in several U.S. cities; visits Spain and Italy where she establishes schools, orphanages, and convents; meets the pope, who commissions her to carry the spirit of God "to the whole world"; *1900* returns to Buenos Aires where she establishes more educational institutions; *August 1901* returns to Genoa in poor health; *1902* visits the Italian convents and travels to Spain, France, and England; returns to the U.S. in August; founds new houses, schools, and orphanages in Denver and other cities; *1905* founds Chicago's Columbus Hospital in the old North Shore Hotel in Lincoln Park; founds orphanages and schools in Oregon and California; celebrates the silver jubilee of her congregation; *1907* visits Italy, France, Spain, and England; awarded the "Grand Prix" by the queen of Italy in recognition of her work among the Italian immigrants; visits Argentina and Brazil; *1909* visits American cities; becomes an American citizen in October; *1910* returns to Italy and is made superior general of the congregation for life; travels to Paris and London; *1911* resides in Rome; *1912-1917* returns to the U.S., where she continues to establish new orphanages and hospitals; *1917* dies on December 22 in Chicago at age sixty-seven and is buried at West Park, New York; *July 7, 1946* declared a saint by Pope Pius XII.

Activities of Historical Significance

Saint Frances Xavier Cabrini was the first American citizen to be elevated to sainthood by the Catholic Church. In her missionary work Mother Cabrini established schools, orphanages, convents, and hospitals throughout Europe, the U.S., and Latin America. Recognized as a vital force for social and spiritual change by the leadership of the Catholic Church, she gave her time and energy unselfishly, bolstered by a simple but powerful faith. At her death, she left behind a legacy of sixty-three foundations of the Missionary Sisters of the Sacred Heart of Jesus (M.S.C.) with a membership of nearly thirteen hundred missionary sisters. Missions established in her honor in China, Australia, and Canada serve the social and spiritual needs of the young and the impoverished through education and the provision of orphanages, health-care facilities, rest homes, and retreat houses.

By Catholic church law, at least fifty years must pass after a candidate's death before he or she may be considered for sainthood. In Mother Cabrini's case, however, Pope Pius XI waived this requirement and the process was initiated in 1928. In September 1933 a church tribunal examined testimony in Chicago regarding Mother Cabrini's virtues and miracles. Two miracles of healing were attributed to her, and miracles have been attributed to her since her canonization.

On November 13, 1938, an official ceremony of beatification for Mother Cabrini was held in St. Peter's Basilica in Rome. At that time the pope extolled her life as a "poem of holiness, activity, intelligence and charity." On December 14 five thousand people gathered at St. Patrick's Cathedral in New York to celebrate the beatification of Blessed Mother Frances Xavier Cabrini.

On July 7, 1946, in St. Peter's Basilica, Pope Pius XII declared Mother Cabrini a saint, the highest honor conferred by the Catholic Church, and in 1950 he proclaimed St. Francis Xavier Cabrini the patroness of all emigrants.

Overview of Biographical Sources

The literature on Mother Cabrini's life and missionary work has grown in both quantity and quality since her death, although none of the current biographies can be considered definitive. Two studies are of particular value: Theodore Maynard, *Too Small a World* (1945), and Giuseppe dall'Ongaro, *Francesca Cabrini, La suora che conquisto' l'America* (1982).

Evaluation of Principal Biographical Sources

Borden, Lucille Papin. *Francesca Cabrini: Without Staff or Scrip*. New York: Macmillan, 1945. (**A, G**) Borden's study is overburdened by excessive biblical digressions which "submerge" the life and career of Mother Cabrini. Borden gives inadequate attention to Mother Cabrini's founding of the Missionary Sisters of the Sacred Heart of Jesus, which was the cornerstone of her missionary work.

Cotter, Marie. *Westward by Command*. Cork: Mercier Press, 1947. (**A, G, Y**) This straightforward and "unadorned presentation" of Mother Cabrini's life story is accurate and well-organized. Suitable for those with little historical or theological background.

Dall'Ongaro, Giuseppe. *Francesca Cabrini, La suora che conquisto' l'America* ("Mother Cabrini, the Nun Who Conquered America"). Milan: Rusconi, 1982. (A, G) Based on extensive research, Dall'Ongaro's biography is notable for a thorough analysis of Mother Cabrini's life within its socio-historical context. The author blends Cabrini's thoughts, ideas, travels, and commitments with the events of the Italian *Risorgimento*. Published only in Italian.

De Maria, Francesca Saverio. *La Madre Francesca Saverio Cabrini, Fondatrice e Superiora Generale delle Missionarie del Sacro Cuore di Gesù, Per una dell sue e figlie.* Turin: Societa' Editrice Internazionale, 1928. (A, G) Written by Cabrini's fellow sister and personal secretary, the biography traces Mother Cabrini's life and career from archival sources. Descriptive and useful, although Theodore Maynard uncovers some inaccuracies. Translated into English and published by the Missionary Sisters of the Sacred Heart (Chicago, 1984).

Di Donato, Pietro. *Immigrant Saint, The Life of Mother Cabrini.* New York: McGraw-Hill, 1960. (A, G, Y) Di Donato, author of *Christ in Concrete* (1937), writes a laudable biography of Mother Cabrini. Despite its "syrupy prose," the book is a serious attempt to show how the work of this Italian-American missionary expresses the soul of the Italian-American immigrant.

Martignoni, Angela. *Madre Cabrini: La Santa delle Americhe* ("Mother Cabrini, the Saint of the Americas"). New York: Vatican City Religious Book Company, 1945. (A) A comprehensive biography. Includes Mother Cabrini's pensieri and fioretti, and discussions of her popes, beatification, and canonization. Recommended for scholars and researchers.

Maynard, Theodore. *Too Small a World.* Milwaukee, WI: Bruce Publishing, 1945. (A, G) Given access to the documents and sources used by the Catholic Church during the beatification process, Maynard's well-written study is highly recommended for scholars and students. Translated into Italian by M. Santi and published by Longanesi in Milan (1971) and by the Missionary Sisters of the Sacred Heart (1987).

Ravetto, Sister Joan Mary. *"Mother Cabrini" by a Daughter of St. Paul.* Boston: St. Paul Editions, 1977. (A, G, Y) This concise but comprehensive biography is intended for students and the general public. As the author states in her short introduction, it is a "humble attempt to depict her most outstanding achievements."

Vian, Nello. *Madre Cabrini* ("Mother Cabrini"). Brescia: Morceliana, 1938. (A, G) Traces the life and career of Mother Cabrini, giving special attention to her activities among Italians abroad. Published only in Italian.

Museums, Historical Landmarks, Societies

Cabrini College (Radnor, PA). A coeducational, four-year, liberal arts college, affiliated with The Catholic University of America.

Mother Cabrini League (Chicago, IL). Established on February 14, 1938, and located at 434 W. Deming Plaza, the league has over 50,000 members. Among many other commitments, it is responsible for the maintenance of the room where Mother Cabrini died, which is located in the Chapel of Saint Frances Xavier Cabrini in Columbus Hospital, Chicago, and is open daily to visitors.

Mother Cabrini Monument (Sant'Angelo Lodigiano, Italy). Erected in 1987 outside the place of her birth.

Motherhouse of the Missionary Sisters of the Sacred Heart (Rome, Italy). Located at Viale Cortina d'Ampezzo 269, the motherhouse is the custodian of part of Mother Cabrini's archives.

St. Cabrini Shrine (Denver, CO). Exhibits videotapes documenting her life.

St. Frances Cabrini Chapel (New York, NY). Mother Cabrini is interred in the chapel of the Missionary Sisters of the Sacred Heart, 701 Fort Washington Ave.

Other Sources

Acta Apostolicae Sedis (Vatican City Archives, Vol. 30, 1938; Vol. 38, 1946) Contain the Vatican official acts of Mother Cabrini's beatification and canonization.

Cicognani, Amleto Giovanni. *Addresses and Sermons, 1938-1942*. Paterson, NJ: St. Anthony Guild Press, 1942. Contains the sermon delivered at the saint's tomb in New York on November 13, 1928, the day of Cabrini's beatification, by Cicognani, the apostolic delegate to the U.S.

DiGiovanni, Stephen Michael. "Mother Cabrini: Early Years in New York." *Catholic Historical Review* (January 1991): 56-77. The article deals with Mother Cabrini's early apostolate among Italian immigrants in New York City. First-hand sources from the Vatican Archives and those of the Congregation of Propaganda Fide reveal the reasons for the coming of Mother Cabrini to the United States.

Lorit, Sergio C. *Frances Cabrini.* New York: New City Press, 1970. Lorit's biography ends with Mother Cabrini's death in 1917, and adds little new information.

Molinari, Paolo, S. I. "Madre Cabrini E Gli Emigrati." In *Civilta' Cattolica* 2 (1968): 555-564. Written on the fiftieth anniversary of her death, the article draws abundantly on Mother Cabrini's notes, travels, letters, and diaries, and underlines her missionary work among Italian immigrants.

Sullivan, Mary Louise. "Mother Cabrini: Missionary to Italian Immigrants." *U.S. Catholic Historian* 6 (Fall 1987): 265-279. This article, an extract from the author's dissertation, deals with Mother Cabrini's missionary work among the Italian immigrants in the U.S.

Pellegrino Nazzaro
Rochester Institute of Technology

ANNA ELLA CARROLL
1815-1894

Chronology

Born Anna Ella Carroll on August 29, 1815, at Kingston Hall in Somerset County, Maryland, the eldest of eight children of Thomas King Carroll and Juliana Stevenson Carroll; although her father was closely related to the Catholic Carrolls of Maryland, he himself was a Protestant; *1830-1831* becomes increasingly committed to the world of politics and law when her father serves as governor of Maryland; *1840* experiencing financial difficulties, her father sells his plantation and half of his slaves, and moves to a smaller plantation, Warwick Fort Manor on the Choptank River; *1845* settles in Washington, D.C., and becomes immersed in Whig politics; *1852* begins long-term correspondence with President Millard Fillmore; *1856* works feverishly for the election of Fillmore as the Know-Nothing candidate for president and is devastated when he loses, carrying only her own state of Maryland; *1858* supports family friend and fellow Know-Nothing Thomas H. Hicks in his successful bid as governor of Maryland; *1861* sounds out members of the Maryland Legislature on the issue of secession and then writes unsigned newspaper articles arguing for Maryland to remain in the Union; later is influential in the election of a Union man, Augustus W. Bradford, to succeed Hicks as governor of Maryland; *July 1861* in reply to a rousing speech in Congress by her friend John C. Breckinridge in support of secession, writes a vigorous and cogent pamphlet, *Reply to the Speech of Hon. J. C. Breckinridge, Delivered in the United States Senate, July 16th, 1861,* that is circulated widely; *August 1861* accompanies Lemuel D. Evans, a Texas Unionist, to St. Louis, where she becomes convinced that the Tennessee River is a more accessible route to the heart of the Confederacy than the Mississippi; *February 1862* General Grant moves up the Tennessee River, taking Forts Donelson and Henry and ultimately breaking the power of the Confederacy in the West; *1863* receives a payment of 750 dollars from the federal government for services, but is indignant at its paltriness; *1870-1881* unsuccessfully pursues her claim for compensation from the federal government for her services as military strategist during the Civil War and specifically as the creator of the Tennessee River strategy; *1881* General Edward Bragg, Democratic congressman from Wisconsin, draws up a bill in the House of Representatives calling for a major general's salary to be awarded retroactively to her; is devastated and becomes physically incapacitated when this bill is replaced by another directing the payment of a mere fifty dollars per month "from and after passage of this act";

mid 1880s the story of her victimization is seized upon by woman suffragists and is written up in many periodicals and newspapers; *1894* an "embittered invalid," dies on February 19 at the home of her sister in Washington, D.C.; is taken by steamer to the Carroll family cemetery plot on the lower Eastern Shore of Maryland.

Activities of Historical Significance

As a journalist, pamphleteer, and what today would be called a lobbyist, Anna Ella Carroll, born into the slave-holding aristocracy of the upper South and subsequently choosing to side with the Union cause at the onset of the Civil War, became, despite formidable Victorian restraints on the creativity of women, one of the most influential women of her time. While her claims as a military strategist may be more dubious than her other accomplishments, she had an undeniably major role in securing Maryland for the Union cause. She was manipulative, but she was also brilliant in her grasp of constitutional law; although her assertiveness irritated some of her correspondents, the force of her reasoning and her tireless polemicizing served to significantly sway public opinion in a crucial border state of severely split allegiances.

Carroll's cooperation was solicited by such political leaders as Governor Thomas H. Hicks of Maryland and Jefferson Davis—although in the case of the latter his overtures were rebuffed. Her greatest friend among presidents was Millard Fillmore after he left office, and although she was also on friendly terms with Presidents Tyler, Pierce, and Buchanan, and Buchanan's vice president John C. Breckinridge, the degree of her friendship with and influence on Abraham Lincoln remains a matter of some controversy. In her later years, Senator Benjamin F. Wade of Ohio was particularly supportive of Carroll in her claim for recognition and remuneration.

The primary argument against crediting her with the Tennessee plan is the fact that other strategists came up with the same idea at the same time. That she was one of many, however, does not effectively eliminate the possibility of partial influence, and the fact that Carroll had regular dealings with Attorney General Edward Bates and Secretary of War Edwin B. Stanton adds credibility to the claim. The sensationalism of the Greenbie plagiarism suit against novelist Hollister Noble in the 1950s was an open invitation for a great many historians to debunk the Carroll legend, but most of the critics, it must be admitted, were male scholars in a field (military history) dominated by males.

In addition to her gender and her tenuous claim as military strategist, two other issues detract from her unqualified enshrinement as an American heroine: her misguided anti-Catholic views, part and parcel of the Know-Nothing movement, and her enduring adherence to the emigration scheme for American blacks. Even these detractions, however, have extenuating, though not redeeming, features—she carefully exempted American Catholics (of which her own grandfather was one) from her indictment, reacting instead to the illiterate Catholic immigrants who she felt were unprepared for the responsibilities of American democracy; and in her resettlement essays she insisted that safeguards be established against the further degradation of the freedmen, even envisioning a plan for the hypothetical emigrants to the Chiriqui Tract of what is now Panama to furnish coal for the United States Navy.

Unquestionably her greatest legacy is the example that she set as a talented career-minded woman. This is impossible to assess with any precision, but she clearly functioned far enough outside the traditional woman's orbit of experience as a writer and swayer of public opinion to inspire successive generations of women struggling for the right to have their own careers in a working world dominated by men.

Overview of Biographical Sources

For many years until the appearance in 1990 of Janet L. Coryell's praiseworthy and even-handed evaluation of Carroll's role in history, *Neither Heroine nor Fool: Anna Ella Carroll of Maryland,* a satisfactory biography had not yet been written. Sarah Blackwell's *A Military Genius: A Life of Anna Ella Carroll of Maryland* (1891-1895) is outdated, and both works by the Greenbies, *My Dear Lady* (1940) and *Anna Ella Carroll and Abraham Lincoln: A Biography* (1952), insist on Carroll's heroism to such a degree that they actually invite skepticism.

Evaluation of Principal Biographical Sources

Blackwell, Sarah Ellen. *A Military Genius: A Life of Anna Ella Carroll of Maryland.* 2 vols. Washington, DC: Judd and Detweiler, 1891-1895. (G) The first volume is an apotheosis by an adoring woman suffragist, and the second volume is an anthology of Carroll's Civil War writings with comments made by Carroll herself.

Coryell, Janet L. *Neither Heroine nor Fool: Anna Ella Carroll of Maryland.* Kent, OH: Kent State University Press, 1990. (G) A balanced appraisal of Carroll's life and work that stresses her importance as a pioneer woman activist while not neglecting an examination of her darker side as manipulator and opportunist.

Greenbie, Marjorie Barstow. *My Dear Lady: The Story of Anna Ella Carroll, The Great, Unrecognized Member of Lincoln's Cabinet.* New York: Whittlesey House, 1940. (G) Going too far perhaps in redressing the injustice done to Carroll's reputation in her own lifetime, Greenbie's treatment is too adulatory for readers' tastes half a century later.

Greenbie, Sydney, and Marjorie Barstow Greenbie. *Anna Ella Carroll and Abraham Lincoln: A Biography.* Manchester, ME: The University of Tampa Press in cooperation with Falmouth Publishing House, 1952. (G) A wholly laudatory amplification of Marjorie Greenbie's book written a dozen years earlier, it calls itself the first definitive biography and offers a more extensive bibliography.

Wise, Winifred Esther. *Lincoln's Secret Weapon.* New York: Chilton House, 1961. (Y) For young adults, this work is only slightly more objective than the works by the Greenbies. Contains a useful biography.

Overview and Evaluation of Primary Sources
The Anna Ella Carroll Papers at the Maryland Historical Society in Baltimore largely deal with her claims for the planning of the Tennessee campaign, but another collection at the same facility, the Cradock, Carroll, Jensen Papers, includes some of her essays. The Hicks Papers at the Maryland Historical Society contain notes made by Carroll on letters that she received from Hicks during the years 1860-1864. About fifty of her letters to Millard Fillmore are among the Fillmore Papers at the State University of New York, Oswego.

Her book, *The Star of the West* (1857), a collection of her journalistic writings combining anti-Catholic polemics with her admiration of William Walker's colonization of Nicaragua and her encouragement of a transcontinental railroad, is at the Enoch Pratt Library in Baltimore. Her longer pamphlets, *The War Powers of the General Government* (1861), at Enoch Pratt Library, and *The Relation of the National Government to the Revolted Citizens Defined* (1862), at the Gilman Storage Facility of the Johns Hopkins University Library, assert the unconstitutionality of the Confederate government and insist that reconstruction is an executive, rather than congressional, responsibility. Her *Reply to the Speech of Hon. J. C. Breckinridge, Delivered in the United States Senate, July 16th, 1861* is available at the Enoch Pratt Library as well as the University of Maryland Library.

Her claim as the architect of the Tennessee-Cumberland River campaign of 1862 is found in many documents and pamphlets, of which the most detailed is the *Petition for Compensation for Services by Anna Ella Carroll, February 14, 1876* in the *House Miscellaneous Documents* (44th Cong., 1st sess.; vol. 9). Charles M. Scott challenged these claims in his *The Origin of the Tennessee Campaign as a Refutation of the Fraudulent Claim of Miss Anna Ella Carroll* (Terre Haute, IN: Moore and Langen, 1889; **A, G**).

Fiction and Adaptations

In 1948 Hollister Noble published a novel, *Woman With a Sword,* covering the Civil War years and emphasizing Carroll's "Tennessee plan." Very much in agreement with the Greenbies' romantic interpretation of the Carroll legend in *My Dear Lady* and *Anna Ella Carroll and Abraham Lincoln: A Biography,* Noble was in fact sued by the Greenbies in 1954 for plagiarism and infringement of copyright. Judgment was eventually made in favor of the defendant because the novel was so different in purpose and treatment from the two biographies. Thirty years later, a softened, insightful, and idealized Carroll appears throughout William Safire's 1987 novel, *Freedom,* about the Civil War and its accompanying suspension of personal liberties. Although Safire takes considerable license with the facts (Carroll is re-created here as the lover of Millard Fillmore), he assiduously compiled an "Underbook" of sources and commentary which contains a significant amount of material on Carroll.

Museums, Historical Landmarks, Societies

Carroll Family Tomb (seven miles southwest of Cambridge, MD). In the cemetery of the restored Old Trinity Church dating from 1676, her tombstone bears the inscription, "A Woman Rarely Gifted—An Able and Accomplished Writer."

Kingston Hall (near Westover, MD). This two-and-a-half-story mansion of twenty-two rooms with an eighteenth-century double veranda and a cupola added later was the home of Governor Thomas King Carroll of Maryland until 1840.

Other Sources

Armstrong, Walter P. "The Story of Anna Ella Carroll." *American Bar Association Journal* 35 (March 1949): 198-200, 275. Offers a modern assessment of the contribution of her Civil War pamphlets.

Boyer, Paul S. "Carroll, Anna Ella." In *Notable American Women 1607-1950: A Biographical Dictionary,* edited by Edward T. Jones. Cambridge: The Belknap

Press of Harvard University, 1974. Remarkably thorough encyclopedic treatment, concluding that her dubious strategic claim has eclipsed the contributions for which she is genuinely deserving of renown, such as the acuity of her constitutional interpretation and her role in the Know-Nothing movement.

Bradley, Sylvia. "Anna Ella Carroll." In *Notable Maryland Women,* edited by Winifred G. Helmes. Cambridge, MD: Tidewater Publishers, 1977. This admiring account of Carroll's life admits that undeniable proof of her role as a Civil War strategist does not seem to exist.

Long, E. B. "Anna Ella Carroll: Exaggerated Heroine?" *Civil War Times* 14 (July 1975): 28-35. Concludes that although she was competent, capable, and thoroughly fascinating, she was a minor figure historically.

Snyder, Charles McCool. "Anna Ella Carroll, Political Strategist and Gadfly for President Fillmore." *The Maryland Historical Magazine* 68 (Spring 1973): 36-63. Availing himself of the only recently discovered Carroll letters to Millard Fillmore, Snyder argues that her work as pamphleteer, propagandist, and political thinker struggling for the freedoms of the twentieth century is truly worthy of admiration.

Jack Shreve
Allegany Community College

JOSHUA CHAMBERLAIN
1828-1914

Chronology

Born Joshua Lawrence Chamberlain in Brewer, Maine, on September 8, 1828, the oldest of five children of Joshua Chamberlain, a farmer, and Sarah Dupee Brastow Chamberlain; *1828-1848* grows up on the family farm and studies at Major Whiting's military academy in Ellsworth; *1848-1862* earns a bachelor's degree from Bowdoin College; studies at the Bangor Theological Seminary while teaching German to young ladies and serving as supervisor of schools in Brewster; *1855* marries Frances Caroline Adams, with whom he has two children; receives a master's degree from Bowdoin and joins the faculty, teaching logic, natural theology, rhetoric, and oratory, as well as modern languages; *1862-1866* enlists in the Union army and is wounded six times while fighting in twenty-four engagements; is frequently decorated and promoted to brevet major general; resigns from the army despite being offered a regular colonelcy on the Rio Grande; *1866-1870* after teaching at Bowdoin and acting as its president while awaiting discharge from the army, is elected governor of Maine with the largest majority to that time; serves four successive annual terms; *1871-1883* serves as president of Bowdoin College where he advances curricular reform; *1874* begins tenure as professor of mental and moral philosophy; *1878* appointed U.S. Commissioner to the Paris Exposition; *1879-1880* commands the Maine militia and keeps order during the electoral/constitutional crisis; *1883-1898* lectures in constitutional and international law at Bowdoin for two years after resigning as president; *1885* moves to Florida to head the Homosassa Company, a real estate development firm, and the Ocala and Silver Springs Railroad; serves as president or director of various firms; *1893* receives the Congressional Medal of Honor for his heroism at the Battle of Gettysburg; *1898* retires to Brunswick, Maine; *1900* appointed surveyor of the port of Portland; *1905* writes Civil War reminiscences after his wife dies; *1913* attends the fiftieth reunion at Gettysburg; *1914* dies in Portland on February 24 of complications of a wound received at Petersburg in 1864.

Activities of Historical Significance

Joshua Chamberlain's finest hour came when he was ordered to hold the extreme left at Little Round Top on the second day of the Battle of Gettysburg. He withstood enemy fire, several attacks, and, with more than a third of his regiment wounded, cleared the slope with a bayonet charge and carried Great Round Top. Many historians have argued that his courageous performance saved the Union army from having its flank rolled up, losing the battle, and, quite possibly, the war.

His vigorous leadership throughout the remainder of the war, despite a near-fatal wound at Petersburg, earned him promotion to major general and led to his selection by Grant to command the parade at Lee's surrender at Appomattox and to his division's selection to lead the Army of the Potomac in the final review in Washington, D.C.

As president of Bowdoin College, Chamberlain modernized the discipline system to treat students in a more adult fashion. He introduced curricular reforms, adding more science, engineering, and modern languages, required military drill for all students, and developed a master's program. These reforms were expensive and unpopular and did not survive his presidency, though they were in tune with broader trends in American higher education.

In his other occupations as well, Chamberlain proved a forceful, active, and imaginative leader. As governor of Maine, he was an influential opponent of prohibition and the establishment of a state constabulary, while he supported capital punishment. As major general of the state militia, he forestalled civil disturbance by taking charge of the capital and imposing order during a difficult and potentially explosive electoral crisis. While U.S. commissioner to the Paris Exposition, he prepared a lengthy report on European education. As surveyor of the port of Portland, he expanded what was intended to be a sinecure by touring Egypt and reporting on administrative methods in use there. Among his many writings, his articles and book on his Civil War experiences remain valuable and moving resources for historians.

Overview of Biographical Sources

Wallace, Willard M. *Soul of the Lion: A Biography of General Joshua Chamberlain*. New York: Thomas Nelson, 1960. (G) Meticulously researched from primary sources, this thorough volume is highly readable but excessively sympathetic and defensive. A disproportionate amount of it is given over to Chamberlain's Civil War experiences, and it is especially thin on the period after he resigned the presidency of Bowdoin.

Overview and Evaluation of Primary Sources

Chamberlain's Civil War reminiscences are notable for their stylistic qualities, reflecting the author's early mastery of pulpit oratory. ''My Story of Fredericksburg appeared in *Cosmopolitan* (1912/1913: 152-159; **G**). "Through Blood and Fire at Gettysburg" was published in *Hearst's Magazine* (June 1913: 899-900; **G**). His posthumously published book, *The Passing of the Armies: An Account of the Final Campaign of the Army of the Potomac, Based Upon Personal Reminiscences of the Fifth Army Corps* (New York: G. P. Putnam's Sons, 1915; **G**) contains an especially moving account of the last parade of Lee's army at Appomattox.

In addition to his published writing, there is a great deal of primary material available. The Chamberlain Collection of the Bowdoin College Library contains fourteen archive boxes of Chamberlain correspondence, photographs, documents, and memorabilia including his Congressional Medal of Honor, while the Bowdoin College Archives, housed in the library, contain materials relating to his association with the school as student, alumnus, faculty member, and president. The Pejepscot Historical Society in Brunswick has newspaper clippings about Chamberlain, some family letters, and his brother's diary of a visit to Gettysburg. The Maine State Archives in Augusta contain correspondence and records from his terms as governor and records of his command of the state militia. For his wartime service, see also *Annual Reports of the Adjutant General of the State of Maine* (Augusta: State of Maine, 1863-1866; **A**). Another valuable collection of letters and documents is held by the Maine Historical Society in Portland. Other significant collections are the Chamberlain File in the National Archives, the Chamberlain Papers in the Library of Congress Manuscript Division, and the Chamberlain Papers in the Frost Family Collection at Yale University.

Fiction and Adaptations

Chamberlain's experience at Gettysburg is brilliantly recreated in Michael Shaara's Pulitzer Prize-winning novel, *The Killer Angels: A Novel About the Four Days at Gettysburg* (1974). Shaara drew on Chamberlain's account of the Little Round Top fighting and added emotionally perceptive detail of his own imagining.

Museums, Historical Landmarks, Societies

Chamberlain House (Brunswick, ME). Located adjacent to the Bowdoin College campus, this home is being restored by the Pejepscot Historical Society as a house museum containing a variety of Chamberlain artifacts.

Pine Grove Cemetery (Brunswick, ME). Chamberlain's grave is located here and bears a Congressional Medal of Honor marker.

Other Sources

Bowdoin College, 1794-1894: Memorial of the One Hundredth Anniversary of the Incorporation of Bowdoin College. Brunswick, ME: Bowdoin College, 1894. A commemorative volume summarizing Chamberlain's presidency.

Hatch, Louis C. *The History of Bowdoin College.* Portland, ME: Loring, Short and Herman, 1927. Puts the best possible face on the opposition to Chamberlain's curricular reforms.

Joshua Lawrence Chamberlain Supplement: The Twelve Days at Augusta. Portland: Maine Historical Society, 1906. Covers Chamberlain's command of the militia during the constitutional crisis of 1879 and 1880.

Maine Gettysburg Commission. *Maine at Gettysburg: Report of the Maine Commissioners.* Portland, ME: Lakeside Press, 1898. Contains a complete account of the fighting at Little Round Top compiled from accounts of survivors.

Pullen, John J. *The Twentieth Maine.* Philadelphia: Longman, 1957. An excellent history of the unit Chamberlain commanded at Gettysburg.

Joseph M. McCarthy
Suffolk University

CESAR CHÁVEZ
b. 1927

Chronology

Born Cesar Estrada Chávez on March 31, 1927, in Yuma, Arizona, the son of migrant workers, Librado and Juana Chávez; attends more than thirty elementary schools, only completing eighth grade; until he enlists in the military, works as a migrant laborer; *1944-1945* serves in the United States Navy; *1948* marries Helen Fabela, with whom he has four daughters and four sons; *1952* joins the Community Service Organization (CSO) in San Jose, California, and leads voter registration drives; *1958* becomes general director of the CSO; *1962* resigns from the CSO after it refuses to create a farm workers union; begins organizing the National Farm Workers Association which later becomes known as the United Farm Works (UFW); *1965* enrolls seventeen hundred families in the UFW; the UFW joins striking Filipino grape pickers in a strike; *1966-1978* spearheads nationwide boycotts of non-union farm produce, such as grapes, lettuce, and citrus fruits, and gains negotiating leverage with growers; *1972* UFW memberships grows to sixty thousand; *1972-1977* the Teamsters Union and UFW compete for autonomy and monopoly over jurisdictional unionization of farm workers; *1977* UFW and Teamsters settle dispute over recruitment of members—they agree that UFW will organize field workers and the Teamsters will work with truck drivers and cannery workers; *1982* UFW and Teamsters' truce is extended and UFW's membership climbs to one hundred thousand.

Activities of Historical Significance

Cesar Chávez's humble beginnings and first-hand experience with labor exploitation prepared him for a career as one of America's most remarkable labor leaders. Prior to assuming the role of union leader, he served in World War II; upon his return, he found it difficult as a high school dropout of Hispanic heritage to escape racial injustice and job discrimination. Thus upon becoming a migrant worker once again, he was a man with a mission. Growing up in a series of migrant labor camps in Arizona and California and attending more than thirty elementary schools, he suffered socio-economic exploitation and as a son of migrant laborers, he understood the related problems and hoped to do something about them.

In 1952 he began as a field representative for the CSO, thereby serving as a link between the organization and the Hispanic community. Within a few years he accepted an appointment as general director and guided the organization through some turbulent periods. Because of his achievements in registering voters and bridging the gap between the CSO and the community, Chávez quickly reached the top of the hierarchy. Nevertheless, he resigned as director in 1962 when the CSO refused to create a farm worker union and no compromise appeared possible. This dispute meant loss of pay and a return to the fields; his experience as CSO director, however, heightened his sensitivity to injustice and renewed his vow to assist his people.

What began as a small-scale effort to enforce the minimum wage law and to better working and living conditions mushroomed into a crusade for an organized labor union and the implementation of collective bargaining. Many Arizona and California growers ignored the state and federal minimum wage laws; they simply devised their own pay scales without any consideration of employees' cost of living or needs. Using the argument of diminished profits, they maintained that they could not afford the increase stipulated by law and remain in business.

Disagreeing with what he perceived to be a thoughtless and illogical business practice, Chávez contended that higher wages served as an incentive for workers to produce higher-yield quality crops. Such process, he argued, augmented profit and decreased overhead expenses due to work slowdowns and poorly picked crops. When the growers refused to negotiate, Chávez mobilized nationwide strikes and boycotts of grapes, wine, and lettuce in an attempt to pressure the growers into signing labor contracts which not only specified worker-employer relations but also recognized the UFW's power of collective bargaining.

The movement was initiated in 1962 when negotiations failed and Chávez decided to educate migrant and agricultural workers about their rights. In 1965, having earned their respect as CSO director, he managed to enroll over seventeen hundred families to join the Filipino grape-pickers strike. Other disadvantaged Asians and African Americans signed on as members and participated in what turned out to be one of the longest labor strikes in American history. The success of this strike and the ensuing consumer boycott thrust Chávez into the national spotlight, and by 1972 his organization had increased to sixty thousand members. By 1982 the UFW's membership had climbed to over one hundred thousand.

Because of the effectiveness of the 1965 boycott, wine producers capitulated early in the struggle, but table grape growers resisted all union efforts until the 1970s. Therefore, the union strategy changed.

The economic security of the growers very much depended upon selling their produce on the world market. Knowing this, Chávez stopped the flow of goods by instituting national and international dock strikes, thereby eroding the staying power of the growers and erecting barriers to trade. Eventually, the boycotts and strikes functioned at both the local and the international levels. Locally some laborers organized work slowdowns and stoppages while others formed human blockades to prevent the transport of produce to the docks and markets. At the international level, foreign laborers exercised even greater control over the mass movement of exported goods. They refused to unload produce considered contraband by the striking American workers. The effects upon the local and international markets were disastrous. Produce rotted at the docks and truckers refused to transport smuggled goods to distributors. The price of crops rose and consumers absorbed the added expense or simply abstained from eating or buying the products. To the detriment of the growers, profits plummeted, and eventually the growers capitulated.

The initial momentum and euphoria that resulted from the success of the strike turned to disillusionment among the workers as they realized their deplorable living conditions had not improved, and Chávez believed he was losing control of his members. The strike had given them a purpose and now they had none. In order to impress upon his members the humanitarian and spiritual importance of their mission, he decided to fast, which he believed would tie their cause to Catholic ritual.

Already his supporters idolized him as a legendary hero, who single-handedly conquered the growers and the Teamsters. Now sympathizers and workers embraced his fast, and he again garnered national attention. The news media reported his every move; religious groups canonized him; university professors and students volunteered to assist the union; Chávez and his cause became the topic of research papers, theses, and dissertations. Satisfied and encouraged by the support he received throughout the fast, he regained his momentum and his popularity increased as he captured the imagination and earned the respect of people other than his followers.

Based on the success of the wine growers boycott, Chávez and his compatriots tightened the boycotts against the table grape growers. In so doing, they ran afoul of the Teamsters Union and jurisdictional conflict divided the two unions. Steady confrontation over which union had the right to organize and represent workers' demands led to property destruction and murder. Pre-arranged by the growers with the Teamsters' support, these intimidation tactics temporarily impeded the progress of the UFW's non-violent struggle.

The ill-feelings and violence continued for years until a truce was arranged in March 1977. A union agreement between the warring factions stipulated that the Teamsters would recruit and organize truck drivers and cannery workers while the UFW would unionize field laborers. Both sides gained satisfactory negotiating leverage with growers and obtained the approval of agricultural workers. With this settlement Chávez and the UFW scored a major victory. Not only did they receive the recognition they sought, but the union joined the AFL-CIO as an affiliate.

In 1978 the growers agreed to a written contract that incorporated the workers' demands, thus ending one of the most controversial labor disputes in California history.

Overview of Biographical Sources

Many authors have attempted to capture the essence of Chávez and his contributions to organized labor. Several innovative techniques were employed to portray the life and achievements of the man of "La Causa." Ruth Franchere's *Cesar Chávez* (1970), written for young adults, consists of a forty-two page narrative with photographs. In *Chávez: Man of the Migrant* (1971), Jean Pitrone introduces his readers to the complexities of Chávez's personality and his unionizing of migrant farm workers. In *So Shall Ye Reap* (1970), Joan London and Henry H. Anderson provide a clear understanding of of Chávez's virtues and vices, and his knowledge of trade unions, agricultural laborers, and California labor history.

Jacques E. Levy presents contemporary insight into the life and accomplishments of Chávez. His work, *Cesar Chávez: An Autobiography of La Causa* (1975), updates speeches and the struggles of the United Farm Workers Union.

Hailed as the most objective and best written biography of Chávez is Ronald B. Taylor's *Chávez and the Farm Workers* (1975). This work, however, is by no means definitive.

In his acclaimed work, *Sal Si Puedes: Cesar Chávez and the New American Revolution* (1969), Peter Matthiessen outlines how Chávez led the 1965 boycott against California grape growers and how his determination led to state reforms.

Other critical biographies on the life of Chávez and the United Farm Workers Union include: Florence M. White, *Cesar Chávez: Man of Courage* (1973); Jan Young, *The Migrant Workers and Cesar Chávez* (1972); Beverly Foddel, *Cesar Chávez and the UFW* (1974); Winthrop Yinger, *Cesar Chávez* (1975); Jean Marie Muller, *Cesar Chávez* (1977); Naurice Roberts, *Cesar Chávez and la Causa* (1986); and Conseulo Roderiguez, *Cesar Chávez* (1991).

Evaluation of Principal Biographical Sources

Franchere, Ruth. *Cesar Chávez*. New York: Crowell, 1970. (Y) This biography uses photographs to explore Chávez and the Hispanic farm laborers. Highly recommended for young adults.

London, Joan, and Henry H. Anderson. *So Shall Ye Reap*. New York: Crowell, 1970. (G) Includes maps and photographs. The authors' scenario of struggling migrants engaged in a hard-won battle for workers' rights earns the sympathy of the audience.

Levy, Jacques E. *Cesar Chávez: An Autobiography of La Causa*. New York: Norton, 1975. (A, G) The author, a labor reporter, re-creates the hardships of Hispanic families, especially Chávez's own family, who are prevented from earning a decent living because of economic exploitation and racism. Levy presents the pains of the outcasts in their own words, including tales of impossible tasks, and unyielding faith in Chávez. Following the chronology of events, he combines the testament of Chávez's family, friends, and enemies to reveal the magnitude of Chávez's life. Because of this stance, critics label the work as biased and one-sided; yet, it will stand as a significant study that details the polarization of unions, employees, and employers.

Matthiessen, Peter. *Sal Si Puedes: Cesar Chávez and the New American Revolution*. New York: Random House, 1969, (A, G) Shows how non-violence and fasting combined with an economic boycott brought about a peaceful revolution. According to Matthiessen, this revolution has resulted in access to clinics, schools, and an increase of wages from two dollars to eight dollars an hour.

Pitrone, Jean. *Chávez: Man of the Migrants*. Staten Island, NY: Alba House, 1971. (G) Illustrates the interdependence of Chávez and his fellow Hispanic farm workers. Pitrone portrays Chávez as the leader who seized the reins of power and unionized migrant farm workers despite overwhelming odds and obstacles. According to the author, the laborers looked to Chávez for guidance as African Americans had turned to Dr. Martin Luther King, Jr., for direction during the 1960s civil rights movement.

Taylor, Ronald B. *Chávez and the Farm Workers*. Boston: Beacon Press, 1975. (G) Helps the reader comprehend why farm workers struggled for so long and continued to fight in face of circumvention of the law, physical and psychological violence, and threats of loss of life and property. Taylor discusses the setbacks and dissension in the union that nearly destroyed the strikers, boycotts, and Chávez.

Overview and Evaluation of Primary Sources

For an overview of the issues of race and exploitation, Chávez in his article, "The California Farm Workers' Struggle" (*Black Scholar* 7 [June 1976]: 16-19; G), and his analytical work, "Harvest of Power" (*Reason* 15 [September 1983]:

19-26; **G**) explains the effects of power, racism, and non-unionization upon minorities, especially African Americans and Hispanics. He reiterates the importance of non-violence and the utilization of civil disobedience as a weapon for socio-economic change. Chávez also stresses the psychological and tangible benefits derived from various forms of empowerment.

Delores Huerta offers another critical explanation from the feminist perspective as well as the Hispanic viewpoint. In her article, "Reflections on the UFW Experience" (*Center Magazine* 18 [July-August 1985]: 2-8; **G**), she explores and documents crucial events and their impact upon Chávez, the workers, and the growers. In a similar vein, Jennie V. Chávez, in "An Opinion: Women of the Mexican-American Movement" (*Mademoiselle* 74 [April 1972]: 82+; **G**), argues the importance of women's roles in the liberation struggle. She chastises Hispanic men for ignoring and not respecting the women's sacrifices and contributions to the movement.

Fiction and Adaptations

Because of Chávez's eminence, organizations, institutions, and the media have interviewed him or invited him to lecture, and numerous recordings and taped interviews exist. "National Farm Workers Convention, California, 1973" is a twenty-six-minute interview with Senator Edward Kennedy and Chávez, with remarks by Sam Kushnor, editor of the labor newspaper *People's World*, and Jose Ramirez with comments by labor journalists. This interview provides an examination of the movement and the farm worker's plight.

In "Creative Non-Violence," a twenty-minute speech taped in 1975 at the Center for Cassette Studies in North Hollywood, Chávez speaks informally about organizing California farm workers using non-violence as a potent weapon.

Chávez reveals his goals for the future—after the grape strike is settled—and his position on Mexican-Americans in politics in a speech given in Santa Barbara, California, in 1971. It is titled, "Strikes and Lockouts," and is available through Santa Barbara's Office of Publisher's Catalog (1971).

Similarly, Chávez speaks of the vital issues in labor history in a seventeen-minute interview with W. Gaylin, "The Farm Workers Fight On."

Other Sources

Dunne, John Gregory. *Delano*. New York: Farrar, Straus and Giroux, 1971. An updated version of Dunne's *Delano: The Story of the California Grape Strike* discusses Chávez's role in the successful Delano, California, strike.

————. "To Die Standing: Cesar Chávez and the Chicanos." *Atlantic Monthly* 227 (June 1971): 39-45. Argues that although the boycott against Bud Antle landed Chávez in jail for the first time, it also launched him into national prominence. Presents Chávez's incarceration as a galvanizing event for emotionally depressed and penniless strikers who made Chávez their champion.

Espinosa, Michael. "Cesar Chávez and La Causa." *School Library Journal* 33 (October 1986): 182. Attributes the farm workers' victories to the stubbornness, faith, and determination of Chávez.

Flynn, Julie. "A Lawsuit Could Ruin the Farmworkers' Union: United Farm Workers Face $1.7 Million Suit." *Business Week* (March 23, 1987): 42. Flynn points out that like many other protesters and dissidents, the farm workers faced the possibility of complete economic ruin, but did not allow such adversity to deter their efforts for economic parity and decent wages.

"A Good Day's Pay for Labor Leaders." *Newsweek* 104 (July 2, 1984): 60. Relates the success of Chávez and the farm workers as a triumph for the labor movement in general.

"Grapes of Wrath." *Economist* 308 (August 20, 1988): 25. Shows how years of strikes and boycotts led to the growth, development, and success of non-unionized farm hands.

Hoffman, Pat. "Cesar Chávez's Fast for Life." *The Christian Century* 105 (October 12, 1988): 895-898. Relates the role of Chávez's fasting in the non-violent struggle of the UFW for decent wages and housing.

Kushner, Sam. *Long Road to Delano.* New York: International Publishing, 1971. Helpful in understanding the major forces behind a century of failed migrants' strikes until the success at Delano, California.

McCarthy, Tim. "UFW Grape Boycott May be Battle for Survival." *National Catholic Reporter* 25, 2 (October 28, 1988): 18. Focuses on the work done in the vineyards around Delano and illustrates how the fires of resistance brought cooperation among migrant workers and fellow employees around the nation and globe.

O'Connell, Mary, et al. "Cause the Bible Tells Me So." *U.S. Catholic* 50 (October 1985): 36-41. Explores the biblical precedent for fasting.

Sly, Julie. "Fast Leaves Cesar Chávez 'Spiritually Strong': Celebrities Vow to Continue Fight." *National Catholic Reporter* 24 (August 26, 1988): 7. Documents fasting as an effective instrument for justice.

Street, Richard S. "It's Boycott Time: Attacks on the California Agricultural Labor Relations Board and the Agricultural Labor Relations Act—In and Out of Court." *The Nation* 240 (March 23, 1985): 330-334. Analyzes in great detail the historical and constitutional precedence of boycotts as non-violent mechanisms for social change.

Thomas, Morgan B. "The Latinization of America." *Esquire* (May 1983): 47-55. Cites ethnicity as a unifying force that Chávez used to mobilize workers into action. He quotes Chávez as saying, "when I was a kid, our identity was strong within our group. We hid our tacos and our tortillas. Today we promote them."

Margaret L. Dwight
University of North Carolina, Charlotte

SHIRLEY CHISHOLM
b. 1924

Chronology

Born Shirley Anita St. Hill on November 30, 1924, in Brooklyn, New York, the daughter of a burlap bag factory worker from British Guiana and a Barbadian seamstress and domestic day-worker; *1924-1934* raised by her grandmother on a farm in Barbados, while her parents struggle in poverty in New York City; *1934-1949* returns to the U.S. and attends Brooklyn public schools; *1942* refuses scholarships from Vassar and Oberlin and chooses Brooklyn College so that she may live at home; *1946* graduates from Brooklyn College; *1949* marries Conrad Q. Chisholm, a private detective of Jamaican origin; *1946-1953* teaches nursery school; *1952* receives master's degree from Columbia University; *1959-1964* supervises ten New York City day-care centers as educational consultant for the New York State Bureau of Child Welfare; *1964-1968* serves in the New York State Assembly as Democratic Representative of the Fifty-fifth District (Bedford-Stuyvesant); *1968* becomes the first black woman ever elected to the U.S. Congress; *1969-1983* serves as representative for the Thirteenth District (Brooklyn); *1972, 1976* member of the Democratic National Committee; *1972* runs unsuccessfully as presidential candidate in the Democratic primary; *1977* divorces Conrad Chisholm; marries Arthur Hardwick, Jr.; *1983* appointed to the Purington Chair at Mt. Holyoke College.

Activities of Historical Significance

Chisholm was the first black woman elected to the United States Congress. After an easy victory in 1968 over James Farmer, former Congress of Racial Equality (CORE) director, Chisholm remained a member of the House of Representatives until her retirement in 1983. While in Congress, she quickly gained a reputation as a maverick, an outspoken critic of the "old boys' network," and one who refused to accept traditional political attitudes and practices. An often recounted anecdote involved the congresswoman challenging her first committee assignment. She broke with tradition when she asked Speaker of the House John McCormack to change her appointment to the rural development and forestry subcommittee of the agricultural committee. As the representative of an inner city district, Chisholm viewed the assignment as an attempt to suppress her. When the speaker seemed reluctant, she stated that she would have "to do my own thing." A startled McCormack replied, "Your own what?" Chisholm received a new assignment.

Chisholm continued to provoke the ire of her colleagues by protesting American involvement in the Vietnam War and refusing to vote for any defense spending. Her feminism caused even more uneasiness in the House, especially among black congressmen who disagreed with Chisholm's assertion that sexism presented a greater problem than racism in America. She supported numerous women's causes, particularly that of reproductive rights, and for a time served as honorary head of the National Association for the Repeal of Abortion Laws. Her refusal to play by unwritten political rules, as well as her often controversial positions, usually left Chisholm without the support she needed from colleagues to enact her programs.

With her outspoken advocacy of the rights of women and minorities, equal employment and educational opportunities, housing and health care reform, Chisholm drew attention to issues that few members of Congress were willing to address. This helped to lay the groundwork for later politicians who would support those issues. She is remembered for her innovative but unsuccessful bid for the Democratic presidential nomination in 1972.

Overview of Biographical Sources

Because there is no biography of Shirley Chisholm written specifically for an adult reading audience, researchers may wish to consult the several children's books about her: Susan Brownmiller, *Shirley Chisholm: A Biography* (1970), James Haskins, *Fighting Shirley Chisholm* (1975), and Sheila Hobson and Harvey Goldenberg, *Fighting Shirley Chisholm: The Story of the First Black U.S. Congresswoman* (1969). Although written in a style appropriate for young readers, these do contain valuable information about Chisholm's life and political career.

Also available are numerous non-scholarly sources, such as articles about Chisholm in newspapers and magazines, which can be located in Susan Duffy's bibliography, *Shirley Chisholm: A Bibliography of Writings By and About Her* (1988).

Evaluation of Principal Biographical Sources

Brownmiller, Susan. *Shirley Chisholm: A Biography*. Garden City, NY: Doubleday, 1970. (Y) Provides many personal anecdotes, showing in particular the importance of education in Chisholm's life. As a young adult, for example, she read a great deal about black heroines, such as the twentieth-century activist and educator Mary McLeod Bethune and nineteenth-century abolitionist Harriet Tubman, whom she adopted as role models. Brownmiller effectively puts Chisholm's life and work into a perspective younger readers can understand.

Duffy, Susan, comp. *Shirley Chisholm: A Bibliography of Writings By and About Her*. Metuchen, NJ: Scarecrow Press, 1988. (A, G) One hundred thirty-five pages of works by and about Chisholm, including speeches, articles, letters, and books. Most entries are simply listed, but a few are annotated. Provides name and subject indexes. Most helpful to researchers are the citations for the hundreds of newspaper articles about Chisholm and the many articles by Chisholm herself. Users should know that some entries contain only a mention of Chisholm, while others contain general material on related subjects, such as blacks in government.

Haskins, James. *Fighting Shirley Chisholm*. New York: Dial Press, 1975. (Y) This book will appeal to more sophisticated young readers because Haskins provides in-depth context and emphasizes Chisholm's adult life. Contains an appendix with her legislative record, and a good bibliography of her speeches.

Hobson, Sheila, and Harvey D. Goldenberg. *Fighting Shirley Chisholm: The Story of the First Black U.S. Congresswoman*. New York: Buckingham Learning Corporation, 1969. (Y) Designed for use in the classroom, this work contains learning exercises to help students understand American government and uses Chisholm's career as an example.

Kuriansky, Joan, and Catherine Smith. *Shirley Chisholm: Democratic Representative from New York*. Washington, DC: Grossman Publishers, 1972. (G) Part of the Ralph Nader Congress Project, Citizens Look at Congress Series, this item focuses on Chisholm's career in Congress.

LeVeness, Frank P., and Jane P. Sweeney, eds. *Women Leaders in Contemporary U.S. Politics*. Boulder, CO: Lynne Rienner, 1987. (A, G) Provides a brief overview of Chisholm's career, with special emphasis on her role as a black female politician, and the problems this caused with male colleagues, black and white.

Overview and Evaluation of Primary Sources

In addition to the following, researchers may also wish to examine Chisholm's speeches and newspaper and magazine articles, using Duffy as a guide. The *Congressional Record* provides Chisholm's debates from the House floor.

Chisholm's book, *Unbought and Unbossed* (Boston: Houghton Mifflin, 1970; **A, G**), is part autobiography, part statement of her political philosophy. This work describes Chisholm's humble and unremarkable early life and her candid views on her political career, colleagues, American democracy, and its shortcomings. Although this and Chisholm's other work have been criticized as politically naive (one reviewer dubbed her book a ''school primer'') and idealistic, her observations—for example, that American democracy does not work because Congress, ''a small group of old men,'' is not representative of the American public—are often valuable for their straightforwardness. The title was Chisholm's campaign slogan in the 1968 congressional race and refers to her neither seeking nor receiving Democratic party machine support.

Chisholm's second work, *The Good Fight* (New York: Harper and Row, 1973; **A, G**), is a short (163 pages plus appendices which include position papers and campaign speeches) account of the 1972 election. Most of the book focuses on her unsuccessful bid for the Democratic presidential nomination, the last third is an examination of George McGovern's loss to Richard Nixon in that race, and the future role of minorities in American politics. As with her first work, *The Good Fight* has been criticized for its unsophisticated political analyses.

In her essay, ''Racism and Anti-Feminism,'' found in *Sociology for the Seventies: A Contemporary Perspective*, edited by Morris L. Medley and James E. Conyers (New York: John Wiley, 1972; **A**), Chisholm uses her political as well as personal experience to compare racism and sexism as similar forms of oppression.

''Interview with Shirley Chisholm'' (1968) consisting of three audio tapes, relates Chisholm's discussion of her childhood, involvement in New York state politics, and her first congressional campaign. It is available at the Schomburg Center for Research in Black Culture at the New York Public Library.

Other Sources

Christopher, Maurine. *America's Black Congressmen.* New York: Crowell, 1971. Covers the lives and careers of black members of Congress, including Chisholm.

Drotning, Philip T., and Wesley South. *Up From the Ghetto.* New York: Cowles, 1970. Focuses on Chisholm's reputation as a political maverick.

Farmer, James. *Lay Bare the Heart: An Autobiography of the Civil Rights Movement.* New York: Arbor House, 1985. Farmer's account of his 1968 contest for Congress against Chisholm.

Ploski, Harry A., and James Williams. *The Negro Almanac: A Reference Work on the African American*. 5th ed. Detroit: Gale Research, 1989. Concise overview of Chisholm's early life, opinions, and career in politics.

Sochen, June. *Movers and Shakers: American Women Thinkers and Activists, 1900-1970.* New York: Quadrangle/*New York Times* Book Company, 1973. Discusses Chisholm's life and career in the context of women's rights and black rights.

Carol Wilson
Washington College
Chestertown, Maryland

JENNIE JEROME CHURCHILL
1854-1921

Chronology

Born Jeanette Jerome on January 9, 1854, in New York City, the daughter of Leonard Jerome, a prominent New York businessman, and Clara Hall Jerome, a member of a wealthy and politically significant New York family; *1854-1874* grows up in New York, Paris, and London; *1874* marries Lord Randolph Churchill, the son of the duke and duchess of Marlborough, in Paris on April 15; gives birth to Winston Spencer Leonard Churchill in England on November 30; *1880* gives birth to her second son, John Strange Spencer Churchill, on February 4; *1895* her husband dies; *1899-1900* organizes and heads a hospital ship during the Boer War; *1900* marries George Cornwallis-West; *1908* writes and publishes *The Reminiscences of Lady Randolph Churchill*; *1909* writes the play *His Borrowed Plumes*; *1912* writes the play *The Bill*; *1913* divorces George Cornwallis-West; *1916* writes and publishes the essay "Small Talk on Big Subjects"; *1918* marries Montagu Porch; *1921* dies on June 29 in London of complications from injuries caused by a fall.

Activities of Historical Significance

Jennie Jerome Churchill's life was focused on the British social order, her marriages, and the career of her oldest son, Winston Churchill. During her years with Randolph Churchill (1874-1895), she identified with Tory democracy. During the Boer War she played a significant role in the formation and administration of a hospital ship that served the British army.

During the Edwardian period, Churchill remarried and pursued literary projects. Her *Reminiscences of Lady Randolph Churchill* was published to a warm reception in 1908; her plays *His Borrowed Plumes* (1909) and *The Bill* (1913) had limited success. She campaigned for her son Winston during his parliamentary elections and was thought to have had some influence in his selection as home secretary. During the last twenty years of her life, Churchill maintained her active social life.

Overview of Biographical Sources

For an individual who is remembered primarily for being the mother of Winston S. Churchill, Churchill has had her share of interested biographers. The earliest full-scale biography was Rene Kraus's *Young Lady Randolph: The Life and Times of Jennie Jerome, American Mother of Winston Churchill* (1943), which was published during Winston Churchill's wartime ministry. While obviously dated, Kraus's book is still of use. Ralph G. Martin's definitive work, *Jennie: The Life of Lady Randolph Churchill* (1969-1971), is still the finest and most scholarly biography available. *Jennie, Lady Randolph Churchill: A Portrait with Letters* (1974), by Peregine Churchill and Julian Mitchell, is an excellent study that centers on Churchill's personal life.

Evaluation of Principal Biographical Sources

Churchill, Peregine, and Julian Mitchell. *Jennie, Lady Randolph Churchill: A Portrait with Letters*. New York: St. Martin's, 1974. (**A, G**) This bibliographic work reproduces an extensive range of letters. The interpretation is balanced, and the work is comprehensive in scope.

Churchill, Randolph S. *Winston Churchill: Youth, 1874-1900*. Boston: Houghton Mifflin, 1966. (**A, G**) This biography of Winston Churchill by his son provides extensive biographical information on Jennie.

Kraus, Rene. *Young Lady Randolph: The Life and Times of Jennie Jerome, American Mother of Winston Churchill*. New York: G. P. Putnam, 1943. (**G, Y**) The author provides an adequate profile of Churchill but fails to treat her subject in a comprehensive manner.

Martin, Ralph G. *Jennie: The Life of Lady Randolph Churchill*. 2 vols. Englewood Cliffs, NJ: Prentice-Hall, 1969-1971. (**A, G**) The most comprehensive and scholarly work available on Churchill, providing excellent documentation and the most thorough bibliography available on the subject.

Morgan, Ted. *Churchill: Young Man in a Hurry, 1874-1915*. New York: Simon and Schuster, 1982. (**A, G, Y**) Morgan's examination of Winston Churchill's early decades provides valuable biographical information on Churchill and her impact on her son's career.

Overview and Evaluation of Primary Sources

Churchill's activities and affairs have been discussed in numerous memoirs, autobiographies, and other primary documents. Perhaps the most significant primary source is her biased autobiography, *Reminiscences of Lady Randolph Churchill* (New York: Century, 1908; **A, G**). This work is of particular value as the autobiography of a prominent woman, as a reflection on the nature of Victorian/Edwardian culture, and for information on her first husband, Lord Randolph Churchill. Winston S. Churchill's *My Early Life* (London: Odhams Press, 1930; **A, G, Y**) is a fascinating book that provides a son's insights into his mother and her activities. Other contemporary accounts are Sir Frederick Ponsonby's *Recollections of Three Reigns* (London: Eyre and Spottiswoode, 1951; **A, G**), Lady Maud Warrender's *My First Sixty Years* (London: Cassell, 1933; **A, G**), the countess of Warwick's *Afterthoughts* (London: Cassell, 1931; **A, G**), and Frank Harris's *My Life and Loves*, edited by John F. Gallagher (New York: Grove Press, 1963; **A, G**).

Museums, Historical Landmarks, Societies

Blenheim Palace (near Woodstock, Oxfordshire, England). Built in 1705, this was the Churchill family residence. Winston was born here, and the Churchill Papers are housed here.

William T. Walker
Philadelphia College of Pharmacy and Science

ELDRIDGE CLEAVER
b. 1935

Chronology

Born Leroy Eldridge Cleaver on August 31, 1935, in Wabbaseka, Arkansas, near Little Rock, the third of six chidlren and the eldest of three sons of Leroy Cleaver, a waiter and piano player, and Thelma Robinson Cleaver, an elementary school teacher; *1945* moves with family to Phoenix when his father takes a new job waiting tables on trains; *1946* moves with family to Los Angeles area when his father takes a job as a waiter on the Super Chief between Los Angeles and Chicago; runs with a Chicano gang while living with family in Rose Hill, a suburb near Pasadena, California; *1947* steals a bike and is arrested as a juvenile; sent to reform school, where he converts to Catholicism; *1954* arrested on a felony charge for selling marijuana; *1957* while out of prison briefly, commits a series of holdups and rapes and continues to deal drugs—all of which he considers suitable "insurrectionary" behavior; *1958* sent to prison for assault with intent to kill during an attempted rape; becomes a Black Muslim in prison; *1964* sides with Malcolm X when Malcolm breaks with Elijah Muhammad; *1965* begins to write as a way to deal with his grief after Malcolm's assassination; *1966* his writing enables his lawyer, Beverly Axelrod, to get him out on parole with a promised job at *Ramparts* magazine in San Francisco; *1967* joins the Black Panther Party for Self Defense, founded the previous October by Huey Newton and Bobby Seale; meets Kathleen Neal, whom he marries in December; party leader Huey Newton imprisoned on charges of killing a police officer; *February 1968* publishes *Soul on Ice* and becomes a celebrity; *April 6, 1968* two days after the assassination of Martin Luther King, Jr., is involved, along with several other Panthers, in a shootout with the Oakland police; released from jail on a writ of *habeas corpus*; *November 27, 1968* ordered to return to prison for parole violations but instead leaves the country for Cuba; *1969* travels to Algiers, where Kathleen joins him; his son, Antonio Maceo, is born; *1970* his second child, Joju, is born; *February 1971* because of letters forged by the FBI and anonymous accusations, splits with Newton and the Black Panther party; *1973* moves with his family to Paris; *1975* designs sex-specific trousers for men only, featuring a codpiece in a contrasting color; returns to the U.S. as a prisoner; housed in the Federal Correctional Center in San Diego, then the Alameda County Courthouse in Oakland; *1976* paroled at the pleading of a wealthy Christian businessman after announcing his conversion to evangelical Christianity; tours the country as an evangelist but has trouble reconciling his image as a preacher with his sex-specific pants; founds the Eldridge Cleaver Crusades; *1978-1987* publishes *Soul on Fire*, an attempt to legitimize his "born again" status; after his Crusades fold, tries a new religion called Christlam, a synthesis of Christianity and Islam; moves into conservative Republican politics; retires from public life as a Mormon convert; *1987* arrested for cocaine possession; *1988* arrested for theft from a residence and placed on probation for three years; divorces Kathleen after a seven-year separation, during which Kathleen attends Yale University and Yale Law School and maintains custody of the children.

Activities of Historical Significance

Eldridge Cleaver has a place in American history for the extreme social and political ideologies that are forcefully articulated in his writings. In 1968 he published *Soul on Ice*, a collection of essays that sold two million copies, was named Book of the Year by the *New York Times*, and was adopted as a primer for the "Second American Revolution" by radicals of the militant pro-civil rights/anti-Vietnam War movement of the late 1960s. As minister of information for the Black Panther party, the short-lived African-American revolutionary group founded in Oakland in 1966, Cleaver published a number of articles in the official organ of the party, the *Black Panther*. Simultaneously, he wrote political essays for the leftist *Ramparts* magazine and tried to put some of his ideas into practice by founding Black House, a cultural center for blacks in the San Francisco area.

Cleaver spent nine years of his adult life in prison for a variety of offenses, including drug dealing and attempted murder. Radical lawyer Beverly Axelrod first secured his release on parole in late 1966 and introduced him to Stew Albert and Jerry Rubin, founders of the "Yippies" (a loose organization of politicized hippies), and Jack Weinberg, leader of the Students for a Democratic Society (SDS). These individuals were influential in providing a theoretical context for many of Cleaver's unorthodox views.

In February 1967, Cleaver met Huey Newton, Bobby Seale, and other members of the newly formed Black Panther party, and fell in with their plans to provide security for Betty Shabbaz, the widow of Malcolm X. Brandishing firearms, the Panthers adopted a policy of confronting the police in the streets of Oakland. In the months that followed, Cleaver became convinced that the Panthers were the vanguard of an imminent violent revolution in the U.S. and joined the group with the intent of fostering a Marxist-Leninist insurrection.

Cleaver espoused the Panther Ten Point Program, written by Newton and Seale, which included demands for liberating all black prisoners on the grounds that they were improperly imprisoned by an oppressive regime; for exempting all black males from the draft on the grounds that they were not protected by the U.S. government; and for calling a United Nations plebiscite to allow African Americans to decide whether to remain Americans or secede as a separate "black colony." The latter terminology derived from Newton and Seale's reading of Franz Fanon's *The Wretched of the Earth*, a black psychiatrist's study of the mentality of colonized blacks in Algeria.

After Newton was imprisoned for his role in a 1967 shoot-out that left a police officer dead, Cleaver worked closely with white radical organizations in an attempt to secure Newton's release. Because of his high public profile, the leftist Peace and Freedom Party (PFP) nominated Cleaver as their presidential candidate in 1968. He chose Jerry Rubin as his running mate, angering the more orthodox socialists of the "Old Left" who dominated the PFP. Cleaver, unlike the PFP, did not take his candidacy seriously; he declared at one point that if he were elected he would not live in the White House, he would "burn the mother . . . down."

The Panthers represented, and Cleaver himself articulated, the anger and militancy of the youth movement of the 1960s. The youth movement rejected the "establishment" as racist and cynical, and condemned the Vietnam War and the draft as fascist and genocidal toward African Americans, who served and were killed in disproportionate numbers. Reading the Ten Point Program and the essays in *Soul on Ice* imparts a solid impression of the mindset of the coalition of young leftist students and ghetto youth who formed this movement. Particularly valuable for understanding white students is the essay "The White Race and Its Heroes," while the black point of view is clearly presented in "Initial Reaction on the Assassination of Malcolm X," "The Black Man's Stake in Vietnam," and "Domestic Law and International Order." The Black Panthers, which lost influence and membership steadily throughout the 1970s, was officially disbanded by Newton in 1980.

Whatever the success or failure of Cleaver's political activism, his lasting achievement is his writing. *Soul on Ice,* which continues to be widely read, will be recorded in American literary and sociological history as the book that popularized radical behavior. Whether or not readers agreed with Cleaver's advocacy of extreme, anti-social, criminal behavior as a response to an oppressive society, they understood the agony of the voice behind it, making *Soul on Ice* a landmark autobiography.

Overview of Biographical Sources

Three biographies are currently available on Cleaver, two of which are by Christian authors who accepted at face value Cleaver's 1976 conversion to "born again'' status: John A. Oliver, *Eldridge Cleaver Reborn* (1977), and George Otis, *Eldridge Cleaver: Ice and Fire!* (1977).

A newer critical biography by Kathleen Rout, *Eldridge Cleaver* (1991), analyzes Cleaver's changing mentality and varied motives at different stages of his career. Cleaver is viewed as a man who requires a belief system that provides coherence to his life, as is shown by his odyssey through Roman Catholicism, Black Muslimism, Marxism/Leninism, evangelical Christianity, political conservatism, and finally Mormonism. One could argue that Cleaver's continual shifting from one ''ism'' to the next eliminates any chance that he is sincere. Rout is understandably skeptical of Cleaver's 1976 conversion to Christianity, but not unsympathetic.

Evaluation of Principal Biographical Sources

Oliver, John A. *Eldridge Cleaver Reborn.* Plainfield, NJ: Logos International, 1977. (**G, Y**) This book was written immediately after Cleaver's announcement that he had ''found Christ'' and accepts his conversion without cynicism: ''The Hound of Heaven is seen pursuing a black kid from the ghetto side of society into black manhood in white America, into prison and beyond, through revolutionary rage into isolated exile, and finally back home, into and out of jail again to speak a new language.''

Otis, George. *Eldridge Cleaver: Ice and Fire!* Van Nuys, CA: Bible Voice, 1977. (**G, Y**) This account by the host of the Christian television show *High Adventure* goes into detail about the events of 1968, including Cleaver's involvement in the shoot-out with the police and his campaign for the presidency. The emphasis, however, is on Cleaver's conversion and includes criticism of the skeptics. The book ends with a pitch for U.S. involvement in Angola and South Africa to save ''our black brothers'' from communism, and a direct plea for funds to cover Cleaver's legal expenses, with the implication that the leftists abandoned him because of his ''decision for Christ''; a post office box number in Berkeley is provided.

Rout, Kathleen. *Eldridge Cleaver.* Boston: Twayne, 1991. (**A, G**) After the Eldridge Cleaver Crusades folded and Cleaver himself was arrested for cocaine possession and robbery, it was obvious that the simplistic ''criminal finds Christ'' interpretation offered by other biographers was inappropriate. Rout makes use of Cleaver's own writings and interviews and articles about him to piece together a more coherent portrait of a complex life. Noting many glaring inconsistencies and the omission of important details about the exile years from the autobiographical

Soul on Fire, Rout strives for a more analytical explanation of Cleaver's behavior. Her opinion is that while it may be true that Cleaver lived in a racist America, that the local police were abusive, and that the FBI violated the rights of many black activists, he nevertheless responded by pursuing criminal behavior and becoming involved with what was ultimately a politicized gang, the Black Panther party. Cleaver seems to have viewed each "conversion" in his life as a new beginning, guaranteed to end a long string of troubles.

Overview and Evaluation of Primary Sources

Cleaver's work, *The Black Moochie*, written in prison and first published in the October and November 1969 issues of *Ramparts* magazine, is a two-part reminiscence of his early years when he ran with the gang in Rosehill. This autobiographical foray conveys a sense of criminal adventure and a terror of the police. A second work, "The Flashlight," is a short story about a character named Stacy, the only black in a Chicano gang, who steals a large flashlight from a wealthy suburban home near Los Angeles. In this story, which was included in *Prize Stories 1971: The O. Henry Awards*, (edited by William Abrams. New York: Doubleday, 1971; **G**), Cleaver uses the flashlight as a symbol of hope for a different and better way of life. Stacy eventually must give up the flashlight and succumb to the fate awaiting him as a drug dealer. The story provides interesting parallels with Cleaver's own drug dealing, his consequent imprisonment, his cycles of finding and losing hope, and his sense of a foreboding, overbearing destiny.

In his semi-autobiographical *Soul on Ice* (New York: McGraw-Hill, 1968; **A, G**), Cleaver makes no attempt to tell the full story of his life; rather, he recounts the development of his socio-political ideas in essay form, from his youth until his parole from prison in 1966. He discusses the social hypocrisy that he observed after passage of the 1954 Supreme Court desegregation decision, *Brown v. Board of Education of Topeka*. He analyzes his decision that rape could be used as an appropriate "insurrectionary act" against the oppressive white man and the "loved/hated Ogre," the white woman. He offers an explication of how the white-controlled government rewrote American history and describes the need for a revolution. The goal of such a revolution would be to place control of all resources in the hands of "The People"; to establish racial and sexual equality; and to return humankind to a primal unity of male/female/white/black.

In Robert Sheer, ed., *Eldridge Cleaver: Post-Prison Writings and Speeches*, (New York: Random House, 1969; **A, G**), the topics covered are political, but self-revelatory. Cleaver is intent on describing the conflicts that existed between himself and the Panthers, on the one hand, and the police and FBI on the other.

In *Soul on Fire* (Waco, TX: Word Books, 1978; **A, G**), Cleaver attempts to fill in gaps left by his other works and to legitimize his 1976 conversion to Christianity. He traces the experience to France in 1975 where he claims to have seen the face of Christ in the moon. But in presenting his childhood and the early Panther days, he jumps around, leaving many unanswered questions, and ends with a passionate declaration of his "calling" as an evangelist and a "New Man." Much of this material is reworked from a failed manuscript entitled "Over My Shoulder."

Many of the details of his life in exile can be found only in the interviews he granted, the most accessible of which is the Curtice Taylor interview in *Rolling Stone* (September 1975). This interview was conducted soon after Cleaver announced his intention to return to the U.S. as a prisoner.

In 1982 Cleaver planned to donate all of his papers to Yale University, which was to establish a Cleaver Collection under the charge of Henry Gates, then an assistant professor there. Subsequently, Cleaver decided to retain the papers as source material for projected works, although he has published nothing since 1978. In 1990 he announced his intention to donate his papers to the Bancroft Library at the University of California, Berkeley.

Fiction and Adaptations

Two movies have approached Cleaver from diametrically opposed viewpoints. The first, *Eldridge Cleaver* (1969) by William Klein, was filmed in Algiers to portray the Black Panther viewpoint, using Cleaver's voice-over on scenes of riots in the U.S. The second film, *The Eldridge Cleaver Story* (1978) by Gospel Films, presents Cleaver as a "born again" Christian who has since withdrawn from circulation.

Other Sources

Bartlett, Laile E. "The Education of Eldridge Cleaver." *Reader's Digest* 109 (September 1976): 65-72. Cleaver discusses the importance of Martin Luther King, Jr., and Christian reformer Walter Rauschenbusch to his developing social thought.

Gates, Skip. "Cuban Experience: Eldridge Cleaver on Ice." *Transition* 49 (1975): 32-44. Relates Cleaver's experiences with Cuban deceit during his seven-month stay in 1968-1969.

————. "Eldridge Cleaver on Ice: Algeria and After." *Ch'Indaba* 2 (1976): 50-57. This is a continuation of the above interview; *Transition* magazine changed its name after the first part was published. Interview contains Cleaver's revelations about the stresses of dealing with multiple problems and personalities in the International Section of the Black Panther party at the new headquarters in Algeria.

Lockwood, Lee. *Conversation with Eldridge Cleaver*. New York: McGraw-Hill, 1970. A book-length interview presenting the essential militant and uncompromising Cleaver of the old days—conducted in Algiers near the beginning of his exile period.

Schanche, Donald. *The Panther Paradox: A Liberal's Dilemma*. New York: David McKay, 1970. The author describes his meetings with Cleaver both in San Francisco and in Algiers and the evolution of his attitude toward him and the Panther organization from a tentative liberal partisanship on the grounds of black oppression to a firm liberal rejection on the grounds of their illiberality and self-destructive inclinations.

Simon, Jaqueline. "Interview with Eldridge Cleaver." *Punto de Contacto/ Point of Contact* 1 (1975): 34-56. The interview that took place at about the time Cleaver supposedly had his vision of Christ in the moon makes no reference to his religious life, but discusses his role as a "tantric guru" and pants designer.

Taylor, Curtice. "Eldridge Cleaver: The *Rolling Stone* Interview." *Rolling Stone* 195 (September 11, 1975): 40+. The first interview in a major periodical since Cleaver's exile began. He shocked Taylor by announcing his "love affair" with the U.S. military and his new conservative values.

Yochelson, Samuel, and Stanton E. Samenow. *The Criminal Personality*. Vol. 1. New York: J. Aronson, 1976. Two psychiatrists reject socio-psycho-economic explanations of criminality; criminal behavior is viewed as learned behavior that must be "unlearned" through a radical transformation of the self. Cleaver read this book in jail in 1976 and referred to it in *Soul on Fire* in 1978; it was probably instrumental in his decision to try being a "born again" Christian to save himself from repeating his criminal patterns.

Kathleen Rout

THOMAS GREEN CLEMSON
1807-1888

Chronology

Born Thomas Green Clemson on July 1, 1807, in Philadelphia, the second of three sons of Thomas Green Clemson, a wealthy merchant, and Elizabeth Baker Clemson; *1814* father dies and his mother petitions the Orphans' Court of Philadelphia to appoint a guardian for her six children; *1822-1824* attends Norwich Academy, forerunner of Norwich University, in Vermont; *1826* sails to Europe where he attends lectures at the Sorbonne; *1827* is admitted to the Ecole des Mines Royale in Paris; *1831* receives diploma as assayer from the Royal Mint of France; *1838* marries Anna Maria Calhoun and works closely with his father-in-law, John C. Calhoun, in ventures in southern agriculture and gold mining; *1844-1852* serves as *chargés d'affaires* to Belgium; assists in the publication of Calhoun's speeches; *1853-1861* purchases a one-hundred-acre farm called "The Home" near Bladensburg, Maryland, and plants, assays, and writes articles on scientific agriculture; is instrumental in the establishment of the Maryland Agricultural College; *1857* King Leopold of Belgium requests Clemson's return to Brussels, but lack of political clout makes this impossible; *1860* appointed superintendent of agricultural affairs after President James Buchanan enlarges the Agricultural Bureau of the Patent Office; sent to Europe to purchase seeds and cuttings to be propagated in the government greenhouse; *March 1861* resigns his position but demonstrates no urgency to abandon his residence in Maryland when that state does not secede from the Union; *June 9, 1861* departs with his son for the South, leaving his wife and daughter behind in Maryland to save his property from confiscation; *July 20, 1861* son, John Calhoun Clemson, enlists in a South Carolina regiment as a private; *spring 1863* travels to Richmond to join the Confederate service, whereupon he is sent to Texas to take charge of the Nitre and Mining Bureau of the Trans-Mississippi Department; *September 9, 1863* son is captured by Union forces at Bolivar, Mississippi, and sent to Johnson's Island in Lake Erie near Sandusky, Ohio; *June 9, 1865* paroled from Confederate service at Shreveport, Louisiana; *May 1866* travels to New York City on business, where he finds no sympathy for the plight of the defeated South; *1871* both of his children die (his daughter probably of tuberculosis and his son in a railroad collision) and Clemson and his wife execute mutual wills with the joint purpose of donating their property, Fort Hill, to the state of South Carolina for an agricultural institution; *1875* Anna Maria Clemson dies suddenly of heart failure; *1888* dies on April 6 at

Fort Hill, and is buried in St. Paul's Episcopal churchyard in what is now Clemson, South Carolina; *1888-1889* son-in-law Gideon Lee challenges the transferral of the Clemson property to South Carolina in the interest of his teenage daughter Floride Isabella, but he loses his case; *1893* Clemson College is opened.

Activities of Historical Significance

An aristocrat by birth and education, Clemson sympathized with the common people and spent a great part of his life advocating their right to education and expressing the conviction that education in the sciences was their primary hope for the future.

Although a native Pennsylvanian, not originally fond of the South and tied to the North by family, property and investments, he chose to side with the Confederacy at the outbreak of the Civil War. While not an opponent of slavery, he nonetheless assumed the disinterested role of labelling the institution as "bad economics" for his adopted state of South Carolina.

As son-in-law of Secretary of State John C. Calhoun, Clemson was appointed *chargé d'affaires* to Belgium by President John Tyler. He continued to serve under presidents Polk and Taylor and became a personal friend of King Leopold I of Belgium. While at his diplomatic post, Clemson sought to promote a direct cotton trade between the American South and the German states through Belgian territory, and he conceived an important treaty of navigation.

A decade later, when the Buchanan administration decided to expand the Agricultural Bureau of the Patent Office and Clemson was appointed to the position of agricultural superintendent, he advised the administration to establish an autonomous bureau of agriculture unaffiliated with the Department of Interior. Clemson was welcomed to this newly created position with enthusiasm, but the administration was hampered by interdepartmental strife and curtailed by the onset of the Civil War. The year following his resignation, Congress acted upon Clemson's recommendation and created a separate executive Department of Agriculture whose secretary would eventually (1889) sit as a member of the president's cabinet.

After the war, Clemson avoided politics, stressing instead the crucial need for South Carolina to reconstruct its agricultural systems. During these years Clemson sounded an impassioned plea in defense of science in education.

Clemson's known promotional activities include his connection with the founding of the Maryland Agricultural College (now the University of Maryland), his support for the Morrill Act (first introduced in 1857 and later vetoed by Buchanan but signed by Lincoln in similar form five years later), his work as superintendent of agricultural affairs, his leadership in the South after the Civil War, and finally his part in the founding of Clemson Agricultural College.

Because the natural sciences were more valued in Europe than in the United States during Clemson's youth, he sought education in France. Afterwards he became a prolific writer on agricultural chemistry, confidently discussing the sources, compositions, and characteristics of various soils, and speculating on such related issues as vegetable anatomy, plant physiology, organic and inorganic constituents of plants, and plant nutrition. The majority of his articles were published in *The American Farmer* between 1855 and 1861. Clemson was ahead of his time in advocating the importance of deep plowing; growing up during a time when great attention was being directed to the rapid depletion of soil along the eastern seaboard, he became a pioneer proponent of the use of fertilizer.

Distinguished as a philanthropist, Clemson was a man of many interests. He played the violin, dabbled in oil painting, purchased paintings in Belgium for the collector William Wilson Corcoran, and collected about forty seventeenth- and eighteenth-century Flemish paintings, which were stored for safety during the Civil War at his uncle's home in Altoona, Pennsylvania, and eventually formed the nuclear holdings of the Rudolph E. Lee Gallery of Clemson University.

Exclusive of the Fort Hill estate which was inherited by his wife alone, the purchasing power of Clemson's property, as bequeathed for the founding of an agricultural college, ranks among the largest benefactions ever made to the state of South Carolina. Considering the different eras and the widely disparate currency values, it could be argued that the amount of Clemson's endowment exceeded the legacies of John Harvard or Elihu Yale to the institutions bearing their names.

Overview of Biographical Sources

There are two biographies of Clemson, written nearly half a century apart, and they complement each other perfectly. *Thomas Green Clemson: His Life and Work* (1937), written by Alester G. Holmes and George R. Sherrill, two Clemson University professors of history and economics, studies primarily his scientific work and public career. Ernest M. Lander, Jr.'s *The Calhoun Family and Thomas Green Clemson: Decline of a Southern Patriarchy* (1983), focuses on Clemson's private life and his difficult relations with his Calhoun in-laws.

Evaluation of Principal Biographical Sources

Holmes, Alester G., and George R. Sherrill. *Thomas Green Clemson: His Life and Work*. Richmond: Garrett and Massie, 1937. (**A, G**) Written with full access to the Thomas G. Clemson Papers at Clemson University, the authors make a frank assessment of the man as diplomat, scientist, and philanthropist.

Lander, Ernest M., Jr. *The Calhoun Family and Thomas Green Clemson: Decline of a Southern Patriarchy.* Columbia: University of South Carolina Press, 1983. (**A, G**) Based primarily on private correspondence, this volume begins with Clemson's entrance into the Calhoun family and proceeds to chronicle in exhaustive detail the family's constant bickering and wrangling. Unfortunately, the author does not examine the social causes of such difficult familial relations.

Overview and Evaluation of Primary Sources

Clemson began writing articles for scientific journals before he finished his studies at the Royal School of Mines. His first article, "Assay and Analysis of Iron Ore (*fer titanné*) from the Environs of Baltimore," appeared in the *American Journal of Science and Arts* when he was twenty-two years old. Most of his articles appeared in *The American Farmer,* but several others were printed in *The United States Agricultural Society Journal* and *DeBow's Review.*

The Thomas G. Clemson Papers are housed at the Robert Muldrow Cooper Library of Clemson University, where they are indexed by the correspondent's last name and date. The earliest sample of his writing is a pocket journal of the years 1832-1837 which Clemson kept while living in Europe. It was donated in 1979 by a distant relative, Charles R. Clemson of Lancaster, Pennsylvania.

Also included in the University's collection of Clemson material are his regular correspondence with his father-in-law, John C. Calhoun, and a microfilm record of his diplomatic activities while in Belgium (which is copied from the original at the National Archives). Although there is little correspondence relating to his agricultural superintendency (1860-1861) or his service in the Confederate government (1863-1865), there is abundant documentation of Clemson's activities as administrator of the Calhoun property, such as his work agreements with the newly freed slaves initiated in order to reestablish the productivity of the plantation.

The Clemson University collection also contains a wealth of biographical and genealogical information on the Clemson and the Calhoun families and a file of published and unpublished papers and addresses about Clemson.

Of related interest are the papers of Charles Leupp, Clemson's New York broker and fellow art collector who committed suicide before the Civil War, housed at Rutgers University Library, and the papers of Clemson's South Carolina financial advisor, Armistead Burt, housed at Duke University Library.

The 1863-1866 diary of Clemson's daughter, Floride, was edited by Ernest M. Lander, Jr., and Charles M. McGee, Jr., and titled *A Rebel Came Home* (Columbia: University of South Carolina Press, 1961; rev. ed. 1989; **A, G**); its prologue is especially valuable to an understanding of Clemson's life and contributions. The diary is interesting in its own right because Floride Clemson, who remained behind in Maryland while her father went South to serve the Confederacy, followed at the end of the war and wrote poignantly of the devastation, impoverishment, and displacement of many of the once affluent Southern families.

Museums, Historical Landmarks, Societies

Fort Hill (Clemson, SC). At the center of the Clemson University campus is the old homestead of both John C. Calhoun and Thomas Green Clemson, preserved as a national landmark. It contains various objects related to Clemson's life, including a number of family portraits.

Clemson Statue (Clemson, SC). There is a large sculpted likeness of Clemson in front of Tillman Hall, the Old Main Building, at Clemson University.

Clemson, SC. The name of this college town in the foothills of the Blue Ridge Mountains was changed from Calhoun to Clemson in 1943. Outside the town is the Thomas Green Clemson Parkway.

Other Sources

Spaulding, E. Wilder. "Clemson, Thomas Green." In *The Dictionary of American Biography,* edited by Allen Johnson. 1927. Reprint; New York: Scribner's, 1964. A pioneering and noteworthy biographical treatment of its subject, written before the appearance of the first full-length biography.

Jack Shreve
Allegany Community College

CAPTAIN JAMES COOK
1728-1779

Chronology

Born James Cook on October 27, 1728, at Mareton in Cleveland, Yorkshire, the second son of James Cook, a Scottish farm laborer, and Grace Vace Cook; *1728-1752* receives only the rudiments of a formal education; helps on the farm and at eighteen is bound as an apprentice to the shipping firm of John Walker at Whitby in North Yorkshire; learns navigation on board Walker's *Freelove* and at twenty is rated able seaman; *1752* promoted to mate; *1755* offered command of a bark; joins the Royal Navy prior to the outbreak of the Seven Years' War between Britain and France; *1755-1763* serves under Sir Hugh Palliser during the war as able seaman, boatswain, and eventually lieutenant; participates in the siege of Louisbourg in Nova Scotia; charts the St. Lawrence River; commands a portion of General James Wolfe's fleet at Quebec; charts Newfoundland after Palliser is made governor there; *1768-1771* commands the first scientific expedition to the Pacific to observe a solar transit of Venus and to search for a hypothetical southern continent, Terra Australes; finds and charts New Zealand; finds and charts the Great Barrier Reef; *1772-1775* sails below latitude 70° south but discovers no trace of Terra Australes; charts Tonga and Easter Island; discovers New Caledonia in the Pacific and the South Sandwich and South Georgia islands in the Atlantic; *1776-1779* as captain and a fellow of the Royal Society, searches for a non-existent Northwest Passage around Canada and a Northeast Passage around Siberia; visits Tasmania, New Zealand, Tahiti, and discovers the Hawaiian Islands; explores Nootka Sound and Vancouver Island off the coast of North America; *1779* on February 14, seeking to recover stolen property, he goes ashore on Hawaii where he shoots a native, reportedly in self-defense, and is stabbed and clubbed to death by outraged islanders.

Activities of Historical Significance

During the Seven Years' War (known as the French and Indian War in America), Cook served as an officer with the British navy, first on blockade duty off the coast of France, and afterward in North America. In 1758 he participated in General James Wolfe's campaign against the French stronghold of Louisbourg, Nova Scotia. The following year, Cook accompanied Wolfe's expedition up the St. Lawrence River to besiege Quebec. In 1760, after the fall of Quebec, Cook produced excellent navigational charts of the St. Lawrence River to aid the British fleet's campaign against Montreal. Cook continued his mapping of the region in the summer of 1762, making thorough surveys of the harbors of Halifax, Grace, and Carbonera Bay, and after the war's end in 1763, he surveyed the entire coast of Newfoundland and the islands of St. Pierre and Miquelon. On August 5, 1766, Cook observed an eclipse of the sun and submitted his report of the event to the Royal Society, which subsequently published it, and commended its scientific accuracy.

On the basis of this report and his proven seamanship, Cook was selected in 1768 by the Royal Society to head an expedition to the South Pacific to transport a group of scientists to observe an important transit of Venus. The expedition was also mandated by King George III to explore geographical regions of potential political importance. Of particular interest to the king was to certify the existence of a temperate Great Southern Continent; this, at a time when no ships had ever sailed beyond the Antarctic Circle.

On August, 25, 1768, Cook sailed from Plymouth, England, on the *Endeavour*, rounded Cape Horn at the tip of South America, and reached Tahiti on April 13, 1769. His progressive dietary theories—feeding his crew on cress, sauerkraut, orange extract, and fresh vegetables—enabled him to make the long voyage, and subsequent voyages, without a single case of scurvy, a disease caused by lack of vitamin C. On Tahiti, Cook and his associates observed the transit of Venus on June 3 and from these observations they were able to determine the exact distance from the earth to the sun.

With the first part of their mission accomplished, Cook sailed west to explore and chart the South Pacific. On October 7, he made land along the east coast of New Zealand, which had not been explored since first discovered by Tasman in 1642. Cook circumnavigated the islands, making detailed charts, then sailed west, charting the two-thousand mile coastline of Australia. Upon returning to England via Djkarta and the Cape of Good Hope at the tip of Africa, he was promoted to commander.

On July 13, 1772, Commander Cook embarked from Plymouth on a more ambitious voyage with two ships—the *Resolution* and the *Adventure*—with orders to find or disprove the existence of the proposed "Lost Continent." Cook was accompanied by artists, naturalists, draftsmen, and astronomers to record the expedition's findings. Cook planned to sail as far south as possible and then eastward, keeping track of his longitude by using a chronometer. He was perhaps the first to use this device thus spurring the beginnings of scientific navigation.

Cook reached the Cape of Good Hope on October 30 and learned that French explorers had reported seeing a continent far to the south. Cook continued his journey into the southern ocean, encountering icebergs and storms. On January 17, 1773, his ships crossed the Antarctic Circle and sailed to within a hundred miles of Antarctica. With hard weather approaching, he returned to New Zealand.

In the spring he continued his voyage and, on January 18, 1774, reached latitude 71°, 10'S—a record for southern penetration that stood unchallenged for nearly fifty years. There he observed an ice barrier backed by the coastline of Antarctica. Turning westward, he rediscovered Easter Island, the Marquesas, the New Hebrides, and discovered New Caledonia. He returned to England via Cape Horn, after having shown that the only large, temperate land masses in the southern latitudes were Australia and New Zealand. Cook was commissioned a post captain on August 9, 1775, and presented to King George III.

In 1777 Captain Cook was asked to conduct a third expedition, this time to find the fabled Northwest Passage, which was thought to connect the North Atlantic with the North Pacific. Leaving Plymouth in July, Cook sailed for New Zealand and then Tahiti. Sailing north from Tahiti, he discovered the Christmas Islands and then the Hawaiian Islands, which he called the "Sandwich Islands."

Cook reached the North American coast in March 1778, where he named "Prince William Sound" and discovered Cook Inlet. He then set out across the North Pacific and reached the Bering Sea, anchoring in the strait where the continents of Asia and North America were only forty miles apart. Charting along the coasts to the far north, he returned to the Aleutian Islands early in August. Except for portions of the northwestern coast of North America, he had now traced the limits of the habitable world, charting thousands of miles of coastline.

He returned to the island of Hawaii for the winter. There, on February 6, 1779, while trying to recover a stolen cutter, Cook fell into a fracas with the Polynesian inhabitants. He shot one of the natives, but as he stood at the water's edge, another stabbed him in the back. His body was dragged ashore and clubbed.

Cook's crew continued the voyage after his death but failed to discover a Northeast Passage, which of course did not exist. The ships returned to England on October 4, 1780, having been away for four years. The Royal Society awarded Cook the Copley Medal, its highest honor, for his methods of preventing scurvy, which saved the lives of countless seamen. The Society also struck a special medal in his honor. Captain James Cook in three voyages had dramatically expanded Europe's knowledge of the world.

Overview of Biographical Sources

The researcher of Cook's life is confronted with a confusing array of sources. The Library of Congress lists over three hundred forty titles in several languages that relate to Cook and his voyages. Notable among the many biographies are: J. C. Beaglehole, *The Life of Captain Cook* (1974); Vice Admiral Gordon Campbell, *Captain James Cook, R.N., F.R.S.* (1936); Hugh Carrington, *Life of Captain Cook* (1939); Sir Joseph Carruthers, *Captain James Cook* (1939); Arthur Kitson, *Captain James Cook, R.N., F.R.S.: "The Circumnavigator"* (1907); Rear Admiral Muir, *Captain James Cook* (1939); and Alan J. Villiers, *Captain James Cook* (released in Britain in 1967 as *Captain Cook: The Seamen's Seaman*). All of these works depend in varying degrees upon Cook's journals, which have been published in various editions.

Evaluation of Principal Biographical Sources

Beaglehole, J. C. *The Life of Captain Cook.* Stanford, CA: Stanford University Press, 1974. (**A, G**) An exhaustive work replete with illustrations and maps. Particularly valuable for its coverage of the Pacific explorations, this biography also includes a listing of manuscripts printed or described in published journals of Cook's Pacific voyages.

Campbell, Gordon. *Captain James Cook, R.N., F.R.S.* London: Hodder & Stoughton, 1936. (**G**) Covers Cook's early years, the period of the Seven Years' War, his three Pacific voyages, and his death. Based on the journals of Cook and others and on sources in England's Public Records Office.

Carruthers, Sir Joseph. *Captain James Cook, R.N.: One Hundred and Fifty Years After.* New York: E. P. Dutton, 1930. (**G**) Focuses on Cook's French competition to discover Terra Australes and seeks to refute charges made against Cook's reputation. A section describes the sesquicentennial celebrations held in honor of Cook's discovery of Hawaii.

Kitson, Arthur. *Captain James Cook, R.N., F.R.S: "The Circumnavigator."* New York: E. P. Dutton, 1907. (**G**) A comprehensive biography that examines Cook's naval career, describes the preparations for his first voyage, and provides narratives of the three voyages. Concludes with an appreciation of Cook's contributions to navigation, cartography, and nutrition.

Lloyd, Christopher. *Captain Cook.* New York: Roy Publishers, 1955. (**G**). An illustrated narrative written in popular style, this book concentrates on Cook's three major voyages and his contributions to hydrography, cartography, and medicine.

Villiers, Alan J. *Captain James Cook*. New York: Scribner's, 1967. (G) A comprehensive life written with verve by a skilled author and competent historian.

Overview and Evaluation of Primary Sources

Unpublished logs and journals of Cook's second and third voyages are in England's Public Records Office (PRO). Also in the PRO are logs and journals of other persons on Cook's second voyage, including First Lieutenant R. Cooper, Second Lieutenant C. Clerke, Third Lieutenant R. Pickersgill, Second Lieutenant A. Kempe, and Midshipman F. Hergest.

Cook's journals, covering every aspect of his expeditions, were collected for the first time in J. C. Beaglehole's, *The Journals of Captain Cook* (4 vols. and portfolio. Cambridge: Cambridge University Press for the Haklyut Society, 1955-1974; A). This massive and masterfully edited series is considered the standard reference work on the three voyages. *A Journal of a Voyage Round the World in His Majesty's Ship "Endeavour" in the Years 1768, 1769, 1770, and 1771* (New York: Da Capo Press, 1967), faithfully reproduces Cook's journal of the first voyage.

Other Sources

Badger, G. M., ed. *Captain Cook: Navigator and Scientist*. London: C. Hurst, 1970. Eight essayists evaluate Cook's relations with the Royal Society and his contributions as a scientist.

Barrow, John, ed. *Captain Cook's Voyages of Discovery*. 1860. Reprint. London: J. M. Dent, 1906. An essential reference on the life and voyages of Cook.

Beaglehole, J. C. *The Death of Captain Cook*. Wellington: Alexander Turnbull Library, 1979. A fine tale extracted from Beaglehole's four-volume edition of Cook's journals.

—————. *The Exploration of the Pacific*. 3d ed. Stanford, CA: Stanford University Press, 1966. Cultural and historical background for Cook's voyages.

Burney, James. *A Chronological History of Discoveries in the South Sea or Pacific Ocean*. 5 vols. London: Luke Hansard for Payne and Foss, 1803-1817. A full treatment of European discovery and mapping of the Pacific Ocean by a member of Cook's crew.

————. *With Captain James Cook in the Antarctic and Pacific: The Private Journal of James Burney, Second Lieutenant of the "Adventure" on Cook's Second Voyage, 1772-1773*. Canberra: National Library of Australia, 1975. Edited by Beverly Hopper. Burney kept this journal of his years aboard the *Resolution* and the *Adventure* during Cook's second expedition. Burney went to sea at the age of ten and was not a polished writer, but he provides an absorbing description of the Antarctic explorations and his experiences in Tasmania, Tahiti, Tonga, and New Zealand. Includes charts.

Fisher, Robin, and Hugh Johnston, eds. *Captain James Cook and His Times*. Seattle: University of Washington Press, 1978. A collection of essays placing Cook's contributions in perspective, addressing Cook's reputation in Spain and Russia, and examining the medical aspects of his work.

Forster, Johann. *A Voyage Round the World in His Majesty's Sloop "Resolution," Commanded by Captain James Cook, During the Years 1772, 3, 4, and 5*. 2 vols. London: B. White, 1777. A very rare book containing firsthand information about the voyage.

Gould, Rupert Thomas. *Captain Cook*. London: Duckworth, 1935. This volume in the Great Lives Series provides a concise overview of Cooks's life and voyages.

Gwyther, John. *Captain Cook and the South Pacific: The Voyage of the "Endeavour" 1768-1771*. Boston: Houghton Mifflin, 1955. An excellent account of Cook's first voyage. The author provides no footnotes but acknowledges that his sources were Cook's journals, other journals, biographies of Cook, and histories of explorations.

Heawood, Edward. *History of Geographical Discovery in the Seventeenth and Eighteenth Centuries*. 1912. Reprint. New York: Octagon Books, 1965. Covers Cook's voyages as well as those of other contemporary explorers.

Holmes, Christine, ed. *Captain Cook's Final Voyage: The Journal of Midshipman George Gelbert*. Honolulu: University Press of Hawaii, 1982. Beautifully illustrated narrative of Cook's visits to the Society Islands, his discovery of Hawaii, and his search for a Northwest Passage.

Hough, Richard A. *The Last Voyage of Captain James Cook*. New York: William Morrow, 1979. A well-illustrated narrative by a fine historian.

Kippis, A. *Captain Cook's Voyages: With an Account of His Life, During the Previous and Intervening Periods.* New York: Knopf, 1934. After brief coverage of Cook's early life, the author assesses the value and effects of the three global voyages.

Lloyd, Christopher, ed. *The Voyages of Captain James Cook Around the World.* New York: Chanticleer, 1949. Lloyd excerpts narratives of the three voyages from Cook's journals, and describes the customs of natives visited, the status of ships and crews, and the work of artists, naturalists, and astronomers on board Cook's ships.

Rickman, John. *Journal of Captain Cook's Last Voyage to the Pacific Ocean.* New York: Da Capo Press, 1967. Rickman reproduces Cook's extensive introduction to his journal of the third voyage, as well as charts of the voyage and woodcuts depicting Cook's ships, his death, and various natives. In his introduction, Cook mentions the discoveries already made by a number of British, Spanish, Dutch, and French explorers, and states the objective of his last voyage is "to compleat the discovery of the Southern Hemisphere."

Rutter, Owen, ed. *Anders Sparrman: A Voyage Around the World with Captain James Cook in H.M.S. "Resolution."* London: Golden Cockrell Press, 1944. Offers commentary on Cook's journal.

Williamson, James A. *Cook and the Opening of the Pacific.* London: Hodder & Stoughton, 1946. Provides useful background information.

Paolo E. Coletta
U.S. Naval Academy (Ret.)

JACOB S. COXEY
1854-1951

Chronology

Born Jacob Sechler Coxey on April 16, 1854, in Selinsgrove, Pennsylvania, to Thomas and Mary Sechler Coxey; leaves public school at fifteen to become laborer in iron mill at Danville, Pennsylvania; *1870-1880* becomes mechanical engineer in rolling mill and enters scrap-iron business; *1881* moves to Massilon, Ohio, and founds Coxey Silica Company (a business he operates until 1929), supplying quarried high-grade sand for use in steel mills; *1885* runs for Ohio state senate on Greenback ticket; *1893* economic panic forces him to lay off forty workers; *March 1894* forms Army of the Commonweal of Christ (dubbed Coxey's Army by the press) and leads these jobless workers in a peaceful protest march to nation's capital to petition Congress for federally sponsored public works to provide jobs for the unemployed; *May 1894* arrested during May Day demonstration in front of Capitol for walking on the grass; his small protest group is dispersed by the police, and he is sentenced to twenty days in jail for trespassing; *November 1894* runs for Congress on Populist party ticket; *1895* testifies at hearing of a subcommittee of the House Ways and Means Committee chaired by Representative William Jennings Bryan; runs for governor of Ohio as a Populist; *1914* leads another march on Washington to protest the creation of the Federal Reserve System and is allowed to present petition to President Woodrow Wilson; *1916* again runs for governor of Ohio, this time as an independent; *1922* secures interview with President Warren G. Harding to call for monetary reform; *1924* runs for Congress as Independent Progressive; *1928* runs for U.S. Senate as Independent Progressive; *1930* seeks Republican nomination for Congress; *1931* wins election as mayor of Massilon, Ohio, and serves a single two-year term; *1932* runs for the presidency as the nominee of the Farmer-Labor party and receives only 7,431 popular votes; *1936* nominated by Farmer-Labor party for the presidency but withdraws to support Union party candidate William Lemke; *1942* runs for Congress as Democrat; *1944* speaks on Capitol steps on the fiftieth anniversary of his first march, and is allowed to deliver the speech he intended to give in 1894; *1951* dies on May 18 in Massilon, Ohio.

Activities of Historical Significance

Jacob S. Coxey was noted for his formation of the Army of the Commonweal of Christ, which was subsequently labeled "Coxey's Army," "Tramps' March on

Washington," an "industrial army," and a "living petition." Coxey led a peaceful protest march of unemployed workers to call attention to the plight of the jobless during the economic depression that followed the Panic of 1893. He called his demonstration "a petition with boots on." His aim was to secure congressional action that would authorize the use of non-interest-bearing bonds by municipalities. The municipalities could then use the bonds as deposits for the loan of legal tender from the Treasury Department. This money would finance local public works projects.

In addition, Coxey wanted Congress to authorize a national road improvement program whereby the federal government would issue $500 million in fiat money (currency not backed by gold) for the purpose of employing jobless workers. His ideas on federally financed public works and currency inflation were considered radical at the time.

In 1894 the very thought of a protest march was considered a dangerous provocation. Coxey and his small band of less than five hundred were forcibly dispersed by police as they paraded in front of the Capitol. Coxey was arrested and sentenced to jail for trespassing on the lawn.

Although Coxey was a man ahead of his time, he lived long enough to see the essence of his ideas on public works and currency inflation come to fruition during the New Deal era of Franklin D. Roosevelt. In 1946 Coxey saw the welfare state concept he advocated become legally embodied in the Employment Act of the Truman administration, which established as permanent policy the federal government's responsibility for maintaining full employment.

Overview of Biographical Sources

In 1894 the press gave wide coverage to Coxey's famous march on Washington. Yet, few full-length studies were ever written about either Coxey or his movement. The first treatment of him and his protest march was *The Story of the Commonweal* (1894) by Henry Vincent, who acted as official historian for Coxey's Army. Donald L. McMurray's *Coxey's Army: A Study of the Industrial Army Movement of 1894* (1929) focuses on the Army of the Commonweal as part of the general unrest among industrial workers during the hard times of 1894. The most recent and most thorough examination of this protest movement is Carlos A. Schwantes's *Coxey's Army: An American Odyssey* (1985). This definitive study supersedes all other works.

Historical studies dealing with the political climate of the 1890s, the Populist movement, industry and organized labor, and the Panic of 1893 provide useful background material for understanding the nationwide makeup of Coxey's Army.

H. Wayne Morgan analyzes the general political outlook of the 1890s in *From Hayes to McKinley: National Party Policies, 1877-1896* (1969). Lawrence Goodwyn's *Democratic Promise: The Populist Movement in America* (1976) provides excellent coverage of the rise of the Populist party. In *The Response to Industrialism, 1885-1914* (1957) Samuel P. Hays explains the problems associated with industrialism. Philip Taft's *The A.F.L. in the Time of Gompers* (1970) and Nick Salvatore's *Eugene V. Debs: Citizen and Socialist* (1982) present the reaction of organized labor.

Works that deal with the Panic of 1893 and its adverse economic repercussions on workers include Charles Hoffmann, *The Depression of the Nineties: An Economic History* (1970); John A. Garraty, *Unemployment in History: Economic Thought and Public Policy* (1978); Leah Hannah Feder, *Unemployment Relief in Periods of Depression: A Study of Measures Adopted in Certain American Cities, 1857 through 1922* (1936); and Roger A. Bruns, *Knights of the Road: A Hobo History* (1980).

Evaluation of Principal Biographical Sources

Murray, Donald L. *Coxey's Army: A Study of the Industrial Army Movement in 1894.* 1929. Reprint. Seattle: University of Washington Press, 1968. (A) Contains very little on Coxey's early years but is thorough on Coxeyism as a national movement. Coxey's views on monetary policy and public works are explained as the author narrates the rise and fall of the Commonweal movement.

Schwantes, Carlos A. *Coxey's Army: An American Odyssey.* Lincoln, NE and London: University of London Press, 1985. (A) The most current and definitive study of the Commonweal of Christ movement. It gives few biographical details of Coxey's early life but is thorough in tracing the origins, makeup, and impact of Coxey's Army. It also forcefully presents the lasting legacy of this protest movement.

Vincent, Henry. *The Story of the Commonweal.* 1894. Reprint. New York: Arno Press and The New York Times, 1969. (A) Written by a participant in the movement, Vincent's book covers Coxey's activities through 1894. While it contains only a brief biographical sketch of Coxey, it delves into the reasons for the formation of the Commonweal of Christ and expounds on Coxey's views relative to public works and currency inflation. It lacks historical perspective but does give a sense of immediacy to this ill-fated movement.

Overview and Evaluation of Primary Sources

The most valuable archival collection on Coxey's Army is the Jacob Sechler Coxey Papers at the Ohio Historical Society in Columbus, Ohio. This collection contains correspondence, pamphlets, campaign documents, and the original manuscript of Coxey's memoirs, "Coxey, His Own Story of the Commonweal: Why the March to Washington in 1894." The memoirs were published as *Coxey's Own Story* (Massilon, OH: Jacob S. Coxey, 1916; A).

Two valuable collections in the Library of Congress in Washington, D.C., are the papers of Grover Cleveland and Ray Stannard Baker. As a reporter, Baker covered Coxey's march and wrote a firsthand account called "Coxey and His Commonweal." Also useful are the Industrial Army File of the Union Pacific Collection housed in the Nebraska Historical Society at Lincoln and Records Group 60 of the Justice Department in the National Archives in Washington, D.C.

Personal accounts by participants are found in Richard W. Etulain, ed., *Jack London on the Road: "The Tramp Diary" and Other Writings* (Logan: Utah State University, 1979; A) and William McDevitt, ed., *When Coxey's "Army" Marched on Washington, 1894* (San Francisco: n.p., 1944; A).

Other personal recollections by Coxey's contemporaries include Samuel Gompers, *Seventy Years of Life and Labor: An Autobiography* (New York: Dutton, 1925; A); Cleveland Hall, "An Observer in Coxey's Camp," *Independent* 46 (May 17, 1894; A); and W. T. Stead, "Coxeyism: A Character Sketch," *Review of Reviews* 10 (July 1894; A).

Other Sources

Austen, Shirley Plumer. "Coxey's Commonweal Army." *Chautauquan* 19 (June 1894): 332-336. A favorable contemporary account of Coxey's objectives and methods of gaining public attention.

————. "The Downfall of Coxeyism." *Chautauquan* 19 (July 1894): 448-452. Details the negative reaction of the Cleveland administration.

Bemis, Edward W. "The Convention of the American Federation of Labor." *Journal of Political Economy* 2 (March 1894): 298-299. Documents the favorable support of organized labor.

Byrnes, Thomas. "Character and Methods of the Men: The Menace of Coxeyism." *North American Review* 158 (June 1894): 696-701. A critical assessment of the "industrial army" movement.

Closson, Carlos C., Jr. "The Unemployed in American Cities." *Quarterly Journal of Economics* 8 (January 1894): 168-217. Describes the economic plight of the unemployed and gives statistical information.

Duryea, Joseph T. "The 'Industrial Army' at Omaha." *Outlook* 159 (May 5, 1894): 780-790. Describes Coxey's movement in Nebraska, focusing on Omaha.

Embry, Bernard H. "Jacob S. Coxey: A Biography of a Monetary Reformer, 1854-1951." Ph.D. diss., Ohio State University, 1973. A very thorough explanation of Coxey's inflationary money policy and his plan for federal funding of public works.

Filler, Louis. "Jacob S. Coxey." In *A Dictionary of a American Social Reform.* New York: Philosophical Library, 1963. Links Coxey to general social reform movements.

Frank, Henry. "The Crusade of the Unemployed." *Arena* 10 (July 1894): 239-244. Outlines the problems faced by the jobless in an era where no unemployment insurance existed.

Garraty, John A., ed. "Jacob Sechler Coxey." In *Encyclopedia of American Biography.* New York: Harper and Row, 1974. A general description of the movement with an emphasis on biographical details.

Hooper, Osman C. "The Coxey Movement in Ohio." *Ohio Archeological and Historical Society* 9 (1910): 155-176. A scholarly account of the origins of Coxey's Army in his home state.

Howard, O. "Significance and Aims of the Movement." *North American Review* 157 (June 1894): 687-696. A supportive contemporary account about the need for government assistance to the unemployed.

Kelley, Charles T. "Are Radicals Insane?" *Current History* 20 (May 1924): 205-210. Links Coxey to socialists and Robert M. La Follette's Progressive movement of 1924.

London, Jack. "A Jack London Diary, Tramping with Keeley through Iowa." *Palimpsest* 7 (May 1926): 129-158. A radical writer's personal account of his activities within the Coxey movement in Iowa.

Reznick, Samuel. "Unemployment, Unrest, and Relief in the United States during the Depression of 1893-1897." *Journal of Political Economy* 61 (August 1953): 324-345. A detailed analysis of economic conditions during the Populist era by a professional economist.

Schapsmeier, Edward L., and Frederick H. Schapsmeier. "Coxey's Army." In *Political Parties and Civic Action Groups*. Westport and London: Greenwood, 1981. Relates Coxey's movement to rural unrest in America during the Populist period.

Schwantes, Carlos A. "Coxey's Montana Navy: A Protest Against Unemployment on the Wageworker's Frontier." *Pacific Northwest Quarterly* 73 (July 1982): 98-107. A description of Coxey's movement among jobless workers in the shipbuilding industry in the Pacific Northwest.

Veblen, Thorstein. "The Army of the Commonweal." *Journal of Political Economy* 2 (June 1894): 459-465. A sympathetic, yet critical, appraisal by a famous contemporary economist.

Voeltz, Herman C. "Coxey's Army in Oregon, 1894." *Oregon State Quarterly* 65 (September 1964): 263-295. Focuses on the rise of the Coxey movement in Portland and other cities in Oregon.

Weaver, James B. "The Commonwealth Crusade." *Midland Monthly* 1 (June 1894): 590-595. A strong defense of the Coxey movement by the former presidential candidate of the Populist party.

Edward L. Schapsmeier
Illinois State University

JAMES MICHAEL CURLEY
1874-1958

Chronology

Born James Michael Curley on November 20, 1874, in Boston, Massachusetts, the son of Michael Curley, a hodcarrier, and Sarah Clancy Curley; *1874-1896* grows up in Boston where he attends Dearborn Grammar School, graduating in 1886, and Boston Evening High School, from which he never graduates; *1898* runs unsuccessfully for the Boston Common Council; *1899* elected to the Boston Common Council; *1900* becomes the youngest ward boss in Boston; *1902-1903* enters the real estate and insurance business with his brother; founds the Roxbury Tammany Club; serves in the Massachusetts House of Representatives; serves ninety days in jail for fraudulently taking a civil service examination for a constituent; *1904-1909* serves as alderman of Boston; marries Mary Emilda Herlihy, with whom he has nine children; *1910-1911* serves as Boston city councilor; *1911-1914* serves in the U.S. House of Representatives; *1914-1934* serves three terms as mayor of Boston (1914-1918, 1922-1926, and 1930-1934); becomes trustee and later president of Hibernia Savings Bank, a position he would return to in his intervals out of elective office; *1924* runs unsuccessfully for governor; *1930* his wife dies; *1934-1937* serves as governor of Massachusetts; *1936* runs unsuccessfully for U.S. Senate; *1937* runs unsuccessfully for mayor of Boston; marries Gertrude Casey Dennis; *1938* runs unsuccessfully for re-election as governor; *1940* runs unsuccessfully for mayor of Boston; *1943-1945* serves in the U.S. House of Representatives; *1945-1949* serves as mayor of Boston; *1947* convicted of mail fraud and serves six months in federal prison; *1949-1955* runs unsuccessfully for mayor of Boston in 1949, 1951, and 1955; *1957* appointed to the State Labor Commission; *1958* dies November 12 in Boston of complications from surgery.

Activities of Historical Significance

A charismatic personality with an orotund speaking style and a dramatic flair, James Michael Curley assumed the role of tribal chieftain deftly articulating and manipulating the grievances of the Boston Irish against the Brahmin ascendancy. Having broken the power of the ward bosses early in his career, he built an immense personal following and made himself the model for political style in Boston and elsewhere.

Curley's accomplishments as an advocate of the urban working class were considerable. As governor he improved old-age pension laws, reduced the work week of employees in state institutions, and began programs for forestation and flood control. His name is associated with the development of Boston City Hospital, the creation of a mile-long public beach in South Boston, and the construction of numerous bathhouses, stadiums, and other recreational facilities, all of which provided jobs for his constituents. His name is also associated with the graft afforded by these projects. Curley remains a symbol of genial corruption, a Robin Hood whose people forgave and even applauded his thievery, of which they were the beneficiaries. He is also remembered for his unabashed roguishness in the playing of political dirty tricks that were ingenious and often hilarious.

Curley was the victim not of his enemies—despite their best efforts—but of his own success. His election as governor defused much of the Irish resentment by forcefully demonstrating the advent of their political ascendancy. At the same time, the growing affluence and education level of the Boston Irish made them less dependent on his largess and less impressed by his demagoguery. A loner in politics, he neglected to develop a structured political organization, and the lack of strategically placed politicians and administrators beholden to him was devastating to him in the period from 1936 to 1955 when he won two elections while losing seven.

Curley's style triumphed over his substance. The style unfortunately lowered the tone of political discourse in Boston and provided a negative model for his own and future generations.

Overview of Biographical Sources

There is only one full-length biography available of Curley, Joseph F. Dineen's *The Purple Shamrock: the Honorable James Michael Curley of Boston* (1949). Curley's earlier career is discussed in Herbert Marshall Zolot's doctoral dissertation, *The Issue of Good Government and James Michael Curley: Curley and the Boston Scene from 1897-1918* (1976). The politician also is treated in numerous books on broader themes such as Boston, political bosses, and demagoguery.

Evaluation of Principal Biographical Sources

Dineen, Joseph F. *The Purple Shamrock: The Honorable James Michael Curley of Boston.* New York: W. W. Norton, 1949. (A, G) Written by a veteran journalist who had prepared articles critical of Curley for national magazines, this volume is based on interviews with Curley and his family and, although Curley used to give autographed copies of it as gifts, it is in no sense an official biography. Frank and searching, it is informed, balanced, and thorough.

Zolot, Herbert Marshall. *The Issue of Good Government and James Michael Curley: Curley and Boston Scene from 1897-1918.* (A) Ann Arbor, MI: University Microfilms, 1976. A doctoral dissertation in political science, this illuminates Curley's early career.

Overview and Evaluation of Primary Sources

An exciting and charismatic speaker, Curley wrote little except for official correspondence. At the end of his life, incensed by Edwin O'Connor's fictional portrayal of him, he produced an autobiography, *I'd Do It Again! A Record of All My Uproarious Years* (Englewood Cliffs, NJ: Prentice-Hall, 1957; **A, G**). Stanley K. Schultz ranked it with *The Autobiography of Lincoln Steffens* (New York: Harcourt Brace & World, 1968) as "one of the most insightful accounts of municipal politics." According to John Henry Cutler, who ghostwrote the book for Curley, the book's rambling, sesquipedalian style reproduces Curley's grandiose conversational manner. A newspaperman, Cutler—who earned a doctorate from Harvard—was keenly aware of the liberties Curley took with the truth and provided some corrections in his later biography of Mayor John Fitzgerald. As he began his own book on Curley, Cutler suffered a stroke that left him unable to write. His valuable insights are being contributed to a Curley biography currently in progress.

The most extensive collection of Curley papers is held by the library of the College of the Holy Cross in Worcester, Massachusetts. The Boston Public Library has an archive of Curley manuscripts and memorabilia, while the Boston Political Archives Section of its Print Department contains photographs and certificates. The Massachusetts Historical Society in Boston has a card catalogue of references to Curley in the papers of Massachusetts residents that it holds.

Fiction and Adaptations

Frank Skeffington, the protagonist of Edwin O'Connor's *The Last Hurrah* (1956) is clearly a characterization of a more benevolent, less threatening Curley. Arthur M. Schlesinger, Jr., called the book "the best novel about urban politics." Spencer Tracy played Skeffington in the well-received film version directed by John Ford and released in 1958.

In the fall of 1991, PBS television aired as part of the American Experience Series a program that follows Curley's life of poverty to his political heights. The program depicts Curley's combative brand of politics; his willingness to exploit ethnic, religious, and class tensions for his own political ends; and his popularity which allowed him to run a winning political campaign from jail.

Museums, Historical Landmarks, Societies

James M. Curley Residence (Boston, MA). Located at 350 The Jamaicaway in Boston's Jamaica Plain section, this elegant brick house, known for the shamrocks carved into its shutters, is maintained by the city of Boston as a headquarters for city-sponsored youth groups and a venue for special events.

Curley Park (Boston, MA). Two life-size statues of Curley, one standing as though addressing a crowd, the other seated casually on a bench, occupy a small park at the corner of Congress and North Streets (Dock Square) behind Boston City Hall next to Faneuil Hall.

Other Sources

Cutler, John F. *"Honey Fitz": Three Steps to the White House: The Life and Times of John F. (Honey Fitz) Fitzgerald.* Indianapolis: Bobbs-Merrill, 1962. This excellent study of John F. Kennedy's maternal grandfather by Curley's ghostwriter includes much that he could not include in *I'd Do It Again!*.

Luthin, Reinhard H. "James M. Curley: The Boston Brahmin-Baiter." In *American Demagogues.* Boston: Beacon Press, 1954. Uses Curley as "a prototype of the urban demagogue who exploited religious and class insecurity for his own political advantage."

Russell, Francis. "The Last of the Bosses." In *The Great Interlude: Neglected Events and Persons from the First World War to the Depression.* New York: McGraw-Hill, 1964. Also in his *The Knave of Boston and Other Ambiguous Massachusetts Characters* (Boston: Quinlan Press, 1987). A highly readable short account.

Schultz, Stanley K. "James Michael Curley." In *Dictionary of American Biography,* Supplement 6. New York: Charles Scribner's Sons, 1980. A careful evaluation by a historian familiar with Boston.

Shanon, William V. "The Legend of Jim Curley." In *The American Irish: A Political and Social Portrait.* 2d ed. Amherst: University of Massachusetts Press, 1989. The best short treatment, summing up Curley as "a self-crippled giant on a provincial stage."

Trout, Charles H. *Boston: The Great Depression and the New Deal.* New York: Oxford University Press, 1977. A thoroughly researched study that develops a picture of Curley as effective in dealing with hard economic times.

Joseph M. McCarthy
Suffolk University

RICHARD CARDINAL CUSHING
1895-1970

Chronology

Born Richard James Cushing on August 24, 1895, in South Boston, Massachusetts, the son of Patrick Cushing, a blacksmith, and Mary Dahill Cushing; *1895-1913* grows up in Boston, attending public schools and the Jesuit-run Boston College High School; *1913-1921* attends Boston College for two years before entering St. John's Seminary in Brighton, Massachusetts; denied the opportunity to study in Rome because of World War I; *1921* ordained a Roman Catholic priest; *1922-1939* assigned to the Boston office of the Society for the Propagation of the Faith to raise money for foreign missions; *1928* appointed director and distinguishes himself through his energy, fund-raising ability, and distinctive pulpit oratory; *1939-1944* serves as auxiliary bishop of the archdiocese of Boston; *1944-1958* becomes archbishop of Boston on the death of William Cardinal O'Connell and embarks on an expansion program that adds more than sixty religious orders, eighty churches, six hospitals, three colleges, and numerous schools and other institutions to the archdiocese; devotes considerable energy to fund-raising; combats the "Boston heresy" of Reverend Leonard Feeney, S.J., who insists that there is no salvation outside the Catholic church; *1958-1970* created a cardinal by Pope John XXIII; founds a missionary society to send priests to Latin America; participates in the Second Vatican Council; figures prominently in American political life by reason of his friendship with John F. Kennedy; suffers from cancer, asthma, shingles, and ulcers; *1970* dies November 2 in Brighton, Massachusetts.

Activities of Historical Significance

Richard Cardinal Cushing is best remembered as a builder and fund-raiser who enormously expanded the archdiocese of Boston as he had earlier in his career increased Boston's contribution to the foreign missions. In addition to building churches, schools, hospitals, and other institutions, Cushing raised money for a wide variety of charities, not all of them Catholic, developed a radio and television apostolate, purchased a large theater in Boston for archdiocesan events, and financed missionary efforts in Peru, Bolivia, and Ecuador. One of the least happy results of all this activity was an overexpansion that could not be sustained, leaving the last five years of his pontificate (and all of his successor's) to be consumed in retrenchment. One of his most visible fund-raising efforts culminated in paying Fidel Castro one million dollars in 1962 to ransom prisoners taken during the Bay of Pigs invasion.

In many ways more important than his expansionist achievements was the influence Cushing exerted in molding the growing Catholic ascendancy in Boston. Unlike some other Irish Catholic leaders, most notably James Michael Curley, Cushing was able to lay aside resentment of the Brahmins, Boston's WASP elite, and reach out to integrate Boston's various ethnic, religious, and racial groups. He resisted religious exclusivity and triumphalism, cultivated friendship and financial support in Boston's Jewish and Protestant communities, and used his influence at Vatican II to promote positive formulations on ecumenism and religious liberty. Through his friendship with John F. Kennedy, his impact was felt in national politics, especially when he defended the separation of church and state and the independence of Catholic politicians from ecclesiastical control.

Cushing's great personal energy made it possible for him to keep a full schedule that kept him accessible to a wide variety of people. Unpretentious, unpolished, with a self-deprecating sense of humor, given to loud and lengthy public addresses, Cushing was more administrator than intellectual; but he was also shrewd and insightful about the nature and needs not only of his own archdiocese, but also of the entire American Catholic church.

Overview of Biographical Sources

Despite his significance as a public figure and the colorful facets of his personality, Cushing has not been the subject of many biographies. Existing biographies are overly dependent on newspaper sources and reverential to the point of hagiography, except for John Henry Cutler's excellent portrayal, *Cardinal Cushing of Boston* (1970).

Evaluation of Principal Biographical Sources

Cutler, John Henry. *Cardinal Cushing of Boston.* New York: Hawthorn Books, 1970. (A, G) Carefully researched and engagingly written by an experienced biographer thoroughly familiar with Boston history and folkways, this work is a true-to-life portrait. For it Cutler interviewed a variety of people who knew Cushing and developed a rich lode of anecdotal information that is very revealing of Cushing's personality and style, not at all like some of the pious tales found in other Cushing biographies.

Dever, Joseph. *Cushing of Boston: A Candid Portrait*. Boston: Bruce Humphries, 1965. (**G, Y**). A novelist and feature writer, Dever helped Cushing write a book on Pope John XXIII and began helping him prepare an informal autobiography. When the project collapsed, he used the talks as the basis for this anecdotal, admiring, and occasionally mildly critical book.

Devine, M. C. *The World's Cardinal*. Boston: Daughters of St. Paul, 1964. (**G, Y**). An undocumented and popular biography prepared from newspaper clippings and limited interviews, this is unabashedly adoring of its subject.

Fenton, John H. *Salt of the Earth: An Informal Portrait of Richard Cardinal Cushing*. New York: Coward-McCann, 1965. (**G, Y**) Another undocumented popular biography by a newspaperman, this work reads like a lengthy press release.

Overview and Evaluation of Primary Sources

Although Cushing turned out many newspaper columns and a few books, these are not particularly revealing of his life. His project of an informal autobiography in 1963 never got beyond the planning stages, and he arranged for the destruction of many of his private papers upon his death. The archives of the archdiocese of Boston contain two linear feet of Cushing's survival correspondence, much of it relating to his elevation to the cardinalate, twelve linear feet of typescripts of his speeches, eleven volumes of appointment books from 1947 to 1970, twenty-four volumes of scrapbooks of newspaper clippings, and four cubic feet of papers relating to Cushing's participation in the Second Vatican Council. They also contain a collection of still photographs and motion pictures, including footage of Cushing's installation as archbishop and some of his foreign trips. Within the past year a previously unknown depository of his papers was donated to the archives and is being catalogued for use.

Fiction and Adaptations

Stephen Fermoyle in Henry Morton Robinson's novel, *The Cardinal* (1950), and the film adaptation by Otto Preminger (1963), is based on Cushing. The character's name echoes the busy market town of Fermoy, five miles from the Irish village of Glanworth, the birthplace of Cushing's father. The title character was supposedly drawn equally from the personalities of Francis Cardinal Spellman, Cushing's predecessor as auxiliary bishop of Boston, and William Cardinal O'Connell.

Museums, Historical Landmarks, Societies

Portiuncula Chapel (Hanover, MA). Located on the grounds of the Cardinal Cushing School and Training Center, a facility founded by Cushing for instruction and treatment of the developmentally disabled, this is an exact replica of the famous shrine in Assisi, Italy, and is the cardinal's burial place.

Other Sources

Cross, Robert D. "Richard Cardinal Cushing." In *Dictionary of American Biography,* Supplement 8, 1966-1970. New York: Charles Scribner's Sons, 1988. An excellent short life and evaluation by a historian of American Catholicism.

Ellis, John Tracy. *Catholic Bishops: A Memoir.* Wilmington, DE: Michael Glazier, 1983. Contains some useful reflections on Cushing as the dean of American Catholic historians.

Fuchs, Lawrence H. *John F. Kennedy and American Catholicism.* New York: Meredith, 1967. Illuminates the friendship of Cushing and Kennedy.

Joseph M. McCarthy
Suffolk University

BEN DAVIS
1904-1964

Chronology

Born Benjamin Jefferson Davis, Jr., in 1904, in Dawson, Georgia, the son of Benjamin Jefferson Davis, Sr., one of the leading African Americans in the Republican party at the time, and Willa Porter Davis; *1904-1922* grows up in Dawson and Atlanta under segregated conditions; *1922-1925* attends and graduates from Amherst College; *1925-1928* attends and graduates from Harvard Law School; *1928-1931* works in newspaper business for the *Baltimore Afro-American* and W. B. Ziff, Inc.; *1932-1933* practices law in Atlanta and is catapulted into prominence and Communist party membership when he takes on the case of Angelo Herndon, one of the key political cases during the Great Depression; *1933-1964* lives in New York and holds various posts in the Communist party as its highest ranking African-American leader; *1943* elected to the New York City Council representing Harlem on the Communist party ticket, the first black Communist so honored; *1945* re-elected to the city council; *1948* indicted by the U.S. Government pursuant with the Smith Act for conspiring to spread the doctrine of Marxism-Leninism; *1949* convicted and as an indirect result is ousted from the City Council; *1951* after failure of his appeal is jailed in federal prison in Terre Haute, Indiana; *1956* released from prison and plunges into an internal party crisis sparked in part by revelations about Josef Stalin at the twentieth Soviet Communist party Congress; *1956-1964* emerges as leader of the hardline faction within the party; his association with Martin Luther King, Jr., helps to justify FBI surveillance of the civil rights leader; *1964* dies August 24, of natural causes in New York City.

Activities of Historical Significance

Ben Davis's political activism was in a sense inherited from his father, who was a top black leader of the Republican party in an era when those African Americans who could vote cast their ballot with the GOP. But after the election of Herbert Hoover in 1928, there was a concerted effort by the GOP to purge black leadership in a "lily-white" effort to appeal to the Democratic party constituency. Shunned by the Democrats and purged by the GOP, Davis turned to the left and joined the Communist party.

Davis's shift in political allegiance occurred after he returned to Atlanta to practice law; one of his early clients was the Communist organizer Angelo Herndon, who had been indicted after leading demonstrations for jobs and relief. Davis handled the trial and assisted on the appeal that eventually led to the U.S. Supreme Court, where Herndon and the First Amendment right to petition were vindicated.

Davis moved to New York during this period and joined the staff of the party newspaper, the *Daily Worker,* and in his lifetime contributed hundreds of articles to the publication. He also became a top party organizer in Harlem and was involved in rent strikes, labor organizing, struggles for improved health care at Harlem Hospital, and the organization of the National Negro Congress. He worked closely with Richard Wright, the well-known African-American novelist (they shared the same party cell), Roy Wilkins, Thurgood Marshall and other NAACP leaders, Adam Clayton Powell (who endorsed Davis as his successor in the city council), and intermittently with A. Philip Randolph. Perhaps Davis's closest political alliance and friendship was with Paul Robeson, whom he met in 1923.

Davis was not the first Communist elected to political office in the United States (Pete Cacchione was elected to the New York City Council representing Brooklyn in 1941), but he was probably the most renowned. During his tenure on the council he advocated rent control and the establishment of more parks, and fought police brutality. Though the Red Scare was dawning, he was re-elected by a wide margin in November 1945; this turned out to be his final electoral victory.

Davis was instrumental in helping the party develop its theoretical position on what was popularly termed the "Negro Question." Members of the American Communist party were of the view that blacks in the United States constituted a nation deserving the right to self-determination, though they stressed that their immediate battle was for equality. There is some controversy as to how much this view was influenced by Moscow; however, foreign influence is probably over-stated in light of the fact that Marcus Garvey and the nineteenth-century African-American leaders before him had reached variations of this thesis and were immensely popular.

The fact that Harlem elected and re-elected a Communist was not only evidence of Davis's popularity but also signified a radical reaction to the Jim Crow laws. With the dawning of the cold war, the atrocious racism inflicted upon blacks became an Achilles' heel in the execution of U.S. foreign policy. How could Washington credibly charge the Soviet Union with human rights violations when African Americans in this country were treated so inhumanely? Jim Crow had to go. But Communists who had become leaders of the black community had to go as well, for they were viewed as the domestic hand of Moscow.

Thus, Davis was convicted of conspiracy in 1949 in the midst of running for re-election. After his appeal to the U.S. Supreme Court failed, he was jailed from 1951 to 1956; it was during this time that *Brown* v. *Board of Education* and the

Montgomery Bus Boycott signaled a new stage in the struggle for racial equality. This was also the time that revelations about Josef Stalin exposed by Soviet party leader Nikita Khrushchev and the Soviet intervention in Hungary in 1956 ignited a raging controversy in the American Communist party about the party's past, present, and future. During these battles, Davis allied with party patriarch William Z. Foster in taking a hard line against some of the changes suggested by a faction led by John Gates. Davis and Foster prevailed in these "party wars" that lasted approximately three years. It was also during this time that the party abandoned their thesis about the "Negro Nation."

Davis's ties to Atlanta were both personal and political. Davis's niece, Jean Carey, married into the family of prominent black leaders Horace Mann Bond and Julian Bond. When Davis gave blood to Dr. Martin Luther King, Jr., after he was stabbed by a deranged woman in Harlem in 1958, the FBI accelerated its already aggressive campaign of surveillance and harassment of King because of his "blood-link" to Davis, a convicted Communist.

Davis also played a role in the outbreak of student activism that helped to break the pall of the "silent 1950s." The effort to bar Davis and other Communist speakers from campuses caused students to organize "free speech" campaigns that set the stage for the explosion at the University of California in Berkeley in 1964. Davis died in 1964 on the verge of this eruption.

Overview of Biographical Sources

Despite his national prominence, Davis's friendship with Paul Robeson and Adam Clayton Powell, and the file on him at FBI headquarters, Davis has been virtually ignored by historians. This stems in part from the controversial nature of his Communist ties (which similarly led to the neglect of Robeson) until Gerald Horne's *Black Liberation/Red Scare: Ben Davis and the Communist Party* (1991).

Evaluation of Biographical Sources

Horne, Gerald. *Black Liberation/Red Scare: Ben Davis and the Communist Party*. Washington, DC: Howard University Press, 1991. (**A, G**) A comprehensive history that includes an overview of Communist party views toward African Americans.

Overview and Evaluation of Primary Sources

Davis wrote hundreds of articles for the *Daily Worker, Political Affairs,* and other left-wing journals over a thirty year period from the 1930s through the

1960s. His papers will soon be deposited in the Schomburg Center of the New York Public Library. Other collections at the Schomburg that include correspondence and information about Davis are the Civil Rights Congress Papers, Frank Crosswaith Papers, Pettis Perry Papers, Hosea Hudson Papers, W. A. Hunton Papers, and Paul Robeson Papers. At New York University the papers of Sam Darcy, Elizabeth Gurly Flynn, and Pete Cacchione include information on Davis, as do the papers of Earl Browder at Syracuse University, Theodore Draper at Emory University, William Patterson and George Murphy at Howard University, Joseph North at Boston University, Eugene Dennis at the State Historical Society of Wisconsin, and W. E. B. Du Bois at the University of Massachusetts.

In addition to his articles, Davis wrote a memoir, *Communist Councilman From Harlem* (New York: International Publishers, 1968; **A, G**).

Other Sources

Both the New York Police Department and the Federal Bureau of Investigation have massive surveillance files on Davis.

Gerald Horne
University of California, Santa Barbara

WALT DISNEY
1901-1966

Chronology

Born Walter Elias Disney on December 5, 1901, in Chicago, Illinois, the fourth
son of Elias Disney, who held various jobs such as carpenter, farmer, and building
contractor, and his wife Flora, a public school teacher; *1906* family moves to
Marceline, Missouri, to farm; *1912* family again relocates to Kansas City, Missouri; develops an early interest in vaudeville and art; *1917* studies art and car-
tooning in Chicago though he interrupts his work and schooling to become an
ambulance driver for the American Red Cross in Europe during World War I;
1919-1922 returns to Kansas City, Missouri, and is employed by a film company
making commercials for cartoon shorts; *1923* moves to Los Angeles, California,
where he establishes a film-making studio in a garage together with Ub Iwerks, an
artist, and his brother Roy as business manager; *1925* marries Lillian Bounds, an
Idaho native; *1928* finally achieves artistic success and renown with screen debut
of Mickey Mouse character in cartoon short "Steam Boat Willie"; *1929-1939*
Silly Symphonies shorts introduce Goofy, Pluto, Donald Duck, and Minnie Mouse;
"Three Little Pigs" short makes screen debut in 1938; brother Roy begins profitable marketing of cartoon products; *1937* produces *Snow White and the Seven
Dwarfs*, one of the most popular films ever released; *1939-1945* creates training
and educational films for the government during war years; studio moves to
Burbank, California; *1940-1942* release of *Fantasia*, *Pinnochio*, and *Dumbo*
(1941); *Bambi* (1942); *1949* release of *Seal Island*, Disney's first nature film;
1950-1955 Disney Studios produces first full-length films using live actors, *Treasure Island* (1950) and *20,000 Leagues Under the Sea* (1954); major animated
productions included *Cinderella* (1950), *Alice in Wonderland* (1951), *Peter Pan*
(1953), and *Lady and the Tramp* (1955); *1955-1966* Disney's productions and
characters appear on weekly television in the *Mickey Mouse Club, Zorro, Davy
Crockett*, and *Disney's Wonderful World of Color*; *1955* opens the first Disneyland
theme park at Anaheim, California; *1964* produces the extremely popular and
successful full-length film *Mary Poppins*; *1966* dies December 15 of cancer in Los
Angeles, California.

Activities of Historical Significance

Although he himself drew only a small number of cartoons, Disney's inspirational and creative genius was instrumental in establishing animated films as an art

form. Disney's figures were colorized, and given human voices and humanized forms. Such memorable and ageless characters as Mickey Mouse, Donald Duck, and the cartoon versions of classic story-book figures created important world-wide characters in popular culture.

A number of animated films were pioneering works. "Steam Boat Willie" (1928) was the first sound cartoon (Disney provided Mickey's voice). *Snow White and the Seven Dwarfs* (1937) was the first full-length animated film as well as the first to utilize human forms in animation. *The Reluctant Dragon* (1941) was the first film to use live individuals and animated figures together. During Disney's lifetime, the Disney Studios garnered a record thirty Academy Awards.

Overview of Biographical Sources

A number of biographies of Disney have appeared. The most important remain Richard Schickel's *The Disney Version* (1968) and Bob Thomas's 1976 study, *Walt Disney*. Though some biographers have pointed to Disney's exacting standards, and at times his inflexibility, all acknowledged his apparently unlimited capacity for creativity, humor, energy, and his lasting contributions to film and popular culture.

Evaluation of Principal Biographical Sources

Ford, Barbara. *Walt Disney: A Biography*. New York: Walker, 1989. (Y) A juvenile biography exploring the major events in the life of Disney and the Disney Studios.

Miller, Diane Disney. *The Story of Walt Disney*. New York: Holt, Henry, 1957. (G) An affectionate biography written by Disney's daughter.

Mosley, Leonard. *Disney's World: A Biography*. Briarcliff Manor, NY: Stein and Day, 1985. (G) This well-researched history of Disney and his studio adds few insights to the picture drawn by earlier biographies.

Schickel, Richard. *The Disney Version; the Life, Times, Art, and Commerce of Walt Disney*. New York: Simon and Schuster, 1968. (A, G) A balanced biography which attempts to provide some insight into Disney's personality. A revised edition with an examination of the company was published in 1985.

Thomas, Bob. *Walt Disney*. New York: Simon and Schuster, 1976. (A, G) The most incisive and comprehensive examination of Disney's life.

Evaluation of Primary Sources

Besides the legacy of the films themselves, there is an extensive Disney archive at the Walt Disney Company headquarters at Burbank, California. This repository, which is available to serious researchers, contains shorts and films, Disney's correspondence, business records, awards, toys, books, photographs, and other personal effects.

Museums, Historical Landmarks, Societies

Disneyland (Anaheim, CA). The first Disney theme park was opened in 1955. It has attracted millions through its exhibits, amusement rides, and entertainment based on Disney characters.

Disneyland (Tokyo, Japan). Opened in 1983, this was the first successful overseas Disney theme park.

Euro Disneyland (Paris, France). This major European complex is being built outside Paris and is expected to open in 1992.

Walt Disney World (Orlando, FL). Although envisioned by Disney, this complex, closely modeled after Disneyland, did not open until 1971, five years after his death. The Orlando location is also the site of EPCOT Center, a permanent world's fair exhibit of future technology, which opened in 1982. Disney World is also the home of the newly opened (1989) Disney-MGM Studios Theme Park.

Other Sources

Bailey, Adrian. *Walt Disney's World of Fantasy*. New York: Everest House, 1982. A recent well-written study which emphasizes the technical success of the Disney Studios.

Finch Christopher. *The Art of Walt Disney: From Mickey Mouse to the Magic Kingdoms*. New York: Abrams, 1973. A good history of the Disney Studios and animation techniques.

Maltin, Leonard. *The Disney Films*. New York: Universe Books, New American Library, 1984. A comprehensive reference book which includes a wealth of information on Disney shorts and films.

Donald J. Richards
Manhattanville College

ALLEN DULLES
1893-1969

Chronology

Born Allen Welsh Dulles on April 7, 1893, in Watertown, New York, the third child of Allen Macy Dulles, a Presbyterian minister and teacher, and Edith Foster Dulles, the daughter of a diplomat and international lawyer; *1893-1909* grows up in Watertown, attending local schools and developing a competitive relationship with older brother John Foster Dulles; *1910-1914* attends Princeton University, graduating with a degree in philosophy and winning the McCosh Prize for his senior thesis on pragmatism; *1914-1915* teaches English at Ewing Christian College in Allahabad, India; *1915-1916* earns a master's degree in international law at Princeton; *1916-1917* joins the diplomatic service and is assigned to Vienna; *1917-1918* serves as an Austria-Hungarian specialist at the U.S. embassy in Berne and develops an enthusiasm for intelligence work; *1918-1919* works for the American Commission to Negotiate Peace in Paris; *1919-1922* serves briefly in Berlin; returns to the United States and marries Martha Clover Todd on October 16, 1920; joins the American mission to Turkey; *1922-1926* serves as chief of the Division of New Eastern Affairs; earns law degree at George Washington University; *1926-1941* practices law as a member of the law firm of Sullivan & Cromwell, headed by brother John Foster Dulles; becomes partner in 1930; *1941-1942* joins the Office of Coordinator of Information (a wartime intelligence organization) and compiles dossiers on leading Nazis; *1942-1945* serves as chief intelligence officer in Switzerland for the Office of Strategic Services; *1945* plays important role in arranging for the surrender of German forces in northern Italy; *1946-1950* resumes law practice with Sullivan & Cromwell; *1948* chairs committee that investigates functions of the newly created Central Intelligence Agency (CIA); *1950-1953* heads CIA's covert operations; becomes deputy director; *1953-1961* serves as director of central intelligence and shapes the course of American intelligence operations during the height of the cold war; *1961* resigns as head of the CIA following the abortive landing at the Bay of Pigs; *1964* serves as member of the Warren Commission that investigates the assassination of John F. Kennedy; *1969* dies on January 29 of pneumonia following several strokes.

Activities of Historical Significance

Allen Dulles presided over the Central Intelligence Agency at the height of cold war tensions and hostility between the United States and the Soviet Union. He shaped and molded the nation's first peacetime intelligence organization, forging it into an important instrument of national policy.

Dulles became attracted to intelligence work while serving as a diplomat in Switzerland during World War I. During the 1930s, while a partner in an international law firm headed by brother John Foster Dulles, he became a leading advocate of American assistance to nations that were opposing Fascist aggression. Following American entry into World War II, Dulles joined what became the Office of Strategic Services (OSS), an intelligence organization that had been created by William J. Donovan at the request of President Franklin D. Roosevelt.

Assigned to neutral Switzerland in 1942, Dulles became OSS's leading European operative. In the most important agent recruitment of the war, he secured the services of a high official in the German foreign office who provided valuable information on diplomatic policy and a wide range of sensitive technical and tactical data. In 1945 Dulles secretly conducted a series of complicated negotiations with SS General Karl Wolff that led to the surrender of German forces in northern Italy.

Returning to his legal practice at the end of the war, Dulles often was consulted on intelligence matters as the nation's first peacetime intelligence organization took shape. In 1948 he chaired a committee that investigated the function of the new Central Intelligence Agency and made recommendations for improvements. In 1950 Dulles joined the CIA to implement some of his recommendations and serve as head of covert operations. Between August 1951 and January 1953, he was the agency's deputy director.

President Dwight D. Eisenhower, who appointed John Foster Dulles secretary of state, placed Dulles in charge of the CIA shortly after he assumed office in 1953. During his eight years as director of central intelligence, Dulles presided over a golden age of covert operations as Eisenhower placed the CIA on the front lines of the cold war. An enthusiastic supporter of covert action, Dulles helped to engineer the overthrow of "unfriendly" governments in Iran and Guatemala. Also, he supported advances in the technical collection of intelligence, especially the development of the high altitude U-2 reconnaissance aircraft. In the end, however, his confidence in the CIA's covert action capability led to the abortive Bay of Pigs invasion—and to his downfall from the recriminations that followed.

During Dulles's tenure as director, the CIA grew into an organization of immense power and prestige. Mysterious and seemingly omnipotent during the 1950s, it would be criticized during the 1970s for what many deemed to be irresponsible behavior. For better or worse, the agency reflected the strengths and weaknesses of Dulles, the man whom Major General Sir Kenneth Strong has termed "the greatest United States professional intelligence officer of his time."

Overview of Biographical Sources

There has been no major biography of Dulles, although various aspects of his career have been covered in a number of volumes. Leonard Mosely, *Dulles: A Biography of Eleanor, Allen and Foster Dulles* (1978), is a collective biography that should be treated with care as it is filled with factual errors and invented happenings. W. H. Brands, Jr., *Cold Warriors: Eisenhower's Generation and American Foreign Policy* (1988), contains a balanced, short sketch of Dulles's career, while Stephen E. Ambrose, *Ike's Spies: Eisenhower and the Intelligence Establishment* (1981), explores the relationship between Dulles and Eisenhower. A full-scale biography of Dulles by R. Harris Smith has been in gestation for a number of years.

Evaluation of Principal Biographical Sources

Ambrose, Stephen E. *Ike's Spies: Eisenhower and the Espionage Establishment.* Garden City, NY: Doubleday, 1981. (**A, G**) Although somewhat critical of Dulles, the author concludes that he gave the CIA "a sense of importance and a sense of mission."

Brands, W. H., Jr. *Cold Warriors: Eisenhower's Generation and American Foreign Policy.* New York: Columbia University Press, 1988. (**A, G**) A fine, brief survey of the topic, containing a balanced portrait of Dulles.

Jeffreys-Jones, Rhodri. *The CIA and American Democracy.* New Haven: Yale University Press, 1989. (**A, G**) This excellent study contains a critical chapter on Dulles's tenure as head of the CIA.

Ranelagh, John. *The Agency: The Rise and Decline of the CIA.* New York: Simon and Schuster, 1986. (**A, G**) An engaging survey of the CIA's checkered past, including a good treatment of the Dulles years.

Smith, Bradley F. *The Shadow Warriors: OSS and the Origins of the CIA.* New York: Basic Books, 1983. (**A, G**) This scholarly account of the OSS contains an extensive treatment of Dulles's wartime activities.

Smith, Bradley F., and Elena Agarossi. *Operation Sunrise: The Secret Surrender.* New York: Basic Books, 1979. (**A, G**) The most-detailed account of Dulles's role in arranging the surrender of German troops in northern Italy.

Smith, R. Harris. *OSS: The Secret History of America's First Central Intelligence Agency.* Berkeley: University of California Press, 1972. (**A, G**) Written by a former intelligence officer, this standard survey of the topic includes considerable information on Dulles's activities with the OSS.

Strong, Sir Kenneth. *Men of Intelligence.* London: Cassell, 1970. (**A, G**) Contains an admiring portrait of Dulles by a fellow intelligence professional.

Overview and Evaluation of Primary Sources
The Papers of Allen Dulles are at the Seeley G. Mudd Manuscript Library, Princeton University. The Mudd Library also houses the Papers of John Foster Dulles. The Records of the Office of Strategic Services can be found in the National Archives, Washington, D.C. Selected items relating to Dulles's CIA career are available at the Eisenhower Presidential Library, Abilene, Kansas. Continuing security restrictions limit the information that can be obtained on Dulles's intelligence work.

Dulles published a number of books that shed light on various aspects of his life. The starting point is *The Craft of Intelligence* (New York: Harper & Row, 1963; **A, G, Y**). Part history, part memoir, part polemic, the volume is a classic in the literature of intelligence (the paperback edition contains material not found in the hardbound version). Dulles discusses important episodes in his wartime service in *Germany's Underground* (New York: Macmillan 1947; **A, G**), and *The Secret Surrender* (New York: Harper & Row, 1966; **A, G**).

Insight into Dulles's early years and his relationship with his siblings can be found in Eleanor Lansing Dulles, *Chances of a Lifetime* (Englewood Cliffs, NJ: Prentice-Hall, 1980; **A, G, Y**).

Other Sources
Dulles, Allen, ed. *Great Spy Stories.* New York: Ballantine Books, 1982. This entertaining collection of stories compiled by Dulles includes a short introduction.

Immerman, Richard H. "Allen Welsh Dulles." In *Dictionary of American Biography,* supplement 8 (1966-1970). Edited by John A. Garraty and Mark C. Carnes. New York: Scribner's, 1988. A fine, brief treatment of Dulles's career.

Leary, William M., ed. *The Central Intelligence Agency: History and Documents.* University: University of Alabama Press, 1984. Reprints "History of the

Central Intelligence Agency,'' written during the mid-1970s by Anne Karalekas for the Senate's Select Committee on Intelligence (Church Committee), as well as other important documents.

O'Toole, G. J. A. *The Encyclopedia of American Intelligence and Espionage.* New York: Facts on File, 1988. This tour-de-force includes entries on Dulles as well as other major intelligence subjects.

Vanderbroucke, Lucien S. "The 'Confessions' of Allen Dulles: New Evidence on the Bay of Pigs." *Diplomatic History* 8 (Fall 1984): 365-375. An interesting interpretation of an article prepared but never published by Dulles. Richard M. Bissell, Jr., Dulles's chief of covert operations, offers a dissenting interpretation in the same volume (377-380).

William M. Leary
University of Georgia

PAUL LAURENCE DUNBAR
1872-1906

Chronology

Born Paul Laurence Dunbar on June 27, 1872, in Dayton, Ohio, to Joshua Dunbar, a plasterer, and Matilda Murphy Dunbar, both former slaves; father had escaped to Canada and returned to fight in the Civil War; *1888* publishes first poem, "Our Martyred Soldiers," in the *Dayton Herald*; *1891* graduates from high school and takes a series of low-paying jobs; *1892* delivers welcoming address to the Western Association of Writers Meeting in Dayton; publishes at his own expense *Oak and Ivy,* a collection of his poems; *1893* meets Frederick Douglass; *1895* meets George Washington Cable and James Whitcomb Riley; *1896* publishes *Lyrics of Lowly Life*; *1897* visits England; *1897* meets Booker T. Washington; *1897-1898* works at the Library of Congress; *1898* marries Alice Ruth Moore; *1898-1900* collaborates with Will Marion Cook on musical plays; *1899* receives honorary master's degree from Atlanta University; falls ill with tuberculosis; *1902* separates from wife; *1906* dies on February 9 in Dayton, Ohio, of tuberculosis.

Activities of Historical Significance

Paul Laurence Dunbar was the son of illiterate former slaves who had intense curiosity about the world around them, and they instilled in their son a love of learning. In his own day, African-American leaders pointed to Dunbar as an example for other blacks to follow. He became a symbol of what blacks could achieve if they were given a chance to succeed in American society. For white audiences, he was first a highly entertaining writer and second a spokesman for African Americans, telling whites about the horrors of racism. He was also the first African American to make a living from his writing. He never carried the role as spokesman of his people well, although in the last years of his life his work began to mature into a blend of entertainment and trenchant social criticism. His premature death from tuberculosis cut short what might have become a profoundly important literary career.

African Americans of Dunbar's day took him into their hearts. They were delighted that he was showing the world at large how blacks could be a positive force in American society, and they believed that his writings were making high art out of their everyday experiences. For decades after his death, they made his writings part of social occasions, including weddings, and other family gatherings.

Although critics of his day, especially William Dean Howells, praised his work, twentieth-century literary critics have taken a different view of Dunbar. Before the 1970s most critics saw Dunbar's works as shallow perpetuations of vile black stereotypes, and they saw Dunbar himself as a traitor to his race. They asserted that Dunbar merely played to white prejudices in exchange for fame.

Thus, in the twentieth century Dunbar became symbolic of two different ideas. The majority of African Americans and a few African-American critics and writers such as Benjamin Brawley and Langston Hughes viewed Dunbar as a romantic genius who had overcome great odds to fulfill his dreams. Viewing him as a role model, they supported attaching his name to a multitude of public buildings, especially schools, where his example was meant to show the value of education.

The intelligentsia that abhorred Dunbar believed him to be a symbol of the corrupting influence of white racism. In exchange for fame and large audiences, they said, Dunbar sold out his own people and fed ignorant whites a stereotypical picture of indolent, unintelligent, comical blacks living happily on white-owned plantations. They believed Dunbar to have harmed black aspirations for social equality by setting a bad example.

This view has been challenged in recent years, particularly since Dunbar's nonfiction has come under close examination. He seems to have written different works for different audiences and to have been ever mindful of his distinct place in the imaginations of African Americans. His nonfiction indicates that he was outspoken about racial divisions and about injustices perpetrated against black Americans by racists. Some critics now suggest that he was using familiar formats for his poetry and fiction about African Americans, but instead of simply cranking out "plantation stories" and "minstrel" works, he was using the old racially prejudiced patterns to present blacks as they really were. That is, Dunbar used literary forms familiar to his white audiences in order to make them more accepting of his revolutionary material. Instead of showing African Americans happy with their servitude to white landowners, he showed lynchings, poverty, and courage against oppression.

At present, many decades after his death, Dunbar still excites passions, and his readers are deeply divided over his merits. Still, there is no denying the special stature he had during his lifetime, and there is no denying his role in the history of African-American literature. He was the first black American creative writer to acquire a broad audience that crossed racial divisions. As such, he demonstrated to publishers that there was a profitable audience available for the writings of other African-American writers. He also became a living demonstration of the great reservoir of talent to be found in black America, and as such he ranked with Frederick Douglass, Booker T. Washington, and other great African-American leaders, nearly all of whom celebrated Dunbar as a glorious figure. Further, he helped sensitize American society and its leaders to issues of great importance to blacks. He was the friend of presidents and participated in the campaigns of William McKinley and Theodore Roosevelt, both of whom knew and respected him. He aspired to transcend race, to show the common humanity of people, and as a result left works that inspired and gave hope to generations of African Americans.

Overview of Biographical Sources

Ever since the publication of Benjamin Brawley's *Paul Laurence Dunbar: Poet of His People* (1936), biographers have had to wrestle with the many contradictions of his life and what his contributions would be to modern times. Brawley attempted to rehabilitate Dunbar's reputation with literary critics, who by the 1930s tended to regard Dunbar with hostility, as someone who had pandered to racist white audiences. This hostility contrasted markedly with the views of most African Americans who held Dunbar in high esteem as a great writer whose work still had great meaning for them. Brawley admired Dunbar and tried to explain in plain terms why the author so often seemed simply to reproduce ugly stereotypes; the times in which he lived forced Dunbar to disguise his more radical social ideas so that they would slip past audiences who were suspicious of accomplished African-American intellectuals. In criticism as well as biographies this has come to be called Dunbar's "mask"—a term borrowed from one of Dunbar's poems.

Since Brawley's book, nearly every biographer who admires Dunbar has felt compelled to write an apology for the unpleasant aspects of Dunbar's accomplishments. These apologies tend to be repetitive, but they serve the purpose of showing that some of what Dunbar wrote is embarrassing in modern terms, although he had compelling reasons for writing as he did. Thus the positive biographical views of Dunbar tend to be more balanced and thoughtful than the negative ones. On the other hand, those biographers who regard Dunbar as a bad example for African Americans to follow have exaggerated Dunbar's use of stereotypes and tend to ignore the popularity of his works in his day.

Evaluation of Principal Biographical Sources

Arnold, Edward F. "Some Personal Reminiscences of Paul Laurence Dunbar." *Journal of Negro History* 17 (October 1932): 400-408. (G) Seeing Dunbar as a great man whose life is worthy of imitation, Arnold unflinchingly tells of the racial prejudice Dunbar endured and manages in a brief space to convey something of the inner strength of the man.

Brawley, Benjamin. *Paul Laurence Dunbar: Poet of His People*. Chapel Hill: University of North Carolina Press, 1936. **(G)** This short biography was written at a time when Dunbar was popular with rank-and-file African Americans and yet detested by many black critics and writers. Thus, it is partly a defense of Dunbar, whom Brawley sees as a pioneer who opened up the literary world to blacks who had been excluded from it.

Cunningham, Virginia. *Paul Laurence Dunbar and His Song*. New York: Dodd, Mead, 1947. **(G)** Long the standard biography of Dunbar, this book focuses on the man rather than his writings. Drawn from many first-hand sources, including interviews with those who had known Dunbar, it shows his life as a triumph of spirit against poverty, racism, and finally a terrible disease. This volume goes a long way toward explaining why Dunbar was so deeply loved by both African Americans and whites even while his writings sometimes contradicted the prejudices of each.

Gayle, Addison, Jr. *Oak and Ivy: A Biography of Paul Laurence Dunbar*. Garden City, NY: Doubleday, 1971. **(G)** This book focuses on the notion that Dunbar was caught in a conflict between a desire for a broad audience and his dismay at racial stereotypes. Gayle provides a short critical biography that shows the growth of Dunbar's art, cut off early by disease.

Hughes, Langston. "Paul Laurence Dunbar: The Robert Burns of Negro Poetry [1872-1906]." In *Famous American Negroes*. New York: Dodd, Mead, 1954. **(Y)** This short biography, part of the Famous Biographies for Young People Series, was written by one of the leading writers of the twentieth century. Hughes is upbeat in portraying Dunbar's rise from the son of an escaped slave to a respected literary figure.

Martin, Jay, ed. *A Singer in the Dawn: Reinterpretations of Paul Laurence Dunbar*. New York: Dodd, Mead, 1975. **(A, G)** A gathering of lectures given at the Centenary Conference on Paul Laurence Dunbar. Includes lectures on racial stereotyping, segregation, Dunbar's tone, subject matter, diction, "attitudes toward black characters," dialect writings, and place among other African-American authors.

McGhee, Nancy B. "Portraits in Black: Illustrated Poems of Paul Laurence Dunbar." In *Stony the Road: Chapters in the History of Hampton Institute*, edited by Keith L. Schall. Charlottesville: University Press of Virginia, 1977. **(A, G)** An informative article that provides background on Dunbar's life and literary relations, as well as on the production of his books. This well-researched piece contains information that would be hard to find elsewhere.

Story, Ralph. "Paul Laurence Dunbar: Master Player in a Fixed Game." *CLA Journal* 27 (September 1983): 30-55. (**A, G**) Sees Dunbar as a pivotal figure in a time of great difficulty for African Americans struggling for equality. Dunbar introduced a more rational, honest view of blacks, but, according to Story, much of his struggle was in vain because he naively did not understand that African Americans were not going to be heard. This essay is brilliantly written, arguing that Dunbar has not yet received a full, wide-eyed examination of his works which include the subjects of "lynchings, racism, and other (still controversial) historical topics the public elementary and secondary schools have artfully avoided for decades."

Wiggins, Lida Keck. "Life of Paul Laurence Dunbar." In *The Life and Works of Paul Laurence Dunbar: Containing His Complete Poetical Works, His Best Short Stories, Numerous Anecdotes and a Complete Biography of the Famous Poet*. Naperville, IL: J. L. Nichols, 1907. (**A, G**) This book is an essential resource on the life and works of Dunbar, with the short biography still a fundamental source of information for researchers. Wiggins portrays Dunbar as a martyred figure torn apart by his efforts to reconcile the cruelties of the world with his idealism.

Overview and Evaluation of Primary Sources

There are three good primary sources on Dunbar, each using some of his letters. Given the openness of Dunbar's revelations in these letters, a fuller edition deserves to be published. Pauline A. Young's "Paul Laurence Dunbar: An Intimate Glimpse," in *Freedomways* (12 [1972]: 319-329; **A, G**), presents letters Dunbar wrote to his future wife. A selection of his letters appears in Jay Martin and Gossie H. Hudson, eds., *The Paul Laurence Dunbar Reader: A Selection of the Best of Paul Laurence Dunbar's Poetry and Prose, Including Writings Never Before Available in Book Form* (New York: Dodd, Mead, 1975; **A, G**). This book has enriched the study of Dunbar by calling attention to his interesting but previously neglected writings. The letters reveal different aspects of Dunbar's character as both private and public man. "Paul Laurence Dunbar: Biography Through Letters" is included in Jay Martin, ed., *A Singer in the Dawn: Reinterpretations of Paul Laurence Dunbar* (New York: Dodd, Mead, 1975; **A, G**). These letters tell primarily of Dunbar's social concerns and are accompanied by Martin's commentary.

The Ohio Historical Society has Dunbar manuscripts in its archives in Columbus. Manuscripts can also be found in the Schomberg Collection of the New York Public Library.

Other Sources

Baker, Houston A., Jr. "Paul Laurence Dunbar: An Evaluation." *Black World* 21 (November 1971): 30-37. Baker argues that any just appraisal of Dunbar must take into account the times in which he lived. Although he has had many detractors since, in his own day Dunbar was honored by African Americans, partly because he was blazing a trail into new realms for black writers and partly because they saw him as a true spokesman for their race.

Bone, Robert. "Paul Dunbar." In *Down Home: A History of Afro-American Short Fiction from Its Beginnings to the End of the Harlem Renaissance.* New York: G. P. Putnam's Sons, 1975. Argues that with so many prejudices still existing in the post-Reconstruction era "it often seemed the better part of valor to blend with one's surroundings." In Dunbar's case, "Protective mimicry consisted (1) of imitating the Plantation School, and (2) utilizing the conventions of the minstrel stage."

Brawley, Benjamin. "Paul Laurence Dunbar." In *The Negro Genius: A New Appraisal of the Achievement of the American Negro in Literature and the Fine Arts.* 1937. Reprint. New York: Biblo and Tannen, 1966. Surveys Dunbar's life and divides his work into poems in traditional English, those in dialect, short stories, and novels. He argues that the writings in dialect are Dunbar's most important ones.

————. "Paul Laurence Dunbar." In *The Negro in Literature and Art in the United States.* New York: Duffield, 1930. Briefly surveys Dunbar's life, then analyzes the poems "Ere Sleep Comes Down to Soothe the Weary Eyes," "The Poet and His Song," "Life," "Lullaby," and "Compensation."

Brown, Sterling. "Dunbar and Traditional Dialect" and "Dunbar and the Romantic Tradition." In *Negro Poetry and Drama and the Negro in American Fiction.* 1937. Reprint. New York: Atheneum, 1969. Comments that Dunbar "is at his best in his picture of the folk life of his day." In the second essay, Brown is concerned with how Dunbar and his black contemporaries dealt with the social ramifications of their work, struggling against stereotypes while trying to create a black cultural identity.

Candela, Gregory L. "We Wear the Mask: Irony in Dunbar's *The Sport of the Gods*." *American Literature* 48 (March 1976): 60-72. Takes sharp issue with negative criticism of Dunbar's writing, believing it to be "misdirected." Shows Dunbar's mastery of language, form, and narrative in *The Sport of the Gods*, noting that if one emphasizes Dunbar's art, then he emerges as an admirable writer. This essay is clearly written and easily accessible to students as well as scholars.

Daniel, Walter C. "Paul Laurence Dunbar: Three Preachers in Search of Them-selves." In *Images of the Preacher in Afro-American Literature*. Washington, DC: University Press of America, 1981. Daniel analyzes the figure of the preacher in the novel *The Uncalled* and the short stories "The Ordeal at Mount Hope" and "The Fruitful Sleeping of the Reverend Elisha Edwards." He notes that only in "The Ordeal at Mount Hope" is the minister necessarily black. In the other works, Dunbar deals with issues of universal significance that transcend race. Daniel sees *The Uncalled* as a daring work that explores the controversial issue of heredity versus environment in the shaping of human beings.

Elder, Arlene A. "Paul Laurence Dunbar: The Triumph of the Tradition." In *The "Hindered Hand": Cultural Implications of Early African-American Fiction*. Westport, CT: Greenwood Press, 1978. Part of the Contributions in Afro-American and African Studies Series, this insightful essay presents Dunbar as a writer in conflict with himself. On the one hand, he had high artistic aspirations, but on the other he was driven by poverty to strive for fame among a large, predominately white audience. Comments that this conflict caused him to compromise his art, so that he never completely fulfilled the promise of his talent. Elder provides close readings of Dunbar's dialect writings, which she considers Dunbar's best work.

Flint, Allen. "Black Response to Colonel Shaw." *Phylon* 45 (September 1984): 210-219. Flint discusses poems about Colonel Robert Gould Shaw by Dunbar, Henrietta Cordelia Ray, and Benjamin Brawley. Shaw commanded the Massachu-setts Fifty-fourth Regiment, which consisted of black troops and which has been the subject of numerous poems, as well as art works and even a popular motion picture, *Glory* (1990). Flint finds Dunbar's "Robert Gould Shaw" to be "start-ling" because of its assertion that Shaw's sacrifice was in vain.

Flusche, Michael. "Paul Laurence Dunbar and the Burden of Race." *Southern Humanities Review* 11 (Winter 1977): 49-61. Suggests that with his successes publishing his works in major magazines Dunbar hoped he would transcend the issue of his race and be valued strictly on the merits of his work. Dunbar's dilemma, as Flusche sees it, was that "only his weak and trivial pieces drew applause," thus discouraging him from writing "strong, significant fiction and poetry." Dunbar ended up writing mostly in the "plantation" tradition which emphasized humorous blacks; this makes his work fundamentally ironic, because even as his stories evoke superficial laughter, they show that underneath the laughter are people living difficult, unfulfilled lives.

Fox, Allan B. "Behind the Mask: Paul Laurence Dunbar's Poetry in Literary English." *Texas Quarterly* 14 (Summer 1971): 7-19. Analyzes poems in order to show how Dunbar used irony to enrich his themes and to undercut the literary conventions that he seemed to be embracing.

Gayle, Addison, Jr. *The Way of the New World: The Black Novel in America*. Garden City, NY: Anchor Press, 1975. Surveys Dunbar's novels as part of a historical study. Gayle sees Dunbar's novels as failures, with *The Fanatics* being "distorted history disguised as fiction."

Gloster, Hugh M. "Paul Laurence Dunbar." In *Negro Voices in American Fiction*. Chapel Hill: University of North Carolina Press, 1948. Gloster sees Dunbar as a formula writer of shallow, amateurish fiction. This piece is typical of the generally hostile critical views of Dunbar that prevailed, with some exceptions, until the 1970s, and it shows why critics who admire his work almost always first defend Dunbar against his detractors before actually analyzing his writings.

Hull, Gloria T. "Alice Dunbar-Nelson (1875-1935)." In *Color, Sex, & Poetry: Three Women Writers of the Harlem Renaissance*. Bloomington: Indiana University Press, 1987. Cherished by feminist critics as well as those interested in African-American literature, Dunbar's wife has become the subject of many critical studies in recent decades. Hull covers the courtship, marriage, and professional relationship of Dunbar and Dunbar-Nelson, and tells of the bizarre aftermath of Dunbar's death, in which Dunbar-Nelson pretended to remain a widow in mourning for her brilliant deceased husband, even while married for a second time.

Jones, Gayle. "Breaking Out of the Conventions of Dialect: Dunbar and Hurston." *Presence Africaine* 144 (1987): 32-46. Examines how Dunbar and Zora

Neale Hurston used the "minstrelsy" tradition in their works containing African American dialect. Although the minstrelsy tradition included offensive black stereotypes, Dunbar and Hurston tried to move beyond the caricatures of blacks to a genuine reflection of black language. Dunbar's short story "The Lynching of Jube Benson" is presented as a striking example of what Dunbar and other turn-of-the-century black writers were trying to achieve.

Larson, Charles R. "The Novels of Paul Laurence Dunbar." *Phylon* 29 (Fall 1968): 257-271. This is one of the most frequently referred to articles on Dunbar. Larson believes that Dunbar's novels reveal a growing social consciousness that did not reach fruition because of his premature death. Asks readers to look beneath the conventions of romance writing in Dunbar's novels to see serious discussions of the issues of African-American civil rights that had developed after the Civil War.

Lawson, Victor. *Dunbar Critically Examined*. Washington, DC: Associated Publishers, 1941. Historical criticism that investigates Dunbar's sources and antecedents. It is typical of most critics' hostility toward Dunbar prior to the 1970s.

Metcalf, E. W., Jr. *Paul Laurence Dunbar: A Bibliography*. Metuchen, NJ: Scarecrow Press, 1975. A thorough listing of works by and about Dunbar. For someone who wishes to study Dunbar in depth, this volume is an excellent resource, covering both primary and secondary publications.

Okeke-Ezigbo, Emeka. "Paul Laurence Dunbar: Straightening the Record." *CLA Journal* 24 (June 1981): 481-496. Wishes to dispel myths that are found in much of the criticism written about Dunbar. While this article examines Dunbar's sources and artistic intent, it also asserts that Dunbar was condescending toward ordinary blacks.

Revell, Peter. *Paul Laurence Dunbar*. Boston: Twayne, 1979. This introductory study is intended primarily for use by students, although professional critics often refer to it. Revell provides chapters on the times in which Dunbar lived, Dunbar's life, poetry in literary English and in dialect, work in theater, short stories, and novels, as well as a concluding summary of his own views on the author.

Turner, Darwin T. "Paul Laurence Dunbar: The Rejected Symbol." In *The Black Novelist*, edited by Robert Hemenway. Columbus, OH: Charles E. Merrill,

1970. Reprinted from *The Journal of Negro History* 52 (January 1967): 1-13. Notes that while still a young man Dunbar became a "symbol of the creative and intellectual potential of the American Negro." Argues that Dunbar's work actually protests inaccurate stereotypes and examines why that protest is often muted.

Wagner, Jean. "Paul Laurence Dunbar." In *Black Poets of the United States: From Paul Laurence Dunbar to Langston Hughes,* translated by Kenneth Douglas. Urbana: University of Illinois Press, 1973. Some critics praise this book as the best one ever written about African-American poetry. Wagner provides a short summary of Dunbar's life, and devotes sections to "Dunbar and the Plantation Tradition," "Race Consciousness and History," "The Poet and His People," and "The Lyricism of Heartbreak." Asserts that Dunbar represents the inner conflicts that develop in the poets who succeed him.

Wakefield, John. "Paul Laurence Dunbar: *The Scapegoat* (1904)." In *The Black American Short Story in the 20th Century: A Collection of Critical Essays,* edited by Peter Bruck. Amsterdam: B. R. Gruner, 1977. Sees Dunbar as hypocritical because his writings contradict what he really believed. Wakefield suggests that Dunbar's careful following of traditional literary forms stemmed from an effort not to offend public opinion.

Williams, Kenny J. "The Masking of the Poet." In *They Also Spoke: An Essay on Negro Literature in America, 1787-1930.* Nashville, TN: Townsend Press, 1970. Works a familiar theme in his analyses of Dunbar: that Dunbar masked his serious ideas with the trappings of conventional writing. In this sensible discussion, Williams places Dunbar in the context of his time and devotes considerable space to in-depth discussions of Dunbar's major works. He presents much evidence to support the belief that Dunbar knew exactly what he was doing when he composed his works in either literary English or in black dialect and that he had sound artistic and social reasons for selecting language, form, and tone for his works. This essay is a good introduction to Dunbar's writings.

Kirk H. Beetz
National University, Sacramento

WYATT EARP
1848-1929

Chronology

Born Wyatt Berry Stapp Earp on March 19, 1848, in Monmouth, Illinois, the third son of Virginia Anne Cooksey Earp, a pioneer housewife, and Nicholas Porter Earp, a restless frontiersman who had once practiced law but was primarily a farmer and land dealer; his older half-brother, four full brothers, and sister all live to maturity; *1848-1864* has a typical childhood in farming communities in Illinois and Iowa; attends village schools; *1861-1865* his father, a Mexican War veteran, and older brothers serve in the Union army during the Civil War; *1864* sets out with most of the family for San Bernardino, California, in a wagon train led by his father; *1865-1868* drives stagecoaches in California and Arizona; *1868* works as section hand for Union Pacific Railroad in Wyoming; *1870* moves to Lamar, Missouri, and is elected town constable, defeating his brother, Newton; marries Willa (or Urilla or Rilla) Sutherland, who dies of typhoid a few months later; *1870-1872* drifts into Indian territory; arrested for horse stealing but escapes into Kansas and becomes a buffalo hunter; *1873* gambles in Hays City and later in Ellsworth; *1874* works as a policeman in Wichita but is dismissed within a year; *1876* goes to Dodge City and joins the police force; *1877* leaves briefly to prospect for gold in the Dakotas, but by summer has gone to Texas to follow the "gambling circuit"; *1878* serves as assistant marshal in Dodge and develops a friendship with John Henry "Doc" Holliday, a man he had recently met in Texas; *1879* travels to Las Vegas, New Mexico, with his common-law wife, Celia Ann "Mattie" Blaylock; operates a tent saloon and gambling hall; *1880* moves to Tombstone, Arizona, with part of his family; works as a Wells Fargo guard and deputy sheriff of Pima County; fails to gain appointment as sheriff when Cochise County is organized; operates a gaming table at the Oriental Saloon in which he holds a minor financial interest; *1881* his brother Virgil Earp, a former U.S. deputy marshal and temporary town marshal, becomes Tombstone's permanent town marshal; a feud develops, pitting the Earps and Doc Holliday against the Clantons and McLaurys; *October 26, 1881* the "Gunfight at the O.K. Corral" occurs; *1882* serves briefly as a deputy U.S. Marshal; *1883-1906* works as gambler, prospector, saloon keeper, detective, bounty hunter, bodyguard, and boxing match referee; drifts throughout the West; *1888* his wife Mattie, whom he deserted, commits suicide at Pinal, Arizona; *c.1897* marries his third wife, Josephine Sarah Marcus; *1906-1929* lives in Los Angeles, where he meets movie greats; spends some time in Parker, Arizona, where he becomes involved in a variety of unsuccessful business ventures; *1929* dies on January 13, in Los Angeles.

Activities of Historical Significance

Although he was much more than a lawman, the historical Wyatt Earp is a relatively unimportant figure. Despite brief stints as a frontier law officer, many of his activities were unsavory if not actually illegal. Until his later years in Los Angeles, his life was largely indistinguishable from that of many frontier drifters, although his cohesive family gave him a social anchor not available to the usual saddle tramp.

The centerpiece of Earp's life was the so-called "Gunfight at the O.K. Corral," a gun battle that took place in an empty lot near the corral along Fremont Street in Tombstone, Arizona. There, Ike and Billy Clanton, Tom and Frank McLaury, and Billy Claiborne fought the Earp brothers (Wyatt, Virgil, and Morgan) and Doc Holliday. There is still disagreement on the reasons for the showdown, although some have labeled it an effort by the Earps and Holliday to cover up their own criminal activities that their adversaries were planning to reveal. More likely, however, animosity occasioned by earlier rough treatment handed the Clantons and McLaurys by Earp and his brothers in the process of "calming" the rowdy element in town caused the gunfight. A more immediate possible cause was a stagecoach robbery in which Ike Clanton apparently became involved. He identified the robbers to Earp for the reward money. Earp, a candidate for sheriff of newly created Cochise County, wanted credit for capturing the robbers, but the deal fell through and Earp was not elected.

When Earp publicly identified Clanton as the informant, Clanton boasted—on the night of October 25, 1881—that he would kill Earp. The next day Tombstone was alive with rumors of an impending shoot-out. Virgil Earp, the town marshal, deputized his brothers and Holliday and they went to arrest the Clantons and McLaurys. In a few seconds Virgil and Morgan were shot, while the McLaurys and Billy Clanton were mortally wounded. Ike and Billy Claiborne fled. As a consequence of the gunfight, several months later Virgil was wounded and Morgan was murdered. Wyatt Earp later killed three men he accused of murdering his brother.

The subsequent depictions of the gunfight in books and movies, together with fictitious events in the Kansas cattle towns of Ellsworth, Wichita, and Dodge City, created the myth of Earp, western lawman. According to this myth, the tall, laconic, rugged, fair, and honest Earp tamed the West with his six-gun, making it livable for decent citizens.

The legend began with the writings of Walter Noble Burns, W. R. Burnett, and Stuart Lake in the late 1920s and early 1930s. It was carried forward by movie makers, who either retold events of the marshal's life in highly imaginative ways or created thinly disguised characters modeled on him. In more recent times television has perpetuated the myth.

The American public has preserved the image of a heroic lawman-protector who, with gun in hand, subdues the lawless element of a frontier community. More than any other document, the Stanley Kramer-Fred Zinnemann movie *High Noon* (United Artists, 1952), which was based on John W. Cunningham's short story, "The Tin Star," epitomizes this yearning. Earp has been suggested as the model for the character Marshal Will Kane, so ably played by the tall, western-born actor, Gary Cooper.

Overview of Biographical Sources

The first publication of importance in the creation of the Earp myth was journalist Walter Noble Burns's semi-fictitious *Tombstone, An Iliad of the Southwest* (1927). However, the book that firmly established Earp as the prototype frontier lawman was Stuart Lake's *Wyatt Earp: Frontier Marshal* (1931), a biography that has since been thoroughly discredited as unreliable. Critics once considered it almost Earp's autobiography; Lake claimed in the preface to have interviewed the marshal in the late 1920s. But in 1941 he revealed that he paid little attention to Earp's reminiscences in writing the book.

Nevertheless, *Frontier Marshal* influenced many of the later accounts of Earp's life. Ramon Adams's three-volume critical western bibliography—*Burrs Under the Saddle* (1964); *Six-Guns and Saddle Leather* (1969); and *More Burrs Under the Saddle* (1979)—lists 369 books about Earp. Adams points out that these biographies, autobiographies, and monographs perpetuate "a great mass of absurdities . . . [and] glaring errors."

No biographical myths go unchallenged for long, however. Frank Waters began the process of "correcting" many of Lake's misstatements in *The Colorado* (1946). His 1960 work, *The Earp Brothers of Tombstone: The Story of Mrs. Virgil Earp*, was a major effort to demolish the Earp legend. During the 1960s Ed E. Bartholomew produced two volumes, *Wyatt Earp, 1848 to 1860: The Untold Story* (1963) and *Wyatt Earp, 1879-1882* (1964), that attempted to chronicle what he termed the "antics and machinations" of this "flotsam of the frontier." Some scholars believe, however, that Waters and Bartholomew exceeded normal critical standards in their debunkings.

Although no comprehensive scholarly biography of Earp exists, two works have appeared that demonstrate meticulous research: Glenn G. Boyer, ed., *I Married Wyatt Earp: The Recollections of Josephine Sarah Marcus Earp* (1976), and Paula Mitchell Marks, *And Die in the West: The Story of the O.K. Corral Gunfight* (1989). Both volumes provide excellent, albeit brief, bibliographies, and Marks's study has the air of scholarly detachment.

Evaluation of Principal Biographical Sources

Bartholomew, Ed E. *Wyatt Earp, 1848 to 1860: The Untold Story*. Toyahvale, TX: Frontier Books, 1963. (**A, G**) Covering Earp's years as a lawman in Dodge City, this study corrects many errors of fact in previous works.

―――――. *Wyatt Earp, 1879-1882: The Man & the Myth: A Sequel to "The Untold Story."* Toyahvale, TX: Frontier Books, 1964. (**A, G**) The second volume of Bartholomew's study, encompassing Earp's Arizona period, it reflects considerable research, but the prose is pedestrian.

Boyer, Glenn G., ed. *I Married Wyatt Earp: The Recollections of Josephine Sarah Marcus Earp*. Tucson: The University of Arizona Press, 1976. (**A, G**) Boyer was a friend of Earp's third wife and acquired two manuscripts by her that form the body of this volume.

―――――. *The Suppressed Murder of Wyatt Earp*. San Antonio, TX: Naylor, 1967. (**A, G**) Deals with the evolution of the Earp myth.

Burns, Walter Noble. *Tombstone: An Iliad of the Southwest*. Garden City, NY: Doubleday, Page, 1927. (**G**) More than a biography of Earp, this is the book that "started" the myth. Burns, a newspaperman who wrote several imaginative western biographies, interviewed Earp. Some scholars consider this to be a work of fiction since Burns invents dialogue and is unreliable on many facts. It served as the basis for the 1942 Paramount movie *Tombstone, The Town Too Tough To Die* (1942).

Hall-Quest, Olga W. *Wyatt Earp, Marshal of the Old West*. New York: Farrar, Straus and Cudahy, 1936. (**Y**) Based on Lake's biography.

Ketchum, Phillip. *Wyatt Earp*. Racine, WI: Whitman Publishing, 1956. (**Y**) Based primarily on Lake's biography.

Lake, Stuart N. *Wyatt Earp, Frontier Marshal*. Boston: Houghton Mifflin, 1931. (**G**) First published serially in the *Saturday Evening Post*, this is the biography that mythologized Wyatt Earp. In something of a self-fulfilling prophecy, Lake labels Earp the "most famous marshal of the old frontier." His claim that Earp was "the most proficient peace officer, the greatest gun-fighting marshal that the Old West knew" is wrong, but indicative of the tone of the biography. Peter Nevill published the book in England in 1952 under the title, *He Carried a Six-Shooter: The Biography of Wyatt Earp*.

Marks, Paula Mitchell. *And Die in the West: The Story of the O.K. Corral Gunfight*. New York: William Morrow, 1989. (**A, G**) An honest, clever, well-researched, and well-written account. Marks focuses her study on the gunfight but provides a great deal of additional information about Earp.

Martin, Douglas D., ed. *The Earps of Tombstone*. Tombstone, AZ: *Tombstone Epitaph*, 1959. (**A, G, Y**) Selection of contemporary newspaper articles from the pro-Earp *Epitaph*.

Turner, Alford E., ed. *The Earps Talk*. College Station, TX: Creative Publishing, 1980. (**A, G, Y**) A collection of interviews and first-person accounts by Earp and relatives that appeared in the San Francisco *Examiner*.

Waters, Frank. *The Earp Brothers of Tombstone: The Story of Mrs. Virgil Earp*. 1960. Reprint. Lincoln: University of Nebraska Press, 1976. (**A, G**) Neither author Waters nor sister-in-law Allie Sullivan Earp had much use for Wyatt Earp. He is described as "an itinerant saloonkeeper, card sharp, gunman, bigamist, church deacon, policeman, bunco artist, and a supreme confidence man." Like all works about Earp, it too contains errors.

Overview and Evaluation of Primary Sources

As might be expected, original research materials pertaining to Earp are scarce. Three collections at the Arizona Pioneers' Historical Society in Tucson contain some items: Earp Family Papers, 1879-1953; Anton Mazzanovich Papers, 1880-1935; and Phillip J. Rasch Papers, 1870-1961. The Mazzanovich and Rasch holdings include correspondence from individuals who knew Earp. The Arizona Collection, 1757-1956, at the Bancroft Library, University of California, Berkeley, contains dictations about him. The Stuart Nathaniel Lake Papers, 1918-1961, Henry E. Huntington Library, San Marino, California, contain fourteen letters written by Earp and other materials relative to him, as do the John P. Clum Papers, University of Arizona Library, Special Collections, Tucson.

Several published memoirs or autobiographies by his associates touch on aspects of Earp's career. William Barclay "Bat" Masterson's *Famous Gunfighters of the Western Frontier* (Houston, TX: Frontier Press, 1957; A, G, Y) is a collection of articles that first appeared in *Human Life Magazine*, 1907, written by a Kansas confederate of Earp and a popular gunfighter in his own right. Three other friends, who recall his exploits, include William S. Hart, *My Life East and West* (Boston: Houghton Mifflin, 1929; A, G); John P. Clum, *It All Happened in Tombstone* (Flagstaff, AZ: Northland Press, 1965; A, G); and George Whitwell Parsons, *The Private Journal of George Whitwell Parsons* (Phoenix, AZ: WPA Statewide Archival and Records Project, 1939; A). Clum was editor of the *Tombstone Epitaph* while Earp was there. W. S. Hart was possibly the most important cowboy star in the early history of American movies and a friend of Earp during the twenties.

Unfavorable, or even hostile, reminiscences include William M. Breakenridge, *Helldorado: Bringing the Law to the Mesquite* (Boston: Houghton Mifflin, 1928; A, G); George Lyttleton Upshur, *As I Recall Them* (New York: Wilson-Erickson, 1936; A, G); and Ben Jaastad, recorder, *Man of the West: Reminiscences of George Washington Oakes, 1840-1917*, edited by Arthur Woodward (Tucson: Arizona Pioneers Historical Society, 1956; A, G, Y). Breakenridge was a Tombstone law officer in its wild and woolly days and was anti-Earp.

Fiction and Adaptations

Novels, movies, and television created the Earp who exists in most people's imagination today. The earliest novel in which he appears is Alfred Henry Lewis's *Sunset Trail* (1905), a fictitious recounting of the deeds of Dodge City's marshal, Bat Masterson. Lewis was famous for a series of books appearing from 1897 to 1908 about "Wolfville," a town modeled on Tombstone.

If Walter Noble Burns's book is considered a nonfiction work, the first important novel about Earp was W. R. Burnett's *Saint Johnson* (1930). The main character is Wayt Johnson, who engages the Northrups and Todds in a gunfight. The novel was poorly received by critics, even though Burnett was the author of the popular novel *Little Caesar*. Three movies titled *Law and Order* (Universal, 1932, 1940, 1953) were based on *Saint Johnson*.

In Tom J. Hopkins's novel *Trouble in Tombstone* (1951), Sam Chambers is the main character, but Earp plays a prominent role in running rustlers out of town and engaging in the gunfight. When Wyatt leaves town, Sam becomes sheriff.

The famed Western writer Will Henry (William Henry Allen) wrote *Who Rides with Wyatt?* (1954), a strange and lovely story. United Artists adapted the tale into the 1969 movie *Young Billy Young*, starring Robert Mitchum. The movie script retains many of Henry's incidents and characters but changes Earp's name.

Two other novels that became movies were: Oakley Hall, *Warlock* (1958), and Robert Kreps, *The Hour of the Gun* (1967). Warlock is the town of Tombstone; the character Clay Blaisdell, played by Henry Fonda (Fox 1959), is a tarnished Earp, presented naturalistically, in Hall's book. Both movie and book versions of *Hour of the Gun* (United Artists, 1967) concern the year following the O.K. Corral gunfight, when Earp tracked down and killed the men who allegedly shot his brothers.

Novels in which Earp plays only a minor part include: Jack O'Connor, *Boom Town* (1938), Lynton Wright Brent, *The Bird Cage: A Theatrical Novel of Early Tombstone* (1945), Clarence Budington Kelland, *Tombstone* (1952), Leslie Scott, *Tombstone Showdown* (1957), James Wyckoff, *John Slaughter's Way* (1963), Jack Slade, *The Man from Tombstone* (1971), and Todhunter Ballard, *The Sheriff of Tombstone* (1977).

In 1916 Wyatt Earp himself played a small part in Allan Dwan's movie *The Half-Breed* (FAF, 1916). Since then twenty-six movies have been made either about Earp or in which a Wyatt Earp character plays a secondary, but often important role. One of these, *Frontier Marshal* (Fox) was filmed twice in 1934 and 1939. Both versions were based on Lake's biography.

In addition to Robert Mitchum, some of Hollywood's greatest actors have portrayed Wyatt Earp on the screen, including Walter Huston, Randolph Scott, Errol Flynn, Henry Fonda, Joel McCrea, Will Geer, Burt Lancaster, James Stewart, and James Garner. Others of note are George O'Brien, Johnny Mack Brown, Richard Dix, Ronald Reagan, Rory Calhoun, Barry Sullivan, Guy Madison, Harris Yulin, and Hugh O'Brian, who made Earp famous on television. A number of outstanding directors and producers have been involved in the Earp movies, among them Darryl Zanuck, John Ford, John Sturges, Walter Mirisch, Hal B. Wallis, Nathan Juran, and Louis King.

Most of the movies are historically inaccurate, but some are excellent films that received outstanding reviews. Aesthetically, the two best are *My Darling Clementine* (Fox, 1946) and *Gunfight at the O.K. Corral* (Paramount, 1957). In *My Darling Clementine*, which is based on Lake's biography, Fonda plays Earp as a courageous champion of law and defender of decency. The only flaw is in the casting of the robust Victor Mature as Doc Holliday.

Burt Lancaster, the star of *Gunfight at the O.K. Corral*, is the ideal Wyatt Earp of legend—tall, dark, handsome, strong, resolute, and stoic. Much of the action takes place in Dodge City and Tombstone. George Scullin's article "The Killer" supplied the story line. Although historically fantastic, it makes a compelling movie, and Kirk Douglas, also unfortunately robust, is convincing as Doc.

The most recent films are an "intellectual" western of weird proportions entitled *Doc* (1971), which centers on Holliday and Earp's relations, and *Sunset* (1988). James Garner, who played Earp in *Hour of the Gun,* portrays him again in *Sunset,* in which Wyatt joins Tom Mix (Bruce Willis) to solve a murder.

A forgettable made-for-television movie, *I Married Wyatt Earp* (Osmond TV-Comworld), starring Marie Osmond as Josephine Sarah Marcus Earp, aired on NBC-TV on January 10, 1983. On September 6, 1955, Hugh O'Brian appeared for the first time in the ABC-TV series, "The Life and Legend of Wyatt Earp." For six seasons and 266 episodes he brought law and order to Ellsworth, Dodge City, and Tombstone, mainly using his "Buntline Special," a Colt-45 with a twelve-inch barrel. The show was ABC's successful answer to "Gunsmoke." Earp also appeared in other TV series, such as ABC's "Maverick," and more recently in a pair of one-hour episodes of CBS's "Paradise." In addition to two movie documentaries—*The Immortal West—And How It Was Lost* (1962) and *The Legendary Champions* (1968)—the gunfight at the O.K. Corral was recalled in Walter Cronkite's "You Are There" (1955) and Timex's "Appointment with Destiny" (1970).

Museums, Historical Landmarks, Societies

Arizona Pioneers Historical Society Museum (Tuscon, AZ). Founded in 1884, this museum contains materials associated with Tombstone and Earp.

Boot Hill Museum (Dodge City, KS). Founded in 1947 and located on famed Boot Hill, Front Street, the museum houses artifacts of the era when Earp served as a member of the city's police force.

Earp, California. Founded as Drennan in 1910, the town was renamed in honor of Earp in 1929.

Helldorado Week (Tombstone, AZ). Held annually since 1929 to commemorate pioneer days. Includes a reenactment of the gunfight at the O.K. Corral.

Tombstone Courthouse State Historical Park (Tombstone, AZ). Founded in 1959, it is housed in the original Cochise County Courthouse. Includes some Earp artifacts.

Other Sources

Chisholm, Joe. *Brewery Gulch.* San Antonio, TX: Naylor, 1949. Good study of the era of Wyatt Earp in southeastern Arizona.

Jahn, Pat. *The Frontier World of Doc Holliday, Faro Dealer from Dallas to Deadwood.* New York: Hastings House, 1957. Good biography of Holliday with a great deal of information on Earp.

Lockwood, Frank C. *Pioneer Days in Arizona: From the Spanish Occupation to Statehood.* New York: Macmillan, 1932. Lockwood interviewed Earp but did not believe the marshal.

Miller, Nyle H., and Joseph W. Snell. *Why the West Was Wild: A Contemporary Look at the Antics of Some Highly Publicized Kansas Cowtown Personalities.* Topeka: Kansas State Historical Society, 1963. Compiled from documents and newspapers. The compilers examined Kansas newspapers and determined Earp's reputation to be nonexistent.

Sonnichsen, C. L. *Billy King's Tombstone: The Private Life of an Arizona Boom Town.* 1942. Reprint. Tuscon: University of Arizona Press, 1972. The author is an authority on the area, but his study includes several errors regarding Earp.

Vestal, Stanley [Walter S. Campbell]. *Queen of Cowtowns, Dodge City: "The Wickedest Little City in America, 1872-1886."* New York: Harper, 1952. Vestal was a prominent western writer and serious researcher, but he accepted Lake's presentation uncritically.

Robert S. La Forte
University of North Texas

JAMES FORTEN
1766-1842
CHARLOTTE L. FORTEN GRIMKÉ
1837-1914

Chronology

Born James Forten on September 2, 1766, in Philadelphia, Pennsylvania, to Thomas Forten, a sailmaker, and his wife Sarah Forten, both descendants of slave immigrants to Philadelphia but themselves born free to free parents; studies for a time, through 1775, at a school conducted by Anthony Benezet, a white Quaker and antislavery writer; *1775* father dies; goes to work to help support his mother; *1781-1782* sails out of Philadelphia as a powder boy on a Revolutionary War privateer, the *Royal Louis,* commanded by Stephen Decatur, Sr.; imprisoned for months on the *Jersey* in New York harbor after the *Royal Louis* is captured by the British; after the Revolution, sails with his sister Abigail's husband, a Mr. Dunbar, to Liverpool and London, where he works as a stevedore and becomes acquainted with the English abolition movement; *1786* having returned to Philadelphia and served an apprenticeship at the sail loft of Robert Bridges, a white sailmaker, becomes foreman of the biracial work force there; *1796* elected a member of the first vestry of the African Episcopal Church of St. Thomas; *1798* buys out the sail loft when Bridges retires; contemporary sources credit him with inventing a device to make large sails on big ships more manageable; *1803* marries Patty Beatte, who dies the next year; *1808-1842* with his second wife, Charlotte Vandine Forten (1784-1884), raises eight children; *1813* publishes a pamphlet of letters against a bill in the Pennsylvania legislature designed to restrict free blacks; *1814* organizes, with Richard Allen and Absalom Jones, a force of hundreds of Philadelphia black men to protect the city during the War of 1812 in the aftermath of the burning of Washington, D.C.; *1817* chairs two meetings called to express concern about the newly-organized American Colonization Society and then to voice opposition to the organization of a branch in Philadelphia; *1830-1842* engages actively, with his wife and five older children, in the abolition movement in Philadelphia and elsewhere, supporting William Lloyd Garrison's publication, *The Liberator*, and participating in the establishment and operation of the American Anti-Slavery Society (1833), the Philadelphia Female Anti-Slavery Society (1833), the American Moral Reform Society (1836), and the Pennsylvania State Anti-Slavery Society (1837); *1842* dies in Philadelphia on March 4 and is buried at the African Episcopal Church of St. Thomas.

Born Charlotte L. Forten in Philadelphia, on August 17, 1837, to Robert Bridges Forten, the son of James Forten, and like his father a sailmaker and abolitionist, and Mary Virginia Woods Forten, who dies in 1840; *1854-1855* after years of being tutored at home when her father refuses to send her to Philadelphia's segregated schools, goes to Salem, Massachusetts, where she graduates from the Higginson Grammar School, a school for both black and white children; *1855* joins the Salem Female Anti-Slavery Society; *1856* graduates from the State Normal School in Salem; *1856-1858* teaches at the Epes Grammar School, the first black teacher of white children in Salem, before resigning because of poor health; *1859-1862* teaches at the Higginson Grammar School in Salem and the Lombard Street School (run by her aunt, Margaretta Forten) in Philadelphia, with interruptions due to bad health; *1862-1864* teaches freedmen at the Penn School, established by Laura Towne on St. Helena Island, during the Civil War, after Union forces occupy portions of coastal South Carolina; *1864* her father, having joined the Union army, dies of typhoid fever on April 25; *1865-1871* serves in Boston as secretary of the Teachers Committee of the New England branch of the Freedmen's Union Commission; *1871-1872* teaches at the Colonel Robert Gould Shaw Memorial School in Charleston, South Carolina; *1872-1873* assists the principal of the Charles Sumner School (which later becomes the M Street High School and then the Dunbar High School) in Washington, D.C.; *1873-1878* works as a clerk in the U. S. Department of the Treasury; *December 19, 1878* marries the Reverend Francis J. Grimké, a former slave, the son of a brother of Sarah and Angelina Grimké, and the new pastor of the Fifteenth Street Presbyterian Church, where she is a member; *1880* their only child, Theodora Cornelia (named for her father's uncle, Theodore Weld), is born January 1 and dies June 30; *1885-1889* lives in Florida where her husband is pastor at the Laura Street Presbyterian Church in Jacksonville, before they return to the Fifteenth Street Presbyterian Church and Washington, D.C., where she resides for the rest of her life; *1894-1898* she and her husband are legal guardians of Angelina Weld Grimké, the daughter of Francis's brother Archibald (and named for the brothers' aunt, Angelina Grimké Weld), while he serves as American consul at Santo Domingo; *1896* is a founding member of the National Association of Colored Women; *1914* dies in Washington, D.C., on July 23, after a long battle with tuberculosis and a year after a debilitating stroke.

Activities of Historical Significance

The overlapping lives of James Forten and Charlotte Forten Grimké, grandfather and granddaughter, stretched from the prelude of the American Revolution through the Civil War and on to the eve of World War I. James Forten was born at a time when, even in the North, most African Americans were slaves. His granddaughter died fifty years after the Emancipation Proclamation. Across the years in between, each in turn worked to promote racial equality.

James Forten was enormously important as an early American abolitionist and civil rights activist. In the aftermath of the organization of the American Colonization Society at the beginning of 1817, he provided leadership that led to the widespread rejection by free black northerners of the idea of emigration to Africa (though Haiti and Canada remained possibilities). The northern free black community remained in America and provided the core of abolitionist support into the 1830s. Forten, his wife and children proved active in promoting equal opportunity regardless of race or sex, in addition to promoting an end to slavery. They worked with the Underground Railroad to assist runaway slaves, and they formed various antislavery societies.

As white northerners began to adopt an abolitionist stance, Forten continued to play a central role. In the 1830s, he supplied much of the subscription money that enabled William Lloyd Garrison to publish his radical paper, *The Liberator*. The Forten home in Philadelphia provided friendship, advice, and hospitality as the Fortens hosted such visiting abolitionists as John Greenleaf Whittier, Garrison, and Sarah and Angelina Grimké. To the extent that Forten fostered Garrison's belief in racial equality and sustained the publication of *The Liberator*, his importance as a pioneer abolitionist is evident. If in fact it was Forten who persuaded Garrison to move beyond the gradualist and colonizationist approach of Garrison's white predecessors, then his role was indeed pivotal.

Charlotte Forten, though she had grown up surrounded by both white and black members of the abolitionist movement, was still a teenager in the late 1850s, and her time for full participation had not yet quite come. By 1862 Union forces had taken control of the Sea Islands off the coast of South Carolina, and thousands of slaves had gained their freedom. Her decision to go South and participate in an effort to address the freed people's material, medical, and educational needs brought her into the midst of an enthusiastic effort by a number of northerners, both black and white, to demonstrate that former slaves could successfully break the shackles of bondage and participate in free communities.

After the war, she lived in Boston for several years working for a freedmen's aid society as a liaison between teachers in black schools in the South and their sources of support in the North. In addition, she taught for a time in black schools in Charleston, South Carolina, and Washington, D.C., and she worked in Washington for the U. S. government. In these various capacities, she reflected the changes in status and in educational and employment opportunities among African Americans in the North as well as the South, while she continued to work in ways consistent with her grandfather's legacy.

In the late 1870s, Charlotte Forten began a new chapter of her life when she married the Reverend Francis James Grimké (1850-1937). Grimké, several years younger than she, was born near Charleston, South Carolina, to a slave woman and a widowed, slaveowning man—the brother of the white abolitionists Sarah and Angelina Grimké. Grimké lived as a small child with his two mixed-race brothers, all nominally slaves but generally treated as free. After their father died, his white son (their half-brother) followed their father's will, for a time, and protected their freedom, until in 1860 he determined to sell them as slaves. Young Francis lost his freedom until late in the Civil War. After the war, he studied in Charleston, graduated from Lincoln University in Pennsylvania, attended law school at Howard University, and, finally, earned a divinity degree at Princeton Theological Seminary. While he and his brother Archibald were at Lincoln University, Angelina and Sarah Grimké discovered the existence of their nephews, acknowledged the relationship, and assisted them in their schooling. After graduating from seminary, Francis Grimké accepted a position at a church in Washington, D.C., and married Charlotte Forten, a member of that church. She became his full partner for the next thirty-five years. During that time, the promises of emancipation, which had seemed so bright in the 1860s, faded, and Grimké took on a role akin to that of James Forten two generations earlier. Beginning in 1909, the Grimké brothers promoted a new civil rights organization, the NAACP.

Overview of Biographical Sources

In mid-twentieth century publications, Ray Allen Billington introduced James Forten, and Anna J. Cooper introduced Charlotte Forten Grimké, as important subjects of historical inquiry. Moreover, Billington edited Charlotte Forten's diaries, and Cooper compiled her other writings. Since that time, various writers have pursued the stories of the Fortens' lives. Esther M. Douty has outlined the lives of James Forten and Charlotte Forten Grimké in two creditable biographies intended for young or general readers, and Julie Winch is writing a scholarly biography of James Forten. A number of short writings for young readers on James Forten can be found in Karen Breen's *Index to Collective Biographies for Young Readers* (4th ed., 1988). Even recent treatments of James Forten and Charlotte Forten Grimké by authorities get some of the facts wrong, and evidence is sparse for such things as marriage dates for James Forten and birth dates for most of his children. Charlotte Forten Grimké's journals provide the most readily available source materials for studies of her life, so it is easy to see why such studies focus on the years she kept those diaries. Written mostly while she was in her teens and twenties, they include the most dramatic period of her life, her year-and-a-half as a teacher in South Carolina during the Civil War.

Scholars have begun to detail the histories of the Philadelphia black community of James Forten's time and that of Washington, D.C., during his granddaughter's life: Julie Winch, *Philadelphia's Black Elite: Activism, Accommodation, and the Struggle for Autonomy, 1787-1848* (1988); Gary B. Nash, *Forging Freedom: The Formation of Philadelphia's Black Community, 1720-1840* (1988); and Constance McLaughlin Green, *The Secret City: A History of Race Relations in the Nation's Capital* (1967); both Winch and Nash contribute fresh information and perspective on James Forten. Other historians have worked up large parts of the stories of black abolitionists in the pre-Civil War years and of the black experience in the war years: Benjamin Quarles, *Black Abolitionists* (1969); James M. McPherson, ed., *The Negro's Civil War: How American Negroes Felt and Acted During the War for Union* (1965); Willie Lee Rose, *Rehearsal for Reconstruction: The Port Royal Experiment* (1964). Readers might consult, too, such sophisticated broader studies as Floyd J. Miller, *The Search for a Black Nationality: Black Emigration and Colonization, 1787-1863* (1975), and Paula Giddings, *When and Where I Enter: The Impact of Black Women on Race and Sex in America* (1984).

Evaluation of Principal Biographical Sources

Billington, Ray Allen, ed. *The Journal of Charlotte L. Forten: A Free Negro in the Slave Era.* New York: Dryden Press, 1953. Reprint. New York: Norton, 1981. (A, G) Billington provides a biographical essay on both Charlotte Forten and her grandfather, James Forten, as well as an edited and annotated version of her journals between 1854 and 1864.

—————. "Charlotte L. Forten Grimké." In *Notable American Women.* Vol. 2. Edited by Edward T. James, et al. Cambridge: Harvard University Press, 1970. (A, G) Interpretive summary by the pioneer student of her life.

—————. "James Forten, Forgotten Abolitionist." *Negro History Bulletin* 13 (October 1949): 31-36, 45. (A, G, Y) An excellent place to begin any study of James Forten's life.

Cooper, Anna J. *Life and Writings of the Grimké Family.* 2 volumes in one. n.p., 1951. (A, G) Few copies of this work exist. Volume 1 is titled *Personal Recollections of the Grimké Family*, while volume 2 is *The Life and Writings of*

Charlotte Forten Grimké. Anna Cooper (1859-1964) was a black Southern educator with a long personal acquaintance with the Grimkés.

Douty, Esther M. *Forten the Sailmaker: Pioneer Champion of Negro Rights*. Chicago: Rand McNally, 1968. **(G, Y)** Carefully researched and sensitively written, this is the fullest study of the life of James Forten.

Stevenson, Brenda, ed. *The Journals of Charlotte Forten Grimké*. New York: Oxford University Press, 1988. **(A, G)** Published as a volume in the series *The Schomburg Library of Nineteenth-Century Black Women Writers*, edited by Henry Lewis Gates, Jr. Stevenson supplies the fullest published scholarly study of Charlotte Forten Grimké, together with the complete and annotated journals.

Evaluation of Biographies for Young People
Chittenden, Elizabeth F. *Profiles in Black and White: Stories of Men and Women Who Fought Against Slavery*. New York: Scribner, 1973. One chapter is on Charlotte Forten. Written on a middle school reading level.

Douty, Esther M. *Charlotte Forten: Free Black Teacher*. Champaign, IL: Garrard, 1971. Focuses on the main years of the journals, 1854-1864. Appropriate for middle school readers and up.

Johnston, Brenda A. *Between the Devil and the Sea: The Life of James Forten*. New York: Harcourt Brace Jovanovich, 1974. A captivating account of the sailmaker and abolitionist. Written on a middle school and up reading level.

Longsworth, Polly. *I, Charlotte Forten, Black and Free*. New York: Thomas Y. Crowell, 1970. A first-person account, based on the 1854-1864 journals. The reading level is middle school and up.

Overview and Evaluation of Primary Sources
James Forten wrote, or contributed to the writing of, a number of letters and petitions related to black Americans, slave and free. Among these are *Letters from a Man of Colour, on a Late Bill before the Senate of Pennsylvania* (Philadelphia: 1813), against a bill that would have imposed new restrictions on free blacks in Pennsylvania, and *An Address to the Humane and Benevolent Inhabitants of the City and County of Philadelphia* (Philadelphia: 1817), in opposition to the newly-

formed American Colonization Society. The address and one of the five letters have been reprinted in Carter G. Woodson, ed., *Negro Orators and Their Orations* (Washington, DC: Associated Publishers, 1925. Reprint. New York: Russell and Russell, 1969; **A, G**). Years later, when a state constitutional convention was on the verge of taking away the right of black men in Pennsylvania to vote, he contributed, with his son-in-law Robert Purvis, to the writing of *Appeal of Forty Thousand Citizens, Threatened with Disfranchisement, to the People of Pennsylvania* (Philadelphia: Merihew and Gunn, 1838; **A, G**). His correspondence with Paul Cuffe (from the 1810s) about emigration to Africa is located in manuscript in the Cuffe Papers at the Free Public Library in New Bedford, Massachusetts, and is reprinted in Sheldon H. Harris, *Paul Cuffe: Black America and the African Return* (New York: Simon and Schuster, 1972; **A, G**). His letters to William Lloyd Garrison (during the 1830s) are in the Garrison Papers in the Boston Public Library, Boston, Massachusetts; some are reprinted in Dorothy B. Porter, ed., "Early Manuscript Letters Written by Negroes," *Journal of Negro History* 24 (April 1939). Various other materials related to his antislavery activities can be found in the Historical Society of Pennsylvania in Philadelphia.

Charlotte Forten kept diaries for most of the period from 1854 to 1864 and again for the Florida years (1885-1889). The manuscript originals are located in the Moorland-Spingarn Research Center at Howard University in Washington, D.C. Ray Allen Billington published an edited version of the 1854-1864 diaries in *The Journal of Charlotte L. Forten: A Free Negro in the Slave Era* (1953. Reprint. New York: Norton, 1981; **A, G, Y**), and Brenda Stevenson has annotated a complete edition, *The Journals of Charlotte Forten Grimké* (New York: Oxford University Press, 1988; **A, G, Y**), as a volume in the series *The Schomburg Library of Nineteenth-Century Black Women Writers*, edited by Henry Lewis Gates, Jr.

From 1856 through the 1890s, Charlotte Forten published poems, essays, and other writings. A lengthy letter she wrote from South Carolina during the Civil War to William Lloyd Garrison, for example, appeared in 1862 in *The Liberator* and is reprinted in Bert James Loewenberg and Ruth Bogin, eds., *Black Women in Nineteenth-Century American Life: Their Words, Their Thoughts, Their Feelings*, (University Park: Pennsylvania State University Press, 1976; **A, G**). Letters she wrote to John Greenleaf Whittier appeared in 1864 in the *Atlantic Monthly* as a two-part essay, "Life on the Sea Islands," reprinted in *Two Black Teachers During the Civil War* (New York: Arno Press, 1969; **A, G**). The teacher who organized the Penn School on St. Helena Island supplies an account of Charlotte Forten's time there in Rupert Sargent Holland, ed., *Letters and Diary of Laura M. Towne: Written from the Sea Islands of South Carolina, 1862-1884* (Cambridge:

Riverside Press, 1912. Reprint. New York: Negro Universities Press, 1969; **A, G**). Charlotte Forten also published her translation of a French novel by Emile Erckmann on the French Revolution, *Madame Thérèse; or, The Volunteers of '92* (New York: Scribner, 1869). Later writings and correspondence can be found in the Francis J. Grimké Papers in the Moorland-Spingarn Research Center at Howard University.

Fiction and Adaptations

John Greenleaf Whittier wrote a poem, "To the Daughters of James Forten" (Charlotte Forten's aunts Margaretta, Harriet, and Sarah). Another poem, "To Keep the Memory of Charlotte Forten Grimké," came from the pen of her niece, Angelina Weld Grimké.

Museums, Historical Landmarks, Societies

Mother Bethel African Methodist Episcopal Church (Philadelphia, PA). The first of the A.M.E. churches, constructed on the site of the founding in 1787 of the Free African Society, and designated a National Historical Landmark by the U. S. Department of Interior.

Penn School Historical District (Frogmore, SC). Site of the Penn School where Charlotte Forten taught during the Civil War. A National Historical Landmark.

Other Sources

Ferry, Henry J. "Francis James Grimké." In *Dictionary of American Negro Biography*, edited by Rayford W. Logan and M. R. Winston. New York: Norton, 1982. Interpretive summary of the life of Charlotte Forten's husband by the author of a full-length but unpublished work, "Francis J. Grimké: Portrait of a Black Puritan" (Ph.D. dissertation, Yale University, 1970).

George, Carol V. R. *Segregated Sabbaths: Richard Allen and the Rise of Independent Black Churches, 1760-1840.* New York: Oxford University Press, 1973. James Forten makes various appearances in this biographical study of one of his longtime friends and allies.

Hornick, Nancy Slocum. "Anthony Benezet and the Africans' School: Toward a Theory of Full Equality." *Pennsylvania Magazine of History and Biography* 99

(October 1975): 399-421. Introduces the teacher and the school that supplied James Forten with all of his limited formal education.

Lewis, Janice Sumler. "The Fortens of Philadelphia: An Afro-American Family and Nineteenth-Century Reform." Ph.D. dissertation, Georgetown University, 1979. The fullest study, though unpublished, of the Forten clan and their activities across the nineteenth century.

Nash, Gary B., and Jean R. Soderlund. *Freedom by Degrees: Emancipation and Its Aftermath in Philadelphia.* New York: Oxford University Press, 1991. Details the halting progress of achieving an end to slavery and of converting freedom into equality in one of the North's major cities.

Oden, Gloria C. *"The Journal of Charlotte L. Forten*: The Salem-Philadelphia Years (1854-1862) Reexamined." *Essex Institute Historical Collections* 119 (April 1983): 119-136. An important critique of R. A. Billington's edition of Forten's diaries, with corrected identifications of the people referred to.

Quarles, Benjamin. *Black Abolitionists.* New York: Oxford University Press, 1969. A pioneering study of the pioneer abolitionists, among them James Forten.

Rose, Willie Lee. *Rehearsal for Reconstruction: The Port Royal Experiment.* Indianapolis: Bobbs-Merrill, 1964. A full and scholarly yet readable account of the enterprise in which Charlotte Forten participated in Civil War South Carolina.

Sterling, Dorothy, ed. *We Are Your Sisters: Black Women in the Nineteenth Century.* New York: Norton, 1984. Charlotte Forten appears throughout this book, often in her own words and sometimes in photographs. So do her parents, aunts (a poem by one of them supplies the book's title), uncles, friends, and husband.

Wilson, Edmund. *Patriotic Gore: Studies in the Literature of the American Civil War.* New York: Oxford University Press, 1962. One brief, bemused chapter concerns the intersecting lives and writings of Charlotte Forten and Thomas Wentworth Higginson at St. Helena Island.

Peter Wallenstein
Virginia Polytechnic Institute and State University

GEORGE III
1738-1820

Chronology

Born George William Frederick on June 4, 1738, at Norfolk House, St. James' Square, London, eldest son of Frederick Louis, Prince of Wales, and Augusta, the daughter of Frederick II, duke of Saxe-Gotha; *1745* Dr. Francis Ayscough, later dean of Bristol, is appointed Prince George's tutor; *1750* Francis Lord North is appointed governor to Prince George; *March 22, 1751* his father, Prince Frederick, dies; *April 18, 1751* is given his own household; *April 19, 1751* becomes Prince of Wales and earl of Chester; Simon Harcourt, earl of Harcourt, replaces North as his governor and Dr. Thomas Hayter replaces Ayscough as his tutor; *1752* household is reorganized because of the resignation of Lord Harcourt, who is replaced by James Waldegrave, earl of Waldegrave, and Dr. Hayter, who is replaced by Dr. John Thomas, bishop of Peterborough; *1755* under prodding from his mother, refuses to marry Sophia Caroline Maria of Brunswick-Wolfenbuttel lest the union benefit Hanover; *1756* appoints John Stuart, earl of Bute, his groom of the stole despite the misgivings of his grandfather, George II; *1756* turns eighteen and George II offers him forty thousand pounds a year and the chance to maintain an establishment separate from that of his mother; refuses the new household while taking the money; *October 25, 1760* upon the death of his grandfather, ascends the throne of Great Britain; *September 8, 1761* marries Charlotte Sophia, the younger sister of Adolphus Frederick IV of Mecklenburg-Strelitz; crowned in Westminster Abbey September 22; *October 5, 1761* accepts the resignation of William Pitt the elder from the cabinet; *June 20, 1762* George, Prince of Wales, is born, the first of fifteen children; *April 19, 1763* struggle with John Wilkes begins with the publication of number forty-five of *The North Briton*; *March 22, 1765* sanctions the passage of the Stamp Act to raise money from the colonies; *January 12, 1766* falls ill and exhibits the first signs of porphyria; *March 18, 1766* assents to the repeal of the Stamp Act; *July 30, 1766* dismisses prime minister and asks William Pitt the elder, now elevated to the peerage as earl of Chatham, to form a government; *May 1767* approves a series of import taxes for the American colonies known collectively as the Townshend Duties; *January 1770* agrees to the repeal of the Townshend Duties except for the tax on tea; *February 8, 1772* the Queen Mother, Princess Augusta, dies; *December 16, 1773* the Boston Tea Party openly defies the government's official policy regarding taxation of the colonies; *April 19, 1775* the American Revolution begins; *July 4, 1776* Declaration of Independence is signed; *July 25, 1777* survives an attack on his life by a madwoman; *May 1778* war is declared on France which is formally allied to the United States; *April 1780* House of Commons passes John Dunning's resolution—"that the influence of the Crown has increased, is increasing, and ought to be diminished"; *June 1780* acts in concert with John Wilkes to stop the anti-Catholic Gordon Riots in London; *October 19, 1781* General Cornwallis surrenders at Yorktown ending the American Revolution; *September 3, 1783* the Treaty of Paris is signed by Great Britain and the United States; *December 19, 1783* William Pitt the younger becomes prime minister; *June 1, 1785* receives John Adams as ambassador of the United States; *August 2, 1786* survives another unsuccessful attack on his life when Margaret Nicholson, a madwoman, attempts to stab him; *June 11, 1788* falls desperately ill, but makes a rapid recovery; *October 22, 1788* falls ill again, exhibiting signs of mental derangement; *March 10, 1789* recovers, but his illness provokes a regency crisis; *January 21, 1790* an insane man throws a stone at him, but fails to injure him; *February 1, 1793* France declares war on Great Britain; *October 29, 1794* escapes injury when his coach is surrounded by a mob as he drives to open parliament; *February 1, 1796* is missed by a stone thrown at the royal carriage; the stone hits Queen Charlotte; *May 15, 1800* while entering the Drury Lane Theater, is fired upon by a madman, John Hadfield, who misses; *February 3, 1801* William Pitt resigns; *February 22-March 2, 1801* becomes seriously ill, and mental alienation is much in evidence; *March 10, 1801* Henry Addington becomes prime minister; *March 27, 1801* the Peace of Amiens is signed; *May 16, 1803* war is renewed with France; *February 27, 1804* resumes his duties after an illness which begins in mid-January and includes mental derangement; *May 10, 1804* William Pitt the younger becomes prime minister again, replacing Addington; *July 1805* due to cataracts goes almost blind; *February 11, 1806* Lord William Grenville becomes prime minister after Pitt's death on January 23, 1806; *October 10, 1810* worried by the serious illness of his daughter, Amelia, becomes mentally deranged; *January 1811* is placed in the care of the Queen, after a regency is established under the Prince of Wales; *November 17, 1818* Queen Charlotte dies; *1820* dies on January 29 and is buried in St. George's Chapel, Windsor on February 16.

Activities of Historical Significance

Almost from the moment of his birth the future George III was surrounded by controversy. The animosity between his father, Frederick Louis, Prince of Wales, and his grandfather, George II, was of long standing, and both men struggled for the ultimate control of this shy and sensitive child who always sought to please those responsible for his care and instruction. Tutors and servants came and went at a dizzying pace, and Prince George's education suffered. In March 1751 his father, whom he loved and admired, died as the result of a freak accident, and the boy was thrust into the center of the family squabble.

George II, seemingly unmoved by the death of his son, now devoted a great deal of attention to his young heir presumptive. The titles of electoral-prince of Brunswick-Luneberg, Prince of Wales, duke of Edinburgh, earl of Chester, and other honors were bestowed upon him in April 1751, including a household staff.

In all things Prince George was guided by his mother, Princess Augusta, and her political advisor, John Stuart, earl of Bute, a man of mediocre intelligence who was rumored to be the princess's lover. They prodded Prince George into refusing the bride whom his grandfather had selected for him in 1755, and then encouraged him to insist the following year that Bute be made his groom of the stole. George was now eighteen years old and entitled to an increase in his annual allowance as well as a residence separate from that of Princess Augusta. He took the proffered forty thousand pounds, but announced to George II that he would prefer to remain with his mother. He passed the remaining years of his grandfather's reign studying the works of politicians such as Henry St. John, Viscount Bolingbroke, and absorbing the ideas of scholars like William Blackstone while remaining completely ignorant of the practical art of governing a modern kingdom. Thus he was not particularly prepared to ascend the throne on October 25, 1760.

The affairs of Great Britain were in the able hands of William Pitt the elder when George III assumed the crown, but he could abide neither his chief minister nor Pitt's deputy, Thomas Pelham-Holles, the duke of Newcastle. He was determined to rid himself of them and end the war with France which was already a triumph for Britain. In the spring of 1761 Lord Bute entered the government as secretary of state for the Northern Department, and it was he, with the Queen Mother's help, who selected a bride for the young king. On September 8, 1761, George III married Princess Charlotte Sophia of Mecklenburg-Strelitz, and two weeks later they were crowned in Westminster Abbey. By October 5, 1761, Pitt resigned from the Cabinet over the question of war with Spain. Newcastle, who had in his day controlled a vast network of patronage, clung to office until the following May when he too surrendered his position. The king then began to heap honors upon Bute. However, the office of first minister granted to Bute on May 26, 1762, was beyond his talents and after barely ten months in office he resigned. Pitt's temporary retirement and Bute's appointment marked the beginning of a decade of political confusion which had dire consequences for the stability of the British Empire. The expertise gained by George III during those critical years should have been acquired when as Prince of Wales he had the opportunity to learn the art of politics from some of the most skilled practitioners of the age.

In 1762, the same year that Bute received the Order of the Garter, George III experienced his first bout with an illness that left doctors baffled. On August 12th his first son, George Augustus Frederick, was born. Over the next twenty-one years George III had eight sons and six daughters, twelve of whom reached adulthood. He was a man of the highest moral principles, and although his marriage was one of state, he and his wife remained faithful to each other.

The one accomplishment of Bute's brief administration was the signing on February 10, 1762, of the Treaty of Paris which ended the French and Indian War and the Seven Years War, and left Great Britain in possession of an empire that spanned the globe and a national debt which seemed equally great. Bute resigned on April 8, 1763, and on April 16th, George Grenville took his place. The king neither liked nor trusted Grenville, so he never gave him his full confidence, a situation which only increased the instability of the government. It was Grenville who encouraged George III to seek punishment for John Wilkes whose scurrilous attacks on the king in number forty-five of the newspaper *The North Briton* caused a sensation. Wilkes was arrested and expelled from the House of Commons, but eventually the use of general warrants to effect an arrest was declared illegal. Wilkes became a public hero, and the king was made to look like a fool.

Attempting to reduce the national debt by requiring the American colonists to absorb the cost of their defense, Grenville persuaded George III to assent to the passage of the Stamp Act on March 22, 1765. Providing for stamps on legal documents, newspapers, pamphlets, dice, playing cards, and almanacs, it was designed to raise substantial revenues for the Crown. Instead, the measure raised a storm of protest in the colonies. By the end of the year the popular Stamp Act Congress, which contained delegates from nine colonies, had forwarded its protests to the government in London. On March 18, 1766, the measure was repealed, but in the Declaratory Act passed that same day the Crown reserved the right to make laws which in all respects were binding in the colonies.

In the midst of the furor over the Stamp Act, George III fell ill and for the first time exhibited the symptoms of porphyria, the mysterious disease which some authorities believe may account for his often erratic behavior and his eventual madness. The disease causes the body to produce a toxin which attacks the nervous system, producing excruciating pain, hyperactivity, partial paralysis, and delirium. The attack in January 1766 was of short duration and relatively mild; each successive reoccurrence was longer and more severe.

Since his accession George III had been trying to rid himself of the great Whig families that had controlled his grandfather and great-grandfather, but no viable alternative had appeared. The old Tory faction of Harley and Bolingbroke, tainted by Jacobitism, had dwindled to a handful of loyal members in Parliament, but a new Tory party was slowly evolving among the new generation of backbenchers. At the beginning of his reign the young king had hoped to govern without regard to party, but his naiveté and inexperience caused him to wander from one group of politicians to another looking for someone strong enough to control the Commons. By the time he found him, the American colonies were on the verge of open rebellion.

In May 1767 George III approved a series of taxes on certain items imported to North America which were collectively known as the Townshend Duties for their author, Charles Townshend, chancellor of the exchequer. Glass, lead, painter's colors, paper, and tea were included as taxable items in the hope that their sale might help raise much needed revenue. The outcry against these new examples of parliamentary tyranny was followed by a boycott of the innumerated articles on the part of all thirteen colonies. Townshend's plan to pay the salaries of royal officials in the colonies with monies raised there was thus a dismal failure. All of the duties were repealed in January 1770, except for the tax on tea.

George III never realized that many of the residents of the thirteen colonies were not bound to Great Britain by ties of blood, culture, or language. Likewise neither he nor his ministers grasped the fact that after a century and a half many of those colonists whose roots were British thought of themselves as Americans and not transplanted Englishmen. Thus Great Britain drifted into a war that nobody wanted, a conflict that would find the most powerful nation on earth diplomatically isolated and defeated by an army dismissed as rabble.

Although gunfire was exchanged on April 19, 1775, in Concord, Massachusetts, the situation was not hopeless if the government in London was willing to negotiate. Unfortunately, neither the king nor North was inclined to give the colonists any latitude. The stunning victories which had characterized Great Britain's performance in the French and Indian War were not repeated as the commanders sent to deal with the rebellious colonists committed one blunder after another. Their poor performance was due to a number of factors not the least being their refusal to adapt to the frontier style of fighting affected by the Americans. Plagued by professional jealousy and the open hostility of the vast majority of the Colonists they lost their early advantage, and soon found themselves trapped in a war they could not win. Like his commanders, George III was bewildered by the unpopularity of the conflict at home. To his enemies the American Revolution was the first stage of another Civil War, and the colonists the true heirs of the Parliamentarians who had defeated Charles I. George III was denounced as a tyrant. Mercenaries were hired to serve in America because it was feared that the American cause was too popular among the lower classes, but many of the foreign soldiers deserted and remained in North America after the war ended.

The proclamation of the Declaration of Independence on July 4, 1776, created a sensation throughout Europe, and in Paris it was regarded as an excellent opportunity for revenge. In one stroke the humiliations suffered by the French at the hands of British diplomats, admirals, and generals could be erased. By May 1778 when war was formally declared on France, the tide was already turning against Great Britain, and public blame was directed at the king whose popularity seemed to evaporate. Then on October 19, 1781, the unthinkable occurred: Lord Cornwallis was trapped at Yorktown and forced to surrender. Britain's effort in America now completely collapsed. The following March, Lord North finally took his leave of the king as the French prepared to host the peace conference that insured America's independence.

The months around the signing of the Treaty of Paris on September 3, 1783, saw a return to the political instability of the preceding decade as well as a series of personal tragedies for the king. The only moments of happiness for him were the birth of his youngest daughter, Princess Amelia, on August 7, 1783, and the appointment of William Pitt the younger as prime minister on December 19th. At long last he had found someone who shared his basic ideas about politics, a minister who was not an old Whig but a new Tory, and a man who could be trusted. Save for a period between 1801 and 1804, Pitt guided the affairs of Great Britain until his untimely death, while George III's health continued to deteriorate. Attempts on his life in the early years of the French revolutionary era as well as the rebellious behavior of his oldest sons had an unsettling effect on the king's sanity. In the early years of his reign George III had tried to take an active role in the political life of the nation, but by 1801, when Pitt resigned, he was more passive. Only when an issue stirred old passions did he rouse himself to oppose the will of his ministers.

The departure of Pitt in 1801 was prompted by the king's stubborn refusal to support Catholic emancipation. By the time Pitt had resumed the position of prime minister on May 10, 1804, George III had experienced several reoccurrences of his illness and had begun to lose his eyesight due to cataracts. Now almost blind, the king paid little attention to affairs of state, and his lifelong passion for art was stilled. By October 1810 the king was almost constantly deranged, and when Amelia died on November 2nd, he had to be restrained at all times lest he injure himself or those responsible for his care. In January 1811 a regency under his son, George, Prince of Wales, was declared, and the king was placed under the care of Queen Charlotte.

On June 2, 1812, the earl of Liverpool became George III's last prime minister, but the king, now totally blind and lost in mental darkness, was completely unaware of the change. From time to time his sanity would return briefly, and he would apologize to his keepers before slipping back into a deranged state. The queen died on November 17, 1818 and the unexpected death of Edward, duke of Kent, on January 23, 1820, was followed on January 29th by that of the king. George III, who is remembered because of the loss of the American colonies, was buried in St. George's Chapel at Windsor without fanfare or pomp on February 16, 1820. He had outlived his unpopularity, and was mourned by subjects from all classes.

Overview of Biographical Sources

Any consideration of the biographical materials relating to George III must begin with a thorough study of Herbert Butterfield's *George III and the Historians* (1959). In three long essays he carefully examines the various approaches which have been taken to King George from the publication of a contemporary account, *History of the Late Minority* (1765), written at the beginning of the reign, to the development of Sir Lewis Namier's technique of structural analysis, and the revolutionary changes it has wrought among scholars of the period. Those works of merit which have appeared since Butterfield's study may be easily catalogued and assigned to the categories which he had already established.

The earliest works which contain biographical data relating to George III are neither friendly to the court nor particularly complimentary to the king. The anonymous *History of the Late Minority* (1765), Edmumd Burke's *Thoughts on the Cause of the Present Discontents* (1770), and William Belsham's *Memoirs of the Reign of George III* (1795) are all quite critical and Belsham is openly hostile to Lord Bute. George III read and agreed with the thesis found in John Adolphus's *History of England* (1802). Concentrating on the years between 1760 and 1783, Adolphus develops a defense of George III which has inspired a host of later apologists, among them Robert Bisset whose *History of the Reign of George III* (1803) was one of the first works to make extensive use of diaries, correspondence, interviews, and state papers.

Immediately after the death of George III books began to appear which sought to examine his life as well as every aspect of his reign. They are for the most part complimentary to George III and critical of his ministers, especially Lord Bute. Edward Holt's *The Public and Domestic Life of His Late . . . Majesty George III* (1820), and Robert Huish's *The Public and Private Life of His Late . . . Majesty George the Third* (1821), fall into this category. A more balanced treatment can be found in Baron Henry Peter Brougham's two volume *Historical Sketches of Statesmen who Flourished in the Time of George III* (1839). While he defends the king's involvement in public affairs and his desire to increase the royal prerogative, Brougham does not attempt to hide the faults of character which lessened George's effectiveness as a ruler. Thomas Smart Hughes also took a favorable view of George III in his *The History of England, from the Accession of George III, 1760, to the Accession of Queen Victoria, 1837* (1846), but he also devotes attention to the role of the House of Commons in the events that shaped the reign; this approach later consumes a great deal of the attention of twentieth-century historians. A particularly popular work in its day, but rather old-fashioned in style, is J. Heneage Jesse's three-volume work, *Memoirs of the Life and Reign of King George the Third* (1867). It is, however, quite sound and its wealth of detail makes it valuable to the serious student. George III was never a figure of romance, but Mary L. Pendered in her *Fair Quaker, Hannah Lightfoot, and her Relations with George III* (1911) tries to alter that, padding her account with gossip and legend.

In 1929 Sir Lewis Namier published *The Structure of Politics at the Accession of George III*, and in 1930 *England in the Age of the American Revolution*. They were the products of an exhaustive study, but they also marked a change in the approach of the professional historian to both research and writing. Namier rejected the work of earlier scholars who either consciously or unintentionally injected contemporary morals and ideas into their consideration of a past era, and demanded that events must always be considered within the context of their own time. This can be accomplished only by a careful analysis of all the available data, and during the first half of the twentieth-century there was an amazing collection of published and manuscript sources available to the scholar. Namier and his associates revolutionized the study of history, and their technique of structural analysis is well-suited to computer technology that is still in the process of development and promises to provide an important new analytical tool.

Modern historians are fascinated by the repeated illnesses of George III and their influence on the course of historical events. In 1941 a noted psychiatrist, Manfred S. Guttmacher, examined the king's mental problems in *America's Last King: an Interpretation of the Madness of George III*. It was well received, but Dr. Guttmacher did not possess data on porphyria, and thus his work had been superseded by more recent studies. Charles Chenevix Trench's *The Royal Malady* (1965) is the first serious study of the king's hereditary illness, but it could have been improved by judicious editing. A far more comprehensive and scholarly work, *George III and the Mad Business* (1969), was written by two physicians, Ida Macalpine and Richard Hunter.

Several general biographies have appeared since Sir Lewis Namier and his associates established a new interpretation of the age of George III. John Cuthbert Long's *George III: The Story of a Complex Man* (1960) seems oblivious to the technique of structural analysis. While offering nothing startling, Stanley Ayling deals with porphyria in his *George the Third* (1972). The best modern biography is John Brooke's *King George III* (1972), while the best short essay is to be found in J. H. Plumb's *First Four Georges* (1956).

Evaluation of Principal Biographical Sources

Ayling, Stanley. *George the Third*. New York: Knopf, 1972. (A, G) While it offers the scholar nothing new, and the author does not attempt to reinterpret available sources, he does deal with the influence of porphyria on the behavior and actions of the king; unfortunately he draws no real conclusions, and simply presents the facts. The bibliography, while not extensive, is nicely balanced between primary and secondary sources and the notes are very useful.

Brooke, John. *King George III*. New York: McGraw-Hill, 1972. (A, G) This is the best modern biography of the king. Written by one of Sir Lewis Namier's closest associates, it contains all of the virtues of structural analysis and none of its faults. Beautifully written, it creates a royal portrait which will please the general reader while delighting the scholar. The notes and the bibliography are extremely valuable.

Chenevix Trench, Charles. *The Royal Malady*. New York: Harcourt-Brace, 1965. (A, G) The author is the first to make extensive use of two unpublished diaries kept by the doctors attending George III during the Regency Crisis of 1788-1789. This book-length study might have better served the scholar as a monograph. A useful work; however, editing would have spared the reader what seems mere gossip.

Fritz, Jean. *Can't You Make Them Behave, King George?* New York: Coward, McCann, and Geoghegan, 1977. (Y) Written for juvenile readers, it nonetheless deals with complex issues, such as the way in which George III viewed his relationship to his subjects, and the effects of porphyria on his behavior.

Lloyd, Alan. *The King Who Lost America: A Portrait of the Life and Times of George III*. New York: Doubleday, 1972. (G) Written for the general reader, but with little attention to balance or scholarship. The final years of the king's life are compressed into brief chapters as seeming afterthoughts. A short bibliography.

Long, John Cuthbert. *George III: the Story of a Complex Man*. New York: Little, Brown, 1960. (G) This work might well have been written in the mid-nineteenth century because of the author's adoption of a tone which relies on gossip and rumor. The remarkable progress made in the study of the reign of George III since 1930 is almost ignored. The bibliography is dated.

Macalpine, Ida, and Richard Hunter. *George III and the Mad Business.* New York: Pantheon Books, 1969. (**A, G**) A detailed treatment of George III's case of porphyria. The authors are physicians and their examination of the manuscript records left by the royal doctors are valuable. A useful bibliography for scholars.

McKelvey, James Lee. *George III and Lord Bute, the Leicester House Years.* Durham: Duke University Press, 1973. (**A, G**) The author concentrates on the years immediately preceding the accession of George III, and the frustration of Lord Bute at being denied a role in politics. It is not the final word on the subject, but essentially a beginning. The bibliography is specialized, but useful.

Plumb, John Harold. *First Four Georges.* New York: Macmillan, 1956 (**G**) While this brief work of 188 pages is intended for the general reader, the scholar will find much of value. Beautifully illustrated, it contains a select bibliography.

Overview and Evaluation of Primary Sources

There are numerous manuscript items relating to George III in private and public collections to which scholars have access, but many items have also been published. Of particular importance are the memoirs and collections of letters which have appeared since the late eighteenth century. Beginning in the year before George III's accession, the *Annual Register, or a view of the history, politics, and literature for the year 1758.* (London, 1759-; **A**) provides the student of contemporary affairs with a compendium of information, and it was friendly to the Court. Equally complimentary to those who surrounded the king was Henry P. Wyndham's edition of the *Diary of the Late George Bubb Dodington, Baron of Melcombe Regis, from March 8, 1749 to February 6, 1761* (Salisbury: E. Easton, 1784; **A**). Dodington was an associate of Bute and the publication of his diary came at a time when the king desperately needed to rebuild public confidence in his government. While a number of historical works appeared during the remaining four decades of the reign containing fragments of correspondence and memoirs, it was not until after the death of George III that editions of primary source materials began to appear in abundance.

Among the first works to be published was James, earl of Waldergrave's *Memoirs* (London: J. Murray, 1821; **A, G**). Governor to King George when he was still

Prince of Wales, Waldergrave did not paint a very complimentary picture of his sovereign. Equally devastating was earl of Oxford, Horace Walpole's *Memoirs of the Last Ten Years of the Reign of George the Second* (London: J. Murray, 1822; **A, G**). William Stanhope Taylor and John Henry Pringle edited the *Correspondence of William Pitt* (London: J. Murray, 1838-1840; **A, G**), making a number of Chatham's letters available to the public for the first time. Sir Denis Le Marchant, edited Horace Walpole's *Memoirs of the Reign of King George the Third* (London: R. Bentley, 1845; **A**). Since the 1920s George III has been able to answer his critics through his own letters which have appeared in a number of collections. Frank A. Mumby edited *George III and the American Revolution; the Beginnings* (London: Houghton, 1924, **A, G**). This volume contains a random selection of letters from the king to a number of prominent politicians, but it is not a major collection. Sir John Fortescue's edition of *The Correspondence of King George III from 1760 to December 1783*, 6 vols. (New York: Macmillan, 1927-1928; **A, G**) was severely criticized for carelessness and lack of understanding, faults which Sir Lewis Namier sought to correct in his *Additions and Corrections to Sir John Fortescue's Edition of the Correspondence of King George the Third*, vol. 1 (Manchester: Manchester University Press, 1937; **A, G**). Far more satisfactory to the general reader and the scholar is Bonamy Dobree's *The Letters of King George III* (London: Cassell, 1935; **A, G**). Romney Sedgwick's introduction to his edition of *Letters from George III to Lord Bute, 1756-1766* (London: Macmillan, 1939; **A, G**) is extremely useful in delineating the character of George III. Beginning where Fortescue wisely stopped, A. Aspinall set new standards of editing with his *The Later Correspondence of George III*, 5 vols. (Cambridge: Cambridge University Press, 1962-1971; **A, G**). The introductory essays are particularly useful. While Horace Walpole could hardly be called objective in his evaluation of the reign of George III, W. S. Lewis's mammoth edition of *Horace Walpole's Correspondence*, 39 vols. (New Haven: Yale University Press, 1937-1974; **A, G**), is nonetheless an important source.

Fiction and Adaptations

George III appears in a number of works as a minor character—sometimes as a villain, sometimes as a figure of fun. In Jean Plaidy's (the pseudonym of Eleanor Hibbert) *Perdita's Prince* (1969), both of these roles are combined. The novel concerns the affairs of the future George IV who led a rather colorful and often scandalous life. George III is the disapproving father who stands in the way of true love. Dredging up gossip and old tales long discarded by reputable historians,

Hibbert chronicles the life of the hapless monarch in her *The Third George* (1969).

From time to time George III has been included as a character in dramatic presentations, but he is rarely treated with candor by authors who usually seek merely to portray the monarch as the loser of an empire or as the poor mad king of Windsor. The exception to this rule is Leonard Wibberley's *1776 and All That* (1975) which presents a charming portrait of George III not as a man, but as a saint.

Museums, Historical Landmarks, Societies

George III sat for all the leading portrait painters of his day, and it is possible to compile a pictorial chronology of his life from youth to old age. Many of these works have been copied, but the originals are for the most part in various royal collections. Some are on view in galleries while others are in royal residences open to the public.

Colonial Williamsburg (Williamsburg, VA). Perhaps the most interesting "monument" of the age of George III, this one mile square living museum in Virginia is dedicated to the study of the late eighteenth century. There are several very fine portraits of George III among the Williamsburg holdings, and an outstanding collection of artifacts and museum-quality pieces can be found in the DeWitt Wallace Decorative Arts Gallery.

Other Sources

Butterfield, Herbert. *George III, Lord North, and the People, 1779-80*. London: British Book Center, 1950. Based entirely on manuscript sources, this volume is at times hard to follow because it assumes a depth of knowledge not present in most students. It is however a masterful and sympathetic study of George III during one of the most critical periods of his life.

Derry, John W. *The Regency Crisis and the Whigs, 1788-9*. Cambridge: Cambridge University Press, 1964. Written by one whose forte is political science and not history, it is nonetheless the final word on the first stage of the collapse of the old Whig faction. While it is not revisionist in its argument, it does present a meticulous analysis of the crisis.

Namier, Sir Lewis. *England in the Age of the American Revolution*. New York: Macmillan, 1930. Using source materials long familiar to scholars, the author reinterprets them using the technique of structural analysis and thereby presents a fresh approach to this critical period.

—————. *The Structure of Politics at the Accession of George III.* 2 vols. 1927. rev. ed. London: Macmillan, 1957. This work introduces the technique of structural analysis to the scholar as well as to the general reader, and led to a complete revision of the interpretation of the world of politics in the late eighteenth century.

Pares, Richard. *King George III and the Politicians.* Oxford: Oxford University Press, 1954. Based largely on printed source materials, these six essays on George III and the politicians who surrounded him offer a fresh interpretation of an often confusing aspect of his reign.

Watson, J. Steven. *The Reign of George III, 1760-1815.* Oxford: Oxford University Press, 1960. Solid and well-researched, this work is considered by many scholars to be the standard modern interpretation of the era. The bibliography is extensive and extremely useful.

White, R. J. *The Age of George III.* New York: Walker, 1968. This useful introduction to the period is well-written and carefully arranged for the general reader as well as the scholar. The bibliography is extensive and quite useful.

Clifton W. Potter, Jr.
Lynchburg College

GEORGE GERSHWIN
1898-1937

Chronology

Born Jacob Gershvin on September 26, 1898, in Brooklyn, New York, the second son of Morris Gershvin (originally Moishe Gershovitz), an immigrant Russian shoemaker, who in America tried his hand at operating a succession of small restaurants, Turkish baths, and other similar enterprises, and Rose Bruskin Gershvin, the immigrant daughter of a Russian furrier; *1898-1909* grows up on Manhattan's Lower East Side, an inattentive student in school who prefers rough-housing with friends on the streets; *1910-1914* quite accidentally becoming aware of music, begins to study the piano aggressively, quickly outgrowing a succession of teachers before spending four years studying with Charles Hambitzer, a young teacher and aspiring composer from Milwaukee; *1914-1920* Anglicizes his name to "George Gershwin"; drops out of the High School of Commerce at age fifteen to work as a fifteen-dollar-a-week piano pounder in Tin Pan Alley, the commercial music publishing district on 28th Street, promoting the sale of other composers' sheet music; also cuts piano rolls, works as an accompanist, tries to sell his own earliest songs, begins compiling notebooks of his ideas, makes numerous valuable contacts, and studies all aspects of the music business; his first attempt at writing a Broadway show, *La-La-Lucille*, is greeted with mixed reviews in 1919, but the next year Al Jolson turns his song "Swanee" into a major hit; *1920-1924* attracts increasing attention as the composer of five successive annual editions of George White's *Scandals* as well as of songs interpolated into other composers' musical reviews; *1924-1931* is suddenly propelled into the front ranks of American com-posers by the sensational popular acclaim that greets *Rhapsody in Blue* (1924), an extended piece for piano and jazz band commissioned by Paul Whiteman and orchestrated by Ferde Grofé; achieves major Broadway hits with *Lady, Be Good* (1924), the second version of *Strike Up the Band* (1927; revised 1930), *Girl Crazy* (1930), and *Of Thee I Sing* (1931); simultaneously continues to explore classical forms with *Concerto in F* (1925), the tone poem *An American in Paris* (1928), and the *Second Rhapsody for Orchestra with Piano* (1931); *1932-1935* begins studying music theory under Joseph Schillinger, in preparation for further serious composi-tion; although he is unable to repeat his previous successes on Broadway, despite an excellent score for *Let 'Em Eat Cake* (1933), he stars in his own weekly radio show for the CBS network throughout much of 1934; with the money thus earned, devotes twenty months to composing and orchestrating a full-length opera, *Porgy and Bess* (1935), which is greeted with rave reviews in Boston but lukewarm notices in New York; *1936-1937* moves to Los Angeles to work on a series of three film musicals; *1937* after several weeks of rapidly deteriorating health, dies of a malignant brain tumor in Los Angeles on July 11 at the age of thirty-eight.

Activities of Historical Significance

George Gershwin was one of the most talented and versatile composers the United States has produced. Although he lacked formal musical training, a fatal flaw in the eyes of some classical music critics and academicians, he had an insatiable hunger for musical knowledge and an uncanny ability to absorb what he heard and read. Even after he achieved international celebrity, he continued to study in an effort to enhance his skills.

From the outset of his career, Gershwin equated success with popular appeal. No doubt, that was to be expected from someone who began in Tin Pan Alley. For him the keys to popular appeal were a melody people could remember, a catchy rhythm, and a clever lyric. He supplied the first two of these ingredients himself; beginning in 1920 his older brother Ira, first as the pseudonymous Arthur Francis and later under his own name, generally supplied the last.

Gershwin demonstrated his ability to write hit songs early in his career. He was only twenty when he composed "Swanee" (1919), and he was able to follow that success with such standards-to-be as "I'll Build a Stairway to Paradise" (1922), "Somebody Loves Me"(1924), "Fascinating Rhythm" (1924), and "Oh, Lady Be Good!" (1924). It was *Rhapsody in Blue* (1924), however, that marked him as more than just another good tunesmith. Paul Whiteman was trying to establish his own sophisticated treatment of popular song and dance melodies (incorrectly identified with jazz) as the characteristic American contribution to the world of music. Commissioning Gershwin to write an extended instrumental piece was a stroke of promotional genius, except that Gershwin's achievement soon overshadowed Whiteman's own. Gershwin was unable to orchestrate his composition himself, so he produced a two-piano score from which Ferde Grofé produced the orchestration and parts. Not content with such dependency, he worked to overcome his lack of formal training. Less than two years later, when Walter Damrosch and the New York Symphony commissioned the *Concerto in F* (1925), Gershwin orchestrated it himself, as he would all his serious compositions thereafter.

Most classical critics were unimpressed with Gershwin's contributions to the concert repertory. They acknowledged his melodic ability and rhythmic inventiveness, but complained that his ideas were poorly worked out. The public did not care and generally embraced each new work with enthusiasm. Gershwin himself seemed to value popular appeal above critical approval. Almost incidentally, he claimed he was not trying to marry jazz to the classics, only to work out his own idiom. And, indeed, his roots were in popular song, not jazz.

In his musical comedies, too, Gershwin was inventive. When he began composing for Broadway, the standard format was a review concocted from disconnected songs matched to the talents of the performers but unrelated to whatever plot there might be. Particularly after he started working with his brother Ira as his lyricist, Gershwin began using his musical numbers to reveal the personalities of the characters who were singing or dancing them and thus integrating the songs into the story. He seldom had effective plot lines to work with, but when he did, as in the political satires *Strike Up the Band* and *Of Thee I Sing*, the results were stunning.

Without question, *Porgy and Bess* was the culmination of Gershwin's career. The opera was based on DuBose Heyward's novel *Porgy*, with Heyward, Heyward's wife Dorothy, and Ira Gershwin all deserving a share of the credit for creating a superb libretto. The story is set in the poverty-stricken black ghetto of Charleston's waterfront, and the opera requires an almost all-black cast; the plot is as much about grand opera, however, as it is about the daily ordeal of African Americans. Nevertheless, the story is compelling and the music the lushest and most complex Gershwin ever wrote. When *Porgy and Bess* opened in Boston in September 1935, both critics and audiences raved, but inexplicably the work was deemed by its producers to be too long. Cut substantially before its opening in New York, the opera was hurt by unfriendly reviews. Virgil Thomson opined, "Gershwin does not even know what an opera is." Still, the opera enjoyed an initial run of 124 performances. Since the Second World War and more especially since the restoration of the original score in 1976, *Porgy and Bess* has become the most frequently performed opera by an American composer. In 1985 it became a staple of New York's Metropolitan Opera.

Had his skill as a composer ever failed him, Gershwin could have continued to thrive as a concert performer. He was a brilliant pianist, although he seldom played any work but his own, whether on the concert circuit or at private parties, where he was much in demand. Beginning with a concert at New York's Lewissohn Stadium in the summer of 1929, he also began to conduct some of his compositions and soon insisted on leading the first performances of his musicals on Broadway.

It is pointless to speculate on the direction Gershwin's career might have taken had he lived longer. The only certainty is that his creative abilities showed no signs of diminishing, right up to his final illness. As much as he disliked the experience of working in Hollywood, the songs he wrote in that last year included "They Can't Take That Away from Me," "They All Laughed," "Let's Call the

Whole Thing Off," "A Foggy Day in London Town," and "Nice Work If You Can Get It"—all classics of their type.

Overview of Biographical Sources

Gershwin has been a favorite subject for biographers. After all, he created a large body of enormously popular music, he symbolized for Jewish Americans an escape from the pervasive anti-Semitism of the interwar years, and he died at a tragically young age. Add to these possibilities the opportunity to spice up any account of his life with speculation about his relationships with women (he was befriended by some of the most beautiful and accomplished women of the day but never married), his apparent self-preoccupation (he was unabashedly his own foremost fan), and the debate over his true place in the American musical pantheon, and his appeal as a subject becomes overwhelming. The first Gershwin biography, Isaac Goldberg's *George Gershwin: A Study in American Music,* appeared, with the composer's help, in 1931. Others have been appearing regularly ever since. The best—those by David Ewen (1970), Charles Schwartz (1973), and Edward Jablonski (1987)—combine an evaluation of his contributions to American music with a narrative of his life, drawing on his surviving letters as well as the reminiscences of his friends and associates.

Evaluation of Principal Biographical Sources

Altman, Frances. *George Gershwin: Master Composer.* Minneapolis: T. S. Denison, 1968. (Y) Written for Denison's Men of Achievement Series, this biography is intended for use by students in grades 4-9. It predictably stresses Gershwin's childhood and early career, then merely summarizes his later successes.

Armitage, Merle. *George Gershwin: Man and Legend.* New York: Duell, Sloan and Pearce, 1958. (A, G) Armitage, a prolific writer, graphic artist, and sometime impresario who produced Gershwin's last concerts and the first posthumous performances of *Porgy and Bess,* stresses Gershwin's growth as a classical musician, noting his interest in the music of Stravinsky, Ravel, Schoenberg, and Berg—all of whom likewise knew and appreciated his own work—and his continuing study of theory and orchestration. This book devotes relatively little attention to the show music, and is more personal reminiscence than formal biography.

Bryant, Bernice. *George Gershwin: Young Composer.* Indianapolis: Bobbs-Merrill, 1965. (Y) Gershwin is a natural subject for inclusion in the Childhood of Famous Americans Series, given the fact that he was working as a professional musician and dabbling in song-writing before he reached adulthood. Bryant, writing a somewhat fictionalized account for elementary school children, emphasizes Gershwin's dedication to learning his craft and concludes the story with the triumphant première of *Rhapsody in Blue.*

Ewen, David. *George Gershwin: His Journey to Greatness.* Englewood Cliffs, NJ: Prentice-Hall, 1970. (**A, G**) Ewen presents a very thorough, highly favorable portrait of Gershwin the composer, with very little attention devoted to his private life.

————. *The Story of George Gershwin.* New York: Holt, Rinehart and Winston, 1943. (**G, Y**) This well-written work is briefer than Ewen's 1970 biography of Gershwin. Ewen succeeds in recreating the musical world into which his subject sought entry. Correspondingly, there is much less analysis of Gershwin's work. Intended for a popular audience, this book would make very effective reading for secondary school students, despite its age.

Goldberg, Isaac, with Edith Garson. *George Gershwin: A Study in American Music.* 1931. Rev. ed. New York: Frederick Ungar, 1958. (**A, G**) George Gershwin assisted Goldberg in the preparation of a series of articles, "Music by Gershwin," for the *Ladies Home Journal,* which Goldberg then expanded into the first edition of this book. Garson added the section on Gershwin's later years. The authors stress Gershwin's strategic role as a popular composer attempting to introduce jazz elements both to Broadway and the concert hall. Presumably, this view reflects their subject's thinking as well.

Jablonski, Edward. *George Gershwin.* New York: G. P. Putnam's Sons, 1962. (**G, Y**) Jablonski is unabashedly a fan of Gershwin. This brief book is well organized, highly readable, and suitable for use by secondary school students.

————. *Gershwin.* New York: Doubleday, 1987. (**A, G**) Basically an expansion of his earlier work, Jablonski's newest volume on Gershwin is well researched and generally readable, despite an excessive number of typographical errors. Jablonski includes an epilogue on the life of Ira Gershwin after 1937, appendices on both brothers' compositions, and an annotated bibliography.

Jablonski, Edward, and Lawrence D. Stewart. *The Gershwin Years.* 1958. Rev. ed. Garden City, NY: Doubleday, 1973. (**A, G**) Slightly revised from the first edition, this combined biography of George and Ira Gershwin is uniformly laudatory. The central theme is the brothers' rise to fame and fortune.

Kendall, Alan. *George Gershwin*. London: Harrap, 1987. **(A, G)** Kendall, an Englishman clearly influenced by Charles Schwartz's biography, offers a critical, often acerbic view of Gershwin's private life. Devotes extensive passages to the composer's self-centeredness, and his apparently unfulfilled relations with women.

Kimball, Robert, and Alfred Simon. *The Gershwins*. New York: Atheneum, 1973. **(A, G)** Begins with a short biographical sketch by John S. Wilson, then offers a wealth of photographs of the Gershwins and their hit shows, sample lyrics by Ira, representative excerpts from George's scores, drawings and paintings (some reproduced in color) by both brothers, and reminiscences of colleagues and friends.

Payne, [Pierre Stephen] Robert. *Gershwin*. New York: Pyramid Books, 1960. **(A, G)** Payne strikes an unusual note by emphasizing the Jewish qualities in Gershwin's music (the use of minor keys). Otherwise, a standard brief account.

Rushmore, Robert. *The Life of George Gershwin*. New York: Crowell-Collier Press, 1966. **(G)** This slender volume is largely drawn from previously published sources, offers little in the way of musical evaluation, and contributes nothing new toward an understanding of its subject.

Schwartz, Charles. *Gershwin: His Life and Music*. Indianapolis: Bobbs-Merrill, 1973. **(A, G)** This large book is the most important volume of musical and bio-graphical scholarship on Gershwin and a perfect example of the classical musical establishment's disdain for his success. Schwartz considers Gershwin a "tune-smith" who "dabbled" in serious musical forms but never outgrew his origins. According to Schwartz, "Gershwin may never have come close to reaching Parnassus in his serious pieces, but that has never mattered to his vast, international public, who after all mold what is acceptable and fashionable by the cumulative strength of their collective dollars. . . . [O]ne cannot overlook his special flair for speaking a musical language they readily understand and savor. . . . Professionals and critics may always find fault with his serious work, but not so the Average Joes of the world." Needless to say, Schwartz takes a jaundiced view of Gershwin's personal foibles as well. Appendices list all of the Gershwin compositions, while the discography and bibliography, dated now, were so complete in 1973 that they became the basis for a separate publication.

Overview and Evaluation of Primary Sources
   The principal primary source for the study of the life and career of George Gershwin is the treasury of materials housed in the Gershwin Archive at the

Library of Congress. The collection includes his musical sketches, original piano scores, and manuscript orchestrations, insofar as these have survived (Gershwin did not orchestrate his own Broadway shows, and the parts were often lost when a show closed), correspondence, photographs of and by the composer, some of his drawings and paintings, and a variety of other memorabilia. After his brother's death, Ira Gershwin devoted a large portion of his life to assembling and annotating these items. The Library of Congress also has a sizable Ira Gershwin Collection. The Museum of the City of New York also possesses a small but significant collection of Gershwin memorabilia.

Immediately after Gershwin's death, Merle Armitage edited a memorial album containing reminiscences of the composer's friends and professional colleagues: *George Gershwin* (London: Longmans, Green, 1938; **A, G**). Among those included are Ira Gershwin, Ferde Grofé, DuBose Heyward, Rouben Mamoulian (who directed the première of *Porgy and Bess*), Todd Duncan (who created the role of Porgy), fellow songwriters Irving Berlin, Jerome Kern, and Harold Arlen, and music critics David Ewen, Olin Downes, Leonard Liebling, and Gilbert Seldes. Oscar Levant, who worked with Gershwin as a musical assistant and rehearsal pianist, and was later recognized as a leading interpreter of Gershwin's music, included a long and witty chapter called "My Life; Or the Story of George Gershwin" in his humorous memoir, *A Smattering of Ignorance* (New York: Doubleday, Doran, 1940; **A, G**). Ira Gershwin's clever volume, *Lyrics on Several Occasions: A Selection of Stage and Screen Lyrics Written for Sundry Situations; And Now Arranged in Arbitrary Categories. To Which Have Been Added Many Informative Annotations & Disquisitions on Their Why & Wherefore, Their Whom-For, Their How; and Matters Associative* (New York: Alfred A. Knopf, 1959; **A, G**), contains a number of interesting comments on how some of Broadway's best songs came to be written and demonstrates conclusively just how integral a part Ira's words played in the Gershwin success story.

Gershwin lived before the invention of the original-cast long-playing record. His songs became standard fare for innumerable artists, however, and individual tunes were recorded by their original interpreters. Charles Schwartz's *George Gershwin: A Selective Bibliography and Discography* (Detroit: Published for the College Music Society by Information Coordinators, 1974; **A, G**) is complete and includes critical notations for some items but is now handicapped by its age. Readers interested in the history of the Broadway musical will want to watch for the appearance of the Library of Congress-Elektra/Nonesuch Records productions of *Girl Crazy, Strike Up the Band,* and *Pardon My English,* based on the original scores and parts that were rediscovered in a Warner Brothers warehouse in New Jersey in 1982.

Fiction and Adaptations

Warner Brothers released *Rhapsody in Blue,* a 139-minute black-and-white feature film, in 1945. Directed by Irving Rapper and starring Robert Alda, the film is purported to be a biography of George Gershwin, but the story is more fiction than fact. It does highlight some of Gershwin's best music, however, and includes Al Jolson, Paul Whiteman, and Oscar Levant playing themselves, so it is not without interest.

An American in Paris, a 113-minute color film released by Metro-Goldwyn-Mayer in 1951, stars Gene Kelly as a struggling American artist living in Paris, who falls in love with a French shop girl, played by Leslie Caron. The rather predictable plot is enhanced by a score employing Gershwin songs and culminates in a famous, imaginatively filmed ballet sequence set to Gershwin's tone poem. The film received the 1951 Academy Award for best picture.

Columbia Pictures' 1959 production of *Porgy and Bess* is a 138-minute color film, starring Sidney Poitier and Dorothy Dandridge in the title roles. Mouthing the singing of Robert McFerrin and Adele Addison, they are too glossy for the ghetto environment of Catfish Row. Brock Peters as Crown and Sammy Davis, Jr., as Sporting Life (singing for themselves) are magnificent, however. Rouben Mamoulian, who directed the original stage production, was engaged to direct the film version, but after disagreements with producer Samuel Goldwyn during pre-production, he was replaced by the heavy-handed Otto Preminger, who simply did not know how to bring the opera to life. This film uses the cut New York version, rather than the complete Boston score, which was not restored until the triumphant Houston Grand Opera production of 1976.

Other Sources

Hitchcock, H. Wiley, and Stanley Sadie, eds. *The New Grove Dictionary of American Music.* 4 vols. London: Macmillan, 1986. The essay on Gershwin presents an excellent summary of his life, a concise analysis of his music, and a useful index to his published works.

Keith Ian Polakoff
California State University, Long Beach

JAY GOULD
1836-1892

Chronology

Born Jason Gould on May 27, 1836, in Roxbury, New York, the son of John Burr Gould, an impoverished hill farmer, and Mary Moore Gould; gains rudimentary education at a local academy; works for a blacksmith and as a clerk in a country store; becomes self-taught surveyor and county mapmaker; publishes local histories; *1857-1867* marries Helen Day Miller of New York City on January 22, 1863; starts business career by operating a tannery in northern Pennsylvania; is briefly a leather merchant in New York City; begins to speculate in railroad securities; *1867-1872* joins with James Fisk and Daniel Drew to control the Erie Railroad; defeats takeover bid by Cornelius Vanderbilt; forges close political ties with New York City's "Tweed Gang"; launches ambitious schemes to expand Erie by acquiring links to the West; precipitates major panic (Black Friday, September 24, 1869) by attempt to corner gold market, and loses control of Erie in resulting backlash; *1872-1883* gains control of the Union Pacific, the Kansas Pacific, the Denver Pacific, the Central Pacific, the Missouri Pacific, the Missouri, Kansas and Texas, the Wabash, the Lackawanna, the Central of New Jersey, and the New York and New England railroads; regains control of the Erie; acquires control of the Western Union Telegraph Company and temporary control of the *New York World* newspaper; *1883-1892* sells off most of his eastern railroads; concentrates upon building a regional system in the Southwest; owns one-half of total railroad mileage in the Southwest (the Missouri Pacific, the Texas & Pacific, the St. Louis Southwestern, and the International & Great Northern railroad systems); becomes major owner of New York City's elevated railroads; *1892* dies on December 2 from tuberculosis at his home on New York City's Fifth Avenue, leaving an estate valued at approximately $72 million.

Activities of Historical Significance

Jay Gould's reputation during his lifetime was of a stock manipulator, corporate wrecker, and political corruptionist who combined the buying and selling of railroads with the purchase of legislators, judges, and government officials and the fleecing of investors. The source of this reputation was the two scandals with which his name became permanently associated. The first was the bitter struggle with Cornelius Vanderbilt for control of the Erie Railroad followed by the collapse of the prices of the line's stocks and bonds because of Gould's issuance of a mass of watered securities in pursuit of his expansionist ambitions. The second was his attempt, in partnership with James Fisk, to corner the gold market and the resulting panic of Black Friday (September 24, 1869). The image of Gould as a despoiler would continue to dominate among journalists, popular biographers, and even historians for many years after his death. Recently, however, business historians have put more emphasis upon his constructive achievements—his attempt (though a failure) to build the Erie into a major east-west trunk line; his reorganization of the finances and management of the Union Pacific Railroad and the Western Union Telegraph Company; and his efforts to rationalize and integrate the operations of the southwestern railroads under his control.

Overview of Biographical Sources

Jay Gould's reputation as a stock manipulator, political corruptionist, and despoiler of investors was firmly set by one of the classics of investigative journalism—the exposé of the Erie Railroad wars and attempted gold corner in Charles Francis Adams, Jr. and Henry Adams, *Chapters of Erie* (1871). The image of Gould as a villain would be reinforced by the hastily assembled biographies published immediately after his death to capitalize upon the accompanying publicity. Among these were Murat Halstead and J. Frank Beale, Jr., *Life of Jay Gould: How He Made His Millions* (1892); John S. Ogilvie, *Life and Death of Jay Gould and How He Made His Millions* (1892); and Trumbull White, *The Wizard of Wall Street and His Wealth* (1892). The same mix of sensationalism with moral denunciation would be recycled, and thereby perpetuated, by such muckraking and debunking accounts as Gustavus Myers, *History of the Great American Fortunes* (1910), Robert I. Warshow, *Jay Gould: The Story of a Fortune* (1928), and Matthew Josephson, *The Robber Barons: The Great American Capitalists* (1934), and by more recent entries directed to the popular audience such as Richard O'Connor, *Gould's Millions* (1962), and Edwin P. Hoyt, *The Goulds: A Social History* (1969). The first step in Gould's rehabilitation came with the publication of Julius Grodinsky's scholarly and detailed examination of Gould's business activities, *Jay Gould: His Business Career, 1867-1892* (1957). An even more positive appraisal is given in railroad historian Maury Klein's exhaustively researched *The Life and Legend of Jay Gould* (1986).

Evaluation of Principal Biographical Sources

Adams, Charles Francis, Jr., and Henry Adams. *Chapters of Erie and Other Essays.* Boston: James R. Osgood, 1871. (A, G) A blistering and brilliant indictment of the chicanery and unscrupulousness Gould displayed in the Erie Railroad wars and in his attempt to corner the gold market. This exposé decisively shaped Gould's reputation for the rest of his life and for many years after his death.

Grodinsky, Julius. *Jay Gould: His Business Career, 1867-1892*. Philadelphia: University of Pennsylvania Press, 1957. (A) Grodinsky describes his work as ''an examination of the policies of a businessman in the field of speculative or equity capital in the free enterprise era between the Civil War and the Theodore Roosevelt Administration.'' Although the plethora of details makes for dull reading, Grodinsky consciously strives to rehabilitate Gould. While acknowledging that Gould's railroads were badly maintained and offered poor service, Grodinsky emphasizes the benefits to consumers, producers, and even, in the long run, the railroad industry from the rate wars that Gould initiated in pursuit of his expansionist ambitions.

Halstead, Murat, and J. Frank Beale, Jr. *Life of Jay Gould: How He Made His Millions*. Philadelphia: Edgewood Publishing, 1892. (A, G) The most solidly based of the swarm of biographies produced to exploit the publicity surrounding Gould's death.

Hoyt, Edwin P. *The Goulds: A Social History*. New York: Weybright and Talley, 1969. (G) Hoyt is a prolific author of popularized biography. Although this work provides the fullest available account of the lives of Gould's children, the emphasis—as in the treatment of Gould himself—is the sensational and scandalous. Hoyt does not include footnotes, a listing of sources, or even a bibliography of secondary works consulted.

Josephson, Matthew. *The Robber Barons: The Great American Capitalists*. New York: Harcourt, Brace, 1934. (G) Presents a sensationalized account of Gould's activities as grist for Josephson's denunciation of big businessmen as crooks and corruptionists. Much of Josephson's so-called research appears lifted from previously published secondary works.

Klein, Maury. *The Life and Legend of Jay Gould*. Baltimore: Johns Hopkins University Press, 1986. (A, G) In producing the most exhaustively researched of the works on Gould, Klein discovered a wealth of new information. Klein blames Gould's negative reputation on sensation-mongering reporters, his personal enemies among New York journalists, and later writers who simply repeated the familiar tales without re-examining the record. By contrast, Klein is admiring, even hero-worshipping. "Few men," Klein argues, "matched the cold realism by which Gould conducted his affairs. . . . He was unfettered by cant, less cowed or deceived by illusions than any other entrepreneur of his age. . . . By any reckoning Gould must be counted among the two or three most important figures in the development of the American industrial economy."

Myers, Gustavus. *History of the Great American Fortunes,* 3 vols. 1910. Reprint. 1 vol. New York: Modern Library, 1936. (A, G) Myers, a socialist penning an indictment of capitalism and capitalists, treats Gould (whom he describes as "a pitiless human carnivore, glutting on the blood of his numberless victims") as demonstrating his thesis: that behind every great fortune lie great crimes.

O'Connor, Richard. *Gould's Millions.* Garden City, NY: Doubleday, 1962. (G) Intended for a popular audience by a prolific journalist turned biographer, this book simply restates the standard portrayal of Gould as villain. The blurb on the dust jacket accurately captures O'Connor's approach: "The Story of Jay Gould's Hundred-Million-Dollar Raid on the American Economy." The only scholarly apparatus is a handful of footnotes.

Ogilvie, John S. *Life and Death of Jay Gould and How He Made His Millions.* New York: J. S. Ogilvie, 1892. (G) One of the biographies based a hasty assembling of newspaper clippings and designed to capitalize upon the publicity accompanying Gould's death.

Warshow, Robert Irving. *Jay Gould: The Story of a Fortune.* New York: Greenberg Publisher, 1928. (G) The work is billed as "the story of one of the greatest financial freebooters of all time" (or alternately "the greatest modern buccaneer"). The author does not pretend to have done independent research; there is not even a list of secondary accounts consulted.

White, Trumbull. *The Wizard of Wall Street and His Wealth; or, The Life and Deeds of Jay Gould.* Chicago: Mid-Continent Publishing, 1892. (G) Another of the hack biographies based upon the sensationalized accounts of Gould's life filling the newspaper columns at the time of his death.

Overview and Evaluation of Primary Sources
While researching his biography, Maury Klein discovered a cache of formerly unknown Gould letterbooks in the possession of great-grandson Kingdon Gould,

Jr. Other Gould papers are at the Manuscript Division, Library of Congress, Washington, D.C., and at Gould's former country home-turned-museum, Lyndhurst, in Tarrytown, New York. This material has to be supplemented by research in contemporary business newspapers and periodicals. The most important for tracing Gould's wheelings and dealings are the *American Railroad Journal, Bradstreet's*, the *Commercial and Financial Chronicle*, the (British) *Railway Journal*, the *Railroad Gazette*, the *Railway Review*, and the *United States Railroad and Mining Register* and its successor from 1875 on, the *Railway World*. Archival and manuscript collections illuminating aspects of Gould's activities include the records of the Chicago, Burlington & Quincy Railroad (Newberry Library, Chicago), the Henry Villard Papers (Baker Library, Harvard Graduate School of Business Administration, Boston), Grenville M. Dodge Papers (Iowa State Department of Archives and History, Des Moines), Western Historical Collection (Denver Public Library), Ralph Ingersoll Papers (Mugar Library, Boston University), James F. Joy Papers (Burton Historical Collection, Detroit Public Library), Erie Railroad Records (Pennsylvania Historical and Museum Commission, Harrisburg), and the Union Pacific Railroad Company Collection (Nebraska State Museum and Archives, Lincoln).

Fiction and Adaptations

As Henry Nash Smith has pointed out ("The Search for a Capitalist Hero: Businessmen in American Fiction" in *The Business Establishment,* edited by Earl F. Cheit [New York: John Wiley, 1964]), many of the late-nineteenth-century novelists writing about businessmen took Jay Gould as the characteristic type. The most important and influential examples of fictional speculators/ stock manipulators modeled upon Gould were Zedekiah Hampton in H. H. Boyeson, *A Daughter of the Philistines* (1883), "Uncle" Jerry Hollowell in Charles Dudley Warner, *A Little Journey in the World* (1889), and Jacob Dryfoos in William Dean Howells, *A Hazard of New Fortunes* (1890).

Museums, Historical Landmarks, Societies

Gould Memorial Library (New York, NY). Gould's daughter Helen (Mrs. Finley J. Shepherd) provided the funds to construct this library at New York University.

Jay Gould Memorial Reformed Church (Roxbury, NY). Built by Gould's daughter Helen, who also purchased the Gould home in Roxbury to be used as a public library for the town.

Lyndhurst (Tarrytown, NY). At her death in 1961, Gould's daughter Anna (the Duchesse de Talleyrand-Perigord) willed Gould's magnificent Gothic castle-like country home to the National Trust for Historic Preservation along with an endowment for its maintenance. The property has been opened to visitors.

Other Sources

Ackerman, Kenneth. *The Gold Ring: Jim Fisk, Jay Gould, and Black Friday, 1869.* New York: Dodd, Mead, 1988. Despite a tendency to breathless prose, Ackerman has done a solid job of research on the attempted gold corner.

Browder, Clifford. *The Money Game in Old New York: Daniel Drew and His Times.* Lexington: University Press of Kentucky, 1986. The most thoroughly documented biography of Drew, a Gould associate in the Erie Railroad wars.

Chandler, Alfred D., Jr. *The Visible Hand: The Managerial Revolution in American Business.* Cambridge: Harvard University Press, 1977. The most insightful and incisive of the histories of the industrial revolution in the United States and the accompanying rise of big business. Includes a balanced appraisal of Gould's role in building the country's railroad and communications infrastructure.

Gordon, John Steele. *The Scarlet Woman of Wall Street: Jay Gould, Jim Fisk, Cornelius Vanderbilt, the Erie Railway Wars, and the Birth of Wall Street.* New York: Weidenfeld & Nicolson, 1988. A readable version, more solidly researched than most, but still largely a rehashing of familiar material.

Klein, Maury. "In Search of Jay Gould." *Business History Review* 52 (Summer 1978): 166-199. An illuminating account of the making and perpetuation of Gould's image "as the supreme villain of his era."

Swanberg, W. A. *Jim Fisk: The Career of an Improbable Rascal.* New York: Scribner's, 1959. A vividly written biography of Gould's partner in the Erie Railroad wars and the attempted corner of the gold market. There are no footnotes; apparently the work rests upon published materials supplemented by contemporary newspaper and periodical stories.

John Braeman
University of Nebraska-Lincoln

BARNARD GRATZ
1738-1801
MICHAEL GRATZ
1740-1811

Chronology

Born Barnard Gratz in 1738, and Michael Gratz in 1740 in Langendorf, Upper Silesia to Solomon Gratz, a moderately successful dry goods merchant and his wife, whose name has not been recorded; *1750-1759* brothers travel to London and then to Philadelphia; reared and educated by their cousin Solomon Henry; serve as apprentices in Henry's lucrative import and export business; *1754* Barnard settles in Philadelphia and works in the counting house of David Franks; *1756-1763* supply British and colonial troops during the French and Indian War; *1759* Michael arrives in Philadelphia and forms the first partnership of B. and M. Gratz; *1760* Barnard marries Richea Myers of New York City; *1761-1767* business grows rapidly as the brothers sell dry goods and hardware to West Indian merchants and import sugar and rum; also engage in coastal trade, buying and selling merchandise in Boston, Newport, New York, and Charleston; *1765* purchase the ship *The Rising Sun* to enter the merchant-shipping business; on October 25 sign the Non-Importation Resolutions to sever commercial relations with British merchants; concentrate on the western movement; *1768* establish a permanent partnership; develop business relations with Joseph Simon and other merchants of the Lancaster Consortium to foster the western trade; send merchandise to William Murray, who directed the first expedition to Illinois; *1769* Michael marries Miriam Simon; brothers send financial aid and merchandise to George Croghan, their agent at Fort Pitt, who unsuccessfully tries to establish settlements south and west of the Ohio River in the Vandalia colony; *1770* Michael buys 9,050 acres of land in the Mohawk Valley from George Croghan to sell to settlers; *1773* contribute to the creation of the Philadelphia Mikve Israel Synagogue and work with David Franks and Joseph Simon to promote the business activities of the newly created Illinois and Wabash Company; *1774* begin to sell lands in Louisville, Kentucky, and recognize the importance of establishing settlements in the Ohio and Mississippi River Valleys; *1776* Barnard directs family store at Pittsburgh, supplying American troops with food, clothes, shoes, blankets, and rifles; *1778* Michael enters business with Carter Braxton, shipping military supplies to American troops; *1779* Barnard becomes secretary of the Illinois and Wabash Company and proposes plans for new settlements in the West; Barnard extends a loan to Edmund Randolph to support the war effort; *1781* provide members of the George Rogers Clark expedition with military supplies; *1799* dissolve the partnership of B. and M. Gratz; *1801* Barnard dies in Baltimore on April 20; *1811* Michael dies in Philadelphia on September 8.

Activities of Historical Significance

Barnard and Michael Gratz were two of the most prominent Jewish merchants in eighteenth-century America, and their success, combined with their assistance to immigrants, encouraged other Jews to settle in the colonies. Having received business training and financial assistance from David Franks, the Gratz brothers succeeded in developing one of the most profitable business firms in colonial Philadelphia. Their business empire was sprawling, for the Gratzes established a network of commissioned agents in colonial coastal cities, the West Indies, and Europe. After the French and Indian War, the Gratzes became "Western Men," working with Simon, Franks, and other members of the Lancaster Group to open up the West for settlement and commercial activity. Their participation in the Vandalia and in the Illinois and Wabash Companies contributed to the gradual settlement of Pittsburgh, Louisville, and other posts in Illinois and Indiana.

As advocates of westward expansion and of republican ideologies, the Gratzes supported the American Revolution. During the War of Independence, they continued to encourage the settlement of western lands, provided the Continental Army with food and military supplies, and raised funds for the patriots. After the British evacuated Philadelphia in 1778, the Gratzes encouraged Jewish patriots who escaped from cities in British hands to come there. They provided them with housing and, in some instances, financial assistance. After the Revolution, the Gratz brothers supported the civic, religious, and political emancipation of Jews in the newly created nation.

Overview of Biographical Sources

There are three major works that contain biographical information on the Gratzes. In *B. and M. Gratz: Merchants in Philadelphia, 1754-1798* (1916), William V. Byars has edited major papers of the Gratzes and details the connections of the Gratzes to the pertinent issues of the times. In *Early American Jewry* (1953), Jacob R. Marcus presents colorful accounts of the careers and achievements of the Gratz brothers during the colonial and early revolutionary eras; He describes the personal qualities of the Gratzes and explains their relations to prominent American business and political leaders. Vivid depictions of the business, civic, and religious leadership roles of the Gratzes also appear in *The History of the Jews of Philadelphia from Colonial Times to the Age of Jackson* (1956) by Edwin Wolf II, and Maxwell Whiteman.

Evaluation of Principal Biographical Sources

Abernethy, Thomas P. *Western Lands and the American Revolution*. New York: Russell and Russell, 1937. (**A, G**) This detailed study emphasizes expansionism as an important factor in colonial America and a major cause of the American Revolution. Abernethy alludes to the involvement of the Gratzes in the Vandalia and Illinois Companies and the importance of their papers for an understanding of westward expansion during the eighteenth century.

Byars, William V., ed. *B. and M. Gratz: Merchants in Philadelphia, 1754-1798*. Jefferson City: Stephens Printing, 1916. (**A, G**) This is the major account of the Gratzes. The multifaceted character of their business emerges as the implicit thesis of the work. Byars provides illuminating accounts of the Gratzes' involvement in the western movement, but his account of their place in the history of the American Revolution is confusing. He devotes minimal attention to their religious views and activities. Contains massively documented footnotes but lacks a bibliography.

Doerflinger, Thomas M. *A Vigorous Spirit of Enterprise: Merchants and Economic Developments in Revolutionary Philadelphia*. Chapel Hill: University of North Carolina Press, 1986. (**A**) The major study of merchants in eighteenth-century America. Doerflinger examines the types, functions, and mentalities of Philadelphia's merchants. Contains a few references to the business operations of the Gratzes and mentions the importance of their papers.

Karp, Abraham, ed. *The Jewish Experience in America: The Colonial Period*. New York: Ktav Publishing, 1969. (**A, G**) A chapter examines the role of the Gratzes as promoters of "the First American West." It details the Gratzes' business connections with Joseph Simon and their Pittsburgh agent, George Croghan. Gives only minimal attention to their business activities during the American Revolution.

Lebeson, Anita L. *Pilgrim People*. New York: Minerva Press, 1975. (**A, G**) In this survey of American Jewish history, Lebeson chronicles the business activities of the Gratzes during the colonial era, briefly examining their rivalry with the firm of Baynton, Wharton, and Morgan for control of western lands. She also calls attention to the fact that in later life Barnard Gratz spoke against religious discrimination in Maryland. Contains a comprehensive bibliography.

Marcus, Jacob R. *Early American Jewry.* 2 vols. Philadelphia: Jewish Publication Society of America, 1953. (**A, G**) These two volumes contain detailed and colorful sketches of American Jews during the colonial and revolutionary periods. The second volume recounts some of the Gratzes' business ventures during the colonial era and details their connections to both Jewish and Christian merchants in Philadelphia and throughout the colonies. Marcus maintains that the Gratzes succeeded in assimilating Jews into American business life and solidifying the Philadelphia Jewish community. Marcus's study, however, neglects the role of the Gratzes during the American Revolution and lacks an adequate bibliography.

—————. *The Colonial American Jew.* 3 vols. Detroit: Wayne State University Press, 1970. (**A**) Marcus's study demonstates that numerous Jews succeeded in various aspects of colonial merchant life and significantly contributed to the cause of the American Revolution. The second volume contains valuable sections on the Gratzes' involvement in the western movement and their role as military contractors during the American Revolution. The third volume contains a fine bibliography.

Saville, Max. *George Morgan: Colonial Builder.* New York: Columbia University Press, 1932. (**A, G**) This readable biography describes the business career of George Morgan and his role in the firm of Baynton, Wharton, and Morgan. The author explains how the firm contributed to western expansion, competed with the Gratzes for frontier trade, and then went bankrupt. Contains adequate documentation.

Simonhoff, Harry. *Jewish Notables in America, 1776-1865.* New York: Greenberg, 1956. (**A, G**) In his short account of the Gratz brothers, Simonhoff describes their business activities and personal qualities. The author perceives Barnard as prudent and conservative in business matters, balancing Michael's aggressiveness. Lacks a bibliography.

Wainwright, Nicholas B. *George Croghan: Wilderness Diplomat.* Chapel Hill: University of North Carolina Press, 1959. (**A, G**) Wainwright portrays Croghan's activities as an Indian trader, colonial military leader, and commissioned agent for land companies. He maintains that the Gratzes deeply trusted Croghan, who served as their agent in Pittsburgh.

Wolf, Edwin, II, and Maxwell Whiteman. *The History of the Jews of Philadelphia from Colonial Times to the Age of Jackson.* Philadelphia: Jewish Publication Society of America, 1956. (**A, G**) This is one of the finest studies of urban Jewish communities in America. Wolf contends that the Gratzes were the most prominent Jewish family in eighteenth-century Philadelphia. In addition to accounts of their business affairs and involvement in the western movement and Revolutionaly War, the study details their leadership role in the Philadelphia Jewish community.

Overview and Evaluation of Primary Sources

The Gratzes' papers are their greatest legacy to the study of eighteenth-century American history. *The Gratz Papers, 1750-1850*, edited by William V. Byars (St. Louis, 1915; **A, G**), available on microfilm from the Missouri Historical Society in St. Louis, consists of letters and other primary materials from numerous archives and libraries. *B. and M. Gratz: Merchants in Philadelphia, 1754-1798*, edited by William V. Byars (Jefferson City: Stephens Printing, 1916; **A, G**) is a selection of the most important letters and documents from *The Gratz Papers.* The primary materials included here are intended to illustrate the importance of the Gratz brothers and their family to the study of the early republic. Important documents include the private ledger of Michael Gratz, correspondence with George Croghan and William Murray about western affairs, and select letters regarding the selling of military supplies, the building of ships, and the extension of loans during the American Revolution. Unfortunately, some valuable primary materials concerning their involvement in other major facets of the American Revolution and their leadership in the Jewish community are not found in this volume.

The Historical Society of Pennsylvania (Philadelphia) holds the Etting and Croghan Collections of the Gratz Papers. There are also important manuscripts in the McAllister Collection of the Library Company of Philadelphia. Yiddish letters of the Gratzes, which reveal very little about their business affairs, are found in the Henry Joseph Collection of the American Jewish Archives in Cincinnati. Other significant primary sources are held by the American Jewish Historical Society (Waltham, MA), the Library of Congress, the State Library of Virginia (Richmond), and the Missouri Historical Society (Jefferson City).

Museums, Historical Landmarks, Societies

Gratz College (Philadelphia, PA). Established in 1897 from funds donated by the Gratz family, this college was intended to foster Jewish education in the Philadelphia vicinity. The library of the college contains a few Gratz papers.

Other Sources

Philipson, David. "Barnard Gratz." In the *Dictionary of American Biography*, edited by Allen Johnson and Dumas Malone. New York: Scribner's, 1931. Philipson's account of Barnard Gratz is terse and accurate, and emphasizes the business acumen and leadership qualities of Michael Gratz.

R. William Weisberger
Butler County Community College

THOMAS WENTWORTH HIGGINSON
1823-1911

Chronology

Born Thomas Wentworth Storrow Higginson on December 22, 1823, in Cambridge, Massachusetts to Stephen Higginson and Louisa Storrow Higginson; *1837* enters Harvard; *1841* graduates second in his class; *1846-1847* attends Harvard Divinity School; *1847* marries Mary Elizabeth Channing and becomes pastor of the Unitarian First Religious Society of Newburyport, Massachusetts; *1849* is requested to leave pulpit because of his abolitionist views and supports himself by writing and lecturing; *1850* makes an unsuccessful run for Congress as a Free-Soil Party candidate; *1852* serves as pastor of a "Free Church" in Worcester, Massachusetts, and remains there until 1861; *1854* called to Boston to help in the liberation of fugitive slave Anthony Burns; *1856* goes to Kansas to help free-soil settlers; publishes *A Ride Through Kansas*; *1858* becomes one of the "Secret Six," the group which financed John Brown's abortive raid on Harper's Ferry; *1862* begins a correspondence with Emily Dickinson in April; accepts the colonelcy of the first black regiment in the Union army, the First South Carolina Volunteers, in November; *May 1864* forced to leave the army because of illness brought on by a minor wound; settles with his wife in Newport, Rhode Island; *1870* publishes the biography, *Margaret Fuller Ossli*, and publishes *Army Life in a Black Regiment*, the memoir of his wartime experiences; *September 1877*, his wife, Mary Elizabeth Channing Higginson dies; *1878* returns to Cambridge and concentrates on writing and working for women's suffrage; *February 1879* marries Mary Potter Thacher; *1880-1881* serves in Massachusetts state legislature; *1888* runs for Congress on the Democratic ticket and loses; *1890* co-edits and publishes the poems of Emily Dickinson; *1890-1911* publishes countless magazine articles and books; *1896* publishes an autobiography, *Cheerful Yesterdays; 1911* dies peacefully of old age on May 9, and his ashes are buried in the Cambridge Cemetery.

Activities of Historical Significance

Thomas Wentworth Higginson was one of those peculiar, even eccentric, characters common to nineteenth-century New England. He did a little bit of everything, beginning life as a minister, becoming renowned as a reformer, dabbling in politics, and also making a mark on the literary scene. Today he is probably best known for his leadership of the first black regiment in the Union army and the book he wrote about it, *Army Life in a Black Regiment*. Literary scholars are also aware of the role he played in subtly discouraging Emily Dickinson from publishing during her lifetime, nonetheless perceiving the power in her work. He edited her first volume of poetry, "regularizing" the punctuation and capitalization to the despair of subsequent generations. His own comments to Dickinson indicate that he saw in her a deep hunger and anger, and was at times profoundly disturbed by her work, a tribute to its strength. His literary works have not stood the test of time very well; they seem dated and overwritten to most contemporary audiences, but he was a popular and widely-read author in his day and a respected literary critic.

His reform impulses were always controversial, especially when it came to the abolitionist movement. He became identified as part of the radical fringe which advocated the use of violence to overthrow the institution of slavery, as seen in his participation in the raid to free Anthony Burns and his financial support for John Brown's raid on Harper's Ferry. Not as well-known is his work for women's suffrage; he was intimate with many of the leading figures of the movement, as demonstrated by his biography of Margaret Fuller, still used by Fuller scholars. He was never able to transmute his ideas to political action; his runs for Congress were unsuccessful, and his brief term in the Massachusetts legislature unremarkable. Higginson's life and career are of exceptional interest for the way in which they touched on so many important issues in nineteenth-century American life: religion, abolitionism, women's suffrage, temperance, literature, and the Civil War. He is, in many ways, a paradigm of the radical and intellectual experience in America during his time.

Overview of Biographical Sources

The biographies of Higginson are as varied as the man himself, reflecting the confusion many scholars feel when trying to categorize the man. It is difficult for biographers to understand his polymath interests and achievements in a time so different from their own. There are two interesting full-length studies by historians and a couple of other works, all with merit. G. Tilden Edelstein, *Strange Enthusiasm: A Life of Thomas Wentworth Higginson* (1970), concentrates on facets of his varied careers. Howard N. Meyer, *Colonel of the Black Regiment: The Life of Thomas Wentworth Higginson* (1967), focuses on Higginson's abolitionism and military career. James W. Tuttleton, *Thomas Wentworth Higginson* (1978), centers on Higginson's merits as an author and critic. An uninspired, yet complete, study of Higginson's life is Anna Mary Wells, *Dear Preceptor: The Life and Times of Thomas Wentworth Higginson* (1963).

Evaluation of Principal Biographical Sources

Edelstein, Tilden G. *Strange Enthusiasm: A Life of Thomas Wentworth Higginson.* New York: Atheneum, 1970. (A, G) This informative study of Higginson concentrates as much on his literary career as on his reform and military activities.

Meyer, Howard N. *Colonel of the Black Regiment: The Life of Thomas Wentworth Higginson.* New York: Norton, 1967. (A, G) This fine work, appearing at the same time as Edelstein's, focuses on Higginson's abolitionism and military career. It reflects the interest on the subject which had grown with the civil rights movement.

Tuttleton, James W. *Thomas Wentworth Higginson.* Boston: Twayne, 1978. (A, G) This volume, one in a series of short studies of American authors, is a fine introduction to Higginson's life and works.

Wells, Anna Mary. *Dear Preceptor: The Life and Times of Thomas Wentworth Higginson.* New York: Houghton Mifflin, 1963. (A, G) This is a full and adequate, if unexciting, account of Higginson's life.

Overview and Evaluation of Primary Sources

Higginson's papers are scattered throughout repositories in the United States: the largest group is at the Houghton Library at Harvard University, with other important collections at the Huntington Library, Kansas State Historical Society in Topeka, the Boston Public Library, Duke University, and the American Academy of Arts and Letters Library. Mary Thacher Higginson, Higginson's second wife, edited a selection of his papers which were published as *Letters and Journals of Thomas Wentworth Higginson, 1846-1906* (Boston: Houghton Mifflin, 1921; A, G). This volume is a representative selection of his works and is sufficient for the average researcher; it is a good introduction and point of departure for the scholar. Higginson's correspondence and journals reflect his sometimes iconoclastic views and idiosyncratic style. She also wrote the memoir, *Thomas Wentworth Higginson; The Story of His Life* (1914. Reprint. Port Washington, NY: Kennikat Press, 1971; A, G), which contains interesting anecdotes and information.

Most of Higginson's published works, consisting largely of collections of his essays, reviews, and occasional pieces for magazines and other periodicals, are dated. While they are available in many libraries, the most important works by far are his autobiography, *Cheerful Yesterdays* (1899. Reprint. New York: Arno Press, 1968; A, G), and his war reminiscences, *Army Life in a Black Regiment* (Boston:

Fields, Osgood, 1870; **A, G**), which records both his struggle to come to terms with his nascent prejudice and his affection for the men under his command. The latter is still widely used in college courses for black and military history, and is available in a reasonably-priced paperback reprint. Of passing interest is *Contemporaries* (Boston: Houghton, Miffin, 1899; **A, G**) sketches of contemporary men and women of letters and historical figures such as Garrison, and *Black Rebellion: A Selection from Travellers and Outlaws* (Boston: Lee and Shepherd Publishers, 1889; **A, G**), a collection of essays on various aspects of black resistance to slavery. He also wrote critical studies of Henry Wadsworth Longfellow and John Greenleaf Whittier and edited many collections of American poetry.

Other Sources

Cornish, Dudley Taylor. *The Sable Arm: Negro Troops in the Union Army, 1861-1865*. New York: Longmans Green, 1956. Cornish's pioneering study has much information on Higginson, his troops, and the use of black troops in general.

Glatthaar, Joseph T. *Forged in Battle: The Civil War Alliance of Black Soldiers and White Officers*. New York: The Free Press, 1990. Glatthaar's new study is also pertinent to Higginson's military career and his role in black military history.

Rossbach, Jeffrey. *Ambivalent Conspirators: John Brown, the Secret Six, and a Theory of Slave Violence*. Philadelphia: University of Pennsylvania Press, 1982. Based on a dissertation, this monograph provides a compelling exploration of the origins of John Brown's raid and concludes that Higginson was the only one of the Secret Six to hold on to the strength of his convictions in advocating the use of violence to overthrow slavery.

Jean V. Berlin
The Correspondence of William T. Sherman
Arizona State University

JIMMY HOFFA
1913-1975

Chronology

Born James Riddle Hoffa on February 14, 1913, in Brazil, Indiana, the son of John Cleveland, a coal miner, and Viola Riddle Hoffa; *1913-1921* raised in Brazil, attends school, the Christian Church of Brazil, and Sunday school; *1920* father dies; assists in household support by delivering laundry his mother takes in; *1922* moves with family to Clinton, Indiana; *1924* moves to working-class west side of Detroit; attends Neinas Intermediate School and works as a delivery boy after school; *1927* quits school at fourteen after completing the ninth grade; becomes full-time stockboy for Frank and Cedar's Department Store; *1930* becomes a freight handler at a grocery warehouse; *1931* organizes the American Federation of Labor Federal Labor Union Local 19341; *1932* becomes a full-time organizer for the International Brotherhood of Teamsters, Chauffeurs, Warehousemen and Helpers of America (IBT) Joint Council 43; *1934* takes membership of Federal Local 19341 into IBT Local 299; *1936* marries Josephine Poszywak; *1937* elected president of IBT Local 299; organizes Central States Driver Council; *1940-1941* chairman, then vice-president of the Central States Drivers Council; *1942* president of the Michigan Conference of Teamsters; *1943* examiner of Teamster books; *1946* president of Teamsters Joint Council 43; *1952* elected an IBT vice-president; *1953* elected president of the Central Conference of Teamsters; *1957* elected international president of the IBT; testifies before the McClellan Government Operations Subcommittee; AFL-CIO expels IBT upon the McClellan Committee's revelations of IBT's alleged organized crime connections; tried for and acquitted of attempting to bribe a Senate Committee investigator; *1964* signs first nationwide trucking contract; increases IBT membership to 2.2 million; convicted of jury tampering, fraud, and conspiracy in the disposition of union benefit funds; *1967* all appeals exhausted, begins thirteen-year prison sentence; *1969* authors *The Trials of Jimmy Hoffa*; *1971* retires IBT positions, awarded $1.7 million by IBT; after spending nearly five years in prison President Richard M. Nixon commutes his sentence; *1972* released from prison; *1975* publishes *Hoffa: The Real Story*; disappears in Detroit, Michigan; *1982* officially declared dead.

Activities of Historical Significance

Possessed of a vibrant, charismatic personality and an instinctive understanding of the use of power, Jimmy Hoffa built the International Brotherhood of Teamsters

(IBT) into a large, powerful organization. He obtained better working conditions, pay, and benefits for hundreds of thousands of workers, in the process bringing nationwide order to the trucking industry. Alleged organized-crime connections and irregularities in the use of the huge amounts of funds collected by the IBT from its members made Hoffa the controversial target of a number of investigations and prosecutions, headed most notably by Attorney General (and later Senator) Robert F. Kennedy. Hoffa's years of hearings and trials became a lightning rod for a continuous and often heated public debate on worker-management relations, the use and misuse of power, the effect of unions on the economy, and the alleged role of organized crime in the U.S. labor movement.

Overview of Biographical Sources

Most biographies that appeared during Hoffa's life (and following his disappearance) sought either to condemn or absolve him. Robert F. Kennedy's *The Enemy Within* (1960), Clark R. Mollenhoff's *Tentacles of Power* (1965), and Walter Sheridan's *The Fall and Rise of Jimmy Hoffa* (1972) were written by officials or reporters involved in government prosecutions of the Teamsters. As with most works composed just after the heat of battle, these books provide a detailed narrative of contemporary events. They retain a sense of immediacy, especially when they describe Hoffa's life and personality, about which the authors often exhibit a certain degree of awe.

Ralph and Estelle James's more academically inclined *Hoffa and the Teamsters: A Study of Power* (1965) examines the process, the substance, and the spirit of the power that go into the creation and operation of a powerful organization. Based on extensive interviews with Hoffa.

Lester Velie's *Desperate Bargain* (1977), an analytical narrative, and Dan Moldea's *The Hoffa Wars* (1979) place Hoffa in the context of union and U.S. politics. They weigh the conflicting evidence and conclude that Hoffa's disappearance was tied in with his alleged political deals with the White House. *Desperate Bargain* does not include some of the material covered by Sheridan, although it would take a massive tome to cover all of the evidence from Hoffa's many trials. *The Hoffa Wars* looks at Hoffa from the view of his greatest source of support, the trucker. In these two books, which appeared just after the administration of Richard M. Nixon, the researcher may recognize a contemporary concern with that controversial presidency.

Steven Brill's *The Teamsters* (1978) and Joseph Franco's *Hoffa's Man* (1987) are firsthand accounts by men close to or affected by Hoffa's career. A law columnist and reporter, Brill's work consists of chapter biographies of a range of people involved with the IBT, from Hoffa to truckers to criminals. After many studies of power based on trial documentation, *The Teamsters* serves to remind the researcher that corruption and courtroom exploits of high officials, whether union, law enforcement, or criminal, ultimately touched the lives of working people on the bottom of the ladder of power. In *Hoffa's Man,* longtime Hoffa aide Franco recounts his observations of his boss. Franco's colorful first-person narrative rips away the genteel courtroom veneer to expose Hoffa's part in the rough power politics that accompanied his career.

Arthur A. Sloane's *Hoffa* (1991) weaves together evidence, personality, and the forces surrounding the Teamsters as he builds on previous biographies, legal records, secondary sources and interviews. Sloane, who wrote his doctoral dissertation on Hoffa, diligently weighs his strengths and weaknesses to present a balanced portrait of a complex man.

In all, the body of Hoffa biography approaches its subject from a variety of angles and furnishes the researcher with an enormous amount of data and opinion. Biographers have just begun to bridge the gap between contemporary commentary and analytical perspective, a process that through the passage of time should bring an ever-deepening understanding of Hoffa.

Evaluation of Principal Biographical Sources

Brill, Steven. *The Teamsters.* New York: Simon and Schuster, 1978. (G) Gives a perspective on the IBT through chapter-length biographies that range from historical figures to current truck drivers. Focuses on organized crime theory of Hoffa's disappearance.

Franco, Joseph, with Richard Hamner. *Hoffa's Man: The Rise and Fall of Jimmy Hoffa as Witnessed by his Strongest Arm.* New York: Prentice-Hall, 1987. (G) A colorful, detailed first-person memoir of a union official close to Hoffa.

James, Ralph, and Estelle James. *Hoffa and the Teamsters: A Study of Power.* New York: Van Nostrand, 1965. (A, G) A painstakingly detailed, topical analysis of the Teamsters, Hoffa, and the nature of power in the labor movement from a sociological perspective. This is one of the more dispassionate examinations of Hoffa and the Teamsters, although it exhibits, as do other works, an awe of Hoffa the man.

Kennedy, Robert F. *The Enemy Within.* New York: Harper, 1960. (G) Written by Hoffa's chief antagonist, this is a firsthand narrative of Kennedy's pursuit of

Hoffa, the Teamsters, and the alleged organized crime connections. A detailed, dramatic, crusading narrative concluding with an election-year political manifesto on the philosophies of vice and justice.

Moldea, Dan. *The Hoffa Wars.* New York: Ace, 1979. (G) Distinguished from other Hoffa works by its view from the trucker's perspective and the union's dissident movement of the 1970s.

Mollenhoff, Clark R. *Tentacles of Power: The Story of Jimmy Hoffa.* New York: World Publishing, 1965. (G) A first-person narrative of the efforts of the author, an investigative reporter, to document corruption in the Teamsters.

Sheridan, Walter. *The Fall and Rise of Jimmy Hoffa.* New York: Saturday Review Press, 1972. (G) A highly detailed account of Hoffa's career and the government's prosecutions, written from firsthand experience and court records by Senator Robert F. Kennedy's chief lieutenant in charge of the Senate Select Committee's investigation into the Teamsters in the late 1950s. Somewhat crusading and polemical, but written in a dramatic, lively style.

Sloane, Arthur. *Hoffa.* Cambridge, MA: MIT Press, 1991. (A, G) Sloane, a professor of industrial relations, has produced the most meticulously researched major study of Hoffa. This is the most balanced, scholarly treatment, fitting Hoffa into the context of his times, the labor movement, and law-enforcement historiography. Because Sloane's is the first of the post-Teamsters-crime investigation era studies since the mid-1970s, it benefits from time, especially in the assessment of the disappearance theories. Sloane's treatment captures Hoffa's personal side, as well as his building of the IBT and tangles with various foes. Complete with photographs, this is the first place to begin any in-depth study of Hoffa, of Teamster practices, and of government intervention into organized crime.

Velie, Lester. *Desperate Bargain: Why Jimmy Hoffa Had to Die.* New York: Reader's Digest Press, 1977. (G) An episodic, at times breathless sketch of Hoffa's life and career that considers conflicting evidence and gives Hoffa a fair hearing. Reflects contemporary controversies concerning the presidential administration of Richard M. Nixon.

Overview and Evaluation of Primary Sources

Most documentation concerning Hoffa rests in voluminous congressional hearings and reports, court proceedings, and IBT files. These have been used extensively by Hoffa's biographers. Reports on congressional hearings are found in the records of the Eighty-Third (1953-1955), Eighty-Fourth (1955-1957), and Eighty-Fifth (1957-1959) Congresses. Records of the McClellan Committees, including fifty-eight volumes of testimony and seven reports, stretch from the Eighty-Fifth through the Eighty-Seventh (1961-1963) Congresses. These are available on microfilm in the Jefferson Building of the Library of Congress. A bound set is shelved in the Adams Building. The Congressional Information Services Index serves as a guide, although the researcher's best route is to call the reference desk for Congressional records for information on which volumes or reels of film to view and their availability.

Court records are located at the Federal Records Center in each of the court districts. Researchers must call the office of the clerk of the court for the case, box, location, and accession numbers. (Most of the books listed above contain lists of cases by number). The clerk's office will then assess the request and make an appointment with the Federal Records Center to have the records readied for viewing. This should be arranged well in advance of the needed date to ensure availability.

Courts most involved with Hoffa include United States Courts for the District of Columbia, served by the Federal Records Center (4205 Suitland Rd., Suitland, MD 20749); the Southern District of New York, served by the Federal Archives and Records Center (Building 22, Military Ocean Terminal, Bayonne, NJ 07002-5388); the Middle District of Tennessee, served by the Federal Archives and Records Center (1557 Saint Joseph Avenue, East Point, GA 30344); and the Northern District of Illinois, Eastern Division, served by the Federal Archives and Records Center (7358 South Pulaski, Chicago, IL 60629).

Records of the International Brotherhood of Teamsters from 1904 to 1955 are at the Wisconsin State Historical Society (816 State Street, Madison, WI 53706). These include eighty-two linear feet of correspondence, reports, and papers of IBT officials and staff, affiliated organizations and bodies, local conferences, and unions and councils. There is an eighty-four-page finding aid. Researchers must obtain written permission from the general president and general secretary treasurer of the IBT at IBT headquarters (25 Louisiana Ave., N.W., Washington, DC 20001) in order to use the records. IBT records from 1955 to the present are in Washington. Access to these also is by written permission of the IBT. Other official records include various federal, state, and local law enforcement agencies. Coverage of contemporary events in the IBT's magazine, entitled *The International Teamster*, assesses their meaning for the union member.

Hoffa's memoirs, *The Trials of Jimmy Hoffa* (as told to Donald I. Rogers) (Chicago: Henry Regnery, 1970; **G**), and *Hoffa: The Real Story* (as told to Oscar

Fraley) (New York: Stein and Day, 1975; G) present a colorful view of his life, the Teamsters, organized crime connections, and federal investigations into the Teamsters. Newspapers and magazines, particularly from the years of hearings and trials, contain voluminous interviews with Hoffa.

Fiction and Adaptations

F.I.S.T. (1978), a motion picture starring Sylvester Stallone, Rod Steiger, and Peter Boyle, somewhat parallels Hoffa's life in its dramatic depiction of a worker's rise from the loading docks to power and prominence in the union, his ethical and legal compromises, and his eventual fate.

Museums, Historical Landmarks, Societies

Wetlands (northeastern New Jersey, between the city of Newark and Newark Bay). Formerly used as a sanitary landfill, this stretch of wetlands has been reputed by some as Hoffa's burial ground. The area is now under development.

Other Sources

ABC News Close-Up. "Hoffa." Segment on Hoffa aired on November 30, 1974.

Friedman, Allen, and Ted Schwarz. *Power and Greed: Inside the Teamsters Epic of Corruption.* New York: Franklin Watts, 1989. The memoir of Teamster vice-president Friedman covers the scope of Teamster history in the twentieth century. Valuable for its view of Hoffa from both the perspective of time and distance. A detailed, clearly written narrative that ties up the loose ends left by most of the works dating to the trial years.

Hendrickson, Paul. "The Fighting Spirit of Jimmy Hoffa's Kids." *Washington Post* (June 17, 1991): C1, C2. Hoffa's children, Barbara Crancer, a judge, James. P. Hoffa, Jr., and foster brother Chuckie O'Brien discuss their efforts to gain access to Hoffa files held by the FBI and other government records that might clarify Hoffa's disappearance. They also reveal family feelings about his betrayal as a father and their determination to clear his name.

Steven Agoratus

OLIVER O. HOWARD
1830-1909

Chronology

Born Oliver Otis Howard on November 8, 1830, in Leeds, Maine, the son of farmer Rowland Bailey Howard and Eliza Otis Howard; *1850* graduates from Bowdoin College and enters West Point; *1854* graduates from West Point and is commissioned a second lieutenant; *1855* on February 14 marries Elizabeth Ann Waite; *1857-1861* teaches mathematics at West Point; *1861* named colonel, Third Maine Infantry; leads a brigade at Bull Run; promoted to brigadier general; *1862* is seriously wounded at the Battle of Seven Pines on June 1, losing his right arm; participates in battles of Antietam and Fredericksburg; promoted to major general; *1863* leads XI Corps, Army of the Potomac, at Chancellorsville, Gettysburg, and Chattanooga; *1864* commands IV Corps, Army of the Cumberland, at the outset of the Atlanta campaign; is wounded at Pickett's Mill on May 27; elevated to command of the Army of the Tennessee in July; *1865* participates in Sherman's advance across the Carolinas; in May is named to head the Bureau of Refugees, Freedmen, and Abandoned Lands; *1869* named first president of Howard University, Washington, D.C.; *1872* serves as peace commissioner to the Apaches; *1874* acquitted by a court of inquiry investigating charges of corruption against the Freedmen's Bureau; *1877* campaigns against Nez Percé; *1878* campaigns against Bannock and Paiute tribes; *1880-1882* serves as superintendent of West Point; *1894* retires from army; *1896* helps found Lincoln Memorial University, becoming managing director in 1898; *1909* dies October 26, in Burlington, Vermont, and is buried in Lake View Cemetery.

Activities of Historical Significance

Oliver Howard, labeled "the Christian Soldier" by contemporaries, was certainly tried by his experiences in the Civil War and Reconstruction. His service with the Army of the Potomac was marked by the poor combat performance of his XI Corps, which broke at Chancellorsville and was driven from the field during the first day of Gettysburg. Characterized as the "German corps" because of the large number of German immigrants in its ranks, Howard's unit never did recover from these defeats until it was transferred to Chattanooga in the fall of 1863. Howard's generalship under William T. Sherman in 1864 and 1865 was solid if unspectacular, as he participated in the Atlanta campaign, the March to the Sea, and the advance through the Carolinas, rising to the command of the Army of the Tennes-see—Ulysses S. Grant's old command.

But it would be peace, not war, which proved Howard's most severe test. In 1865 he was appointed head of the Bureau for Refugees, Freedmen, and Aban-doned Lands—usually called the Freedmen's Bureau—to assist blacks in the transition from slavery to freedom. Over the next several years Howard struggled to protect blacks from white violence and intimidation, provide relief to the poor and destitute, and defend the bureau from President Andrew Johnson, who sought to cripple it whenever possible. Howard's performance has received mixed reviews from historians, who acknowledge his good intentions while questioning some of his policies.

In some respects, it is a disservice to Howard that he is best remembered today for his service as head of the Freedmen's Bureau. Overlooked is his service on the frontier, especially in the Nez Percé conflict, and his involvement in higher educa-tion. He helped establish Howard University in 1869 and Lincoln Memorial University in 1896, playing major roles in the administration of both institutions in their early years.

Overview of Biographical Sources

Despite Howard's prominence in the Civil War and Reconstruction, biographers have not flocked to study him, and a recent survey of important American military commanders on the frontier omitted him altogether. John A. Carpenter's study, *Sword and Olive Branch: Oliver Otis Howard* (1964), still stands alone as the only complete scholarly biography of Howard. Carpenter views his subject positively, and at times seems a little too eager to justify Howard's behavior. On the whole, however, it is a successful biography within its limits. William S. McFeely, *Yankee Stepfather: General O. O. Howard and the Freedmen* (1968), studies Howard's service as head of the Freedmen's Bureau and suffers from exactly the opposite problem: a tendency to be over-critical and excessively harsh. It is marred by presentism, measuring Howard's actions according to twentieth-century stan-dards, and an unrealistic notion of what the bureau could achieve. McFeely dis-counts the obstructionist behavior of Andrew Johnson, although the president severely curtailed Howard's freedom of action. However, some of McFeely's criticisms ring true, especially those outlining the limits of Howard's vision for the freedmen. Oddly enough, in light of Howard's key role in determining federal policy toward the freedmen after the Civil War, there exists no complete study of his management of the Freedmen's Bureau.

Evaluation of Principal Biographical Sources

Carpenter, John A. *Sword and Olive Branch: Oliver Otis Howard*. Pittsburgh: University of Pittsburgh Press, 1964. (**A, G**) A largely sympathetic and favorable portrait of Howard; the standard modern biography.

McFeely, William S. *Yankee Stepfather: General O. O Howard and the Freedmen*. New Haven: Yale University Press, 1968. (**A, G**) Severely although not always unjustly critical of Howard's tenure as head of the Freedmen's Bureau.

Overview and Evaluation of Primary Sources

The major collection of Howard's papers is at the Bowdoin College Library. Other collections are housed at Howard University and Lincoln Memorial University. Essential to any study of Howard's tenure as head of the Freedmen's Bureau is Record Group 105 at the National Archives; other sections of the archives include additional Howard material. Howard told his own story in the *Autobiography of Oliver Otis Howard*, 2 vols. (New York: Baker and Tailor, 1907; **A, G**). Other Howard writings include *Nez Percé Joseph* (New York: DaCapo, 1972 [1881]; **A, G**); *General Taylor* (New York: D. Appleton, 1892; **G**), a biography of Zachary Taylor; *My Life and Experiences Among Our Hostile Indians* (New York: DaCapo, 1972 [1907]; **A, G**), and *Famous Indian Chiefs I Have Known* (Lincoln: University of Nebraska Press, 1989 [1908]; **A, G**). A good bibliography of Howard's writings is in Carpenter's biography.

Museums, Historical Landmarks, Societies

Fredericksburg and Spotsylavania National Military Park (Fredericksburg, VA). Within the park's boundaries are the battlefields of Fredericksburg and Chancellorsville. The path of Jackson's flanking march and the position of XI Corps on May 2 are clearly marked.

Gettysburg National Military Park (Gettysburg, PA). A statue of Howard is located at the east slope of Cemetery Hill, where he rallied the retreating Army of the Potomac on July 1. The ground defended by the XI Corps is clearly marked.

Howard University (Washington, DC). Named after its first president, the university has some of Howard's papers.

Lincoln Memorial University (Harrogate, TN). More devoted to the study and commemoration of Abraham Lincoln, the university has a library well-stocked with books on the sixteenth president and his times. Some Howard items are also on display.

Other Sources

Bentley, George R. *A History of the Freedmen's Bureau.* Philadelphia: University of Pennsylvania Press, 1955. A fairly comprehensive study of the Bureau's operations, although seriously dated.

Bremner, Robert H. *The Public Good: Philanthropy & Welfare in the Civil War Era.* New York: Knopf, 1980. A chapter on the Freedmen's Bureau discusses its links to other efforts to provide relief and assistance during the war.

Cox, LaWanda, and John Cox. "General O. O. Howard and the 'Misrepresented Bureau.' " *Journal of Southern History* 19 (November 1953): 427-456. One of the first efforts to rehabilitate Howard's reputation as a protector of black rights.

Nieman, Donald G. *To Set the Law in Motion: The Freedman's Bureau and the Legal Rights of Blacks, 1865-1868.* Millwood, NY: KTO Press, 1979. Clearly sets forth the obstacles Howard faced as commissioner of the Freemen's Bureau; a useful corrective to McFeely's biography.

Peirce, Paul S. *The Freedmen's Bureau.* 1904. Reprint. New York: Haskell House, 1971. An early study of the bureau's operations, arguing that it was used to advance the Republican party in the South—a view since discredited.

Brooks Donohue Simpson
Arizona State University

JULIA WARD HOWE
1819-1910

Chronology

Born Julia Ward on May 27, 1819, in New York City, to Samuel Ward, Jr., a well-to-do banker, and Julia Rush Cutler Ward; *1824* mother dies; *1839* father dies; *1841* meets future husband Samuel Gridley Howe, a reformer and teacher of the blind; *1843* marries Howe; *1844-1850* gives birth to four children; *1850* separates from her husband for a year because of marital friction; lives in Rome with two of her children; *1854* gives birth to her fifth child; *1854* publishes her first book, *Passion-Flowers*, a collection of poems; *1857* publishes *Words for the Hour*, a collection of poems; *1857* her play, *Leonora: or the World's Own*, is produced at the Lyceum Theatre in New York; *1859* gives birth to her sixth child; *1860* publishes a travel book, *A Trip to Cuba*; *1862* son Samuel dies of diphtheria; publishes the "Battle Hymn of the Republic" in the February issue of the *Atlantic Monthly*; *1868* co-founds the New England Woman Suffrage Association; *1868-1877* presides over the New England Woman Suffrage Association; *1870* helps found *Woman's Journal*; *1870-1872* tries unsuccessfully to organize an international women's peace movement; *1870-1878* presides over the Massachusetts Woman Suffrage Association; *1871* presides over the New England Women's Club; *1873* helps found the Association for the Advancement of Women; *1876* husband dies January 9; *1881* becomes president of the Association for the Advancement of Women; *1883* publishes biography, *Margaret Fuller*; *1891* helps found the American Friends of Russian Freedom; *1891-1893* again presides over the Massachusetts Woman Suffrage Association; *1893-1898* is director of the General Federation of Women's Clubs; *1898-1910* again presides over the New England Woman Suffrage Association; *1908* becomes the first woman elected to the American Academy of Arts and Letters; *1910* dies of pneumonia on October 17 in Newport, Rhode Island.

Activities of Historical Significance

Julia Ward Howe was a genteel lady who affected the manners of the English aristocracy. This combined with her marriage to one of her time's most renowned philanthropists, Samuel Gridley Howe, should have placed her among the social elite of Boston and New York. Yet, while she lived in Boston, she was an outcast. She had a sharp, pungent wit that she often used on people before she thought about what she was saying. This alienated members of high-society who expected a woman of her class to be quiet and deferential to others.

Her marriage was also less than idyllic. Her husband was abusive and held strict views about a woman's place. He expected his wife to stay at home and mind the children and otherwise not involve herself in the outside world. This narrow role of dutiful wife was far too restricting for Howe, however, and she and her husband bickered bitterly over her conduct. She wrote and published both poetry and articles about the major issues of the day. This seems to have infuriated her husband, who resented sharing the limelight with his wife.

Howe's writings about social issues eventually made her a well-known figure in the eastern United States, but it was one of her poems that made her a nationally known and admired figure. The February 1862 issue of the *Atlantic Monthly* included her poem "Battle Hymn of the Republic." Its simple, straightforward sentiments captured the imaginations of readers. It was soon set to music and sung at political and social gatherings throughout America. It is said that Abraham Lincoln wept when he first heard it; families of a nation torn apart by the Civil War took comfort in its assurances of the justness of their cause; and soldiers sang it as they marched.

Howe used her fame to help promote her favorite cause: that of civil rights for women. After the Civil War, she devoted her life to advocating women's right to higher education and to promoting women's suffrage. When America's leading feminists learned of Howe's devotion to women's rights, they were delighted, because her popularity with average Americans could bring many new supporters to their cause. It turned out that Howe was an able leader. When given the presidency of the newly formed New England Woman Suffrage Association, she traveled widely in America campaigning for women's right to vote and helping to organize sister associations throughout the country. Although Howe is best remembered for the "Battle Hymn of the Republic," in her own day she was a powerful influence on the shape and direction of women's roles in politics and society.

Overview of Biographical Sources

Howe's turbulent life receives its best coverage in Deborah Pickman Clifford's *Mine Eyes Have Seen the Glory* (1979). This book provides valuable details about Howe's personal life and her struggles to assert herself in a social environment that was more concerned with how fashionable a woman was than with the merits of her mind. Furthermore, Clifford offers a worthwhile account of Howe's importance to the social causes of her day. As the title suggests, the publication of the "Battle Hymn of the Republic" played a pivotal role in Howe's life; biographers have generally portrayed the event as that which enabled Howe to assume a public leadership role that previously had been denied to her. Most biographers gloss over her troubles with her husband, although his resistance to her intellectual and social pursuits was one of her greatest obstacles.

Evaluation of Principal Biographical Sources

Clifford, Deborah Pickman. *Mine Eyes Have Seen the Glory: A Biography of Julia Ward Howe.* Boston: Little, Brown, 1979. (A, G) Focuses on Howe's private life, but nevertheless gives a good account of her public activities. Clifford portrays Howe as an insecure person who overcame the tragic deaths of close family members, as well as her husband's insistence that she abandon all activities outside the home, to become one of nineteenth-century America's most important women.

Hall, Florence Howe. *The Story of the Battle Hymn of the Republic.* 1916. Reprint. Freeport, NY: Books for Libraries Press, 1971. (G) This historical account relates how the poem "Battle Hymn of the Republic" came to be written. The author, Howe's daughter, sees its roots forming in the antislavery movement of the early 1800s. With the advent of the Civil War, Howe composed the poem to express her belief that the Union was on a crusade to eradicate a terrible evil, slavery. Hall traces the popularity of the poem after it was published, noting how Union troops took it up as their song, singing it to the tune of "John Brown's Body." Hall records notes written by her mother in which she explains that she was appalled when she heard the awful lyrics of "John Brown's Body" that were set to such beautiful music. A friend suggested that she could write better lyrics, and so she wrote the "Battle Hymn of the Republic" to be sung to the music she'd heard.

Richards, Laura E., Maud Howe Elliott, and Florence Howe Hall. *Julia Ward Howe: 1819-1910.* 2 vols. Boston: Houghton Mifflin, 1916. (G) This book, written by three of Howe's daughters, won the first Pulitzer Prize for biography in 1917. Although the biography is a flattering one, it contains valuable information about Howe's ancestry and family. The authors reveal no doubts about the place of their mother in history; they regard her as a great leader and a fine writer.

Richards, Laura E. *Two Noble Lives: Samuel Gridley Howe, Julia Ward Howe.* Boston: Dana Estes, 1911. (G) This is a loving account of the Howes, revealing only a few childish pranks to slightly darken their otherwise saintly lives.

Schriber, Mary Suzanne. "Julia Ward Howe and the Travel Book." *New England Quarterly* 62 (June 1989): 264-279. (**A, G**) Offers a survey from a feminist perspective of how women writers of nineteenth-century America broke into publishing travel books. Schriber covers Howe's *A Trip to Cuba* and *From the Oak to the Olive: Records of a Pleasant Journey,* detailing the obstacles Howe overcame and how she went about composing her travel books.

Tharp, Louise Hall. *Three Saints and a Sinner: Julia Ward Howe, Louisa, Annie and Sam Ward.* Boston: Little, Brown, 1956. (**G**) In this well-written book, Tharp gives an account of Howe's familial relationships. She treats Howe's marriage as "a curious and sad situation," asserting that many of Howe's social causes were picked up from her husband.

Overview and Evaluation of Primary Sources

There are four principal primary sources for information on Howe's life. The most valuable of these is Howe's *Reminiscences: 1819-1899* (Boston: Houghton, Mifflin, 1899; **A, G**). In this book, Howe tells of the restrictions put on her because she was a woman and explains how she tried, not always successfully, to overcome them. She downplays her troubles with her husband but does note his objections to women leading public lives. The book is admirable for how it reveals Howe's active mind; the liveliness of the autobiography is suggestive of why Howe was such a captivating figure in nineteenth-century America. Howe's two travel books offer views of two periods in her life. *A Trip to Cuba* (Boston: Ticknor and Fields, 1860; **G**) tells of her impressions of her journey there, and *From the Oak to the Olive: A Plain Record of a Pleasant Journey* (Boston: Lee and Shepard, 1868; **G**) tells of an 1867 trip to Europe. Another source is Florence Howe Hall, ed., *Julia Ward Howe and the Woman Suffrage Movement* (Boston: Dana Estes, 1913; **A, G**). Hall offers a brief history of Howe's participation in the women's suffrage movement, then presents a selection of Howe's writings on the rights of women. These writings are scholarly, and they provide details of Howe's view of the feminist movement and suggest that she saw herself as an interpreter of the aspirations of the women of her time.

The Howe Papers at Harvard University's Houghton Library contain her journals, many of her letters, and other manuscripts. Much of this collection is uncatalogued and is in need of a thorough study of its contents. The Julia Ward Howe Papers at Radcliffe's Schlesinger Library include letters and scrapbooks. The Library of Congress's Julia Ward Howe Papers contain some letters.

Other Sources

Boyer, Paul S. "Howe, Julia Ward." In *Notable American Women 1607-1950: A Biographical Dictionary*. Cambridge, MA: Belknap Press, 1971. A well-written summary of Howe's life and career.

Kirk H. Beetz
National University, Sacramento

ROBERT MAYNARD HUTCHINS
1899-1978

Chronology

Born Robert Maynard Hutchins on January 17, 1899, in Brooklyn, New York, the second of three sons of William James Hutchins, a Presbyterian pastor and college president, and Anna Laura Murch Hutchins; *1899-1915* grows up in Brooklyn and, after 1907, in Oberlin, Ohio, where his father takes a professorship; *1915-1919* studies at Oberlin College before joining the U.S. Army; sees action in the Ambulance Corps on the Italian front; wins the croce di guerra; *1919-1927* attends Yale University, earning his bachelor's degree in 1921; marries Maude Phelps McVeigh, a sculptor and author, with whom he has three daughters; after teaching English and history for a year at the Lake Placid School, becomes secretary to the Yale Corporation; earns his law degree and lectures at the Yale School of Law; *1927-1929* is professor of law and dean of the Yale School of Law; *1929-1951* serves as president of the University of Chicago, and chancellor after 1945, where he champions the introduction of a "great books" curriculum and is instrumental in bringing the atom bomb project to the university; becomes director of the *Encyclopedia Britannica,* a position he holds until 1974; *1948* divorces Maude and marries Vesta Orlick; *1951-1954* serves as associate director of the Ford Foundation, responsible for eighty-nine million dollars in educational grants; *1954-1977* serves as chief executive officer of the Fund for the Republic and of the Center for the Study of Democratic Institutions, becoming president of both after 1975, and attracting a variety of scholars to Santa Barbara, California, to discuss problems of public policy; *1977* dies on May 14 in Santa Barbara of kidney failure.

Activities of Historical Significance

Robert Maynard Hutchins was a tireless educational innovator, committed to the promotion of free and rigorous public discussion. Through a long and varied career he successfully created and maintained a national debate on higher education and defended the central role of nonconformity and protest in American society.

In his first major position, Hutchins made Yale a center of experimentation in legal education. Espousing legal realism, the notion that law is not an independent system of logical rules but a mode of government that must consider social facts and arrive at socially desirable outcomes, Hutchins introduced required economics, history, and philosophy courses in the law school and attracted reformist professors, most notably future Supreme Court Associate Justice William O. Douglas. In pursuit of academic excellence, Hutchins doubled the size of the faculty while reducing the size of the student body.

At Chicago, Hutchins took the offensive against academic specialization, vocationalism, and professionalism. He implemented the Chicago Plan, integrating the last two years of high school with the first two years of college in a general education continuum, introduced a curriculum based upon prolonged exposure to the great books of Western culture, and deemphasized athletics, social activities, and pre-professional training. During his tenure, the longest of a University of Chicago president, he displayed an impressive talent for fund-raising, and was instrumental in bringing Harold Urey, Enrico Fermi, and others to the university where they carried out the first controlled nuclear chain reaction.

At the Ford Foundation, Hutchins was attacked for aiding liberal causes and projects. When he became head of the Fund for the Republic, he set it on an agenda of opposition to right-wing intimidation and McCarthyism, financing studies of loyalty programs, blacklisting, and the nature of domestic communism. This led to the Center for the Study of Democratic Institutions' focus on the preservation of civil liberties by means of continuous discussion, the production of studies on the media, science, technology, and war, and to the publication of the highly successful *Center Magazine*.

Overview of Biographical Sources

There are two biographies about Hutchins, Harry S. Ashmore's *Unseasonable Truths: The Life of Robert Maynard Hutchins* (1989) and Frank L. Kelly's *Court of Reason: Robert Hutchins and the Fund for the Republic* (1981). Fortunately, his life and career are treated in several works on colleagues and the various institutions for which he worked.

Evaluation of Principal Biographical Sources

Ashmore, Harry S. *Unseasonable Truths: The Life of Robert Maynard Hutchins*. Boston: Little, Brown, 1989. (**A, G**) An experienced author who did lengthy and meticulous research in the voluminous materials available on Hutchins, Ashmore was also Hutchins's colleague at the Fund for the Republic, and as a result is able to give the quality of a personal memoir to his portrait. This biography realistically portrays the subject's personality while carefully assessing his life work.

Kelly, Frank L. *Court of Reason: Robert Hutchins and the Fund for the Republic*. New York: Free Press, 1981. (A, G) An officer of the Fund for the Republic for nineteen years, Kelly presents a public relations specialist's view of his subject. The book enthusiastically portrays Hutchins, but suffers from the author's eagerness to make his side of the story clear regarding their disagreements.

Overview and Evaluation of Primary Sources

Hutchins authored hundreds of articles and books, most of which originated as speeches for various occasion. His notions on the role of higher education in American life are best presented in *The Higher Learning in America* (New Haven: Yale University Press, 1936; A, G), *The Conflict of Education in a Democratic Society* (New York: Harper & Bros., 1953; A, G), and *The University of Utopia* (Chicago: University of Chicago Press, 1953; A, G). His advocacy of the great books curriculum is most usefully presented in *The Great Conversation* (Chicago: Encyclopedia Britannica, 1952; A, G) and *The Learning Society* (New York: Praeger, 1968; A, G).

Beyond Hutchins's published writings, there is a wealth of material available in archives. The University of Chicago Archives, located in the University of Chicago Library, contains Hutchins's personal Yale papers and files that he maintained after he left Chicago as well as papers pertaining to his years as president and chancellor at Chicago. The library's Special Collections has the privately printed memoirs of Carroll Mason Russell, the wife of a trustee, *The University of Chicago and Me, 1901-1962*. The university also holds papers of a number of people who served at Chicago with Hutchins. The Hutchins Library at Berea College in Kentucky has family correspondence, the Douglas Papers at the Library of Congress contain his correspondence with Supreme Court Justice William O. Douglas, and the Time-Life Archives in New York have his correspondence with Henry Luce. The Beinecke Rare Book and Manuscript Library at Yale contains his correspondence with Thornton Wilder and the Yale University Library and Law School Library have official materials relating to Hutchins's years at Yale. The Adlai Stevenson Papers at Firestone Library, Princeton University, contain Hutchins correspondence with Stevenson; the Fund for the Republic Archives are also at Princeton. Archives of the Ford Foundation, including oral history materials, and of the Center for the Study of Democratic Institutions are housed at the University of California at Santa Barbara.

Hutchins is mentioned in a number of autobiographies by those who knew or worked with him, including Mortimer J. Adler, *Philosopher at Large: An Intellectual Autobiography* (New York: Macmillan, 1977; A, G); William O. Douglas, *Go*

East Young Man: The Early Years (New York: Random House, 1974; **A, G**); John U. Nef, *The Search for Meaning: The Autobiography of a Nonconformist* (Washington, DC: Public Affairs Press, 1973; **A, G**); and T. V. Smith, *A Non-Existent Man: An Autobiography* (Austin: University of Texas Press, 1962; **A, G**).

Other Sources

Cohen, Arthur A. *Humanistic Education and Western Civilization.* New York: Holt, Rinehart, and Winston, 1965. Collection of essays by colleagues Mortimer Adler, Scott Buchanan, and William O. Douglas illuminates Hutchins's ideas.

Gideonse, Harry D. *The Higher Learning in a Democracy: A Reply to President Hutchins' Critique of the American University.* New York: Farrar and Rinehart, 1937. An economics professor at Chicago, Gideonse opposed Hutchins in campus discussions and articulated the sentiments of faculty opposed to the curricular reforms advocated by Hutchins.

Hyman, Sidney. *The Lives of William Benton.* Chicago: University of Chicago Press, 1969. Fund-raiser, University of Chicago vice-president, and owner of the *Encyclopedia Britannica,* Benton worked with Hutchins for many years.

Jones, Dorothy V. *Harold Swift and the Higher Learning.* Chicago: University of Chicago Library, 1985. Swift was chairman of the Board of Trustees of the University of Chicago and instrumental in hiring Hutchins.

Macdonald, Dwight. *The Ford Foundation: The Men and the Millions.* New York: Reynal, 1956. Macdonald disliked Hutchins and this biases his evaluation of the work of the Ford Foundation.

Reeves, Thomas C. *Freedom and the Foundation: The Fund for the Republic in the Era of McCarthyism.* New York: Knopf, 1969. An outsider's account, this is a useful corrective for some of Kelly's views of events.

"Robert M. Hutchins, Long a Leader in Education Change, Dies at 78." *New York Times* (May 16, 1977). A lengthy, accurate, and useful obituary.

Tannler, Albert M. *One in Spirit: A Retrospective View of the University of Chicago.* Chicago: University of Chicago Library, 1973. Covers Hutchins's Chicago years somewhat uncritically.

Ward, F. Champion, ed. *The Idea and Practice of General Education: An Account of the College of the University of Chicago.* Chicago: University of Chicago Press, 1950. The best description of the "Chicago Plan" in action.

Joseph M. McCarthy
Suffolk University

HELEN KELLER
1880-1968

Chronology

Born Helen Keller on June 27, 1880, in Tuscumbia, Alabama, to Arthur, a lawyer and newspaper editor, and Kate Keller; *1882* falls ill in February, losing both sight and hearing; *1889* her parents consult the Perkins School for the Blind to find out whether she can be educated; *1887* on March 3, Anne Mansfield Sullivan, a student at the Perkins Institute, arrives to become Helen Keller's teacher; on April 5, Keller makes the connection between Sullivan's finger-spelling and the objects the spelling describes; *1888* visits Perkins Institute for first time—in following visits learns to read Braille; *1890* begins to learn to talk; *1894-1896* attends the Wright-Humason School for the deaf; *1896* enters the Cambridge School for Young Ladies, a college preparatory school; *1903* the publication of *The Story of My Life* marks the beginning of Keller's efforts to make a living as a professional writer—her writing did not bring in enough money; *1904* graduates *cum laude* from Radcliffe College; *1905* Sullivan and John A. Macy marry, with John joining Keller's household; *1906* Keller is appointed to the Massachusetts Commission for the Blind; *1910-1913* trains speaking voice under Charles A. White of the New England Conservatory of Music; *1913* with the aid of an interpreter, Keller goes on the lecture circuit; *1914* makes national lecture tour; Polly Thompson becomes her secretary; *1915* becomes member of the first board of directors of the Permanent Blind Relief War Fund; *1918* appears in Hollywood dramatization of her life, *Deliverance*; *1920-1924* tours as a vaudeville act; *1923* becomes a public representative for the American Foundation for the Blind; *1931* wins a five thousand dollar prize from *Pictorial Review* for raising two million dollars for the American Foundation for the Blind; *1933* is elected to the National Institute of Arts and Letters; *1936* Anne Sullivan Macy, Keller's beloved "Teacher," dies on October 20; *1938* receives the Gold Key from the National Education Association; *1941* receives Scroll of Honor from the International Federation of Women's Clubs; *1946* fire destroys Keller's home, taking with it her notes, memorabilia, and the first manuscript of *Teacher: Anne Sullivan Macy*; *1951* receives Shotwell Memorial Award of the American Association of Workers for the Blind; *1952* is made chevalier of the French Legion of Honor; *1960* Polly Thompson dies; *1962* health begins to markedly decline and she largely withdraws from public life; *1964* receives Presidential Medal of Freedom; *1968* dies June 1 in Easton, Connecticut, after a series of strokes.

Activities of Historical Significance

Helen Keller was of great interest to psychologists, who wished to know how she experienced the world without being able to see or hear. One of these psychologists wrote that Keller had neither remarkable intellect nor exceptional talent. However, he wrote, her spirit and desire to live life to its fullest were extraordinary. It was apparently this aspect of her personality that enabled her to overcome her terrible handicaps. Throughout her long career as advocate for the rights of handicapped people, Keller was charismatic and attracted many to her cause.

Born without handicaps, Keller fell ill in 1882 with a disease that was never properly diagnosed; consequently she lost both her sight and hearing. Her parents tried to raise her normally, but they spoiled her. She became an uncontrollable, selfish child, lost in her own world. Eventually, her parents consulted eye and ear specialists, and on the recommendation of Alexander Graham Bell, they contacted the Perkins School for the Blind, then one of the world's most famous institutions for educating blind children. The Perkins school sent to them one of its students, Anne Mansfield Sullivan.

As a child, Sullivan herself had lost most of her sight to disease. Her mother died and her father abandoned his family, so she was institutionalized and neglected. During an investigation of her institution, Sullivan managed to convey to an investigator that she wanted to go to school. She was sent to the Perkins school, which specialized in educating handicapped people. She underwent an operation that returned much, but not all, of her eyesight, and in 1887, with only six years of education, was sent to the Kellers to teach their unruly child.

Sullivan's miserable childhood made her a zealot, determined that children should not be deprived of an education simply because of physical handicaps. Although Keller was unpleasant and even nasty to work with, Sullivan kept after her relentlessly, trying to get the little girl to make the connection between the finger signals she drummed into Keller's hand and the objects that these signals described. Finally, at a moment that has since become celebrated in film and theater, Keller made the connection.

People would later accuse Sullivan of putting ideas into Keller's head that were not Keller's own. They suggested that much of what Keller had to say was actually Sullivan's work—that Keller was too disconnected from physical reality to comprehend the sophisticated ideas that she was purported to express. Psychologists largely disagree with this view. Although some of them have concluded that Keller's descriptions of many of her experiences were more fantasy than reality, they tended to agree that she knew what she was saying and could fully grasp difficult abstract ideas. Thus, they believe that her advocacy of socialism and civil rights for handicapped people were born of her own studies and desires.

Keller's attending a college preparatory school and then Radcliffe was part of her effort to stand as much as she could on her own in the world. These schools were not specialized for the teaching of blind or deaf people; they were primarily attended by young women who lacked Keller's handicaps. Her charismatic personality worked its magic on her classmates, who honored her as one of their best compatriots. Her graduation from Radcliffe was one of her greatest triumphs.

After graduation, Keller faced the problem of earning a living. A proud person, she wished to make her way in the world without charity. She wanted to use her hard-won education to its best advantage, so she tried in vain to support herself as a professional writer. The reading public wanted books about the remarkable blind and deaf woman, but Keller wanted to discuss the leading political and social issues of the day. Her advocacy of socialism alienated much of her audience; her frank discussions of disease and handicaps repelled others. Desperate for money, she turned to lecturing. Sullivan had labored to teach Keller how to speak aloud, but Keller never managed to speak in a manner that was understandable to people who did not know her well. For her lectures, she relied on interpreters. As with her writing, her lectures did not supply enough money to support her, so she made one of the most controversial decisions of her life and turned to the stage. She and Sullivan performed a vaudeville act, re-enacting how she was taught. Many people were outraged, believing that Keller was degrading handicapped people by trivializing her own difficult life for theater audiences. Nonetheless, her act earned interim money until she got a job as a representative for the American Foundation for the Blind.

Some social historians credit Keller with the early success of the American Foundation for the Blind because her fame brought money, and political support to the organization. Although the organization was primarily concerned with blindness, Keller saw herself as an advocate for all handicapped people, and she campaigned for social barriers to be eliminated. A tireless campaigner, she tried to make her life an example of what any handicapped person could do if allowed to try. She wrote books, acted in movies, and spoke with an independence of mind, not shrinking from confrontation with those who disagreed with her. When she died in 1968, she was world famous; she left behind a powerful organization for serving the needs of blind people and the message that it is wrong to deny handicapped people the help they need to become fully functioning members of society.

Overview of Biographical Sources

Upon publication of *The Story of My Life,* Keller captured the imagination of the American people. Her classic story of overcoming seemingly insurmountable odds has always appealed to readers, but biographers who have written full-length accounts of Keller's life have approached their subject in different ways. Nella Braddy, *Anne Sullivan Macy: The Story Behind Helen Keller* (1933), is interested primarily in Keller's teacher, Anne Sullivan, whom Braddy sees as the more important story hidden behind Keller's public one. Van Wyck Brooks, *Helen Keller: Sketch for a Portrait* (1956), reveals Keller's life as exactly what it seems—a story of courage and accomplishment. For him, Keller's independent life is a triumph of the human spirit. Joseph Lash's *Helen and Teacher: The Story of Helen Keller and Anne Sullivan Macy* (1980), exhaustively investigates the details of Keller's life, trying to create a full, well-rounded picture of a human being, with flaws as well as merits.

Evaluation of Principal Biographical Sources

Braddy, Nella. *Anne Sullivan Macy: The Story Behind Helen Keller.* Garden City, NY: Doubleday, Doran, 1933. (A, G) Through her work with Helen Keller, Anne Sullivan Macy became a famous educator; her techniques for educating blind children were widely discussed, and in general she was treated as one of America's leading experts on teaching. Braddy portrays her as someone driven by deep psychological pain and fierce anger. In this biography, Macy comes across as an heroic figure; Keller, too, seems larger than life.

Brooks, Van Wyck. *Helen Keller: Sketch for a Portrait.* New York: E. P. Dutton, 1956. (A, G) This work was a best seller, going through three printings in its first year of publication. Brooks brings to his audience the wit and incisive psychological insight that have made all of his biographies popular reading. This passionate perspective is not a scholarly treatise; it is intended for general audiences and lacks footnotes and a bibliography. The real-life story of Helen Keller is reminiscent of a fairy tale, and Brooks treats it as such, portraying Keller as a little girl who was lost in a nightmarish world but who overcame all odds.

Lash, Joseph P. *Helen and Teacher: The Story of Helen Keller and Anne Sullivan Macy.* New York: Seymour Lawrence, 1980. (A, G) Part of the Radcliffe Biography Series, this is the most exhaustive study of Keller's life, which Lash sees as intertwined with that of Macy. Researchers are likely to be disappointed at the book's lack of scholarly apparatus. In any case, this is the most definitive biography of Keller to date. Researchers will value its wealth of detail about the activities of Keller and Macy; others will enjoy the clear prose and the emphasis on the humanity of two figures who are often portrayed as larger than life.

Evaluation of Biographies for Young People

Bigland, Eileen. *Helen Keller.* New York: Wronker, Philips, 1967. This volume, ideal for young adults, covers most of Keller's life.

Davidson, Margaret. *Helen Keller.* New York: Scholastic Book Services, 1969. A biography for early readers.

Hickok, Lorena A. *The Story of Helen Keller.* New York: Grosset and Dunlap, 1958. Suited to early readers, this is a notably well written account of Keller's life.

―――――. *The Touch of Magic: The Story of Helen Keller's Great Teacher, Anne Sullivan Macy.* New York: Dodd, Mead, 1961. This is an insightful account suited to junior high and high school readers.

Peare, Catherine Owens. *The Helen Keller Story.* New York: Crowell, 1959. This book is appropriate for junior high school readers.

Waite, Helen Elmira. *Valiant Companions: Helen Keller and Anne Sullivan Macy.* Philadelphia: Macrae Smith, 1959. This work provides accounts of the lives of both women and is well suited to junior high school readers.

Overview and Evaluation of Primary Sources

Keller wrote *The Story of My Life* (1903. Reprint. Garden City, NY: Doubleday, 1954; **G, Y**) while she was still in college. Long a favorite of young readers, this book describes in clear prose what it was like to grow up without being able to see or hear. It shows that whatever her handicaps, Keller still had a normal emotional life, full of the playfulness and frustration that are typical of childhood and youth. Of particular interest is her effort to explain to sighted and hearing people how she experiences reality. Although psychologists and others have made much out her descriptions of her internal world, this book is intended for general audiences and is a pleasure to read.

Her later book *Midstream: My Later Life* (New York: Crowell, 1929. Reprint. New York: Greenwood Press, 1968; **G**) is more complex. Keller provides reminiscences of her youth—meeting Mark Twain, for instance—and an account of the growth of her mind. Also included are accounts of the intellectual passions of her life, including her work on behalf of socialism and the American Foundation for the Blind. In *The World I Live In* (New York: Century, 1908; **G**) Keller explains how she experiences the world. She covers her senses, especially touch, but also describes what she suggests may be indescribable: how she sees and hears. She likens much of her life to a waking dream. In *Teacher: Anne Sullivan Macy: A Tribute by the Foster-Child of Her Mind* (Garden City, NY: Doubleday, 1956; **G, Y**), Keller tells of her experiences with Anne Sullivan Macy, whom she affectionately referred to as "Teacher." This account is largely told through personal anecdotes. Of Macy, she says, "She was never the 'schoolmarm' portrayed in some of the articles I have read. She was a lively young woman whose imagination was kindled by her accomplishments with little Helen to unique dreams of molding a deaf-blind creature to the full life of a useful, normal human being."

Keller's *My Religion* (London: Hodder and Stoughton, 1927; **A, G**) tells about her spiritual life. She was a follower of Emanuel Swedenborg's New Church doctrines. Swedenborg had taken upon himself the mission of explaining the spiritual reality behind the Bible. Keller herself had found the Bible baffling, and for her Swedenborg's explanations revealed the true meaning behind the Bible's "barbarous creeds." She was particularly troubled by the conflicting views in the Bible's portrayal of a vengeful God and a loving Jesus; through Swedenborg's views of a spiritual realm that was subtly connected with the material, Keller gained a belief in Jesus as a representative of the essentially loving nature of God.

Philip S. Foner, ed., *Helen Keller: Her Socialist Years* (New York: International, 1967; **A, G**) consists of essays that to some critics represent a dark side of Keller's life: her defense of Soviet communism and Lenin. Under the influence of H. G. Wells's *New Worlds for Old,* Keller formed the belief that socialism could lift children out of poverty and help all people lead lives of dignity. To Keller, poverty led to diseases that could cause blindness and worse in children, and she wanted no one to endure her own hardships if they could be avoided.

Fiction and Adaptations

William Gibson's play, *The Miracle Worker* (1957), received its greatest acclaim as a 1962 motion picture, directed by Arthur Penn. Anne Bancroft received an Academy Award as best actress for her role of Sullivan, and Patty Duke won best supporting actress for her portrayal of Keller. Penn was nominated for an Academy Award for best director, and Gibson was nominated for best screenplay adapted from another medium. The motion picture has become a classic, with emotionally charged scenes and brilliant performances. Gibson has commented, with a tone of annoyance, that people often refer to this work as being about Helen Keller, rather than about Sullivan.

Gibson comments in his "Author's Note" to *Monday after the Miracle* (1983) that he does not want this play to be seen as a sequel to *The Miracle Worker.* The events take place twenty years after *The Miracle Worker.* Sullivan is portrayed as bitter, regarding herself as a mere adjunct to her famous pupil. She meets her future husband John Macy and tries to build a new life for herself. This work has a more melancholy tone than *The Miracle Worker*, covering as it does lost dreams and missed opportunities.

Other Sources

Keeling, Kara K. "The Story of My Life." In *Beacham's Guide to Literature for Young Adults*, Vol. 3. edited by Kirk H. Beetz, et al. Washington, DC: Beacham Publishing, 1990. This article provides background on Keller's life and an analysis of Keller's *The Story of My Life*. It includes study aids and suggestions for further research.

Koestler, Frances A. "The Perfect Symbol." In *The Unseen Minority: A Social History of Blindness in the United States*. New York: David McKay, 1976. Keller is mentioned often in this book, and a chapter is devoted to her. Koestler examines Keller as a public figure who used her fame to further the needs of the blind. This volume illustrates Keller's significance in the history of the development of civil rights for handicapped people.

Kirk H. Beetz
National University, Sacramento

JAMES LONGSTREET
1821-1904

Chronology

Born James Longstreet on January 8, 1821, in Edgefield District, South Carolina, the son of James Longstreet and Mary Anna Dent Longstreet; *1833* father dies and family moves to Somerville, Alabama, from Augusta, Georgia; *1838* is admitted to West Point; *1842* graduates fifty-fourth in a class of sixty-two; breveted second lieutenant of Fourth Infantry with which he serves at Jefferson Barracks, Missouri; *1845* promoted to full rank of second lieutenant and assigned to Eighth Infantry at St. Augustine, Florida; *1845-1847* serves in Mexican-American War; is wounded at Chapultepec and breveted captain and then major; *1848* marries Maria Louise Garland, daughter of General John Garland; *1848-1858* serves at various western posts; *1858* promoted to full rank of major in Paymasters Corps; *1861* resigns from United States Army on June 1 and is appointed brigadier-general in the Confederate army on June 17; *1861* earns the rank of major-general for his skillful use of troops under Joseph E. Johnston at the Battle of First Manassas; *Spring 1862* serves with Johnston at Yorktown; commands the rearguard action at Williamsburg on May 5; criticized for his behavior at Seven Pines on May 31; *June 25-July 1, 1862* wins Lee's confidence with his conduct during the Seven Days Battle around Richmond; *August 18, 1862* sent to reinforce Stonewall Jackson near Orange County Courthouse; *August 30, 1862* joins in action at Battle of Second Manassas with great effect; *October 11, 1862* promoted to lieutenant-general after his role in the Battle of Antietam on Lee's recommendation; *December 13, 1862* engages in most of the defensive fighting at the Battle of Fredericksburg; *Late February 1863* fails to seize initiative in his first semi-independent command during the Suffolk Campaign; *July 1-4, 1863* plays controversial role in the Confederate defeat at the Battle of Gettysburg; *September 1863* performs well at the Battle of Chickamauga; *October 1863* is unable to break Thomas's defenses at Chattanooga and is very critical of Braxton Bragg; *November 1863* suffers defeat when he attempts to take Knoxville; *May 1864* rallies A. P. Hill's corps during the second day of the Battle of the Wilderness and is wounded; *November 1864* returns to duty; *April 9, 1865* surrenders his corps at Appomattox; *1865-1867* works for an insurance company and a cotton factory in New Orleans; *1869* nominated surveyor of the port of New Orleans by Ulysses S. Grant; *1875* moves to Gainesville, Georgia; *August-December 1877* "Gettysburg Series," attacking his behavior at the Battle of Gettysburg, appears in *Southern Historical Society*

Papers; *1880* appointed United States minister to Turkey; *1881* returns to Georgia as federal marshall; *1884* removed as marshall amid widespread rumors of corruption; *1889* wife dies; *1896* publishes his memoirs, *From Manassas to Appomattox*; *1897* appointed United States commissioner of railroads; marries Helen Dortch; *1904* dies January 2, of pneumonia, and is buried in the Alta Vista Cemetery in Gainesville, Georgia.

Activities of Historical Significance

James Longstreet was, for a long time, the Confederate general that southerners loved to hate. All of their frustration and bitterness about defeat was directed toward this somewhat taciturn corps commander, who was unable to defend himself effectively against such eminent detractors as Jubal Early and John B. Gordon after Lee's death. Most of the controversy about Longstreet focuses on his role in the Confederate defeat at Gettysburg: Longstreet was allegedly slow in responding to Lee's orders. In defending himself, Longstreet pointed out what he saw to be mistakes in Lee's generalship and his belief that prompt obedience to Lee's orders would bring disaster to the Confederate army. But in criticizing Lee, he brought down on his head the wrath of the southern people, who had been schooled ever since Lee's death to believe in the virtual sainthood of the Confederate army's supreme commander and the sanctity of all his decisions. Ironically, Lee himself took all blame for the loss at Gettysburg and never expressed anything but confidence in and admiration for Longstreet during the rest of the war and until the day he died. He even brought Longstreet back to his command for the Battle of the Wilderness and referred to him affectionately as "my old war horse."

Longstreet's military contribution to American history was an advanced understanding of defensive tactics, predictions about the horrific nature of trench warfare which he believed would become widespread, and brilliant command of his corps. In some ways, his military contribution is similar in scope to William T. Sherman's. After the war, Longstreet occasioned much controversy by his espousal of the Republican party, Reconstruction, and his kinsman Ulysses S. Grant. No small measure of his later unpopularity was due to these factors.

Overview of Biographical Sources

The information on Longstreet is of widely varying quality. Too much of it consists of biased and unreliable accounts written by southerners who believed the distortions of Early and others. The biographies are generally more accurate and less biased. Recent publications make a more balanced assessment of Longstreet and his contributions, perhaps in light of studies that found Lee to be less than infallible. Any researcher should be very careful of which biographies he consults.

Evaluation of Principal Biographical Sources

Eckenrode, Hamilton J., and Bryan Conrad. *James Longsteet, Lee's War Horse*. Chapel Hill: University of North Carolina Press, 1936. (**A, G**) The first biography of Longstreet, this study admits Lee's weaknesses, but also pins the responsibility for multiple Confederate defeats on Longstreet.

Connelly, Thomas L., and Barbara L. Bellows. *God and General Longstreet: The Lost Cause and the Southern Mind*. Baton Rouge: Louisiana State University Press, 1982. (**A, G**) Similar in effect to Connelly's book on Lee, this book eloquently defines Longstreet's place in southern history.

Piston, William Garret. *Lee's Tarnished Lieutenant: James Longstreet and His Place in Southern History*. Athens: University of Georgia Press, 1987. (**A, G**) This well-written interpretive biography reflects the culmination of historical revisionism on Longstreet and has a particularly valuable bibliographical essay evaluating the writings about him.

Sanger, Donald Bridgman, and Thomas Robson Hay. *James Longstreet: I. Soldier and II. Politician, Officeholder, and Writer*. Baton Rouge: Louisiana State University Press, 1952. (**A, G**) The importance of this study stems from Sanger's careful, well-reasoned review of Longstreet's military career, the impact of which was lessened by Hay's lukewarm assessment of his postwar career.

Overview and Evaluation of Primary Sources

The largest collection of Longstreet papers available to the public were given to the Georgia Department of Archives and History in Atlanta by his descendants. There is also a small collection at Duke University and a letterbook from the years 1863-1865 at the Texas Archives and the University of Texas Library at Austin. While his papers are of great interest and importance to scholars of Longstreet, Lee, and the Southern military experience, researchers can get most necessary information from his published memoirs. Scholars might also wish to look at the Donald Bridgman Sanger Papers at the Library of Congress, which contain his notes and research for his work on Longstreet.

Longstreet's own surprisingly literate memoirs, *From Manassas to Appomattox: Memoirs of the Civil War in America* (Philadelphia: J.B. Lippincott, 1896; **A, G**), tell his side of the story and reflect his stubborn, unpopular character. This volume sheds light on the man and the controversy surrounding him through the author's tone and the information he imparts. Longstreet's wife, Helen Dortch Longstreet, in *Lee and Longstreet at High Tide* (1904. Reprint. New York: Kraus Reprint, 1969; **A, G**), defends her husband in a response to attacks on the general during his final illness; this volume carried little weight with his critics.

Fiction and Adaptations

Michael Shaara's Pulitzer Prize-winning novel, *Killer Angels* (1975) focuses on the Battle of Gettysburg. Longstreet is one of the main characters, depicted as seeing the ultimate futility of both the battle and the Southern cause. Robert Skimin's peculiar counterfactual novel, *Gray Victory* (1980) portrays Jeb Stuart on trial for treason for his role at the Battle of Gettysburg in a victorious Confederacy; Longstreet plays an important role. *House Divided* (1947), the best-seller by Longstreet's nephew, Ben Ames Williams, depicts him as a kind, generous family man, but a short-tempered, overbearing general. Williams's successful sequel, *The Unconquered* (1953), perpetuates the negative public image of Longstreet.

Museums, Historical Landmarks, Societies

Antietam National Battlefield (Sharpsburg, MD). Site of the battle where Longstreet earned a promotion for his actions.

Appomattox Court House National Historical Park (Appomattox, VA). Longstreet surrendered with Lee to Grant at this National Park Service site.

Chickamauga and Chattanooga National Military Park (Chattanooga, TN). Site of two of Longstreet's important battles.

Fredericksburg and Spotsylvania National Military Park (Fredericksburg, VA). Location of Longstreet's strong defensive stand at Fredericksburg and the Wilderness Battlefield, where he was wounded.

Gettysburg National Military Park (Gettysburg, PA). This well-run National Park Service site devotes much time to Longstreet's controversial actions.

Manassas National Battlefield Park (Manassas, VA). Longstreet fought well in both of the battles here.

Richmond National Battlefield Park (Richmond, VA). Site of the battles that Longstreet fought during the Seven Days Campaign.

Other Sources

Freeman, Douglas Southall. *Lee's Lieutenants.* 3 vols. New York: Scribner's, 1942-1944. Freeman's anti-Longstreet bias is very evident, but his scholarship and prose are wonderful.

Tucker, Glenn. *High Tide at Gettysburg.* Rev. ed. Dayton, OH: Press of the Morningside Bookshop, 1973. One of the first studies of the battle to dismiss the charges against Longstreet and maintain that he was only trying to serve Lee.

————. *Lee and Longstreet at Gettysburg.* New York: Bobbs-Merrill, 1968. Tucker elaborates on his defense of Longstreet and concludes he was one of the finest commanders of the war.

Jean V. Berlin
The Correspondence of William T. Sherman
Arizona State University

LOUIS XVI
1754-1793

Chronology

Born Louis-Auguste of the royal house of Bourbon on August 23, 1754, at Versailles, France, the son of Louis-Ferdinand, the dauphin, Louis XV's only son, and Maria Josepha of Saxony; *1760* begins studies under private tutors, receiving a solid academic education and acquiring the knowledge of several languages; *1761* becomes second in line to the French crown after the death of his eldest brother; *1765* becomes the new dauphin and heir to the throne at age eleven after his father dies; *1770* marries Marie Antoinette, the daughter of Emperor Francis I and Maria Theresa of the house of Habsburg-Lorraine; *1774* ascends the throne of France at the age of nineteen upon the death of his grandfather; *1775* crowned in traditional splendor at Rheims Cathedral in Champagne; *1776* begins covert support of American colonists in revolt against England upon the advice of Vergennes, his cautious but able foreign affairs minister; although reluctant to support the colonies because of the need for economy and domestic reforms, establishes the fictitious Roderique Hortalez and Company to supply arms to Americans; begins naval rearmament; Necker serves as his financial advisor and borrows money to support growing involvement in the American War of Independence; U.S. Congress appoints Silas Deane, Benjamin Franklin, and Arthur Lee to go to Europe to gain support; *1777* recognizes American independence after news of Burgoyne's surrender at Saratoga on December 17; *1778* on February 6 signs a formal treaty of friendship and commerce with the colonies, as well as a defensive alliance which precipitates war with the English; receives Franklin, Deane, and Lee in a public audience on March 20; appoints Conrad-Alexandre Gérard French minister to the U.S.; French government aims to regain international prestige and restore the balance of power by defeating the English who had humiliated France in the Seven Years' War; *1778* in August a French fleet under Count d'Estaing participates in Franco-American expedition against Newport but fails due to weather and lack of coordination; d'Estaing departs to help French forces in the West Indies; *1779* Charles III of Spain, at the urging of Vergennes, declares war on England to regain Gibraltar, but has no interest in recognizing American independence; *1780* Catherine II of Russia organizes the League of Armed Neutrality in response to British attacks on neutral shipping; other European nations join within the next two years; France sends a six thousand man expeditionary force to America under Rochambeau, but the greatest French contribution is its navy; *1781* Admiral de Grasse and his ships set up a naval blockade at Yorktown

while a combined American-French army force the surrender of British general
Cornwallis; spends over 1,066 million livres (a skilled worker earned about one
livre a day) to aid Americans and fight the British, subsequently pushing the
government deeper into debt; Necker opposes continued expenditure and publishes
a justification of his administration, the *compte rendu,* purporting to show his
financial talent but concealing the mounting deficit; Necker falls from power due
to ministerial intrigue; *1782* French and Americans conduct separate peace talks
with the British; the U.S. forces concessions from the British and on November 30
signs a preliminary peace with Britain contingent upon the end of Franco-British
hostilities; *1783* peace signed by the British, French, Spanish, and Americans on
January 20; France achieves little from its victory; its hope to weaken the British
by gaining control of U.S. trade never materializes as most American trade remains with the British; the war undermines France's financial strength, preparing
the way for the financial and political crisis which would shortly follow; appoints
Calonne finance minister, who, unlike Necker, does not call for budget cuts but
initiates pump priming to restore public confidence in the economy until the ever-
looming deficit forces action; *1787* persuaded by Calonne to support a wide series
of reforms including taxing all landowners; forced by the opposition of nobles and
clergy, who are largely tax-exempt, to act on Calonne's advice and call the Assembly of Notables to rubberstamp royal policies; the defiant assembly denounces
Calonne; bows to opinion and replaces Calonne with Loménie de Brienne, a member of the Assembly of Notables; *1788* forced by the rejection of Parlement and
resulting bankruptcy to call the Estates-General for the first time since 1614-1615;
1789 opens Estates-General on May 5; intransigence of members of the Third
Estate lead to its transformation into a National Assembly; attempts to quash this
by royal session of June 23, but the assembly refuses on the grounds that it cannot
take orders; mob action in Paris and the fall of the Bastille precipitates collapse of
royal authority; on August 4 the National Assembly renounces feudal rights and
declares the equality of all citizens; the National Assembly adopts the Declaration
of the Rights of Man and the Citizen on August 26; escorted to the capital on
October 5-6 by an angry mob which has marched from Paris to Versailles; becomes a captive of the Revolution; *1790* promises to defend constitutional liberties
before the National Assembly; the National Assembly institutes a Civil Constitution of the Clergy and forces priests to swear allegiance; *1791* the pope condemns
the Civil Constitution of the Clergy; decides to flee with the royal family but their
flight is stopped at Varennes on June 21; placed under greater surveillance and
temporarily suspended by the National Assembly; reinstated in July; signs the
Constitution of 1791 making France a constitutional monarchy; fear for the safety

of the royal family leads the emperor and the king of Prussia to issue the Declaration of Pillnitz promising allied intervention if other European powers agree; *1792* France declares war on Austria and Prussia, and as war turns against the French, the duke of Brunswick's Manifesto, promising protection for the royal family in the event of violence, inflames the capital; on August 10 a revolutionary mob invades the Tuileries and the royal family flees to the nearby Legislative Assembly as members of the Swiss Guards are murdered; the Legislative Assembly succumbs to revolutionary pressure, suspends the monarchy, and authorizes a new National Convention; the royal family is imprisoned in the Temple; on September 21 the new Convention abolishes the thousand-year-old monarchy and declares France a republic; tried for treason; *1793* guillotined on January 21; Marie Antoinette is guillotined on October 16.

Activities of Historical Significance

Louis XVI, France's last absolute monarch, was a key participant in the most momentous political event of his time, the French Revolution. This event brought about the destruction of the privileged classes of the Ancien Regime and the reshaping of a more democratic society, as well as the downfall of the monarchy and the proclamation of the first French republic. However, Louis had reigned since 1774, some fifteen years before the Revolution, and his actions need to be separated into two sections: attempted reforms in his early reign and support of the American Revolution, and his later reign in which he became the symbolic victim of the French Revolution.

Louis XVI ascended the throne at age nineteen, with no experience in government. His grandfather, Louis XV, like earlier kings had excluded his heir from the royal council. This lack of experience was coupled with an education that did little to prepare the king for political realities. He was well read and of average intelligence, but his tutors had impressed upon him the traditional principles of absolute monarchy as well as a naive paternalism toward his people. He was a prisoner of the Versailles system, raised at court without knowledge of the world around him. Moreover the young king was unsure of himself. This was made worse by sexual incapacity in his marriage to Marie Antoinette. A target of jokes at court, the king did not consummate his marriage until 1777, after seven years of marriage. Louis XVI remained shy and introspective, and suspicious of the motives of others.

Despite these drawbacks, his reign began on a positive note. The monarch was a kind and good-natured young man who desired the well-being of his subjects. Although raised a sincere Christian, he opposed religious fanaticism and shared in the eighteenth century's enlightened humanitarianism. A moral man, he kept no mistresses but was faithful to his frivolous and impolitic young bride. He was a frugal man, and unlike other members of the royal family, he did not gamble, dance, or attend the theater. In principle he was not opposed to reform; he was interested in the technological advances of his century, desiring to promote overseas exploration, intrigued by the first aviation experiments of the Montgolfier brothers, and he was a collector of scientific instruments.

His greatest failure was his lack of direction. Unsure of himself, he needed a close relationship with a strong minister like his ancestor Louis XIII had found in Cardinal Richelieu. Louis XVI's closest equivalent was the count de Maurepas, an ex-minister who served as the king's *éminence grise* until his death in 1781. A master of court intrigue, Maurepas engineered the dismissal of ministers like Turgot and Necker if he felt they challenged his authority. The king's ministers embarked upon a checkered program of reform. Turgot, the controller general of finance during the first two years of the reign, attempted to free trade, promote agriculture, cut expenditures, and abolish archaic institutions like guilds. Necker, in his first ministry (1776-1781), continued this policy of fiscal retrenchment by eliminating fiscal offices and trying to reorganize government accounting procedures and the mechanism of taxation. Even Calonne, the controller who embarked upon a frenzy of deficit financing, proposed calling an Assembly of Notables to endorse new taxes upon the largely immune privileged groups as well as other reforms such as the elimination of internal customs barriers.

In other areas Louis' reign was marked by accomplishment. Several able secretaries of state sought to continue Choiseul's efforts to build a strong navy, which the king eagerly supported—he was one of the few French monarchs to recognize the importance of a navy. The result was a respectable naval force which challenged the British during the American War of Independence. Ministers such as Saint-Germain sought similar reforms in the army.

However, Louis' greatest success remained in the area of foreign affairs. He ably supported his talented foreign minister, Vergennes, who sought to erase the humiliation suffered by France during the Seven Years' War. Vergennes bears much of the responsibility for French involvement in the American Revolution. A career diplomat, his foreign policy was not motivated by crude revenge against the British, but by deliberate calculation and an attempt to restore Europe's balance of power. France's defeat in the Seven Years' War had disturbed the international order. Traditionally, France was the axis among the great powers and protected a client network of minor powers. Now France had lost prestige and position. The first partition of Poland in 1771 by Russia, Prussia, and Austria had demonstrated the consequences of this decline.

Vergennes had hoped for a reconciliation with England, but had found England contemptuous of France. If France could fight a preventive war against the British and reduce their strength to a position of equality with France, it would be possible for the old international system to be restored. France's policy was a traditional mercantilist one: the French believed that Britain's monopoly of trade with its colonies maintained the British economy and navy, and if France could seize this trade, England would be weakened. Louis XVI had to be won over to this position because he was reluctant to intervene on behalf of the rebels of a fellow monarch and because he was interested in domestic reform. The triumvirate of Maurepas, Vergennes, and Sartine, the navy minister, supported this foreign policy, and only Turgot had reservations. Convinced that France's fiscal problems should have priority and that American independence would bring few advantages, Turgot opposed intervention, but did not present his views strongly enough. Widespread opposition to his reforms among the privileged classes soon led to his dismissal. Jacques Necker, a Swiss banker and Louis' financial advisor, financed the American intervention through loans at high interest rates.

American interests at the French court were represented by three commissioners—Silas Deane (later replaced by John Adams), Benjamin Franklin (until February 1779 when Franklin was named minister plenipotentiary to the French court), and Arthur Lee. Franklin was the most effective of the Americans. Well known among intellectuals for his scientific interests, he was quickly lionized by French society, and was invited to dine with nobles and meet with intellectuals. His simple dress stunned high Parisian society. He reflected both a Quaker image of simplicity and virtue popularized by Voltaire and Rousseau's idea of a "backwoods philosopher," a self taught natural man. During obligatory visits to members of the royal family, Marie Antoinette went out of the way to converse with Franklin during lulls in her cardplaying, a ritualized feature of court life. As ambassador, Franklin regularly attended court on Tuesdays and, like other diplomats, took part in court life, dressing in mourning for the death of Maria Theresa, the queen's mother, and paying his respects at the birth of a royal infant. His compatriot John Adams even thought him servile in his attention to the royal family.

Franklin played two important roles as commissioner to France; his elderly patriarchal nature reassured the upper classes that the American Revolution did not threaten the social order, and by living at Passy, not far from Versailles, he was able to meet frequently with Vergennes, who disliked the other American commissioners.

Vergennes was a realist who recognized that aiding the Americans made the avoidance of war with Britain difficult. He proceeded cautiously by limiting fiscal and military aid to the Americans while Louis grew accustomed to the idea. Moreover, time was needed for France to prepare for war. Supposedly the French wavered over the issue of war and peace until Burgoyne's surrender at Saratoga in 1778 convinced the French that the American cause was viable. While the American commissioners tried to bluff the French with the possibility of a compromise with the British unless the French signed an alliance, in reality Vergennes awaited a naval buildup before committing France to a stronger position. He also hoped to bring the Spanish, ruled by Charles III, a fellow Bourbon, into the alliance. Spanish intervention was important because of its large navy. Not until 1782 did the British regain their naval position. This provided the crucial edge for the Americans and French at Yorktown.

By the time of preliminary peace negotiations in 1782, however, the balance had shifted against the French. The military situation worsened with Admiral de Grasse's defeat at the Battle of Saintes in the West Indies and England's regaining supremacy of the seas. The French were also at the limit of their financial ability to continue the war. Finally, in eastern Europe, Russia and Austria threatened the dismemberment of Turkey, a French client. Thus Vergennes was willing to accept America's separate negotiations with Lord Shelburne. While the Americans gained advantageous terms, the French were ready to accept any reasonable settlement to escape from their dangerous situation. France gained little from the war; the hoped-for American trade remained in British hands and the revolt popularized democratic ideals in France. Worst of all, French involvement burdened France with a huge war debt that overwhelmed the government deficit.

The actual influence of America upon the French Revolution is a complex question. Traditionally many French (and following their example, American) historians have seen the origins of the French Revolution in class terms. Other historians, however, have seen the French Revolution and the American Revolution as part of a larger struggle, the so-called "Age of Democratic Revolution," or "Atlantic Revolution," in which western European society drew upon a common treasure of Enlightenment ideas in their attacks upon an archaic political and social system. America's struggle is seen as the most important before the French Revolution, but there were other episodes, such as those in Geneva as early as 1763. Proponents argue that both America and France were influenced by the same currents in western European intellectual thought. The American Revolution did not originate ideas like political liberty and the equality of man, government by consent, natural rights, rule by law, separation of powers, and the sovereignty of the people; all were concepts familiar to European thinkers.

Such historians speak of the importance of the United States as a model. Until 1776 change was a matter of theoretical speculation, but the American example demonstrated that existing political authority could be overthrown and institutions rebuilt according to rational, enlightened principles. The American Revolution showed that slow, gradual reform was not the only route to change; direct action was also possible. It also illustrated that a liberal republic could triumph over a traditional monarchical system. Indeed, after 1776 there was a dramatic surge in French writings about America. The French government itself fostered this publicity, permitting the publication of books and journals favorable to its ally even though it represented diametrically opposite political principles, in order to gain support for French intervention.

The influence of these ideas, while centered in a literate elite, gradually widened. French literacy increased dramatically in the eighteenth century. It is estimated that almost forty percent of the French male population could read and write (this figure was much higher in Paris). While books were expensive, more than the weekly wages of a working man, there were subscription societies and reading rooms with low fees as well as more elite organizations like literary societies.

Some historians have argued that there was a more direct American influence on the French Revolution. It has been estimated that at least thirty-eight French army officers who served in America later played some role in the French Revolution. The marquis de Lafayette is the most prominent; he came to America not to participate in an idealistic cause, but he acquired a taste for liberty and political change from his American experience and returned a convert to France. Other officers, however, such as Axel von Fersen with his attachment to Marie Antoinette and the court, took a different course.

A number of revolutionaries were familiar with the American model even though they had not served in America, namely Mounier, Mirabeau, Condorcet, and even Marat and Robespierre. Brissot, the leader of the Girondins and a foe of Robespierre, for example, founded a Gallo-American society and visited America before 1789. Moreover, French revolutionary methods also exhibited themselves in forms used earlier by the Americans, namely, constitutional conventions, written constitutions, a declaration of rights, committees of correspondence, public safety, surveillance, political clubs, and even loyalty oaths. These forms, however, later took on a French context. In addition, French revolutionaries were familiar with American political institutions but frequently rejected them as French models. For example, a number of revolutionary thinkers condemned America's reliance upon a "Gothic" system of common law and archaic institutions like bicameralism and a system of checks and balances. Writers like Mirabeau, Turgot, and Condorcet argued that these were unnecessary, claiming that bicameral legislature implied the preserving of privileged elites and contradicted the idea of the sovereignty of the people. A crucial moment in the French Revolution occurred when the Estates

General evolved into the National Assembly. Proponents argued that the older form, representing the three estates, thwarted the national will where representatives of the people should meet in common and legislate for the common good. Unlike the American system where representatives reflect the wishes of their constituents, French revolutionary thinkers argued that such a system was incompatible with the general will. Nor were checks and balances necessary. When the legislative body spoke for the nation, other bodies by nature, whether executive or judicial, must be subordinate.

The French and American revolutions differed not only in interpretation of principles such as representation and legislative authority, but in fundamental forms. The United States had a more open class structure and lacked a hereditary aristocracy; consequently America never experienced the elements of class struggle as sharply as France. Generally more prosperous than France and with open frontiers, America did not face such extremes of wealth and poverty. While American mobs were often violent, and the colonies experienced sharp political conflicts and considerable emigration, it did not develop France's militant egalitarian stance. In part this was because America fought a foreign power, albeit a mother country, while France fought against its own citizens. Moreover, America did not face a struggle against an established church and a traditional religious life, while in France the Catholic church took an early opposition to the course of the Revolution. The government under the Convention openly adopted the policy of the Terror, deliberate intimidation of its opponents. The bloodshed of the French Revolution has been exaggerated, however; it has been estimated that about forty thousand people were executed although hundreds of thousands were arrested. Yet France saw provincial atrocities such as at Nantes where two thousand prisoners were taken to the river in barges and then drowned. The bloodshed associated with the Revolution provoked a widespread revulsion, both in France and in other countries, including America.

The financial crisis contributed to by the American Revolution proved the French monarchy's undoing. While Great Britain with its smaller size bore a national debt of the same magnitude without problems, the French government was not so successful. The government faced three essential problems. Government finance largely remained in the hands of financiers or tax farmers who collected indirect taxes for a price and kept the left-over money, and loaned it back to the government at high rates of interest. In addition, the heavy burden of taxation upon the lower orders meant that even the government recognized that little additional taxes could be raised from this source. Finally, the privileged orders, the clergy and nobility, had vigorously opposed past efforts to tax them and largely escaped direct taxation.

This resistance manifested itself through two routes: aristocratic influence on members of the royal family at court as well as the Parlement of Paris and other sovereign courts obstructing royal reforms. The Parlement of Paris claimed to represent the voice of the nation in the absence of an Estates-General. When Calonne revealed the disastrous state of French finances to the king, Louis XVI reluctantly went along with his idea of circumventing the Parlement by consulting a specially chosen Assembly of Notables. The resistance of this body and the continued hostility of Parlement forced the government to call an Estates-General, which had not been summoned since 1614.

The king foresaw that such a meeting would curb his powers, but circumstances permitted few other options, for his ministers were themselves unsure what to advise. The result was that the government let itself be carried along by events, reluctantly accepting changes such as the transformation of the Estates General into a National Assembly. In his last effort to act as an absolute monarch Louis XVI tried holding a royal session on June 23, 1789, nullifying the National Assembly and proposing a moderate reform program. When the National Assembly refused to adjourn, the king backed down and let them remain.

There are various explanations for the king's failure to act against this defiance. Louis had always been a king who needed time to make decisions. Despite the pejorative term of Bourbon absolutism, all of the Bourbon monarchs consulted their advisors. The royal ministers were divided; some like Necker supported the changes, and other more conservative members, backed by the royal family, resisted. The King was paralyzed by this conflicting advice on how to deal with the situation. Louis could not count on liberal clerical and noble delegates who had gone over to the National Assembly. A show of military force posed problems. He was a humane man who had bent to public opinion in the past and disliked the idea of force. Nor was the government certain of the loyalty of its troops. The king capitulated for the time being but also gave in to conservative councils, including that of the queen and his brother Artois, to move troops closer to Paris. Louis' motives are unclear; he only admitted that the forces were to maintain order. Rioting broke out in Paris as crowds sought to defend themselves. The fall of the Bastille was the most visible sign of the government's failure to maintain order. While a stronger, self-made man such as Napoleon would not have hesitated to use force, even if it meant bloodshed and division within the army, neither the king nor his general Broglie had the stomach for this type of solution. Louis ordered the withdrawal of troops and made an appearance at the city hall in Paris where he accepted the revolutionary cockade to the shouts of the crowd. Yet he remained deeply ambivalent about the Revolution and called upon the Flanders Regiment to protect the royal family. A banquet was held to welcome the regiment, at which, it was rumored, the revolutionary cockade had been trampled. An angry mob marched on Versailles and escorted the royal family back to Paris making it a prisoner of the Revolution.

The absolute monarchy was thus destroyed; the National Assembly set out to sweep away the old society of privileged orders and erect a constitutional monarchy, but the issue of constitutional monarchy was never tested in France. If Louis had cooperated, a limited monarchy might have developed, as time has a way of changing political structures. The monarchy might even have strengthened its relationship with the legislature. However, Louis XVI never completely accepted the revolutionary changes. Raised with the principles of divine right monarchy in which the king enjoyed theoretically unlimited powers and was accountable only to God, the tradition-bound king could not adjust to such changes. Forced by events, the king responded by reluctantly agreeing under pressure to reforms which he did not in his heart accept. The king's conscience was also affected by the National Assembly's confiscation of church property and its reorganization under the Civil Constitution of the Clergy, which was established without consulting the pope.

The king's played a dangerous double game: pretending to accept reforms while working for outside forces to come to his aid. Increasingly he and the queen put their hope in foreign action and they corresponded with the rulers of Austria and Prussia. The crowned heads of Europe were reluctant to intervene to restore Louis' absolute power, in part because it was in their own interest to see France weakened by political crisis. However, the abortive royal family's flight to Varennes and their resulting protective custody brought matters to a head. It was clear that Louis XVI was a prisoner and international action was necessary.

The king's attempt to escape doomed the constitutional monarchy for it implied that he could not be trusted. The growing republican movement gained impetus and war added new problems. While many saw imminent war with Austria and Prussia as a means of regenerating France and rooting out traitors, the king also favored the war for he hoped that victorious allied troops would restore the monarchy. The French army, racked by desertion and its numbers augmented by raw, inexperienced volunteers, was no match for the allied forces. As foreign troops invaded France, radicals within the Legislative Assembly elected under the new constitution sought scapegoats and denounced traitors. The duke of Brunswick's Manifesto promising vengeance upon Paris if it harmed the royal family sparked an angry sansculotte mob which invaded the Tuileries Palace on June 20. The king's calm dignity dispersed the crowd, but as bad news continued to arrive from the front, further agitation erupted, and another mob attacked the Tuileries on August 10, massacring the retreating Swiss Guards as the royal family fled to the nearby National Assembly for protection. As crowds roamed Paris pulling down royalist symbols, the Legislative Assembly suspended the monarchy and called for a new National Convention to decide the future form of government. The royal family was imprisoned in the Temple, a medieval fortress.

The new Convention abolished the monarchy on September 21, 1792. The real question—what to do with Louis—reflected the power struggle between the two revolutionary factions of the Girondins and the more radical Jacobins. The Convention condemned the king to death by a vote of 361 to 360 (who voted either against death or in delaying the penalty). Although his lawyers attempted an appeal, the king was guillotined on January 21 and his body placed in a common grave.

The trial and execution of Louis XVI removed him as a focus of counterrevolution, and his trial as a common citizen removed the last vestiges of divine right monarchy. Kings were no longer regarded as sacred figures representing the divine order, but as lesser beings responsible to the nation. This visible desacralization of political power had a profound impact all over Europe, striking a death blow to the arbitrary rule of kings. Coupled with the American Revolution it meant that new republican states provided a model for future change.

Overview of Biographical Sources

Louis XVI still suffers from the lack of a definitive biography. He was a silent and uncommunicative figure who has never attracted biographers, as has the more romantic figure of Marie Antoinette. Moreover, even his more recent French biographers base their work upon memoirs and other printed sources rather than upon an examination of manuscript sources.

Views of Louis XVI largely have been shaped by reactions to the French Revolution. Reviled during his lifetime by anonymous pamphleteers, the king was accused of vices ranging from cruelty and impotence to being a cuckold and a drunkard. With the coming of the Restoration, Louis XVIII, who had belittled his brother during his lifetime, reburied the king's remains at St. Denis, and the government exalted the memory of the martyr king. Bourbon apologists glorified the courage of the king, while defenders of the church proclaimed the king as one of their own—an enemy of the free thinking Enlightenment who suffered martyrdom for his defense of a church despoiled by the atheistical Revolution. However, others, like the novelist Stendahl, welcomed the liberating effects of the Revolution.

Conservatives attempted to justify Louis' actions. Even in the early days of the Revolution, the Englishman Edmund Burke in his *Reflections on the French*

Revolution (first published in 1790 some six months before the king's flight to Varennes) sympathized with the king whose reign, Burke wrote, had been one of concession to his subjects culminating in a sharing of authority. Burke argued that the king did not deserve the insulting treatment accorded him during the course of the Revolution. The conservative Catholic apologist, Joseph de Maistre, in his *Considerations sur la France* (1797), described the king as an innocent sustained by his religion, and maintained that he had committed no crime, but was betrayed.

Nineteenth-century liberals like Hippolyte Taine and François Guizot were in favor of the Revolution but felt that it had gone too far in the Terror. Guizot, a minister of Louis-Philippe's July Monarchy, judged the king as kindly and sincere, but commented that his weakness was a result of "the long standing debt of absolute power corrupted and corrupting." Taine, who lived to see the Paris Commune of 1870, was repulsed by popular rule and saw Louis XVI as no despot but a benevolent and gentle man.

Jules Michelet, a contemporary of Guizot, was a Romantic democrat and nationalist who was harsh in his attacks of the monarchy and the established church. He saw evil less in Louis XVI than in the institution of kingship. However, to Michelet, the king was feeble, indecisive, and insignificant, incapable of reforming France, and the priests had made him into a martyr to perpetuate their control over human minds.

As republicanism established itself in nineteenth-century France, historians developed canons of scholarship and controlled the educational establishment. Resolutely republican, these historians devoted much attention to the Revolution. Alphonse Aulard, for many years the dean of French revolutionary historians, noted in his *The French Revolution, a Political History, 1789-1804* (English translation, 1910) that while well intended, the king was incapable; weak, the creature of whim, Louis XVI did not know how to act as king of a revolution. Although the nation was royalist, his actions drove France into republicanism.

This view of the king as a weak and indecisive monarch dominated academic history, although with the growth of leftist and Socialist historians less attention was placed upon individual action and more on Marx's inevitable class struggle. Albert Mathiez, a great admirer of Robespierre, saw the king as playing only a minor role. In his *The French Revolution* (English translation, 1911) the king comes across as a fat, common man swayed by the queen and aristocratic factions. If the king had mounted his horse and led his troops, he might have saved his power, but, according to Mathiez, Louis XVI was incapable of such heroic action. For the Communist Albert Soboul, whose views are recorded in *The French Revolution 1787-1799* (English translation, 1974), social factors become dominant. The king remained honorable and well-intended, but unobtrusive, weak, and hesitant, the control of the Revolution outside of his hands. In Georges Lefebvre's magistral two-volume work, *The French Revolution* (English translation, 1962), the king largely disappears, subsumed by the court. Lefebvre remarks that after 1789 France had no government until 1793.

Royalist and conservative writers following the tradition of Jacques Bainville in the twentieth century have developed a more sympathetic portrait of the king. Pierre Gaxotte, *The French Revolution* (English translation, 1931), praised the king's good qualities and his sound judgement in foreign affairs, but confesses that the king was less able in domestic matters. Bernard Faÿ in his biography, *Louis XVI or the End of a World* (English translation, 1968), aimed at a major restoration of the king's reputation in international affairs and downplayed the Revolution to a minor part of his book. Other monarchists, particularly Paul and Pierrette Girault de Coursac, are extravagant in their praise of the executed monarch, blackening Marie Antoinette along the way.

However, old-fashioned Jacobins such as Claude Manceron offer antidotes to this positive picture. His *Les Hommes de la liberté* (five volumes of which are in English translation: *Twilight of the Old Order*, 1977; *Wind from America*, 1979; *Their Gracious Pleasure*, 1980; *Toward the Brink*, 1983; and *Blood of the Bastille*, 1990) does not hesitate to criticize the king with old libels, describing him as the "walking image of degeneracy" who beat lame dogs senseless, shot cats on Versailles roofs, and was a glutton for food and drink.

Evaluation of Principal Biographical Sources

Bosher, J. F. *The French Revolution.* New York: W. W. Norton, 1988. (A) Although a work on the Revolution as a whole, Bosher devotes considerable space to the king's reign before 1789. Argues that the king's virtues and his humane enlightened vision helped bring about the revolution, and the attempt at a constitutional monarchy failed, in part, because of the same "benevolent weakness" of the government to use force to maintain order.

Dull, Jonathan R. *A Diplomatic History of the American Revolution.* New Haven: Yale University Press. 1985. (A, G) The most readable and reliable synthesis of diplomacy during the American Revolution. Its strength lies in its focus on all participants, not only the U.S., but also major European powers. Attention is paid to eastern Europe. Includes an excellent annotated bibliography.

—————. *The French Navy and American Independence. A Study of Arms and Diplomacy, 1774-1787.* Princeton: Princeton University Press, 1975. (A) Highly recommended work for its detailed and masterful examination of Vergennes as well as the French navy's relationship to French foreign policy.

Faÿ, Bernard. *Louis XVI, or the End of a World*. London: W. H. Allen, 1968. (G) An English translation of the 1966 French edition, this polemical account provides a highly favorable view of a devout and honest upholder of monarchical principles who becomes a victim of a selfish, short-sighted nobility, a hollow church, and the dangerous ideas of the Enlightenment espoused by Masons and other freethinkers. Concentrates on the early period of the king's reign and downplays the Revolution.

Hazen, Charles Downer. *Contemporary American Opinion of the French Revolution*. Gloucester, MA: Peter Smith, 1964. (A) An older work that focuses primarily on the views of Jefferson and Gouverneur Morris as well as American public opinion.

Higonnet, Patrice. *Sister Republics. The Origins of French and American Republicanism*. Cambridge: Harvard University Press, 1988. (A) Stimulating if somewhat one dimensional essay examining the origins of the American (individualistic) and French (communal) approach to revolution and their effects upon the revolution in each country. While not everyone would fully agree with the interpretation, this work is highly recommended.

Jordan, David P. *The King's Trial. Louis XVI vs. the French Revolution*. Berkeley and Los Angeles: University of California Press, 1979. (A, G) An accurate narrative account of Louis's trial which focuses on the political issues involved, the struggle between the Girondins and the Jacobins, and the course of the Revolution, while providing details on the royal defense.

Lever, Evelyne. *Louis XVI*. Paris: Fayard, 1985. (A, G) This balanced French language biography of the king is based upon printed accounts rather than archival sources. A sympathetic account by a French scholar, it presents a deft psychological portrait of the king whose indecision and lack of self confidence is blamed on a "castrating" familial and educational upbringing.

Kennett, Lee. *The French Forces in America, 1780-1783*. Westport, CT: Greenwood Press, 1977. (A) Part of the Contribution in American History Series, this useful work studying the role of French soldiers in America was written by a military historian equally adept in French and English sources.

Padover, Saul K. *The Life and Death of Louis XVI.* 1939. Reprint. New York: Pyramid Books, 1963. **(A, G)** Written by a New York liberal professor of the 1930s, this well-documented, sympathetic account portrays the king as an unenlightened monarch out of touch with the legitimate needs of his subjects. A bit old-fashioned, it remains the best scholarly account in English.

Overview and Evaluation of Primary Sources

Louis XVI was a reticent man who rarely put thoughts to paper. His celebrated *Journal,* edited by L. Nicolardot (1873), is more a calendar where the king jotted down notes to himself than a diary. On only a few occasions such as the birth of his children does the king add much detail and this is mostly dry inventory.

Several documentary surveys of the French Revolution, such as J. H. Stewart, ed., *Documentary Survey of the French Revolution* (New York: Colliers Macmillan, 1951; **A**), or the more recent John Hardman, *The French Revolution. The Fall of the Ancien Regime to the Thermidorian Reaction 1785-1795* (New York: St. Martin's, 1982; **A**), contain extracts of various letters and declarations of the king relating to the Revolution.

Mercy-Argenteau, Austrian ambassador at the French court, left a remarkable set of correspondence with the Viennese court which has been edited in different scholarly editions by Alfred Arneth, Jules Flammermont, and Auguste Geffroy. This often unflattering correspondence about the king is the basis for any serious study of Louis XVI's marriage. An English translation and selection from this correspondence has appeared in print with the rather sensational title of *Secrets of Maria Antoinette,* edited by Olivier Bernier (New York: Doubleday, 1985; **G**).

Numerous memoirs of the period survive, written by figures at the court and royal officials such as the duke of Croy, the abbé de Veri, Saint-Priest, and Barentin, and by participants in the Revolution such as Bailly and Roederer. These accounts need to be treated with care for they are not always accurate and each figure has his or her own complaints. Unfortunately many of these memoirs have no English editions. However, the following brief list contains memoirs of varying degrees of importance: A. F. Bertrand de Molleville, the king's minister of the marine in 1791, *Private Memoirs Relative to the Last Year of the Reign of Louis the Sixteenth,* 2 vols. (Boston: J. B. Millet, 1909; **A**); Madame de Campan, a lady in waiting to Marie Antoinette, *Memoirs of Maria Antoinette,* 3 vols. (New York: P. F. Collier, 1910; **G**); François Hue, a gentleman in waiting of Louis XVI, *The Last Years of the Reign and Life of Louis XVI* (London: Cadell and Davies, 1806; **G**); Count Louis-Philippe de Ségur, a moderate royalist and diplomat, *Memoirs and Anecdotes of the Count de Ségur* (New York: C. Scribner's Sons, 1928; **G**);

and the duchess de Tourzel, *Memoirs of the Duchess de Tourzel, governess of the Children of France during the years 1789, 1790, 1791, 1792, 1793, and 1795,* 2 vols. (London: Remington, 1886; **G**). The French economic minister Jacques Necker also has provided his account of the Revolution, *On the French Revolution,* 2 vols. (London: Cadell and Davies, 1797; **A, G**).

American views on the French monarch vary in quality. Leonard W. Labaree, et al., eds., *The Papers of Benjamin Franklin,* (New Haven: Yale University Press, 1959-; **A**), consisting of twenty-eight volumes to date, provide only a brief mention of Louis XVI. In general Franklin described the king's treatment of Americans as "generous and magnanimous," and depicted him as a young and benevolent defender of an oppressed people. The American position was to appeal to the French generosity for a noble cause. Arthur Lee's account of the royal audience of March 20, 1778, is reprinted in volume twenty-six of Franklin's *Papers* as well as the French version from the duc de Croy's memoirs.

John Adams also presents a brief account of this audience in L. H. Butterfield, ed., *Diary and Autobiography of John Adams,* 4 vols. (Cambridge: Belknap Press of Harvard University Press, 1961; **A**). Adams agreed with Franklin's view of the king's generosity, yet he was harsher than Franklin in his treatment of Marie Antoinette, noting her expensive clothes and artificial elegance. Thomas Jefferson and later Gouverneur Morris were American ministers in France during the French Revolution. Jefferson in his *Works,* edited by Paul Leicester Ford, 12 vols. (New York: G. P. Putnam's Sons, 1904-1905; **A**), and the more recent *Papers,* edited by Julian P. Boyd, et al., (Princeton: Princeton University Press, 1950-; **A**), consisting of twenty-four volumes to date, speaks repeatedly of the king as a good man who desired the best for his people but who was led astray by the dissolute Marie Antoinette. He favored the king's exile to America, and Marie Antoinette's confinement to a convent. Morris was more of a conservative; in his *Diary of the French Revolution by Gouverneur Morris,* 2 vols. (Boston: Houghton Mifflin, 1939; **A, G**), he relates the opening session of the Estates-General which he witnessed, and observes the Revolution's course. He believed that France's monarchy was rooted in history and a limited constitutional monarchy was in France's best interests. He encouraged Lafayette to support the monarchy, but he believed that Louis XVI was a weak individual swept along by events.

Documents relating to the king's trial have been edited by Albert Soboul, *Le Procès de Louis XVI* (Paris: Julliard, 1966; **A**). The second half of Michael Walzer's *Regicide and Revolution, Speeches at the Trial of Louis XVI* (Cambridge: Cambridge University Press, 1974; **A**) contains transcripts of various speeches by such revolutionary figures as Condorcet, Paine, Robespierre, and Saint-Just.

Katherine Prescott Wormeley has translated the letters of Louis XVI's sister during the royal family's imprisonment at the Temple and included the journal of the king's valet, Cléry, as well as the account of Louis XVI's daughter the duchess d'Angoulême, in *The Life and Letters of Madame Elizabeth de France* (New York: P. F. Collier, 1901; **A, G**). The Folio Society has published a more readily available edition of Cléry's journal as well as an account of the priest who accompanied the king to his execution, *A Journal of the Terror, Being an account of the occurrences in the Temple during the confinement of Louis XVI, by M. Cléry, the King's valet-de-chambre, together with a description of the last hours of the King by the Abbé de Firmont* (London: Folio Society, 1955; **A, G**).

Fiction and Adaptations

Triumph Films, a division of Columbia Pictures, has released the 1982 French film, *La Nuit de Varennes,* with English subtitles. This fictitious account describes the efforts of the eighteenth-century writer Restif de la Bretonne to uncover the truth of the royal family's flight by taking a stagecoach which follows their route. This highly recommended movie is a vivid and poignant account of the reactions of different French people and it culminates in a brief glimpse of the captured king.

The bicentennial of the French Revolution has been commemorated by a joint Franco-American film, co-directed by Richard Heffron and Robert Enrico. Released in a French version in October and November 1989, *La Révolution française* is divided into two parts: *les Années lumière* and *les Années terribles.* Jean-François Balmer portrays Louis XVI sympathetically and the American actress Jean Seymour plays Marie Antoinette. The film is due to be released in an English language version, perhaps as a television miniseries.

Museums, Historical Landmarks, Societies

Basilica of St. Denis (St. Denis, France). In this royal sepulchre just outside of Paris, the presumed bodies of Louis XVI and Marie Antoinette were reinterred during the Restoration.

Carnavalet Museum (Paris). This museum of the history of the city of Paris contains furniture and souvenirs from the royal family's residence in the Temple.

Hôtel de Ville (Paris). The Paris city hall, rebuilt after burning in the 1870 Commune, where Louis XVI was received by city fathers on visits to the city before the Revolution and where Louis XVI accepted the red-white-and-blue revolutionary cockade shortly after the fall of the Bastille.

Place de la Concorde (Paris). Execution site of Louis XVI near the present day statue of the city of Brest.

Place de la Bastille (Paris). Site of the ancient fortress symbolizing royal authority in Paris. Its seizure by Parisian crowds on July 14, 1789, paralyzed the government and assured the continuation of the Revolution.

Square du Temple (Paris). Site of the medieval tower of the Knights Templar where the royal family was imprisoned under the Convention. Louis XVI came from here to his execution. Napoleon tore the building down to prevent it from becoming a royalist shrine.

Tuileries Gardens (Paris). Site of the palace in which the royal family resided after being escorted from Versailles in October 1789. The palace burned during the Paris Commune of 1870. Nearby was the *Manège* where the Legislative Assembly met. The royal family fled there for refuge on August 10, 1792, after an angry crowd invaded the Tuileries Palace.

Varennes, France. Town where Louis XVI and royal family were stopped when they tried to flee from Paris.

Versailles Palace (Versailles, France). Splendid palace of Louis XIV, residence of the court, and seat of government before the Revolution. Louis XVI was born, married, and ruled from here. The Opera was erected for his marriage celebration. The Petit Trianon and the Hameau of Marie Antoinette are in the gardens. Vergennes also had offices at Versailles.

Other Sources

Doyle, William. *Oxford History of the French Revolution.* Oxford: Clarendon Press, 1989. A detailed up-to-date synthesis of the French Revolution. While it contains little biographical material on the king, it provides an excellent overview of the Revolution.

Dull, Jonathan R. *Franklin the Diplomat: The French Mission.* Philadelphia: American Philosophical Society, 1982. This slim monograph is the best scholarly appraisal of Franklin's strengths and weaknesses as a diplomat at the French court.

Murphy, Orville T. *Charles Gravier, Comte de Vergennes: French Diplomacy in the Age of Revolution, 1719-1787.* Albany: State University of New York Press,

1982. The only English language biography of Louis XVI's foreign minister. Although it devotes considerable attention to Vergennes's early diplomatic career, it is less helpful on the American Revolution than Dull's work on the French navy.

Shama, Simon. *Citizens. A Chronicle of the French Revolution.* New York: Alfred Knopf, 1989. This riveting narrative of the Revolution focuses not upon economic and social structures, but upon human response to the momentous event. Contains helpful background on Louis XVI's reign before 1789.

Douglas Clark Baxter
Ohio University

JAMES RUSSELL LOWELL
1819-1891

Chronology

Born James Russell Lowell on February 22, 1819, in Cambridge, Massachusetts, the son of the Reverend Charles Lowell and Harriet Traill Spence Lowell; *1834* enters Harvard College, graduating in 1838; *1839-1840* studies law at Dane College; *1841* publishes first volume of poems, *A Year's Life*; *1844* marries Maria White, with whom he has four children; *1846* publishes first *Bigelow Paper*; *1848* publishes *Poems: Second Series*, *The Bigelow Papers: First Series*, *The Fable for Critics*, and *The Vision of Sir Launful*; *1853* his wife dies; *1856* becomes editor of the *Atlantic Monthly*; marries Frances Dunlap on September 16; *1861* resigns editorship of the *Atlantic Monthly*; *1862-1863* writes second series of *Bigelow Papers*; *1863* with Charles Eliot Norton, becomes co-editor of the *North American Review*, a post he holds until 1868; *1865* on July 21, delivers "Commemoration Ode" at Harvard; *1868* publishes *Under the Willows and Other Poems*; *1870* publishes *Among My Books: Second Series*; *1877-1880* serves as minister to Spain; *1880-1885* serves as minister to the Court of St. James in London; *1885* second wife dies; *1891* dies August 12 and is buried in Mount Auburn Cemetery.

Activities of Historical Significance

The range of James Russell Lowell's activities is remarkable. In the nineteenth century he stood at the forefront of American men of letters, keeping company with Longfellow, Whittier, Hawthorne, Emerson, and Holmes. His poetry, although not enduring, was popular in its time; his literary criticism, although sometimes excessively discursive, once commanded attention. An uncertain liberal republicanism so evident in his *Bigelow Papers*, a masterpiece of political satire against Southern pretensions during the Civil War era, gave way to a stiff conservatism in his later years. His diplomatic service was a compliment to his prominence as a literary man, not a recognition of diplomatic ability. In many ways, Lowell tells us more about the tastes of his times than he does about the timeless truths explored in great literature.

Lowell's literary legacy, as one might expect, is mixed. Recognized as one of the most important poets and critics of his time, his conventional approach has not worn well with critics. In many ways, *The Bigelow Papers* is the most enduring of his works because of its value to American historians. Lowell's reputation is due in part to the diversity of genres which he attempted to master. Poet, satirist, critic, editor, diplomat, and teacher—his multifaceted career and contributions were more honored in his time than by posterity.

Overview of Biographical Sources

Lowell's biographers have engaged in some rather heated controversy over the value of his contributions to American life and letters. Moreover, nearly all efforts combine biographical narrative with literary criticism; at times this dual function obscures as much as it illuminates. Early studies, including biographies by Scudder (1901), Hale (1899), and Greenslet (1901), sometime err in their effusive praise and stanch defense of Lowell. Beatty and Howard have responded with studies which are sometimes unduly and unfairly critical. Duberman and Wagenknecht present balanced, thoughtful analyses. Other brief evaluations are cited in the bibliographies of Duberman and Wagenknecht.

Evaluation of Principal Biographical Sources

Beatty, Richmond C. *James Russell Lowell*. Nashville, TN: Vanderbilt University Press, 1942. (A, G) Complaining of the New England bias of much previous Lowell scholarship, Beatty's own southern roots are all too clearly exposed.

Duberman, Martin B. *James Russell Lowell*. Boston: Houghton Mifflin, 1966. (A, G) In many ways the best biography, because Duberman evaluates Lowell in historical context and explores the tensions in his public and private life.

Greenslet, Ferris. *James Russell Lowell: His Life and Work*. Boston: Houghton Mifflin, 1905. Reprint. Detroit: Gale Research, 1969. (A, G) Although based largely in part on Scudder's study, this is by far the best of the early studies, and favorable to Lowell.

Hale, Edward Everett. *James Russell Lowell and His Friends*. 1899. Reprint. New York: AMS Press, 1969. (A) Chiefly valuable now as a collection of primary sources, this biography reflects the veneration accorded to Lowell in the nineteenth century.

Heymann, C. David. *American Aristocracy: The Lives and Times of James Russell, Amy and Robert Lowell*. New York: Dodd, Mead, 1980. (G) Part biography, part literary criticism, Heymann's narrative is not firmly grounded in historical context, displays some shoddy research, and offers occasionally facile comments on Lowell's writings.

Howard, Leon. *A Victorian Knight-Errand: A Study of the Early Career of James Russell Lowell.* Berkeley: The University of California Press, 1952. (A, G) A detailed study of Lowell's pre-Civil War career, focusing on using literary works as biographical sources; unsympathetic to its subject.

McGlinchee, Claire. *James Russell Lowell.* New York: Twayne, 1967 (G) A brief and somewhat uncritical introduction to Lowell's life and work.

Scudder, Horace E. *James Russell Lowell,* 2 vols. Boston: Houghton Mifflin, 1901. (A) The "authorized" biography, this valuable compendium of information is marred by the problems typical of such works.

Wagenknecht, Edward. *James Russell Lowell: Portrait of a Many-Sided Man.* New York: Oxford University Press, 1971. (A, G) More of a sketch than a full-blown biography, Wagenknecht's study is discerning in its criticism and enjoyable to read.

Overview and Evaluation of Primary Sources
Lowell's papers reside at Harvard University's Houghton Library. The best guide to the papers is contained in Martin Duberman's bibliography, which also lists other depositories containing Lowell's correspondence. These include the Library of Congress, the National Archives, the Massachusetts Historical Society, the Morgan Library, and the University of Virginia. Charles Eliot Norton, ed., *Letters of James Russell Lowell,* 2 vols. (Boston: Houghton, Mifflin, 1893; A, G) presents a large number of letters, but Lowell's entire correspondence deserves treatment by modern documentary editors.

Lowell's writings are voluminous. Short guides are in the bibliographies of Wagenknecht, Duberman, and McGlinchee. Although by no means complete, *The Writings of James Russell Lowell,* 11 vols. (Boston: Houghton Mifflin, 1890; A) contain most of Lowell's works. Some of Lowell's pre-Civil War political writings can be sampled in William B. Parker, ed., *The Anti-Slavery Papers of James Russell Lowell,* 2 vols. (Boston: Houghton Mifflin, 1902; A, G). Among the most enjoyable pieces are "A Fable for Critics," a satirical characterization of America's most prominent literary figures, the "Commemoration Ode," which captures the tragedy and bravery of sacrifice, and *The Bigelow Papers.* Thomas Wortham, ed., *James Russell Lowell's "The Bigelow Papers" (First Series): A Critical Edition* (DeKalb: Northern Illinois University Press, 1977; **A, G**) makes available Lowell's commentary on the Mexican War.

Museums and Historical Landmarks

Elmwood (Cambridge, MA). Lowell's house, although privately owned, is a National Historic Landmark.

Other Sources

Aaron, Daniel S. *The Unwritten War: American Writers and the Civil War.* New York: Knopf, 1973. Makes clear how American writers, including Lowell, struggled with the implications and legacy of conflict.

Fredrickson, George M. *The Inner Civil War: Northern Intellectuals and the Crisis of the Union.* New York: Harper and Row, 1965. An influential survey of the reaction of many Northern intellectuals, including Lowell, to the Civil War.

Kaplan, Lawrence S. "The Brahmin as Diplomat in Nineteenth-Century America: Everett, Bancroft, Motley, Lowell." *Civil War History* 19 (March 1973): 5-28. Suggests that Lowell and his fellow writers were inferior diplomats, unprepared for the tasks before them.

Livingston, Luther Samuel. *A Bibliography of the First Editions in Book Form of the Writings of James Russell Lowell.* New York: Ben Franklin, 1968. A useful research tool for students of Lowell's literary career.

Brooks Donohue Simpson
Arizona State University

JACQUES MARQUETTE
1637-1675
LOUIS JOLLIET
1645-1700

Chronology

Jacques Marquette was born on June 1, 1637, in Lyon, France, the sixth and last child of Nicolas and Rose Marquette; *1654* makes commitment to become a Jesuit priest; *1656* begins teaching at a Jesuit college in Auxere, France; *1657* studies philosophy at Pont-a-Mousson; *1659-1664* teaches at Jesuit colleges in France (Reims, Charleville, Langres, and Pont-a-Mousson); *1666* receives ordination at Toul, France, and sets out for Quebec where he arrives on September 20; leaves in November for Trois Rivieres to study Indian languages; *1668* appointed to the mission among the Ottawas and later founds the mission at Sault Ste. Marie; *1669* meets Louis Jolliet; *1671* founds the mission of St. Ignace on the Straits of Mackinac; *1672* appointed with Jolliet to explore Mississippi River; *May 17, 1673*, sets out with Jolliet on the exploration and returns to Green Bay on September 30; *1674* founds a mission among the Illinois Indians; *May 18, 1675*, dies on the Père Marquette River in Illinois.

Louis Jolliet was born on September 21, 1645 near Quebec, the third of four children of Jean Jolliet, a wheelright carpenter, and Marie Jolliet; *1655* studies at the Jesuit seminary in Quebec; *1667* goes to France to continue his studies; *1668* abandons religious studies; returns to Quebec to begin trading venture with his brother Adrien and embark on a career of hydrography and exploration; *1673* explores the Mississippi River with Marquette; *1675* marries Claire-Françoise Bissot and with her raises four children; *1679* explores Hudson Bay; *1680* granted Anticosti Island at the mouth of the St. Lawrence River as reward for his services to France; *1694* explores Labrador; *1696* returns to France and appointed royal hydrographer in Canada; opens school to teach mapmaking; *1700* dies in the summer just outside Montreal.

Activities of Historical Significance

Father Marquette was a conscientious and pious missionary to the Indians and founded several missions in New France. Louis Jolliet was an expert hydrographer and explorer throughout the St. Lawrence region. Yet for both men, their fame rests almost exclusively on being the first white men to explore the upper Mississippi River. De Soto discovered and surveyed the southern regions of that river for Spain in the 1640s, but as yet the great river of the north was not known to be the same and, in fact, was hoped by Marquette and Jolliet to be a westward passage to the Pacific Ocean. They explored downriver until it was joined by the Arkansas River. Having determined that it was the Mississippi River De Soto had discovered and fearing Spanish aggression, they returned to New France. Tragically, all of Jolliet's notes and maps were destroyed on the return trip, and the journal of the less proficient Marquette was the only source of information that survived. This journal, and its authorship, has proven a source of controversy for historians. Marquette died within a year of returning from the trip, but Jolliet continued to serve New France in exploration and mapmaking. Nevertheless, the fame of these two men is linked in their joint exploration of the Mississippi River.

Overview of Biographical Sources

It should not be surprising that Marquette has received more biographical attention than Jolliet since Marquette's journal of the voyage survived whereas Jolliet's was lost. Nevertheless, it is striking that virtually all of the biographical work has been done by members of the Catholic faith.

Despite the contributions of Marquette as a missionary and Jolliet as a mapmaker, the main emphasis in historical writing has centered on their joint exploration. In this, the main historiographic debate has centered on Marquette. Repplier, *Pere Marquette, Priest, Pioneer, and Adventurer* (1927), and Donnelly, *Jacques Marquette, S.J., 1637-1675* (1968), argue that the journal that survived was largely the work of Marquette, who was an integral part of the mission. Steck, in each of his works (see below), has insisted that Marquette was not a Jesuit and, in fact, did not go with Jolliet on the voyage, and, therefore, the journal was not his. Hamilton's critical study, *Marquette's Explorations: The Narratives Reexamined* (1970), has hopefully settled this dispute, and restored Marquette to his rightful place as an active participant in the journey.

Evaluation of Principal Biographical Sources

Delanglez, Jean. *Louis Jolliet: 1645-1700.* Chicago: Institute of Jesuit History, 1948. (A) This work makes much use of primary material and is a good study of Jolliet. This collection of ten articles is coherently organized and well-written. It offers the scholar's conclusions and a total assessment, something not found in the individual articles.

Derleth, August William. *Father Marquette and the Great Rivers.* New York: Farrar, Straus and Cudahy, 1955. (G, Y) A simple, straightforward story without nuance or depth. A pleasure to read, it is primarily for those taking their first look at Marquette.

Donnelly, Joseph P. *Jacques Marquette, S.J., 1637-1675.* Chicago: Loyola University Press, 1968. (A) Written to celebrate the tercentennial of the Marquette-Jolliet expedition, this study offers the best scholarly biography of Marquette. It includes an excellent genealogy and bibliography, and is authoritative without being dogmatic.

Eifert, Virginia. *Louis Jolliet, Explorer of Rivers.* New York: Dodd, Mead, 1962. (A, G, Y) A readable biography that covers all aspects of Jolliet's life. His roles as hydrographer and explorer of all New France are emphasized, though the book possesses a slightly tragic undertone.

Grandbois, Alain. *Born in Quebec; a Tale of Louis Joliet.* Montreal: Palm Publishers, 1964. (G, Y) This is an English translation of a French Canadian work. The poetic license used by the author to fill in gaps where original materials are lacking limits its use for historians, though it offers a nice story based on reliable sources.

Hamilton, Raphael. *Father Marquette.* Grand Rapids, MI: Eerdman's, 1970. (A, G) Part of the Great Men of Michigan Series, this brief biography is a good starting point for the scholar looking for facts only.

————. *Marquette's Explorations: the Narratives Reexamined.* Madison: University of Wisconsin Press, 1970. (A, G) Hopefully, this study settles the dispute as to the authorship of the journal in Marquette's favor. It is an able discussion of both sides of the story, as well as an examination of the primary material. Marquette emerges from Hamilton's examination as Jesuit and author, his reputation intact.

Kelly, Regina. *The Picture Story and Biography of Marquette and Joliet.* Chicago: Follett Publishing, 1965. (Y) A handsome book for younger readers. It offers the story, embellished to be sure, through captivating illustrations.

Repplier, Agnes. *Pere Marquette, Priest, Pioneer, and Adventurer.* New York: Doubleday, Doran, 1929. (A, G) Repplier's book focuses on the zest of the missionary, stressing the story told in the *Jesuit Relations*. Though brief, it is still descriptive and compares Marquette with other missionary explorers.

Steck, Francis. *Essays Relating to the Jolliet-Marquette Expedition*. Privately printed, 1953. (A) This is a privately printed document designed to supplement the author's 1927 dissertation and rebut the arguments made by Repplier. The book is argumentative and direct; it offers a one-sided look at Marquette but little else.

————. *Marquette Legends*. New York: Pageant Press, 1960. (G) This is a popularized version of the *Essays*. It is free of the bibliographic arguments, ponderous footnotes, and aggressive attitude, but still seeks to remove Marquette from any historical significance in the exploration of the Mississippi River.

————. *The Jolliet-Marquette Expedition, 1673*. Washington, DC: Catholic University of America Press, 1927. (A, G) This well-documented work stresses conflict between church and state. The author concludes that the voyage was not a discovery of the Mississippi River, that Jolliet was the leader of the expedition, and that Marquette did not write the narrative normally attributed to him. In fact, Steck seriously doubts if Marquette even went on the mission.

Thwaites, Reuben G. *Father Marquette*. New York: D. Appleton, 1902. This volume in the Appleton's Life Histories Series is written from the point of view of Marquette as the hero of the Mississippi Valley. It concentrates on his work in the wilderness, and relies almost exclusively on the *Jesuit Relations*, and Marquette's *Journal*. It tells Marquette's story in his own words. (A, G)

Overview of Primary Sources

The Voyages of Marquette in the Jesuit Relations, edited by Reuben G. Thwaites (Ann Arbor, MI: Ann Arbor Microfilms International, 1966; A, G), includes the often disputed journals of Marquette in both French and English. It is excerpted from *The Jesuit Relations and Allied Documents*, 73 vols. (Cleveland: Burrows Brothers; A, G), also edited by Thwaites. Volumes 50-60 contain material relevant to Marquette. Francis Steck has edited *Facsimile Reproductions to Accompany Essays Relating to the Jolliet-Marquette Expedition, 1673* (privately printed, 1954; A), a compilation of selected documents he uses to assert that Marquette was not the author of the journal attributed to him. Jolliet's journal of the journey was lost on the return trip; therefore, there is no primary material relating directly to Jolliet.

Other Sources

Hamilton, Raphael N. "The Marquette Death Site: The Case for Ludington." *Michigan History* 49 (September 1965): 228-248. This article and those below by May and Stebbins discuss the discovery of Marquette's death site.

Kellogg, Louise Phelps. "Jacques Marquette" and "Louis Jolliet." In *Dictionary of American Biography*, edited by Allen Johnson and Dumas Malone. New York: Charles Scribner's Sons, 1928-1936. Both articles are informative and offer good brief accounts, even though the bibliographic information is dated.

May, George S., ed. "The Discovery of Father Marquette's Grave at St. Ignace in 1877, as Related by Father Edward Jacker." *Michigan History* 42 (September 1958): 267-287.

Stebbins, Catherine L. "The Marquette Death Site." *Michigan History* 48 (December 1964): 333-368.

Daniel Dean Roland

THURGOOD MARSHALL
b. 1908

Chronology

Born Thoroughgood Marshall on July 2, 1908, in Baltimore, Maryland, to William Marshall, a writer and one-time chief steward at the Chesapeake Bay Boat Club, and his wife Norma, a schoolteacher; grows up in Baltimore; *1925-1930* attends Lincoln University, Oxford, Pennsylvania; *1929* marries Vivian Burey, with whom he has two sons; *1930* graduates with honors from Lincoln University; rejected by the University of Maryland Law School because of his race; *1933* graduates from Howard University Law School; returns to Baltimore to begin private practice; begins his work with the National Association for the Advancement of Colored People (NAACP); *1935* wins *Pearson v. Murray*, which requires the admission of the first African American student to University of Maryland Law School; *1940* becomes head of the NAACP Legal Defense and Education Fund; *1944* wins *Smith v. Allwright*, which finds racially restricted state primaries a violation of voting rights; *1946* wins *Morgan v. Virginia*, which invalidates racial segregation on interstate transportation; *1946* awarded Springarn Medal by the NAACP; *1948* wins *Shelly v. Kraemer*, which ends racially restrictive real estate covenants; *1954* wins *Brown v. Board of Education of Topeka*, which finds separate educational institutions for the races unconstitutional; *1955* Vivian Marshall dies in February; wins *Lucy v. Adams*, requiring the admission of the first African American student to the University of Alabama; marries Cecelia Suryat in December; *1958* wins *Cooper v. Aaron*, which orders the immediate desegregation of Little Rock, Arkansas, schools; *1960* acts as consultant to the Constitutional Conference on Kenya held in London; *1961* heads U.S. delegation at the celebration in April of the independence of Sierra Leone; *1961* appointed to the Second U.S. Circuit Court of Appeals by President John F. Kennedy; *1965* appointed solicitor general of the United States by President Lyndon B. Johnson, thus becoming the first African American to hold the position; *1967* appointed justice of the U.S. Supreme Court by President Johnson, becoming the first African American to sit on the Court; *1967-1991* serves as associate justice of the Supreme Court; *1991* resigns from an increasing conservative Supreme Court, citing age as the reason.

Activities of Historical Significance

As the head of the NAACP Legal Defense and Education Fund, Marshall argued some of the most important civil rights cases in U.S. history before the Supreme

Court. The most important was *Brown v. Board of Education of Topeka*. In its decision the Supreme Court overturned *Plessy v. Ferguson* (1896), which held that providing separate facilities for the races was constitutional. In *Brown* the Court found that "separate educational facilities are inherently unequal." The decision, while not the first attacking *Plessy*, put an end to the legality of segregation and opened the modern civil rights movement. Marshall's record before the Supreme Court was impressive; he won twenty-nine of the thirty-two cases he argued.

Marshall was nominated to the Second Circuit Court of Appeals on September 23, 1961, by President Kennedy, but was not confirmed by the Senate until September 1962. In 1965 he became the first African American to serve as solicitor general, the government's lawyer before the Supreme Court. In this position he continued his impressive string of legal victories, finishing his tenure with fourteen wins and five losses. Among the victories were two important civil rights cases in which the Court extended legal protection to include actions of private citizens; formerly, only governments actions were protected under the law.

Marshall remained solicitor general until 1967 when President Lyndon B. Johnson selected him to sit on the U.S. Supreme Court, the first African American to hold that honor. Throughout his tenure on the Court, Marshall remained a consistent proponent of civil rights. His majority opinions on criminal matters defined the rights and limitations of both the government and defendants. Because the judicial appointments to the Court by Presidents Nixon, Reagan and Bush gave it a more conservative cast, Marshall dissented with greater regularly, voting with what is termed the "liberal minority."

In 1987 Marshall opened a controversy over the nature of the Constitution which had the effect of reinvigorating the study of its creation and early history. He argued that the Constitution was flawed from its inception because the founding fathers did not include protection of rights for African Americans or women. He argued that these flaws led to the Civil War and necessitated a number of constitutional amendments. Marshall's view, expressed in the Constitution's bicentennial year, challenged many Americans' popular belief that the document was a perfect instrument of government. The debate brought out new ideas about the foundation of American government and the intentions of the founding fathers.

Overview of Biographical Sources

The majority of works that treat Marshall's life and career focus on his legal career and the civil rights movement rather than on his personal life. Although there is not yet a definitive work on his life, a number of works give good professional overviews.

Richard Kluger's *Simple Justice* (1976) gives the most information about Marshall's career while providing some facts about his family. The biographical entry in *Current Biographical Yearbook* (1989) covers all aspects of his life and may contain the most complete information in print. Randall Bland's *Private Pressure on Public Law* (1973) examines the effects of Marshall's life on his legal career. The 1978 supplement to Leon Friedman's *The Justices of the United States Supreme Court, 1789-1969* (1969) covers some aspects of Marshall's early life but emphasizes his work on the Court. *Congressional Quarterly's Guide to the United States Supreme Court* (1979) contains a biographical sketch that deals primarily with his legal career.

Evaluation of Principal Biographical Sources

Bland, Randall. *Private Pressure on Public Law: The Legal Career of Thurgood Marshall*. Port Washington, NY: Kennikat Press, 1973. (A) Bland's study uses Marshall as an example to show that the U.S. constitutional system "works." It contains a great deal of valuable information about Marshall and provides background for the major cases that he was involved in up to his appointment to the Supreme Court.

Clark, Ramsey. "Thurgood Marshall." In *The Justices of the United States Supreme Court: Their Lives and Major Opinions, The Burger Court 1969-1978*. Vol. 5. Edited by Leon Friedman. New York: Chelsea House, 1978. (A) The article in this supplement updates MacKenzie's treatment cited below. It covers Marshall's work on the Court between 1967 and 1978, including the opinions he authored during his first ten terms. It is excellent for those studying Marshall's Supreme Court career.

Kluger, Richard. *Simple Justice*. New York: Alfred Knopf, 1976. (A, G) This study traces Marshall's legal career and personal background up to the *Brown v. Board of Education* case and is one of the few sources for extensive background on Marshall and his family. Kluger continues with a thorough explanation of the case and an analysis of its far-reaching effects on American law and society. Kluger concludes with a summary of Marshall's career through his early years on the Supreme Court.

MacKenzie, John. "Thurgood Marshall." In *The Justices of the United States Supreme Court 1789-1969: Their Lives and Major Opinions*. Vol. 4. Edited by Leon Friedman. New York: Chelsea House, 1969. (A) Focuses on Marshall's legal career up to 1969. MacKenzie provides an excellent examination of the cases he worked on as a lawyer, judge, and solicitor general.

Moritz, Charles, ed. "Thurgood Marshall." In *Current Bibliography Yearbook 1989*. New York: H. W. Wilson, 1989. (A, G) This is among the best of the general biographies and covers Marshall's professional and personal life. It provides a quick reference to the major cases of Marshall's career.

Tushnet, Mark. "Thurgood Marshall." In *Encyclopedia of the American Constitution*, edited by Leonard Levy, et al. New York: Macmillan, 1986. A concise sketch of Marshall's life with emphasis on his work on the Supreme Court.

Williams, Juan. "Marshall's Law." *Washington Post Magazine* (January 7, 1990): 12-19, 27-29. (A, G) This is a review of the career of Marshall that emphasizes the pre-Supreme Court period. An insert in the article discusses Marshall's private life, which makes this a rare and useful piece.

Witt, Elder, ed. *Congressional Quarterly's Guide to the United States Supreme Court*. Washington, DC: Congressional Quarterly, 1979. This reference volume includes a short outline of Marshall's life and is a good starting point for further research.

Overview and Evaluation of Primary Sources
    The majority of primary sources focus on Marshall's professional career and are found in law libraries. These sources include interviews, introductions, tributes, congressional hearings, manuscripts, and articles.
    Interviews provide a first-hand account of Marshall's judicial and social concerns. The *Washington Post* published Joseph Mohbat's interview with Marshall when he was solicitor general ("It's an Old Shoe Job to Marshall," December 26, 1965; G). The interview treats Marshall's motives for moving from the NAACP to government service and touches briefly on his early life. Two synopses of a 1987 television interview with Marshall have been published by legal journals. Gary Hengstler, "Marshalling His Views: Justice's Controversial Comments Break Twenty Year Silence," appeared in the *American Bar Association Journal* 74 (March 1, 1988: 36; A, G). This synopsis gives Marshall's personal views on presidents, Chief Justice Rehnquist, and the Constitution. A synopsis by Carl Rowan, "Justice Marshall: Candor on the Court, Meese, Life," *Legal Times* (December 14, 1987: 8; A, G), gives Marshall's attitudes about the Constitution's

guarantees of privacy. These synopses give some understanding of how Marshall views the world and his work.

The introduction to a Thurgood Marshall Symposium issue of the *Arkansas Law Review* 40 (Spring 1987, 1-3; **A, G**) covers the major highlights of his life and career and the most important legal cases in which he was involved. It serves as a basis for understanding the breadth of his experience and the importance of his work. The issue contains three tributes to Marshall. Justice William Brennan stresses Marshall's work on the Court, while Wiley Branton and P. A. Hollingsworth discuss his importance to the civil rights movement, especially during the 1950s. These latter tributes offer personal accounts of the effect of Marshall's work on the lives of African Americans.

Marshall has written numerous articles and speeches on the Constitution and its history. "The View from the Inside," published in *The Bill of Rights Journal* 22 (December 1989: 1-4; **A, G**), discusses the Court's handling of civil rights cases and projects its future direction. A 1986 speech on the death penalty and its implementation was published by the *Columbia Law Review*, 86 (January 1986: 1-8; **A**).

A speech that Marshall gave in 1987 helped spark a debate among constitutional scholars. The speech was reprinted in various forms in a number of legal journals: "The Constitution's Bicentennial: Commemorating the Wrong Document?" *Vanderbilt Law Review* 40 (November 1987: 1337-1342; **A, G**); "The Constitution: A Living Document," *Howard Law Journal* 30 (Fall 1987: 915-920; **A, G**); "Constitution: Defective from the Start." *Legal Times* (May 11, 1987: 15; **A, G**); and, "Those the Constitution Left Out," *Judges Journal* 26 (Summer 1987, 18-22; **A, G**). Marshall's speech called the Constitution imperfect from the beginning, a differing view from that prevailing during the Constitution's bicentennial celebration. The speech clarifies Marshall's view of the Court's role in the continuing evolution of the Constitution.

Marshall has appeared before three confirmation hearings in the U.S. Senate. Transcripts of these hearings can be found in the *Congressional Record* for the years of the appointments. The Senate Judiciary Committee's confirmation hearings for Supreme Court justices have been published separately since 1916. Roy Mersky and J. Myron Jacobstein complied *The Supreme Court of the United States: Hearings and Reports on Successful and Unsuccessful Nominations of United States Supreme Court Justices by the Senate Judiciary Committee, 1916-1975.* (Washington, DC: William S. Hein, 1979; **A**). This hearing gives a vivid picture of social atmosphere in the U.S. during the mid-1960s, especially the concerns of some senators over appointing an NAACP lawyer to the Court. It provides some biographical data, including Marshall's official biography.

The hearings on Marshall's appointment to the Second Circuit Court of Appeals are printed in *Nomination of Thurgood Marshall* (U.S. Congress, Senate. Committee on the Judiciary's Special Subcommittee on Nominations. 87th Cong., 2nd sess., 1962; A). The hearing focused on Marshall's leadership of the NAACP Legal Defense Fund and reveals some senators' views on race issues.

The hearings on his appointment as solicitor general are published as *Nomination of Thurgood Marshall to be Solicitor General of the United States* (U.S. Congress, Senate. Committee on the Judiciary. 89th Cong., 1st sess., 1965; A). Unlike the 1962 hearings, this hearing lasted a single day, after which the nomination was sent to the full Senate with a favorable recommendation. These hearings can also be obtained on microfiche from the Congressional Information Service under the reference numbers (87) S1532-3 and (89) 1700-2 respectively.

A number of special collections contain material by or about Justice Marshall. The Manuscript Division of the Library of Congress (Washington, D.C.) contains the National Association for the Advancement of Colored People Records, 1909-1930, and the Arthur Barnett Springarn, founder of the NAACP, Papers, 1911-1964. The Moorland Springarn Research Center at Howard University (Washington, D.C.) has an index of references to Marshall for the manuscript correspondence that it holds.

Fiction and Adaptations

In April 1991 ABC aired a six-hour, two-part film based on Marshall's litigation of a South Carolina school board that eventually was combined with four similar cases and taken to the Supreme Court as *Brown v. Board of Education. Separate But Equal* begins in Clarendon County, South Carolina, where a minister and black school principal, Rev. J. A. DeLaine, was denied bus service for his students, some of whom walked six miles to school. The laws of seventeen states recognized the principle of "separate but equal." Sensing impending federal government intervention, Governor Jimmy Byrnes immediately appropriated seventy-five million dollars to upgrade the Negro schools, but Marshall, as chief counsel for the NAACP, challenged that equal facilities do not provide equal opportunities or self-esteem.

Sidney Poitier came out of retirement to play the lead as Marshall, making his first television appearance since 1955. Burt Lancaster, in his last performance, plays John W. Davis, the distinguished lawyer who had argued a hundred and thirty-eight cases, both liberal and conservative, before the Supreme Court and who, here, argues the case for school segregation. Richard Kiley plays Chief Justice Earl Warren, and Tommy Hollis plays Harry Biggs, Sr., whose request for a bus for his son started the process that led to the landmark decision desegregating schools through busing. Ed Hall plays a convincing J. A. DeLaine, whose first request was for "just one bus, even the oldest."

Museums, Historical Landmarks, Societies
Enoch Pratt Free Library-Maryland Room, African-American Collection (Baltimore, MD). The Library maintains a file on Justice Marshall, a Maryland native.

Garmatz Federal Building (Baltimore, MD). The building contains a bronze statue of Marshall, sculpted by Reuben Kramer and erected in 1980.

United States Supreme Court (Washington, DC). The Court library maintains a collection on the lives and works of justices.

Other Sources
Blaustein, Albert, and Roy Mersky. *The First Hundred Justices: Statistical Studies on the Supreme Court of the United States.* Hamden, CT: Archon, 1978. Compares the first one hundred individuals to serve on the Supreme Court in such matters as background, profession, and judicial opinions and dissents.

Cox, Archibald. *The Court and the Constitution.* Boston: Houghton Mifflin, 1987. Discusses the relationship of the Supreme Court to the Constitution. Cox covers Marshall's work for civil rights both before and after joining the Court.

Diamond, Raymond. "No Call to Glory: Thurgood Marshall's Thesis on the Intent of a Pro-Slavery Constitution." *Vanderbilt Law Review* (January 1989): 93-131. This scholarly examination of Marshall's thesis about the nature of the Constitution finds that he has many valid points.

Douglas, William O. *The Court Years, 1939-1975: The Autobiography of William O. Douglas.* New York: Random House, 1980. This interesting account of the Court and its members by a former justice includes his opinions of Marshall.

Kohlmeier, Louis. *"God Save this Honorable Court!"* New York: Scribner's, 1972. Kohlmeier examines the conflict between the executive and the Congress over the Supreme Court during the Johnson and Nixon administrations.

Lytle, Clifford. *The Warren Court and Its Critics.* Tucson: University of Arizona Press, 1968. This work is a study of the critics of the Warren Court's decisions, beginning with *Brown v. Board of Education.* It details the response of the critics to these decisions and their attempts to limit the Court's influence.

Ripple, Kenneth. "Thurgood Marshall and the Forgotten Legacy of *Brown v. Board of Education.*" *Notre Dame Lawyer* 55 (Fall 1980): 471-484. Discusses the strategy used in overturning *Plessy v. Ferguson* and how it has influenced Marshall during his tenure on the Court. Ripple finds him to be a pragmatist who understands both his own and the Court's limits.

Schwartz, Herman, ed. *The Burger Years: Rights and Wrongs in the Supreme Court, 1969-1986.* New York: Viking, 1987. This anthology of essays examines the influence of the Court under Chief Justice Warren Burger. It gives a good overview of the early interpretations of the influence of the Court during these years.

Simon, James. *In His Own Image: The Supreme Court In Richard Nixon's America.* New York: David McKay, 1973. Simon examines Nixon's first term and the effect of his four Supreme Court appointments. During this period Justice Marshall went from voting with the majority to being a leading dissenter.

Woodward, Bob, and Scott Armstrong. *The Brethren: Inside the Supreme Court.* New York: Simon and Schuster, 1979. Studies the inner workings of the Court from 1969 through the 1975 term, which include Marshall's first sessions on the Court.

Donald E. Heidenreich, Jr.
Kemper College

GEORGE MASON
1725-1792

Chronology

Born George Mason (the fourth of that name in Virginia) on December 11, 1725, on a plantation in Prince William County, later Fairfax County, Virginia, the first of three children of George Mason, a planter and officeholder, and Ann Thomson Mason, *1735* his father dies on March 5, and his mother looks after the family holdings until he reaches adulthood; continues his studies, and is particularly interested in his uncle's law books; *1748-1785* serves as a vestryman of Truro Parish; *1749-1792* serves as a partner and treasurer of the Ohio Company, a group with interests in western lands; *1750* marries sixteen-year-old Anne Eilbeck, a neighbor from the Maryland side of the Potomac River, on April 4, with whom he has twelve children, nine of whom survive; *1754-1779* serves as a trustee of the town of Alexandria; *1758* moves into his new family home, Gunston Hall, when it is sufficiently completed; *1763-1765* opposes the Proclamation Line of 1763, the Sugar Act of 1764, and the Stamp Act of 1765; *1764-1789* is a member of the Fairfax County court (after a previous, inactive stint from 1747 to 1752); *1769* contributes to the Virginia Nonimportation Resolutions (against the Townsend duties on imported goods); *1773* his wife dies on March 9, three months after the birth and death of twin sons; compiles and annotates "Extracts from the Virginia Charters" (in defense of the territorial claims of the Ohio Company and the Virginia colony); *1774* writes the Prince William County Resolves and the Fairfax County Resolves (in response to the Boston Port Act); *1775-1776* participates as a member of the third and fifth Revolutionary conventions in Virginia; *1776* writes drafts of the Virginia Declaration of Rights and the new state's constitution; *1776-1780* participates actively in the new Virginia House of Delegates; *1780* marries Sarah Brent on April 11; *1782* attacks the unrepublican nature of local government in Virginia; *1785* participates in the Mount Vernon Conference, composed of delegates from Virginia and Maryland, which leads to the Annapolis Convention of 1786 and the Philadelphia Convention of 1787; *1787* represents Virginia in the Philadelphia Convention and then writes his "Objections" to the proposed constitution that results; *1787-1788* represents Fairfax County again in the House of Delegates; *1788* represents Stafford County in the Virginia Convention, where he is a leading opponent of ratification of the proposed U.S. Constitution; *1790* declines appointment to the U.S. Senate; *1792* dies October 7, at Gunston Hall, where he is buried.

Activities of Historical Significance

George Mason's historical importance derives primarily from his activities in the events leading to the Declaration of Independence, especially during the middle months of 1776. In addition, he continued his involvement as a member of the Philadelphia convention of 1787 and Virginia's ratifying convention of 1788.

Mason proved to be of critical importance in drafting the Fairfax County Resolves in 1774, which called for a "Congress of Delegates" from all the colonies to coordinate their response to the British Parliament's passage of the Boston Port Act and other Intolerable Acts. The First Continental Congress soon met and accepted his central proposals. He participated in the third and last of the five "conventions" of 1775 and 1776, in which Virginians moved toward a decision to declare independence from Great Britain. In 1776 he took the leading role, first, in drafting a Declaration of Rights, and then, in drafting a constitution for the new state. The Declaration of Rights provided Thomas Jefferson with much of the material from which he wrote the Preamble to the Declaration of Independence. It also provided a model for other states, and after the U.S. Constitution went into effect, for the new nation's Bill of Rights.

His leadership did not end at the point of Virginia's declaring independence. In his most sustained involvement in public affairs outside his home county, Mason served in the new state's House of Delegates from 1776 through 1780. There he worked on major questions relating to Virginia's western lands, support for George Washington's army against the British, the revision of the former colony's legal system, and the relations between church and state.

Mason is perhaps best known for his criticism of the proposed U.S. Constitution in 1787 and 1788. He objected to portions of it, refused to sign it at the conclusion of the Philadelphia Convention in 1787, and, with Patrick Henry, led the opposition to its ratification in the Virginia Convention of 1788. He objected that the proposed new government would be too weak, in that the Constitution denied it the power to end slave imports until twenty years had passed. Yet, in various other respects, he feared that the proposed new government might prove too powerful. The Constitution lacked a bill of rights with such guarantees as freedom of the press and trial by jury, and he wished to amend such major provisions as those on tariff acts and the federal judiciary.

While embodying the transforming ideas of the American Revolution, Mason also reflected the material interests of large slaveholders from the upper South. To understand his position on questions related to slavery, it is essential to distinguish between slavery and the slave trade. Although Mason harbored deep reservations about the system of slave labor, he himself continued to work his plantation with a large force of slaves, and he did not grant them freedom. The major complaint that he voiced about slavery concerned the continued importation of slaves into the new nation from Africa and the Caribbean. Mason could, in a single sentence, voice both opinions—in support of slavery in Virginia yet against the international slave trade—as he did at the 1788 convention when he complained about the proposed U. S. Constitution: "though this infamous traffic be continued, we have no security for the [slaves] that we have already."

Overview of Biographical Sources

Though not the subject of as much historical investigation as his contemporaries who acted more widely on the national scene, Mason has by no means been neglected. One of his descendants, Kate Mason Rowland, rescued him from relative obscurity when she published a two-volume biography, complete with many of his writings, in 1892, at the centenary of his death. The two major modern scholars of Mason are Helen Hill Miller and Robert A. Rutland. Throughout the twentieth century, Mason has generally been treated as a major figure in Revolutionary Virginia whose major roles occurred in events that led to the writing of Thomas Jefferson's Declaration of Independence. Today, he is widely recognized as a political thinker, writer, consultant, and actor who, though his actions were largely confined to the colony and then to the Commonwealth of Virginia, had enormous impact on the wider events of the revolutionary era. And yet writers on Mason routinely demonstrate how difficult it is to state his positions on slavery, the slave trade, and a bill of rights, and to relate these positions to his own time and to modern times.

Evaluation of Principal Biographical Sources

Copeland, Pamela C., and Richard K. MacMaster. *The Five George Masons: Patriots and Planters of Virginia and Maryland.* Charlottesville: Published for the Board of Regents of Gunston Hall by the University Press of Virginia, 1975. (A, G) This book, which accords the most space to Virginia's fourth George Mason, introduces dates for his birth and his father's death.

Henri, Florette. *George Mason of Virginia.* New York: Crowell-Collier, 1971. (G, Y) A competent, accessible biography for young and general readers.

Hill, Helen. "George Mason." In *Dictionary of American Biography.* Vol. 12, edited by Dumas Malone. New York: Charles Scribner's Sons, 1933. (A, G) An early interpretive summary by Mason's major biographer.

————. *George Mason: Constitutionalist.* Cambridge: Harvard University Press, 1938. Reprint. Gloucester, MA: Peter Smith, 1966. (A, G) A fine scholarly study of Mason in his major public role.

Miller, Helen Hill. *George Mason: Gentleman Revolutionary.* Chapel Hill: University of North Carolina Press, 1975. (A, G) The fullest biography, replete with illustrations.

————. *George Mason of Gunston Hall.* Lorton, VA: Board of Regents of Gunston Hall, 1958. (G) A condensed version of the author's *George Mason: Constitutionalist.*

————. *George Mason: The Man Who Didn't Sign.* Lorton, VA: Board of Regents of Gunston Hall, 1987. (G) A brief treatment of Mason at the 1787 Philadephia Convention and the 1788 ratifying convention.

Rowland, Kate Mason. *The Life of George Mason, 1725-1792, Including His Speeches, Public Papers, and Correspondence.* 2 vols. New York: G. P. Putnam's Sons, 1892. (A, G) The pioneering study. Rowland incorporates lengthy quotations from letters and other writings.

Rutland, Robert A. *George Mason and the War for Independence.* Williams-burg, VA: Virginia Independence Bicentennial Commission, 1976. (G) A fine introduction to Mason's activities from 1765 through 1781.

————. *George Mason: Reluctant Statesman.* Baton Rouge: Louisiana State University Press, 1961. (A, G, Y) A readable short biography by the editor of Mason's papers. Contains no notes.

Overview and Evaluation of Primary Sources

The place to begin with Mason's writings is Robert A. Rutland, ed., *The Papers of George Mason, 1725-1792,* 3 vols. (Chapel Hill: University of North Carolina Press, 1970; A, G). To track his path through the documentation from the various Revolutionary-era conventions, one may consult William J. Van Schreeven, Robert L. Scribner, and Brent Tarter, eds., *Revolutionary Virginia: The Road to Independence,* 7 vols. (Charlottesville: University Press of Virginia for the Virginia Independence Bicentennial Commission, 1973-1983; A, G); Max Farrand, ed., *The Records of the Federal Convention of 1787,* 4 vols. (New Haven: Yale University

Press, 1911-1937; rev. ed., 1966; **A, G**); and David Robertson, ed., *Debates and Other Proceedings of the Convention of Virginia . . . June, 1788*, 3 vols. (Petersburg, VA: Hunter and Prentis, 1788-1789; **A**). The story of ratification in Virginia is told in three magisterial volumes, *Ratification of the Constitution by the States: Virginia*, which are volumes 8-10 in the series *The Documentary History of the Ratification of the Constitution*, edited by John P. Kaminski, et al. (Madison: State Historical Society of Wisconsin, 1988-1991; **A, G**).

Fiction and Adaptations

Mason is the subject of a historical novel, *Glimpse of Glory: George Mason of Gunston Hall* (1954), by Marian Buckley Cox. "George Mason of Gunston Hall," a twenty-nine-minute video, is a 1989 Theater Wagon of Virginia Production, suitable for high school, college, and general audiences. Robbins Gates plays Mason as, in 1789, he reads the Bill of Rights as proposed by Congress, and explains why, in his view, these proposed amendments are "necessary" but "not enough." "George Mason," a forty-eight-minute black-and-white motion picture, dramatizes Mason's fight for a bill of rights to the U.S. Constitution. Produced as a sixteen-mm filmstrip by Robert Saudek Associates in 1965 in the Profiles in Courage Series, and released in video in 1983 by Zenger Video, it is suitable for high school and college audiences. "George Mason, Conservative Revolutionary," is a seventeen-minute color video produced by the Virginia Department of Education. In 1991 Gunston Hall released a new video on Mason—a twelve-minute version for orientation at Gunston Hall and a half-hour version that is available to organizations and schools; produced by Robert Cole and narrated by Roger Mudd, it includes as speakers Virginia governor Douglas Wilder and Mason biographers Helen Hill Miller and Robert A. Rutland. Gunston Hall has also prepared detailed booklets about Mason, one designed for elementary school teachers and their students, another for high schools. These can serve as a manual to accompany the new film, prepare students for visits to Gunston Hall, or substitute for such visits.

Museums, Historical Landmarks, Societies

George Mason University (Fairfax, VA). Located in northern Virginia, the university carries Mason's name and promotes his legacy. An annual lecture series at the university has led to the publication, by the George Mason University Press, of various titles, among them *The Legacy of George Mason*, edited by Josephine F. Pacheco (1983); *The First Amendment: The Legacy of George Mason*, edited by T. Daniel Shumate (1985); *Federalism: The Legacy of George Mason*, edited by

Martin B. Cohen (1988); *Separation of Powers in the American Political System: The Legacy of George Mason*, edited by Barbara B. Knight (1989); and *The Will of the People: The Legacy of George Mason*, edited by George R. Johnson (1990).

Gunston Hall (near Lorton, VA). Open daily to visitors, Mason's home offers an excellent introduction to life in Tidewater Virginia in the colonial and revolutionary eras. Books related to Gunston Hall include *"Enchanted Ground": George Mason's Gunston Hall*, with text by Joanne Young and photographs by Taylor Lewis (1980); it is a brief, recent, illustrated introduction to Mason's family home. A new volume is in preparation by Donald Taylor for publication in late 1991. An older, architectural study, with a brief text by Harry R. Connor and with photographs by Kenneth Clark, is *Gunston Hall, Fairfax County, Virginia* (1930). A chapter on Gunston Hall is contained in Rosamond Randall Beirne and John Henry Scarff, *William Buckland, 1734-1774: Architect of Virginia and Maryland* (1958, 1970).

Other Sources

Breen, T. H. *Tobacco Culture: The Mentality of the Great Tidewater Planters on the Eve of Revolution*. Princeton: Princeton University Press, 1985. An effort to comprehend the dynamic relationship between the private lives and the public concerns of the leaders of Virginia's revolutionary generation.

Buckley, Thomas E. *Church and State in Revolutionary Virginia, 1776-1787*. Charlottesville: University Press of Virginia, 1977. Notes Mason's participation in the political struggle in Virginia over the relations between church and state.

Horrell, Joseph. "George Mason and the Fairfax Court." *Virginia Magazine of History and Biography* 91 (October 1983): 418-439. Corrects all previous accounts of Mason's roles in local government and politics from 1747 to 1790.

Kulikoff, Allan. *Tobacco and Slaves: The Development of Southern Cultures in the Chesapeake, 1680-1800*. Chapel Hill: University of North Carolina Press, for the Institute of Early American History and Culture, 1986. The fullest study of economic and cultural patterns, and of the social worlds of black and white Virginians, in Mason's time and place.

McColley, Robert. *Slavery and Jeffersonian Virginia*. 2d ed. Urbana: University of Illinois Press, 1973. Introduces the world of the slaves on Virginia's plantations, during the revolution and contends that "the true emancipators" were Quakers and Methodists, not the big (Episcopalian) planters.

Main, Jackson T. "The One Hundred." *William and Mary Quarterly* 11 (3rd Series, July 1954): 354-384. A descriptive survey of Virginia's hundred leading late eighteenth-century families, among them that of George Mason, who in the 1780s owned thousands of acres of land and more than one hundred slaves.

Mayer, Henry. *A Son of Thunder: Patrick Henry and the American Republic.* New York: Franklin Watts, 1986. Contains a spirited, discerning, and well-written account of the efforts of Patrick Henry and Mason to keep Virginia from ratifying the U.S. Constitution before major changes had been made in it.

Selby, John E. *The Revolution in Virginia, 1775-1783.* Williamsburg, VA: Colonial Williamsburg Foundation, 1988; distributed by the University Press of Virginia. The major book on Virginia in the American Revolution, it places Mason's participation in its full context.

Smith, Daniel Blake. *Inside the Great House: Planter Family Life in Eighteenth-Century Chesapeake Society.* Ithaca: Cornell University Press, 1980. A rich study of the private lives of the gentry families of Mason's time and place.

Sydnor, Charles S. *Gentlemen Freeholders: Political Practices in Washington's Virginia.* Chapel Hill: University of North Carolina Press, 1952. Reprinted as *American Revolutionaries in the Making.* New York: Crowell-Collier, 1962. A masterful brief recreation of the political world of late eighteenth-century Virginia.

Peter Wallenstein
Virginia Polytechnic Institute and State University

N. SCOTT MOMADAY
b. 1934

Chronology

Born Navarro Scotte Mammeday on February 27, 1934, near Lawton, Oklahoma, the son of Natachee Mammeday of Cherokee descent and Alfred Morris Mammeday of Kiowa descent; *1935* moves with family to northern New Mexico and is subsequently raised on Navajo, Apache, and Jemez Pueblo reservations; *1952* graduates from Augusta Military Academy in Virginia and matriculates at the University of New Mexico; *1956* begins study of law at the University of Virginia and meets writer-in-residence William Faulkner; *1958* graduates from the University of New Mexico with a bachelor's degree in political science and begins a brief teaching career on the Jacarilla Apache Indian Reservation in New Mexico; *1959* marries Gaye Mangold and wins a fellowship in creative writing from Stanford; *1963* earns a doctorate in English from Stanford and accepts a position at the University of California at Santa Barbara; *1965* edits *The Complete Poems of Frederick Goddard Tuckerman*; *1966* wins a Guggenheim Fellowship and moves to Amherst, Massachusetts, to study the poetry of Emily Dickinson; *1968* publishes the novel *House Made of Dawn*; *1969* wins a Pulitzer Prize for *House Made of Dawn*; is initiated into the Gourd Dance (Taimpe Society) of the Kiowas; accepts position at the University of California at Berkeley; publishes the prose poem *The Way to Rainy Mountain*; *1972* serves as visiting professor at New Mexico State University at Las Cruces and edits *American Indian Authors*; *1974* joins the faculty at New Mexico State University at Las Cruces; *1976* publishes *The Gourd Dancer*, a book of poetry and *The Names: A Memoir*; *1981* joins faculty at the University of Arizona at Tucson; *1989* publishes a novel, *The Ancient Child*.

Activities of Historical Significance

Scott Momaday's Pulitzer Prize for his novel *House Made of Dawn* (1968) is a watershed in Native-American literary history in particular and in modern Native-American history in general. For the first time, a Native American's aesthetic and intellectual achievement was not only appreciated by academics, literary critics, and art critics, but also was publicly acclaimed by a significant institution. Indeed Momaday's honor signified potential honor for all Native-American artists, both living and dead.

But Momaday himself seems to have achieved more meaningful self-definition as a Native American in a white man's world through the composition of two autobiographical works, *The Way to Rainy Mountain* (1969) and *The Names: A Memoir* (1976). While developing these works—essentially the stories of both his racial and his personal quests for cultural identity—Momaday came to know the almost mystical value of the oral history of the Kiowa and other tribes, especially those of the Pueblo culture of the Southwest. Greeted with relatively warm, if often puzzled, reviews, these books reminded Native Americans of the possibilities of the historical recovery and preservation of their cultures. Paradoxically, these two personal works achieve an almost epic ideal: they capture the ethos of a people.

Momaday's other significant activities include his serious work as a visual artist. Since the early 1970s, Momaday has devoted as much time and creative energy to drawing and painting as to prose and verse. In 1979 he presented a one-man show at the University of North Dakota and subsequently in Minneapolis, Minnesota, and Norman, Oklahoma. Momaday has also shown in galleries in Santa Fe and Phoenix. In 1979 Morningside College awarded Momaday an honorary doctorate in fine arts (one of several honorary degrees he has received), and in 1981 the Fifth Annual Exhibition of Art from the Earth in Norman, Oklahoma, presented him with an award in contemporary art. His paintings, illustrations, and etchings, like his prose and poetry, often probe the ritualized spirit of a people as they examine the individual's harmony with the past and with the land. Thus, Momaday, like William Faulkner and Robert Penn Warren, informs all of his art with the seminal relationships of history confronted by the creative imagination. This achievement explains why the Kiowas, early in Momaday's career, initiated him into the Gourd Dance—a very high honor indeed from the people perhaps most respected by Momaday himself.

Overview of Biographical and Critical Sources

Since the mid-1970s Momaday has attracted a growing critical appreciation, especially for his fiction, but he has yet to attract a definitive biographer. As several scholars would attest, a potential problem facing any biography is the secret rites and beliefs of the Kiowa tribe of Oklahoma and of the Pueblo tribes of the Southwest, spiritual paths followed by Momaday as a person and as an artist. So guarded are the Jemez, for instance, that they turned down much-needed revenue from a producer who wanted to shot a film of *House Made of Dawn* on their reservation. Momaday, of course, has one foot in the Native-American world and the other in the white man's world, maintaining that both cultures can learn much from each other. Nevertheless, probing Momaday's Native-American identity presents a formidable challenge for his future biographer.

Fortunately, two autobiographical works and several readable and accurate biographical sketches are readily accessible. Anyone seriously interested in Momaday's biography must first turn to his autobiographical works, *The Way to Rainy Mountain* (1969) and *The Names: A Memoir* (1976). Martha Scott Trimble's *N. Scott Momaday* (1973) devotes several pages to a very general—and now dated—biographical introduction. Matthias Schubnell's *N. Scott Momaday* (1985) offers the best biographical sketch available to date. Schubnell's trenchant analysis of Momaday's relationship to mentor and friend Yvor Winters is especially helpful. *Approaches to Teaching Momaday's "The Way to Rainy Mountain"* (1988), edited by Kenneth M. Roemer, also offers some useful biographical aid.

Evaluation of Principal Biographical and Critical Sources

Roemer, Kenneth M., ed. *Approaches to Teaching Momaday's "The Way to Rainy Mountain."* New York: Modern Language Association of America, 1988. (**A, G**) While basically designed as a teaching aid, this volume offers several cogent critical essays as well as a brief, accurate biographical sketch.

Schubnell, Matthias. *N. Scott Momaday: The Cultural and Literary Background.* Norman: University of Oklahoma Press, 1985. (**A, G**) The best general study of Momaday to date, Schubnell's work includes a lengthy biographical sketch, the most accurate, thorough, and thoughtful one available. Schubnell discusses the life of Momaday's parents—artists and teachers in their own right—and traces their influence on their son's life and art. Schubnell also provides a helpful annotated bibliography of secondary sources.

Trimble, Martha Scott. *N. Scott Momaday.* Boise: Boise State College, 1973. (**A, G, Y**) One of the earliest comprehensive studies of Momaday, this monograph remains useful only for biographical details of his early life and career.

Overview and Evaluation of Primary Sources

Defying conventional generic classification and therefore requiring close and patient reading, Momaday's *The Way to Rainy Mountain* (Albuquerque: University of New Mexico Press, 1969; New York: Ballantine, 1969; **A, G**) retells Kiowa myth with an overlay of autobiographical experimentation, especially through memories of childhood.

Momaday's later work, *The Names: A Memoir* (New York: Harper and Row, 1976; **A, G, Y**), certainly is autobiographical, although Momaday experiments with fictional and somewhat difficult artifices as he seeks to establish personal identity through searches of family and tribal pasts. In this powerful work, Momaday again recalls a childhood among the Pueblo tribes of the Southwest and a family's history in the traditions of the Kiowa. Just as the Native American's search for meaningful identity is a major theme of *House Made of Dawn*, it also resonates in Momaday's personal search in *The Names*. More broadly, from perusing *The Names*, one discovers that the act of naming is as profoundly significant for the Kiowa and for the Southwest Native Americans as it was for the ancient Hebrews, bearing many of the same implications for personal definition.

Other Sources

Bruchac, Joseph. "The Magic of Words: An Interview with N. Scott Momaday." In *Survival This Way: Interviews with American Indian Poets.* Tucson: University of Arizona Press, 1987. An interview that is especially helpful for understanding Momaday's own theories of creativity. Other interviews in the collection provide useful comparisons.

Chambers, D. D. C. "Momaday, N. Scott." In *Contemporary Novelists,* edited by James Vinson. New York: St. Martin's Press, 1976. A brief and somewhat dated biographical sketch along with general summaries of his themes.

Evers, Lawrence J. "The Killing of a New Mexico State Trooper: Ways of Telling an Historical Event." In *Critical Essays on American Literature,* edited by Andrew Wiget. Boston: G. K. Hall, 1985. A perceptive analysis of Momaday's transformation of historical fact into fiction in *House Made of Dawn*.

King, Tom. "A MELUS Interview: N. Scott Momaday—Literature and the Native Writer." *MELUS: The Journal of the Society for the Study of the Multi-Ethnic Literature of the United States* 10 (Winter 1983): 66-72. Useful interview for interesting perspectives by Momaday on his heritage, literary and otherwise.

Kroeber, Karl. "Technology and Tribal Narrative." In *Narrative Chance: Postmodern Discourse on Native American Literature,* edited by Gerald Vizenor. Albuquerque: University of New Mexico Press, 1989. A cogent discussion of modern technology's impact on Native-American cultural identity, with special emphasis on Momaday's *House Made of Dawn*.

Lincoln, Kenneth. "Tai-Me to Rainy Mountain: The Making of American Indian Literature." *American Indian Quarterly* 10 (Spring 1986): 101-117. Presents the development of Momaday's *Way to Rainy Mountain* as a window on the Native American's special modes of creativity.

Trimble, Martha Scott. "N. Scott Momaday." In *Fifty Western Writers: A Bio-Bibliographic Sourcebook,* edited by Fred Erisman and Richard W. Etuslain. Westport, CT: Greenwood Press, 1982. A relatively full biographical sketch and still useful summaries of scholarship, critical trends, and annotated bibliographical aids.

Velie, Alan R. *Four American Indian Literary Masters: N. Scott Momaday, James Welch, Leslie Marmom Silko, and Gerald Vizenor.* Norman: University of Oklahoma Press, 1982. Contains a discussion of *House Made of Dawn*, Momaday's poetry, and Momaday's autobiographical pieces from disparate perspectives. Various interpretations of other Native-American writers provide myriad social and cultural contexts for comparisons.

John T. Hiers
Valdosta State College

DWIGHT L. MOODY
1837-1899

Chronology

Born Dwight Lyman Moody in Northfield, Massachusetts, on February 5, 1837, the son of Edwin Moody, a brick mason, and Betsey Horton Moody, and the descendant of one of the original settlers of Hartford, Connecticut; *1837-1854* baptized in the local Unitarian church; father dies when he is four years old; attends school until age thirteen; works on nearby farms and in neighboring towns; *1854-1856* leaves home to seek fortune in Boston; works in shoe store owned by two of his mother's brothers; begins attending the Mount Vernon Congregational Church; undergoes conversion experience; received into full church membership; *1856-1860* leaves for Chicago; becomes a financially successful traveling salesman for wholesale shoe firm; active in Plymouth Congregational Church; organizes the North Market Sabbath School and develops broad-based program of evangelistic services, prayer meetings, home-visitation, recreation, and welfare work; resigns from business to devote full time to serving as an independent city missionary; *1860-1873* organizes an army and navy branch of the Chicago Young Men's Christian Association (which later became a branch of the United States Christian Commission) to promote the spiritual, physical, and intellectual well-being of Union army soldiers; marries Emma C. Revell (the daughter of a Chicago ship-builder and the sister of future religious book publisher Fleming H. Revell); establishes his own non-denominational church; becomes president of the Chicago Young Men's Christian Association and builds Farwell Hall as the first association building in the country; is active in promoting national organization of Sunday school workers and association leaders; visits Great Britain twice to meet with religious activists there and study their methods; *1873-1881* makes first evangelistic tour of Great Britain accompanied by organist and singer Ira Sankey and achieves tremendous success; moves back to Northfield; tours the U.S., holding revival meetings in city after city; establishes the Northfield Seminary (later Northfield School for Girls) as a school for girls of limited means; establishes a similar school for boys, Mount Hermon School, near Northfield; begins annual conference of Christian workers at Northfield Seminary; *1881-1899* undertakes two-year evangelistic campaign in Great Britain; tours the U.S. and Canada, holding revival meetings; visits Palestine; establishes the Chicago Bible Institute (later the Moody Bible Institute) to train men and women without college degrees who wish to become home or foreign missionary workers; organizes the Bible

Institute Colportage Association (which grows to become the Moody Press) for the publication of low-priced religious books; promotes the spread on college campuses of the Young Men's Christian Association and the Student Volunteer Movement, an organization of college students committed to foreign missionary service whose slogan is "the evangelization of the world in this generation"; *1899* dies at Northfield on December 22 from heart failure.

Activities of Historical Significance

Dwight L. Moody remained throughout his life a layman who never sought ordination. He reflected and gave further impetus to the increasingly important role being taken by laymen in church and religious affairs. By temperament a kindly and conciliatory personality, Moody was successful in working with churchmen and religious activists of widely differing views. At the same time, he had the drive and organizational abilities that would have made him a highly successful businessman if he had stayed in that sphere. He thus could, and did, win the confidence of prominent business leaders, who generously contributed to the support of his projects. Never money-hungry, Moody was scrupulous in refusing to profit personally from his religious labors. He and Ira Sankey, for example, turned over the royalties from the sale of their highly popular hymnbooks to an independent board of trustees, who devoted the funds mostly to the endowment of the Northfield schools.

Moody's preaching was forceful and direct, featuring short sentences and the language of daily life. Rather than relying upon the threat of fire-and-brimstone to win converts, he emphasized the message of God's fatherly love. Although periodic revivals in individual churches and even groups of churches had become a fixture of evangelical Protestantism by 1875, Moody pioneered in adapting the revival to large urban centers by applying the techniques of business corporate enterprise. Critics have argued that Moody's pietistic concern with winning souls had strongly conservative implications for the church's role in society. Although he was aware of, and sympathized with, the plight of the lower class in Britain and the U.S., Moody emphasized that society could be reformed only by the moral and spiritual regeneration of individuals via revivals. As a premillenialist, he inclined toward a pessimism that was largely hostile to "progress" during his day. Accordingly, most of Moody's later admirers have belonged to the "fundamentalist" side in the split that took place within American Protestantism between conservatives (or "fundamentalists") and liberals (or "modernists").

Moody was probably more responsible than any other individual for the continued strength and vitality of evangelical Protestantism in the U.S. despite the vast social changes sweeping over the country during his life. The Student Volunteer Movement that grew out of his efforts to promote Christianity on the nation's college campuses would supply many of the foreign missionaries sent abroad by American Protestant churches in the late nineteenth and early twentieth centuries. His legacy continues to this day. The Young Men's Christian Association—which Moody did so much to expand—remains a significant part of life in communities across the United States even if largely shorn of its explicitly religious orientation. The Moody Bible Institute in Chicago and the Moody Press are key parts in the institutional infrastructure of present-day American evangelical Protestantism.

Overview of Biographical Sources

Moody has attracted the continuing attention of biographers. His death stimulated the publication of an array of hastily assembled hagiographical exercises, such as J. Wilbur Chapman, *The Life and Work of D. L. Moody* (1900), and A. P. Fitt, *The Shorter Life of D. L. Moody* (1900). The most substantial of those accounts was by his older son, William R. Moody. First published in 1900 under the title *The Life of Dwight L. Moody,* the work was expanded, revised, and corrected for its reissuance in 1930 as *D. L. Moody.* Most of the biographies in the following years would rely largely upon William R. Moody for their facts. Gamaliel Bradford's *D. L. Moody: A Worker in Souls* (1927) reflects the debunking mood among American intellectuals in the 1920s. More reverential were Charles R. Erdman, *D. L. Moody: His Message for To-Day* (1928); A. P. Fitt, *Moody Still Lives: Word Pictures of D. L. Moody* (1936); Richard E. Day, *Bush Aglow: The Life Story of Dwight Lyman Moody, Commoner of Northfield* (1936); and Richard K. Curtis, *They Called Him Mr. Moody* (1962). J. C. Pollock's *Moody: A Biographical Portrait of the Pacesetter in Modern Mass Evangelism* (1963) is based upon extensive independent research in primary sources in this country and Great Britain and is the first serious attempt at a systematic examination of all of Moody's career. But the work suffers from overly sentimental writing, the author's hagiographical attitude toward Moody, and his lack of a grasp of the larger historical context. Stanley N. Gundry, *Love Them In: The Proclamation Theology of D. L. Moody* (1976), is a thorough examination of Moody's theological position. The most satisfactory biography, at least in terms of scholarly standards, is James F. Findlay, Jr., *Dwight Moody: American Evangelist 1837-1899* (1969). A complete listing (up to its date of publication) with accompanying brief descriptions of the writings about Moody is in Wilbur M. Smith, *An Annotated Bibliography of D. L. Moody* (1948).

Evaluation of Principal Biographical Sources

Bradford, Gamaliel. *D. L. Moody: A Worker in Souls.* New York: George H. Doran, 1927. (A, G) A provocative "psychograph" of Moody—a strongly Freudian-influenced mix of psychological analysis with biographical data drawn from the available published works. There is no question that Bradford came to scoff; but he ended up impressed by, even admiring of, Moody.

Chapman, J. Wilbur. *The Life and Work of Dwight L. Moody.* New York: W. E. Scull, 1900. (G) A hastily compiled exercise in hagiography written in the immediate aftermath of Moody's death.

Curtis, Richard K. *They Called Him Mr. Moody.* Garden City, NY: Doubleday, 1962. (A, G) Although Curtis did undertake some independent research in the primary sources, the work still rests largely upon prior accounts and remains within the eulogistic tradition.

Day, Richard E. *Bush Aglow: The Life Story of Dwight Lyman Moody, Commoner of Northfield.* Philadelphia: Judson, 1936. (G) Eulogizes Moody as the greatest of Protestant fundamentalist leaders.

Erdman, Charles R. *D. L. Moody: His Message for To-Day.* Chicago: Fleming H. Revell, 1928. (G) Another admiring fundamentalist-inspired account.

Findlay, James F., Jr. *Dwight L. Moody: American Evangelist 1837-1899.* Chicago: University of Chicago Press, 1969. (A, G) The most exhaustively researched and scholarly of Moody biographies. Findlay is sympathetic but balanced. He successfully conveys how much Moody's success was due to the power of his personality, and simultaneously does an excellent job of placing Moody's evangelism within the larger context of American social and religious history.

Fitt, A. P. *The Shorter Life of D. L. Moody.* Chicago: Biblical Colportage Association, 1900. (A, G) A brief account by Moody's son-in-law and an official of the Moody Bible Institute that places him firmly on the fundamentalist side in the widening split between fundamentalism and modernism. The same approach is taken in A. P. Fitt, *Moody Still Lives: Word Pictures of D. L. Moody* (New York: Fleming H. Revell, 1936).

Gundry, Stanley N. *Love Them In: The Proclamation Theology of D. L. Moody.* Chicago: Moody Press, 1976. (A) A thorough analysis of Moody's theological position. Gundry documents how Moody was in his basic views a fundamentalist—except in one crucial respect, his strong opposition to controversy. And he shows that while disapproving of liberalism in the abstract, as a pragmatic activist Moody sought to maintain ties with influential liberals in hopes of avoiding conflict that might interfere with the effective preaching of the Gospel.

Moody, William R. *The Life of D. L. Moody.* New York: Fleming H. Revell, 1900. (A, G) Although its hasty writing resulted in factual errors, this account by Moody's older son is the most substantial, reliable, and balanced of the treatments published in the immediate aftermath of his death. An expanded, revised, and corrected edition was published as *D. L. Moody* (New York: Macmillan, 1930).

Pollock, J. C. *Moody: A Biographical Portrait of the Pacesetter in Modern Mass Evangelism.* New York: Macmillan, 1963. (A, G) Pollock, an English Anglican rector, did extensive research in the primary sources in the U.S. and Great Britain and was the first writer to make a serious attempt to deal systematically with Moody's entire career. But the work suffers from Pollock's tendency to write breathless prose, to get bogged down in the details of Moody's day-to-day doings, and to see persons and events largely through Moody's eyes. Nor is Pollock sufficiently attuned to how Moody fits in the context of his time.

Smith, Wilbur M. *An Annotated Bibliography of D. L. Moody.* Chicago: Moody Press, 1948. (A, G) This complete (up to the date of publication) listing with brief accompanying descriptions of the writings about Moody is indispensable for students of his life and work.

Overview and Evaluation of Primary Sources

The most important of Moody's surviving personal papers were collected and preserved by the members of his immediate family. The collection begun by his daughter Emma Fitt and expanded by his granddaughter, Emma Moody Fitt Powell, is in Emma Powell's possession in East Northfield, Massachusetts. It contains family and other letters to and from Moody, Emma Moody's diary of 1873-1875, sermon outlines, and scrapbooks of newspaper clippings. The collection of May Moody, the wife of Moody's older son, has some of Moody's earliest letters plus materials gathered by William R. Moody when preparing his father's biography. The collection was split up after her death. Some materials, including the diary of D. W. Whittle, May Moody's father and D. L. Moody's long-time confidant, went to the Moody Bible Institute in Chicago; the other part is at the Northfield School for Girls, Northfield, Massachusetts. Another granddaughter, Mrs. Frank R. Smith, deposited in the Manuscript Division, Library of Congress, Washington, D.C., her collection of papers (including the correspondence between Moody and his cousin Ambert Moody, the general manager of Moody's affairs at Northfield during his last years).

Outside the family, the largest group of manuscripts is at the Moody Bible Institute, Chicago—most importantly the Bible Institute Correspondence, consisting primarily of correspondence between Moody and institute superintendent Reuben A. Torrey and its business manager, A. F. Gaylord. Important for the founding of the institute are the papers of Nettie Fowler McCormick, McCormick Family Collection, State Historical Society of Wisconsin, Madison; for Moody's association with the Young Men's Christian Association, the archives of the Chicago YMCA at its downtown headquarters and the records in the Historical Library at the YMCA's headquarters in New York City; and for Moody's impact on the college campuses, the John R. Mott Papers, Yale Divinity School, New Haven, Connecticut.

Contemporary eulogistic accounts of Moody and his evangelistic work include William H. Daniels, *D. L. Moody and His Work* (Hartford, CT: American Publishing, 1875; A, G); Rufus W. Clark, *The Work of God in Great Britain under Messrs. Moody and Sankey, 1873-1875, with Biographical Sketches* (New York: Harper and Brothers, 1875; G); and Edgar J. Goodspeed, *A Full History of the Wonderful Career of Moody and Sankey in Great Britain and America* (New York: H. S. Goodspeed, 1876; G). Probably the most valuable is the one by Daniels, a Methodist minister in Chicago who gives information about Moody's earliest days in that city not found elsewhere. Impressions and recollections (not always factually accurate) by associates include Henry Drummond, *Dwight L. Moody: Impressions and Facts* (New York: McClure, Phillips, 1900; A, G), by one of Moody's closest allies in Great Britain; John V. Farwell, *Early Recollections of Dwight L. Moody* (Chicago: Winona Publishing; A, G), by a wealthy Chicago businessman who was one of Moody's earliest financial backers; and Ira Sankey, *My Life and the Story of the Gospel Hymns* (New York: Bigelow & Main, 1906; A, G), by the organist and singer who accompanied Moody on his most successful revivals. The book by his younger son, Paul D. Moody, *My Father: An Intimate Portrait of Dwight Moody* (Boston: Little, Brown, 1938; A, G), contains valuable recollections of personal and family life and provoked much controversy by suggesting that Moody was not the hard-line fundamentalist that many of his admirers had pictured him.

The most important sources, however, for tracing Moody's public career are the newspapers and periodicals published by the evangelical denominations during his lifetime. The most important are: *The Congregational Herald; The Congregation-alist; The Advance; New York Observer; New York Evangelist; Zion's Herald; The Interior; New York Christian Advocate; Northwestern Christian Advocate; Western Christian Advocate; The Evangelist Record; The Record of Christian Work;* and *Northfield Echoes.*

Museums, Historical Landmarks, Societies
The Moody Museum (Northfield, MA). On the campus of the Northfield Mt. Herman School, the museum contains scrapbooks of letters and clippings.

Moody Bible Institute (Chicago, IL). The Moodyana Collection contains some memoribilia.

Other Sources
Marsden, George M. *Fundamentalism and American Culture: The Shaping of Twentieth-Century Evangelicalism 1870-1925.* New York: Oxford University Press, 1980. An excellent scholarly account of the rise of fundamentalism, with a balanced appraisal of Moody's relationship to the movement.

McLoughlin, William G., Jr. *Modern Revivalism: Charles Grandison Finney to Billy Graham.* New York: Ronald Press, 1959. A first-rate piece of scholarship indispensable for appreciating Moody's place in the development of nineteenth-and twentieth-century Anglo-American evangelical Protestantism.

Parrington, Vernon Louis. *Main Currents in American Thought.* Vol. 3, *The Beginnings of Critical Realism in America: 1860-1920.* New York: Harcourt, Brace, 1927-1930. Exemplifies the hostility toward Moody and his brand of revivalism by the dominant progressive school of American historical writing in the years between the two world wars.

Powell, Emma Moody. *Heavenly Destiny: The Life Story of Mrs. D. L. Moody, By Her Granddaughter, Emma Moody Powell.* Chicago: Moody Press, 1943. A eulogistic biography of D. L. Moody's wife, but valuable for showing her extremely important behind-the-scenes influence upon her husband.

Robertson, Darrel M. *The Chicago Revival, 1876: Society and Revivalism in a Nineteenth-Century City.* Studies in Evangelicalism, no. 9. Metuchen, NJ: Scarecrow Press, 1989. An in-depth analysis of Moody's 1876 revival in Chicago that is perceptive on the reasons for his success.

Weisberger, Bernard. *They Gathered at the River: The Story of the Great Revivalists and Their Impact upon Religion in America.* Boston: Little, Brown, 1958. A sprightly and readable, but somewhat superficial, history of revivalism in the United States.

John Braeman
University of Nebraska-Lincoln

PAUL ELMER MORE
1864-1937

Chronology

Born on December 12, 1864, in St. Louis, the fourth son and seventh of eight children of Enoch Anson More, a small businessman and active member of the local Presbyterian church, and Katherine Hay More, a pious and stern moral influence on the children; strong Calvinist leanings of the parents suggest the New England roots of the More genealogy in the U.S.; is a shy and withdrawn young man whose intellect is much more evident than his social skills as he attends the public schools in St. Louis; *1883* enters Washington University in St. Louis and discovers interests in Oriental and Classical languages; graduates *cum laude* from Washington University and takes teaching position at Smith Academy in St. Louis; *1890* publishes first book, *Helena and Occasional Poems*; *1891* completes master's degree at Washington University; *1892* enters Harvard University where he and Irving Babbitt constitute the entire class in Sanskrit; they will soon become the two major principals of the intellectual movement known as the New Humanism; comes increasingly under the intellectual influence of Babbitt; *1895* begins teaching Sanskrit and classical literature at Bryn Mawr, having decided not to pursue a doctoral degree; *1900* marries Henrietta Beck, a long-time friend from his St. Louis neighborhood; joins the literary staff of the *Independent*; *1903* becomes literary editor of the New York *Evening Post*; *1904* publishes the first volume in the long series of the *Shelburne Essays*; *1906* becomes literary editor of the *Nation* and then in 1909 the editor of that publication; *1914* resigns from the *Nation* and moves to Princeton, New Jersey, to pursue work as an independent scholar; immerses himself in study of Greek literature; *1917* publishes *Platonism*, the first of his several contributions on this subject; arranges with Princeton University to teach courses on Greek and Patristic philosophy; *1919* elected to the American Academy of Arts and Letters; *1924* visits England and parts of the Continent at a time of increasing interest in religion and an intellectual shift from humanism to Christianity; *1930* Norman Foerster edits *Humanism and America,* which includes essays from More and Babbitt and which marks the high point of interest in the New Humanism movement; C. Hartley Grattan and rivals of the New Humanists answer the same year with *The Critique of Humanism*; is nominated for a Nobel Prize in literature by friends and suppporters but the award is given to Sinclair Lewis; *1934* publishes *The Skeptical Approach to Religion*, an intellectual defense of Christianity; *1937* dies March 9 in Princeton, New Jersey.

Activities of Historical Significance

Paul Elmer More and Irving Babbitt were the two key figures of the New Humanist movement, an important chapter in the intellectual history of conservatism in the U.S. Other participants included Stuart Sherman, Norman Foerster, Robert Shafer, Gorham Munson, and G. R. Elliott. Whereas Babbitt provided the movement its sharp and often rigorous intellectual outline, More gave it critical finesse and breadth of view. Babbitt and More, both highly learned men, contrasted sharply in personalities. Babbitt was dynamic and forceful, an engaging and popular teacher; More was quiet and withdrawn, content to cultivate his garden and read the Greeks. They won themselves the nicknames, respectively, "The Warring Buddha of Harvard" and "The Hermit of Princeton."

The New Humanists decried the loss of standards, the shallow spiritual quality of American life, its pervasive materialism, and its soft humanitarian sentimentalism. They generally ascribed to intellectual change the development of these tendencies, citing especially the pernicious influences of romanticism and naturalism. Both influences, they believed, had eroded a view of life that defined human nature in terms of a dualism of the spirit. Babbitt and More argued that in each individual an expansive and undisciplined spirit pursues hedonistic, materialist, and emotional excesses and must be disciplined by a counterforce, a moral power that pulls the individual in the direction of humanist restraint. The New Humanists believed that the ability to exercise this counterforce to one's natural, or lower instincts depended on an imaginative grasp of a universal, higher humanity, as portrayed especially in the great, classical works of literature.

More's writings do not necessarily reflect such an intellectual outline in so stark a form. His literary criticism, as conveyed in the several volumes of the *Shelburne Essays,* shows that the dualistic philosophy constitutes a recurring framework of his judgments, but does not function universally or inflexibly in his critical essays. Nonetheless, the notion of an ideal human self, and the ability of any writer or artist to depict it imaginatively, did provide More a working framework for his discussion of literature. He criticized literature that was merely reflective of an idiosyncratic personality or failed to transcend the historical conditions that inspired it. The explicit formulations of More's dualism appear in his *Studies of Religious Dualism,* the sixth volume of the *Shelburne Essays.*

More and the New Humanists shared in a cultural phenomena that antedated the war years and became quite pronounced in the 1920s—the so-called revolt of the intellectuals. Artists and writers of all kinds evidenced their discontent with the state of American society and culture. They recoiled from the dominance of business and the alleged excessive materialism of the population. They believed that American moralism, a legacy of Puritanism, and the prevalence of commercialism, had conspired to deprive the arts of their needed place in the life of the nation. Intellectuals also generally recoiled from democracy, especially in the evident philistinism they attributed to the average man and woman. Individuals such as Van Wyck Brooks, Randolph Bourne, A. J. Nock, and H. L. Mencken gave vivid expression to these discontents and the collection of essays edited by Harold Stearns in *Civilization in the United States* (1922) showed the breadth of categories to which they applied.

If More and the Humanists participated in the revolt of the intellectuals, they were nonetheless set apart from many of its standard laments. In More's case, this distinction was most evident in his efforts to render an appreciative assessment of American literary tradition. Critics such as Brooks and Mencken had dismissed the generality of American literature, from the Puritans through the romantic era at least, as essentially useless. They faulted writers for their aloofness from the real life of the country and for their retreat into moral idealism. But it was just this quality of American letters that More admired. He praised the Puritan tradition and judged it the most useful, lasting influence in American culture. In writers like Hawthorne, Thoreau, and Whitman, More saw a healthy moral instinct at work within the raw materials of American life and history. Although More considered himself an admirer of Emerson, he saw in the Concord sage the beginnings of a soft romanticism that yielded to individual whim and encouraged followers to achieve their humanity on too easy terms.

More also opposed the naturalistic influence in American literature. As the cultural impact of Darwinism gained acceptance in the late nineteenth century its literary reflections induced various critical reactions. Mencken welcomed Theodore Dreiser as an important departure from the idealistic strain in American letters. He described Dreiser as a writer who portrayed life in its fatalistic character and who imposed on his material no overriding moral law. More disagreed with Dreiser's philosophy and refused to yield to any critical interpretation of literature in which blood and environment are the major determinants of the human condition. In addition, it must be said that More dismissed much of contemporary writing because he found it vulgar and distasteful. His description of John Dos Passos's novel *Manhattan Transfer* as "an explosion in a cesspool" became one of the most quoted lines in the anti-Humanist commentary.

In his views on society and politics More was unabashedly elitist, in the sense, especially, that he endorsed the legitimacy of class and rank and would trust all social improvement to a natural aristocracy. More defended the rights of property unapologetically and categorically. He was outspoken against any humanitarianism that took the form of sentimental indulgence of special groups and their alleged deprivation or that translated into schemes for the political reform of society. At a time when the American university was expanding its curricular program to include new subjects and to emphasize professional training, More adhered to an older idea of higher education based on the classics. He looked to a small group of special students to master their own souls through the study of Greek literature, and to constitute an authentic leadership class in the United States.

More held to such opinions rather consistently from the time he came under the influence of Babbitt. The one change that was important in his intellectual career, and that set him apart from Babbitt, was More's move to religion. Whereas he and Babbitt had once upheld an empirical dualism, without an appeal to the supernatural, More increasingly found religious faith indispensable to his own peace. His late writings reflect his intellectual adherence to the premises of theism and to the forms of Christianity. More also accepted religion on pragmatic grounds, arguing against Babbitt that only religious faith, as opposed to empirical humanism, could withstand the otherwise triumphant combination of the expansive instinct. More became especially interested and active in the Anglican religious tradition, but declined an offer of confirmation made by an Episcopalian bishop as More was near death.

Overview of Biographical Sources

More has not received a great deal of scholarly attention, though there are several books that reliably cover his life and thought. Robert Shafer provided the first full study of More with his *Paul Elmer More and American Criticism* (1935). Robert M. Davies provided another overview of More with his *The Humanism of Paul Elmer More* (1958), which gives much attention to his Platonism. Another appreciative account is Arthur Hazard Dakin, *Paul Elmer More* (1960). Somewhat more judgmental is Francis X. Duggan's *Paul Elmer More* (1966). A work that deals comprehensively with More's literary criticisms is Stephen L. Tanner, *Paul Elmer More: Literary Criticism as the History of Ideas* (1987). J. David Hoeveler, Jr.'s *The New Humanism: A Critique of Modern America, 1900-1940* (1977) treats More within the larger framework of the New Humanism movement.

Evaluation of Principal Biographical Sources

Dakin, Arthur Hazard. *Paul Elmer More*. Princeton: Princeton University Press, 1960. (A, G) Dakin used the extensive More correspondence in writing a biography that is full of personal reflections and details of More's life. While scholarly, it is also a very readable account.

Davies, Robert M. *The Humanism of Paul Elmer More*. New York: Bookman Associates, 1958. (A) Davies deals with several aspects of More's thought, but especially values More's contribution to Greek scholarship.

Duggan, Francis X. *Paul Elmer More*. Boston: Twayne, 1966. (A) Duggan discusses More in terms of the different categories of his thought—criticism, social views, Platonism and Christianity, and Humanism and naturalism—and finds that More's study of the intellectual history of ancient Greece is the most important of his work. It is an engaging and very useful study.

Hoeveler, J. David, Jr. *The New Humanism: A Critique of Modern America, 1900-1940*. Charlottesville: University Press of Virginia, 1977. (A) Makes Babbitt the central intellectual figure of the New Humanism but sees More providing some subtle illustrations of Babbitt's dualistic philosophy.

Shafer, Robert. *Paul Elmer More and American Criticism*. New Haven: Yale University Press, 1935. (A). A sympathetic and apologetic account written by one of the members of the New Humanist party. The book reflects the critical warfare of the times.

Tanner, Stephen L. *Paul Elmer More: Literary Criticism as the History of Ideas*. Provo, UT: Brigham Young University Press, 1987. (A) The best introduction to More as a literary critic. Tanner treats More's criticism as a somewhat self-contained enterprise and he stresses the continuity of theme in the larger range of More's critical writings.

Overview and Evaluation of Primary Sources

More's main contributions remain his graceful essays about literature and his studies of Greek philosophy. Nearly all of his essential writings can be found in his eleven volumes of the *Shelburne Essays,* his four volumes of *The Greek Tradition,* and his late *New Shelburne Essays.*

Shelburne Essays: First Series (Boston: Houghton Mifflin, 1904; A) contains some of More's important essays on American literature, with contributions on Thoreau, Hawthorne, and Emerson, and additional essays on Tolstoy and Carlyle. *Shelburne Essays: Second Series* (Boston: Houghton Mifflin, 1906; A) offers More's essays on Shakespearean and Elizabethan sonnets, Hazlitt, Lamb, and Meredith. *Shelburne Essays: Third Series* (Boston: Houghton Mifflin, 1905; A) is another wide-ranging volume, with essays on Whittier, Scottish novels and history,

Swinburne, Browning, Byron, and Sterne. *Shelburne Essays: Fourth Series* (Boston: Houghton Mifflin, 1906; A) contains essays on Keats, Franklin, Whitman, Blake, and Milton. *Shelburne Essays: Fifth Series* (New York: G. P. Putnam's Sons, 1908; A) has More's reflections on Dickens and Longfellow. *Studies of Religious Dualism: Shelburne Essays, Sixth Series* (Boston: Houghton Mifflin, 1909; A) is one of More's most important volumes. It contains the essay "The Forest Philosophy of India," a critical piece for More's appreciation of humanistic, non-supernatural religion. Other essays deal with the Bhagavad Ghita, Saint Augustine, Pascal, Plato, and Rousseau. *Shelburne Essays: Seventh Series* (Boston: Houghton Mifflin, 1910; A) has essays on Shelley, Tennyson, William Morris, William James, and an especially significant one on criticism. *The Drift of Romanticism: Shelburne Essays, Eighth Series* (Boston: Houghton Mifflin, 1913; A) has a wonderful set of epigrams that More wrote under the heading "Definitions of Dualism." It also contains his essays on Cardinal Newman, Pater, Nietzsche, and Thomas Huxley. For More's political thought, *Aristocracy and Justice: Shelburne Essays, Ninth Series* (Boston: Houghton Mifflin, 1915; A) is the most important volume in this series. Subjects include "Natural Aristocracy," "Property and Law," "The New Morality," "Academic Leadership," "Disraeli and Conservatism," and "The Philosophy of Law." *With the Wits: Shelburne Essays, Tenth Series* (Boston: Houghton Mifflin, 1921; A) has pieces on Beaumont and Fletcher, Swift, Pope, and "Decadent Wit." *A New England Group and Other: Shelburne Essays, Eleventh Series* (Boston: Houghton Mifflin, 1921; A) has a key More essay, "The Spirit and Poetry of Early New England," and other essays on Jonathan Edwards, Emerson, Charles Eliot Norton, and Henry Adams.

In his series titled *New Shelburne Essays* More offered *The Demon of the Absolute* (Princeton: Princeton University Press, 1928; A), which contains essays that reflect More's recoil from the chill of rationalistic and scientific thinking and convey his lament at the decline of judgment in artistic criticism. *The Skeptical Approach to Religion: New Shelburne Essays*, vol. 2 (Princeton: Princeton University Press, 1934; A) is one of More's most important late books, the one in which he tries deliberately to defend Christianity to the "skeptic," the modern individual who is disinclined to accept any system of belief derived from dogmatic truth. *On Being Human: New Shelburne Essays*, vol. 3 (Princeton: Princeton University Press, 1936; A) contains an illuminating essay by More on his friend and colleague Babbitt.

More's literary criticism will certainly be of the greatest interest to the contemporary student, but those with a special interest in the classics will benefit from More's extensive writing on Greek philosophy and literature. As the chronology of his late works indicates, More followed his interest in Platonism into his

Christian apologetics. One should begin with *Platonism* (Princeton: Princeton University Press, 1917; A) and then move to the series titled *The Greek Tradition*. It begins with *The Religion of Plato* (Princeton: Princeton University Press, 1921; A). *Hellenistic Philosophies: The Greek Tradition,* vol. 2 (Princeton: Princeton University Press, 1923; A) follows, then *The Christ of the New Testament: The Greek Tradition,* vol. 3 (Princeton: Princeton University Press, 1924; A). *Christ the Word: The Greek Tradition,* vol. 4 (Princeton: Princeton University Press, 1927; A) concludes the series.

An important document in More's religious thinking is his introductory essay, "The Spirit of Anglicanism," in *Anglicanism: The Thought and Practice of the Church of England, Illustrated from the Religious Literature of the Seventeenth Century,* edited by More and Leslie Cross (London: Morehouse, 1935; A). For some interesting biographical reflections see More's essay "Marginalia, Part I" *American Review* 8 (November, 1936: 1-30; A). Finally, The Paul Elmer More Papers, in the Department of Rare Books and Special Collections, Princeton University, has numerous interesting letters by More to many noted individuals.

Other Sources

Bart, Peter J. "The Christianity of Paul Elmer More." *Catholic World* 135 (1932): 542-547. Contrasts More's views with Catholic theology.

Eliot, T. S. "Second Thoughts about Humanism." *Hound and Horn* 2 (1929): 225-233. Eliot sympathized with the New Humanism (he was a student of Babbitt at Harvard) but believed it must embrace theism.

Lora, Ronald. *Conservative Minds in America.* Chicago: Rand-McNally, 1971. Places Babbitt and More in the context of American intellectual conservatism.

Mercier, Louis A. *The Challenge of Humanism.* New York: Oxford University Press, 1933. An early, sympathetic treatment.

Ruland, Richard. *The Rediscovery of American Literature: Premises of Critical Taste, 1900-1940.* Cambridge: Harvard University Press, 1967. Usefully places More and the New Humanists within the context of American literary criticism.

J. David Hoeveler, Jr.
University of Wisconsin-Milwaukee

REINHOLD NIEBUHR
1892-1971

Chronology

Born Karl Paul Reinhold Niebuhr on June 21, 1892, in Wright City, Missouri, the son of Gustav Niebuhr, a minister in the German Evangelical Church of North America, and Lydia Hosto Niebuhr; *1892-1907* raised in Wright City and Lincoln, Illinois; *1907-1910* attends Elmhurst College, which was then a boarding school; *1910-1913* attends Eden Theological Seminary in St. Louis; *1913* ordained into ministry of German Evangelical Synod; *1913-1915* attends Yale Divinity School from which he receives a bachelor's and master's degree; *1915-1928* serves as minister of Bethel Evangelical Church in Detroit, Michigan, where he gains national visibility as a writer and lecturer on both religious and secular affairs; *1921* joins the Fellowship for a Christian Social Order, which he serves as traveling secretary; *1923-1940* serves on editorial board of *Christian Century*; *1926* serves as contributing editor of the Fellowship of Reconciliation's unofficial journal *World Tomorrow*; *1928-1934* serves as editor of *World Tomorrow*; becomes biweekly columnist for the *Detroit Times,* a Hearst daily newspaper catering to a working-class clientele; *1931* helps form the Fellowship of Socialist Christians (later becomes Frontier Fellowship, and, in 1951, Christian Action); *1931* marries British theological student Ursula Keppel-Compton; *1933* elected chairman of the executive council of the Fellowship of Reconciliation; *1928-1960* appointed to faculty of Union Theological Seminary, New York, first as associate professor of the philosophy of religion and in 1930 as professor of applied Christianity; *1929-1940* member of Socialist party; is a congressional candidate in 1932; *1935* founds quarterly *Radical Religion* (renamed *Christianity and Society* in 1940); *1939-1945* serves on the Federal Council of Churches' Commission on a Just and Durable Peace; *1939* delivers Gifford Lectures, University of Edinburgh; *1940* elected chairman of the American Friends of German Freedom; *1941* founds *Christianity and Crisis* to combat pacifism and isolationism of *Christian Century*; serves as co-chairman of editorial board until 1966; *1941* elected chairman of the Union for Democratic Action, a group of ex-Socialists who endorse Roosevelt's foreign policy; *1941-1951* becomes contributing editor of *Nation*; *1944* elected vice chairman of the Liberal party of New York State; *1944* elected treasurer of the American Christian Palestine Committee, a pro-Zionist body; *1947* elected to executive board of the Americans for Democratic Action; *1971* dies on June 1 of a pulmonary embolism in Stockbridge, Massachusetts.

Activities of Historical Significance

From the 1920s through the 1960s, Reinhold Niebuhr was America's most prominent native-born theologian. Professor at New York's Union Theological Seminary, Niebuhr was a major proponent of "Christian realism," a theology that stresses the limits of human potential; finds that moral choices frequently lie between evils, not between good and evil; and denies that any community based on self-sacrificing love could ever exist in the world. Niebuhr believed that the tragic character of all human life firmly limits the possibility of perfect justice, although ethical imperatives still make the quest for justice necessary.

A bitter social critic during his pastorate in Detroit (which, contrary to common opinion, was not a working-class congregation), Niebuhr accused American Protestantism of the 1920s of building "a little paradise on Earth in which people are decent but not kind, and honest but not sacrificial." When he arrived at Union in 1928, the tall, bald, sharp-eyed minister appeared, in the words of biographer Richard Fox, to be "an uncouth country bumpkin with dubious credentials, an indecorous pulpit style, a nasal midwestern twang, and a growing reputation for political radicalism." Yet this totally unselfconscious man was a magnetic figure to hundreds of Union students and was revered among secular intellectuals as well.

At Union he soon changed his mind about numerous matters. In the early 1930s, he abandoned his pacifism, and by the time of Pearl Harbor, he was an ardent interventionist. During the cold war, he strongly backed the American "containment" policy, but warned against any accompanying messianism and moralism, particularly in dealing with Asia. Once a professional dissenter, by 1942 he was calling for curbs on civil liberties, ironically at the very time the FBI was launching its first nationwide investigation into Niebuhr's own loyalty. The man who said in 1933 that a Socialist regime in the U.S. might have to maintain itself by force ended up an advocate of liberal Democratic politics.

It was, in part, out of this political transformation that his theology evolved. Religiosity, Niebuhr kept stressing, was no sign of virtue. Rather genuine faith involves piercing "a mystery of grace, beyond the conscious designs and contrivances of men." It means realizing one's finitude, something that even involves acknowledging the evils that necessarily result from all efforts to do good. Human achievements are always possible, but they contain the seeds of their own destruction. The higher the good attained, the greater the potential for evil.

Overview of Biographical Sources

Typical of early treatment of Niebuhr is that of Englishman David Richard Davies, *Reinhold Niebuhr: Prophet from America* (1948), whose theme is revealed in his subtitle. The first major biography, June Bingham's *Courage to Change: An Introduction to the Life and Thought of Reinhold Niebuhr* (1961), is an uncritical treatment though rich in narrative. Paul Merkley's *Reinhold Niebuhr: A Political Account* (1975) and Ronald Stone's *Reinhold Niebuhr: Prophet to Politician* (1972) go into greater depth on his thought, but are also admiring in tone. A far more revisionist treatment is found in Richard Wightman Fox, *Reinhold Niebuhr: A Biography* (1985), from which all serious Niebuhr interpretation must begin.

Evaluation of Principal Biographical Sources

Bingham, June. *Courage to Change: An Introduction to the Life and Thought of Reinhold Niebuhr.* New York: Charles Scribner's Sons, 1961. (A, G) The best of the early attempts at Niebuhr's life, written by an ardent student and disciple, it uses extensive unpublished sources and interviews. Bingham offers perceptive remarks on his writing style and his philosophical fascination with paradox, and presents long quotations from a variety of publications and correspondence. Though possessing a general chronological organization, the book is eclectically organized. There are no scholarly footnotes. Bingham worked under severe constraints—Niebuhr's own domineering presence and the disapproval of Niebuhr's wife—and found it difficult to maintain any critical distance. Given such handicaps, as well as the adulatory tone and inevitable lack of perspective, the book is a remarkable achievement, one that captures much of the man and his time.

Fackre, Gabriel. *The Promise of Reinhold Niebuhr.* Philadelphia and New York: Lippincott, 1971. (A, G) An important synthesis of Niebuhr's life and thought.

Fox, Richard Wightman. *Reinhold Niebuhr: A Biography.* New York: Pantheon, 1985. (A, G) Meticulously researched, Fox's critical and analytical biography is grounded in the Niebuhr Papers at the Library of Congress, numerous interviews, oral history collections, and even some 635 pages of FBI reports. In his clear and subtle study, Fox keeps his distance from Niebuhr, something quite difficult to do. He portrays Niebuhr as the prophet who sought influence, the German-American who was a lifelong Anglophile, a liberal crusader against liberalism. The book contains a healthy amount of demythologizing. For example, Fox notes how this much revered man would personalize an issue, taking the initiative in breaking off friendships with people who had become his intellectual foes. He would present polar opposites in simplistic terms, then offer the Christian alternative. Too many of his books, argues Fox, were "quickies," disjointed and vague, and little deserving the attention given them.

Markley, Paul. *Reinhold Niebuhr: A Political Account*. Montreal: McGill-Queens University Press, 1975. (**A, G**) Stresses the early and middle periods of Niebuhr's life. Thoroughly researched, this book tends to exaggerate the consistency in Niebuhr's role as "Cold Warrior."

Patterson, Bob E. *Reinhold Niebuhr*. Waco, TX: Word Books, 1977. (**A, G**) Part of the Makers of the Theological Mind Series, this volume is a concise and well-written account that argues Niebuhr's relevance to a later generation.

Stone, Ronald. *Reinhold Niebuhr: Prophet to Politician*. Nashville: Abington Press, 1972. (**A, G**) Written by one who knew Niebuhr in his final days at Union, this study stresses the well-known mature thought of Niebuhr's later years. Exaggerates Niebuhr's detachment from cold war ideology.

Overview and Evaluation of Primary Sources

The Reinhold Niebuhr Papers are deposited at the Library of Congress. Crucial are the files relating to June Bingham, Will Scarlett, Floyd Brown, and Samuel Press. Niebuhr interviews conducted in 1953 and 1954 are deposited with the Columbia University Oral Research Office. Valuable Niebuhr correspondence lies in the Arthur M. Schlesinger, Jr., Papers, John F. Kennedy Presidential Library, Waltham, Massachusetts; John Baltzer Papers, archives of Eden Theological Seminary, Webster Groves, Missouri; Waldo Frank and Lewis Mumford Papers, University of Pennsylvania; and Kirby Page Papers, Southern California School of Theology, Claremont, California.

Niebuhr's only effort at autobiography is contained in Charles W. Kegley, ed., *Reinhold Niebuhr: His Religious, Social and Political Thought* (2d ed. New York: Pilgrim Press, 1984; **A, G**). Entitled "Intellectual Autobiography," it devotes only three pages to his personal formation and contains some inaccuracies. Almost as thin is his introduction, "Changing Perspectives," in *Man's Nature and His Communities: Essays on the Dynamics and Enigmas of Man's Personal and Social Existence* (New York: Charles Scribner's Sons, 1965; **A, G**). Niebuhr's letters to and from his wife Ursula, written between 1931 and 1949, are collected in *Remembering Reinhold Niebuhr* (San Francisco: Harper, 1991; **A, G**), edited and introduced by Ursula M. Niebuhr.

Niebuhr was one of America's most prolific theologians. Until the 1940s, he was chiefly known as a critic of liberal Protestantism and the capitalist economic system. For his earliest essays, see William G. Chrystal, ed., *Young Reinhold Niebuhr: The Early Writings, 1931-1941* (St. Louis: Eden Publishing House, 1977;

rev. ed. New York: Pilgrim Press, 1982, **A, G**). In *Does Civilization Need Religion?: A Study in the Social Resources and Limitations of Religion in Modern Life* (New York: Macmillan, 1923; **A, G**), based on articles and reviews written for the *Christian Century*, Niebuhr argues that a liberal Christian has to be rational in rejecting "superstition and magic," but irrational in pursuing love and self-sacrifice. His *Leaves from the Notebook of a Tamed Cynic* (Chicago: Willett, Clark, and Colby, 1929; **A, G**) reveals his efforts to become a prophet without succumbing to the sin of pride. In his addresses delivered to the New York School of Social Work, *The Contribution of Religion to Social Work* (New York: Columbia University Press, 1932; **A, G**), Niebuhr stresses the conflict between the religious ideal of love and the political ideal of justice.

By the early 1930s Niebuhr was entering his most radical political phase. In *Moral Man and Immoral Society: A Study of Ethics and Politics* (New York: Charles Scribner's Sons, 1932; **A, G**), he points out the actual roles of power and self-interest in human affairs and stresses the impossibility of achieving real social change without force. In his most Marxist book, a collection of twenty essays entitled *Reflections on the End of an Era* (New York: Charles Scribner's Sons, 1934; **A, G**), Niebuhr finds capitalistic civilization doomed. His *Interpretation of Christian Ethics* (New York: Harper and Brothers, 1935; **A, G**) seeks to place his brand of realism between liberal and conservative Christianity. Perfect love, he asserts, is an impossible possibility, but Christians must nonetheless act in history. *Beyond Tragedy: Essays on the Christian Interpretation of History* (New York: Charles Scribner's Sons, 1937; **A, G**) contains fifteen "sermonic essays" focusing on the Christian claim of ultimate hope beyond the failures, clashes, and contradictions of life. *Christianity and Power Politics* (New York: Charles Scribner's Sons, 1940; **A, G**) attacks Christian pacifism. By placing a premium on non-participation in conflict, perfectionism sentimentalizes the Christian faith and betrays its deepest insights.

Beginning in the 1940s Niebuhr ventured more into abstract theology while tempering his indictment of American society. *The Nature and Destiny of Man*, 2 vols. (New York: Charles Scribner's Sons, 1941-1943; **A**), based on his Gifford Lectures, offers the most mature and learned exposition of his theology. *The Children of Light and the Children of Darkness: A Vindication of Democracy and a Critique of Its Traditional Defense* (New York: Charles Scribner's Sons, 1944; **A, G**) presents his famous dictum that man's capacity for justice makes democracy possible while his inclination for injustice makes its necessary. *Discerning the Signs of the Times: Sermons for Today and Tomorrow* (New York: Charles Scribner's Sons, 1945; **A, G**), based on sermons delivered to university audiences, stresses the persistence of sin within every level of human advancement. *Faith and*

History: A Comparison of Christian and Modern Views of History (New York: Charles Scribner's Sons, 1949; **A**) attacks Arnold Toynbee's views of history and calls for a return to Christian belief in innate and divine redemption.

During the 1950s Niebuhr often focused on the meaning of the American mission, something accentuated by the nation's intensive cold war involvement. In *The Irony of American History* (New York: Charles Scribner's Sons, 1952; **A, G**), Niebuhr juxtaposes the "innocent" nation of the Puritan and Jeffersonian forefathers with a twentieth-century world power whose very strength necessitates participation in a struggle where such "innocence" is impossible. *Christian Realism and Political Problems* (New York: Charles Scribner's Sons, 1953; **A, G**), a collection of ten political and theological articles, includes his famous "Augustine's Political Realism." Here Niebuhr finds history remaining morally ambiguous to the end, with the possibility of ultimate tragedy overshadowing all human effort. *The Self and the Dramas of History* (New York: Charles Scribner's Sons, 1954; **A**) contrasts the Hellenic and Hebraic ways of looking at God, man, and the universe. *Pious and Secular America* (New York: Charles Scribner's Sons, 1957; **A, G**) is a series of occasional papers that covers a variety of topics, ranging from the cold war and the predicament of American blacks to evangelist Billy Graham and the matter of converting the Jews.

In his final productive years, Niebuhr continued focusing on America's role in global politics. *The Structure of Nations and Empires* (New York: Charles Scribner's Sons, 1959; **A, G**) stresses that while the United States had more power than any empire in history, it would find it difficult to exercise that power in a world of autonomous nations. *A Nation So Conceived: Reflections on the History of America from Its Early Visions to Its Present Power* (New York: Charles Scribner's Sons, 1963; **A, G**), written with historian Alan Heimert, covers transformations in America's sense of national identity. *Man's Nature and His Communities: Essays on the Dynamics and Enigmas of Man's Personal and Social Existence* (New York: Charles Scribner's Sons, 1965; **A**) contains three essays on historic conceptions of community. *The Democratic Experience* (New York: Praeger, 1969; **A, G**), co-authored by political scientist Paul Sigmund, warns Americans against extolling liberty at the expense of community and justice.

Niebuhr's works have frequently been anthologized; see, for example, D. B. Robertson, ed., *Love and Justice: Selections from the Shorter Writings of Reinhold Niebuhr* (Philadelphia: Westminster, 1959; **A, G**); D. B. Robertson, ed., *Essays in Applied Christianity* (New York: Meridian, 1959; **A, G**); Harry R. Davis and Robert C. Good, eds., *Reinhold Niebuhr on Politics: His Political Philosophy and Its Application to Our Age as Expressed in His Writings* (New York: Charles Scribner's Sons, 1960; **A, G**); Ronald Stone, ed., *Faith and Politics* (New York:

Braziller, 1968; (**A, G**); Ursula M. Niebuhr, ed., *Justice and Mercy* (New York: Harper and Row, 1974; **A, G**); and Robert McAfee Brown, ed., *The Essential Reinhold Niebuhr: Selected Essays and Addresses* (New Haven: Yale University Press, 1986; **A, G**).

For listings of Niebuhr's writings, see D. B. Robertson, *Reinhold Niebuhr's Works: A Bibliography* (Boston: G. K. Hall, 1979; rev. ed.; Lanham, MD: University Press of America, 1983; **A, G**); Priscilla Richards, ''A Bibliography of Works about Reinhold Niebuhr,'' *Bulletin of Bibliography* 38 (October-December 1981: 179-188; **A, G**); Charles W. Kegley, *Reinhold Niebuhr: His Religious, Social and Political Thought* (New York: Pilgrim Press, 1984; **A, G**).

Other Sources

Becker, William H. ''Reinhold Niebuhr: From Marx to Roosevelt.'' *Historian* 35, 4 (1973): 539-550. Shows Niebuhr's offering a Marxist critique of the New Deal as late as 1938, but argues that by 1943 he grudgingly accepted the capitalist system.

Carnell, Edward John. *The Theology of Reinhold Niebuhr*. Rev. ed. Grand Rapids, MI: Eerdmans, 1960. Appreciative critique by a noted conservative.

Chatfield, Charles. *For Peace and Justice: Pacifism in America, 1914-1941*. Knoxville: University of Tennessee Press, 1971. Puts Niebuhr's intellectual odyssey in the context of the pacifist movement.

Doenecke, Justus D. ''Reinhold Niebuhr and His Critics.'' In *Proceedings of the Kanuga Conference for Faculty Episcopalians, 1990*, edited by Manning M. Petillo, Jr. Hendersonville, NC: Kanuga Conferences, 1990. Stresses arguments developed against Niebuhr's interventionism in the years 1939 to 1941.

''Faith for a Lenten Age.'' *Time* 51 (March 8, 1948): 70-79. This unsigned article by Whittaker Chambers provides an unusually clear and sensitive picture aimed at the general reader.

Gilkey, Langdon. ''Reinhold Niebuhr: A Biography—A Critical Review Article.'' *Journal of Religion* 68 (April 1988): 263-276. Finds Fox, in his biography, misunderstanding Niebuhr and his teaching.

Handy, Robert T. *A History of Union Theological Seminary in New York.* New York: Columbia University Press, 1987. Puts Niebuhr in the context of his seminary.

Harland, Gordon. *The Thought of Reinhold Niebuhr.* New York: Oxford University Press, 1960. First delineates the structure of Niebuhr's theological ethic, then analyses his view on such issues as politics, economics, and war. His clear exposition often fails to interpret Niebuhr's theology in the broader context of his life, however.

Harries, Richard, ed. *Reinhold Niebuhr and the Issues of Our Time.* Grand Rapids, MI: Eerdmans, 1986. Contributions by such prominent Niebuhr students as Richard Wightman Fox.

Hofmann, Hans. *The Theology of Reinhold Niebuhr.* Translated by Louise Pettibone Smith. 1954. Reprint. New York: Charles Scribner's Sons, 1956. Niebuhr's student examines his writings in chronological order, thus enabling the reader to see the development of his thought. Not as useful as Harland while possessing the same limitations.

Landon, Harold R. *Reinhold Niebuhr: A Prophetic Voice in Our Time.* Greenwich, CT: Seabury Press, 1962. Valuable contributions by theologians Paul Tillich and John C. Bennett and political scientist Hans Morgenthau.

Marty, Martin E. "The Lost Worlds of Reinhold Niebuhr." *American Scholar* 45, 4 (1976): 566-572. Sees dynamic relationship between Niebuhr's inner theological and outer political worlds.

McCann, Dennis. *Christian Realism and Liberation Theology: Practical Theologies in Creative Conflict.* Maryknoll, NY: Orbis, 1981. Finds Niebuhr's thought more realistic and faithful to Christian tradition than today's liberation theology.

Meyer, Donald. *The Protestant Search for Political Realism.* Berkeley: University of California Press, 1960. In an extensive and admiring treatment, Meyer shows Niebuhr's ambivalence toward Marxism even in his most radical phase.

Scott, Nathan A., Jr. *The Legacy of Reinhold Niebuhr.* Chicago: University of Chicago Press, 1974. Essays originally published in the *Journal of Religion* (October 1974) by leading scholars, many of whom knew Niebuhr personally.

Shinn, Roger Lincoln. "Reinhold Niebuhr." In *Encyclopedia of Religion*. Vol. 10. Edited by Mircea Eliade. New York: Macmillan, 1987. Succinct essay stressing the development of Niebuhr's thought.

Thompson, Dennis L. "The Basic Doctrines and Concepts of Reinhold Niebuhr's Political Thought." *Journal of Church and State* 17, 2 (1975): 275-299. A helpful survey of Niebuhr's teachings on such topics as love, power, justice, and community.

Justus D. Doenecke
New College of the University of South Florida

GEORGIA O'KEEFFE
1887-1986

Chronology

Born Georgia Totto O'Keeffe on November 15, 1887, in Sun Prairie, Wisconsin, a small town near Madison, the second of seven children of Ida Totto O'Keeffe, an Episcopalian and descendent of Hungarian nobility and Dutch ancestry, and Francis Calixtus O'Keeffe, a second generation farmer of Irish Catholic ancestry; *1891-1903* attends local one-room grammar school; boards at Sacred Heart Academy in Madison for one year where art teacher chides her for drawing too small; attends Madison High School for one year; takes art lessons with her sisters in Sun Prairie, at boarding schools, and high school; *1903* moves with her family to Williamsburg, Virginia; *1903-1905* boards at Chatham Episcopal Institute, Chatham, Virginia; receives diploma with special art award and prize for watercolor; *1905-1906* attends Art Institute of Chicago; studies with John Vanderpoel; returns to Virginia for summer; has serious bout with typhoid fever; *1907-1908* studies with William Merritt Chase at the Art Students League, New York; visits exhibit of Rodin drawings at Alfred Stieglitz's 201 Fifth Avenue Gallery; wins Chase Still Life Prize to attend summer art school at Lake George, New York; *1908-1910* works as free-lance commercial artist in Chicago to support herself; family moves to Charlottesville, Virginia; substitutes for former Chatham art teacher Elizabeth May Wills; *1912* attends University of Virginia summer school for women where she studies advanced art with Alon Bement who introduces her to works by Arthur Wesley Dow, both of whose ideas influence her work; teaches as supervisor of drawing for Amarillo, Texas, school system; *1913* joins National Woman's Party and remains member for thirty years; teaches drawing in summer school at University of Virginia through 1916; *1914* attends Teachers College, Columbia University, studying with Arthur Dow at Alon Bement's suggestion; begins friendship with Anita Pollitzer which lasts nearly to the end of Anita's life; *fall 1915-March 1916* teaches art at Columbia College, South Carolina, where she does a series of original charcoal drawings after feeling too influenced by her art teachers; sends some of these drawings to Anita Pollitzer who shows them to Alfred Stieglitz against O'Keeffe's wishes; Stieglitz praises drawings as original, honest expressions from a woman; begins correspondence with Stieglitz; her mother dies; *March-June 1916* studies at Teachers College; *May 23-July 5, 1916* Stieglitz hangs her drawings and watercolors along with Charles Duncan's and Rene Lafferty's work at 291 Gallery which causes a stir among patrons of the gallery; *1916-1918* heads art department of West Texas State Normal College in Canyon; loves the wide open spaces of Texas and feels at home there; *April 3-May 14, 1917* Stieglitz hangs her first solo exhibition at 291 (and the last as the gallery is closing); arrives in New York after the show is dismantled, and Stieglitz rehangs it for her; begins modeling for Stieglitz's photographs; *1917* travels with her sister Claudia to Colorado making a detour into New Mexico; *1918* takes leave of absence from teaching due to illness; lives with a female friend in Waring and San Antonio, Texas; *June 1918* returns to New York to paint with financial assistance from Stieglitz and lives with his niece; Stieglitz moves into the same apartment after leaving his wife and takes some of his most erotic photographs of O'Keeffe; *August-October 1918* stays at Lake George with Stieglitz and his family, the first of many annual vacations there through the 1920s; *November 1918* her father dies; *1919* paints series of music-inspired pictures; *1921* Stieglitz's photographs of O'Keeffe are shown for the first time in an exhibition of his work at the Anderson Galleries, New York; *1923* Stieglitz presents a large solo exhibition of one hundred pictures by O'Keeffe at the Anderson Galleries; *1924* marries Stieglitz and does first large flower paintings; *1925* Stieglitz presents the "Seven Americans" exhibition at the Anderson Galleries which includes work by Charles Demuth, Arthur G. Dove, Marsden Hartley, John Marin, Georgia O'Keeffe, photographer Paul Strand, and himself; causes a sensation with her large flower paintings, the soft and feathery curves and rhythms of the paintings seem to be charged with feminine sensuality and are shocking to a public not used to seeing anything like them, especially by a woman painter; *1926* addresses the National Woman's Party Convention in Washington, D.C.; Dorothy Norman begins to visit Stieglitz's gallery and by 1929 is a daily visitor; *1929* visits New Mexico with Rebecca Strand as a guest of Mabel Dodge Luhan in Taos; *1929-1930* paintings included in an exhibition at the Museum of Modern Art; *1930* after visit to Taos, continues to paint New Mexican themes; Dorothy Norman becomes a model for Stieglitz's photography; *1933* hospitalized in New York for a nervous breakdown; *1934* returns to New Mexico for summer; continues to summer regularly in New Mexico and lives other months with Stieglitz in New York; Stieglitz's health begins to decline; *1940* buys adobe house (Rancho de los Burros or Ghost Ranch) near Abiquiu, New Mexico; *1943* first large retrospective of her work held at Art Institute of Chicago and the first time the institute featured a woman; *1945* buys property in Abiquiu, which becomes her home and studio; *1946* retrospective of her work held at Museum of Modern Art, New York; Stieglitz dies in a New York hospital; *1946-1949* catalogues Stieglitz's large collection of art and large collection of his own photographs and distributes them to museums; prepares two exhibitions from the collections; *1949* moves permanently to New Mexico; paints

New Mexico themes and travels extensively; *1953* visits Europe for the first time; *1960* retrospective exhibition held at Worcester Art Museum, Worcester, Massachusetts; *1963* elected to the American Academy of Arts and Letters; *1966* elected to the American Academy of Arts and Sciences; retrospective exhibition at Amon Carter Museum of Western Art, Fort Worth, Texas; *1970* large retrospective at the Whitney Museum of Art, New York; *1971* begins losing central vision; *1973* Juan Hamilton becomes her assistant and traveling companion, teaching her to make pottery; with the help of Hamilton, publishes first book, *Georgia O'Keeffe,* in which she describes her own paintings; *1978-1979* exhibition of photographs "Georgia O'Keeffe: A Portrait by Alfred Stieglitz" shown at the Metropolitan Museum of Art, New York; *1984* moves to Santa Fe to be close to medical help; *1986* dies on March 6 in Santa Fe at age ninety-eight.

Activities of Historical Significance

The artistic impact of Georgia O'Keeffe on the American consciousness is still being assessed. Her unusually straightforward thinking was odd for a woman in the 1910s and 1920s, and her vision of what she wanted to do kept her on a track from which she rarely wavered. O'Keeffe herself said in 1926 that she is the type of person who comes to quick and positive decisions. When she said at age twelve that she "was going to be an artist," her goal held throughout her life. Indeed, her work was her life, unlike the conventional domestic role played by the women of the time. Her independent spirit and unwavering belief in herself and what she wanted to do has become a model for women especially after the 1960s when she and her work were rediscovered after falling out of favor with the public for a couple decades.

O'Keeffe cared little about what people or the critics thought. Her early drawings of 1915 and 1916 were so unique that other artists could find no outside influence in them. She was not interested in European art movements but instead wanted to be an American artist. She developed a highly personal "language" of expression and when her large flower paintings were shown, the public was shocked at her daring colors and forms which were often interpreted as erotic. The flowers became her signature works; they are still fresh and appealing nearly seventy years later and enjoy immense popularity. By 1936 she was ranked by a noted art critic along with Cézanne, Gauguin, Matisse, and others as a master of modern art. In fact O'Keeffe was lucky enough to live through early acclaim, a period of lesser favor, and finally a resurgence of interest and honors for her works. She resisted labels of any kind but at one point said, "I suppose you have the right to call me a romantic painter."

O'Keeffe was a supporter of feminism throughout her life; by 1929 she was called an ardent feminist and in 1944 wrote Eleanor Roosevelt chiding her lack of support for the Equal Rights Amendment. She lived her life as she wanted, making some hard choices: she decided not to have children, to preserve her focus on her work, and she stayed with Stieglitz when he was having an affair with Dorothy Norman. Her life with Stieglitz flourished due to their close artistic relationship, which is best understood by exploring some references on Stieglitz as well. In their early years together, O'Keeffe was highly creative and productive but as time progressed she began to need her own space, undominated by his energetic and powerful presence. She became independent in her own right and her work began to overshadow Stieglitz's toward the end of his life.

Stieglitz supported O'Keeffe's work from the first time he saw it; he had an eye for art, as O'Keeffe once said "his eye was in him," always composing, attentive to form, light, shape, and not needing to travel to exotic places in search of subjects. He hung her works every year in his galleries and this constant exposure, along with his controversial photographs of her, helped to shape her image for the public. O'Keeffe was just as determined to project her own image, however, often struggling to maintain her identity as an artist and an individual and not just a woman artist. Her paintings were unique in their differing perspectives and their wedding of opposites: abstract and concrete forms, hard and soft edges, bold and delicate color, and forms of life and forms of death. She did not choose to sign her works, feeling that the subject matter would speak for her. O'Keeffe had always commanded a good price for her work, and by 1987 one of her paintings brought 1.9 million dollars at auction.

Overview of Biographical Sources

As a result of O'Keeffe's protective stance toward her work and life, especially after her move to New Mexico, biographical sources of book length began appearing only toward the end of her life. The first, Laurie Lisle's *Portrait of an Artist* (1980), published when O'Keeffe was ninety-three, outraged O'Keeffe as an intrusion on her privacy. Lisle's work, though not encompassing O'Keeffe's final six years or the estate settlement, is an excellently crafted account considering the information available to her. The thoughtful selection of photographs reveals O'Keeffe in striking settings at various times in her life. Although numerous newspaper and magazine articles were written about O'Keeffe and her art (the Cleveland Museum of Art has an extensive clipping file of fascinating materials), she herself said little about her work until her commentary on representative works, *Georgia O'Keeffe* (1976), was published with the help of Juan Hamilton.

Stieglitz guarded O'Keeffe's paintings from art dealers, the general public, and anyone he thought unworthy, often refusing to sell a piece if he did not like a patron. O'Keeffe absorbed this attitude and a similar one of carefully portraying her ideas in print. After Stieglitz died in 1946, she lost his protection, but continued these attitudes. In addition to her desire for privacy, there was and still is limited access to some of her personal papers.

Before Lisle's work, the 1943 Art Institute of Chicago catalogue essay by Daniel Catton Rich contained more biographical information than anything previously written. O'Keeffe seemed to trust him, and Rich realized how closely intertwined her life and work were. An outstanding work by Jan Garden Castro, *The Art and Life of Georgia O'Keeffe* (1985), is splendidly produced and illustrated with color plates. The most substantial biography is *Georgia O'Keeffe, A Life* (1989) by historian Roxanne Robinson. The book makes fascinating reading about the highly complex, intelligent, and talented woman. Published posthumously through the efforts of William Pollitzer, Anita Pollitzer's nephew and literary executor, *A Woman on Paper: Georgia O'Keeffe* (1988), edited by Clive Giboire, is a testimony to a unique friendship that soured at the end of Pollitzer's life when O'Keeffe refused to allow her to publish it. Another source is *Lovingly Georgia: The Complete Correspondence of Georgia O'Keeffe and Anita Pollitzer* (1990), edited by Clive Gibiore. A book young people may enjoy is Beverly Gherman, *Georgia O'Keeffe, the Wideness and Wonder of Her World* (1986).

Much of the biographical material on O'Keeffe before 1980 was contained in essays in catalogues accompanying her major retrospective exhibitions: The Art Institute of Chicago, *Georgia O'Keeffe* (1943), with a thorough text by Daniel Catton Rich; The Museum of Modern Art, New York (1946); Worcester Art Museum, Worcester, Massachusetts, *An Exhibition by Georgia O'Keeffe* (1960), with text by Daniel Catton Rich; Amon Carter Museum of Western Art, *Georgia O'Keeffe, An Exhibition* (1966), text by Marsden Hartley; and the Whitney Museum of Art, New York, *Georgia O'Keeffe* (1970), text by Lloyd Goodrich and Doris Bry, a long time associate and O'Keeffe expert. With text by Jack Cowart and Juan Hamilton, and letters of O'Keeffe selected and edited by Sarah Greenough, research curator at the National Gallery and respected scholar, *Georgia O'Keeffe: Art and Letters* (1987-1988) was published for the National Gallery of Art's complete retrospective of O'Keeffe's best works. Many of her paintings are magnificently reproduced along with some 125 letters and three essays uncovering the private side of O'Keeffe who had become a remote and somewhat romanticized icon of American painting. The most recent biography is Benita Eisler, *O'Keeffe and Stieglitz: An American Romance* (1991), which is the most thorough treatment of their passionate professional and personal relationship.

Evaluation of Biographical Sources

Castro, Jan Garden. *The Art and Life of Georgia O'Keeffe*. New York: Crown, 1985. (**A, G**) Castro throws light on O'Keeffe's personality and relationships, as well as her art, by including extensive information from those who knew her well. Includes splendid color reproductions of a variety of works, some seldom seen, such as the portrait of Beauford Delaney, Blue B, and Three Shells.

Eisler, Benita. *O'Keeffe and Stieglitz: An American Romance*. Garden City, NY: Doubleday/Talese, 1991 (**A, G**). Eisler portrays this relationship as a tug-of-war, with each partner fueling the other's artistic and sexual urges. First her mentor and patron, then her lover and husband, and finally her betrayer, Stieglitz inspired the passion that characterizes the color and themes of O'Keeffe's painting. This tumultuous, troubled romance, laced with infidelities and lesbianism, is graphically exposed. If the author's approach is racy, it is also fascinating reading as a love story.

Gherman, Beverly. *Georgia O'Keeffe, the Wideness and Wonder of Her World*. New York: Atheneum, 1986. (**Y**) Written for young people, this is a sympathetic view O'Keeffe's life and works.

Giboire, Clive, ed. *A Woman on Paper: Georgia O'Keeffe*. New York: Simon and Schuster, 1988. (**A, G**) This incomparable look at O'Keeffe's relationship with one of her closest friends contains correspondence from 1914 to 1955 and enlightening commentary by Anita Pollitzer.

Lisle, Laurie. *Portrait of an Artist*. New York: Washington Square Press, 1980. (**A, G**) Although O'Keeffe herself was outraged at the intrusion on her private life that this biography represented, this volume is a fine work, warm and moving, yet dispassionate. The portrait that arises is of a woman of great character and determination with her attendant frailties and strengths well documented. Includes photographs of the artist throughout her life.

Robinson, Roxanne. *Georgia O'Keeffe, A Life*. New York: Harper & Row, 1989. (**A, G**) This volume, produced after her death, is the most definitive biography of O'Keeffe to date. With extensive, rich detail Robinson creates a readable text, balanced and perceptive, though sometimes lapsing into her own subjective views. Includes extensive endnotes, bibliography, and index.

Overview and Evaluation of Primary Sources

Archival materials can be found in abundance in two main institutions, the Archives of American Art, Smithsonian Institution, Washington, D.C., and the Beinecke Rare Book and Manuscript Library, Yale University, New Haven, Connecticut. The Archives of American Art has correspondence between O'Keeffe and Andrew Dasburg, Arthur G. Dove, Caroline Fesler, Russell Vernon Hunter, Aline M. Liebman, Elizabeth McCausland, and Cady Wells, among others. When O'Keeffe executed Stieglitz's estate, she deposited all of his papers and their nearly eighteen hundred letters (they sometimes wrote twice a day when she was in Taos) at the Beinecke Library. The collection contains upwards of fifty thousand items including thousands of letters, family photographs, other papers, and five hundred of Stieglitz's photographs from 1922 to 1937. The materials, which take up a whole room of files, are still being catalogued and received from the O'Keeffe estate. There is restricted access to the O'Keeffe-Stieglitz letters, some of which have never been seen, until twenty-five years after O'Keeffe's death. Material in this collection is a treasure of information on early twentieth-century America. In addition, the Carl Van Vechten Gallery of Fine Art, Fisk University, Nashville, Tennessee, has O'Keeffe's painting *Radiator Building-Night New York* (1927), her papers and correspondence with the black author and lecturer Jean Toomer (1894-1967), and one hundred art works and photographs from Stieglitz's collection.

Doris Bry, ed., *Some Memories of Drawings* (New York: Atlantis Editions, 1974; **A, G, Y**), is O'Keeffe's spontaneous and sometimes humorous account of her drawings. *Georgia O'Keeffe* (New York: Viking Press, 1976; **A, G, Y**) contains the artist's comments on her own paintings and why she painted the way she did. *A Portrait by Alfred Stieglitz* (New York: Viking Press, 1978; **A, G**) is a collection of Stieglitz's photographs of O'Keeffe with an introduction by the artist.

Clive Giboire, *Lovingly Georgia: The Complete Correspondence of Georgia O'Keeffe and Anita Pollitzer* (New York: Simon and Schuster, 1990; **A, G**), contains about two hundred letters between O'Keeffe and Pollitzer and dozens of sketches. He shows Pollitzer's energetic and unflagging support of O'Keeffe and her work over fifty-three years of letter writing.

Museums, Historical Landmarks, Societies

The largest collection of O'Keeffe paintings, twenty-nine works, is in the Metropolitan Museum of Art, New York; other large collections are in the Phillips Collection, Washington, D.C.; the Museum of Modern Art, New York; the Whitney Museum of American Art, New York; and the National Gallery of Art,

Washington, D.C. Museums receiving several paintings from her estate were: the Art Institute of Chicago, the Boston Museum of Fine Arts, the Brooklyn Museum, the Cleveland Museum of Art, the Philadelphia Museum of Art, the Metropolitan Museum of Art, New York, the Museum of Modern Art, New York, and the National Gallery of Art, Washington, D.C.

Other Sources

Bry, Doris. *Georgia O'Keeffe in the West*. New York: Alfred A. Knopf, 1989. Contains fine reproductions of her New Mexican era paintings with a perceptive essay by Bry, an O'Keeffe expert and long-time associate.

Calloway, Nicholas, ed. *Georgia O'Keeffe, One Hundred Flowers*. New York: Alfred A. Knopf, 1987. A coffee-table volume with magnificent reproductions of her best flower paintings and a brief and laudatory essay by the editor.

Chave, Anna C. "O'Keeffe and the Masculine Gaze." *Art in America* 78 (January 1990): 114-125. A penetrating assessment of O'Keeffe as an audacious painter of the female experience which raises some controversial issues for mostly male critics.

Decker, Andrew. "The Battle Over Georgia O'Keeffe's Multimillion-Dollar Legacy." *Art News* 86 (January-May 1987): 120-127. A look at the dispute between the O'Keeffe family and Juan Hamilton who was left virtually all of O'Keeffe's estate according to a will drafted in 1984 when O'Keeffe was ninety-six and Hamilton had been her companion and helper for twelve years.

Greenough, Sarah. "The Letters of Georgia O'Keeffe." *Antiques* 132 (November 1987): 1110-1117. An assessment of O'Keeffe's way with words which was quite effective in evoking images and metaphors in a direct, clear style.

Greenough, Sarah, and Juan Hamilton. *Alfred Stieglitz, Photographs and Writings*. New York: Calloway Editions, 1983. An excellent overview of Stieglitz's life and relationship with O'Keeffe.

Luhan, Mabel Dodge. "Georgia O'Keeffe in Taos." *Creative Art* (June 1931): 407-410. A fresh look at O'Keeffe's first summer in New Mexico by another unusual and independent woman.

Lynes, Barbara Buhler. *O'Keeffe, Stieglitz and the Critics, 1916-1929*. Ann Arbor, MI: UMI Research Press, 1989. A knowledgeable study of the interactions of art critics, many of whom disagreed with each other, and the relationship between O'Keeffe and Stieglitz, showing much of the struggle O'Keeffe had in forging her own identity and that of her work.

Peters, Sarah Whitaker. *Becoming O'Keeffe: The Early Years*. New York: Abbeville, 1991. Peters explores O'Keefe's artistic collaboration with Stieglitz by comparing his lyrical photographs of Lake George (New York) with her spiritual landscapes of the same scenes. Peters also argues that his photography changed as his portraits of her became less obsessive and more objective. Once O'Keefe began returning to New Mexico, the influences on her art become more diverse, reflecting the styles of art nouveau and Kandinsky. Richly illustrated.

Tomkins, Calvin. "The Rose in the Eye Looked Pretty Fine." *The New Yorker* (March 4, 1974): 40-66. An excellent and balanced profile of O'Keeffe who was known to be sometimes abrasive and abrupt in manner.

Webb, Todd. *Georgia O'Keeffe, the Artist's Landscape*. Pasadena, CA: Twelvetree Press, 1984. Photographs of O'Keeffe and her surroundings by a friend and occasional travelling companion.

Wilson, Edmund. "The Stieglitz Exhibition." *The New Republic* (March 18, 1925): 97-98. Written by a well-known art critic, this review is a highly charged response to O'Keeffe's flower paintings and abstractions. It contains his often quoted comment that she "outblazes the other painters," all men, and admits that America has produced a woman painter comparable to the country's best woman poets and novelists.

Young, Mahonri Sharp. *Painters of the Stieglitz Group: Early American Moderns*. New York: Watson-Guptil, 1974. Focuses on the painters in the Stieglitz "stable," including O'Keeffe.

Evelyn E. Hunt
Cleveland State University

JAMES OGLETHORPE
1696-1785

Chronology

Born James Edward Oglethorpe on December 22, 1696, in London, the fifth son of Lady Eleanor Wall and Sir Theophilus Oglethorpe; baptized the following day at St. Martin's in the Fields Church, London; grows up on the family estate, Westbrook Manor in Surrey, but spends part of each year in London, where his mother is associated with supporters of the exiled Stuarts (Jacobites); *1713* receives commission as lieutenant in Queen Anne's First Regiment of Foot Guards but is not active; *1714* spends brief period at Eton; enters Corpus Christi College, Oxford, but stays only a few months; joins the imperial forces of Prince Eugene of Savoy in France; sees action against the Turks in the Danubian campaign and at the siege of Belgrade; campaigns against the Spanish in Sicily; *1719* returns to England where he disavows intrigues of his mother and sisters in Jacobite politics; *1722* elected to Parliament as member for Haslemere, the traditional family seat, which he retains for thirty-two years; *1729* advocates penal reform and chairs committee to investigate prisons; opposes imprisonment for debt; writes brief book, *The Sailor's Advocate,* to oppose the practice of impressment; meets Dr. Thomas Bray, leader of the Society for Propagation of Gospel and the Society for Propagation for Christian Knowledge; befriends John Viscount Percival (later earl of Egmont); *1730* elected chair of expanded Bray Associates group which petitions the Privy Council for permission to found a charity colony in America; *June 1732* George II grants land between Altamaha and Savannah Rivers to Oglethorpe-Percy group as "Georgia" trustees for twenty-one year period; trustees determine to prohibit slavery and liquor, and to limit the size of landholdings in the new colony; *November 1732* Oglethorpe sails with first shipload of colonists aboard the ship *Anne*; *1733* reaches colony site on Savannah River in February; assumes leadership, chooses Savannah town site, and directs settler activities; signs treaty with Lower Creeks and secures friendship of Chief Tomochichi; *May 1734* returns to England, bringing Chief Tomochichi with him, to stimulate interest in the new colony called Georgia, and to appeal for military support; *December 1735* returns to colony with 490 colonists; others, including many religious refugees, also come to the colony; *February 1736* settles about two hundred Scotch Highlanders at Darien; constructs Fort Frederica on St. Simon's Island; *November 1736* returns to England with encouraging reports for trustees; *1738* returns to Georgia with five transports and about seven hundred soldiers, carrying a royal commission as captain general of Georgia and South Carolina forces; prepares Georgia defenses when England and Spain go to war; *1739* leads force from Georgia into Florida without decisive result; *1740* leads a stronger force, including eleven hundred Native Americans, in invasion of Florida; captures two Spanish forts but abandons siege of St. Augustine in July; *1742* repels Spanish assault on Fort Frederica at the Battle of Bloody Marsh; *1743* fails again to take St. Augustine and withdraws to Georgia; criticized by Parliament for financial problems in the colony and denied further subsidies; *July 1743* leaves Georgia for England, never to return; *September 15, 1744* marries Elizabeth Wright at Westminster Abbey; *1745* promoted to major general and leads British troops against pretender Charles Stuart (Bonnie Prince Charlie); relieved of command after dispute with the duke of Cumberland, commander of British forces; *1746* faces court martial and is acquitted but denied active command; *1749* elected Fellow of Royal Society; devotes time and money to charitable institutions, such as the Foundling Hospital and Westminster Infirmary; works with friend Sir Hans Sloane to organize the British Museum; *1754* loses his parliamentary seat; *1755* serves with Prussian army against French forces in Europe, using an assumed name; *1761* returns to England; *1765* promoted to general in British army; *1767-1784* associates with literary and artistic luminaries in London; *1785* calls socially on John Adams, the first American minister to Britain; dies in London on June 30.

Activities of Historical Significance

James Edward Oglethorpe was foremost among the group of English trustees who visualized and planned the colonization of Georgia, and he was the only trustee to come to America to implement the plan. Although the initial Georgia "experiment" foundered, Oglethorpe is today remembered as the father of Georgia. Through his dual roles as trustee and director of the colony, Oglethorpe served as a focal point for several recurrent themes of English colonial expansion. The Georgia colony was envisioned as a haven for those fleeing religious persecution, such as Salzburger Lutherans and Moravians; it was also seen as a place where the deserving poor could make a new start, as a homeland for Europe's Jews, and as a buffer colony to insulate South Carolina from Spanish Florida and hostile Native-American tribes. It is doubtful that anyone could have transformed the colony of Georgia into both the "Garden of Eden" and the "Gibraltar of America." But to Oglethorpe's credit, the colony did fulfill, at least in part, each of these intentions.

Oglethorpe, more than any of his fellow trustees, defended the principles on which Georgia was founded. For him, the ideals of abolition, prohibition, land reform, and fair dealings with the Native-American tribes could not be compromised without admitting to the failure of the colony. Other trustees, however, began to oppose Oglethorpe's "high-mindedness" on economic and political grounds and worked to undermine his authority and support for the colony. When Oglethorpe returned to England, the noble ideals were abandoned one by one.

While in America, Oglethorpe devoted much of his attention to the military defense of the new colony. He strengthened fortifications, procured troops— often at his own expense—and forged alliances with neighboring Native-American tribes. His offensive incursions into Florida against the Spanish were only moderately successful, but the decisive repulse of the Spanish attack at the Battle of Bloody Marsh (1742), was due primarily to his skill and leadership. Oglethorpe's determination and commitment to principles left a lasting mark on the early settlement of America.

Overview of Biographical Sources

Oglethorpe was not well-served by his early biographers. Most of the numerous existing biographies are eulogistic and fail to adequately capture the personality or spirit of Oglethorpe. The first biographies of the founder of Georgia appeared in the 1840s when two New England Unitarian ministers published biographies: Thaddeus M. Harris, *Biographical Memorials of James Oglethorpe, Founder of the Colony of Georgia in North America* (1841), and William B. O. Peabody, *Life of James Oglethorpe, the Founder of Georgia* (1846). These works are highly laudatory and frankly admit the paucity of source materials. Of the two, Harris presents a more balanced view and is less prone to accept legendary stories as fact; Peabody appears to depend heavily on Harris and suspends any pretense of critical judgement—Oglethorpe is exalted; those who opposed him are debased; and there is little consideration of a possible middle ground.

Robert Wright, in *Memoir of General James Oglethorpe* (1867), adopts a laudatory tone but does attempt to uncover the facts surrounding Oglethorpe's English reform efforts as well as his Georgia experiences. Wright laments the lack of source materials, but is more successful than the earlier writers. A generation later, Henry Bruce, *Life of General Oglethorpe* (1890), offers an easier style, but makes no real improvements in content. Errors of fact, even in fundamentals such as Oglethorpe's correct birth date, are present in all of these early biographies.

These works also foreshadow the tendency by later writers to concentrate on single facets of Oglethorpe's character or beliefs, usually to serve a didactic purpose. Thus, Harriet C. Cooper's *James Oglethorpe, The Founder of Georgia* (1904) stresses his ban on liquor in early Georgia as a forerunner of prohibition. A more scholarly work, Leslie F. Church, *Oglethorpe: A Study of Philanthropy in*

England and Georgia (1932), emphasizes charity and philanthropy as the keys to Oglethorpe's life. Amos A. Ettinger's *James Edward Oglethorpe: Imperial Idealist* (1936) was the first biography to meet modern standards of scholarship, but Ettinger offers little interpretation or evaluation.

Phinizy Spalding's *Oglethorpe in America* (1977) is by far the most academically sound work on Oglethorpe. Spalding not only provides a realistic portrait of the man but offers a reasonable analysis of his purposes and motivations.

Evaluation of Principal Biographical Sources

Blackburn, Joyce. *James Edward Oglethorpe*. New York and Philadelphia: J. B. Lippincott, 1970. (Y) A careful study in a lively style that emphasizes Oglethorpe's American years and his humanitarianism. Military aspects are secondary. This is the best available work for a juvenile audience.

Bruce, Henry. *Life of General Oglethorpe*. New York: Dodd, Mead, 1890. (G) A volume in the Makers of America Series. Although this work rests on archival research in England and America, the author laments the lack of primary materials, especially personal correspondence. Factual accuracy is sought, but overall the author is too laudatory and fails to bring his subject to life. This volume was the first on Oglethorpe to include a bibliography.

Church, Leslie F. *Oglethorpe: A Study of Philanthropy in England and Georgia*. London: Epworth Press, 1932. (A, G) This study was the first to make extensive use of primary materials, and it includes a full bibliography. Church is too narrowly focused on philanthropy as his subject's primary motivation.

Cooper, Harriet C. *James Oglethorpe, The Founder of Georgia*. New York: Appleton, 1904. (Y) From Appleton's Historic Lives Series, this book is frankly written "to extend to the uttermost the inspiring effect of the character" of its subject. It is a relatively late example of tendencies most early Oglethorpe biographers revealed. Modern young people would not find it of much interest.

Ettinger, Amos Aschbach. *James Edward Oglethorpe: Imperial Idealist*. Oxford: Clarendon Press, 1936. (A, G) For many years this was the standard study and it is still a good starting point for work on Oglethorpe. It is fully documented and represents sound scholarship at its best. The subtitle suggests the theme but this is not forced. In general, Ettinger offers a balanced treatment of the phases of Oglethorpe's life but provides fullest coverage of his career in England.

—————. *Oglethorpe: A Brief Biography* [1929]. Reprint. Macon, GA: Mercer University Press, 1984. (**A**) This short biography won the Beit Prize in Colonial History for 1929 at Oxford and retains value even though Ettinger wrote his full study later. This work condenses Oglethorpe's career and includes sound judgments without the extensive notes and digressions that at times interrupt the flow of the author's 1936 biography.

Garrison, Webb B. *Oglethorpe's Folly: The Birth of Georgia*. Lakemont, GA: Copple House, 1982. (**G**) Based on a wide range of sources, primary and secondary, this is an obvious attempt to find the true Oglethorpe. Although Garrison occasionally lapses into academic methodology, this is still the best popular study of Oglethorpe. Illustrated and includes an excellent bibliography.

Spalding, Phinizy. *Oglethorpe in America*. Chicago: University of Chicago Press, 1977. (**A, G**) The best overall study of Oglethorpe available. Even though the focus is on the American phase of his life, the author convinces readers that the English background has been considered in terms of relevance for Oglethorpe's work in Georgia. Spalding has made thorough use of all available sources. The final chapter presents a good summary of Oglethorpe's contributions to American settlement and a comprehensive analysis of his character.

Wright, Robert. *A Memoir of General James Oglethorpe, One of the Earliest Reformers of Prison Discipline in England and the Founder of Georgia in America*. London: Chapman and Hall, 1867. (**G**) The first full-length study of Oglethorpe. Wright aimed for objectivity but was unable to overcome his admiration for his subject. Still, Wright avoided the pitfalls of later biographers.

Overview and Evaluation of Primary Sources
There is no major collection of personal papers to document Oglethorpe's life and work. There are, however, numerous references to his career in official documents and correspondence housed in the University of Georgia Library, the Georgia Department of Archives and History, the Library of Congress, and other repositories. These materials include documents of the British Colonial Office from the British Public Record Office that have been copied or transferred to microfilm.

A major source for both Oglethorpe and early Georgia is the twenty-volume Phillipps Collection of Egmont Manuscripts at the University of Georgia. Duke University houses a collection of Oglethorpe papers, as well as the Georgia Miscellaneous Papers, dated 1727-1753. At Yale's Beinecke Library the Boswell Papers contain much Oglethorpe material, especially on his post-Georgia years.

Among primary material for the study of Oglethorpe and early Georgia are those compiled by Allan D. Candler and Lucian L. Knight, *The Colonial Records of the State of Georgia*, 26 vols. (Atlanta: Department of Archives, 1904-1916; **A, G**); Kenneth Coleman and Milton L. Ready have continued this series and have recently published a manuscript from the Georgia Department of Archives and History as *Original Papers and Correspondence to the Trustees, James Oglethorpe and Others, 1732-1735* (Athens: University of Georgia Press, 1982; **A, G**)

The earl of Egmont, the most important of the trustees next to Oglethorpe, left diaries that are invaluable for studying the early settlement of Georgia. These are available in separate publications: *Manuscripts of the Earl of Egmont: Diary of Viscount Percival, Afterwards First Earl of Egmont*, 3 vols., edited by R. A. Roberts (London: Historical Manuscripts Commission, 1920-1923; **A, G**); and a long-missing part of the original diary, *The Journal of the Earl of Egmont. Abstract of the Trustees Proceedings for Establishing the Colony of Georgia, 1732-1738*, edited by Robert G. McPherson (Wormsloe Foundation Publication Number Five; Athens: University of Georgia Press, 1962; **A, G**). Further trustee correspondence, including eighty letters from or to Oglethorpe, may be found in Mills Lane, ed., *General Oglethorpe's Georgia: Colonial Letters, 1733-1743*, 2 vols. (Savannah, GA: Beehive Press, 1975; **A, G**).

Museums, Historical Landmarks, Societies

Chippewa Square (Savannah, GA). Contains a nine-foot bronze statue of Oglethorpe sculpted by Daniel Chester French and dedicated November 23, 1910.

Other Sources

Ivers, Larry E. *British Drums on the Southern Frontier: The Military Colonization of Georgia, 1733-1749*. Chapel Hill: University of North Carolina Press, 1974. An excellent study with much information on Oglethorpe's military actions in America.

Jackson, Harvey H., and Phinizy Spalding, eds. *Forty Years of Diversity: Essays on Colonial Georgia*. Athens: University of Georgia Press, 1984. Important essays on a variety of topics during the era of Oglethorpe and the trustees. Spalding's piece on Oglethorpe's quest for an American Zion is especially insightful.

Alan S. Brown
Western Michigan University

FREDERICK LAW OLMSTED
1822-1903

Chronology

Born Frederick Law Olmsted on April 26, 1822, in Hartford, Connecticut, the first of two sons born to Charlotte Law Hull and John Olmsted, a successful dry-goods merchant; *1826-1836* receives primary education at various boarding schools in rural Connecticut; *1837* poor vision prohibits continued education; *1842* attends lectures at Yale University after his eyesight improves; *1843-1844* journeys to China as a cabin boy on the bark *Ronaldson*; *1844-1845* studies scientific farming in Connecticut and New York; *1848-1854* works as a farmer on Staten Island, New York; *1850* takes walking tour through the British Isles and western Europe; *1851* visits landscape architect and horticulturist Andrew Jackson Downing at Newburgh, New York; *1852* publishes first book, *Walks and Talks of an American Farmer in England*; *1852-1854* travels through the American South as a corre-spondent for the *New York Times*; *1855-1856* becomes part-owner and editor of *Putnam's Monthly Magazine*; publishes *A Journey in the Seaboard Slave States, with Remarks on Their Economy*, the first of a series of books about his observa-tions traveling in the antebellum South; *1857* publishes the second book of the series, *A Journey Through Texas; or A Saddle-Trip on the Southwest Frontier with a Statistical Appendix*; after *Putnam's* fails, becomes superintendent of Central Park in New York City; collaborates with British architect Calvert Vaux on the competitive design for the park that they first call "Greensward"; *1858* wins design competition and is appointed chief architect of Central Park; *1859* marries Mary Cleveland Perkins Olmsted, the widow of his younger brother; *1860* publish-es third book in the series about the antebellum South, *A Journey in the Back Country*; *1861* is named general secretary of the U.S. Sanitary Commission, which later serves as a prototype for other volunteer organizations such as the American Red Cross, the Salvation Army, and the YMCA; publishes *The Cotton Kingdom: A Traveller's Observations on Cotton and Slavery in the American Slave States*, his final travel record of the Old South; *1863* helps start *The Nation* magazine; resigns from positions on the Sanitary Commission and Board of Commissioners of Central Park and is named a director of the Mariposa Mining Company in California; *1864-1865* prepares "The Yosemite Valley and the Mariposa Big Trees: A Preliminary Report, 1865"; reappointed landscape architect to the Board of Commissioners of Central Park; *1866* with Vaux, draws up landscape plan for the Columbia Institute for the Deaf and Dumb (Gallaudet University), Washington, publishes various landscape plans, including that of the University of California at Berkeley; *1868* draws plan for the suburban community of Riverside, Illinois; *1869* advises Boston officials on park planning; *1871* collaborates with architect Henry Hobson Richardson on the design for the state hospital for the mentally ill, Buffalo, New York; *1874* consults on park planning in Montreal; draws plan for the Arnold Arboretum, Boston; *1875* prepares landscape plan for U.S. Capitol; *1876* with Richardson, prepares plans to complete the construction of the New York State Capitol, Albany; *1877* prepares design for Mount Royal Park, Montreal; *1878* exhibits plan for the city of Buffalo at the Paris Exposition; *1879* proposes improvements to Boston's Back Bay; becomes involved in efforts to conserve Niagara Falls; *1880* collaborates with architectural firm of McKim, Mead and White on the construction of the home of William Drew Washburn in Minneapolis; submits proposal for the Anson Phelps Stokes estate, Newport, Rhode Island; *1883* submits plans for Belle Isle Park, Detroit; *1884* proposes scheme for the construction of West Roxbury Park and Wood Island Park, Boston; participates in campaign to preserve the Adirondack region; *1886* consults on the campus plan for Groton School, Groton, Massachusetts; *1887* issues proposal for an interconnecting park system in Boston; *1888* engaged by George Washington Vanderbilt in the construction of the colossal Biltmore Estate, Asheville, North Carolina; provides campus plan for Stanford University; *1889* draws landscaping plan for the grounds of the Alabama State Capitol, Montgomery; recommends park system for Rochester, New York; *1890* advises on site selection for the World's Columbian Exposition, Chicago; *1891* submits plan for a system of parks for Louisville, Kentucky; *1893* consults on the site plan for the Cotton States and International Exposition in Atlanta; collaborates on the campus plan for Columbia University, New York; receives honorary doctor of laws degrees from Harvard and Yale universities; *1894* prepares report on a park system for Cincinnati; *1895* plans the campus design for Union College, Schenectady, New York; submits plan for the design of Pinehurst, North Carolina, James Walker Tuft's community for tuberculosis invalids; retires from professional practice because of increasing illness; participates in founding the American Society of Landscape Architects, chartered in 1898; *1896* becomes permanently incapacitated; *1903* dies on August 28 in a cottage on the grounds of the McLean Asylum, Waverley, Massachusetts, which he designed many years earlier.

Activities of Historical Significance

Frederick Law Olmsted's work as a landscape architect and conservationist set a standard of excellence that continues to influence those who follow in his footsteps. He was active in conservation projects nationwide, including Niagara Falls and the Adirondack region of upstate New York. His forethought helped persuade Congress to set aside the Yosemite Valley as a national park and to begin designating a national park system for the entire nation. As a landscape architect, Olmsted planned parks for almost every major American city of his day and demonstrated that it was possible to plan the development of the environment rather than to rely on the discretion of unscrupulous businessmen and irresponsible politicians. Olmsted worked in both the public and private sectors. He viewed the art of landscape design as a civilizing force in the rapid physical development of late nineteenth-century urban America. Central Park in New York City, Riverside outside Chicago, Prospect Park in Brooklyn, Druid Hills in Atlanta, the grounds of the U.S. Capitol, and many other public and private projects that bear his mark continue to stand as a testament to his thoughtful planning and careful treatment of the environment. By 1900, largely because of his efforts, landscape architecture emerged as a recognized profession in America.

Overview of Biographical Sources

Olmsted, a man whose life spanned the last seventy-five years of the nineteenth century and whose interests and accomplishments ranged widely, has attracted the attention of many writers and scholars. But most have shied away from the challenge of undertaking a full-scale, exhaustive biographical analysis of this complex American. To date, only two comprehensive works, both of which capitalize on the wealth of available primary source material, have been published. Laura Wood Roper's massive biography, *FLO: A Biography of Frederick Law Olmsted* (1973), is the result of a thirty-year interest in Olmsted. Roper emphasizes Olmsted's firm belief that the environment—be it urban, suburban, or rural—could be manipulated for the physical and spiritual enrichment of people. Roper had the advantage of interviewing and corresponding with Frederick Law Olmsted, Jr., about various aspects of his father's life. Her biography, therefore, not only depicts Olmsted's development as a professional planner and environmental designer but delves deeply into his personal life as well. The other major analysis of Olmsted is by the accomplished biographer Elizabeth Stevenson. *Park Maker: A Life of Frederick Law Olmsted* (1977), like Roper's exhaustive biography, provides a sympathetic look at its subject. Stevenson closely traces Olmsted's career from agriculturalist to landscape architect and provides an engaging interpretation of how his travels through the antebellum South helped influence his subsequent work as a maker of parks.

Evaluation of Principal Biographical Sources

Fabos, Julius G., Gordon T. Milde, and Michael V. Weinmayr. *Frederick Law Olmsted, Sr.: Founder of Landscape Architecture in America.* Amherst: University of Massachusetts Press, 1968. (**A, G**) This abundantly illustrated volume contains the designs of many of Olmsted's most well-known projects. Far more exhibitory than biographical, it was published under the supervision of the American Society of Landscape Architects and the Harvard University Graduate School of Design in conjunction with a national traveling exhibition of Olmsted's work.

Fein, Albert. *Frederick Law Olmsted and the American Environmental Tradition.* New York: George Braziller, 1972. (**A, G**) This concise, profusely illustrated book places Olmsted's work as a planner and environmentalist in the historical context of the late nineteenth century.

Johnston, Johanna. *Frederick Law Olmsted: Partner with Nature.* New York: Dodd, Mead, 1975. (**Y**) A juvenile biography that includes an index and a bibliography.

Kalfus, Melvin. *Frederick Law Olmsted: The Passion of a Public Artist.* New York: New York University Press, 1990. (**A, G**) Volume eighteen of the American Social Experience Series, this study was derived from the author's doctoral dissertation at New York University.

Mitchell, Broadus. *Frederick Law Olmsted: A Critic of the Old South.* 1924. Reprint. New York: Russell and Russell, 1968. (**A, G**) This is primarily an examination of Olmsted as a literary figure and social critic of the South.

Noble, Iris. *Frederick Law Olmsted: Park Designer.* New York: J. Messner, 1974. (**Y**) Noble presents a good synthesis for young readers of Olmsted's activities and ideals concerning the value of open space within the urban environment.

Roper, Laura Wood. *FLO: A Biography of Frederick Law Olmsted.* Baltimore: Johns Hopkins University Press, 1973. (**A, G**) This is a detailed, well-written analysis by an author who obviously admires her subject.

Stevenson, Elizabeth. *Park Maker: A Life of Frederick Law Olmsted.* New York: Macmillan, 1977. (**A, G**) Stevenson's extensively researched volume provides an extraordinarily vivid portrait of Olmsted and of some of his collaborators, such as Calvert Vaux and Henry Hobson Richardson.

Todd, John Emerson. *Frederick Law Olmsted*. Edited by Arthur Brown. Boston: Twayne, 1982. (G) This short, well-documented study in Twayne's World Leader Series should appeal to readers less interested in detail and scholarly interpretation.

Overview and Evaluation of Primary Sources

Olmsted's extraordinarily objective travel accounts of life in the antebellum South serve as one of the very best primary sources available. These books include *A Journey in the Seaboard Slave States, with Remarks on Their Economy* (1856. Reprint. Westport, CT: Negro Universities Press, 1968; A, G); *A Journey Through Texas; or, A Saddle-Trip on the Southwestern Frontier with a Statistical Appendix* (1857. Reprint. Austin: University of Texas Press, 1969; A, G); *A Journey in the Back Country* (1860. Reprint. New York: Schocken Books, 1970; A, G); and *The Cotton Kingdom: A Traveller's Observations on Cotton and Slavery in the American Slave States*, 2 vols. (1861. Reprint. New York: Alfred A. Knopf, 1953, with an introduction by Arthur M. Schlesinger; A, G).

Hospital Transports (Boston: Ticknor and Fields, 1863; A) is Olmsted's personal memoir of the embarkation of the sick and wounded from the Virginia peninsula during the bloody summer of 1862. It was published at the request of the U.S. Sanitary Commission when Olmsted served as its general secretary. Also noteworthy is a paper he delivered to a meeting of the American Social Science Association, *Public Parks and the Enlargement of Towns* (1870. Reprint. New York: Arno Press, 1970; A).

Even though Olmsted wrote widely and is responsible for literally thousands of plans and reports, he never published an autobiography. He did, however, take care to maintain copies of the documents he produced. Some of these are housed in the Manuscript Division of the Library of Congress, Washington, D.C., but most are maintained in the offices of Olmsted Associates, Brookline, Massachusetts. Other documents pertaining to Olmsted's life and work may be found at the John M. Olin Library, Cornell University, Ithaca, New York; the Henry M. Huntington Library, San Marino, California; the Sterling Memorial Library, Yale University, New Haven, Connecticut; and the Stanford University Archives, Stanford, California.

This vast array of primary source material is currently being edited into a projected twelve-volume chronological compilation of Olmsted's work published under the general title *The Papers of Frederick Law Olmsted* (Baltimore: Johns Hopkins University Press, 1977-; A). To date only four volumes have been completed: Charles Capen McLaughlin, ed., *The Formative Years, 1822-1852* (1977); Charles Capen McLaughlin and Charles Eliot Beveridge, eds., *Slavery and the*

South, 1852-1857 (1981); Charles Eliot Beveridge and David Schuyler, eds., *Creating Central Park, 1857-1861* (1983); and Jane Turner Censer, ed., *Defending the Union: The Civil War and the United States Sanitary Commission, 1861-1863* (1986).

Many of Olmsted's now-familiar ideas about the importance of parks within the urban environment have been edited by S. B. Sutton in *Civilizing American Cities: A Selection of Frederick Law Olmsted's Writings on City Landscapes* (Cambridge: M.I.T. Press, 1971; **A, G**). Albert Fein, *Landscape into Cityscape: Frederick Law Olmsted's Plans for a Greater New York City* (Ithaca, NY: Cornell University Press, 1967; **A, G**), compiles the landscape architect's planning projects and pamphlet publications for the city of New York. Also noteworthy in its selection of Olmsted's writings is Frederick Law Olmsted, Jr., and Theodora Kimball, *Forty Years of Landscape Architecture: Frederick Law Olmsted, Sr.*, 2 vols. (New York: G. P. Putnam's Sons, 1922, 1928; **A, G**). The original Olmsted-Vaux plan for Central Park may be found in the Arsenal, Central Park.

Fiction and Adaptations

Helen Yglesias's *Family Feeling* (1967) is an inventive novel about a Jewish family living in New York during the 1950s. The main character fantasizes about telling the life story of Olmsted via film. In so doing, she recounts many biographical facts and portrays him in a remarkably lifelike manner. Yglesias employs several direct quotations from Olmsted that enhance the credibility of her work by revealing the humanity and philosophical nature of the famous landscape designer.

Museums, Historical Landmarks, Societies

Biltmore Estate (Asheville, NC). Magnificent Vanderbilt estate with historic house and expansive gardens designed by Olmsted. Open to the public.

Frederick Law Olmsted National Historic Site (Brookline, MA). The National Park Service maintains the clapboard house, named Fairstead, where Olmsted lived from 1883 to 1898. The house is open to the public. Olmsted's original firm, Olmsted Associates, continues to operate from a Brookline office.

Riverside National Historic District (Riverside, IL). Gardens and expansive parks designed by Olmsted. Open to the public. Also the site of the Frederick Law Olmsted Society, whose purpose is to encourage the development of landscaped parks.

Other Sources

Barlow, Elizabeth, and William Alex. *Frederick Law Olmsted's New York*. New York: Praeger Publishers, 1972. Published in connection with an exhibition at the Whitney Museum of American Art.

Beveridge, Charles Eliot. "Frederick Law Olmsted's Theory of Landscape Design." *Nineteenth Century* 2 (Summer 1977): 38-43. An intellectual analysis, by one of the associate editors of *The Papers of Frederick Law Olmsted*, of the ideals Olmsted maintained when he created many of his landscape masterpieces.

Blodgett, Geoffrey. "Frederick Law Olmsted: Landscape Architecture as Conservative Reform." *Journal of American History* 62 (March 1976): 869-887. Blodgett confronts those who argue that Olmsted was a reformer who brought significant social change to late nineteenth-century American cities.

Cecil, William A. V. *Biltmore: The Vision and Reality of George W. Vanderbilt, Richard Morris Hunt, and Frederick Law Olmsted*. Asheville, NC: Biltmore Estate, 1972. Detailed photographic volume compiled by George Washington Vanderbilt's grandson that depicts Olmsted's collaboration with architect Richard Morris Hunt in the construction of the baronial Biltmore estate.

Clark, Thomas H. "Frederick Law Olmsted on the South, 1889." *South Atlantic Quarterly* 3 (January 1904): 11-15. Unique work in that it denotes Olmsted's post-Civil War attitude about the South. Except for the collection of essays edited by White and Kramer cited below, little attention has been given this subject.

Fisher, Irving D. *Frederick Law Olmsted and the City Planning Movement in the United States*. Ann Arbor, MI: University Microfilms International, 1986. Scholarly examination of how Olmsted's philosophy for improving the urban environment merged with the City Beautiful Movement of the late nineteenth and early twentieth centuries.

Heidrich, Robert W. *Riverside: A Village in a Park*. Riverside, IL: Frederick Law Olmsted Society, 1970. Published to commemorate the designation of Riverside as a National Historic Landmark, this brief volume documents Olmsted's creation of one of the nation's first planned suburbs.

Kelly, Bruce, Gail Travis Guillet, and Mary Ellen W. Hern. *Art of the Olmsted Landscape*. New York: New York City Landmarks Preservation Commission,

1981. Published in conjunction with an exhibition of the same title at the Metropolitan Museum of Art, New York.

Lewis, Robert. "Frontier and Civilization in the Thought of Frederick Law Olmsted." *American Quarterly* 29 (Fall 1977): 385-403. Asserts that the controversial themes of social progress and social control were central to Olmsted's theory of civilization.

Maxwell, William Quentin. *Lincoln's Fifth Wheel: The Political History of the United States Sanitary Commission.* New York: Longmans, Green, 1956. Chronicles Olmsted's role as the commission's general secretary and relates how he continuously pressured the Army Medical Corps to upgrade its efforts to care for Union soldiers wounded during the Civil War.

Newton, Norman T. *Design on the Land: The Development of Landscape Architecture.* Cambridge: Harvard University Press, 1971. Surveys the evolution of landscape architecture both abroad and in the United States, giving dutiful attention to the role Olmsted played in the development of this profession.

Ranney, Victoria Post. *Olmsted in Chicago.* Chicago: R. R. Donnelley, 1972. One of the associate editors of *The Frederick Law Olmsted Papers* examines Olmsted's planning activities in and around Chicago, as well as his involvement in the site selection and landscape design for the 1893 World's Columbian Exposition.

Reed, Henry Hope, and Sophia Duckworth. *Central Park: A History and Guide.* New York: Clarkson N. Potter, 1967. Discusses the work of Olmsted and Calvert Vaux in their design of America's first urban park. Two walking tours of Central Park are outlined.

Roper, Laura Wood. "Frederick Law Olmsted and the Port Royal Experiment." *Journal of Southern History* 31 (August 1965): 272-284. Concerns Olmsted's interest in the federal government's attempt to upgrade the status of African Americans living on South Carolina's Sea Island during the Civil War.

―――――. "Frederick Law Olmsted and the Western Free-Soil Movement." *American Historical Review* 56 (October 1950): 58-64. Details Olmsted's involvement in the Free-Soil movement in west Texas.

—————. " 'Mr. Law' and *Putnam's Monthly Magazine:* A Note on a Phase in the Career of Frederick Law Olmsted." *American Literature* 26 (March 1954): 88-93. Surveys Olmsted's brief experience as a partner in a New York publishing firm and as an editor of a principal mid-nineteenth-century periodical.

Russell, Carl P. *One Hundred Years of Yosemite: The Story of a Great Park and Its Friends.* Berkeley and Los Angeles: University of California Press, 1947. Standard history of Yosemite that includes the role that Olmsted played in its incorporation as a national park.

Scheper, George L. "The Reformist Vision of Frederick Law Olmsted and the Poetics of Park Design." *New England Quarterly* 62 (September 1989): 369-407. Views Olmsted's environmental accomplishments against the strong late nineteenth-century currents of liberal reform, romantic transcendentalism, and the moral influence of the feminist movement.

Smithson, Robert. "Frederick Law Olmsted and the Dialectical Landscape." *Artform* 11 (February 1973): 62-63. Argues the relationship of an Olmstedian park to other aspects of the physical landscape.

Tyre, Peg. "Olmsted Avenue." *New York* 20 (February 2, 1987): 22. Illustrated analysis of Olmsted's design for Brooklyn's Eastern Parkway.

White, Dana F., and Victor A. Kramer, eds. *Olmsted South: Old South Critic/New South Planner.* Westport, CT: Greenwood Press, 1979. Collection of essays that focus on Olmsted's influence as an observer of the antebellum South and as a planner of the postwar South.

Wurman, Richard Saul, Alan Levy, and Joel Katz. *The Nature of Recreation: A Handbook in Honor of Frederick Law Olmsted.* Cambridge: M.I.T. Press, 1972. Interesting catalog-like volume in which the authors apply many of Olmsted's open space theories to various contemporary recreational needs.

Zaitzevsky, Cynthia. *Frederick Law Olmsted and the Boston Park System.* Cambridge: Harvard University Press, 1982. Oversized, profusely illustrated history of Olmsted's landscape artistry in Boston.

Howard L. Preston

WILLIAM PATTERSON
1891-1980

Chronology

Born William Patterson in San Francisco, California, on or about August 27, 1891 (official birth records were destroyed in the San Francisco earthquake and fire of 1906), the son of James Edward Patterson, a ship's cook and steward, dentist, and Seventh Day Adventist missionary, and Mary Patterson, a domestic worker; *1891-1919* grows up and attends school in the San Francisco Bay area; *1917* arrested for protesting World War I and joins National Association for the Advancement of Colored People (NAACP); *1919* graduates from Hastings School of Law of the University of California and travels to Pittsburgh to render legal assistance during the big steel strike; *1920* moves to New York City, befriends Paul Robeson, begins law practice; *1926* travels to Massachusetts to protest persecution of the Italian anarchists Nicola Sacco and Bartolomeo Vanzetti, and is arrested; joins the Communist party; *1927* travels to Europe and the Soviet Union, *1928* participates in the Sixth Congress of the Communist International in Moscow which proclaims that U.S. blacks are a nation deserving the right of self-determination; decides to remain abroad for three years of activism and study of anti-imperialism; *1931* returns to the U.S. and becomes leader of the International Labor Defense (ILD) which spearheads the defense of the Scottsboro Nine—black youths arrested wrongly for rape of a white woman; *1938* after spending seven years in a world-wide campaign seeking to free the Nine, moves to Chicago to become associate editor of the *Daily Record*, a labor-oriented newspaper; *1940* with Paul Robeson and others, meets with major league baseball executives to press for integration; *1940* becomes full-time operative for the Communist party in Chicago and founds the Abraham Lincoln School which is geared toward education of workers; *1946* helps to found the Civil Rights Congress (CRC); *1956* CRC folds under government pressure; becomes an operative once more for the Communist party, in which he remains until his death in 1980; in that capacity he emerges as a key advisor to the Black Panther party, which is organized in Oakland in 1966; *1980* dies March 5th in New York City after a prolonged illness.

Activities of Historical Significance

William Patterson was one of the premier left-wing African-American leaders of the twentieth century. Like his good friends Paul Robeson and Ben Davis, he too was an attorney. He wielded his legal skills in some of the key political cases in U.S. history, including that of Sacco and Vanzetti, who were arrested for alleged involvement in a payroll robbery that led to the killing of two guards. When Patterson travelled to Massachusetts to campaign for their freedom, he encountered other leftists like Mother Bloor, John Howard Lawson, and Dorothy Parker. He was arrested three times and was threatened with commitment to an insane asylum; writers Edna St. Vincent Millay, John Dos Passos, and Mike Gold were arrested with him and the noted civil libertarian Arthur Garfield Hays served as his attorney. At that juncture he joined the Communist party.

Patterson led the campaign to free the Scottsboro Nine, black youths arrested wrongly for raping a white woman in Alabama in 1931. This case, which combined an explosive mixture of race and sex, captured international headlines, though it required a number of landmark U.S. Supreme Court decisions before the defendants were released. This case also marked a noted conflict between the International Labor Defense (ILD), the organization headed by Patterson, and the NAACP, as to who would spearhead the campaign to free the defendants. The ILD handled numerous well-known cases, particularly during the 1930s, including the case of Tom Mooney, another celebrated political prisoner. After leaving the ILD Patterson moved to Chicago; there he married Louise Thompson, a political activist, who was a close friend of Langston Hughes and a key participant in the Harlem Renaissance.

Perhaps the zenith of Patterson's political career occurred during his tenure as leader of the Civil Rights Congress (CRC). The CRC emerged in 1946 as a result of a merger among the National Negro Congress, the ILD, and the National Federation for Constitutional Liberties. It was organized to combat the growing "Red Scare" and a rising tide of racial violence that marked the conclusion of World War II. An early case of note handled by the CRC was that of Willie McGee, a black truck driver in Mississippi, arrested wrongly for the rape of his white female lover; caught in a compromising position with her, she chose to charge him with rape rather than face the wrath of her community and her spouse. This case was fought in the courts and the streets between 1946 and 1951, when McGee was executed.

Patterson championed McGee's case as a global cause célèbre and, along with other CRC cases, highlighted one of the major contradictions of the era: how could Washington credibly charge Moscow with human rights violations when the U.S. imposed atrocious Jim Crow laws upon its black citizens? The sharpening of this contradiction led inexorably to *Brown v. Board of Education* in 1954, which held *de jure* segregation to be unconstitutional and set the stage for the civil rights push that followed shortly thereafter.

The CRC also led the campaign to free Rose Lee Ingram (a black woman sharecropper put on trial after participating in the killing of her white male landlord who had assaulted her sexually), the Martinsville Seven (black youth in Virginia accused of raping a white woman), Wesley Robert Wells (a California prisoner facing a lengthy sentence after assaulting a prison guard), the Trenton Six (black defendants accused of murdering a white merchant during a robbery), the Communist party Eleven (top leaders of the party convicted of spreading the doctrines of Marxism-Leninism), Julius and Ethel Rosenberg (Jewish-American Communists accused of passing on the "secret" of making atomic bombs to the Soviet Union), and numerous other cases across the country.

Not only was the CRC the major organization fighting racist and political repression in the post-World War II era, in many areas of the country it was the only organization acting through the judicial system. Patterson, as the CRC's leader, frequently appeared in *Time,* the *New York Times,* and other major news publications, and his actions were widely covered by the media when he filed a petition with the United Nations charging the U.S. government with genocide against African Americans. This petition, which Paul Robeson and W. E. B. Du Bois helped promote, captured headlines worldwide and was part of the pressure that led to the collapse of Jim Crow after World War II.

The CRC worked closely with the National Lawyers Guild and created important constitutional precedents in cases like *Stack v. Boyle* and *Dennis v. U.S.* However, the Communist leadership of the CRC, symbolized by Patterson, was not viewed benignly by the authorities and the CRC was dismantled in 1956 under the combined pressure of the Subversive Activities Control Board, the F.B.I., the government of the state of New York, and the Internal Revenue Service.

After the demise of the CRC, Patterson became embroiled in internecine conflicts within the Communist party, sparked by revelations about Josef Stalin made at the Twentieth Congress of the Communist party of the Soviet Union in 1956 by Nikita Khrushchev. Patterson leaned toward the "hard-line" faction led by his long-time friend and fellow Communist attorney, Ben Davis. During that post-1956 period he held a number of high-level posts within the party, including editor of the *Daily Worker* and head of the New York State Communist party. He resided in Harlem where he also served as an unofficial advisor to the Black Panther party until his death in 1980.

Overview of Biographical Sources

Despite his prominence in some of the most important civil rights and civil liberties cases in the United States during the twentieth century, Patterson has not attracted the attention of a biographer. This stems in part from the controversial nature of his Communist ties. However, Gerald Horne's *Communist Front? The Civil Rights Congress, 1946-56* (London: Associated University Presses, 1988) adequately covers the CRC phase of his life.

Evaluation of Biographical Sources

Horne, Gerald. *Communist Front? The Civil Rights Congress, 1946-56*. London: Associated University Presses, 1988. (A, G) Horne traces the rise and decline of the Civil Rights Congress (CRC), which was formed in 1956 at the initiative of the Communist party-USA and other left-liberal forces. The CRC's primary goal was to combat Jim Crowism and the gathering Red Scare repression. The CRC was the primary organization during the cold war that mobilized against the Smith Act trials and their domestic equivalent. The organization was soon driven out of business by severe pressure from the government, which deemed it a "communist front."

Overview and Evaluation of Primary Sources

Patterson was the author of numerous articles in the *Daily Worker* and the party journal *Political Affairs*; these articles shed considerable light on the evolution of his thought. He also authored a memoir, *The Man Who Cried Genocide* (New York: International Publishers, 1971; A, G), which is particularly revelatory about his early years in the San Francisco Bay area but much less so about his post-1956 years. Patterson's papers, which he donated to Howard University, are indispensable to an understanding of not only the Communist party but also the civil rights movement. Other collections at Howard that include correspondence and information about Patterson are the George Murphy Papers and Paul Robeson Papers. The Schomburg Center of the New York Public Library contains the Civil Rights Congress Papers, the W. A. Hunton Papers, the Paul Robeson Papers, the Pettis Perry Papers, and the Hosea Hudson Papers, all of which include information on Patterson. At New York University the papers of Sam Darcy, Elizabeth Gurley Flynn, and Pete Cacchione contain information on Patterson, as do the papers of Earl Browder at Syracuse University, Theodore Draper at Emory University, Joseph North at Boston University, Eugene Dennis at the State Historical Society of Wisconsin, W. E. B. Du Bois at the University of Massachusetts, John Daschbach at the University of Washington, and the NAACP Papers at the Library of Congress.

Other Sources

Both the New York Police Department and the Federal Bureau of Investigation have massive surveillance files on Patterson. Other works that examine cases like Scottsboro, such as Dan T. Carter's *Scottsboro: A Tragedy of the American South* (Baton Rouge: Louisiana State University Press, 1969) speak of Patterson's role but, again, the controversial nature of his Communist ties often hamper an objective evaluation of him.

Gerald Horne
University of California, Santa Barbara

ROBERT E. PEARY
1856-1920

Chronology

Born Robert Edwin Peary on May 6, 1856, in Cresson, Pennsylvania, the only son of Charles Peary, a manufacturer of barrel heads and staves, and Mary Wiley Peary; *1859-1873* following his father's death in 1859, moves to Cape Elizabeth, Maine, where he grows up and graduates from Portland High School; *1873-1877* attends Bowdoin College in Brunswick, Maine, graduating second in his class with a degree in civil engineering; works as a county surveyor in Fryeburg, Maine; *1877-1879* employed as a cartographic draftsman with the U.S. Coast and Geodetic Survey in Washington, D.C.; *1881-1884* joins the Corps of Civil Engineers of the U.S. Navy with the rank of lieutenant and serves at various naval stations; *1884-1885* assigned as assistant engineer on a project to survey a route for a canal through Nicaragua; *1886* makes first expedition to Greenland while on leave from the navy; *1887-1888* returns to Nicaragua as engineer in charge of the Canal Survey; marries Josephine Diebitsch when assignment is completed; *1888-1891* studies about Arctic while serving at various naval posts; *1891-1892* explores northern coast of Greenland; *1893-1897* makes three expeditions to Greenland and develops plans to reach the North Pole; *1898-1902* reaches 84°17' north latitude on polar expedition and carries out extensive series of explorations in the High Arctic; *1905-1906* comes within 174 miles of the North Pole in his second attempt to reach this goal; *April 6, 1909* claims to have reached the North Pole; *1910-1919* engages in dispute with Dr. Frederick Cook over polar exploits; retires to Eagle Island, Maine; interested in aviation and serves as president of Aero League of America; *1920* dies on February 20 of pernicious anemia in Washington, D.C., and is buried at Arlington National Cemetery.

Activities of Historical Significance

Robert E. Peary ranks as one of the greatest Arctic explorers in history. He mounted several expeditions to Greenland, where he conducted extensive explorations of the northern coast and established the territory's insularity. Determined to become the first man to reach the North Pole, he made three assaults on his goal, claiming success on April 6, 1909.

Driven by a fierce desire for public recognition, Peary became a prominent figure in Arctic exploration following a series of trips to Greenland between 1891 and 1897. He made his first attempt to cross the Arctic ice and reach the North Pole at the turn-of-the century. A second effort followed in 1905 to 1906. Learning from his failures, Peary perfected a transportation system that emphasized the use of small parties travelling on sledges drawn by dogs. Adopting Eskimo methods and costume, he used the native people as an essential element of his expeditionary parties. On March 1, 1909, Peary set out for his objective with 23 men (including 17 Eskimos), 133 dogs, and 19 sledges. After the trail breakers turned back, Peary struck out for his goal with Matthew Henson (his black servant and skilled associate) and four Eskimos. On April 6, 1909, Peary announced that they had reached the North Pole.

Peary's claim soon became mired in controversy. Dr. Frederick A. Cook, a surgeon on Peary's 1891 expedition to Greenland, returned from the Arctic shortly before Peary and stated that he had reached the Pole a year earlier. Although most respected authorities rejected Cook's claim, the dispute over who reached the pole first would not die. Later, Peary's claim itself came into question when researchers discovered that his navigational methods had left a great deal to be desired. Nonetheless, even those who doubt that Peary reached the Pole place him in the first rank of Arctic explorers.

Overview of Biographical Sources

Three major biographies of Peary have been published, all admiring and none written by a professional historian. Fitzhugh Green, *Peary: The Man Who Refused to Fail* (1926), casts Peary in a heroic mold; it belongs in the category of hagiography. William Herbert Hobbs, *Peary* (1936), is more comprehensive but not more critical in its treatment of the "great man." The most recent study, John Edward Weems, *Peary: The Explorer and the Man* (1967), is by far the best. Weems was the first biographer to have access to Peary's papers. While presenting Peary in the most favorable possible light, his detailed examination of the explorer's life contains much valuable information. There remains a need for a scholarly biography of this important and controversial figure in Arctic exploration.

Evaluation of Principal Biographical Sources

Berton, Pierre. *The Arctic Grail*. New York: Viking-Penguin, 1988. (G, Y) By a popular Canadian historian, this spritely written account of the quest for the Northwest Passage and the North Pole includes an unflattering portrait of Peary the man, especially in his treatment of the Eskimos. Berton argues that Peary never reached the pole, but notes that his exploits remain admirable. "Without mechanical aid," Berton emphasizes, "he got further north than had any human being before him—*and he got back.*"

Green, Fitzhugh. *Peary: The Man Who Refused to Fail.* New York: Putnam, 1926. (**G, Y**) An admiring and uncritical study by a physicist and sometime Arctic explorer, this was the first major biography of Peary.

Hobbs, William Herbert. *Peary.* New York: Macmillan, 1936. (**G, Y**) Written by a geologist familiar with Greenland, this flattering portrait of Peary remained the standard biography for thirty years.

Hunt, William R. *To Stand at the Pole.* New York: Stein and Day, 1981. (**A, G, Y**) After examining the most recent evidence on the subject, Hunt concludes that Cook was "a liar." He portrays Peary as a legitimate explorer who probably did not reach the North Pole but came close to his goal.

Mirsky, Jeannette. *To The Arctic!* New York: Knopf, 1948. (**A, G, Y**) Although somewhat dated, especially in its treatment of the Peary-Cook controversy, this remains a fine, well-written, balanced account of Arctic exploration.

Rawlins, Denis. *Peary at the Pole: Fact or Fiction?* Washington, DC: Luce, 1973. (**A, G**) This detailed critique of the topic concludes, in somewhat strident language, that Peary never reached his goal. Rawlins argues: "The sum total of Peary's claim to the North Pole: no witnesses, no specific scientific yield, and a 'method' of aiming which no one familiar with Arctic Ocean ice conditions could possibly take seriously."

Weems, John Edward. *Peary: The Explorer and the Man.* Boston: Houghton Mifflin, 1967. (**A, G, Y**) The author of several historical novels, Weems was the first person to be granted access to the Peary Papers. This sympathetic but sometimes unflattering portrait of the man makes a strong case for Peary's attainment of the North Pole.

Wright, Theon. *The Big Nail.* New York: Day, 1970. (**A, G**) This detailed examination of the feud between Peary and Cook has little sympathy for Peary's claim to have reached the North Pole. "The perpetuation of the myth that Peary discovered the North Pole," Wright concludes, "has no possible justification in fact or tradition."

Overview and Evaluation of Primary Sources

The most important collection of primary sources is the Papers of Robert E. Peary, housed in the Center for Polar Archives at the National Archives, Washington, D.C.

Peary's books include *Northward Over the "Great Ice,"* 2 vols. (New York: Stokes, 1898; **A, G, Y**), which records his expeditions to Greenland; *Nearest The Pole* (New York: Doubleday, 1907; **A, G, Y**), a chronicle of his polar expedition of 1905-1906; and *The North Pole* (New York: Stokes, 1910; **A, G, Y**), an account of his triumph ghostwritten by A. E. Thomas.

Memoirs by individuals who accompanied Peary on his polar expeditions include Robert A. Bartlett, *The Log of "Bob" Bartlett* (New York: Putnam, 1928; **A, G, Y**); George Borup, *A Tenderfoot with Peary* (New York: Stokes, 1911; **A, G, Y**); Matthew A. Henson, *A Negro Explorer at the North Pole* (New York: Stokes, 1912; **A, G, Y**); and Donald B. MacMillan, *How Peary Reached the North Pole* (Boston: Houghton Mifflin, 1934; **A, G, Y**).

Robert E. Keely, Jr., and G. G. Davis, *In Arctic Seas: The Voyage of the "Kite" with the Peary Expedition* (Philadelphia: Hartranft, 1892; **A, G**), provides firsthand information on Peary's Greenland expedition of 1891-1892, while Josephine Diebitsch Peary, *My Arctic Journal* (New York: Contemporary Publishing, 1893; **A, G, Y**), offers the recollections of Peary's wife, the first white woman to spend a winter in the Arctic.

Fiction and Adaptations

Cook & Peary: The Race to the Pole, a made-for-television movie, appeared on CBS in December 1983. Starring Richard Chamberlain as Cook and Rod Steiger as Peary, it dramatized the controversy between the two men from Cook's perspective. Needless to say, Peary appeared as the villain of the piece. Movie critic Leslie Halliwell summed up this docudrama as a "stiff and not entirely reliable account of still mysterious doings in remote places."

Museums, Historical Landmarks, Societies

The National Geographic Society (Washington, DC). Collection contains artifacts from Peary's polar expeditions, some on permanent display in Explorers' Hall.

The Peary-MacMillan Arctic Museum (Brunswick, ME). A small but active museum at Bowdoin College that features artifacts from Peary's last expedition, Eskimo carvings, and a small collection of photographs.

The Peary Memorial (Cape York, Greenland). A granite shaft, capped with steel, with white stone P's on its sides for "Peary" and "Pole," erected at the tip of Cape York, south of Thule, by Josephine Peary in 1932.

U.S.S. Peary (DD-226). Shortly after Peary's death, the U.S. Navy named a destroyer after him. Commissioned on October 20, 1920, it operated in Asian waters for the next two decades. The *Peary* was sunk in the harbor of Darwin, Australia, by Japanese carrier planes on February 19, 1942.

Other Sources

Davies, Thomas D. "New Evidence Places Peary at the Pole." *National Geographic* 177 (January 1990): 44-60. This summary of an exhaustive investigation by the Navigation Society attests to the longevity of the polar controversy, which remains as vigorous in the last decade of the twentieth century as it was in the first. Using information on ice movements, soundings, and noon sightings, plus an effort to determine the elevation of the sun from shadows in photographs taken during the 1909 expedition, the foundation concludes that Peary indeed reached the North Pole.

Herbert, Wally. "Did He Reach the Pole?" *National Geographic* 174 (September 1988): 387-413. Veteran explorer Herbert, an admirer of Peary, examined all the evidence and concludes that Peary likely missed the pole because wind-driven ice carried him west of his goal.

Marmer, H. A. "Robert Edwin Peary." In *Dictionary of American Biography,* vol. 14, edited by Dumas Malone. New York: Scribner's, 1934. Written more than fifty years ago, this remains the best brief survey of Peary's career.

Stafford, Edward Peary. "The Peary Family." *National Geographic* 174 (September 1988): 417-421. Peary's grandson has written an interesting account of his meeting in Greenland with the descendants of the two children that resulted from Peary's union with the Eskimo woman Aleqasina.

William M. Leary
University of Georgia

JACKSON POLLOCK
1912-1956

Chronology

Born Paul Jackson Pollock on January 28, 1912, in Cody, Wyoming, the youngest of five sons of Stella May McClure Pollock, a seamstress, and LeRoy Pollock, a mason; *1912-1924* family makes a series of moves to farms in Phoenix, Arizona; San Diego, Chico, and Janesville, California, and finally settles in Riverside, near Los Angeles; *1926* oldest brother Charles studies with Thomas Hart Benton at Art Students League in New York City; *1927-1929* moves with family to Los Angeles and enrolls at Manual High School, where he is expelled from school each year; *1930* goes with brothers Charles and Frank to New York and enrolls in Thomas Hart Benton's class at the Art Students League; *1931-1932* studies mural painting with Benton; *1933-1934* father dies on March 6, 1933; spends time with Benton and his wife and son; *1935* included in a group exhibition in February at the Brooklyn Museum; joins the mural division of the Federal Art Project of the Works Progress Administration (WPA); *1936* begins seven years of work for the easel division of the WPA; *1937* submits to psychiatric counseling for alcoholism; visits the Bentons in Kansas City; *1938* dropped from the WPA payroll for absenteeism; receives further treatment for alcoholism in New York Hospital; rehired in November by the WPA; *1939* begins Jungian psychoanalysis; *1940* registers for draft but classified 4-F; *1941* begins friendship with Lee Krasner; *1942* included in show held at McMillen Inc.; assigned by the WPA to Krasner's window-display project; Krasner comes to live with him; *1943* WPA program ends; gets 150 dollar monthly contract from Peggy Guggenheim and a commission to do a mural for her home; begins treatment with a homeopathic physician, which continues until he dies; Guggenheim sponsors his first one-man show at Art of This Century; *1944* "The She-Wolf" is purchased by Museum of Modern Art; *1945* buys a farmhouse in Springs, Long Island; marries Lee Krasner; *1946* included in "Annual Exhibition of Contemporary American Paintings," Whitney Museum of Modern Art, New York; creates his first "allover" poured painting; *1947* signs contract with art dealer Betty Parsons; uses knives, sticks, and trowels in experiments with sand and broken glass added to thick layers of paint; *1948* represented in Venice Biennale; receives grant from Ebsen Demarest Trust Fund; treated for alcoholism by Dr. Edwin Heller and stops drinking in late fall; *1949* gets new contract with Betty Parsons; *1950* paints mural for Geller House in Lawrence, Long Island; refuses to participate in the exhibition "American Painting

Today 1950'' at the Museum of Modern Art because of the jury's antipathy to advanced art; allows Hans Namuth to film him at work; resumes drinking; *1951* begins two years of biochemical treatment for alcoholism in September; included in "Bienal de São Paolo," Museu de Arte Moderna, São Paolo, Brazil; *1952* holds solo exhibition at Studio Janis Gallery; Bennington College puts on first Pollock retrospective; *1955* undertakes analysis with Ralph Klein in New York; *1956* Lee Krasner goes to Europe; on August 11 Pollock dies in a car crash.

Activities of Historical Significance

Pollock's accomplishment as an artist will always remain problematic to many people. He was an inadequate draftsman who struggled with many personal demons—alcoholism, sexual insecurities, poverty—while groping his way toward a form of expression that satisfied him and finally received critical acclaim.

By 1946 he had created the first of many "allover" paintings. This is the term used to describe works that abandon depth and cover a surface evenly with unbroken forms, compelling the viewer to grasp the total composition. "Allover" paintings must be judged on their own terms rather than as representations of the visible world. Pollock was fortunate that an articulate critic, Clement Greenberg, championed this phase of his work and helped educate a naive public to Pollock's unique genius. Greenberg's praise of Pollock had a radical political motive in that Greenberg perceived Pollock's departure from mimesis as an egalitarian force. Greenberg's political theories created a controversial climate for Pollock's work, making objective evaluation difficult.

In 1947 Pollock began his famous "drip" paintings. (Although some critics insist they are poured rather than dripped, the term "drip" seems to have won out in the vocabulary of art historians.) His technique was sensational. He put a canvas on the floor and a stick in a paint can, tilting the can so that paint would run down the stick and onto the canvas. By this means Pollock was able to manipulate the angle of the can and experiment with many kinds of paints. It is commonly said of these "drip" paintings, in which line predominates over color and form, that they are drawings done with a stream of paint rather than a pencil. The streaming paint, following its own free path, is substituted for more conventional draftsmanship.

Another critic, Harold Rosenberg, complicated the critical response to Pollock's works by declaring in 1952 that American painters were treating their canvases as arenas in which to play out their personal psychodramas. Although Pollock was not mentioned by name, he took the criticism personally and was gravely offended by the image Rosenberg presented of artists as crude figures circling their canvases and throwing pigments at them. From this portrayal came the term "action painting," which became the phrase most laymen associate with abstract expressionism.

One of Pollock's fellow abstract artists, Willem de Kooning, attempted to explain what Pollock was doing: "Every so often a painter has to destroy painting. Cezanne did it. Picasso did it with cubism. Then Pollock did it. He busted our idea of a picture all to hell." Although Pollock's long-term critical reputation is uncertain, his importance in the evolution of modern art is well established.

Overview of Biographical Sources

There are four standard biographies of Pollock, supplemented by Ruth Kligman's memoir, *Love Affair*, (1974), and Jeffrey Potter's *To a Violent Grave: An Oral Biography of Jackson Pollock* (1987). Kligman was with Pollock when he died in a car wreck, and her memoir is important. Potter's oral biography is an engrossing source of testimony about Pollock. B. H. Friedman's *Jackson Pollock: Energy Made Visible* (1972) was the most important biographical source until the publication of Potter's oral biography, which was followed in the next four years by three excellent studies of Pollock's life. Another useful work that depicts the general scene of abstract expressionism is John Gruen's *The Party's Over Now: Reminiscences of the Fifties—New York's Artists, Writers, Musicians, and Their Friends* (1967. Reprint. 1989).

Evaluation of Principal Biographical Sources

Friedman, B. H. *Jackson Pollock: Energy Made Visible*. New York: McGraw-Hill, 1972. (A, G) Friedman met Pollock a year before the artist's death, when Friedman was twenty-eight and Pollock forty-three, and his biography has a personal flavor. The introduction describes their first meeting, when the drunken Pollock arrived at Friedman's house in the tow of Ben Heller, an art collector. After a nap, the belligerent Pollock settled down, and eventually he and Friedman made the obligatory extended visit to the nearby Cedar Bar, the favored hangout for Pollock and many others from the art world.

Landau, Ellen G. *Jackson Pollock*. New York: Abrams, 1989. (A, G) Landau stresses the myth that grew up around Pollock, identifying him with Marlon Brando in *A Streetcar Named Desire* and James Dean in *Rebel Without a Cause*. Pollock thus fits into the picture of a generation of alienated rebels in the 1950s. This beautiful, lavish book contains many excellent color reproductions of Pollock's work.

Naifeh, Steven, and Gregory White Smith. *Jackson Pollock: An American Saga.* New York: Clarkson Potter, 1989. (**A, G**) Naifeh and Smith's Pultizer Prize-winning work is huge—934 pages with notes—as compared to the other biographies, each of which is under three hundred pages. The work is greatly detailed and will probably be the standard biography for a long while. Even though it is detailed, Naifeh and Smith's account is readable, and contains many candid snapshots and illustrations in addition to the sixteen color reproductions of Pollock paintings. The selected bibliography and the copious notes are a useful source for scholars.

Solomon, Deborah. *Jackson Pollock: A Biography.* New York: Simon and Schuster, 1987. (**A, G**) Solomon is less concerned to advance the Pollock myth than other biographers. Her biography provides an excellent introduction to the life and a reasonable approach to the work. Highly recommended to Pollock beginners who have seen some of the paintings and want a balanced overview.

Overview and Evaluation of Primary Sources

Pollock expressed himself through his paintings rather than through published writing. His personal papers are in the Archives of American Art, part of the Smithsonian Institution in Washington, D.C. A few brief statements occur in a wide range of sources. *American Artists on Art from 1940 to 1980,* edited by Ellen Johnson (New York: Harper and Row, 1982; **A, G**) has ten pages of Pollock's statements. "Unframed Space," *The New Yorker* 26 (August 5, 1950: 16; **A**) contains remarks by Pollock and Lee Krasner. Selden Rodman conducted an interview with Pollock in Springs, Long Island in 1956, *Conversations with Artists.* (New York: Devin-Adair, 1957; **A, G**). Hans Namuth and Paul Falkenberg produced a 1951 docomentary film, *Jackson Pollock,* that shows the artist at work. The film is distributed by Film Images, New York; the typescript for the narration is in the Museum of Modern Art Library in New York.

Museums, Historical Landmarks, Societies

The following collections include works by Pollock: Amsterdam, The Netherlands: *Stedelijk Museum;* Andover, MA: Phillips Academy, *Addison Gallery of American Art;* Baltimore, MD: *Baltimore Museum of Art;* Bloomington, ID: *Indiana University Art Museum;* Bologna, Italy: *Galleria Communale d'Arte Moderna;* Boston, MA: *Museum of Fine Arts;* Buffalo, NY: *Albright-Knox Art Gallery;* Cambridge, MA: Harvard University, *Fogg Art Museum;* Chicago, IL: *Art Institute of Chicago;* Dallas, TX, *Dallas Museum of Fine Arts;* Dusseldorf, West

Germany: *Kunstsammlung Nordrhein-Westfalen;* East Hampton, NY: *Guild Hall;* Edinburgh, Scotland: *Scottish National Gallery of Modern Art;* Hartford, CT: *Wadsworth Atheneum;* Helena, MT: *Montana Historical Society;* Houston, TX: *Sarah Campbell Blaffer Foundation;* Iowa City, IA: *University of Iowa Museum of Art;* Kansas City, MO: *William Rockhill Nelson Gallery of Art* and *Mary Atkins Museum of Fine Arts;* Kurashiki City, Okayama Prefecture, Japan: *Ohara Museum;* London, England: *Tate Gallery;* New Haven, CT: *Yale University Art Gallery;* New Orleans, LA: *New Orleans Museum of Art;* New York City: *Metropolitan Museum of Art, Solomon R. Guggenheim Museum, Whitney Museum of American Art;* Norfolk, VA: *Chrysler Museum;* Omaha, NB: *Joslyn Art Museum;* Ottawa, Canada: *National Gallery of Canada;* Paris, France: *Musée National d'Art Modern;* Pittsburgh, PA: *Carnegie Institute, Museum of Art;* Providence, RI: *Rhode Island School of Design, Museum of Art;* Purchase, NY: State University of New York College at Purchase, *Neuberger Museum;* Rio de Janeiro, Brazil: *Museu de Arte Moderna do Rio de Janeiro;* Rochester, NY: University of Rochester, *Memorial Art Gallery;* Rome, Italy: *Galleria Nazionale d'Arte Moderna;* St. Louis, MO: *Shoenberg Foundation, Washington University Gallery of Art;* San Antonio, TX: *Mario Koogler McNay Art Institute;* San Francisco: *San Francisco Museum of Modern Art;* Seattle, WA: *Seattle Art Museum, Virginia Wright Foundation;* Stockholm, Sweden: *Moderna Museet;* Stuttgart, West Germany: *Staatsgalerie Stuttgart;* Tehran, Iran: *Tehran Museum of Contemporary Art;* Tel Aviv: *Tel Aviv Museum;* Tokyo: *National Museum of Western Art;* Tucson, AZ: *University of Arizona Museum of Art;* Utica, NY: *Munson-Williams-Proctor Institute;* Venice, Italy: *Peggy Guggenheim Foundation;* Washington, DC: *Hirshhorn Museum and Sculpture Garden, National Gallery of Art, National Museum of American Art, Phillips Collection;* West Palm Beach, FL: *Norton Gallery and School of Art, Art Museum of the Palm Beaches.*

Other Sources

Frank, Elizabeth. *Jackson Pollock.* New York: Abbeville Press, 1983. An excellent critical introduction to Pollock's art, with one hundred reproductions, many in color. Reprints Pollock's statements about art from various sources, and includes a brief "Notes on Technique," a detailed "Chronology" by Anna Brooke, and an important and useful list of Pollock's exhibitions. A helpful book for scholars.

O'Connor, Francis Valentine, and Eugene Victor Thaw, eds. *Jackson Pollock. A Catalogue Raisonné of Paintings, Drawings, and Other Works.* 4 vols. New

Haven: Yale University Press, 1978. This indispensable catalogue, includes such excellent supplementary material as an account of "Jackson Pollock's Library"; a superbly informative documentary chronology of Pollock's life, generously illustrated; and a list of "Collectors and Former Owners." A well-made set that is vital to the scholar and a pleasure for the browser.

O'Hara, Frank. *Jackson Pollock*. New York: George Braziller, 1959. An appreciation by a poet. Many illustrations but only a few in color.

Robertson, Bryan. *Jackson Pollock*. New York: Abrams, 1960. A long collection of prints and commentary.

Frank Day
Clemson University

ADAM CLAYTON POWELL, JR.
1908-1972

Chronology

Born Adam Clayton Powell, Jr., on November 29, 1908, in New Haven, Connecticut, the only son of Adam Clayton Powell, a minister, and Mattie Fletcher Powell; *1930* graduates from Colgate University; *1932* receives his master's degree from Columbia University; *1933* marries Isabel Washington, whom he divorces in 1943; *1935* receives his doctorate of divinity from Shaw University; *1937-1960* pastors Abyssinian Baptist Church in Harlem; *1941* elected to the New York City Council; *1942* founds, publishes, and edits *People's Voice*; *1945* marries Hazel Scott, whom he subsequently divorces after the birth of their son, Adam Clayton Powell III; *1944* elected to U.S. Congress; serves from the Seventy-ninth through the Eighty-ninth Congress; *1947* receives his doctorate of law from Virginia Union University; *1960* marries Yvette Diago, with whom he has a son, Adam Diago Powell; *1967* appointed chairman of the Committee on Education and Labor; Congress moves to exclude him from continuing congressional duties; *1969* U.S. Supreme Court rules that Congress's exclusion is unconstitutional and that he be seated; *1970* defeated by Charles Rangel; *1972* dies April 4 in Miami, Florida, of cancer.

Activities of Historical Significance

To residents of Harlem, Adam Clayton Powell, Jr., was unerringly direct in his approach to human and civil rights. Although he was considered kind and compassionate, his virtues and vices were never confused with idealism. The harsh realities of prostitution, police brutality, drug abuse, and gambling forced him to deal with street life in Harlem as his father had. And he made a difference, though he did not win every battle or salvage every cause. The bourgeois pulpit politician identified with the masses when he prayed with them at the altar of Abyssinian Baptist Church. Together, they forged an unshakable bond that saw them through the hardest of times. United as a religious and political force under Powell's tutelage, the church and the community fought institutionalized racism. Using the Bible and the scales of justice, Powell managed to successfully mix politics and religion, two volatile subjects.

Powell instilled "black pride" and raised black consciousness, and his church emerged as the center of Harlem's African-American community. In its multipurpose role, the church functioned as house of worship, educational institution, community and social service agency, job training and placement office, and child care center. Assisted by federal and state funds, Powell and the church helped to ameliorate some of the poverty, hunger, malnutrition, and homelessness that plagued Harlem.

Powell also engaged in the politics of non-violence to guarantee economic parity and fair play. He popularized the economic boycott as a mechanism for social change. Using economic pressures, he spearheaded selective campaigns to end segregated jobs, hospitals, housing, public facilities, and accommodations. By withholding rent from slumlords, evictions decreased and living conditions somewhat improved, and he insisted that African Americans fill mid-level jobs in industries doing business in the black community.

Having benefitted from economic empowerment, residents responded to Powell's political rhetoric. Seizing the moment, Powell organized black Harlem into a political base to affect change and to control electoral decisions. He registered significant numbers of his congregation and the community as voters, and got some elected or appointed to office. This political base allowed Powell to operate independent of whites' endorsements and finances. As James Q. Wilson observed, "Powell provided the leadership and the Abyssinian Baptist Church furnished the infrastructure of human and financial resources necessary for success at a time when blacks were denied access to party mechanism and when those very mechanisms were collapsing."

Powell's public policies were shaped by a dynamic mixture of influences, including the black theology espoused by his minister-father and the economic nationalism advocated by Booker T. Washington and Marcus Garvey's Universal Negro Improvement Association. Politically, Mahatma Ghandi and Jesus Christ taught him social activism through non-violent protest and the National Association for the Advancement of Colored People (NAACP) showed him how to use the judicial system to overcome injustice. W. E. B. Du Bois's Pan-Africanism molded his views of the Third World, and remnants of the Harlem Renaissance affected his socio-cultural inclinations.

Often, Powell did what was expedient to gain lasting and effective results for his people. To achieve his objectives, he wore no specific party label and owed no allegiance to anyone except members of his race. The *People's Voice,* the newspaper that he founded, published, and edited, reported that he "always liked the guy who was nationally a Democrat, locally a Republican, theoretically a Socialist, but practically a Communist." His coalition accepted members without regard to race, religion, or national origin. Prominent party leaders appointed a number of black officials after consulting with Powell in exchange for the African-American vote.

Employing these concepts and tactics, Powell wrought lasting changes and permanently transformed local politics in New York City. Powell tackled the New York City Council and was victorious when he presented it with documented cases of hospital abuse, negligence, and discrimination. Next, he demanded the hiring of qualified African-American physicians and health officials. His articulate defense angered the council but yielded positive results, and his constituency applauded his triumph.

His boldness earned him a seat on the city council as the first African American ever elected to that post. Freed from financial worries and unswayed by political machines, Powell upset the political status quo. His exposure of racketeering, nepotism, and political bosses destroyed the closed society and racial conformity. Until Powell's crusade, a system of kickbacks and bribes persisted despite investigations into organized crime. He uncovered decades of dishonest government and attacked political machines.

Besieged by Powell's one-man army, Jim Crowism was thrown on the defensive. All facets of institutionalized racism came under his scrutiny. For example, he alleged that discriminatory hiring practices existed at the city's colleges. Although inquiries into the matter did not substantiate the charge, they nevertheless led to the employment of more African-American professors. Thus, Powell's action on the city council served a two-fold purpose: the exposure of corruption and the monitoring of civil rights.

His courage and commitment endeared him to his constituency and catapulted him into national prominence. In 1944, he became the first black congressman elected from the Northeast. Like New York, national politics in the 1940s had roots deeply embedded in the racial doctrine of white supremacy. Slowly, through legislative reforms initiated by Powell, *de facto* and *de jure* segregation was defeated.

Powell, who was born into wealth and privilege, called national attention to institutional racism on the federal level. Soon after his election to Congress, he issued a challenge to end separate dining facilities for blacks and whites and to admit African Americans to the press gallery. Once that was achieved, Powell then attached ''riders'' to every important piece of legislation introduced in the House in order to dismantle all forms of racial discrimination. Within five years he initiated over sixty pieces of legislation that were enacted into law. Most of them dealt with human and civil rights, such as health care, minimum wage, school segregation, housing, affirmative action, and lynching. His chairmanship of the powerful House Committee on Education and Labor greatly assisted in these accomplishments. Even more striking, as recalled by former attorney general Ramsey Clark, was the fact that ''his personal force, the power that he accumulated in the Congress, probably isn't equaled by a single member in the [black] Caucus, even now, and that's amazing.''

The establishment of the Federal Employment Commission designed, to eradicate discriminatory hiring practices, along with the 1964 Civil Rights Act, the 1965 Voting Rights Act, and the 1968 Fair Housing Act raised great hope in the black community for a new era of racial fairness. These laws provided the opportunity for African Americans to demonstrate what oppressed people could do given equal opportunity in an open society.

Powell's elections as councilman and congressman symbolized several meaningful historic events in local, state, and national politics. First, those elections represented a gigantic step in the political advancement of blacks. Second, from those decades onward, African Americans used the vote to gain economic parity and racial equality. And third, his election to Congress gave him a platform from which to denounce international racism.

Heralded as a hero at home, Powell earned the respect of the Third World community, played a pivotal role in world affairs, and proved himself an astute student of geopolitics. He made Pan-Africanism and foreign aid to developing countries the major topics on his international agenda. He denounced apartheid and called for economic sanctions against all colonizers. In addition, he advocated independence for African nations and supported unpopular leaders, such as Fidel Castro and Kwame Nkrumah. His crusade for human rights and the methods employed to draw attention to these issues often ran counter to American foreign policy.

Powell's audacity in formulating foreign policy and attempting diplomatic negotiations outraged presidents and congressmen alike. From Franklin Roosevelt to John Kennedy, they dismissed him as unskilled in international affairs or merely ignored him. They sought to embarrass or undermine his credibility abroad; in some instances, embassy officials, upon instructions from the State Department, denied him diplomatic courtesies routinely accorded to congressmen.

Powell's lavish lifestyle and reported affairs did little to offset negative opinions or to ease political doubt. His sexual liaison with Corrine Huff, the former Miss Ohio and his personal secretary, stirred even more controversy. His critics used this affair to publicly attack his morals and claimed that it showed his unsuitability as a representative of the American people and government.

Powell's opponents used his lifestyle and political tactics as weapons to defeat him. He aroused the wrath of both Democrats and Republicans for his use of riders to delay or defeat legislation. Both parties seized every opportunity to expose any weakness or perceived malfeasance in office. For instance, they accused Powell of excessive absenteeism during roll call and at times when bills he introduced were being considered. In addition, congressional members sought to have him impeached on charges of income tax evasion, fraud, and the embezzlement of public funds. They and local adversaries persuaded prominent African Americans to oppose him for re-election or to sue him for libel. Powell barely survived the barrage of attacks on his character and career.

Finally in 1970 his brand of politics cost him his House seat. Questionable campaigning and "black power" advocacy proved his downfall. Many critics viewed him as a self-serving militant; others labeled him an opportunist who exploited human misery for political gain. Some alleged that he cried racism to confuse issues that were unrelated to discrimination. While all of these factors contributed to Powell's political demise, the redistricting of Harlem to include additional white voters posed the most serious threat. The dilution of black voting strength ensured the election of the less radical and flamboyant African American, Charles B. Rangel, who was more acceptable to conservative New Yorkers. In the final analysis the agitation that had sustained Powell evaporated when other prominent African-American leaders challenged his leadership with less provocative forms of social protest. Although, removed from city hall and the halls of Congress, he remained politically active, fighting for racial equality until his death in 1972.

Overview of Biographical Sources

For a man as revered and hated as Powell, it is curious that no definitive biographies have been written. Perhaps the preoccupation with his private life, sex scandals, divorces, and marriages limited reports to sensational accounts printed in newspapers and journals. However, the most recent biography, Charles V. Hamilton's *Adam Clayton Powell: The Political Biography of an American Dilemma* (1991), is by far the most balanced. *Newsweek* reporter Claude Lewis in his piece, *Adam Clayton Powell: The Inside Story of the Congressman From Harlem* (1963), tries to judge Powell fairly by weighing the two great influences in his life—the Abyssinian Baptist Church and his Harlem neighborhood. In his analysis, he asks two pertinent questions: what did Powell contribute? And, what did he leave unresolved in the fight for civil rights?

Capeci Dominic, *The Harlem Riot of 1943* (1977), provides a biographical sketch of Powell in the context of his role as a mediator. Sources that document some aspects of Powell's civil rights activities, the racial problems that he confronted in Harlem, and his representation of African Americans in the U.S. House of Representatives are Ed Edwin and Neal Hickey, *Adam Clayton Powell and the Politics of Race* (1965); Philip Bradley, et al., *Fair Employment Legislation in*

New York State, Its History Development and Suggested Use Elsewhere (1946); Claude McKay, *Harlem: Negro Metropolis* (1940); Edwin R. Lewinson, *Black Politics In New York* (1974); *Ebony's Pictorial History of Black Americans* (1971); Roi Ottley, *The Negro in New York: An Informal Social History* (1964); Gilbert Osafsky, *The Making of a Ghetto* (1966); John H. Johnson, *Harlem, the War and Other Addresses* (1942); Herbert Garfinkle, *When Negroes March: The March on Washington Movement in the Organizational Politics of FEPC* (1959); Jesse Guzman, ed., *Negro Year Book: A Review of Events Affecting Negro Life, 1941-46* (1986); James Weldon Johnson, *Black Manhattan* (1968); Kenneth B. Clark, *Dark Ghetto: Dilemmas of Social Power* (1965); John Henrik Clarke, *Harlem: A Community in Transition* (1964); and Richard Dalfume, *Desegregation and the U.S. Armed Forces: Fighting on Two Fronts, 1939-53* (1969).

Evaluation of Principal Biographical Sources

Edwin, Ed, and Neal Hickey. *Adam Clayton Powell and the Politics of Race.* New York: Fleet, 1965. **(A, G)** Illustrates how white supremacy and legal segregation affected every facet of African-American life and how Powell allied with different factions to attack discrimination. The authors contend that Powell never accepted communism as a solution because it was antireligious; therefore, Powell sought solutions to race issues within the democratic framework of the Constitution, particularly the Bill of Rights. Rewarding for serious students of race relations in the United States.

Hamilton, Charles V. *Adam Clayton Powell: The Political Biography of an American Dilemma.* New York: Antheneum, 1991. **(G)** Professor of government at Columbia University and author of *The Black Preacher in America,* Hamilton presents a sympathetic portrait of Powell as a leader who instilled in black Americans a sense of self-worth. He pictures Powell as the self-appointed keeper of the civil rights flame until Martin Luther King, Jr., became a more acceptable symbol for the movement. Hamilton follows Powell's career from newspaper columnist and city council member to watchdog of the Kennedy administration and ally of Lyndon Johnson. This is a spirited account of a dynamic personality, emphasizing Powell's achievements rather than the controversy surrounding his personal life. Includes photographs.

Lewis, Claude. *Adam Clayton Powell: The Inside Story of the Congressman from Harlem.* New York: Gold Medal Books, 1963. **(A, G)** Lewis compares Powell to a twentieth-century Br'er Rabbit, who expressed the contempt and hostility African Americans felt for the dominant class. While he acknowledges that Powell was intelligent, handsome, privileged, and wealthy, he also asserts that he was not very scrupulous. Without Powell's personal papers a complete interpretation of his personal and political life is impossible. Nevertheless, this volume is valuable from a journalistic perspective, although it lacks comprehensive documentation.

Overview and Evaluation of Primary Sources

The constant criticism and distortions by contemporary biographers and journalists prompted Powell to give his own account in *Adam by Adam: The Autobiography of Adam Clayton Powell, Jr.* (New York: Dial Press, 1971; A, G), which was characterized by critics as self-serving. Of particular interest is Powell's reply to Claude Lewis's *Adam Clayton Powell: The Inside Story of the Controversial Congressman From Harlem* (Greenwich, CT: Fawcett, 1963; A, G), on the subjects of his personality, style, and development. According to Powell, his book is an insightful and corrective view of the fearless lion in Congress, the dedicated man of God, and the leader marching African Americans forward. He blames many of his problems on his adversaries, who used African-American lackeys to try to destroy him because of his tenacious stance on racial equality and his criticism of complacent bureaucrats.

Powell fails to analyze the political significance of his defeat in 1970 by New York assemblyman Charles Rangel. Minor weaknesses aside, however, this autobiography documents Powell's substantial accomplishments as councilman and congressman in the field of human and civil rights. In his own words, he candidly reveals his difficulties with marriages, pastoring, income tax evasion charges, and civil rights initiatives and gains. By providing previously unpublished personal correspondences and political documents, Powell adds credibility to his story.

Powell's *Marching Blacks: An Interpretive History of the Rise of the Common Black Man* (New York: Dial Press, 1945; rev. ed. 1973; A, G) contains the personal feelings and positions that Powell took on critical race issues. Also of note is the central focus on economic repression, racism, and police brutality in Harlem. For a deeper understanding of African-American politics and protest in New York City, this book is essential.

Invaluable for understanding race relations at the state and national levels is the newspaper founded and edited by Powell, the *People's Voice* (1942-1943). Powell used this protest-oriented paper to serve his political career and to inform the Harlem community about critical issues. All the issues of this newspaper are on microfilm at the Schomburg Center of the New York Public Library.

Powell's *Upon This Rock* (New York: Abyssinian Baptist Church, 1949; G) narrates the history of the Abyssinian Baptist Church. It details the inception, growth, and achievements of Abyssinian as one of the largest Protestant churches in the nation and one of the most affluent African-American churches. It also tells how father and son hunted down sinners and rooted out sin. As Powell acknowledged, "My father was a radical and a prophet and I am a radical and a fighter."

Keep the Faith Baby (New York: Trident, 1967; G) is the printed version of Powell's fiery speech; *Marching Black: An Interpretive History of the Rise of the Common Man* (New York: Dial, 1972; A, G) is Powell's explanation of why the "New Negro" had to take his protest to the streets to gain respect and equality.

The *Proceedings of the City Council of New York* (1940-1944), located in the Municipal Reference Library, also gives insight into his life and tenure as a city councilman. The *Journal of the United States House of Representatives* (1944-1970) and the *Congressional Record* contain bills introduced and argued in the House by Powell during his thirty years tenure. *The New Image: A Prospectus for the Future* (Washington, DC: Government Printing Office, 1962; A) outlines the broad reforms in education that Powell proposed while chair of the powerful House Committee on Education, in the Eighty-seventh Congress.

Fiction and Adaptations

Adam Clayton Powell (1990) is a dramatic portrait of the flamboyant Harlem minister and politician who became one of the most powerful and controversial figures of his time. Using archival sources, still photographs, and live interviews, the producer reconstructs Powell's life, beliefs, and achievements and shows how financial calamities and an affluent lifestyle led to political ruin. This fifty-three minute production by PBS presents a balanced view of Powell's life and times.

Recordings of some of Powell's speeches are available. They include: "Rep. Adam Clayton Powell, Jr., Faces the Nation," February 28, 1965, and January 14, 1968 (*Encyclopedia Americana*/CBS Audio Resource Library, 1972); "Powell v. McCormack," which deals with the 1969 seating of Powell in Congress (National Archives record services); and selected sermons including "Burn, Baby, Burn," "Death of Any Man," "One Day," and "Keep the Faith Baby" (Michigan State University, 1987).

Museums, Historical Landmarks, Societies

Adam Clayton Powell, Jr., Boulevard (New York, NY). This boulevard in Harlem serves as a reminder of Powell's rise to political power and his vigorous struggle against racism in American life.

Adam Clayton Powell, Jr., State Office Building (New York, NY). This tallest structure in Harlem is a tribute to Powell. Much of his political activity took place here.

Two schools named in his honor memorialize the fiery passion of the man who served as chairman of one of the House's most powerful committees, advocating quality, non-discriminatory education.

Other Sources

Garland, Phyl. "I Remember Adam." *Ebony* (March 1990): 56-63.

Kesselman, Louis C. "The Fair Employment Practice Movement in Perspective." *Journal of Negro History* 29 (January 1944): 24-31. Considers Powell within the larger context of civil rights.

Library of Congress, Washington DC. The FBI files compiled on Powell over many years provide a detailed account of the investigations into alleged charges of income tax evasion and the confrontations of Hazel and Adam Powell with the Internal Revenue Service. Also contained in these files is the investigation of embezzlement of federal funds for anti-poverty programs awarded to the Abyssinian Baptist Church while he was pastor.

Lee, Daniel A. "The Political Career of Adam Clayton Powell: Paradigm and Paradox." *Journal of Black Studies* 4 (December 1973): 115-138. Provides perspective on Powell's life and career.

Myrdal, Gunnar, et al. *An American Dilemma: The Negro Problem and Modern Democracy.* 2 vols. New York: Harper and Brothers, 1944. Still stands as a classic in understanding black leadership and the politics of race in America.

Schomburg Center, New York Public Library. The center contains a wealth of material, including the Civil Rights Vertical File of newspaper clippings that deal with pro- and anti-Powell sentiments, marital scandals, congressional campaigns, tax evasion, libel suits, and a brief history of the Abyssinian Baptist Church. Also includes anniversary programs and sketchy biographical materials on his parents, a chronicle of his political achievements, and campaign literature.

Wilson, James Q. *Negro Politics: The Search For Leadership*. New York: The Free Press, 1960. Wilson examines Powell within the context of his time in order to draw conclusions about the phenomenon of race and politics in America.

Margaret L. Dwight
University of North Carolina, Charlotte

ELVIS PRESLEY
1935-1977

Chronology

Born Elvis Aron Presley on January 8, 1935, in Tupelo, Mississippi, the only surviving child (a twin brother, Jesse Garon, died a few hours after birth) of Gladys and Vernon Presley, laborers; *1946* sings "Old Shep" in Mississippi-Alabama Fair and Dairy Show talent contest and wins second prize; *1948* family moves to Memphis, Tennessee; *1953* graduates from Humes High School; records two songs at the Memphis Recording Service; *1954* meets Sam Phillips of Sun Records and records "That's All Right Mama" and "Blue Moon of Kentucky," his first commercial releases; makes first concert appearance, in Memphis; *1954-1956* performs at concerts and shows throughout the southeast and southwest; *1955* RCA buys song rights from Sun Records; makes first television appearance on regional broadcast of "Louisiana Hayride"; *January 1956* appears on national television on Tommy and Jimmy Dorsey's "Stage Show"; appears later in the year on shows hosted by Milton Berle, Steve Allen, and Ed Sullivan; makes first recordings for RCA-Victor; has first number-one hit, "Heartbreak Hotel"; *March 1956* Colonel Tom Parker becomes his manager; records first album, *Elvis Presley*, which becomes history's first "gold" record; *April 1956* makes first appearance in Las Vegas, but show is not well received; *August 1956* begins filming *Love Me Tender*, first of over thirty motion pictures: *October 1956* receives draft notice; *1957* buys Graceland, his Memphis residence for the rest of his life; *March 1958* enters U.S. Army; *June 1958* "Hard Headed Woman" becomes first single to sell a million copies; *August 1958* mother dies; *October 1958* stationed in Germany where he meets his future wife, Priscilla Beaulieu; *1960* discharged from army as sergeant; *1961* performs in Hawaii in his last concert for seven years; *1961* Priscilla Beaulieu moves into Graceland; *1961-1968* makes motion pictures and records in studio; *1967* marries Priscilla; *1968* daughter is born; television "comeback special" broadcast; *1969-1977* tours frequently, with two engagements a year in Las Vegas; *1972* separated from wife; divorced in 1973; *1977* dies August 16 at Graceland of cardiac arrythmia brought on by heavy use of prescription drugs.

Activities of Historical Significance

Elvis Presley was one of the most influential singers and performers of the twentieth century. His thirty feature films, scores of gold albums, and tens of millions in record sales attest to his popularity, and even today his fans continue to draw inspiration from his life. While many fans have practically deified him, others maintain that Presley allowed himself to be manipulated by his manager, staff, and admirers into an artificial lifestyle that diluted his talents and eventually killed him. These contrary opinions also exist in the material written about him.

To understand Presley's importance and originality, it is necessary to place him within the context of the history of American popular music. From the 1920s through the early 1950s, American popular music was composed of three primary strains, that reflected the economic and social divisions in American society. Mainstream, or middle-class, popular music consisted primarily of dance tunes and songs derived from musical comedies. Rural America preferred the "hillbilly music" based on the ensemble sound of such Appalachian folk groups as the Carter Family or the individual approach of troubadours such as Mississippi Jimmie Rodgers and the then-current favorite, Hank Williams, who were heard at local dances or over the radio. Black music changed during this period from the rural blues sung by such singers and guitarists as Blind Lemon Jefferson to the classic, concert-like vocal performances of vocalists such as Bessie Smith, and finally into the more up-tempo, urban-oriented music of T-Bone Walker and Muddy Waters. A fourth, secondary strain, gospel, which emphasized ensemble singing, was based on the black spiritual. The popularity of gospel was confined for the most part to the churches—both black and white—of the South.

By the 1950s, mainstream American popular music, mostly sentimental ballads and novelty songs, was boring. The most vital and interesting kind of music was black urban blues, which had by then acquired the name rhythm and blues. Racial prejudice, however, made many whites uncomfortable listening to black music unless it was "covered," or re-recorded by a white performer or group. The early careers of singers such as Pat Boone, Georgia Gibbs, and the Macguire Sisters were launched by this "cover work."

Recognizing the absurdity of these conditions, Sam Phillips of the small Sun Record Company in Memphis, Tennessee, hoped to find a white performer who could sing black music without sounding pretentious or ridiculous. He found such a person in Presley, whose background enabled him to unite disparate musical strains. His boyhood in Mississippi and Tennessee had exposed him to hillbilly music; he had grown up listening to rhythm and blues over black radio stations; and he knew gospel music from church services. Even more important, Presley had the talent to present the resulting musical fusion with unforgettable impact. Youngsters loved his wild, energetic performances; conservative adults regarded his style as vulgar and obscene; but few could ignore his stage presence and compelling voice.

Ironically, at the start of his career, Presley wanted to establish himself as a "straight" ballad singer. One of his early hits, "It's Now or Never" (a re-working of "O Sole Mio"), is performed in a style reminiscent of such mainstream singers as Tony Martin and Vic Damone. However, he balanced his mainstream ballads with many covers of songs written or performed by black musicians, among them Arthur "Big Boy" Crudup ("That's All Right, Mama") and Big Mama Thornton ("Hound Dog"). For the first time, however, the cover versions matched the originals in emotional intensity. Presley also drew on the gospel tradition from the start of his career, winning his only Grammy Award for one of several early albums of religious music. He later added gospel quartets—first the Jordanaires and then the Imperials and the Stamps—as backup groups for his secular records.

As a result of Presley's work in the mid-1950s, two new types of music emerged. The first, "rockabilly," was a mixture of hillbilly and rhythm and blues. Rockabilly infused the work of other Sun performers such as Carl Perkins, Roy Orbison, Johnny Cash, and Jerry Lee Lewis. As a result, hillbilly was gradually transformed into "country and western," and acquired a much wider audience.

The second genre, rock-and-roll, also evolved out of rhythm and blues; as rock's popularity spread, mainstream white culture began to accept black performers, such as Chuck Berry and Little Richard, as well as gospel-influenced singers, such as Sam Cooke and Aretha Franklin. Presley was not the only force behind these changes in popular music, but he certainly was the dominant one. Rock stars from Bob Dylan to the Beatles have cited Elvis as an early influence. Moreover, Presley was not merely a singer but a personality whose rise from obscurity while retaining the common touch uplifted many people. The singer had a genuinely spiritual side, as he investigated many kinds of religions and practiced faith healing. He regarded his talent and success as gifts from God which, if he were to keep them, had to be shared with others. He wanted to entertain as many people as possible and bring happiness into their lives; so he drove himself to perform, shared his wealth with strangers, and became a sacred figure to many people. Critics panned the concerts of his last years, but his fans did not care because they enjoyed simply being in his presence and bathing in his charisma. At his death, they apotheosized him like a Roman emperor, and there are those people who say that they pray to Elvis to intercede with God for them. Those critics who say that Presley could have been a better musician or actor ignore the fact that he became a figure of spiritual dimensions.

Overview of Biographical Sources

Biographical material on Presley falls into one of three categories. Most common are adulatory books written by uncritical admirers—often not biographies at all, but rather collections of pictures padded with a chronology, bibliography, or simple text. Sean Shaver's *Life of Elvis* (1979) fits this category, with Paul Lichter's *The Boy Who Dared to Rock* (1978) the best of the type.

Accounts of Elvis's life that attempt to debunk the performer's public image by revealing unpleasant details about his personal life are also common. Often openly biased, these books are usually as untrustworthy as the idolatory biographies of Presley. Albert Goldman's *Elvis* (1981) is the most famous, or infamous, representative of this approach, and several books by Elvis's close associates also attack the singer.

Fewest in number are books that attempt to view Elvis's life and contributions objectively. Jerry Hopkins's *Elvis: A Biography* (1971) and *Elvis: The Final Years* (1980), and Patsy Guy Hammontree's *Elvis Presley: A Bio-Bibliography* (1985) are the best of the more academically oriented works.

Evaluation of Principal Biographical Sources

Goldman, Albert. *Elvis*. New York: McGraw-Hill, 1981. (G) The author is a former university professor who also wrote rock music reviews for *Life* magazine. In his reviews he revealed an antipathy for rock music and its adherents, and in this book—based largely on the revelations of one of Elvis's inner circle of bodyguards and friends—Goldman attacks not only Presley but also his music and his fans. The material on Elvis's drug use is not new, and Goldman's information about Elvis's sex life seems more embarrassing than shocking. Neither scholarly nor objective.

Hammontree, Patsy Guy. *Elvis Presley: A Bio-Bibliography*. Westport, CT: Greenwood Press, 1985. (A, G) Part of a series of "bio-bibliographies" of popular culture figures. Hammontree covers all elements of the singer's career and is the first writer to attempt to define his effect on his fans beyond his music and films. The most-balanced book written on Elvis since his death and a good reference source.

Hopkins, Jerry. *Elvis: A Biography*. New York: Simon and Schuster, 1971. (A, G, Y) The first serious book written about Elvis, and still one of the best. Because this biography was written before Elvis's death, it lacks the moralizing and tendentious tone of later studies.

————. *Elvis: The Final Years*. New York: St. Martin's, 1980. (A, G, Y) Hopkins takes the story of Elvis to its conclusion. More sensational than his first book, this study is still more objective than most accounts written shortly after the singer's death.

Lichter, Paul. *The Boy Who Dared to Rock: The Definitive Elvis.* New York: Dolphin Books, 1978. (**G, Y**) Although this book by one of Elvis's most avid fans does contain a brief biographical section, its most important section is a discography of American records, foreign records, and bootlegs, with pictures of the record sleeves and album covers. Complete only to 1978.

Marsh, Dave. *Elvis.* New York: Rolling Stone Press, 1982. (**A, G, Y**) The author, one of the editors of *Rolling Stone* magazine, is a major rock critic who believes that the singer's career began to fade after he left Sun Records. More critical analysis than a biography.

Shaver, Sean, with Hal Noland. *The Life of Elvis.* Memphis, TN: Timur, 1979. (**G, Y**) Elvis as seen through the eyes of a devoted fan. Many photographs of Elvis on tour.

Vellenga, Dirk, with Mick Farren. *Elvis and the Colonel.* New York: Delacorte, 1988. (**A, G**) The author is a Dutch rock critic who focuses on Colonel Tom Parker's mysterious European origins. Not to be confused with another book by the same title by Elvis fan May Mann, which is of little interest to the researcher.

Overview and Evaluation of Primary Sources

Presley wrote no autobiography and gave very few interviews after his discharge from the army. Snippets from interviews have been collected in *Elvis Presley in His Own Words,* edited by Mick Farren and Pearce Marchbank (London and New York: Quick Brown Fox, 1977; **G, Y**). A better guide to this material is Patsy Guy Hammontree's chapter "Interviews" in *Elvis Presley: A Bio-Bibliography* (1985), which attempts to separate authentic comments from material that may have been paraphrased or fabricated by reporters.

Numerous family members and associates have written books that exploit their association with the singer. The most famous of these is *Elvis: What Happened?* by Red West, Sonny West and Dave Hebler, as told to Steve Dunleavy (New York: Ballantine, 1977; **G**). This book was the first to reveal the extent of the singer's drug use and to focus on the seamier side of his nature; it is worth noting that the authors had been fired from Presley's entourage, and the desire for revenge may have tainted their account.

Becky Yancey's *My Life With Elvis,* with Cliff Linedecker (New York: Warner Books, 1977; **G**), is the work of Vernon Presley's secretary, who had little to do with Elvis; Vester Presley, Elvis's uncle, does not reveal much more in the book he wrote with Deda Bonura, *A Presley Speaks* (Memphis, TN: Wimmer Brothers Books, 1978; **G**). Ed Parker, one of Presley's karate training friends, attempts to answer West, West, and Hebler in his *Inside Elvis* (Orange, CA: Rampart House, 1978; **G**). Elvis's stepmother Dee Stanley, who married Vernon shortly after the death of Gladys Presley, presents her side of the story in *Elvis, We Love You Tender* (New York: Delacorte, 1979; **G**), a book that is largely self-serving.

Elvis, Portrait of a Friend (New York: Bantam, 1979; **G**) has three sections—two written from the points of view of Presley's intimate friend, Marty Lacker, and his wife Patsy, and the third section written by the "as told to" author of the book, Leslie Smith. The Lackers' sections present an interesting and fairly balanced account of life at Graceland, as does Marian Cocke's *I Called Him Babe* (Memphis, TN: Memphis State University Press, 1979: **G**), written by Presley's nurse. Alfred Wertheimer's *Elvis '56: In the Beginning* (New York: Collier, 1979; **G**) is a collection of photographs that Wertheimer took of Presley at home and on tour just before the singer achieved national stardom. Larry Geller, Elvis's former hairdresser, gives his views in *The Truth About Elvis* (New York: Jove, 1980; **G**). Geller encouraged the singer's investigation of spiritualism and mysticism until other associates forced him to leave the singer's entourage.

Elvis's wife, Priscilla Beaulieu Presley, explores their marriage in *Elvis and Me* (New York: Putnam's, 1985; **G**). She is remarkably free of rancor and candidly discusses Elvis's drug use, which, she reveals, began quite early in his career. In *Are You Lonesome Tonight?* (New York; Villard, 1987; **G**), Lucy de Barbin (with Dary Matera) tells the story of her romance with the singer that began in 1953, resulted in the birth of a daughter, and lasted until Presley's death.

Fiction and Adaptations
Elvis himself wanted to be a successful film performer even more than he wanted fame as a singer. Unfortunately, the many films he appeared in merely exploited his popularity; critics agree that the movies mark the nadir of Elvis's career. *Jailhouse Rock* (1957), with an amusing screenplay and lively characterization, and *King Creole* (1958), adapted from a novel by Harold Robbins, are considered the best; the worst include at least twenty others, such as *Harum Scarum* (1965), with Elvis cavorting in a Hollywood Middle East, and the last, *Change of Habit* (1970), costarring Mary Tyler Moore as a nun. Two documentaries made after Elvis's acting career had ended—*Elvis: That's the Way It Is* (1970)

and *Elvis on Tour* (1972)—are of greater interest than the films, as is the film biography *This Is Elvis* (1981) that was approved by his manager, Colonel Tom Parker.

Presley's life has proved a fertile subject for fictional portrayals. Perhaps the first was the satirical figure of Conrad Birdie in the Broadway musical "Bye, Bye Birdie" (1962), which was made into a film the following year. "Elvis Presley" appears as a character in the novels *Stark Raving Elvis* by William McCranor Henderson (1984) and *Elvis—the Novel* by Keith Baty and Robert Graham (1984); the play "Are You Lonesome Tonight?" by Alan Bleasdale (1985); and the film *Heartbreak Hotel* (1988). Presley is also the subject of three made-for-television movies: *Elvis and the Beauty Queen* (1981), an account of his relationship with girl friend Linda Thompson; *Elvis and Me* (1986), a dramatization of Priscilla Presley's book; and *Elvis* (1979), the story of the young, struggling Elvis, which led to a half-hour dramatic series, *Elvis,* on the ABC television network during the 1989-1990 season. Many popular songs, such as Don McLean's classic "American Pie," contain references or allusions to Presley. Also, hundreds of Elvis imitators continue to perform his songs as "tributes to the king."

Museums, Historical Landmarks, Societies

Birthplace (Tupelo, MS). Elvis's birthplace on Old Saltillo Road is now part of a city park that also contains an Elvis Presley Civic Center and Memorial Chapel.

Elvis Aron Presley Memorial Highway (Highway 78, TN). The Presley family traveled Highway 78 when moving from Tupelo to Memphis in 1948.

Fan Clubs. At least forty Elvis Presley fan clubs exist. Three of the largest are: Elvis Special Photo Association, founded in 1969, has about 1,000 members and is based in Pacifica, California; We Remember Elvis, founded in 1982, has 750 members and is located in Pittsburgh, Pennsylvania; King of Our Hearts Elvis Presley Fan Club, founded in 1968 in San Jose, California, commemorates his life through charitable activities.

Graceland (Memphis, TN). Elvis's home at 3764 Elvis Presley Boulevard is one of the South's main tourist attractions. Visitors make a tour of the house, which is filled with Elvis memorabilia, and end in the meditation garden where Elvis is buried along with his father, mother, and paternal grandmother. Across the street is a shopping center where souvenirs include bottles of whiskey shaped like Elvis during various periods of his career.

Other Sources

Escott, Colin, and Martin Hawkins. *Catalyst: The Sun Records Story*. London: Aquarius Books, 1975. An account of the musical and social background that nurtured Elvis.

Harbinson, W. A. *The Illustrated Elvis*. New York: Grossett & Dunlap, 1975. This discussion of Elvis's career by a British rock critic presents itself as a biography, but is really an extended meditation on the meaning of the singer's life. The many photographs are poorly reproduced.

Lichter, Paul. *Elvis in Hollywood*. New York: Fireside Books, 1975. A complete account of Elvis's films with many illustrations.

Marcus, Greil. "Elvis: Presliad." In *Mystery Train*. New York: Dutton, 1976. A careful analysis of Presley's career with emphasis on the early, "rockabilly" period by one of the most thoughtful and thorough rock critics.

Sauers, Wendy. *Elvis Presley: A Complete Reference*. Jefferson, NC: McFarland, 1984. In addition to a complete discography, filmography, and bibliography, this book also includes an exhaustive chronology, an account of the singer's death and funeral, a list of all his concerts from 1969 to 1977, many photographs, and copies of his birth, marriage, and death certificates. Indispensable.

Tharpe, Jac. L., ed. *Elvis: Images and Fancies*. Jackson: University Press of Mississippi, 1979. A collection of serious scholarly essays on all elements of the Presley phenomenon.

Whisler, John A. *Elvis Presley: Reference Guide and Discography*. Metuchen, NJ: Scarecrow Press, 1981. Contains bibliographies, filmographies, and discographies. Two unusual features are a periodical index listed by subject and an index of song titles, helpful for locating items in the discography. Complete only to 1981, but valuable.

Jim Baird
University of North Texas

JOSEPH PULITZER
1847-1911

Chronology

Born Joseph Pulitzer on April 10, 1847, in Mako, Hungary, the son of a Jewish grain merchant, Philip Pulitzer (or Politizer), and his Roman Catholic wife, Louise Berger Pulitzer; *1847-1865* grows up in Budapest, Hungary; leaves home at seventeen in search of military adventure; goes to the United States to join the Union army in the Civil War; serves in the First New York (Lincoln) Cavalry regiment; settles in St. Louis, Missouri, after being mustered out; *1865-1873* becomes secretary of the Deutsche Gesellschaft; gets job as reporter for Carl Schurz's German-language daily newspaper, the *Westliche Post,* and in 1871 becomes its part-owner; becomes naturalized American citizen; *1869-1871* is elected to the lower house of the Missouri legislature; shoots and slightly wounds prominent lobbyist; becomes one of the three police commissioners for St. Louis; *1872* is active in the Liberal Republican movement and serves as secretary of the convention nominating Horace Greeley for president; joins Democratic party; *1873-1877* sells his interest in the *Westliche Post,* purchases the bankrupt *St. Louis Staats-Zeitung* and makes a big profit by selling its Associated Press membership; is a delegate to the Missouri constitutional convention; studies law and is admitted to the bar; is active in Democratic party politics; runs unsuccessfully for Congress; marries Kate Davis; *1878-1883* purchases the *St. Louis Dispatch,* merges with the *Post* to form the *St. Louis Post and Dispatch* (later the *St. Louis Post-Dispatch*) and becomes its sole owner; *1883-1890* purchases *New York World* from Jay Gould, builds circulation and turns the paper into a large moneymaker by innovative techniques; is elected to Congress from New York but resigns after brief service; founds the *Evening World*; suffers from worsening health that leaves him almost totally blind and abnormally sensitive to noise; formally retires as editor of the *World*; *1890-1898* still maintains complete control of *World* papers despite blindness; cuts price of morning *World* to one cent; engages in feverish circulation war with William Randolph Hearst and enters upon most extreme sensationalist phase; plays leading role in stirring up public opinion for war with Spain; *1899-1903* moves to transform *World* papers from sensationalistic rags aimed at a primarily working-class audience into more respectable journals of news and opinion; *1903* pledges funds to establish a school of journalism at Columbia University; provides in will for the school and for "prizes or scholarships for the encouragement of public service, public morals, American literature, and the advancement of education''; *1911* dies on October 29 on his yacht in the harbor of Charleston, South Carolina.

Activities of Historical Significance

Joseph Pulitzer was more responsible than any other individual for the shape of the modern American newspaper. He pioneered, first at the *St. Louis Post-Dispatch* and then more significantly at the *New York World,* techniques that became the standard practice of mass circulation newspapers. One technique was the sponsorship of self-promotional ''stunts'' (e.g., the *World*'s sending Nelly Bligh around the world to beat the eighty-day record that novelist Jules Verne had set for Phineas Fogg). Other techniques associated with Pulitzer that would be widely copied include the ''feature'' story; large-size and multi-column headlines; slangy, colloquial, and simple language; emphasis upon the ''lead'' paragraph to summarize the most vital information in a story; the lavish use of illustrations, such as cartoons, sketches, and pictures; the daily sports page; and the sensational exploitation of sex, crime, and tragedy. Pulitzer saw the daily newspaper not simply as a vehicle for information but also as entertainment for people who lived otherwise drab and cramped lives and who had little or no interest in developments in government, business, or high culture. The importance of the entertainment function of the newspaper was most apparent in the rapid growth of the *Sunday World,* which included romantic fiction and poetry, and was closer to an illustrated magazine than the traditional newspaper.

Most of these innovations were not in a strict sense originated by Pulitzer. What he did was to exploit to their fullest potential devices that others had tried partially or half-heartedly. His genius lay in grasping the significance for the newspaper business of broad social changes that were underway in the late nineteenth century. The role of women was changing and they were becoming consumers and determiners of household expenditures, which in turn increased their attractiveness to advertisers. Pulitzer consciously strove to attract women to his newspaper with stories and features on domestic life, fashion, beauty, culture, recipes, and etiquette. The *World* introduced the first women's advice column in 1883 as a series of letters from city cousin Edith to country cousin Bessie.

A second social change was the growing number of people commuting to work by buses and street railways. Many of the changes in layout that he introduced at the *World* were motivated—at least in part—by a wish to adapt to the needs of riders of public transit. Perhaps most importantly, Pulitzer perceived the potential of the market provided by the growing urban working class, many of whose members were recent immigrants. On taking over the *World,* Pulitzer declared that the paper would be the spokesman not of the aristocracy of money but of "the aristocracy of labor." But he simultaneously shied from taking radical stands that might appear to threaten the aspirations of his readers to rise within the system.

At the same time, Pulitzer was responsible for revolutionary changes in the business side of newspaper publishing. He recognized that the key to newspaper profitability was advertising. And he pushed to boost circulation to attract advertisers. Most papers before Pulitzer had limited advertising to agate-size type, partly because of the limits custom placed on the amount of space that should be allotted to advertising, partly because of the belief that large advertisements were "unfair" to the smaller advertisers who constituted the backbone of advertising revenue. Pulitzer did away with the traditional penalties on advertisers who used illustrations or broke column rules. He further rationalized newspaper business practice and the relationship between newspapers and advertisers by initiating the practice of selling advertising space on the basis of actual circulation and at fixed prices.

Pulitzer's bitter circulation war with William Randolph Hearst in the latter half of the 1890s led him into his most extreme sensationalist, or "yellow journalism," phase. The *World* did much to stir up the public outrage over Spanish behavior in Cuba that brought on the war with Spain. But after that conflict, Pulitzer began to move the *World* toward the upscale end of the market. By the time of his death, the *World* papers had become highly regarded for their news and opinion, political independence, defense of free speech, opposition to Tammany Hall, attacks upon political corruption and trusts, and freedom from advertiser domination. When *Editor & Publisher* in 1934 polled newspapers about who was the greatest American editor of all time, the overwhelming majority picked Pulitzer.

Pulitzer's will stipulated that his papers could not be sold but should be carried on in his spirit. His eldest son Ralph became president of the Press Publishing Company, the publisher of the *World* papers. Ralph Pulitzer did much to increase the papers' stature by hiring talented reporters and writers, expanding foreign coverage, and developing the "opposite editorial page" (or op-ed); but he lacked his father's talent for business. With the papers suffering mounting losses, Ralph withdrew from their management in 1930 in favor of his youngest brother, Herbert. The following year, the heirs succeeded in breaking Pulitzer's will in court and the *World* papers were sold to the Scripps-Howard chain. The morning and Sunday *World* were killed; the evening *World* was merged with the *Telegram* to form the *New York World-Telegram*. The *St. Louis Post-Dispatch* remained under the management of the middle son, Joseph Pulitzer, Jr., who was succeeded on his death in 1955 as editor and publisher by his son, Joseph Pulitzer III.

Pulitzer had an exalted opinion of the duties and responsibilities of the journalist. In 1903 he announced his intention of establishing a school of journalism at

Columbia University to promote the professionalization of the newspaper business. He gave one million dollars for this purpose to Columbia before his death; he left another million dollars in his will. The school, which opened its doors in September 1912, would become the stimulus of, and model for, the establishment of similar institutions in the United States and abroad. The income from five hundred thousand dollars of the gift to Columbia was earmarked for what became the Pulitzer Prizes—prestigious annual awards for outstanding work in journalism and American history, biography, literature, and drama (with prizes in poetry and music added later).

Overview of Biographical Sources

There is no satisfactory scholarly full-scale biography of Pulitzer. The nearest approximation, a 1950 Columbia University doctoral dissertation by William Robinson Reynolds, has not been published. Don C. Seitz's *Joseph Pulitzer: His Life & Letters* (1924) remains valuable because of its author's first-hand knowledge of Pulitzer from his long service as a *World* staffer and executive and his access to Pulitzer's letters and memoranda. James W. Barrett, *Joseph Pulitzer and His World* (1941), is a biography aimed at the general reading public by another former *World* staffer. Barrett's account did not, even at the time of its publication, supply much in the way of new information about Pulitzer himself, but did carry the story of the *World* up to its demise. A series of articles by George S. Johns (1931-1932) surveys Pulitzer's St. Louis years; Julian S. Rammelkamp's *Pulitzer's Post-Dispatch 1878-1883* (1967) is a fuller and more perceptive study that shows how Pulitzer experimented at the *St. Louis Post-Dispatch* with the techniques that he would elaborate upon more fully at the *World*. The single most important work on Pulitzer as a newspaper innovator is George Juergens, *Joseph Pulitzer and the New York World* (1966), which does an outstanding job of analyzing how, during a brief two-year period, Pulitzer multiplied the *World*'s circulation and transformed the paper into a large moneymaker. The most solidly based attempt at a comprehensive portrait—including substantial research in the Pulitzer Papers—is W. A. Swanberg, *Pulitzer* (1967); but even Swanberg admits that his volume is not a definitive biography.

Evaluation of Principal Biographical Sources

Barrett, James W. *Joseph Pulitzer and His World.* New York: Vanguard Press, 1941. (G) This work by the former city editor of the *World* carries the story of the *World* up to 1931, but fails to add much in the way of new information or analysis in its treatment of Pulitzer himself. Its straining for vividness, staccato prose style, and what a reviewer aptly termed "a chronic excess of the historical or hysterical present tense" makes for irritating reading.

Johns, George S. "Joseph Pulitzer: Early Life in St. Louis and His Founding and Conduct of the Post-Dispatch up to 1883." *Missouri Historical Review* 25 (January 1931): 201-218; (April 1931): 404-420; (July 1931); 563-575; 26 (October 1931): 54-67; (January 1932): 163-178; (April 1932): 267-280. (**A, G**) A survey of Pulitzer's St. Louis years.

Juergens, George. *Joseph Pulitzer and the "New York World."* Princeton, NJ: Princeton University Press, 1966. (**A, G**) An excellent scholarly account of how, during the years 1883 to 1885, Pulitzer increased the circulation of the *World* tenfold through the introduction of new techniques that would be widely copied. Juergens emphasizes Pulitzer's success in appealing to the city's immigrant working-class population. Despite the narrow time span covered, the work is indispensable for understanding how Pulitzer revolutionized the face and practices of American journalism.

Rammelkamp, Julian S. *Pulitzer's Post-Dispatch 1878-1883.* Princeton, NJ: Princeton University Press, 1967. (**A, G**) A first-rate account of how Pulitzer first developed his style as a journalist—a mix of sensationalism with reform. Rammelkamp shows how Pulitzer's years with the *St. Louis Post-Dispatch* laid the foundations for his later success with the *World.*

Reynolds, William Robinson. "Joseph Pulitzer." Ph.D. dissertation. Columbia University, New York, 1950. (**A**) The most thorough attempt at a full biography, but never published.

Seitz, Don C. *Joseph Pulitzer: His Life & Letters.* New York: Simon & Schuster, 1924. (**A, G**) A hero-worshiping account by a long-time *World* staffer and executive who rose to be second in the newspaper's hierarchy only to Pulitzer himself. As such, he was not simply privy to upper-level decisions, but was an astute student of Pulitzer's personality and mind. Includes extensive excerpts from Pulitzer's letters and memoranda.

Swanberg, W. A. *Pulitzer.* New York: Scribner's, 1967. (**A, G**) The most solidly based of the published biographies—including substantial research in the Pulitzer Papers at Columbia University and the Library of Congress. But even

Swanberg admits that the "enormous scope of Joseph Pulitzer's efforts in journalism, politics, social reform, philanthropy, education and self-preservation would make a definitive biography assume encyclopedic proportions. This book has a more modest aim—to show the man himself as clearly as possible within moderate space, and to illustrate his methods and achievements only in some of their more outstanding instances."

Overview and Evaluation of Primary Sources

The most important sources for Pulitzer's career remain the files of the *Post-Dispatch* and *World* newspapers. While no large newspaper is the product of simply one man, Pulitzer's papers were to a remarkable degree the reflection of his guiding hand. There are two collections of Pulitzer Papers, mostly dating from after 1890 when his ill health and blindness forced him to rely upon a daily barrage of memoranda to his staff to run things. One, comprising approximately twenty-five thousand pieces, is in Special Collections, Columbia University Library, New York; the other, less than half as large in size, is in the Manuscript Division, Library of Congress, Washington, D.C.

Other manuscript collections containing Pulitzer letters include the Chauncey M. Depew Papers, Yale University Library, New Haven, Connecticut; Don C. Seitz Papers, Manuscript and Archives Division, New York Public Library; and the papers of Grover Cleveland, Carl Schurz, and William C. Whitney, Manuscript Division, Library of Congress. Don C. Seitz's *Joseph Pulitzer: His Life & Letters* (1924, see above) includes extensive excerpts from Pulitzer's letters and memoranda. Pulitzer's personality is perceptively conveyed by one of the last secretary-companions upon whom he relied after his blindness—Alleyne Ireland, whose *Joseph Pulitzer: Reminiscences of a Secretary* (New York: Mitchell Kennerley, 1914) was reissued as *An Adventure with a Genius: Recollections of Joseph Pulitzer* (New York: E. P. Dutton, 1920; **A, G**). An astute contemporary pen-portrait is James Creelman, "Joseph Pulitzer—Master Journalist" (*Pearson's Magazine* 21 [March 1909]: 229-256; **A, G**).

Fiction and Adaptations

A program titled "The Story of Joseph Pulitzer," presented by the Institute of Democratic Education in cooperation with the Boston Radio Network as part of the series "Lest We Forget These Great Americans," is available on cassette from the National Center for Audio Tapes.

Museums, Historical Landmarks, Societies

The two lasting monuments to Pulitzer are the Columbia University School of Journalism and the annual Pulitzer Prizes. For the story of the first, see: Richard T. Baker, *A History of the Graduate School of Journalism, Columbia University [Bicentennial History of Columbia University]* (New York: Columbia University Press, 1954), and Heinz-Dietrich Fischer and Christopher G. Trump, eds., *Education in Journalism: The 75th Anniversary of Joseph Pulitzer's Ideas at Columbia University, 1904-1979.* (Bochum, West Germany: Studienverlag Dr. N. Brockmeyer, 1980); for the second: John Hohenberg, *The Pulitzer Prizes: A History of the Awards in Books, Drama, Music, and Journalism, Based on the Private Files over Six Decades* (New York: Columbia University, 1974).

Other Sources

King, Homer W. *Pulitzer's Prize Editor: A Biography of John A. Cockerill, 1845-1896.* Durham, NC: Duke University Press, 1965. (A) A workmanlike biography of John A. Cockerill, one of Pulitzer's closest and most important associates until their break in 1891. Pulitzer brought Cockerill in as managing editor of the *St. Louis Post-Dispatch* and took Cockerill with him in the same capacity when he purchased the *World*.

Mott, Frank Luther. *American Journalism, A History: 1690-1960.* 3d. ed. New York: Macmillan, 1962. Generally regarded as the standard history of the American newspaper.

Schudson, Michael. *Discovering the News: A Social History of American Newspapers.* New York: Basic Books, 1978. Does an excellent job of explaining how Pulitzer revolutionized American journalism.

Swanberg, W. A. *Citizen Hearst: A Biography of William Randolph Hearst.* New York: Charles Scribner's Sons, 1961. Probably the most accurate and solidly based of the many biographies of Pulitzer's chief rival for newspaper circulation leadership in New York City. Includes a detailed account of their bitter feud in the 1890s.

John Braeman
University of Nebraska, Lincoln

WALTER RAUSCHENBUSCH
1861-1918

Chronology

Born Walther Rauschenbusch (adopts name Walter in his early forties) on October 4, 1861, in Rochester, New York, to August Rauschenbusch, a professor at Rochester Theological Seminary, and Caroline Rhomp Rauschenbusch; *1879* graduates from Rochester Free Academy after attending Pfafflin's private school; *1879-1883* attends classical gymnasium in Gütersloh, Germany, from which he graduates with first honors; *1885* receives bachelor's degree from the University of Rochester; *1886* graduates from Rochester Theological Seminary; ordained to the Baptist ministry; becomes pastor of Second German Baptist Church, New York City; *1889-1891* edits *For the Right*, a reformist paper; *1890* marries Pauline Ernestine Rother, a German teacher from Milwaukee; *1891* travels in Germany and England, studying reform; *1892* establishes the Brotherhood of the Kingdom with six young Baptist ministers; *1897* chairs New Testament interpretation in the German Department, Rochester Theological Seminary; *1902-1918* becomes Pettengill Professor of Church History at Rochester Theological Seminary; *1908* researches in Kiel and Marburg; *1918* dies of cancer on July 28 in Rochester.

Activities of Historical Significance

More than any theologian, Walter Rauschenbusch was responsible for moving the Baptist church towards a new sense of the social implications of Christianity. During the progressive era, he was the most renowned exponent of the "social gospel." Claiming that God's redemptive purpose reaches to institutions as well as to individuals, he called upon a ministry concerned with saving souls to change economic and social conditions as well. Both church and nation, asserted Rauschenbusch, must be reformed to make them responsive to the divine will.

"The primary and comprehensive aim of Christianity," he said, was the concept of the Kingdom of God, which he defined as "the spread of the spirit of Christ in the political, industrial, scientific, and artistic life of humanity." As individuals meet Christ, they are freed from sin and made channels of God's action in all society. To advance Jesus's reign of love and justice on earth, Rauschenbusch founded the Brotherhood of the Kingdom, a group of Baptist clergy that held summer conferences for two decades at Marlborough-on-the-Hudson. He was influential in the Federal Council of Churches and was president of the Religious

2716

Citizenship League, an interfaith group devoted to such causes as woman suffrage and the prohibition of child labor.

His pastorate at the Second German Baptist Church, just north of New York's "Hell's Kitchen" and only a few blocks west of the Tenderloin, gave him first-hand experience with poverty. In his articles for the paper *For the Right*, he called for an eight-hour work day, municipal ownership of utilities, a single tax, and socialization of the railroads. When in 1897 he moved to Rochester, he became involved in such various civic causes as school reform, utilities rates, and the closing of saloons.

Strongly influenced by such reformers as Henry George and Richard Ely, Rauschenbusch started questioning the capitalist structure of society. He considered himself a socialist, accepting the Marxist tenets of class struggle and surplus value but opposing the atheism and materialism he found within the movement.

Near the end of his life, his opposition to American entry in World War I brought rebuke, and during the middle decades of the twentieth century, neo-orthodox theologians found his optimism naive and his doctrine of sin deficient. However, Martin Luther King, Jr., cited Rauschenbusch as a major influence on his thinking, and comparisons are made between him and today's liberation theologians.

Overview of Biographical Sources

Although Rauschenbusch received many tributes at the time of his death, a full-scale biography did not appear until 1942. Dores R. Sharpe's *Walter Rauschenbusch*, closely identifies with its subject, is richly documented, and is still valuable despite its age. Paul Minus's *Walter Rauschenbusch: American Reformer* (1988), offers more perspective and reflects fifty years of new findings.

Evaluation of Principal Biographical Sources

Minus, Paul M. *Walter Rauschenbusch: American Reformer.* New York: Macmillan, 1988. (A, G) The first major biography to appear in almost half a century, it is based primarily upon the Rauschenbusch Papers. Minus speculates that Rauschenbusch's sympathy for the weak first stemmed from sympathy for his mother, whom he felt was abused by his authoritarian father. Though strongly admiring of his subject, Minus claims that Rauschenbusch exhibited a "moral blind spot" in his espousal of Anglo-Saxon supremacy. The book contains more narrative than analysis and does not place him in the context of American theological liberalism; the bibliography is superb, however.

Sharpe, Dores R. *Walter Rauschenbusch*. New York: Macmillan, 1942. (**A, G**) This first full-scale biography, introduced by Harry Emerson Fosdick, was written by his former student and confidential secretary, who was selected for the task by Rauschenbush's widow, family, and colleagues. Sharpe drew upon letters, sermons, lectures, and diaries. Detailed and sympathetic, it contains a wealth of rich and lengthy quotations difficult to find elsewhere. Though lacking perspective, it captures Rauschenbusch's spirit in ways other biographers miss.

Overview and Evaluation of Primary Sources

Some 107 linear feet of Rauschenbusch Papers are located in the American Baptist-Samuel Colgate Historical Library, Rochester, New York. Further materials can be found at the North American Baptist Seminary, Sioux Falls, South Dakota (successor to the German Department of Rochester Theological Seminary); the Rockefeller Archive Center in North Tarrytown, New York (John D. Rockefeller, Sr. helped support his ministry); the Valley Stream Baptist Church, Valley Stream, New York (successor to the Second German Baptist Church); Cornell University; and Yale University. Rauschenbusch wrote a biography of his father, *Leben and Wirken von August Rauschenbusch* (Cleveland, OH: n.p.: 1901), in which he gives some account of his own life as well. Fragments of a Rauschenbusch autobiography exist in the Ambrose Swasey Library of Colgate Rochester Divinity School/Bexley Hall/Crozer Theological Seminary.

Rauschenbusch's first major piece of writing was never published. Discovered close to half a century after his death in the archives of the American Baptist Historical Society, *The Righteousness of the Kingdom* (Nashville and New York: Abingdon Press, 1968; **A, G**) is edited by Max L. Stackhouse with an introduction by Robert T. Handy. It proclaims that Christianity is revolutionary, demanding a radical restructuring of thought and society. Rauschenbusch catapulted into fame with the publication of *Christianity and the Social Crisis* (New York: Macmillan, 1907; rev. ed. edited with introduction by Robert D. Cross; New York: Harper and Row, 1964; **A, G**), where he calls upon Christians to create a new social order. He discusses the mission of Jesus and the early prophets, indicts contemporary capitalistic society, and stresses that corrective action is within reach, especially for the expanding professional and business classes. In *Christianizing the Social Order* (New York: Macmillan, 1912; **A, G**), his major statement on a better social order, Rauschenbusch advocates taxation of unearned income, regulation of industry, abolition of monopolies, state ownership of natural resources and vital public services, aid for the disadvantaged, and the right of labor to organize. His short book for college seniors, *The Social Principles of Jesus* (New York: Association

Press, 1916; **A, G**), stresses the need to make every social institution an instrument of God's purpose. In his most theologically sophisticated work, *A Theology for the Social Gospel* (New York: Macmillan, 1917; **A, G**), Rauschenbusch emphasizes that in so far as any institution or form of collective behavior thwarts God's purposes, it is part of a kingdom of evil. Followers of Christ know conflict and can anticipate only partial realizations of the Kingdom of God. Other volumes include such devotional works as *For God and the People: Prayers of the Social Awakening* (Boston: Pilgrim Press, 1910; **G**), and *Dare We Be Christians?* (Boston: Pilgrim Press, 1914; **G**).

For convenient collections of essays, see Benjamin E. Mays, comp., *A Gospel for the Social Awakening: Selections from the Writings of Walter Rauschenbusch*, with an introduction by C. Howard Hopkins (New York: Association Press, 1950; **A, G**); Benson Y. Landis, comp., *A Rauschenbusch Reader: The Kingdom of God and the Social Gospel*, with an introduction by Harry Emerson Fosdick (New York: Harper, 1957; **A, G**); and Winthrop Hudson, ed., *Walter Rauschenbusch: Selected Writings* (New York: Paulist Press, 1984; **A, G**).

Other Sources

Aiken, John R., and James R. McDonnell. "Walter Rauschenbusch and Labor Reform: A Social Gospeller's Approach." *Labor History* 11 (1970): 131-150. Roots Rauschenbusch's failure to influence the labor movement in his appeal to a professional elite and his lack of understanding of the collective nature of the movement.

Bowden, Henry Warner. "Walter Rauschenbusch and American Church History." *Foundations* 9 (1966): 234-250. Based on notes from Rauschenbusch's lectures, Bowden reveals the reformer's views on American church history and church union.

Cauthen, Kenneth. *The Impact of American Religious Liberalism.* New York: Harper and Row, 1962. Sophisticated chapter on Rauschenbusch's finding the theoretical formulations of religious doctrines ranking far above his schemes for the reorganization of society.

Davis, R. Dennis. "The Impact of Evolutionary Thought on Walter Rauschenbusch." *Foundations* 21 (1978): 174-192. Shows how Rauschenbusch interpreted the struggle for existence in light of cooperation and used Spencerian categories to advance his concept of the Kingdom of God.

Gorrell, Donald K. *The Age of Social Responsibility: The Social Gospel in the Progressive Era, 1900-1920*. Macon, GA: Mercer University Press, 1988. Places Rauschenbusch in the context of general reform.

Handy, Robert T. "Walter Rauschenbusch." In *Ten Makers of Modern Protestant Thought*, edited by G. L. Hunt. New York: Association Press, 1958.

————. "Walter Rauschenbusch in Historical Perspective." *Baptist Quarterly* 20 (1964): 313-321. This leading church historian puts Rauschenbusch in the general framework of reform.

Hopkins, C. Howard. "Walter Rauschenbusch and the Brotherhood of the Kingdom." *Church History* 7 (June 1938): 138-156. An able description of what Rauschenbusch hoped to accomplish through his small cadre of Christian reformers.

————. *The Rise of the Social Gospel in American Protestantism, 1865-1915*. New Haven: Yale University Press, 1940. Classic account devoting an entire chapter to Rauschenbusch. Finds his books the most significant American religious works of his time.

Hudson, Winthrop S. *The Great Tradition of the American Churches*. New York: Harper and Row, 1953. In his chapter on Rauschenbusch as "the lonely prophet," Hudson finds the Baptist theologian honored by people who little understood his message. No sentimental optimist, Rauschenbusch denied the inevitability of progress and affirmed the doctrine of original sin.

————. "Walter Rauschenbusch and the New Evangelism." *Religion in Life* 30 (1961): 412-430. A general survey of Rauschenbusch's career. Advances the claim that he never allowed his interest in social Christianity to obscure the centrality of personal religion.

Hutchison, William R. *The Modernist Impulse in American Protestantism*. Cambridge: Harvard University Press, 1976. Finds Rauschenbusch more in the line of religious liberalism than a later neo-orthodox generation would admit. Argues that Rauschenbusch always found individual salvation secondary to that of society.

Jaehn, Klaus. *Rauschenbusch: The Formative Years*. Valley Forge, PA: Judson Press, 1976. Includes a discussion of his seminary experiences.

Marney, Carlyle. "The Significance of Walter Rauschenbusch." *Foundations* 2 (January 1959): 13-26. A penetrating evaluation, praising Rauschenbusch's teachings on the kingdoms of God and evil, but criticizing his concepts of sin, the church, Christ's atonement, the transcendence of God, and progress in history.

Massanair, Ronald Lee. "The Sacred Workshop of God: Reflections on the Historical Perspective of Walter Rauschenbusch." *Religion in Life* 40 (1971): 257-266. Claims Rauschenbusch believed in socially transmitted sin, linked the Kingdom of God to the ongoing movement of history, and saw Jesus as stressing the transformation of society far more than the transformation of the individual.

Moehlman, Conrad H. "Walter Rauschenbusch and His Interpreters." *The Crozer Quarterly* 23 (January 1946): 39-49. This prominent church historian stresses less positive aspects of Rauschenbush's thought.

Niebuhr, Reinhold. "Walter Rauschenbusch in Historical Perspective." *Religion in Life* 27 (1958): 527-536. This major leader of Protestant neo-orthodoxy praises Rauschenbusch for insisting on the social relevance of the Christian faith but finds his understanding of love and justice too naive.

Noble, David W. *The Paradox of Progressive Thought*. Minneapolis: University of Minnesota Press, 1958. In a chapter devoted to Rauschenbusch, Noble finds him exemplifying one form of the "progressive" doctrine of progress.

Stackhouse, Max L. "The Continuing Importance of Walter Rauschenbusch." In *The Righteousness of the Kingdom*. Nashville and New York: Abingdon Press, 1968. Defends Rauschenbusch against charges that he overestimated the teaching power of the gospel, ignored the need for organizational instrumentalities, avoided the question of salvation, and was a shallow sentimentalist.

————. "The Formation of a Prophet: Reflections on the Early Sermons of Walter Rauschenbusch." *Andover-Newton Quarterly* 9 (1969): 137-159. Analysis of newly discovered sermons. Shows that the early Rauschenbusch was not a social radical by training, theology, or intention but had radicalism thrust upon him by service in the New York slums.

Strain, Charles R. "Toward a Generic Analysis of a Classic of the Social Gospel: An Essay-Review of Walter Rauschenbusch, *Christianity and the Social Crisis*." *Journal of the American Academy of Religion* 46 (1978): 525-543. By using tools of literary analysis, Strain explains why Rauschenbusch's classic book was so popular.

Ward, Harry F. "Walter Rauschenbusch." In *Dictionary of American Biography*. Vol. 15. New York: Charles Scribner's Sons, 1935. Succinct, appreciative sketch by a political rival.

Justus D. Doenecke
New College of the University of South Florida

HIRAM REVELS
1827(?)-1901

Chronology

Born Hiram Rhoades Revels on September 27, 1827 (some scholars give his birth date as 1822; no records are now available), in Fayetteville, North Carolina, to free parents, whose names are unknown, the father a preacher, and the mother possibly of Scottish descent; *1835* attends private school for blacks in Fayetteville; *c. 1844* works as a barber in Lincolntown, North Carolina; *1844-1846* attends Quaker seminary near Liberty, Indiana, and prepares for ministry in African Methodist Episcopal Church; *1845-1850* preaches and lectures in Indiana, Ohio, and Illinois; *1849* ordained as elder in Indiana Conference of A.M.E. Church; *early 1850s* marries Phoeba A. Bass of Zanesville, Ohio; *1850-1857* continues to lecture and teach blacks in Missouri, Kansas, Kentucky, and Tennessee; *1856-1857* attends Knox Academy (later Knox College) as a scholarship student; *1857* becomes pastor of A.M.E. Church and high school principal in Baltimore; *1861-1863* helps organize two Union regiments of black soldiers in Maryland; *1863* teaches in a black high school in St. Louis; *1864* becomes chaplain of a Union regiment in Mississippi; establishes churches in Jackson; *Winter 1865* leaves A.M.E. Church and becomes minister in African-Methodist Episcopal Church North in Leavenworth, Kansas; *Early 1867-1868* continues work for A.M.E. Church North in Louisville, Kentucky, New Orleans, and finally Natchez, Mississippi; *1868* appointed to Natchez city council; *November 1869* elected state senator (Republican) to Mississippi legislature; *January 20, 1870* chosen U.S. senator by legislature; *February 20, 1870* sworn in as first black senator; *March 4, 1871* upon completion of his term, returns to Natchez; chosen by Governor James L. Alcorn to be president of Alcorn Agricultural College, a newly-established black institution near Rodney, Mississippi; *1874* resigns Alcorn presidency under pressure from Republican Governor Adelbert Ames and resumes career as a minister; *1876* reappointed by Democrat governor as president of Alcorn College; *1882* resigns in order to become assistant pastor in Holly Springs, Mississippi; *1901* dies on January 16 in Aberdeen, Mississippi.

Activities of Historical Significance

When Hiram Revels presented his credentials to the U.S. Senate on February 23, 1870, the body debated for three days as to whether Revels was entitled to take his seat. The real issue was not Revels's credentials or even the readmission of Mississippi to the Union after the Civil War, but the fact that Revels was black. He had been elected by the Mississippi legislature to serve as Mississippi's first U.S. senator since Jefferson Davis had resigned in 1861. Much of the attention then and now devoted to Revels results from his historic role as the first African-American in the U.S. Congress. Although Revels served creditably as senator, some scholars believe that he has been honored more than he deserves. Others denigrate him because they claim he failed to advance black rights significantly.

Although Revels pursued a moderate political course throughout his life, he tried to improve blacks' welfare in practical ways. At a time when few southern blacks were free, let alone educated, Revels persistently sought further education for himself. He then tried to elevate the status of other African Americans by organizing schools and churches; during the Civil War he helped recruit black soldiers. Up until 1868, however, Revels had never been active in politics. This apolitical background, along with his stately bearing, made him a suitable compromise candidate in 1870 when the Mississippi legislators (of whom only one-third were freedmen) chose their first post-Civil War senator. Not surprisingly, the African American was chosen for the shorter, unexpired term, while two whites were elected to regular terms. As U.S. senator, Revels spoke rarely and voted consistently with the Republican party. He gave two civil rights speeches, arguing that Georgia, with its unreconstructed government, should be denied admission, and that the District of Columbia public schools should become integrated.

Choosing to return to Mississippi after his Senate term, Revels gratefully accepted the position as president of Alcorn College, but once again he found himself under the influence of whites who made up Alcorn's board of trustees. He has been most strongly criticized for turning against Republicans in the 1875 election, one that was marked with violence and voter intimidation from white Democrats. Revels broke with Radical Republicans in his district's congressional race, and endorsed the Independent Republican G. Wiley Wells whom the Democrats supported. In an attempt to justify his stand, Revels wrote President Ulysses S. Grant to explain that he had deserted the Republican party because the party's "unprincipled adventurers" had attracted the support of unwitting blacks. He insisted that he had remained a good Republican and that whites in Mississippi would "guarantee to my people every right and privilege guaranteed to an American citizen." Some historians assert that Revels turned against Republicans in order to regain his Alcorn College presidency; and indeed he was reappointed by Ames's successor.

As senator and educator, Revels often temporized on issues (such as segregated southern schools), and catered to whites' opinions. Although his belief that whites would treat blacks as equals seems naive, he merits attention for several reasons. First, against the taunts and doubts of white senators who thought no black should vote, much less govern, he served with dignity in the Senate. A neophyte senator for only a thirteen-month term, Revels should not be criticized for few speeches or unsuccessful legislation. Most importantly, Revels exemplifies both the attainments and weaknesses of moderate, persevering African Americans of his time. He chose not to become a civil rights advocate. His career illustrates the plight of intelligent, well-meaning, yet uncertain African Americans during Reconstruction.

Overview of Biographical Sources

Only two sources—Julius Eric Thompson's *Hiram R. Revels 1827-1901: A Biography* (1982) and Elizabeth Lawson's *The Gentleman From Mississippi* (1960)—treat Revels exclusively. As a minor but symbolically important figure, he is usually briefly and neutrally presented, as in W.E.B. Du Bois's *Black Reconstruction in America* (1964), John Hope Franklin's *From Slavery to Freedom* (1988), and Eric Foner's *Reconstruction* (1988).

Evaluation of Principal Biographical Sources

Thompson, Julius Eric. *Hiram R. Revels 1827-1901: A Biography.* New York: Arno Press, 1982. (A) Thompson's study is the only full-length treatment of Revels, and the only source to evaluate him critically. Because of the paucity of first-hand materials on Revels, Thompson had to draw on secondary sources on black education, the ministry, and Mississippi politics to re-create the environment in which Revels lived. Through no fault of Thompson's, the biography reveals more about this milieu than about Revels himself. Thompson concludes that Revels was basically cautious and timid throughout his life, "a conservative who because of the securities of his life found it difficult to make realistic decisions concerning Black people."

Lawson, Elizabeth. *The Gentleman From Mississippi.* New York: n.p., 1960. (A, G) In a brief (63 pages), sympathetic study of Revels as U.S. Senator, Lawson dispels several myths, but does not satisfactorily explain his controversial switch to the Democratic party in 1875.

Overview and Evaluation of Primary Sources

Primary materials on Revels are scarce. Most of his papers were destroyed in a series of fires. The best source on Revels's congressional career is the *Congres-*

sional Globe, 41st Congress, Second and Third Sessions, which contain the record of the debate on Revels's credentials, as well as his remarks and speeches during his short term. His speech arguing for desegregated schools in the District of Columbia is included in *The Voice of Black America,* edited by Philip S. Foner (New York: Simon and Schuster, 1972; **A, G**). Revels's testimony to the Boutwell committee about the election of 1875, as well as his controversial letter to Grant, can be found in *Senate Report 527* (serial set 1669-70) for the 44th Congress, 1st session. An excerpt from Revels's autobiography, supposedly dictated to a daughter (in the Carter G. Woodson Collection in the Manuscript Division, Library of Congress), has been printed in Emma Lou Thornbrough, editor, *Black Reconstructionists* (Englewood Cliffs, NJ: Prentice-Hall, 1972; **A, G**). Revels's four letters to Charles Sumner are available in the *Papers of Charles Sumner* (Cambridge, England: Chadwyck-Healey, 1988; **A, G**), edited by Beverly Wilson Palmer. Besides the Carter G. Woodson Collection, clippings, speeches and family letters (around seventeen items) are in the Schomburg Collection at the New York Public Library.

Other Sources

Christopher, Maurine. *Black Americans in Congress.* New York: Thomas Y. Crowell, 1976. Chapter one is a largely sympathetic survey of Revels's career.

Hosmer, John, and Joseph Fineman. "Black Congressmen in Reconstruction Historiography." *Phylon* (June 1978): 97-107. This useful overview cites studies containing exaggerated claims of black achievement as well as those treating blacks condescendingly. The writers argue that the fact that blacks in this period were "docile" and "ineffective" makes greater the need to study them.

Lynch, John R. *The Facts of Reconstruction.* 1913. Reprint. New York: Neale, 1968. Lynch's first-hand description of the 1870 Mississippi state legislature provides the basis for other accounts of Revels's role in that body.

Wharton, Vernon Lane. *The Negro in Mississippi.* Chapel Hill: University of North Carolina Press, 1947. Two chapters of Wharton's book present an excellent analysis of Mississippi politics from 1870 to 1875, including an assessment of Revels's influence.

Beverly Wilson Palmer
Pomona College

PAUL REVERE
1734-1818

Chronology

Born Paul Revere in December 1734 and baptized January 1, 1735, in Boston, Massachusetts, the third of twelve children of Paul Revere (originally named Apollos Rivoire), a French-born gold and silversmith, and Deborah Hitchborn, of Boston; attends North Grammar School, and apprentices with his father, who dies in 1754; *1756* serves in French and Indian War as second lieutenant of artillery on Massachusetts expedition against Crown Point; returns to Boston and resumes work as gold- and silversmith; *August 17, 1757* marries Sarah Orne of Boston, with whom he will have eight children; *1760-1765* joins St. Andrews Masonic Lodge, an association important in his business and personal life; becomes successful gold and silversmith with upper- and middle-class clientele; develops a reputation as engraver of copperplates for prints, a talent he will later use for his well-known Boston Massacre work; *1765* becomes a member of the North End Caucus, is active with Sons of Liberty, and is an associate of Samuel Adams, James Otis, Joseph Warren, John Hancock, and other leaders of opposition to British policies; *1768* makes famous "Liberty" silver punchbowl to honor Massachusetts assemblymen who oppose Townshend Acts; *1773* his wife dies, and he marries Rachel Walker, with whom he will have eight more children; participates in the Boston Tea Party in December and is chosen by popular leaders to carry news of this event to New York and Philadelphia; *1774* is chosen official courier between the Massachusetts Provincial Assembly and the Continental Congress; *1775* is a member of a committee to monitor activities of British troops in the Boston area and on April 16 rides to Concord to warn of British plans to raid munitions stored there; on night of April 18-19 makes his famous ride to alert patriots of British march to Lexington and Concord, and rescues trunk of important patriot correspondence and papers; *1776* serves as lieutenant colonel of artillery in Massachusetts forces and as commander of detachment on Castle Island in Boston Harbor; *1779-1782* takes part in Massachusetts expedition to Penobscot River mouth, the failure of which brings on investigations and much recrimination among officers involved; is suspended from military duties when disgruntled naval officers accuse him and others of disobedience and cowardice; demands a court-martial to clear name and is finally absolved of charges and vindicated after a military court meets; *1783-1788* at war's end he tries various mercantile enterprises in Boston but relies mainly on craft as silversmith for his livelihood; *1789* takes an active and important role in securing ratification of the federal constitution in Massachusetts; continues work as silversmith but adds to reputation and displays versatility by developing a foundry for casting heavy ironware; *1792* begins to cast bells and is highly successful in this enterprise; *late 1790s* begins manufacture of bolts, spikes, nails, and copper fittings for naval vessels, including the US *Constitution* ("Old Ironsides"); *1800* builds a mill for rolling copper at Canton and produces copper sheathing and boiler plates for ships at his works, Revere Copper and Brass; *1818* dies on May 10 in Boston, a successful industrialist and esteemed silversmith.

Activities of Historical Significance

It is an irony of history that Paul Revere, one of early America's most versatile and talented individuals, is chiefly remembered by modern Americans for his role as a courier during the era of the Revolution. Recognition for his midnight ride of April 18-19, 1775, immortalized in Henry Wadsworth Longfellow's 1863 poem, has overshadowed attention Revere rightfully deserves in other contexts, for in his long and productive life he displayed a variety of talents, and his career helps highlight several themes in the nation's history.

Revere was an effective political activist and organizer, an acknowledged leader of the Boston mechanics and artisans. His value in this context was known and appreciated by Sons of Liberty associates such as Samuel Adams, James Otis, Joseph Warren, and John Hancock. During the pre-revolutionary crises he also used his talent as an engraver to reproduce political cartoons that helped encourage popular resistance to British policies. An outstanding example of this was his 1770 copperplate engraving of the Boston Massacre—surely one of the most effective propaganda devices used by the patriot party in Massachusetts. He created one of his best-known pieces, the famous "Liberty" punchbowl, to commemorate the ninety-two assemblymen who refused to rescind the 1768 Massachusetts Circular Letter. Revere was a participant in the Boston Tea Party and also served as an official courier for the Massachusetts Provisional Assembly, making several rides to New York and Philadelphia on official business before the famous April 18, 1775, midnight ride to Lexington. At Lexington, he succeeded in warning Samuel Adams and John Hancock of the impending British attack, but British troops prevented him from reaching Concord. During the war years he served as lieutenant colonel of Massachusetts artillery and was judged to have served honorably despite his involvement in the ill-fated Penobscot expedition of 1779.

After the Revolution he continued his public service role and worked diligently for ratification of the federal Constitution in Massachusetts. His major activities, however, were in the business world, where he built on his reputation as a master silversmith. He showed his versatility when he developed skills as a foundryman, and with his son Joseph Warren Revere established a reputation in casting bells. All told, the Revere foundry produced about four hundred bells for church and other uses throughout America and abroad.

Revere's next industrial venture involved work with copper, from which he made a great variety of bolts, spikes, fittings, and accessories for naval vessels, including the famous Old Ironsides. But his major contribution in this field was his skill in making copper sheathing, then much-needed for sailing vessels. Assured of government interest and a federal loan, Revere built a copper-rolling mill at Canton, Massachusetts—the forerunner of the famous Revere Copper and Brass company. Here, copper sheathing and copperplate for a variety of uses were produced in great quantities—at least three tons a week by 1813. When he died in 1818, Revere was one of the country's first large-scale industrialists, and products of his silversmith's art were already being sought as collector's items.

Overview of Biographical Sources

Revere was not lost to history after the American Revolution, and his memory was recalled in an occasional sketch such as appeared in the *New England Magazine* in 1832. But it was not until the 1863 appearance of Longfellow's poem that his midnight ride achieved legendary status. Interest in Revere was again aroused at the centennial of the fighting at Lexington and Concord. The first full-scale biography of Revere did not appear until 1891, when Elbridge H. Goss produced his two-volume *Life of Colonel Paul Revere*. This work, frankly laudatory but not uncritical, still has value, especially for the amount of primary material it prints. No other Revere biography appeared until two studies were published early in the twentieth century. These, Charles F. Gettemy, *The True Story of Paul Revere* (1905), and Emerson G. Taylor, *Paul Revere* (1930), offered little insight or additional knowledge to the Revere story. The most recent Revere biography, by Esther Forbes, *Paul Revere & The World He Lived In* (1942), is still the best after almost fifty years and clearly merits the Pulitzer Prize it was awarded. Many other works—biographies and special studies dealing with Massachusetts's role in the coming of the Revolutionary War and with Boston leaders such as Joseph Warren, Samuel Adams, and James Otis—contain details regarding Revere's activities during this era. The same is true for works dealing with the Stamp Act, the Townshend Acts, the Boston Tea Party, and the Coercive Acts. An excellent example, replete with references to Revere, is Arthur B. Tourtellot, *Lexington and Concord: The Beginning of the War of the American Revolution* (1959).

Evaluation of Principal Biographical Sources

Forbes, Esther. *Paul Revere & The World He Lived In*. Boston: Houghton Mifflin, 1942. (**A, G**) The most authoritative and recent biography. Clearly written and based on a thorough knowledge of available materials, this Pulitzer Prize winner does not romanticize or mythologize its subject. Forbes presents Revere in the context of his era and with insight that brings both the man and age alive.

Gettemy, Charles Ferris. *The True Story of Paul Revere*. Boston: Little, 1905. (**G**) A short biography written with the intent of moving beyond the romantic and legendary treatment of Revere. Based on primary materials, it does well in placing Revere within the context of his era and locale. It is straightforward and factual but fails to add much to prior accounts.

Goss, Elbridge H. *The Life of Colonel Paul Revere*. 2 vols. Boston: Joseph George Cupples, 1891. (**A, G**) The earliest full-scale biography, this was for many years a chief source of information for Revere's career since the author aimed to print "letters, documents, and items of interest, not otherwise available." It is fulsome in praise of Revere but not uncritically so, and still has value for the primary materials it prints. Goss clearly shows Revere as an important leader of the Boston "mechanics" and artisan classes, and succeeds in showing Revere beyond Longfellow's depiction. The two volumes have been reprinted by Ayer Publishers of Salem, New Hampshire, and by Irvington Publishers of New York.

Taylor, Emerson. *Paul Revere*. New York: Mitchell, Dodd and Mead, 1930. (**G**) This laudatory work attempts to move beyond previous studies and show Revere in terms of modern values but really adds little to what Goss and Gettemy presented for earlier generations. It is well written but overbalanced toward the revolutionary era in that Revere's career as industrialist is covered only briefly.

Weisberger, Bernard A. "Paul Revere: The Man, the Myth, and the Midnight Ride." *American Heritage* 28 (April 1977): 24-37. (**A, G**) An excellent article by a gifted historian, this account provides an imaginative and insightful introduction to Revere's entire career. The discussion of Revere's business activities after the war is especially valuable.

Evaluation of Biographies for Young People

Brandt, Keith. *Paul Revere: Son of Liberty*. Mahwah, NJ: Troll Associates, 1982. A biography for students in grades four through six.

Forbes, Esther. *America's Paul Revere*. Boston: Houghton Mifflin, 1946. A brief condensation for younger readers of Forbes's earlier book. Events leading up to the American Revolution and Revere's role in these events are discussed without hyperbole. Of particular value is Forbes's treatment of Revere as silversmith, foundryman, and copper and brass manufacturer.

Fritz, Jean. *And Then What Happened, Paul Revere?* New York: Putnam, 1973. An amusing biography for students in grades two through six.

Graves, Charles P. *Paul Revere: Rider for Liberty*. Champaign, IL: Garrard, 1964. This biography is for students in grades two through five.

Stein, R. Conrad. *The Story of Lexington and Concord*. Chicago: Children's Press, 1983. Stein recounts Revere's famous midnight ride for grades three through six.

Stevenson, Augusta. *Paul Revere: Boston Patriot*. New York: Bobbs-Merrill, 1984. As part of the Childhood of Famous Americans Series, Stevenson's book emphasizes Revere's early years.

Overview and Evaluation of Primary Sources

As might be expected, the bulk of the primary sources for Revere are located in Boston and begin with the Revere Family Papers held by the Massachusetts Historical Society. Among these sixteen volumes are letterbooks, invoices, ledgers, loose manuscripts, memoranda books for the Boston workshop, and records dealing with the copperworks at Canton. The Grand Lodge of Masons and St. Andrews Lodge, Boston, also have Revere materials, including an account book for 1784-1793. Newspaper collections at the Boston Public Library are another important source for Revere's life and include the *Boston News-Letter, Independent Chronicle*, and *Massachusetts Sentinel*. For the famous April 1775 ride to Lexington, see Edmund S. Morgan, ed., *Paul Revere's Three Accounts of His Famous Ride* (Boston: Massachusetts Historical Society, 1968; **A, G, Y**). This work traces the history of each of the accounts and provides historical notes by a careful scholar. A map and several facsimile pages are included. The Paul Revere Memorial Association, Boston, holds some Revere letters and miscellaneous memorabilia. Numerous letters and documents relating to Revere's family, business, and military activities—including his diary of the Penobscot expedition—are printed in Elbridge H. Goss's biographical study.

Fiction and Adaptations

By far the most famous creative interpretation of Revere's deeds is Henry Wadsworth Longfellow's "Paul Revere's Ride," which opens *Tales of the Wayside Inn* (1863), a collection of narrative poems that Longfellow loosely modeled after Geoffrey Chaucer's *Canterbury Tales*. In a country torn by civil war, the poem achieved extraordinary popularity and turned Revere into a national hero.

Museums, Historical Landmarks, Societies

Boston Museum of Fine Arts (Boston, MA). Houses two famous portraits of Revere, one by J. S. Copley and the other by Gilbert Stuart. The museum also holds the best collection of Revere's silver.

Granary Burial Ground (Boston, MA). A bronze tablet placed at the entrance gate indicates this cemetery as the site of Revere's grave.

Paul Revere Mall (Boston, MA). This spot, in Boston's North End, features an equestrian statue sculpted by Cyrus Dallin and placed in 1940.

Paul Revere Memorial Association (Boston, MA). This organization, founded in 1908, maintains the Revere House.

Revere House National Historic Landmark (Boston, MA). Bought by Revere in 1770, this seventeenth-century dwelling at 19 North Square is the oldest standing structure in Boston. Period furnishings include five pieces of Revere's furniture.

Other Sources

Boatner, Mark Mayo, III. "Paul Revere." In *Encyclopedia of the American Revolution*. New York: David McKay, 1966. A good account that primarily deals with Revere as the leader of "mechanics" but covers his military and post-revolutionary life as well.

Brigham, Clarence P. *Paul Revere's Engravings*. 1954. Rev. ed. New York: Atheneum, 1969. The authoritative work on its subject, useful for evaluating one aspect of Revere's role in pre-revolutionary crises.

Brown, Richard D. "Paul Revere." In *The Encyclopedia of American Biography*, edited by John A. Garraty and Jerome L. Sternstein. New York: Harper &

Row, 1974. A brief sketch with emphasis on Revere's creativity, versatility, and innovative talents.

Buhler, Kathryn C. *American Silver, 1655-1825, in the Museum of Fine Arts*. 2 vols. Boston: The Museum of Fine Arts, 1972. Important for illustrations and discussions of Revere as silversmith. Includes photographs and descriptions of his major works, such as the "Liberty" punchbowl. By a leading authority.

Leehey, Patrick, et al. *Paul Revere—Artisan, Businessman, and Patriot: The Man Behind the Myth*. Boston: Paul Revere Memorial Association, 1988. This work, distributed by the American Association for State and Local History, is a series of five essays on Revere in his various roles and also contains the complete catalogue of a Revere exhibition at the Museum of Our National Heritage, Lexington, Massachusetts, held 1988-1989. Includes a good bibliography, as well as descriptions and photos of the exhibits.

Alan S. Brown
Western Michigan University

EDMUND RUFFIN
1794-1865

Chronology

Born January 5, 1794, in Prince Edward County, Virginia, to George Ruffin, a planter, and Jane Lucas Ruffin,; *1810* studies at the College of William and Mary; *1812-1813* volunteers to fight in the War of 1812; *c. 1813* marries Susan Travis; *1821* publishes his study of soil fertilization in *The American Farmer*; *1823-1826* member of Virginia state legislature; *1832* publishes *Essay on Calcareous Manures*; *1833-1842* publishes *Farmers' Register*; *1841-1842* edits *Bank Reformer*; *1843* travels to South Carolina and prepares a report on agriculture; *1844* returns to Virginia and moves from Petersburg to Hanover County, north of Richmond; *1852* accepts presidency of the Virginia State Agricultural Society; *1853-1859* publishes several defenses of slavery; *April 12, 1861* fires first shot at Fort Sumter; *1865* crushed by the news of Confederate defeat, kills himself on June 17.

Activities of Historical Significance

Edmund Ruffin defended the South yet sought to change it. Usually recognized as one of the most prominent and fervent advocates of Southern secession, Ruffin was also important because of his efforts to convince southern planters to employ scientific methods in farming. His advocacy of agricultural reform, first broached in 1818, became the dominant force in his life for several decades. By the 1840s, having realized that he had lost the battle to change the South, he began to channel his energies toward the cause of Southern independence, writing extensively on slavery while pushing for secession whenever possible.

In 1861 Ruffin became a prophet honored in his own time for his advocacy of Southern independence (although not for his cause of agricultural reform). He was allowed the honor of firing the first shot at Fort Sumter on April 12. Yet the course of the war crushed his spirit, as the Southern nation he had long dreamed of was defeated. On June 17, 1865, he killed himself, but not before making clear "my unmitigated hatred to Yankee rule—to all political, social, & business connection with Yankees, & to the perfidious, malignant, & vile Yankee race."

Overview of Biographical Sources

Avery Craven set the standard for future biographers of Ruffin. His biography, *Edmund Ruffin, Southerner: A Study in Secession* (1932), which makes Ruffin into the prototypical Southern extremist, is an absorbing story, conflating as it did with Craven's argument that hotheads on both sides led the nation into war in 1861. Oddly enough, however, his discussion of Ruffin's interest in scientific agriculture strikes a blow to the concept of the tradition-bound Southerner. Betty L. Mitchell's biography, *Edmund Ruffin: A Biography* (1981), by taking Ruffin at essentially face value, becomes more of a narrative (albeit a highly readable one) than an interpretation or analysis. William M. Mathew, *Edmund Ruffin and the Crisis of Slavery in the Old South: The Failure of Agricultural Reform* (1988), disputes the conclusions of Craven and Mitchell that Ruffin had much of an impact on Southern agriculture and suggests that slavery made such reforms difficult to implement. The works of Daniel F. Allmendinger, *Ruffin: Family and Reform in the South* (1990), and Drew Faust, *A Sacred Circle: The Dilemma of the Intellectual in the Old South, 1840-1860* (1977), are the most absorbing, for in them Ruffin emerges as a human being, whose political beliefs were shaped by personal experiences.

Evaluation of Principal Biographical Sources

Allmendinger, David F., Jr. *Ruffin: Family and Reform in the Old South.* New York: Oxford University Press, 1990. (**A, G**) Draws suggestive connections between Ruffin's public and private life in an account notable for its clear, engaging prose.

Craven, Avery. *Edmund Ruffin, Southerner: A Study in Secession.* New York: D. Appleton, 1932. (**A, G**) Long the standard biography, this well-crafted narrative is still worth reading.

Faust, Drew Gilpin. *A Sacred Circle: The Dilemma of the Intellectual in the Old South, 1840-1860.* Baltimore: The Johns Hopkins University Press, 1977. (**A**) This study of Ruffin and his contemporaries, William Gilmore Simms, James Henry Hammond, Nathaniel Beverley Tucker, and George Frederick Holmes, traces their efforts to create a distinct Southern culture based upon the defense of slavery and with themselves as the leading explicators of Southern identity. Faust argues that these five men were trying to reassert the primacy of the status of the Southern intellectual in society.

Mathew, William M. *Edmund Ruffin and the Crisis of Slavery in the Old South: The Failure of Agricultural Reform.* Athens: University of Georgia Press, 1988. (**A**) Argues that Ruffin's plans for agricultural reform were thwarted by an indifferent South and the institution of slavery.

Mitchell, Betty L. *Edmund Ruffin: A Biography*. Bloomington: Indiana University Press, 1981. (A, G) This well-written narrative concentrates on Ruffin's advocacy of secession and the Civil War.

Overview and Evaluation of Primary Sources

The two main collections of Ruffin's papers are at the Library of Congress and the Virginia Historical Society, Richmond. Other collections are at the University of Virginia, Charlottesville; the University of North Carolina, Chapel Hill; and the Virginia State Library, Richmond. Essential for any study of Ruffin is his diary; William K. Scarborough has completed the three-volume edition of *The Diary of Edmund Ruffin* (Baton Rouge: Louisiana State University Press, 1972-1989; A, G). For other writings by Ruffin, consult *Incidents of My Life: Edmund Ruffin's Autobiographical Essays* (Richmond: Virginia Historical Society, 1990; A, G), edited by David Allmendinger, and *Anticipations of the Future, to Serve as Lessons for the Present Time* (1860; reprint; Freeport, NY: Books for Libraries Press, 1972; A), a speculative novel about sectional politics which holds some surprising parallels to what has actually happened. Other Ruffin pieces appear in *Farmers' Register, American Farmer*, and *DeBow's Review*; a good bibliography appears in Allmendinger's biography of Ruffin.

Other Sources

Genovese, Eugene. *The Political Economy of Slavery*. 1965. Reprint. New York: Vintage Books, 1967. This controversial study, designed to show the precapitalist bent of slaveholders, found troublesome Ruffin's attempt to apply science to the practice of plantation slavery.

McCardell, John. *The Idea of a Southern Nation: Southern Nationalists and Southern Nationalism, 1830-1860*. New York: W. W. Norton, 1979. Although it spends relatively little time on Ruffin, this book does what it can to make the case for the existence of Southern nationalism before 1860.

Brooks Donohue Simpson
Arizona State University

ELIZABETH BAYLEY SETON
1774-1821

Chronology

Born Elizabeth Ann Bayley on August 28, 1774, probably in New York City, the second of three daughters of the prominent physician-surgeon, Richard Bayley, and Catherine Charlton Bayley, who died when Elizabeth was three years old; *1774- 1794* grows up unwelcome and often away from the home of her stepmother Charlotte Barclay Bayley; taught French and piano at Mama Pompelion's; *January 25, 1794* marries William Magee Seton, a bank clerk and merchant, oldest son of a banker and assistant superintendent of the port of New York; *1795* gives birth to Anna Maria; *1796* gives birth to William; *1797* helps found a society to aid destitute, widowed mothers; *1798* gives birth to Richard Bayley; mothers five younger sisters of her husband after the death of the elder Seton; *1799-1801* assists husband after bankruptcy of Seton-Maitland firm; *1800* gives birth to Catherine; *1802* gives birth to Rebecca; *1803* her husband dies in Italy where she becomes interested in Roman Catholicism; *1805* converts to Catholicism; *1806-1807* fails in attempts to run a school and boarding house to support her family; *1808* begins small Catholic school for girls on Paca Street, Baltimore; *1809* founds Sisters of Charity of St. Joseph; *1810* receives first female day students in Emmitsburg, Maryland; *1821* dies of tuberculosis on January 4, in Emmitsburg, where she is buried; *1959* named Venerable; *1963* entitled "Blessed"; *1975* proclaimed first American-born saint.

Activities of Historical Significance

A widowed Catholic convert and one of the most influential Catholic women of the nineteenth century, Elizabeth Seton founded the American Sisters of Charity. She began her educational and charity work in an effort to support herself and her five children after the death of her husband and estrangement from her Episcopal relatives because of her conversion to Roman Catholicism. Seton succeeded in spite of organizational, monetary, and health difficulties, sustained by her practical genius, her disciplined resilience, Christian commitment, and generous friends. Seton laid the foundation for the nineteenth-century parochial school system in America by founding a girls' academy, training teachers in a religious community, preparing textbooks for classroom use, translating religious books from French, and writing her own hymns and spiritual treatises. Her sisters opened orphanages in Philadelphia (1814) and New York City (1817) before her death. Today, the Emmitsburg community remains active; St. Joseph School became a college for women. The Sisters of Charity, who trace their origins to Seton's foundation, serve in North and South America, Italy, Japan, and on the island of Formosa.

Overview of Biographical Sources

Until Annabelle M. Melville published the definitive, scholarly biography, *Elizabeth Bayley Seton* (1951), biographies of Seton consisted of collections of her writings with added commentary, often marred by sentiment and error. The earliest biography, Charles White's *Life of Mrs. Eliza A. Seton* (1853, 1879), served as a model for subsequent works, including *Elizabeth Seton* (1927), written in French by Helene B. De Barberey, and translated by Joseph B. Code. Code later enlarged upon his translation, adding an admiring commentary, more Seton letters, and an account of Seton's death written by her priest-confessor. This version went into a fourth printing in 1957.

Joseph Dirvin, a promoter of Seton's cause for canonization, based his 1962 biography, *Mrs. Seton: Foundress of the American Sisters of Charity*, upon all earlier sources to produce a lively but unscholarly work. Ellin M. Kelly's *Numerous Choirs: The Seton Years 1774-1821* (1981), the first volume of her history of the American religious order of the Sisters of Charity, gives a comprehensive chronicle of Seton and her times. In its careful description of historical context, it serves as a companion volume to *Elizabeth Ann Seton: A Self Portrait* (1986) by Sister Marie Celeste, who describes Seton's family and associates in a style Seton herself might have used to write an "autobiographical" biography.

Evaluation of Principal Biographical Sources

Celeste, Marie. *Elizabeth Ann Seton: A Self Portrait.* Libertyville, IL: Franciscan Marytown Press, 1986. (**A, G**) With minimal intrusion, this scholar-biographer quotes from and explains Seton's own writings thereby allowing her to tell her own story. Celeste probes Seton's ancestry more than any other biographer but gives less attention to the social and political context of Seton's life in this "spiritual biography" that includes an account of Seton's 1975 canonization ceremony. Includes scholarly, informative footnotes, an extensive bibliography, and an index.

De Barbarey, Helene Bailly, and Joseph B. Code. *Elizabeth Seton.* 1927. Reprint. Emmitsburg, MD: Mother Seton Guild Press, 1957. (**A, G**) Code's expanded English translation of De Barberey's work was reprinted for the fourth time in 1957 and served as the best available English biography until the publication of Melville's work. This extended collection of Seton's own writings contains factual errors uncovered and corrected by Melville. Brief footnotes and index.

Dirvin, Joseph I. *Mrs. Seton: Foundress of the American Sisters of Charity.* New York: Farrar, Straus and Cudahy, 1962. **(A, G, Y)** Prepared for the general reader, Dirvin's personal biography includes long quotations from Seton and vivid narration with slight attention to historical context. The author often pauses to moralize or contemplate religion and spirituality in order to defend Seton's goodness in every aspect of her life. Dirvin's analysis is stronger when he probes Seton's emotional stresses as the widowed, impoverished mother of five children. Perfunctory footnotes for essential sources, bibliography, and detailed index.

Kelly, Ellin, ed. *Numerous Choirs: A Chronicle of Elizabeth Bayley Seton and Her Spiritual Daughters,* Vol. 1, *The Seton Years: 1774-1821.* Evansville, IN: Mater Dei, 1981. **(A, G)** Succinct facts and events of American political, military, and Catholic Church history are arranged in sequence and woven into a readable chronicle of each year of Seton's life. Seton's letters and diaries are edited to maintain a factual tone. Brief footnotes, index, and appendix of the evolving rules and constitution of the religious order.

Melville, Annabelle M. *Elizabeth Bayley Seton.* New York: Scribner's, 1951. **(A, G)** This scholarly, definitive biography balances historical accuracy with the author's admiration for her subject and makes use of most extant sources including earlier biographies. Melville weaves historical context with confirmed details of Seton's life but tries too hard to remove the taint of strong sympathy. Includes ample footnotes, complete bibliography, and helpful index.

White, Charles. I. *Life of Mrs. Eliza A. Seton.* New York: P. J. Kenedy, 1853. Rev. ed. 1879. **(A, G)** Inclusive of many of Seton's letters and journal entries, this almost worshipful biography is intent on proving Seton's piety and religious spirit. After White's death, the publishers added a summary history of the expansion of the sisterhood established by Seton through 1879 when the American sisters affiliated with the Sisters of Charity of Saint Vincent de Paul in France and adopted their religious habit. Includes footnotes and statistics on American Sisters of Charity.

Overview and Evaluation of Primary Sources

Seton recorded her own life in more than twelve volumes of lively, heartfelt, witty, and demanding letters, journals, and meditations. During her short lifetime, the journal she kept at Leghorn, Italy, when her husband died was published without her permission as *Memoirs of Mrs. S.* (Elizabeth, NJ: Isaac Kollock, 1817; **A, G**). Robert Seton, her grandson who became a bishop, published some inaccurate commentary and a collection of her writings as *Memoir, Letters and Journal of Elizabeth Seton*. 2 vols. (New York, 1869; **A, G**). These less accessible publications have been made available in a recent book carefully edited by Ellin M. Kelly, *Elizabeth Seton: Selected Writings* (New York: Paulist Press, 1986; **A, G**). This edition presents some previously unpublished letters and published documents with all the flaws and eccentricities of their originals and a helpful list identifying individuals mentioned in the letters and journals. It also includes a succinct biography of Seton's spiritual growth by Annabelle Melville. Seton's letters to her widowed friend Julia Sitgreaves Scott were collected with informative background commentary by Joseph Code in *Letters of Mother Seton to Mrs. Julianna Scott* (New York: Father Burgio Foundation Press, 1960; **A, G**). These letters convey Seton's simple, practical goodness, her strong faith and affection, her pleas for money and for her friend's conversion to Catholicism, along with details of her daily life with her children.

Several archives contain valuable resources for biographical study of Seton: St. Joseph Provincial House in Emmitsburg, Maryland (open by appointment only); the University of Notre Dame; Baltimore Archdiocese; the Convent of St. Elizabeth, Convent Station, New Jersey; the Sisters of Charity of Mount St. Joseph, Ohio; the Sisters of Charity of Seton Hill, Greensburg, Pennsylvania; and the Sisters of Charity of Mount St. Vincent, Bronx, New York.

Fiction and Adaptations

Numerous pamphlets have been written about the life of Saint Elizabeth Seton in English, Spanish, German, French, Italian, Swiss, and Portuguese. Adapted for children are biographies by Charlotte Baecher, *A Child's Life of Elizabeth Seton* (1961) and Mary Louise Callahan, *Little Birds and Lilies* (1955), and a coloring book (1961).

Three biographical novels have been published: Clare Seramur, *Courageous Calling* (1961); Sigrid Van Sweringen, *As the Morning Rising* (1936) and *White Noon* (1939).

Biographical facts form the basis for a three-act play, *Elizabeth of New York* (1975), by Sr. Francis Maria Cassidy, and a two-hour television play, *A Time for Miracles*, by Henry Denker (broadcast December 21, 1980, on ABC). Kate Mulgrew played a handsome, pleasant but dispassionate Seton in this rather stiff, sometimes romantic and violent television drama.

Museums, Historical Landmarks, Societies

Museum of Old Cathedral of Saint Francis Xavier (Vincennes, IN). The Brute Memorial Library displays one of Mother Seton's Bibles and other books she gave to her confessor, Reverend Simon Gabriel Brute, first bishop of Vincennes.

National Shrine of Saint Elizabeth Ann Seton (Emmitsburg, MD). Includes many Seton exhibits and a visitors' center founded in 1975 and run by the Sisters of Charity of St. Vincent de Paul. The "Stone House" is a restoration of Seton's 1809 residence and school. It was moved to its present location in 1979. A replica of the larger and more comfortable White House (1810) now stands approximately where the original was completed as a residence for Seton, her three daughters, the Sisters of St. Joseph, the children who boarded, and their classroom. Among places open to the public are a replica of the classroom with original embroidered samplers made by the first students and sisters, the chapel, the room where Mother Seton died, and a mortuary chapel (1846) where Seton's remains were placed until the completion of the Seton Shrine Chapel (1976).

Paca Street House (Baltimore, MD). A restoration of the original home and school building of the small group of women who first joined Mother Seton.

Shrine of St. Elizabeth Ann Seton (New York, NY). The home of the Seton family at 7 State Street is now a part of the Church of Our Lady of the Rosary, designated a shrine by the late Cardinal Spellman.

Other Sources

Code, J. B. "Elizabeth Ann Bayley Seton." In *Dictionary of American Biography,* edited by Dumas Malone. New York: Scribner's, 1935. As the editor of Seton's letters to Julia Scott, the translator of De Barbarey's biography, and promoter of Seton's cause for sainthood, Code presents a concise biography but sometimes uncritical estimate of her historical contributions.

Gretchen R. Sutherland
Cornell College

ALAN B. SHEPARD, JR.
b. 1923

Chronology

Born Alan Barlett Shepard, Jr., on November 18, 1923, in East Derry, New Hampshire, the son of a career military officer; *1923-1929* spends early life in New England; *1929-1940* attends primary and secondary public schools in East Derry and Derry, New Hampshire; *1940-1941* attends Admiral Farragut Academy in Toms River, New Jersey; *1941-1944* attends the U.S. Naval Academy, graduating with a bachelor's degree; *1944-1946* serves on the destroyer USS *Cogswell* in the Pacific in World War II; *1946-1947* receives flight training in Corpus Christi, Texas, for commission as a navy aviator; *1947-1950* serves several tours aboard aircraft carriers in the Mediterranean and on shore with Navy Fighter Squadron Forty-Two; *1950* attends the U.S. Navy Test Pilot School at Pautuxent River, Maryland; *1951-1953* participates in flight testing several weapons systems including the F2H3 "Banshee" fighter; *1953-1956* serves as a test pilot and as squadron operations officer on the carrier USS *Oriskany; 1957* assigned to the commander of the Atlantic Fleet as aircraft readiness officer; *1959* named as one of the original seven Project Mercury Astronauts by the National Aeronautics and Space Administration; *May 5, 1961* becomes the first American in space when a Redstone launch vehicle lifts him in his Mercury capsule, *Freedom 7,* into a suborbital flight from Cape Canaveral, Florida, to a landing point 302 statute miles down the Atlantic Missile Range; *1963* designated as chief of the Astronaut Office for NASA after an inner ear disorder forces his removal from flight status; *1969* restored to full flight status and resumes activity as an astronaut; *January 31-February 9, 1971* commands *Apollo 14,* the third lunar landing mission; *September-December 1971* serves as a delegate to the twenty-sixth United Nations General Assembly; *1971* promoted to rear admiral by the navy, the first astronaut to achieve flag rank; *1971-1974* continues as chief of the Astronaut Office until retirement from NASA and the navy; *1974-present* resides in Houston, Texas, were he is president of Windward Coors Company; *1979* receives from President Jimmy Carter the Medal of Honor for gallantry in the astronaut corps.

Activities of Historical Significance

Alan Shepard's exploits as an astronaut were among the most significant scientific endeavors of the recent past. His actions as the first American to ride a rocket into space made him not only a celebrity, a result of the American people's interest in manned spaceflight and NASA's deft public relations, but also a frontiersman in the same mold as Lewis and Clark. He did not undertake these missions alone, but nevertheless his achievements symbolize the technological revolution which began seriously in the 1960s. They marked the onset of a new, great age of discovery, the exploration of the "new frontiers"—in space, under the ocean, and at the poles. His exploits made him a hero and a rallying symbol for the United States.

His actions as one of the seven Mercury astronauts for the American space program served to unify a nation behind the great opportunities attendant with the exploration of space. His May 5, 1961, suborbital Mercury mission confirmed that the United States could successfully launch a human into space. It was an enormously significant event for a nation that had been recently shocked by several outstanding space exploits from its closest rival, the Soviet Union—the 1957 orbiting of the *Sputnik* satellite and the Yuri Gargarin space flight—and there was much impetus to rescue national honor in the United States' own space program. The flight made Shepard a national hero, but his stoical persona and public countenance also served to solidify his stature among Americans as a role model.

Shepard's other important space flight took place a decade later, from January 31 to February 9, 1971. After battling a medical disorder that kept him off flight status for several years, Shepard commanded *Apollo 14* on a lunar landing mission at a critical time, just a few months after the near-tragic *Apollo 13* mission in which the lunar lander had been used as a lifeboat by the crew. His successful mission served as a tremendous boost to national spirit. The achievements of *Apollo 14* were many: the first use of the Mobile Equipment Transporter; the placement of the largest payload ever in lunar orbit; the longest stay on the lunar surface (thirty-three hours); the longest lunar surface extravehicular activity (nine hours and seventeen minutes); the first use of shortened lunar orbit rendezvous techniques; the first use of color television on the lunar surface; the first extensive orbital science period conducted in lunar orbit; and the first lunar golf game as Shepard, an avid golfer, surprised and delighted Americans by smuggling a golf club on board the spacecraft, then shooting a lunar hole-in-one.

Overview of Biographical Sources

There are no full-length biographies on Shepard written for an adult audience, but there are works appropriate for young people. In addition to several article-length works, most of the published material containing information on his life and experiences are broader studies profiling other people as well. At the time of the

Mercury program several books appeared on the astronauts: Joseph N. Bell, *Seven Into Space: The Story of the Mercury Astronauts* (1960); Martin Caiden, *The Astronauts: The Story of Project Mercury, America's Man-in-Space Program* (1960); and Shirley Thomas, *Men of Space: Profiles of the Leaders in Space Research, Development, and Exploration*, vol. 3 (1961). A later collection of sketches on the astronauts, including those on later missions, is Congressional Research Service, Library of Congress, *Astronauts and Cosmonauts Biographical and Statistical Data* (1989). Tom Wolfe's *The Right Stuff* (1979) is a brilliant and eminently readable account of the Mercury program with emphasis on the personality of the astronauts, including Shepard. Several good articles on Shepard with information on his later career were written by A. J. Hall, "Climb Up Cone Crater," *National Geographic* (July 1971); Louden Wainwright, "The Old Pro Gets His Shot at the Moon," *Life* (July 31, 1970); and R. M. Henry, "Alan Shepard, Reaching for the Stars," *All Hands* (April 1982).

Evaluation of Principal Biographical Sources

Bell, Joseph N. *Seven Into Space: The Story of the Mercury Astronauts*. Chicago: University of Chicago Press, 1960. (**A, G**) A routine account of all Mercury astronauts written before a single American manned space flight took place. Shepard is profiled along with his six colleagues.

Brennen, Dennis. *Adventures in Courage*. New York: Reilly and Lee, 1968. (**G**) Includes a lengthy portrait of Shepard and his astronautical experiences.

Caiden, Martin. *The Astronauts: The Story of Project Mercury, America's Man-in-Space Program*. New York: Dutton, 1960. (**G**) Popular account sensationalizing the Mercury astronauts, of which Shepard was a leading figure.

Congressional Research Service, Library of Congress. *Astronauts and Cosmonauts Biographical and Statistical Data*. Washington, DC: Government Printing Office, December 1989. (**A, G**) A short profile of the astronaut containing basic information.

Hall, A. J. "Climb Up Cone Crater." *National Geographic* 140 (July 1971): 136-148. (**A, G**) Although this account centers on the *Apollo 14* lunar mission, Shepard was the mission commander and is prominently profiled.

Henry, R. M. "Alan Shepard, Reaching for the Stars." *All Hands* (April 1982): 6-11. (G) A retrospective story of Shepard's "heroic" career written for a navy audience and published in a service magazine.

"Shepard's Space Saga." *Naval Aviation News* 42 (June 1961): 20-23. (G) A photo essay on Shepard's historic Mercury flight.

Thomas, Shirley. "Alan B. Shepard, Jr." In *Men of Space: Profiles of the Leaders in Space Research, Development, and Exploration*. Vol. 3. Philadelphia: Chilton, 1961. (A, G) Written a decade before the Apollo mission, this uncritical account chronicles Shepard's life only through his Mercury space flight, but is useful because of the level of detail.

Wainwright, Louden. *The Astronauts*. New York: Time-Life, 1960. (G) This semi-biographical account of the lives of the Mercury astronauts is a significant source of the myths surrounding the early years of the American manned space program and was largely responsible for making heroes of the astronauts.

————. "The Old Pro Gets His Shot at the Moon." *Life* (July 31, 1970). (G) Feature story, complete with the trademark *Life* photo spread, of Shepard and his 1971 lunar landing shot. Describes much about his life between the 1961 Mercury mission and the Apollo flight.

Wolfe, Tom. *The Right Stuff*. New York: Farrar, Straus, and Giroux, 1979. (G) A sweeping, popularized chronicle of the test pilots who made the postwar super-sonic revolution and the space program a reality. Emphasizing the cool courage of such men, those with "the right stuff," Wolfe describes in unforgettable terms how Chuck Yeager broke the sound barrier and other exploits through the Mercury manned spaceflight program. Prone to hyperbole, Wolfe nonetheless describes in generally accurate terms the activities of Shepard and other astronauts in the early space program.

Evaluation of Biographical Sources for Young People
Cipriano, Anthony J. *America's Journeys into Space: The Astronauts of the United States*. New York: Wanderer Books, 1979. This volume, illustrated by William Joffe Numeroff, contains biographical sketches of all the astronauts up to that time, emphasizing their courage and devotion to duty. Shepard is the first profiled.

Crocker, Chris. *Great American Astronauts*. New York: Watts, 1988. Includes a recent sketch of Shepard's career for a young audience.

Faber, Harold, and Doris Faber. "Alan Shepard: First American in Space." In *American Heroes of the 20th Century*. New York: Random House, 1967. An adequate profile of Shepard emphasizing the heroic aspects of his mission as the first American to ride a rocket into space.

Leipold, L. Edmond. *Famous Scientists and Astronauts*. New York: Denison, 1967. This book contains a sketch of Shepard, portraying him as a modern American hero.

————. *Heroes of Today—The Astronauts*. New York: Denison, 1973. Largely a rehash and updating of Leipold's earlier work on Shepard, this volume casts the astronaut in a heroic image and adds information on his Apollo mission.

Newton, Clarke. *Famous Pioneers of Space*. New York: Dodd, 1963. Profiles several people involved in the space program, including Shepard.

Shelton, William Roy. *Flights of the Astronauts*. Boston: Little, Brown, 1963. Contains a comprehensive account of Shepard's Mercury mission.

Smaus, Jewel, and Charles B. Spangler. *America's First Spaceman*. Garden City, NY: Doubleday, 1962. A biography of Shepard which describes him as a hero and role model.

Westman, Paul. *Alan Shepard: The First American in Space*. New York: Dillon Press, 1979. This biography, illustrated by Todd Grande, emphasizes the difficulties in the conquest of space and the importance of men like Shepard who were willing to risk their lives attempting to further knowledge.

Overview and Evaluation of Primary Sources

Shepard has written several autobiographical accounts and a technical paper. *We Seven* (New York: Simon and Schuster, 1962; **A, G**), written, according to the titlepage, by "The Astronauts Themselves" recounts the experiences of each of the seven Mercury astronauts. It is especially useful for its description of the public image of the astronaut corps early in the space program. Shepard wrote three sections of the book: "The Urge to Pioneer," "What to Do Until the Ship

Comes," and "A Range Around the World." Shepard also wrote, although he had some help from staff writers, "The Astronaut's Story of the Thrust into Space," *Life* (May 19, 1961; **G**). NASA made this and profiles by the other Mercury astronauts possible through a deal with Time-Life, which stipulated that proceeds would go to the astronauts as an insurance policy against failures in the space program, and features on each man appeared at strategic intervals. This one, timed to coincide with Shepard's Mercury flight, described in detail the preparations for the mission. Shepard also wrote "A Pilot's Story," *National Geographic* 130 (September 1961: 432-44; **A, G**), about his life and especially his suborbital Mercury space flight. Shepard also published one technical work: *Training by Simulation* (Washington, DC: Smithsonian Publication No. 4597, January 1965; **A**), the printed version of the first Edwin A. Link lecture delivered at the Smithsonian Institution, February 19, 1964. In it Shepard describes the development of pilot training using flight simulators.

Shepard has left no large collection of manuscript materials for the scholar seeking primary resources, but for anyone working on the early manned space program there are several collections that should be reviewed, each containing some Shepard material. The NASA History Division, NASA Headquarters, Washington, D.C., has biographical files on virtually every important person involved with the agency, and there are several on Shepard. The Johnson Space Center, Houston, Texas, has archives which contain Shepard materials, as does the Special Collections Department at nearby Rice University library, which maintains the Project Apollo archival materials. The Smithsonian Institution's National Air and Space Museum and the Manuscript Division of the Library of Congress, both in Washington, D.C., also have some materials concerning the astronaut.

Fiction and Adaptations

The most significant fictional work dealing with the space program is James A. Michener's *Space* (1982), a masterful novel describing the lives of several fictional characters involved in the American space program. As a novel it is superb, and it also contains many facts about the methods of experimentation, program management, NASA operations, and associated subjects.

A fine screen adaptation of *The Right Stuff* was released in 1981. A cast of then relatively unknown actors depicted the development of aeronautics and astronautics from 1947 through the Mercury program. Scott Glenn gave a strong performance as Alan Shepard. A box-office hit, the film also won an Academy Award for special effects.

Museums, Historical Landmarks, Societies

Johnson Space Center Museum (Houston, TX). Run by NASA, this museum contains many displays related to the manned space flight program. Alan Shepard's career, as one of the key astronauts, is depicted in several exhibits.

National Air and Space Museum (Washington, DC). Part of the Smithsonian Institution, this outstanding museum, which chronicles the development of flight, contains several exhibits relating to the Mercury program, including capsules, spacesuits, and memorabilia.

Spaceport U.S.A. (Cape Canaveral, FL). Run by NASA, this museum depicts the development of the manned space flight programs, with considerable attention placed on Project Mercury and Shepard's place in it.

Other Sources

Atkinson, Joseph D., Jr., and Jay M. Shafritz. *The Real Stuff: A History of the Astronaut Recruitment Program.* New York: Praeger, 1985. A useful survey of the methodology used to recruit and train astronauts. Although not limited to the Mercury selection, as the first recruitment program there is considerable discussion of Shepard's selection and training.

Swenson, Loyd S., Jr., James M. Grimwood, and Charles Alexander. *This New Ocean: A History of Project Mercury.* Washington, DC: National Aeronautics and Space Administration, 1966. An outstanding history of the Mercury program written under the auspices of NASA. Although broader in scope, it has significant information on the selection and training of the astronauts as well as detailed discussions of each space mission.

Wilson, K. T. "The Recovery of American Manned Spacecraft, 1961-1975." *Spaceflight* 24 (April 1982): 179-184. This article describes the recovery of thirty-one American spacecrafts after splashdown. Considerable discussion of the methods employed with the recovery of Shepard's Mercury capsule.

Roger D. Launius
NASA Chief Historian

PHILIP H. SHERIDAN
1831-1888

Chronology

Born Philip Henry Sheridan on March 6, 1831, probably in Albany, New York, the son of John and Mary Sheridan, soon moves with family to Somerset, Ohio; *1848* enters West Point; *1853* graduates from West Point and is dispatched to the frontier; *1861* serves in several staff positions after outbreak of Civil War; *1862* commissioned colonel, Second Michigan Cavalry; advances to brigadier general, distinguishing himself at Perryville (October 8) and Stones River (December 21-January 2, 1863); *1863* promoted to major general; fights in the battles of Chickamauga (September 19-20) and Chattanooga (November 23-25); *March 1864* placed in command of the Cavalry Corps, Army of the Potomac; *May 5-6, 1864* participates in the Battle of the Wilderness; *May 7-8, 1864* fights in the Battle of Spotsylvania before setting off on a series of raids south toward Richmond; *August 1864* is placed in command of Union forces in the Shenandoah Valley, defeating Confederate forces at Winchester (September 19), Fisher's Hill (September 22) and Cedar Creek (October 19), while laying waste to the Shenandoah valley; *1865* plays a leading role in Grant's Appomattox campaign, striking blows at Five Forks (April 1), Sayler's Creek (April 6) and Appomattox Court House (April 9), where his horsemen cut off Lee's retreat and force the surrender of the Army of Northern Virginia; dispatched to Rio Grande in May to guard the frontier with Mexico; *1866-1867* plays a major role in the military supervision of Reconstruction in Louisiana until his removal as commander of the Fifth Military District in August 1867; *1868-1869* as commander of the Department of the Missouri, subdues tribes in a series of campaigns along the southern plains; *1869* promoted to lieutenant general and placed in command of the Division of the Missouri; *1870-1871* serves as military observer during Franco-Prussian War; maintains order in Chicago after the fire in October 1871; *1874-1875* conducts Red River War; *1876-1877* campaigns against the Sioux; *1883* is appointed general-in-chief, United States Army; *1888* completes his autobiography; promoted to full general; dies August 5 at Nonquitt, Massachusetts, and is buried at Arlington National Cemetery.

Activities of Historical Significance

Next to Ulysses S. Grant and William T. Sherman, Philip H. Sheridan ranks as one of the North's most successful commanders, overshadowing the substantial contributions of George H. Thomas and George G. Meade to the success of the Union on the battlefield. In part this is because Sheridan won with flair and dash; his ride from Winchester to Cedar Creek was immortalized in song, verse, and art. Such an image obscures both Sheridan's shortcomings and skills as a commander—skills that may have made him Grant's favorite subordinate. At Stones River Sheridan's division saved the Army of the Cumberland from defeat; at Chattanooga it was his men who broke the seemingly impregnable Confederate position on Missionary Ridge. Sheridan's victories in 1864 were crucial to bolstering Northern morale on the eve of the presidential election, going far to assure Abraham Lincoln a second term, while denying the Shenandoah Valley to the Confederacy. In the Appomattox campaign Sheridan played a critical role; his victory at Five Forks forced Robert E. Lee to evacuate Petersburg and Richmond, breaking nearly ten months of siege warfare; after smashing Lee's rear guard at Sayler's Creek, his rapid movement corralled the Confederate commander at Appomattox, forcing him to surrender to Grant.

After the Civil War Sheridan remained a controversial and colorful figure. His supervision of Reconstruction in Louisiana and Texas during a rather tumultuous time earned him the praise of Republicans and blacks and the scorn of President Andrew Johnson, who removed him in 1867. In 1875 President Grant dispatched Sheridan to restore order to New Orleans in the wake of an attempted coup by white supremacists, but Sheridan's recommendation that white terrorists be treated as "banditti" outraged those northerners who had grown indifferent to the fate of the Reconstruction experiment. Sheridan also played a major role in directing the efforts of the United States Army to subdue frontier tribes, although he is not recognized as an Indian fighter.

Overview of Biographical Sources

Although Sheridan played a major role in the military operations of the Civil War, there is no modern scholarly biography of the general's entire life. Rather, studies tend to concentrate on his Civil War career, his involvement in Reconstruction, and his activities on the frontier. Richard O'Connor, *Sheridan the Inevitable* (1953), and Joseph Hergesheimer, *Sheridan: A Military Narrative* (1931), while highly readable, are dated on Sheridan the Civil War leader; Joseph Dawson, *Army Generals and Reconstruction: Louisiana, 1862-1877* (1982), and William Richter, "General Phil Sheridan, the Historians, and Reconstruction," *Civil War History* 33 (June 1987), provide contrasting evaluations of his service in Louisiana and Texas during Reconstruction; and Paul Andrew Hutton's *Phil Sheridan and His Army* (1985) is preeminent among explorations of Sheridan's role in the Indian wars.

Sheridan's historical importance still demands a full-scale biography that integrates all of these activities and focuses on his personality.

Evaluation of Principal Biographical Sources

Burr, Frank A., and Richard J. L. Hinton. *The Life of General Philip H. Sheridan: Its Romance and Reality.* Providence, RI: J. A. and R. A. Reid, 1888. (A) An early tribute to Sheridan and the best of the first biographies.

Davies, Henry E. *General Sheridan.* New York: D. Appleton, 1909. (A, G) An astute examination of Sheridan's military career, written by a former subordinate.

Frost, Lawrence A. *The Phil Sheridan Album: A Pictorial Biography of Philip Henry Sheridan.* Seattle, WA: Superior, 1968. (A, G) An engrossing pictorial account of Sheridan's life, although some of the portraits verge on redundancy.

Hergesheimer, Joseph. *Sheridan: A Military Narrative.* Boston: Houghton Mifflin, 1931. (A, G) A colorful, if dated, biography of Sheridan's military exploits during the Civil War.

Hutton, Paul A. *Phil Sheridan and His Army.* Lincoln: University of Nebraska Press, 1985. (A, G) Clearly the best examination of Sheridan's post-Civil War activity. While it concentrates on Sheridan's responsibilities on the frontier, several chapters address his involvement in Reconstruction politics and other aspects of the United States Army from 1865 to 1888.

Hutton, Paul A., ed. *Soldiers West: Biographies from the Military Frontier.* Lincoln: University of Nebraska Press, 1987. (A, G) Included in this work is Hutton's short introduction to Sheridan's military career on the frontier.

O'Connor, Richard. *Sheridan the Inevitable.* Indianapolis: Bobbs-Merrill, 1953. (A, G) A very readable biography, but badly in need of updating.

Rister, Carl C. *Border Command: General Phil Sheridan in the West.* Norman: University of Oklahoma Press, 1944. (A, G) A concise account of Sheridan's frontier campaigns, dated in light of recent literature.

Weigley, Russell. "Philip H. Sheridan: A Personality Profile." *Civil War Times Illustrated* 7 (July 1968): 4-11. (G) A good, brief introduction to Sheridan.

Overview and Evaluation of Primary Sources

Major collections of Sheridan's correspondence are located at the Library of Congress, the Chicago Historical Society, and the Huntington Library. The general tells his own story in *Personal Memoirs of Philip Henry Sheridan* (2 vols. New York: Charles L. Webster, 1888; **A, G**), an account which stops at 1871. These memoirs fall far short of the standard set by Sheridan's comrades Grant and Sherman. The National Archives contains much material relating to Sheridan; for Sheridan's correspondence with Grant, refer to *The Papers of Ulysses S. Grant,* edited by John Y. Simon (18 vols. to date. Carbondale: Southern Illinois University Press, 1967-; **A, G**).

Museums, Historical Landmarks, Societies

Appomattox Court House National Historical Park (Appomattox, VA). The site of the final confrontation between the Army of the Potomac and the Army of Northern Virginia and the surrender of Robert E. Lee to Ulysses S. Grant. After blocking Lee's route west, Sheridan was present at the surrender in the parlor of Wilmer McLean's farmhouse.

Arlington National Cemetery (Arlington, VA). Sheridan's grave, marked by a dark pyramid, is in a group of trees just outside the front entrance to the Arlington mansion, within sight of the graves of John and Robert Kennedy.

Cedar Creek Battlefield (Middletown, VA). At present, Civil War enthusiasts and others are engaged in an endeavor to save this battlefield site. Belle Grove, owned by the National Trust for Historic Preservation, served as Union headquarters during the battle.

Chicamauga and Chattanooga National Military Park (Chattanooga, TN). Of most interest is the position on Missionary Ridge which Sheridan attacked on November 25, 1863.

Five Forks (Intersection of Virginia S.R. 613 and 627, near Interstate 85). Another target of preservation efforts, the road junction was at the center of the Confederate position.

Perryville Battlefield State Park (Perryville, KY). This small battlefield park is located thirty-five miles southwest of Lexington. Sheridan's position, the Turpin House, is located due west of Perryville.

Sailor's Creek Battlefield State Park (Farmville, VA). Also known as Sayler's Creek, this battlefield saw the crushing of Lee's rear guard by Sheridan's cavalry and two infantry corps.

Sheridan Circle (Washington, DC). Located just west of Dupont Circle on Embassy Row, the circle contains a statue of Sheridan, mounted on his horse Rienzi, rallying his soldiers at Cedar Creek.

Smithsonian Institution (Washington, DC). Sheridan's horse, Rienzi, is preserved on display in the Museum of American History.

Stones River National Battlefield (Murfeesboro, TN). Sheridan's stand here may have saved the Army of the Cumberland from disaster.

Fiction and Adaptations

A recreation of Sheridan's ride appeared in D. W. Griffith's film, *Abraham Lincoln* (1930); otherwise, "Little Phil" has had to play second fiddle to his subordinate George Custer in two movies, *Santa Fe Trail* (1942), where David Bruce played Sheridan, and *They Died with Their Boots On* (1942), with John Litel as Sheridan. Neither motion picture bears much resemblance to reality. More recently, Dean Stockwell played Sheridan on *Son of the Morning Star* (1990), a television movie portrayal of the life of George Armstrong Custer. Douglas C. Jones's *The Court-Martial of George Armstrong Custer* (1976) features Sheridan in its interesting "what-if" about Little Big Horn, while Bruce Catton's *Banners at Shenandoah* (1955) is a fictional account of one of Sheridan's soldiers who serves as a spy for the general; it is intended for young readers. Thomas Buchanan Read's "Sheridan's Ride," reprinted in Lewis's *The Guns of Cedar Creek*, a poem written in the immediate aftermath of Cedar Creek, became almost as well-known as Tennyson's "Charge of the Light Brigade," although Sheridan believed that what listeners liked most about the poem was the description of his horse, Rienzi.

Other Sources

Catton, Bruce. *Grant Takes Command*. Boston: Little, Brown, 1969. Sets Sheridan's operations within the larger context of Grant's Virginia campaign.

Dawson, Joseph G. *Army Generals and Reconstruction: Louisiana, 1862-1867*. Baton Rouge: Louisiana State University Press, 1982. An excellent study of Sheridan's activities in Louisiana during Reconstruction.

Grant, Ulysses S. *Personal Memoirs of U. S. Grant*. 2 vols. New York: Charles L. Webster, 1885-1886. Makes clear Grant's admiration for his subordinate, overlooking Sheridan's faults.

Lewis, Thomas A. *The Guns of Cedar Creek*. New York: Harper and Row, 1988. More valuable for its personality sketches than for its account of the battle itself, Lewis's fast-paced narrative suffers from occasional factual errors.

————. *The Shenandoah in Flames: The Valley Campaign of 1864*. Alexandria, VA: Time-Life Books, 1987. A colorful pictorial history of Sheridan's most important Civil War campaign.

Marshal, S. L. A. *Crimsoned Prairie: The Wars between the United States and the Plains Indians during the Winning of the West*. New York: Scribner, 1972.

Rable, George C. *But There Was No Peace: The Role of Violence in the Politics of Reconstruction*. Athens: University of Georgia Press, 1984. Contains a discussion of the New Orleans riot of 1866 and the attempted coup of 1875, incidents of Louisiana Reconstruction in which Sheridan played a prominent role.

Richter, William L. "General Phil Sheridan, the Historians, and Reconstruction." *Civil War History* 33 (June 1987): 131-154. Argues that efforts to rehabilitate Sheridan's Reconstruction services are misguided because the hero of Cedar Creek's "stubborn, single purpose of punishing the South lacked a Lincolnian sense of compassion and emphasized only hatred."

Simpson, Brooks D. *Let Us Have Peace: Ulysses S. Grant and the Politics of War and Reconstruction, 1861-1868*. Chapel Hill: University of North Carolina Press, 1991. Contains a discussion of Sheridan's activities on the Mexican border and in Louisiana following the Civil War, emphasizing his relationship to Grant and Andrew Johnson.

Stackpole, Edward J. *Sheridan in the Shenandoah*. Harrisburg, PA: Stackpole, 1961. Long the standard account of the operations during the fall of 1864.

Starr, Stephen A. *The Union Cavalry in the Civil War: The War in the East from Gettysburg to Appomattox, 1863-1865*. Baton Rouge: Louisiana State University Press, 1981. A fine operational history of the mounted army of the Union calvary under Sheridan's command.

Utley, Robert M. *Frontier Regulars: The United States Army and the Indian, 1866-1891.* New York: Macmillan, 1973. The standard account of the frontier wars after Appomattox.

Wert, Jeffry D. *From Winchester to Cedar Creek: The Shenandoah Campaign of 1864.* 2d ed. New York: Simon and Schuster, 1989. The best account of Sheridan's valley campaign available.

Brooks Donohue Simpson
Arizona State University

JEDEDIAH S. SMITH
1799-1831

Chronology

Born Jedediah Strong Smith on January 6, 1799, in Bainbridge, New York, the sixth child of Jedediah and Sally Strong Smith, both of old New England pioneer stock; *1799-1811* spends early life in the upper Susquehanna Valley; *1811-1817* lives with family in Erie County, Pennsylvania, and attends school; *1817-1821* pioneers with family in the Western Reserve of Ohio; *1821* moves to northern Illinois; *1822* travels to St. Louis in the spring to seek work that would take him into the Oregon country where he would be able to become a trapper; *June 1822-Spring 1823* makes first trip up the Missouri River, working for William H. Ashley, and travels as far as the mouth of the Musselshell River; *Spring 1823* carries an urgent message to Ashley in St. Louis about the need for additional horses; *June 1, 1823* survives battle at the Arikara tribal villages in which thirteen traders are killed; *October 1823* mauled by a bear and scarred for life, hereafter he wears his hair long to hide the scars; *Winter 1823-1824* stays in the Wind River Valley (present-day Dubois), Wyoming; *February-March 1824* travels down Sweetwater River to mouth of the Big Sandy River and over South Pass, the effective discovery of this significant route over the continental divide; *October 1824* meets Hudson Bay Company's Snake Country expedition and travels with them to Flathead Post; *1825* becomes a partner of Ashley and the leader of field parties; *1826* Smith, David E. Jackson, and William L. Sublette buy out Ashley and form their own company; *1826-1827* undertakes a significant exploration from Cache Valley to the Southwest in search of new trapping grounds, via Great Salt Lake southward onto the Colorado Plateau and along the Colorado River to the Mohave Desert and from there to San Gabriel, California; returns through the San Joaquin Valley and turns east across the mountains via the American River; *July 3, 1827* arrives at the rendezvous in the Great Basin as the first white American to cross the Sierra Nevada from west to east; *1827-1828* retraces route to southern California, travelling by ship from San Gabriel to San Francisco and then north by land into Oregon; *July 13, 1828* party is attacked by American Indians on the Umpqua River and all but four out of eighteen are killed; leads survivors to Fort Vancouver; *Summer 1828* returns to rendezvous in Great Basin by travelling through Hudson Bay Company trapping lands; *1828-1829* leads additional trapping parties into the upper Rockies; *1830* retires from fur trade and enters the Santa Fe supply trade; *April 10, 1831* leaves Independence, Missouri, with a wagon train bound for Santa Fe, New Mexico; *1831* killed by Comanches on May 27, while searching for water for the wagon train on the Santa Fe trail.

Activities of Historical Significance

Smith's explorations of the Rockies and Far West in the 1820s rank as some of the most significant expeditions of the nineteenth century. His skill as a frontiersman, as well as his undeniable ambition to develop a preeminent position for his company in the fur trade, combine with these expeditions to establish Smith as a heroic figure in the American West. In addition, his stoic personality and religious countenance became a model for his fellow fur traders.

In 1824 Smith effectively discovered South Pass (in present-day Wyoming) which had earlier been traversed but forgotten by returning Astorians. The importance of this discovery cannot be overestimated. It provided a route for trappers to cross the Rockies into the Great Basin without using the Missouri River. It also allowed settlers to take their wagons on an easy route along the Platte and Sweetwater Rivers, then cross the mountains at South Pass on their way to Oregon or California. It made possible the great overland migrations along the Oregon Trail that began in the 1840s.

Jedediah Smith's 1826-1827 expedition travelled overland from the Great Basin to California and back. Undertaken to locate new trapping grounds, the expedition explored the Great Salt Lake and moved southward onto the Colorado Plateau. Pioneering along the Colorado River, Smith journeyed to the Mohave Desert and visited San Gabriel, California, where he made contact with Spanish officials. He explored northward through the San Joaquin Valley and then turned eastward across the Sierra Nevada range, the first record of an eastward crossing, via the American River. By the time of Smith's return to the rendezvous the next summer, he had acquired more geographical knowledge about the Far West than any other American.

Smith's last great expedition took place in 1827 to 1828 when he retraced his route to southern California. He then moved northward along the West Coast, travelling by ship from San Gabriel to San Francisco, and eventually to Fort Vancouver, the Hudson Bay Company outpost in the Oregon territory. In the summer of 1828 he returned to the Great Basin trappers' rendezvous. Once again, Smith's efforts led to the rapid expansion of geographical knowledge, but he also gave U.S. authorities information about the strength of Spanish and British claims on the region.

In summary, Smith must be credited with being the first to find and recognize the natural gateway to the Oregon country through South Pass; the first overland traveler to reach California; the first white man to cross the Sierra Nevada; and the first to travel overland from California to the Columbia. Unlike most other explorers of the nineteenth century, Smith's expeditions were not sponsored by the federal government but were the byproduct of efforts to further his company's fur-trading business.

Overview of Biographical Sources

In the nineteenth century Smith's activities were overshadowed by explorers with lesser accomplishments but greater public relations abilities, most particularly Kit Carson and John Charles Frémont. Both men, who joined together in some exploring parties, had the benefit of talented chroniclers who brought their names to the attention of the American public. They became legendary western figures, while the quiet and presumably shy Smith was all but forgotten. Among the trappers of the Far West, however, Smith was an acknowledged leader, a blazer of trails, and a maker of history. His proper place in the story of western exploration began to be recognized in the early twentieth century through the efforts of Harrison C. Dale, *The Ashley-Smith Explorations and the Discovery of a Central Route to the Pacific, 1822-1829* (1918, 1941), and Maurice L. Sullivan, *Jedediah Smith, Trader and Trail Breaker* (1936). These men began to study Smith's journals in detail and piece together the crazy-quilt of interrelationships and activities of the early mountain men. By far the most significant biography of Smith is Dale L. Morgan's masterful *Jedediah Smith and the Opening of the West* (1953), which carefully analyzes the fragments of Smith's life within the context of the fur trade industry in the Far West. Smith is also discussed in numerous other accounts of the Western fur trade.

Evaluation of Principal Biographical Sources

Carter, Harvey L. "Jedediah Smith." In *The Mountain Men and the Fur Trade of the Far West*, edited by LeRoy C. Hafen. Glendale, CA: Arthur H. Clark, 1971. (A, G) This is an excellent short account of Smith's life, raising most of the major issues and providing a concise discussion of his explorations and accomplishments.

Goetzmann, William H. *Exploration and Empire: The Explorer and the Scientist in the Winning of the American West*. New York: Alfred A. Knopf, 1966. (A, G) This Pulitzer Prize-winning history deals with the largest issues in the exploration of the American West, but devotes considerable attention to Smith's activities.

Hall, James. "Captain Jedediah Strong Smith: A Eulogy of That Most Romantic and Pious of Mountainmen, First American by Land into California." *Illinois Monthly Magazine* 22 (June 1832): 393-398. (A, G) A fine account of Smith's life written not long after his death.

Miller, Helen Markley. *Jedediah Smith on the Far Frontier*. New York: G. P. Putnam's Sons, 1971. (Y) This biography, written for young readers, depicts Smith as a virtuous hero who earned his reputation on the western frontier. It is illustrated by Ted A. Xaras.

Morgan, Dale L. *Jedediah Smith and the Opening of the West*. Indianapolis: Bobbs-Merrill, 1953. Reprint. Lincoln: University of Nebraska Press, 1964. (A, G) In this standard biography of Smith, Morgan blends a rich understanding of the overall fur trade with information about Smith and his career. It presents Smith as a Jacksonian capitalist, seeking to use the expanding fur trade as a basis for advancing his fortunes. While a dedicated explorer, like a true young man of business, Smith pursued those expeditions as a means of enhancing his business opportunities by opening new trapping areas and discovering more efficient routes of travel.

Neihardt, John G. *The Splendid Wayfaring: The Exploits and Adventures of Jedediah Smith and the Ashley-Henry Men*. New York: Macmillan, 1920. Reprint. Lincoln: University of Nebraska Press, 1970. (A, G) This is an early popular discussion of the Rocky Mountain fur trade during its heyday in the 1820s, emphasizing the career of Jedediah Smith. It is a readable but unsophisticated work.

Smith, Alson J. *Men Against the Mountains: Jedediah Smith and the South West Expedition of 1826-1829*. New York: John Day, 1965. (A, G) A popular, well-written account of Smith's activities during one period of significant trailblazing. It is based on the scholarly work of Dale Morgan, Harrison Dale, and Maurice Sullivan.

Sullivan, Maurice L. *Jedediah Smith: Trader and Trail Breaker*. New York: Press of the Pioneers, 1936. (A, G) After years of studying Smith's explorations, Sullivan distilled his knowledge into this biography. While it is a significant and readable biography, its style is flamboyant and perhaps elevates Smith beyond his place in the history of the West. Sullivan died after the book was completed but before it appeared in print. Accordingly, a brief foreword and bibliographical notes were added by Rufus Rockwell Wilson. Illustrations by Howard Simon.

Sunder, John E. *Bill Sublette, Mountain Man.* Norman: University of Oklahoma Press, 1959. (**A, G**) A fine biography of one of Smith's fur trading partners.

Overview and Evaluation of Primary Sources

There have been several works containing accounts of Smith's activities. Perhaps the earliest was Harrison C. Dale's *The Ashley-Smith Explorations and the Discovery of a Central Route to the Pacific, 1822-1829* (Cleveland: Arthur H. Clark, 1918. Rev. ed. Glendale, CA: Arthur H. Clark, 1941; **A, G**). For years one of the major sources for Smith's activities, Dale rescued Smith from obscurity and established him as a force in the exploration of the American West. One of his major themes was the relationship among fur trading, economics, and exploration. It is an edited work containing an account by William H. Ashley of his trip down the Green River in 1824-1825; a fragmentary journal of Harrison G. Rogers, who accompanied Smith in 1826-1829; and a letter from Smith to William Clark written in 1827 briefly describing some of his Southwest expedition. Following on Dale's heels, Maurice S. Sullivan published *The Travels of Jedediah Smith* (Santa Ana, CA: Fine Arts, 1934; **A, G**), an important book which contained a transcript of Smith's original journal, copied by a friend, Samuel Parkman, in 1831.

A giant in the scholarship of Smith, as he was in the trans-Mississippi West in general, Dale L. Morgan edited two significant books on the trapper and explorer. Teaming with Carl I. Wheat, he coedited *Jedediah Smith and his Maps of the American West* (San Francisco: California Historical Society, 1954; **A, G**). This book published Smith's maps of the West and analyzed their importance for subsequent cartography and knowledge about the geography of the region. Morgan also edited *The West of William H. Ashley . . . Recorded in Diaries of Ashley and his Contemporaries, 1822-1838* (Denver: Old West, 1964; **A, G**), an excellent edit of Ashley's fur trade activities with significant attention to Smith's operations.

Recently, George R. Brooks edited *The Southwest Expedition of Jedediah S. Smith: His Personal Account of the Journey to California, 1826-1827* (Glendale, CA: Arthur H. Clark, 1977. Reprint. Lincoln: University of Nebraska Press, 1989; **A, G**), which contains portions of the recently discovered journal of Smith's California trip.

Smith left no large collection of manuscript materials, but for anyone researching the trans-Mississippi western fur trade all roads lead to the Missouri Historical Society, Jefferson Memorial Building-Forest Park, St. Louis, Missouri, which holds thousands of items on the subject. Especially significant are the papers of Smith, and of William L. Sublette and William H. Ashley, both for a time Smith's partners. There are also some Smith letters at the Kansas Historical Society,

Topeka, and a manuscript at the Jennewein Western Collection, Dakota Wesleyan University, Mitchell, South Dakota.

Fiction and Adaptations

Smith has been the subject of only a few fictional works. The most significant is John G. Neihardt, *The Song of Jed Smith* (1941), a most difficult book to categorize. It is an epic poem of Smith's exploits, and while accurate in most respects it takes some literary license. It is the third volume, but the last completed, of Neihardt's epic work, *A Cycle of the West*, which told the story of certain heroic aspects of westward expansion. The books of poetry in this series included: *The Song of Three Friends* (1919), *The Song of Hugh Glass* (1915), *The Song of Jed Smith* (1941), *The Song of the Indian Wars* (1928), and *The Song of the Messiah* (1935).

Only a few adult novels have been written about Smith. Olive Woolley Burt's *Jedediah Smith: Fur Trapper of the Old West* (1951) is an unsophisticated work glorifying the exploits of the trapper. Merritt P. Allen wrote *The Sun Trail* (1943), an escapist work that took the minds of readers off the horrors of World War II. Neither of these works is particularly useful.

Fictional books written for young people which use Smith as a role model include: Olive Woolley Burt, *Jed Smith: Young Western Explorer* (1963), a revision of her, *Young Jed Smith: Westering Boy* (1954), part of the Childhood of Famous Americans Series; and Frank Brown Latham, *Jed Smith: Trail Blazer* (1952).

Famous Trailblazers of Early America: Jedediah Smith by Doyce Y. Nunis, Jr., (1973) is a filmstrip, designed for classroom use, describing the life and career of Jedediah Smith as a mountain man and trapper who explored the upper Mississippi River, the Rocky Mountains, the Mohave Desert, and other parts of the West.

Museums, Historical Landmarks, Societies

Jefferson National Expansion Memorial (St. Louis, MO). An excellent museum dedicated to the trans-Mississippi West, it contains several exhibits relating to the fur trade and Smith's role in the exploration of the region.

Other Sources

Chittenden, Hiram M. *The American Fur Trade of the Far West.* 2 vols. New York: Francis P. Harper, 1902. An exhaustive recounting of the origins, development, and decline of the fur trade that was so much a part of Smith's life.

Cleland, Robert Glass. *This Reckless Breed of Men: The Trappers and Fur Traders of the Southwest.* New York: Alfred A. Knopf, 1950. Reprint. 1963. A fine general description of the fur trade in the southern Rockies, describing some of the activities of Smith in the region.

Farquhar, Francis P. "Jedediah Smith and the First Crossing of the Sierra Nevada." *Sierra Club Bulletin* 28 (June 1943): 36-53. A concise discussion of his significant 1828 expedition across the Sierra Nevada.

Merriam, C. Hart. "Earliest Crossings of the Deserts of Utah and Nevada to Southern California: Route of Jedediah S. Smith in 1826." *Quarterly of the California Historical Society* 2 (July 1923): 228-236. A useful description of the epic 1826 exploring party.

————. "Jedediah Smith's Route Across the Sierra in 1827." *Quarterly of the California Historical Society* 3 (April 1924): 25-29. Another worthwhile description of a single Smith exploring party.

Wood, Raymond F. "Jedediah Smith: A Protestant in Catholic California." *Pacific Historian* 21 (1977): 68-79. A fine description of the difference of religions between the Catholic Californians and the Protestant Smith.

Roger D. Launius
NASA Chief Historian

JOSEPH STORY
1779-1845

Chronology

Born Joseph Story on September 18, 1779, in Marblehead, Massachusetts, to Dr. Elisha Story, a medical doctor, and Mehitable Pedrick Story; *1795* enters Harvard College; *1798* graduates from Harvard; studies law under eminent Massachusetts jurist Samuel Sewell, then under Samuel Putnam; *1801* passes bar and opens a law practice in Salem, Massachusetts; *1804* marries Mary Lynde Oliver on December 9; she dies the following June; *1805-1808* serves in Massachusetts state legislature; *1808* on August 27 marries Sarah Waldo Emerson; is elected to the United States House of Representatives; *1811* elected speaker, Massachusetts state legislature; on November 15 is nominated associate justice of the Supreme Court by James Madison, and is confirmed three days later; *1816* writes majority opinion in *Martin v. Hunter's Lessee*; *1829* appointed professor of law at Harvard; *1832* publishes first of his *Commentaries* on American law; *1837* issues dissent in *The Charles River Bridge v. The Warren Bridge*; *1841* writes majority opinion in *United States v. Amistad*; *1842* delivers majority opinion in *Swift v. Tyson* and *Prigg v. Pennsylvania*; *1845* dies September 10 and is buried in Mount Auburn Cemetery.

Activities of Historical Significance

As a jurist and scholar Joseph Story played a preeminent role in the creation of an American legal tradition in the early republic. Among his most critical Supreme Court opinions was his majority opinion in *Martin v. Hunter's Lessee* (1816), which established the appellate jurisdiction of the Supreme Court over state court decisions; *United States v. Amistad* (1841), which declared free, slaves who had mutinied against the crew of a Spanish slave trader; *Swift v. Tyson* (1842), which declared that federal courts were not bound to follow state law in reviewing common-law decisions; and *Prigg v. Pennsylvania* (1842), which, while striking down a Pennsylvania "personal liberty law" prohibiting the seizure and removal of fugitives as a violation of the Fugitive Slave Act of 1793 and the Constitution, also stated that enforcement of the Constitution's fugitive slave clause was up to the federal government. This last declaration encouraged northern states to pass laws forbidding state officials from assisting in the arrest and return of fugitive slaves. These decisions helped build the foundations of federal judicial power, and establish groundwork to deter slavery consistent with the Constitution. Story's most notable dissent came in *The Charles River Bridge v. The Warren Bridge* (1837), when he held that the charter extended to the Charles River Bridge Company had been impaired by another charter to the Warren Bridge Company.

As important as were Story's contributions on the bench, they were matched by his role in the education of American lawyers and by his commentaries on American law that became benchmark authorities. He was instrumental in making Harvard Law School preeminent in the training of American lawyers.

Overview of Biographical Sources

Story's biographers are a small but dedicated lot, devoting themselves to rescuing Story from the shadow of the more famous John Marshall. Gerald T. Dunne's pioneering effort, *Justice Joseph Story and the Rise of the Supreme Court* (1970), laid out much of the terrain; James McClellan, *Joseph Story and the American Constitution* (1971), carefully examines Story's constitutional thought and deserves consideration; and R. Kent Newmyer's biography, *Supreme Court Justice Joseph Story: Statesman of the Old Republic* (1985), rich with information and analysis, is a fine tribute to its subject. Story's biographers view him favorably, although Newmyer highlights that Story was not always a selfless statesman. Perhaps the only reasons more scholars have not focused on Story's blurring of professional ethics (as with his correspondence with Daniel Webster about *Dartmouth College v. Woodward*, a case that Webster would argue before, among others, Story) is because Story was not alone in engaging in such questionable communication.

Evaluation of Principal Biographical Sources

Dunne, Gerald T. *Justice Joseph Story and the Rise of the Supreme Court.* New York: Simon and Schuster, 1970. (**A, G**) The first scholarly, full-length biography of Story, this study remains helpful, although it has been eclipsed as the definitive life by Newmyer's biography.

McClellan, James. *Joseph Story and the American Constitution.* Norman: University of Oklahoma Press, 1971. (**A**) A careful and approving analysis of Story's Cconstitutional views, relating them to natural law theory.

Newmyer, R. Kent. *Supreme Court Justice Joseph Story: Statesman of the Old Republic.* Chapel Hill: University of North Carolina Press, 1985. (**A, G**) The best and most complete biography of Story, grounded in an appreciation of the republican ideology which Story tried to preserve and promote as legal scholar and jurist.

Schwartz, Mortimer D., and John G. Logan, eds. *Joseph Story: A Collection of Writings By and About an Eminent American Jurist*. New York: Oceana Publications, 1959. (**A**) A selection of primary source material exploring different facets of Story's life.

Overview and Evaluation of Primary Sources

Major collections of Story's papers are at the Library of Congress; the Massachusetts Historical Society, Boston; the University of Texas, Austin; and the University of Michigan, Ann Arbor. Other collections are at the New York Historical Society; Yale University; the Essex Institute, Salem, Mass.; Harvard University; Philadelphia's Free Library; the Huntington Library; and the Pierpont Morgan Library, New York. William Wetmore Story, ed., *Life and Letters of Joseph Story* (2 vols.; Boston: Little, Brown, 1851; **A**) and Charles Warren, ed., *The Story-Marshall Correspondence, 1819-1831* (New York: New York University School of Law, 1942; **A**) contain valuable material. Four numbers of the *Proceedings of the Massachusetts Historical Society,* second series (14 [1900-1901], 15 [1901-1902], 49 [1915-1916], and 53 [1919-1920]) reprint Story's correspondence. A bibliography of Story's voluminous writings is in Newmyer's biography, including the dozen volumes of *Commentaries,* which first appeared between 1832 and 1845.

Other Sources

Freyer, Tony. *Harmony & Dissonance: The Swift & Erie Cases in American Federalism*. New York: New York University Press, 1981. Explores the ramifications of Story's decision in *Swift v. Tyson* (1842) that federal courts were not compelled to follow state law in common-law litigation—a decision eventually reversed in *Erie v. Tompkins* (1938).

Haskins, George L., and Herbert A. Johnson. *Foundations of Power: John Marshall, 1801-15. The Oliver Wendell Holmes Devise History of the Supreme Court of the United States,* vol. 2. New York: Macmillan, 1981. A massive study of the early years of the Marshall Court and Story's early tenure on the bench.

Horwitz, Morton J. *The Transformation of American Law, 1780-1860*. Cambridge: Harvard University Press, 1977. An important study, showing how court decisions helped create a favorable environment for economic growth and business enterprise. Includes discussions of several of Story's decisions, including *Swift v. Tyson.*

Jones, Howard. *Mutiny on the Amistad: The Saga of a Slave Revolt and its Impact on American Abolition, Law, and Diplomacy.* New York: Oxford University Press, 1987. An account of *United States v. Amistad* (1841), in which Story's majority opinion declared that the slaves who had overthrown the captain and crew of the Spanish slave ship *Amistad* were free.

Kutler, Stanley I. *Privilege and Creative Destruction: The Charles River Bridge Case.* Philadelphia: J. B. Lippincott, 1971. A study of the classic contest between property rights and public welfare, defined in terms of economic opportunity. Kutler's criticism of Story's dissent in this case is extreme; Newmyer's biography provides a useful and informed corrective.

Morris, Thomas D. *Free Men All: The Personal Liberty Laws of the North, 1780-1861.* Baltimore: Johns Hopkins University Press, 1974. Sets *Prigg v. Pennsylvania* in context of northern efforts through legislation to hamper southern attempts to recover fugitive slaves.

Newmyer, R. Kent. *The Supreme Court under Marshall and Taney.* Arlington Heights, IL: Harlan Davidson, 1968. A short interpretive study of the Supreme Court during Story's career.

Swisher, Carl B. *The Taney Period, 1836-64. The Oliver Wendell Holmes Devise History of the Supreme Court of the United States,* Vol. 5. New York: Macmillan, 1974. Covers Story's final years on the Court, when he shook Marshall's shadow to establish his own legacy.

White, G. Edward. *The Marshall Court and Cultural Change, 1815-35. The Oliver Wendell Holmes Devise History of the Supreme Court of the United States,* Vols. 3 and 4 (combined). New York: Macmillan, 1988. A careful examination of the heyday and decline of the Marshall Court.

—————. *The American Judicial Tradition: Profiles of Leading American Judges.* New York; Oxford University Press, 1976. Includes a chapter discussing Story, Lemuel Shaw, and James Kent and the evolution of the concept of property rights in Jacksonian America.

Brooks Donohue Simpson
Arizona State University

J. E. B. STUART
1833-1864

Chronology

Born James Ewell Brown Stuart on February 2, 1833, on Laurel Hill plantation in Patrick County, Virginia, to Archibald Stuart, a farmer, and Elizabeth Letcher Stuart; *1848-1850* attends Emory and Henry College; *1850* enters West Point; *1854* graduates thirteenth in a class of forty-six and is appointed second lieutenant in the Mounted Rifles in Texas; *March 1855* transferred to the First U.S. Cavalry in Kansas where he spends much of the next six years; *November 14, 1855* marries Flora St. George Cooke, daughter of Colonel Philip St. George Cooke; *December 20, 1855* promoted to first lieutenant; *summer 1859* while in the East, takes sealed message to Colonel Robert E. Lee from Washington and then accompanies him to Harper's Ferry where he recognizes John Brown; *January 15, 1861* writes to Jefferson Davis, asking for a position in the Confederate army; *May 1861* appointed colonel of Virginia infantry and captain of Confederate cavalry; *July 1861* plays important role in the victory of First Manassas at the head of the First Virginia Cavalry; *September 1861* promoted to brigadier general; *July 1862* Stuart's cavalry plays a significant role at the Seven Days Campaign, but his foolhardy behavior loses the strategically valuable Evelington Heights; *August-September 1862* excels at Second Manassas and is appointed major general; *October 1862* conducts an abortive raid into Pennsylvania; *December 13, 1862* fights well and dumfounds critics at the Battle of Fredericksburg; *winter 1862-1863* holds the Rappahannock Line; *June 9, 1863* leads troops at the Battle of Brandy Station, Virginia; *July 2, 1863* arrives at the Battle of Gettysburg later than expected and questionably has a role in Lee's defeat by depriving him of accurate information; *May 1864* while trying to get between Sheridan's troops and Richmond, is wounded on May 11 by a dismounted Union cavalryman; *May 12, 1864* dies in Richmond and is buried there in the Hollywood Cemetery.

Activities of Historical Significance

Jeb Stuart is one of the most romantic figures to have emerged from the Civil War, perhaps because he died before Appomattox and had no peacetime career. His prowess as a cavalry leader and organizer was unquestioned, although his excessive self-regard and consequent foolhardiness led him to lose strategic ground or, with tragic consequences in the case of Gettysburg, arrive too late to participate constructively in reconnaissance or battle. Nonetheless, his death was a blow, both for the military strength of the South and for the morale of his troops. Lee, when told of his death, sorrowfully remarked that Stuart "never brought me a false piece of information," and "I can scarcely think of him without weeping." In the years after the Civil War, as the myth of the "Lost Cause" took root in many Southerners' hearts, Stuart became an important symbol of the chivalry, panache, and idealism of the Old South as they remembered it. In many ways, Stuart's life and myth say as much about the South after the Civil War as before and during it.

Overview of Biographical Sources

There are several Stuart biographies, as befits such a dashing, swaggering figure; they range from pedestrian to excellent. Emory M. Thomas, *Bold Dragoon: The Life of J. E. B. Stuart* (1986) is by far the best, but Burke Davis, *Jeb Stuart: The Last Cavalier* (1957) is also of value, and they are both easily found in libraries and bookstores.

Evaluation of Principal Biographical Sources

Davis, Burke. *Jeb Stuart: The Last Cavalier*. New York: Rinehart, 1957. (**A, G**) Davis, the author of many popular books on the Civil War, has produced an accurate and enjoyable account of Stuart as a romantic military figure.

De Grummond, Lena Young, and Lynn de Grummond. *Jeb Stuart*. Philadelphia: Lippincott, 1962. (**G**) An adequate, albeit pedestrian biography with no outstanding interpretive features.

Thomas, Emory M. *Bold Dragoon: the Life of J.E.B. Stuart*. New York: Harper & Row, 1986. (**A, G**) This most recent biography is by far the finest; Thomas combines compelling prose, first-rate research, and excellent analysis of Stuart as a Southern symbol.

Thomason, John William. *Jeb Stuart*. New York: Charles Scribner's Sons, 1930. (**A, G**) The first of the full-length, well-researched works, it has been largely superseded by Davis and Thomas, both of which offer stronger interpretations.

Overview and Evaluation of Primary Sources

Most of Stuart's papers remain in private or family hands. Many others are under restricted access, which obviously hinders primary research beyond a certain point. Two hundred and sixty-six pieces of correspondence to and from Stuart, including over one hundred pieces from Lee, are in the collection of the Huntington Library. Additional collections of varying sizes are in the Library of Congress, the Petersburg National Military Park Library, and the Virginia Historical Society Collections, including some family papers on deposit by Colonel James Ewell Brown Stuart IV. Other Stuart items are to be found in the collections of Southern military leaders of the period, or are printed in the *Official Records*. What letters that are available reflect Stuart's flamboyant personality.

Fiction and Adaptations

Michael Shaara's Pulitzer Prize winning novel, *The Killer Angels* (1975), focuses on the Battle of Gettysburg, and Stuart is only a peripheral character. Robert Skimin's peculiar novel, *Gray Victory* (1988), about a victorious Confederacy has Stuart on trial for treason for his role in the defeat at Gettysburg.

Museums, Historical Landmarks, Societies

Antietam National Battlefield (Sharpsburg, MD). This battlefield, administered by the National Park Service, is in an excellent state of preservation with many instructive markers.

Brandy Station Battlefield (intersection of routes 20 and 15 at Brandy Station, near Culpeper, VA). This privately owned battlefield is the site of one of the last spectacular Confederate cavalry stands under Stuart's leadership.

Fredericksburg and Spotsylvania National Military Park (Fredericksburg, VA). Part of the National Park Service's series of Civil War Sites, this complex includes the ground where Stuart distinguished himself militarily.

Gettysburg National Military Park (Gettysburg, PA). Although Stuart's cavalry played only a minor role in the battle owing to its late arrival, the battlefield is still of significance.

Manassas National Battlefield Park (Manassas, VA). This site, part of which was saved from developers by intensive lobbying, is the site of two of Stuart's important battles.

Richmond National Battlefield Park (Richmond, VA). Site of the Seven Days Battle where Stuart distinguished himself.

Other Sources

Freeman, Douglas Southall. *Lee's Lieutenants.* 3 vols. New York: Charles Scribner's Sons, 1942-1944. Freeman's monumental study contains much material on Stuart.

McClellan, Henry Brainerd. *I Rode with Jeb Stuart; The Life and Campaigns of Major General J.E.B. Stuart.* Bloomington: Indiana University Press, 1958. This memoir written by one of Stuart's subordinates contains much primary information.

Mosby, John Singleton. *Mosby's War Reminiscences and Stuart's Cavalry Campaigns.* New York: Pagent, 1958. The controversial associate of Stuart has much of value to say about his comrade-in-arms.

Jean V. Berlin
The Correspondence of William T. Sherman
Arizona State University

MOTHER TERESA
b. 1910

Chronology

Born Agnes Gonxha Bojaxhiu on August 26, 1910, in Skopje, now in Yugoslavia, the third child of Albanian parents, Nikola Bojaxhiu, a prosperous building contractor and grocer, and Dranafile Bernai Bojaxhiu, a housewife; *1916-1927* attends elementary school at the Sacred Heart Church and the local state gymnasium; joins the Sodality of the Blessed Virgin Mary; joins the church choir and the Albanian Catholic Choir of Skopje; *1919* father dies at the age of forty-five and his business partner takes all of the assets; mother starts a business of handcrafted embroidery and the family prospers again; *1928* goes to Paris, via Zagreb, to join the Sisters of the Institute of the Blessed Virgin Mary, commonly called the Sisters of Loreto; in September is sent to Loreto Abbey, Rathfarnham, Dublin, Ireland, where she learns English; in mid-November is sent to India to the Bengal Mission; novitiate and training take place in the town of Darjeeling; *1931* takes vows of poverty, chastity, and obedience in Darjeeling: becomes Sister Mary Teresa of the Child Jesus, after St. Thérèse of Lisieux, the French Carmelite nun patroness of missionaries; *1933-1946* in Calcutta teaches geography and history in the schools of the Sisters of Loreto; teaches in Bengali, her fourth language; *1938* becomes principal of the school; joins the Entally's Sodality of the Blessed Virgin; *1939* becomes head of the Daughters of St. Anne, a community of Indian nuns who teach in the Bengali school; with Hindu girls visits patients in the Nilratan Sachar hospital and the poor and destitute of the Moti Jihl slums; *August 16, 1946* witnesses the Day of the Great Killing between the Muslims and Hindus of Calcutta; *1946* confides to the Jesuit father Celeste Van Exem her desire to leave the Sisters of Loreto to work in the slums; *1947* spends the year in Asansol (about three hours from Calcutta) for health reasons; Archbishop of Calcutta Ferdinand Perier consents to her writing the mother general of Loreto to ask to be released from the congregation; *1948* permission for "secularization" is granted on February 2, and the request for "exclaustration" on April 2; leaves for Patna, in the state of Bihar, on August 16, to join the Medical Mission Sisters at Holy Family Hospital where she learns the basic skills for caring for the sick among the city's poor; meets Jacqueline de Decker, a Belgian graduate of the University of Louvain (in 1953 de Decker will accept Mother Teresa's request to head the Sick and Suffering Co-Workers); leaves Patna for Calcutta in December and with five rupees starts her work in Moti Jihl and Til-Jala *bustees* (old workers' housing);

1949 lives with the Gomes family; within a few months ten young women join her; takes Indian citizenship; *1950* Archbishop Perier expresses willingness to recognize her group as a congregation; she writes the first draft of the constitution and calls the congregation the Missionary Sisters of Charity; adds a fourth vow, "to give wholehearted and free service to the poorest of the poor," to the traditional vows of poverty, chastity, and obedience; congregation is approved by the Vatican on October 7, but restricted to the diocese of Calcutta; becomes Mother Teresa, foundress of the Missionaries of Charity; *1953* congregation moves into a new house which becomes the Motherhouse of the Missionaries of Charity; in April, in the Cathedral of the Most Holy Rosary, takes her final vows and the first sisters take their first vows; Father Edward Le Joly, a Belgian Jesuit missionary, is chosen confessor and spiritual director of the novices and postulants; *1955-1958* opens Nirmala Shishu Bhavan (the Children's Home of the Immaculate) for abandoned, homeless, and unwanted children; the Nirmal Hriday (the Immaculate Heart of Mary), a home for the dying at Kalighat; a leprosarium at Gobra; mobile leprosy clinics at Howrah, Tiljala, Dhappa, and Moti Jihl; and a leprosy dispensary at Titagarh; launches citywide collections with the theme "touch the leper with your compassion"; starts Mother and Child Clinics and several schools; receives food and assistance from the United States government through the Catholic Relief Services, Church World Service, CARE, the American Women's Club of Calcutta, and Food for Peace; *1959-1964* the first foundations outside Calcutta are established in the cities of Ranchi, Delhi, Jhansi, and in time spread throughout India; leaves India for the first time on August 9, 1960; goes to Las Vegas, Nevada, for the national convention of the National Council of Catholic Women, then to Washington, D.C., New York, London, Frankfurt, Aachen, Munich, Dachau, Geneva, and finally to Rome to request that the Missionaries of Charity receive pontifical approval; in Rome meets Pope John XXIII, Cardinal Gregory Agagianian, and, for the first time in thirty years, her brother Lazar; receives the Padmashree Award in New Delhi and the Magsaysay Awards, sponsored by the Rockefeller Brothers Fund, in Manila; *1963* the Missionary Brothers of Charity are founded; appoints Father Robert Antoine, a Jesuit, in charge of the postulants; *1964* Pope Paul VI visits India and donates to the missionary a white Cadillac, a gift from Notre Dame University, used during the trip; sells it for almost half million rupees (current value about $28,000) and opens new houses; *1965* the Vatican issues the *Decretum Laudis* (Decree of Praise) to the Missionaries of Charity; the congregation numbers three hundred sisters; *1966* the Missionaries of Charity establish their first foundation outside of India, in Venezuela; *1969* International Association of Co-Workers, composed of Hindus, Christians, Buddhists, Jains, Jews, Parsis, Muslims, and all people of "good will," is approved by the Vatican; opens Shanti

Nagar (the Town of Peace) for lepers, in the district of Burdwan, in the suburbs of Calcutta; *1971-1990* the Missionaries of Charity, with the collaboration and help of the Missionary Brothers of Charity and the International Association of Co-Workers, establish new foundations and houses throughout the world, serving millions of needy people; *1971* awarded the Pope John XXIII Peace Prize, the Good Samaritan Award at the National Catholic Development Conference, Boston, the Joseph F. Kennedy, Jr., Foundation Award, the John F. Kennedy International Award, and the Jawaharlal Nehru Award for International Understanding; receives an honorary doctorate from the Catholic University of America, Washington, D.C.; *1973* receives the Templeton Prize for Progress in Religion from Prince Philip, Duke of Edinburgh; receives the "Mother et Magistra" Award in the United States; *1974* receives an honorary doctorate from St. Francis Xavier University in Antigonish, Nova Scotia; in July appears before the U.S. Senate Committee on Foreign Relations on the twentieth anniversary of the Food for Peace program; *1975* on the twenty-fifth anniversary of the founding of the Missionaries of Charity, there are nearly two thousand Sisters serving in more than eighty houses throughout the world; receives the Albert Schweitzer Prize at the University of North Carolina at Wilmington; is honored by the Food and Agriculture Organization of the United States (FAO) when they issue the Ceres Medal in recognition of her "love and concern for the hungry and the poorest of the poor"; in December, appears on the cover of *Time* magazine, as the focus of an article entitled "Messengers of Love and Hope: Living Saints"; *1976* receives honorary doctorates from Iona College, New Rochelle, New York, and the University of Visva-Bharati, Bengal; *1979* receives the Nobel Peace Prize and the People's Prize from the Norwegian nation; receives the Balzan International Prize from Italy's President Sandro Pertini; receives India's highest civilian award, the Bharat Ratna, the Jewel of India; receives an honorary doctorate from Temple University; *1980* the Indian Government issues a commemorative stamp to honor her receipt of the Nobel Peace Prize; *1981* receives an honorary doctorate from the Catholic University of the Sacred Heart in Rome; *1982* receives honorary doctorates from Harvard and Georgetown universities and from the University of Alberta in Edmonton; *1983* is awarded the Order of Merit, one of England's highest honors, by Queen Elizabeth II; *1985* the number of Sisters reaches twenty-four hundred, with 370 houses on five continents, including East and West Berlin and some Eastern European countries; the entire congregation is divided into nineteen regions worldwide; *October 11, 1986* miraculously escapes injury in an airplane crash in Tanzania; *1987* receives the United States Presidential Medal of Freedom from President Ronald Reagan; *1988* visits the areas of Armenia devastated by the earthquake; *September 8, 1989* suffers a heart attack and is admitted to Woodlands

Nursing Home in Calcutta; receives a pacemaker and in October is released from the hospital; *1990* at the age of seventy-nine, sends her resignation as head of the Missionaries of Charity to Pope John Paul II; the election for her successor is scheduled for September 8, but the Sisters of the Missionaries of Charity reject her resignation; at the present there are some three thousand sisters, six hundred brothers, and over three million co-workers scattered in eighty-seven countries.

Activities of Historical Significance

Mother Teresa is a universal figure, as a result of her work among the poor, the destitute, the sick, the abandoned, the crippled, and the lepers throughout the world. As the Catholic church's ambassador of good will, charity, and peace, she has attended hundreds of international congresses and meetings. Her efforts have been recognized with countless honorary degrees and awards, including the Nobel Peace Prize (1979), the United States Medal of Freedom (1987), and Great Britain's Order of Merit (1983).

September 10 is celebrated by the Missionaries of Charity as Inspiration Day to mark the major event in the life of Mother Teresa. On that same day in 1946, on the train from Calcutta to Darjeeling, she received God's call to follow Him into the slums, "to serve Him in the poorest of the poor, those who had no whereon to lay their heads." That day also represents the foundation of the congregation of the Missionaries of Charity. The constitution of the Missionaries of Charity refers to this event as "when the Holy Spirit communicated God's will to Mother Teresa." Mother Teresa expressed a wish that all the houses of the Missionaries of Charity be adopted spiritually by the convents of contemplative nuns. Within a year, some four hundred monasteries throughout the world agreed to spiritually join a house of the Missionaries of Charity. Newsletters, prayers,and information are exchanged periodically. In addition, the Missionaries of Charity are directly tied with other organizations with similar goals of charity and service, such as the International Co-Workers, the Sick and Suffering Co-Workers, and the Missionaries of Charity Brothers. Mother Teresa's message to the world is simple: God can do wonders working through humble instruments. She stated in the constitution, "a Missionary of Charity must be a missionary of love. She must be full of charity in her soul and spread that same charity to the souls of others, Christians and non-Christians." Spiritually, Mother Teresa is conscious that God has chosen her to work for the glory of Christ. Like St. Paul she proclaimed: "Christ lives in me, acts in me, through me, inspires me, directs me. I do nothing; He does it all." The Eucharist and Jesus are the center of the spiritual life of the Missionaries of Charity. Christ's phrase "I Thirst" is inscribed in all chapels of the congregation, implying the congregation's thirst for love. The Missionaries of Charity are not a contemplative order; they go out on the street every day to dutifully help those less fortunate. Thus the Sisters have been nicknamed "the running Sisters." The *New York Times* called Mother Teresa a "secular saint." She embraces all the people of the world as "her people" without distinction; to her "the poor is an ambassador of Christ." In presenting Mother Teresa the Pope John XXIII Peace Prize, Pope Paul VI called her "the apostle of brotherhood and the messenger of peace."

Mother Teresa's first personal and direct contact with the United States was in October 1960, when she participated in the convention of the National Council of Catholic Women, attended by three thousand delegates nationwide. She was invited to address the convention in Las Vegas by the Catholic Relief Service, which had been actively involved in helping poor women and children worldwide, including India. The theme of Mother Teresa's speech was that the love of mothers for their children is universal and knows no limits. Referring to the assistance her program received from the Catholic Relief Fund, she added, "This is what your help has done for Indian mothers. It has helped to draw out of these good mothers the best in them." American involvement in "The Works for Peace" program represented one of the most far-reaching U.S. Catholic relief efforts overseas. From Las Vegas, Mother Teresa traveled to Peoria, Chicago, Washington, D.C., and New York City where she sought help from the World Health Organization for the lepers of India.

Mother Teresa's apostolate and missionary work was well known in the United States long before her arrival in Las Vegas and her appeal to the United Nations. Patricia Burke Kump of Minneapolis wrote to Mother Teresa in 1958 expressing her desire to become associated with her missionary work. Kump had been impressed by an article that appeared in *Jubilee* in 1958 which explained Mother Teresa's apostolate and missionary work in the slums of Calcutta. By 1961 Kump had formed a small group of people, composed mostly of doctors and their wives, who were interested in Mother Teresa's programs. Mother Teresa gave them her permission to become Co-Workers, and on December 8, 1971, the American branch of Co-Workers was formed, with Kump as the first chairperson. The group spread the ideas and the apostolate of Mother Teresa, made new associates, and raised funds for the Missionaries of Charity.

In 1970 Terence Cardinal Cooke, archbishop of New York, asked Mother Teresa to establish a house in the city. It was opened in the South Bronx in 1971 to serve poverty-stricken African Americans and Hispanics. Poverty, lack of skill, and low self-esteem had condemned most of them to live in destitution, plagued by crime and drugs. Mother Teresa promised to be "a bridge between those who have and those who have less."

In August 1976 Mother Teresa addressed the Forty-first Eucharistic Congress assembled in Philadelphia. The main celebrant was Cardinal Karol Wojtyla, later Pope John Paul II. Among the thousands who attended were Dom Helder Camara, archbishop of Olinda-Recife, Brazil, and the Rev. Pedro Arrupe, superior general of the Jesuits. Camara and Mother Teresa teamed together and spoke on love and justice, violence and oppression.

By 1985 Mother Teresa had established sixteen houses of the Missionaries of Charity in the United States whose mission was "to serve the poorest of the poor." Even in the United States, the country of plenty, the work and presence of Mother Teresa's missionaries of Charity, though a "drop in the ocean," as she says, is seen as God's call to all people to join and love each other, regardless of race, color, religion, or nationality, thus embodying the Christian spirit of justice and equality for all.

Overview of Biographical Sources

In the past two decades the literature on Mother Teresa has grown steadily. Although none of the current biographical studies is definitive, two are of particular value: Edward Le Joly, *Mother Teresa of Calcutta, a Biography* (1983), and Eileen Egan, *Such A Vision Of The Street; Mother Teresa—The Spirit and the Work* (1985). Both are excellent works documenting in comprehensive details her spirituality and extraordinary accomplishments. Important, too, are the works by Brother Angelo Devananda, *Mother Teresa: Contemplative in the Heart of the World* (1985) and *Jesus the Word to be Spoken, Prayers and Meditations for Every Day of the Year: Mother Teresa* (1986). Both reflect Mother Teresa's spirituality, simplicity, and humility. Most of the other works draw systematically from these fundamental sources and tend to be hagiographical and devotional.

Evaluation of Principal Biographical Sources

Doig, Desmond. *Mother Teresa, Her People and Her Work.* New York: Harper & Row, 1976 (**A, G**) A compendium of the many articles that appeared in the *Statesman*, India's leading newspaper. With a forward by Indira Gandhi, the work contains expressive photographs by Raghu Rai of Mother Teresa and the Missionaries of Charity in Calcutta.

Devananda, Angelo. *Mother Teresa: Contemplative in the Heart of the World.* Ann Arbor, MI: Servant Books, 1985. (**A, G**) Brother Angelo Devananda joined the Universal Brothers of the Word, founded by Mother Teresa, in 1975. This book concentrates on her life and spiritual commitment and is highly recommended for spiritual guidance. Contains selections from Mother Teresa's writings and teachings.

Egan, Eileen. *Such A Vision Of the Street; Mother Teresa—The Spirit and the Work.* New York: Doubleday, 1985. (A, G) Written by one of Mother Teresa's Co-Workers and former inspector for Catholic Relief Services in India, this excellent work covers the life, career, and accomplishments of Mother Teresa from Skopje to 1984. The material is well organized and contains details not available in other biographies.

Le Joly, Edward. *Servant of Love, Mother Teresa and her Missionaries of Charity.* San Francisco: Harper & Row, 1977. (A, G) Not a complete biography of Mother Teresa but a depiction of the origins of the congregation. The author is the confessor and spiritual director of the novices and postulants of the Missionaries of Charity. It covers Mother Teresa's work from the founding of the congregation to its twenty-fifth anniversary. Inspired by Mother Teresa herself, the work explains the objectives of her apostolate. The book was published in England under the title *We Do It For Jesus, Mother Teresa and her Missionaries of Charity* (London: Darton, Longman and Todd, 1977).

―――――. *Mother Teresa of Calcutta, A Biography.* San Francisco: Harper & Row, 1984. (A, G) This biography, though not definitive, is by far the best in its insight of the spiritual ascendancy of Mother Teresa. The author draws on conversations with and recollections by Mother Teresa. Mother Teresa's actions, messages, spirituality, and apostolate are described in clear prose. Highly recommended for students, researchers, and theologians.

Luis, Jose, Balado Gonzalo, and Janet N. Playfoot, eds. *My Life for the Poor, Mother Teresa of Calcutta.* South Yarmouth, MA: John Curley, 1985. (A, G) The authors narrate the story of Mother Teresa's life using her own words and statements. In the preface, Brother Andrew states that this is perhaps the "nearest thing to an autobiography by Mother Teresa herself." The book is in large print.

Mary, Mother of Reconciliations: Mother Teresa of Calcutta and Brother Roger of Taize. New York and Mahwah, NJ: Paulist Press, 1989. (A, G) First published in England by A. R. Mowbray, Oxford, this booklet offers the personal reflections of Mother Teresa and Brother Roger on the Virgin Mary.

Muggeridge, Malcolm. *Something Beautiful for God, Mother Teresa of Calcutta.* London: Collins, 1971. (A, G) The author interviewed Mother Teresa for the British Broadcasting Company in 1966, went to Calcutta in 1969, and put together a brilliant and touching television documentary on Mother Teresa and the Congregation of the Missionaries of Charity called *Something Beautiful for God.* This book contains a transcript of the BBC interview and examines the objectives of the documentary. Translated in several languages and printed in Braille, it is also available on audio-cassette. The book's royalties are donated to Mother Teresa's work.

Murthy, Srinivasa B. *Mother Teresa and India.* Long Beach, CA: Long Beach Publications, 1983. (G) This book, in manuscript form, attempts to compare Mother Teresa's apostolate and spirituality to the values of Hinduism.

Porter, David. *Mother Teresa, The Early Years.* Grand Rapids, MI: William B. Eerdmans, 1986. (G, Y) This volume, with an introduction by Malcolm Muggeridge, is an abridged translation of *Mother Teresa: the First Complete Biography* by Kush Gjerji, an Albanian priest and Mother Teresa's cousin. The work is limited in its scope and content.

Rae, Daphne. *Love Until It Hurts.* San Francisco: Harper & Row, 1981. (A, G) A tribute to Mother Teresa and to the men and women of the Missionaries of Charity who work at Shishu Bhavan, Nirmal Hriday, and the leprosariums. A chapter is dedicated to the issue of abortion. Contains several photographs.

Speakman, Paula. *Love Without Boundaries, Mother Teresa of Calcutta.* Translated by Georges Gorrée and Jean Barbier. Huntington, IN: Our Sunday Visitor, 1974. (G, Y) In less than one hundred pages Speakman traces Mother Teresa's life and activity up to 1965.

Spink, Kathryn. *The Miracle of Love, Mother Teresa of Calcutta, Her Missionaries of Charity and Her Co-Workers.* San Francisco: Harper & Row, 1981. (A, G, Y) This straightforward presentation of Mother Teresa's life and career is based on information and recollections provided by Ann Blaikie and Jacqueline de Decker. A section of the book covers the apostolate of the Missionaries of Charity and the Co-Workers. The book is intended for a general audience and includes photographs. The appendix contains, among other things, Mother Teresa's Nobel Prize speech and the Vocation of the Missionaries of Charity.

————. *I Need Souls Like You: Sharing in the Work of Mother Teresa Through Prayer and Suffering*. San Francisco: Harper & Row, 1984 (A, G) Deals with the Sick and Suffering Co-Workers. As a close friend of de Decker, Spink draws mostly from de Decker's correspondence with Mother Teresa through the years. The book is also published in England under the title *A Chain of Love, Mother Teresa and her Suffering Disciples* (London, 1984).

Evaluation of Biographies for Young People

Leigh, Vanora. *Mother Teresa*. New York: The Bookwright Press, 1986. Illustrated by Richard Hook, this volume is part of the Great Lives Series written for young people.

Reilly Giff, Patricia. *Mother Teresa, Sister to the Poor*. New York: Viking Penguin, 1986. Part of the Women of Our Time Series, this is a short narrative of Mother Teresa's life.

Sebba, Anne. *Mother Teresa*. London: Franklin Watts, 1982. This highly recommended and well-presented children's book is illustrated by Paul Crompton.

Shrady, Maria. *The Mother Teresa Story*. New York and Mahwah, NJ: Paulist Press, 1987. Illustrated by Frederick Shrady, this volume presents the story of Mother Teresa in a popularized style.

Overview and Evaluation of Primary Sources

Mother Teresa's speeches, writings, and vocations are often included in the text or appendixes of biographical sources (see above). In addition, a few compilations of her meditations, writings, and letters exist. Angelo Devananda, *Jesus the Word to be Spoken, Prayers and Meditations for Every Day of the Year: Mother Teresa* (Ann Arbor, MI: Servant Books, 1986; A, G), collects 366 "words of wisdom" drawn from Mother Teresa's instructions, meditations, anecdotes, writings, and letters in an important volume for scholars and theologians. The appendix contains the Rule of Life and the Covenant of the Universal Brothers of the Word. Dorothy H. Hunt, ed., *Love: A Fruit Always in Season, Daily Meditations by Mother Teresa* (San Francisco: Ignatius Press, 1987; A, G), is a collection of published and unpublished interviews, reflections, and speeches that constitute the themes of Mother Teresa's daily meditations; the material is arranged according to the events of the liturgical calendar. Kathryn Spink, *Life in the Spirit, Reflections, Meditations and Prayers* (San Francisco: Harper & Row, 1983; **A, G**), with a preface by Ann Blaikie, contains Mother Teresa's thoughts and prayers. The book is also published in England under the title *In the Silence of the Heart* (London, SPCK, 1983). Georges Gorrée and Jean Barbier, eds. and trans., *The Love of Christ, Spiritual Counsels, Mother Teresa of Calcutta* (San Francisco: Harper & Row, 1982; **A, G**), translated from the French *Tu M'Apporte L'Amour* (Paris, 1975), contains the most significant words spoken or written by Mother Teresa. Some of the material is unpublished and supplied by the Missionaries of Charity. It is valuable in understanding the concrete and incarnational spirituality of Mother Teresa.

Fiction and Adaptations

Mother Teresa, a 1986 documentary directed by Ann and Jeanette Petrie, edited by Tom Haneke, with music by Suzanne Ciani, was released by Petrie Productions. The documentary is now on videotape and is released by Today Home Entertainment.

Malcolm Muggeridge's *Something Beautiful for God* is a television documentary for the BBC based on interviews with Mother Teresa in 1966 and a visit to Calcutta in 1967. The transcript of the film has been published in a book which contains additional commentary on the film's objectives. The book is available in audio-cassette format.

Museums, Historical Landmarks, Societies

The Sick and Suffering Co-Workers. This organization, founded by Mother Teresa in 1952, is headed by Jacqueline de Decker, called by Mother Teresa "my second self." Its mission is to call upon the sick to obtain, through prayer and sacrifice, graces for the apostolate of the Missionaries of Charity.

The International Associate of Co-Workers. A group that originated in 1954, their task is to work with the handicapped, the lonely, and the sick in the same spirit as the Missionaries of Charity.

The Missionary Brothers of Charity. This branch, founded in 1964, works with men, lepers, and orphaned, abandoned, and crippled boys. Father Ian Travers-Ball, an Australian Jesuit, originated the program, becoming Brother Andrew.

Pellegrino Nazzaro
Rochester Institute of Technology

GEORGE HENRY THOMAS
1816-1870

Chronology

Born George Henry Thomas on July 31, 1816, in Southampton County, Virginia, the son of John Thomas, a farmer, and Elizabeth Rochelle Thomas; *1836* enters West Point and rooms with William T. Sherman; *1840* graduates and is commissioned second lieutenant in the Third Artillery in Florida; *1844* promoted to first lieutenant; *1845-1847* assigned to Braxton Bragg's light battery and sees action in Mexican-American War where he is breveted captain and then major for gallantry at Monterey and Buena Vista; *1851-1854* serves as instructor of artillery at West Point; *November 17, 1852* marries Frances Lucretia Kellog of Troy, New York; *November 1, 1860* granted a twelve-month leave of absence; *April 14, 1861* chooses to fight for the Union, rejoins his regiment at Carlisle, Pennsylvania, and is promoted to lieutenant colonel; *November 1861* assumes command of the First Division of the Army of the Ohio having been made a brigadier general of volunteers in August; *April 1862* promoted major general of volunteers; *1863* holds firm at the Battle of Chickamauga; is given command of the Army of the Cumberland on October 16 and is ordered to hold Chattanooga; is victorious at the Battle of Chattanooga in late November; promoted to brigadier general in the regular army on December 31; *1864* plays vital role in Sherman's Atlanta campaign; goes to Nashville in October to head new western army to oppose Hood while Sherman goes on the March to the Sea; refuses Grant's orders to conduct an offensive at the end of November because he believes the troops are not strong enough to win a decisive victory, but changes his mind in December after pressure from Grant and wins a decisive victory; *1865* promoted to major general in the regular army and receives the thanks of Congress; *1865-1868* commands military district made up of Kentucky, Tennessee, Mississippi, Alabama, and Georgia; *1868* refuses President Johnson's offer of brevet promotions to lieutenant general and general because he believes he is being used against Grant; also refuses to be a presidential candidate; *June 1869* assumes command of the Military Division of the Pacific at San Francisco; *1870* dies on March 28 of apoplexy in San Francisco and is buried in Troy, New York.

Activities of Historical Significance

George Henry Thomas was one of the most important defensive generals of the Union forces during the Civil War. He spent much of his time fighting in the western theater of the war, which may have been less glamorous and appreciated, but which produced most of the outstanding Union leaders. He was also notable for making the decision to fight for the Union although he was from Virginia and had spent much of his early military career in various parts of the South. After he made this decision, his sisters in Virginia never communicated with him again and refused to admit they had a brother who had fought against the Confederacy. However, Thomas's brother remained in contact with him, and his wife and her family were Northerners who welcomed his decision. Later in the war, Thomas came to feel that Grant and Sherman did not sufficiently appreciate his talents and that they took credit for many of his achievements. The fact does remain, however, that Thomas was generally unable to initiate a successful aggressive action although he was rarely beaten when he took a strong defensive stand. One of his popular nicknames, the "Rock of Chickamauga," reflects both the strength and inflexibility that prevented him from becoming as aggressive a leader as Grant or Sherman. After the war, he did his best to uphold Reconstruction in his military district but was repeatedly frustrated by the government's refusal to believe his reports of Ku Klux Klan atrocities and so, was reluctant to take independent action against them. His last command promised to be a less stressful one, but he died before he could make his mark there.

Overview of Biographical Sources

Most of Thomas's biographers have shared the view that he was a neglected and unappreciated military figure and that Grant and Sherman rose to their heights of prominence at his expense. They credit him with participating in every great Union scheme of the war, including Sherman's March to the Sea. As a result, there is no truly satisfactory, unbiased biography of Thomas available, and none published any later than the 1960s. Most of them, however, are accurate in their facts and comprehensive in their scope, and several read well and convincingly. Although biased, the available biographies are still useful.

Evaluation of Principal Biographical Sources

Cleaves, Freeman. *Rock of Chickamauga, the Life of General George H. Thomas*. Norman: University of Oklahoma Press, 1948. (A, G) This well-written and entertaining account is probably the best place to begin.

Coppee, Henry. *General Thomas*. New York: D. Appleton, 1897. (A, G) Written by a former artillery officer under Thomas's command, this work includes much important information gleaned from men who knew and fought with Thomas.

Johnson, Richard W. *Memoir of Major-General George H. Thomas.* Philadelphia: J. B. Lippincott, 1881. **(A, G)** This was one of the earliest works on Thomas and also contains much valuable primary material.

McKinney, Francis F. *Education in Violence: The Life of George H. Thomas and the History of the Army of the Cumberland.* Detroit: Wayne State University Press, 1961. **(A, G)** In the most recent of the biographies, McKinney tries to place Thomas's career in a wider military perspective.

O'Connor, Richard. *Thomas, Rock of Chickamauga.* New York: Prentice-Hall, 1948. **(A, G)** While published in the same year as Cleaves's study, this biography is episodic and overwritten.

Piatt, Don. *General George H. Thomas, a Critical Biography.* Cincinnati: R. Clarke, 1893. **(A, G)** Completed after Piatt's death by Henry V. Boynton, this book uses Thomas to make Grant look bad.

Thomas, Wilbur D. *General George H. Thomas, the Indomitable Warrior.* New York: Exposition Press, 1964. **(A, G)** The author has set out to resurrect Thomas at the expense of Grant and Sherman.

Van Horne, Thomas Budd. *The Life of Major-General George H. Thomas.* New York: Scribner's, 1882. **(A, G)** This former chaplain depicts Thomas in a righteous, sanctimonious light.

Overview and Evaluation of Primary Sources

There is no collection of Thomas's personal papers as he and his wife destroyed all of them. As a result, the documentary record is virtually nonexistent for the years of his life preceding the Civil War. Many of his military writings and dispatches are available in the pertinent National Archives Record Groups, along with the papers of his colleagues during the war. Some are reprinted in the *Official Records.* But reconstructing his private life with any degree of certainty is difficult and therefore adds to the distortion of the accounts of his life.

Museums, Historical Landmarks, Societies

Chickamauga and Chattanooga National Military Park (Chattanooga, TN). The location of many of Thomas's battles during the fall and winter of 1863.

Kennesaw Mountain National Battlefield Park (near Marietta, GA). This National Park Service installation marks the site of one of the battles of the Atlanta campaign in which Thomas participated.

New Hope Church Battlefield (New Hope, GA). This privately owned land is the site of another battle in the Atlanta campaign.

Stones River National Battlefield (Murfreesboro, TN). This battle from December 31, 1862, to January 2, 1863, was one of the many that would lead to the campaign for Chattanooga the following fall.

Jean V. Berlin
The Correspondence of William T. Sherman
Arizona State University

PAUL TILLICH
1886-1965

Chronology

Born Paul Johannes Oskar Tillich on August 20, 1886, in the village of Starzeddel, East Prussia, the son of Johannes Oscar Tillich, a Lutheran pastor and diocesan superintendent of the Prussian Territorial church, and Mathilde Dürselen Tillich; *1891-1898* grows up in Schönfleiss; *1898-1901* attends humanistic gymnasium at Königsberg; *1901-1904* attends Friedrich Wilhelm Gymnasium in Berlin; *1904-1909* studies theology at the Universities of Berlin, Tübingen, Halle, and again at Berlin; presides over the Wingolf Society, a famous Christian student fellowship at Halle; *1909-1910* attends Domstift Cthedral school; *1910* awarded doctorate degree from University of Breslau; *1910-1912* serves as vicar in Nauen, near Berlin; *1912* awarded the degree of Licentiate of Theology from Halle; ordained minister of the Evangelical Church of the Prussian Union, Berlin; *1912-1914* serves as assistant preacher of the Old Prussian United Church in the Maobit or worker's section of Berlin; *1914* marries Margarethe ("Grethi") Wever, whom he divorces in 1921; *1914-1918* serves as field chaplain on the western front; receives two Iron Crosses, one of them First Class, for courageous service; suffers three mental collapses and begins to question the traditional concept of God; *1919-1924* awarded Privatdozent in theology, University of Berlin; *1920* helps found Kairos Circle, Berlin, a group of Christian and non-Christian intellectuals; *1924* marries Hannah Werner, an art teacher; *1924-1925* serves as associate professor of theology, University of Marburg; *1925-1929* serves as professor of philosophy and religious studies, Dresden Institute of Technology; *1929-1933* serves as professor of philosophy, University of Frankfurt; *1932* appointed dean of the philosophy faculty; suspended for being anti-Nazi; *1933-1955* serves in various positions at Union Theological Seminary, New York, culminating as professor of philosophical theology; *1936-1951* serves as chairman of Self-Help for Emigrés for Central Europe, a refugee aid society; *1939* elected to the Philosophy Club, thus ranking him among the twenty-five leading philosophers in the United States; *1940* becomes active in the New York Psychology Group; becomes American citizen; *1941-1943* serves on the editorial board of *The Protestant*; *1948* travels to Europe; *1953-1954* delivers Gifford Lectures, University of Aberdeen; travels through Europe again; *1955-1962* serves as professor, Harvard University; *1958* travels to Europe; awarded Hanseatic Goethe Prize; *1960* visits Japan; *1962* awarded Peace Prize of the German Publishers Association in Frankfurt; *1962-1965* serves as

Nuveen Professor of Theology, Divinity School, University of Chicago; *1963* visits
Israel and Egypt; *1965* dies October 22 of a heart attack in Chicago.

Activities of Historical Significance

One of the truly great theologians of the twentieth century, Paul Tillich began
his career in Germany, where he focused on the relationship of the church to the
Socialist movement. As a member of a Socialist group called the Kairos Circle,
Tillich proclaimed a new *kairos,* or divine breakthrough, in the form of religiously
grounded socialism. By 1925, he was exploring the relationship of Christianity to
psychoanalysis and the visual arts, in particular expressionist painting. Arriving in
the United States in 1933 as a refugee from Nazi Germany, Tillich soon gained
international recognition for his explorations in religious philosophy.

Tillich created a theological revolution by forming an entirely new theological
system and a new vocabulary to go with it. Denying that religion simply adheres
to a series of propositions or reverence for a supernatural power, Tillich defined
religion as the state of being grasped by an "ultimate concern," something possessed by every person, even an atheist, for generic man is inherently *homo
religious.* Most religious commitments, however, are idolatrous, for people have a
proclivity to give unreserved allegiance to that which is limited and finite. People
continually face "existential" disappointment, which means that their doubt and
uncertainty can never be removed. Humanity is, he said, filled with wonder at the
phenomena of "being," which is simple astonishment that things are; one remains,
however, fearful of "non-being," the darker knowledge that things might not be.
All "religious" efforts to gain salvation by human effort—such as legalism,
asceticism, and mysticism—ultimately fail.

To Tillich, sin is no mere transgression of religious law, nor a single immoral
act; rather it is a universal state of estrangement in which one finds oneself
alienated from oneself, others, and God, something implied in various mythical
accounts—the expulsion from Paradise, the story of Cain and Abel, the failure of
the Tower of Babel. To Tillich, Adam before the Fall symbolizes the "dreaming
innocence" of undivided potentialities, whereas the Fall itself represents the
inevitable loss of this innocence through the knowledge, power, and guilt that
comes through self-actualization.

Traditionally, God has been conceived as the originator and ruler of the universe, the sole, perfect, omnipresent, omnipotent being. Tillich denied that God is
"a being alongside or above others," because that would be limiting God to
categories of finitude, especially space and substance. Rather "the God above
God" is "the Ground and Power of being" or "Being itself." Yet Tillich asserted

that redemption is available, for Christ has brought about a new state of things as "the New Being." Though concretely embodied in a personal historical experience and subject to the limits of time and space, the New Being in Jesus as the Christ heals all existential conflicts. Empowered by the "Spiritual Presence" traditionally known as the Holy Spirit, the believer receives grace. Tillich defined grace not as a virtue or state of perfection but as rather "being grasped in the totality of our being by the ground of our being." Salvation, rooted in the Latin *salvus* or healed, means the reuniting of that which is estranged, "giving a center to what is split."

Tillich drew from a variety of theologians. Second-century Logos theologians claimed that God was manifest to people of all religions and cultures; Augustine stressed the immediate mystical union with God, Anselm of Canterbury a direct awareness of God's presence, and Martin Luther the experience of divine acceptance through faith alone. Tillich found in Jacob Böhme the dialectical relationship between God as ground of being and eternal abyss and in Friedrich Schleiermacher the feeling of absolute dependence (which became Tillich's "ultimate concern"). Søren Kierkegaard focused on the inevitability of guilt through self-actualization and on the object of religious faith as a matter of infinite trust.

Throughout Tillich's work lies a strong anti-authoritarian strain. Although acknowledging "Catholic substance," that which preserves the tradition of Christianity and its sacrificial message, Tillich gave particular attention to what he called "the Protestant Principle," a concept rooted in the Pauline and Lutheran doctrine of justification by faith. If one lives by this principle, one rejects the identification of the object of one's ultimate concern with any human form of authority, including biblical writings, the liturgical and creedal theological traditions of any church, and Protestantism itself. It is, said Tillich, presumptuous of any "conditional" institution, such as church or state, to claim to speak for "the unconditional," namely God. Even to say that "God exists" is blasphemy, for it involves putting limits on what is fundamentally unlimitable and putting conditions on what is fundamentally unconditional. God remains above and beyond all such theological formulations.

In Tillich's eyes doubt remains an inevitable part of faith. Doubt is "existential," and is inevitably part of the predicament in which all humans live. Indeed, the Protestant Principle "does not accept any truth of faith as ultimate, except the one that no one possesses it."

Overview of Biographical Sources

David Hopper's *Tillich: A Theological Portrait* (1968) was the first book to cover Tillich's life and thought for the general reader. Yet for a detailed biography, with focus on his personal life, one must consult volume one of Wilhelm and Marion Pauck's *Paul Tillich: His Life and Thought* (1976). (The second volume was never completed.) More intimate and controversial pictures were given by Tillich's widow Hannah in *From Time to Time* (1973) and *From Place to Place* (1976) and by his personal friend, psychologist Rollo May, in *Paulus: Reminiscences of a Friendship* (1973). Most work on Tillich, however, remains centered on his philosophical and theological ideas and is highly sophisticated.

Evaluation of Principal Biographical Sources

Hopper, David. *Tillich: A Theological Portrait.* Philadelphia and New York: Lippincott, 1968. (A) A pioneering effort, bringing to light some of the more controversial aspects of Tillich's work. Included are accounts of important incidents in Tillich's German years, including his break with pro-Hitler theologian Emanuel Hirsch. Hopper claims that Tillich's most basic philosophical categories were essentially defined before World War I, and that his subsequent thought represents "variations on the theme."

Pauck, Wilhelm, and Marion Pauck. *Paul Tillich: His Life and Thought.* Vol. 1, *Life.* New York: Harper and Row, 1976. (A, G) This definitive life of Tillich is based on a myriad of sources, including research in the Harvard and Göttingen archives, interviews with his family, friends, and colleagues, and many conversations with Tillich himself. Revealed is little-known material concerning Tillich's complex relationship with his dominating yet continually beloved father; his feeling for his sisters and how they affected his future relationships with women; his tragic first marriage and turbulent second; and his baptism by fire as a military chaplain. Also shown is his love of the arts; his enthusiastic involvement in the half-decadent, half-ethereal world of the Weimar Republic; and his dilemma as an émigré professor forced to straddle between philosophy and theology. This volume contains no hagiography; the authors often compare Tillich unfavorably to other scholars. The projected second volume was never published.

Overview and Evaluation of Primary Sources

Tillich's papers are located in the Paul Tillich Archive, in the Andover-Harvard Theological Archive. His German papers and materials are located in Göttingen.

For Tillich's autobiographical writings, see N. A. Razetski and Elsa L. Tamley, trans., *The Interpretation of History* (New York: Scribner's, 1936; A); "Autobiographical Reflections," in C. W. Kegley and R. W. Bretall, eds., *The Theology of*

Paul Tillich (New York: Macmillan, 1952. Reprint. New York: Pilgrim Press, 1982; **A**); "Author's Introduction," in James Luther Adams, ed. and trans., *The Protestant Era* (Chicago: University of Chicago Press, 1948; **A**). His *On the Boundary: An Autobiographical Sketch* (New York: Scribner's, 1966; **A, G**) is a freshly translated revision of the autobiographical material in *The Interpretation of History*, which focuses on his early life in Germany. The first chapter of the posthumously published *My Search for Absolutes* (New York: Simon and Schuster, 1967; **A, G**) includes a slightly modified version of "Autobiographical Reflections." Tillich's *My Travel Diary, 1936: Between Two Worlds* (New York: Harper and Row, 1970; **A, G**), edited with an introduction by Jerald C. Brauer and translated by Maria Pelikan, centers on a trip to Europe.

For a bittersweet and candid view by Tillich's widow, with a description of his frequent infidelities, see Hannah Tillich, *From Time to Time* (New York: Stein and Day, 1973; **A, G**). The book is a mélange, mixing autobiographical sketches with her own prose and poetry. Her book *From Place to Place* (New York: Stein and Day, 1976; **A, G**) covers travels in later life.

In *Paulus: Reminiscences of a Friendship* (New York: Harper and Row, 1973; **A, G**), the psychoanalyst and Tillich student Rollo May, who was his closest friend for thirty years, presents personal reminiscences, flashbacks of Tillichian biography, and psychological insights. Seeing Tillich's erotic life in a less derogatory light than his widow, May finds him a highly sensitive person stemming from the loss of his mother at age seventeen. Thenceforth he engaged in a passionate quest for knowledge while suffering periods of melancholy, loneliness, and anxiety. In some ways May confirms Hannah's portrait, but he interprets husband Paul as a great thinker who felt in his own being the power of evil, or to use Tillich's own phrase, the "demonic."

Henry Sloane Coffin, president of Union Seminary, gives his recollections of Tillich in *A Half Century of Union Theological Seminary, 1895-1945: An Informal History* (New York: 1954; **A, G**). Two German collections of Tillich's works exist: Renate Albrecht and Margot Hahl, eds., *Paul Tillich: Ein Lebensbild in Documenten* (1980), and Renate Albrecht, ed., *Gesammelte Werke*, 14 vols. (Stuttgart: Evangelisches Verlagswerk, 1959-1975; **A**). By 1983, six supplementary volumes had been published.

Tillich's early work was translated in the 1970s and 1980s: *The Construction of the History of Religion in Schelling's Positive Philosophy: Its Presuppositions and Principles* and *Mysticism and Guilt-consciousness in Schelling's Philosophical Development* (translated with an introduction and notes by Victor Nuovo; Lewisburg, PA: Bucknell University Press, 1975; **A**). Tillich's first major publishing success came with *The Religious Situation* (1925; translated by H. Richard Niebuhr; New York: Henry Holt, 1932; **A**), a call for a "realism based on faith," arising out of his interest in Expressionist art. His most important political book, *The Socialist Decision* (1933; translated by Franklin Sherman with introduction by John Stumme; Lanham, MD: University Press of America, 1977; **A**), attacks communism and national socialism as forms of "political romanticism" while reaffirming "the socialist principle" as realistic and humanistic. He finds Marx moving from flexibility to dogmatism, from an early dialectical view to lifeless materialism and narrow empiricism. In *The Interpretation of History* (see above), Tillich reveals his concern with the tension between Nature and God, form and matter, the divine and the demonic, and the absolute and the relative.

Much of Tillich's work is collected in various anthologies. *The Protestant Era* (see above) is an excellent collection of essays representative of his theology during his German period. Drawn from twenty years of his writing, this volume contains suggestions that the Protestant era might end, but that the prophetic and critical power of the Protestant spirit of principle would remain. James Luther Adams, ed. and trans., *What is Religion?* (New York: Harper, 1969; **A**), a series of Tillich's early essays, reveals his early efforts at synthesis between religion and the philosophy of religion. James Luther Adams, ed., *Political Expectation* (New York: Harper, 1971; **A**), contains articles and addresses written from 1923 to 1965. The anthology explores utopianism, the rights and limits of governmental power, and the relative merits of Marxist and Christian views of man. Adams's introduction discloses Tillich's early Socialist activities. Tillich sees Protestantism as a prophetic critical spirit, then calls into question all human ventures in light of the transcendent. *On Art and Architecture,* edited by John Dillenberger in collaboration with Jane Dillenberger; translated from German texts by Robert L. Scharlemann (New York: Crossroad, 1987; **A**), gives his opinions on aesthetics from 1920 to 1965. Robert W. Kimball, ed., *Theology of Culture* (New York: Oxford University Press, 1959; **A**), is an assemblage of Tillich's writings on the religious dimension of existentialism, psychoanalysis, politics, sociology, education, and the arts. For a general mélange of Tillich's writings, see *The Essential Tillich: An Anthology of His Writings* (New York: Macmillan, 1987; **A, G**), edited with an introduction by F. Forrester Church.

Tillich was introduced to much of the American public through his sermons. These are collected in *The Shaking of the Foundations* (New York: Charles Scribner's Sons, 1948; **A, G**); *The New Being* (New York: Charles Scribner's Sons, 1955; **A, G**); *The Eternal Now* (New York: Charles Scribner's Sons, 1963; **A, G**); and *Theology of Peace* (Louisville: Westminster/John Knox, 1990; **A, G**), edited by Ronald H. Stone.

In *The Courage to Be* (New Haven: Yale University Press, 1952; **A, G**), containing the text of his Terry Lectures at Yale, Tillich claimed that while neurotic anxiety is often curable, existential anxiety is inevitable. To Tillich, true courage includes the audacity to be both one's self and part of society, and to allow one's self to be upheld by the creative power of being in which every person participates. *Love, Power and Justice* (New York: Oxford University Press, 1954; **A, G**) shows how these three major elements become either sentimentalized or brutalized when any one falls apart from the other two, either in personal or social morality. *The Dynamics of Faith* (New York: Harper, 1957; **A, G**) is the best introduction to the basic theological views he had often repeated earlier; topics include history, science, and scripture. *Morality and Beyond* (New York: Harper and Row, 1961; **A, G**) claims that *agape* love in a unique moment can break the prison of any absolute moral law, even if such law is vested with the authority of sacred tradition.

Tillich's *magnum opus* was his *Systematic Theology*. The first volume (Chicago: University of Chicago Press, 1951; **A**) explores the themes of reason and revelation, being, and God. Volume two, subtitled *Existence and the Christ* (Chicago: University of Chicago Press, 1952; **A**), represents the first part of his Gifford Lectures and contrasts man in the fallen world with the biblical picture of Jesus as the Christ as the "New Being." Volume three, subtitled *Life and the Spirit and History and the Kingdom of God* (Chicago: University of Chicago Press, 1963; **A**), stresses his conviction that every theologian implies a philosophical position when using biblical language. *Christianity and the Encounter of the World Religions* (New York: Columbia University Press, 1963; **A**), based on the Bampton Lectures at Columbia, emphasizes the universal element in Christianity as well as its openness to other religions. Jerald C. Brauer, ed., *The Future of Religions* (New York: Harper and Row, 1966; **A**), combines eulogies to Tillich by theologians Brauer, Wilhelm Pauck, and Mircea Eliade with four of his own essays on non-Western religions, the death-of-God theology, and the Reformed theologian Karl Barth. *My Search for Absolutes* (see above) draws upon religious and humanistic philosophies to find absolutes, show their validity, and reveal their limitations. In his *A History of Christian Thought: From Its Judaic and Hellenistic Origins to Existentialism* (New York: Simon and Schuster, 1968; **A**), one of Tillich's students, Carl E. Braaten, edits and introduces lectures originally delivered at Union Theological Seminary in 1953 and the Divinity School of the University of Chicago in 1963.

There are several guides to Tillich research. Each Tillich work up to 1952, excluding book reviews, is listed in Kegley and Bretall (see above). For a thirty-page bibliography of Tillich's works, see Walter Leibrecht, ed., *Religion and Culture: Essays in Honor of Paul Tillich* (New York: Harper, 1959; **A, G**). Included are all Tillich publications from 1958, including book reviews and prefaces. R. C. Crossman has edited *Paul Tillich: A Comprehensive Bibliography and Key Word Index of Primary and Secondary Writings in English* (Metuchen, NJ: The Scarecrow Press, 1986; **A, G**), which contains Tillich's own English-language essays as well as books, articles, dissertations, and reviews on Tillich. John J. Carey, "Tillich Archives: A Bibliographical and Research Report," in *Theology Today* 35 (April 1975: 46-55), describes various Tillich manuscript holdings.

Museums, Historical Landmarks, Societies

Paul Tillich Park (New Harmony, IN). Tillich is buried in this park, which he had dedicated in 1963.

Such societies as the North American Paul Tillich Society, the German Paul Tillich Gesellschaft, and the French Association Paul Tillich continue to explore his thought.

Other Sources

Adams, James Luther. *Paul Tillich's Philosophy of Culture, Science, and Religion.* New York: Harper and Row, 1965. Tillich's first outstanding interpreter focuses on his early writing.

Adams, James Luther, Wilhelm Pauck, and Roger Lincoln Shinn, eds. *The Thought of Paul Tillich.* New York: Harper and Row, 1985. Seventeen scholars contribute rich and diverse essays.

Ambruster, C. J. *The Vision of Paul Tillich.* New York: Sheed and Ward, 1967. Stresses Tillich's efforts to unite religion and culture.

Brown, D. MacKenzie, ed. *Ultimate Concern: Tillich in Dialogue.* New York: Harper and Row, 1965. A transcript of a seminar conducted in the winters of 1963 and 1964 at the University of California, Santa Barbara, for graduate and senior students. Gives Tillich's views on major religious and political systems.

Bulman, Raymond F. *A Blueprint for Humanity: Tillich's Theology of Culture.* Lewisburg, PA: Bucknell University Press, 1981. Philosophical critique of Tillich's views on culture and humanism.

————. "Paul Tillich." In *Dictionary of American Biography,* Supplement 7. New York: Charles Scribner's Sons, 1981. Standard account.

Carey, John J. *Theonomy and Autonomy: Studies in Paul Tillich's Engagement with Modern Culture.* Macon, GA: Mercer University Press, 1984.

Hammond, Guyton B. *The Power of Self-Transcendence: An Introduction to the Philosophical Theology of Paul Tillich.* St. Louis: Bethany Press, 1966.

Handy, Robert T. *A History of Union Theological Seminary in New York.* New York: Columbia University Press, 1987. Places Tillich in his immediate intellectual milieu.

Hiltner, Seward. "Tillich the Person: A Review Article." *Theology Today* 30 (January 1974): 382-388. In examining works by Rollo May and Hannah Tillich, Hiltner finds both May and Tillich extremely narcissistic.

Kantonen, T. A., ed. *Paul Tillich: Retrospect and Future.* Nashville: Abingdon, 1966. Essays assessing Tillich's strengths and weaknesses.

Kegley, C. W., and R. W. Bretall, eds. *The Theology of Paul Tillich.* New York: Macmillan, 1952. Perceptive essays from a variety of perspectives.

Kelsey, David H. *The Fabric of Paul Tillich.* New Haven: Yale University Press, 1967. In an excellent work for the specialist, Kelsey presents Tillich's views on biblical authority, religious symbols, and verbal icons.

Leibrecht, Walter, ed., *Religion and Culture: Essays in Honor of Paul Tillich.* New York: Harper, 1959. Twenty-four appreciative essays by philosopher Karl Jaspers, psychologist Eric Fromm, and such theologians as Karl Barth, Emil Brunner, Rudolf Bultmann, Reinhold Niebuhr, and Gabriel Marcel.

Lyons, James R., ed. *The Intellectual Legacy of Paul Tillich.* Detroit: Wayne State University Press, 1969. Essays by J. H. Randall, Jr., Roger Shinn, and E. A. Loomis.

McKelway, Alexander J. *The Systematic Theology of Paul Tillich: A Review and Analysis.* Richmond, VA: John Knox Press, 1964. Critique based on the thought of the Swiss theologian Karl Barth.

Newport, John P. *Paul Tillich.* Waco, TX: Word Books, 1984. Sets forth with clarity essentials of Tillich's theology.

O'Meara, Thomas A., and Celetin D. Wiesser, eds. *Paul Tillich in Catholic Thought.* Dubuque, IA: The Priory Press, 1964. Fifteen authors show the diversity of Roman Catholic response.

Scharlemann, Robert P. "Paul Tillich." In *The Encyclopedia of Religion.* Vol. 14, edited by Mircea Eliade. New York: Macmillan, 1987.

————. *Reflection and Doubt in the Thought of Paul Tillich.* New Haven: Yale University Press, 1969. In a superior study, Scharlemann finds Tillich in a philosophical quest for the nature of being itself.

Smith, John. "Paul Tillich." In *Thirteen for Christ,* edited by Melville Harcourt. New York: Sheed and Ward, 1963. A clear and authoritative exposition of Tillich and his American experience.

Stone, Ronald H. *Paul Tillich's Radical Social Thought.* Richmond: John Knox, 1980. Places Tillich in the context of the Frankfurt School.

Stumme, John R. *Socialism in Theological Perspective: A Study of Paul Tillich, 1918-1933.* Missoula, MT: Scholars Press, 1978.

Tait, Gordon. *The Promise of Tillich.* Philadelphia and New York: Lippincott, 1971. An able introduction to Tillich's thought.

Tavard, George. *Paul Tillich and the Christian Message.* New York: Scribner's, 1962. A Roman Catholic critique focusing on Tillich's Christology.

Thomas, J. Haywood. *Paul Tillich: An Appraisal.* Philadelphia: Westminster Press, 1963. Sympathetic yet critical. Uses tools of logical analysis.

"To Be or Not To Be." *Time* 73 (March 16, 1959): 46-52. Able effort to explain Tillich's thought to the general reader.

Justus D. Doenecke
New College of the University of South Florida

ALEXIS DE TOCQUEVILLE
1805-1859

Chronology

Born Alexis Charles Henri Maurice Clérel de Tocqueville on July 29, 1805, in Paris, to Herve de Tocqueville, a member of the nobility and an administrator, and Louise Le Peletier de Rosanbo; *1827* appointed magistrate at Versailles; *1830* supports July Monarchy; *1831-1832* with Gustave de Beaumont visits the United States, ostensibly to inspect American penal reforms; *1833* Beaumont and Tocqueville publish their findings; visits England; *1835* publishes volume one of *Democracy in America*; visits England again; marries Mary Mottley in October; *1839* wins election to the Chamber of Deputies on second try; *1840* publishes volume two of *Democracy in America*; *1841* elected to the *Académie francaise*; *1848* attacks French regime just prior to the outbreak of revolution; becomes member of the Constituent Assembly; helps draft constitution of the Second Republic; *1849* serves as member of the Legislative Assembly; serves briefly as minister of foreign affairs; *1851* is imprisoned in the aftermath of Louis Napoleon's coup d'etat of December 2; *1856* publishes first part of *The Ancien Regime and the Revolution*; *1859* dies April 16 at Cannes, France.

Activities of Historical Significance

In 1831 Alexis de Tocqueville and Gustave de Beaumont arrived in the United States to examine America's prisons. But Tocqueville, having recently witnessed a revolution in France, was interested in broader issues: the impact of democracy upon American life and institutions, and the value of the American experience and the nature of its democratic government and society. His findings, presented in the two volumes of *Democracy in America*, elevated him to a position of prominence as a social and political analyst and thinker. In many ways his reflections on American society still remain essential reading; and his description of Jacksonian America, although disputed by some scholars, remains influential.

Tocqueville perceived American democracy as the harbinger of a new political and social order. Yet while he wrote penetratingly of the impact of a democratic ethos on culture and politics, studies of American social and economic structure during the years of Tocqueville's visit produce a more ambiguous portrait of the character and quality of democracy in America. American scholars often overlook Tocqueville's political career in France and his observations on European society and politics. There he tried to build upon the foundation laid during his trip to America to create a new democratic order for France. It is in this light that *Democracy in America* is best understood.

Tocqueville's writings have spawned a major body of scholarship, including a journal devoted to his life and thought. They continue to provide a point of departure for discussions of American democratic society.

Overview of Biographical Sources

There is extensive literature on Tocqueville as political theorist, much of which reflects upon his life history. But until André Jardin's biography, there was no full-length study of his life; most scholars were more interested in what he thought than in what he did and how he lived. Jardin's study, *Tocqueville: A Biography* (1988), focuses on Tocqueville's concern with democratic governance. George Pierson's account of Tocqueville and Beaumont's experiences in America, *Tocqueville and Beaumont in America* (1938), makes for very interesting reading, and clarifies the sources of Tocqueville's information.

Evaluation of Principal Biographical Sources

Gargan, Edward T. *De Tocqueville*. New York: Hillary House, 1965. (A, G) A short introduction to Tocqueville by a student of his political career in France.

Jardin, André. *Tocqueville: A Biography*. New York: Farrar, Straus and Giroux, 1988. (A, G) The first full life of Tocqueville by the general editor of his works. A well-written study, it highlights links between Tocquevile's life and work as he sought to structure a concept of aristocratic liberalism and governance.

Mayer, J. P. *Alexis de Tocqueville: A Biographical Study in Political Science.* 1939. Reprint. New York: Harper and Row, 1960. (A, G) A concise analysis by one of the leading scholars on Tocqueville. Those looking for a brief introduction to Tocqueville's life and thought should consult it.

Pierson, George Wilson. *Tocqueville and Beaumont in America*. New York: Oxford University Press, 1938. (A) A detailed recounting of where Tocqueville and Beaumont went and to whom they talked. Fascinating for its insights into the source material for *Democracy in America,* suggesting some of the biases which inform that work.

Overview and Evaluation of Primary Sources

Yale University holds the largest collection of Tocqueville material in the United States, including much material relevant to the writing of *Democracy in America*. The greatest single depository is at the Bibliotheque de l'Institut in Paris. Some revealing letters are in James Toupin and Roger Boesche, trans., *Selected Letters on Politics and Society* (Berkeley: University of California Press, 1985; **A, G**). Also worth reading is J. P. Mayer, ed. *The Recollections of Alexis de Tocqueville* (New York: Columbia University Press, 1949; **A**).

To Americans, Tocqueville's most important work is the two-volume *Democracy in America*, edited by J. P. Mayer (New York: Harper and Row, 1966; **A, G**). A definitive edition of Tocqueville's works is underway; several volumes have been translated into English, including the edition of *Democracy in America* cited above. Other Tocqueville writings available in English include *Journey to America*, edited by J. P. Mayer and translated by George Lawrence (Garden City, NY: Doubleday, 1971; **A, G**); *The Old Regime and the French Revolution,* translated by Stuart Gilbert (Garden City, NY: Doubleday, 1955; **A, G**); *On the Penitentiary System in the United States and Its Application in France* (with Beaumont; Carbondale: Southern Illinois University Press, 1979; **A**); and *The European Revolution & Correspondence with Gobineau,* translated and edited by John Lukacs (1959; Rpt. Gloucester, MA: Peter Smith, 1968; **A**). Students interested in recent scholarship on the Frenchman should consult the pages of *The Tocqueville Review*.

Other Sources

Boesche, Roger. *The Strange Liberalism of Alexis de Tocqueville.* Ithaca, NY: Cornell University Press, 1987. Suggests certain tensions and ambivalences in Tocqueville's thought by examining it against its historical backdrop.

Drescher, Seymour. *Dilemma of Democracy: Tocqueville and Modernization.* Pittsburgh: University of Pittsburgh Press, 1968. Shows how Tocqueville's notions of democracy were challenged by the onset of industrialization.

Hereth, Michael. *Alexis de Tocqueville: Threats to Freedom in Democracy.* Durham, NC: Duke University Press, 1986. Examines Tocqueville's quest to create a stable democratic social order in theory and practice, including a provocative discussion of his support of the French conquest of Algeria.

Lamberti, Jean-Claude. *Tocqueville and the Two Democracies.* Translated by Arthur Goldhammer. Cambridge: Harvard University Press, 1989. Compares Tocqueville's thoughts on democracy and revolution in France and the U.S.

Lerner, Max. *Tocqueville and American Civilization*. 1966. Reprint. New York: Harper and Row, 1969. A brief but incisive examination of Tocqueville's observations on America.

Lively, Jack. *The Social and Political Thought of Alexis de Tocqueville*. Oxford: Clarendon Press, 1962. A careful study of *Democracy in America* in terms of the meaning of Tocqueville's political concepts and the relationship between them.

McCarthy, Eugene J. *America Revisited: 150 Years After*. Garden City, NY: Doubleday, 1970. Presidential candidate McCarthy attempts to trace Tocqueville's steps through America and comment on the contemporary importance of his observations about democratic systems of government.

Reeves, Richard. *American Journey: Travelling with Tocqueville in Search of Democracy in America*. New York: Simon and Schuster, 1982. Another effort to use Tocqueville as a basis for looking at twentieth century America. Reeves actually retraced Tocqueville's journey, interviewing people as he went.

Schleifer, James T. *The Making of Tocqueville's Democracy in America*. Chapel Hill: University of North Carolina Press, 1980. A detailed account of the drafting of *Democracy in America*, tracing the evolution of the author's ideas through a careful examination of the text.

Zeitlin, Irving M. *Liberty, Equality, and Revolution in Alexis de Tocqueville*. Boston: Little, Brown, 1971. A short critical introduction to Tocqueville's works, comparing Tocqueville to Marx, and questioning his portrait of American society as democratic.

Zetterbaum, Marvin. *Tocqueville and the Problem of Democracy*. Stanford, CA; Stanford University Press, 1967. Reflecting the influence of Leo Strauss and Allan Bloom in his analysis, Zetterbaum argues that Tocqueville was unable to resolve the interplay of self-interest and democratic order. For Tocqueville, unrestrained self-interest led to democracy's destruction, while restriction of the exercise of self-interest places undemocratic restraints on people.

Brooks Donohue Simpson
Arizona State University

ALBION TOURGÉE
1838-1905

Chronology

Born Albion Winegar Tourgée on May 2, 1838, in Williamsfield, Ohio, the only child of Valentine Tourgée, a farmer, and Louise Emma Winegar Tourgée; *1859* enters Rochester University, receiving his bachelor's degree in 1862; *1861* enters Union army (27th New York Infantry) and is wounded at Manassas on July 21; *1862* commissioned first lieutenant, 105th Ohio Infantry; wounded at Perryville, October 8; *January 1863* captured in Murfessboro, Tennessee; exchanged after four months; *May 14, 1863* marries Emma L. Kilbourne; *December 1863* resigns commission; *1864* admitted to bar; *1865* moves to Guilford County, near Greensboro, North Carolina; *1868* delegate to the North Carolina constitutional convention; assists in codifying state's law and legal procedure; appointed state superior court judge (a post he holds until 1874); *1874* publishes *Toinette: A Tale of the South*; *1879* leaves North Carolina; publishes *Figs and Thistles* and *A Fool's Errand*; *1880* publishes *The Invisible Empire* and *Bricks Without Straw*; *1882* publishes *Our Continent*; *1884* contributes columns to the Chicago *Inter-Ocean*; *1886* publishes *The Veteran and His Pipe*; *1891* helps found National Civil Rights Association; *1895* edits *Basis: A Journal of Citizenship*; *1896* serves as counsel for Homer Plessy in *Plessy v. Ferguson*; *1897* appointed as foreign consulate to Bordeaux, France; *1905* dies May 21 in Bordeaux; buried at Mayville, New York.

Activities of Historical Significance

Albion Tourgée's career is a standing rebuke to old notions of Yankee carpetbaggers who traveled South after Appomattox to plunder and profit from the Confederacy's defeat. No one who is familiar with the man can quarrel with his sincere humanitarianism, his commitment to black equality, or his understanding of the warping impact of racism upon Southern society. The twice-wounded Civil War veteran came to North Carolina in 1865 to seek opportunity and to help rebuild the South; by 1867 he had become convinced that racism and Southern intransigence were blocking the road to progress and renewal. Joining the Republican party, he did what he could as a member of the 1868 state constitutional convention and as state superior court judge to protect blacks from terrorism. By 1879, having risked life and career on behalf of the cause, he decided to abandon the South but not his beliefs.

Tourgée devoted himself to examining the impact of race and Reconstruction on Southern society in a series of novels. The most notable of these, *A Fool's Errand*, appeared within months of his return to the North in 1879. While Tourgée attacked Southern racism, his books also implicated Northern naiveté and sectional differences as contributing to the failure of Reconstruction to protect and preserve the legal and political equality of blacks. Unlike many other white Northerners who lost their interest in advocating black equality, Tourgée continued to battle for his beliefs, most notably as the lawyer representing Homer A. Plessy in *Plessy v. Ferguson*, the 1896 Supreme Court decision which endorsed "separate but equal" facilities for blacks and whites.

Overview of Biographical Sources

Historians of Reconstruction neglected Tourgée's biography for some time, because they were not apt to view sympathetically the endeavors of white Northerners who assisted in the rebuilding and renewal of the South after the Civil War; they were especially cynical about the Northerners' advocacy of black equality. Roy F. Dibble's 1921 study, *Albion W. Tourgée,* reflects these assumptions. With the advent of the civil rights movement of the 1950s, marked by the Supreme Court's decision to endorse desegregation in *Brown v. Board of Education* (1954), it seemed only just to reexamine the career of the man who had argued and lost *Plessy v. Ferguson*, the decision that *Brown v. Board of Education* overturned. Theodore A. Gross's *Albion W. Tourgée* (1963) examines Tourgée's works, and while Gross is sympathetic to the goal of black equality, he still adheres to an interpretation of Tourgée as a carpetbagger apologist for Reconstruction. Otto H. Olsen, in his *Carpetbagger's Crusade: The Life of Albion Winegar Tourgée* (1965), presents the first favorable biography of Tourgée in line with the revolution in Reconstruction historiography, which took place in the 1950s and 1960s. Richard Current's *Those Terrible Carpetbaggers: A Reinterpretation* (1988) follows the basic outlines of Olsen's account.

Evaluation of Principal Biographical Sources

Current, Richard N. *Those Terrible Carpetbaggers: A Reinterpretation*. New York: Oxford University Press, 1988. **(A, G)** Examines Tourgée as one of ten representative carpetbaggers in a work that is objective yet sympathetic, a necessary corrective to timeworn stereotypes of venal Yankees.

Dibble, Roy F. *Albion W. Tourgée.* New York: Lemcke and Buechner, 1921. (A) Hostile to Tourgée, Dibble's biography neglects Tourgée's experiences in North Carolina.

Gross, Theodore L. *Albion W. Tourgée.* New York, 1963. (A, G) A discussion of Tourgée's writings, especially his fictional accounts of Reconstruction. Slim as a biographical source.

Olsen, Otto H. *Carpetbagger's Crusade: The Life of Albion Winegar Tourgée.* Baltimore: Johns Hopkins University Press, 1965. (A, G) The best account of Tourgée's career, and especially detailed on his experiences during Reconstruction. Reflects recent scholarship on Reconstruction.

Overview and Evaluation of Primary Sources

Tourgée's papers are collected at the Chautauqua County Historical Museum in New York. They have been exploited by Tourgée's various biographers, most notably Theodore L. Gross, Otto Olsen, and Richard Current. Material on Tourgée during the Civil War and Reconstruction is scattered throughout the National Archives; the Martin B. Anderson Papers at the University of Rochester and several collections at Duke University and the Southern Historical Collection at the University of North Carolina also contain material on Tourgée. Olsen's bibliographical essay in *Carpetbagger's Crusade* provides an expanded commentary on manuscript sources.

Tourgée's most important work is *A Fool's Errand: A Novel of the South During Reconstruction,* edited by George Fredrickson (New York: Harper and Row, 1966; A, G). When critics challenged the factual accuracy of *A Fool's Errand,* Tourgée replied with *The Invisible Empire* (1880. Reprint. Baton Rouge: Louisiana State University Press, 1989; A, G). Originally produced as an appendix to later editions of *A Fool's Errand,* it is readily available again in this edition edited by Otto H. Olsen. Tourgée's other works include *Toinette: A Tale of the South* (New York: Ford, 1874; A, G), an attack upon Southern chivalry and civilization; *Figs and Thistles* (New York: Fords, Howard and Hulbert, 1879; A, G), about political corruption; *Bricks Without Straw* (New York: Fords, Howard and Hulbert, 1880; A, G), relating the status and situation of the freedmen; *John Eax and Mamelon; or, the South without the Shadow* (New York: Fords, Howard, and Hulbert, 1882; A, G), on Southern society; *Hot Plowshares* (New York: Fords, Howard, and Hulbert, 1883; A, G), an exploration of race and identity; *An*

Appeal to Ceasar (New York, 1884; **A, G**), a cry for federal aid to education as the solution to racial prejudice; *The Veteran and His Pipe* (Chicago and New York: Belford, Clarke, 1886; **A, G**), a set of short pieces reflecting on the war and Reconstruction.

Museums, Historical Landmarks, Societies

Chautauqua County Historical Museum (Westfield, NY). Tourgée and Grace Bedell (the little girl who advised Lincoln to grow a beard) are Chautauqua's most memorable residents. Tourgée's papers are held by the society; he lived in nearby Mayville.

Other Sources

Aaron, Daniel. *The Unwritten War: American Writers and the Civil War.* New York: Alfred A. Knopf, 1973. Devotes a chapter to Tourgée's works on Reconstruction, focusing on his emphasis on race.

Ealy, Margaret, and Sanford E. Marovitz. "Albion Winegar Tourgée (1838-1905)." *American Literary Realism* 8 (1975): 53-80. The best bibliography of Tourgée's works available.

Lofgren, Charles A. *The Plessy Case: A Legal-Historical Interpretation.* New York: Oxford University Press, 1987. In this complete study of a critical Supreme Court decision, Lofgren includes a careful analysis of Tourgée's brief.

McPherson, James M. *The Abolitionist Legacy: From Reconstruction to the NAACP.* Princeton, NJ: Princeton University Press, 1975. A study of the continuing battle for civil rights in the late nineteenth century.

Wilson, Edmund. *Patriotic Gore: Studies in the Literature of the American Civil War.* New York: Oxford University Press, 1962. Includes an examination of *A Fool's Errand* as part of a larger discussion about fictional treatments of the postwar South.

Brooks Donohue Simpson
Arizona State University

AMERIGO VESPUCCI
1454-1512

Chronology

Born Amerigo Vespucci on March 14, 1454, in Florence, Italy, the third son of five children of Nastagio Vespucci, a notary (later to serve in the Florentine government in a position of authority in the field of finance, rising to the post of chancellor of the exchange); unlike his two university-educated brothers, receives his education at the home of a paternal uncle, Giorgio Antonio, a Dominican friar; studies Latin, mathematics, astronomy, cosmography, and geography, reading extensively in his uncle's vast library, and preparing for a career in commerce; *1478* travels to Paris to serve as secretary to another relative, his cousin Guido Antonio Vespucci, appointed Florentine ambassador to the court of Louis XI that same year; *1480* returns to Florence; *1482* his father dies; assumes control of family affairs; *1483-1499* becomes manager of the household of a branch of the Medicis, the ruling family of Florence; travels to Spain on behalf on his employers on at least two occasions; *1491* settles in Seville, where he marries a local woman, Maria Cerezo; becomes associated with Giannetto Berardi, an Italian outfitter of ships and supplier for the Spanish Crown who resides in Seville; *1495* after Berardi dies, commissioned by the monarchs to fulfill the terms of their unfinished contract; *1499* inspired by reports of overseas successes from Spanish and Portuguese explorers, decides to join a trans-Atlantic expedition led by Alonso de Hojeda in search of Asia in the dual capacity of astronomer and merchant; *1499* sets sail from the Spanish port of Cadiz on May 18; the expedition stops at the Canary Islands off the coast of Africa, and sails west and then south; sights land after twenty-four days of navigation, possibly at Surinam or French Guyana, continues southeasterly to the South American coast of northern Brazil, the mouth of the Amazon River, and the Equator, before turning northward to the northern coast of South America and the Caribbean Islands; *1500* arrives in Cadiz in June loaded with few of the expected luxury goods, but with a cargo of pearls and two hundred slaves; plans a second expedition from Seville intended to continue exploration of the Brazilian coast, but his license is revoked on the grounds that he is a foreigner; goes to Portugal, where he secures royal support for a three-ship expedition; *1501* sails from Lisbon on May 13; reaches the coast of Brazil and travels south toward Patagonia; realizes that traditional assumptions of reaching Asia by sailing west are incorrect; develops insights, reflected in the 1502 Cantino world map, that this landmass (America) was a continent previously unknown to

Europeans; *1502* returns to Spain; *1505* receives citizenship; *1508* appointed pilot major of the Board of Trade (*Casa de Contratación*), the public authority with exclusive responsibility for all overseas trade and travel; *1512* dies on February 22, in Seville.

Activities of Historical Significance

Amerigo Vespucci was born at the start of Europe's great drive to expand overseas. He was a contemporary of Christopher Columbus (1451?-1506), John Cabot (1450-1498), Vasco da Gama (1469?-1524), and Pedro Alvares Cabral (1460?-1526?), to name a few of the many great figures associated with this remarkable historical period. Motivated by advances in technology and cartography, these navigators and explorers sought new routes to the legendary East, a land associated with luxury goods, gems, and spices. Columbus and Cabot sailed westward, while da Gama and Cabral expected to reach Asia by circumnavigating Africa. All were inspired by the writings and maps of the Egyptian mathematician and astronomer Ptolemy (2nd century A.D.) whose *Geography* became an important reference book for educated Europeans and travelers of the fifteenth century. Ptolemy's book included a carefully executed calculation of the size of the earth as well as descriptions and lists of its continents, oceans, and other geographic points of interest. One such place was the Cape of Cattigara, the southernmost point of Ptolemy's version of the map of Asia. Cattigara was Vespucci's original destination when he set sail in 1499. Instead, he reached the northern coast of South America.

On his second voyage, under the auspices of the Portuguese government, Vespucci traveled along the Atlantic coast of South America, perhaps as far south as Patagonia. The geographic details he encountered during this venture must have persuaded him that this landmass did not coincide with the continent of Asia described in Ptolemy's *Geography* and that in fact the land appeared to block his initial intent to reach Asia by following a westerly route from Europe. He concluded, therefore, that the land before him was a new world. Vespucci's fame is based, to a large extent, on this important insight. Columbus, on the other hand, never gave up the notion that he had reached Asia.

Vespucci's legacy, however, is replete with controversy, much of it surrounding his specific role in the complex process of the European discovery of America. At the heart of the problem is the question of whether his contribution was noteworthy enough to merit naming the continent after him. The word "America" first appeared on a map drawn by Martin Waldseemüller, a professor of geography, in 1507 to distinguish the continent described by Vespucci from the continents of Asia, Europe, and Africa, acknowledged by Ptolemy and traditional European geography. Although Waldseemüller was familiar with the trans-Atlantic achievements of Columbus, he nonetheless honored Vespucci as the first to recognize that what lay across the Atlantic was a new world. The detractors of Vespucci on this point would argue that Columbus deserves the credit, and that the continent should have been named after him instead. Columbus, however, did not partake in this controversy; he died in 1506 before the new map was published and was thus spared whatever indignity arose from the choice of a name. It is not even clear that the two ever met, although most serious historians believe that they corresponded and might have known and collaborated with each other. There is no evidence that Columbus resented Vespucci or that he felt that they were in direct competition; in other words, the presumed rivalry between the two was created neither by Columbus nor by Vespucci while Columbus was alive.

A second area of disagreement about Vespucci concerns the possibility that he, rather that Columbus, was the first European to discover the American mainland along the northern coast of South America. This could only be possible if Vespucci had made an ocean crossing before Columbus's third in June 1498, at which time Columbus sailed along the Caribbean coast of Venezuela. While Vespucci's 1499 trip is well documented, and he did visit this region at the time, little is known about his activities between 1496 and 1499, fueling speculation that he might indeed have preceded Columbus to the mainland.

This historical uncertainty is due mostly to a document attributed to Vespucci himself, believed to have been written in 1504, addressed to Pero Soderini, government chief of Florence, entitled *Letter from Amerigo Vespucci on the Islands Newly Discovered During his Four Voyages* (*Lettera di Amerigo Vespucci delle isole nouvamente trovate in quatri suoi viaggi*; 1505). In this text, the author claims to have made four voyages across the Atlantic, in the first of which, around 1497, he reached the northern coast of South America, turning north to the Caribbean mainland of Central America, continuing north to the Yucatan Peninsula and the Gulf of Mexico, before returning to Europe.

In spite of the fact that Vespucci was an avid letter writer, the general consensus among historians is that this particular document is a forgery. There is little evidence to support the idea that Vespucci had any part in the composition of the letter, attributing its authorship instead to any number of enterprising publishers supplying fictional accounts as well as news of exotic new worlds to an eager European reading public. Moreover, there has been no way to authenticate the letter's contention that the first and fourth trips in 1497 and 1503-1504 actually took place.

Vespucci's earlier 1501 Atlantic crossing, however, has remained an important personal achievement and has withstood the serious scrutiny of scholars for many generations. The best source of information is a second letter also attributed to Vespucci, the *Mundus Novus*. It is addressed to Piero Francesco di Medici, Vespucci's Florentine patron, and appeared in print for the first time in 1504. In the text of the letter Vespucci gives a careful description of the coast of South America, several accurate and insightful astronomical observations and calculations, and, most important of all, suggests the revolutionary idea that America was a new continent. By daring to do so, Vespucci challenged the long-standing yet incorrect scientific tradition of the Ptolemaic world view and introduced new evidence based on experience and observation. He inspired future generations of explorers, travelers, geographers, cartographers, and astronomers to confirm his insights, thus serving to energize and refocus the navigational ventures of his contemporaries. The clearest outcome of Vespucci's conclusions was that the exploration and exploitation of America became an end in itself rather than a step for reaching Asia.

Overview of Biographical Sources

Vespucci's gift for self-promotion and his penchant for letter writing made him rather well known during his lifetime. In fact, much of what is known about his whereabouts during the most active and historically important period of his life comes from his own correspondence. He wrote letters to employers, business associates, relatives, and acquaintances. It might have been the abundance of genuine epistolary material that led to the controversy about Vespucci's preeminence in America.

Inflated claims about Vespucci, whether initiated by him or by his admirers such as Waldseemüller, were quickly attacked, primarily in Spain, by those coming forward in defense of Columbus's legacy and reputation. The earliest and most important advocate of Columbus was the Spanish Dominican friar Bartolomé de Las Casas (1474-1566), the eloquent and distinguished historian of the first colonial generation in America. In his *History of the Indies (Historia de las Indias,* begun in 1527 and completed some thirty years later), he denounces the account of Vespucci's 1497 voyage, his presumed first, and dismisses it as false. He also suggests that the proper name for the new continent should be "Columba" after Columbus who discovered it, or "Gracia" (Grace), which Columbus had originally named it.

Las Casas's challenge to the authenticity of the account of Vespucci's first voyage was largely ignored outside of Spain until the eighteenth century, when an Italian abbot, Angelo Bandini, discovered in 1745 one of Vespucci's letters in a

Florentine library. The content of this letter vindicated Las Casas's assertion that there was no voyage in 1497. This discovery reawakened interest in Vespucci, and twentieth-century researchers have continued to find new documents such as letters and letter fragments.

Secondary material on Vespucci is ample, the majority of it published in the nineteenth and early twentieth century. Much of this research has been produced by non-English speaking scholars, most of them Italian, Spanish, and Portuguese. An annotated bibliographical listing, consisting of one hundred and fifty pages, appeared in José Alberto Aboal Amaro's *Amerigho Vespucci. Ensayo de bibiliografía crítica* (1962). The goal of many of the titles included in this bibliography is to reiterate or attempt to confirm either or both controversial issues surrounding the figure of Vespucci: the voyage of 1497 and the naming of the continent. Vespucci's most vehement defender in Spanish language historiography has been the erudite Roberto Levillier. In his numerous publications, the Argentine scholar argues that Vespucci is indeed deserving of all the praise he has received, and that he made all the voyages attributed to him. Two of his best known works are *América la bien llamada*, ("America, the Properly Named"; 1948) and *Américo Vespucio. El Nuevo Mundo* ("Amerigo Vespucci. The New World"; 1951). One of the most recent accounts of Vespucci's historical activities, though not strictly a biography, is Vicente D. Sierra's *Amerigo Vespucci. El enigma de la historia de América* ("Amerigo Vespucci. The Question of the Discovery of America"; 1968) published in Madrid in Spanish. In this work the author examines in some detail the nature of the Vespuccian debate and gives a sober and well-considered assessment of Vespucci's contributions based on available primary materials. The book also contains an extensive collection of useful facsimiles of contemporary maps and charts. Sierra's conclusions agree with the thrust of modern scholarship on the subject.

For reasons not altogether clear, Vespucci had not attracted much attention among English-speaking scholars. In the United States, George Tyler Northup published an English translation of Vespucci's *Letter to Piero Soderini* (1916), and Frederick Julius Pohl wrote a biography entitled *Americo Vespucci. Pilot Major* (1944).

Historical interest in Vespucci, even among western Europeans, has diminished in the second half on the twentieth century, a loss of popularity possibly due to the fact that researchers have already reached a consensus on the most important aspects of his career. Nevertheless, new approaches might come to light, as in the case of Columbian scholarship, on the occasion of the quincentenary celebration of Vespucci's voyage of 1499.

Evaluation of Principal Biographical Sources

Arciniegas, Germán. *Amerigo and the New World*. New York: Alfred A. Knopf, 1955. (**A, G**) An entertaining account of the life of the Florentine navigator, at times too imaginative for the serious scholar. The noted scholar and Columbia native, Arciniegas, argues vehemently against the findings of current scholarship, that Vespucci did make all the four voyages attributed to him, and that his detractors have attempted to discredit him for nationalistic reasons. Arciniegas is especially critical of Las Casas's anti-Vespuccian position. This narrative history is an easy book to read, rich in the details of fifteenth-century Florentine life.

Parry, J. H. *The Discovery of South America*. London: Paul Elek, 1979, (**A, G**) A serious and clearly written general account of the early experiences of Europeans in America. Parry considers Vespucci an opportunist, yet gives him credit for adding to Europe's understanding of geography and navigation. The author, an expert in North-American maritime history, has published a number of important studies on various aspects of European, especially Spanish, expansion. This particular book contains important and handsome reproductions of both artistic and scientific renderings of first impressions of the New World by European artists and travelers during the early stages of discovery.

Pohl, Frederick, J. *Amerigo Vespucci. Pilot Major*. 1944. 2d ed. New York: Octagon Books, 1966. (**A, G**) Argues that Vespucci wrote neither of the two controversial letters attributed to him, the *Letter* and the *Mundus Novus*. English translations of the two letters are published in this volume. By denying Vespucci authorship of the disputed documents, and claiming that "less is more" in this case, Pohl attempts to prove that Vespucci did make the 1499 voyage and that he deserves the honor of having the continent named after him for being the first to recognize its uniqueness. This is a serious biography of Vespucci, less imaginative than Arciniegas's and more focused on Vespucci's mature years.

Zweig, Stefan. *Amerigo, A Comedy of Errors in History*. New York: Viking Press, 1942. (**G**) This work echoes the opinion of a number of Latin American historians hostile to the legacy of the Spanish empire in America and the European pride in their colonial empire in the New World by asserting that the continent's discovery by the early navigators resulted from accident rather than design. The Austrian novelist and amateur historian believes that Vespucci's letters, and the *Letter from Amerigo Vespucci on the Islands Newly Discovered During his Four Voyages,* in particular, were actually written by Vespucci himself but discredited not for their uncertain authorship but for their inaccuracies and false claims.

Overview and Evaluation of Primary Sources

The most important collection of primary material about the life and career of Vespucci is his letters. These have been edited, published, and translated from the early part of the sixteenth century until the present, and have appeared in a number of publications over the years. An English version of the account of Vespucci's presumed four voyages is *The First Four Voyages of Amerigo Vespucci, Reprinted in Facsimile and Translated from the Rare Original Edition (Florence 1505-06)* (London: Bernard Quaritch, 1893; A). Materials related to his travels and career are collected and translated in C. R. Markham, *The Letters of Amerigo Vespucci and Documents of his Career* (London: Hakluyt Society, 1894; A). George Tyler Northup edited and translated the two best known Vespucci letters, *Amerigo Vespucci; Letter to Piero Soderini, Gonfaloniere. The Year 1504* (Princeton: Princeton University Press, 1916; A) and *Mundus Novus: Letter to Lorenzo Pietro di Medici* (Princeton: Princeton University Press, 1916; A).

Museums, Historical Landmarks, Societies

Portrait (Florence, Italy). A contemporary portrait of Vespucci and his family, painted by the Florentine muralist Domenico Ghirlandajo (1449-1494), hangs in the Church of Ognissanti.

Portrait (Florence, Italy). The most often reproduced portrait of Vespucci, by an anonymous painter, hangs in the Uffizi Gallery.

Portrait (New York, NY). A second painting of the explorer, the current location of which is unknown, by Sandro Botticelli (1444?-1510), is available in reproduction from the Frick Art Reference Library.

Other Sources

Las Casas, Bartolomé de. *History of the Indies*. Translated and edited by Andrée Collard. New York: Harper and Row, 1971. This is an abridged edition of the monumental work first published in its entirety in Spanish in 1875. Las Casas is Columbus's first and most ardent defender, and this work gives the reader a clear view of the importance assigned to the American discoveries by the contemporaries of Vespucci.

Harrisse, Henry. *The Discovery of North America*. 1892. Reprint. Amsterdam: N. Israel, 1969. This classic study is a highly erudite and difficult to read account of the various European efforts to explore and colonize the American mainland. Harrisse's greatest contribution lies in his insistence on drawing conclusions about authentic primary materials and dismissing much that was propagandistic or self-serving.

Vigneras, Louis Andre. *The Discovery of South America and the Andalusian Voyages*. Chicago: University of Chicago Press, 1976. An appendix of this serious and well-researched book is devoted to Vespucci's second voyage under the sponsorship of the Spanish Crown. The author examines in detail all material relevant to the various individuals who participated in that expedition, the conflicts and misleading claims that arose from it, and includes a set of very useful maps charting the course of this and other early voyages.

Clara Estow
University of Massachusetts at Boston

JOHN WAYNE
1907-1979

Chronology

Born Marion Michael Morrison on May 26, 1907, in Winterset, Iowa, the oldest son of Clyde L. Morrison, a pharmacist, and Mary Brown Morrison, both of Irish extraction; *1907-1914* spends early life in Winterset and Earlham, Iowa; *1914-1916* lives near Lancaster, California, where his father unsuccessfully tries farming; *1916-1925* lives in Glendale, California; attends the local high school and plays football; *1925-1928* attends the University of Southern California on a football scholarship; by this time is well-known by his nickname "Duke"; *1925-1928* works summers as a propman on the Fox Pictures lot, a job arranged for him because of his football ties at USC; plays in crowd scenes in several movies; *1928-1930* continues working for Fox in the props department; *1930* unexpectedly cast as a lead in *The Big Trail,* a sprawling western about a wagon train, directed by Raul Walsh; the film is a box-office disaster; takes his stage name, John Wayne; slips into making "B" movies; *1931-1939* becomes the king of "B" movies, most of which are westerns, and in the process learns about acting and film-making; *1939* stars in *Stagecoach,* a masterpiece of the genre, directed by John Ford, and establishes himself as a first-class film star; *1942-1945* makes several important films about World War II—*Flying Tigers* (1942), *Reunion in France* (1942), *The Fighting Seabees* (1944), *Back to Bataan* (1945), and *They Were Expendable* (1945)—all of which were designed to boost the spirits of wartime America; *1947* becomes so popular that he is able to break out of the studio-controlled star system and form his own film production company; produces and stars in *Angel and the Badman* (1947); *1948-1952* makes films with John Ford—*Fort Apache* (1948), *Three Godfathers* (1949), *She Wore a Yellow Ribbon* (1950), *Rio Grande* (1951), and *The Quiet Man* (1952)—and several other memorable movies, *Red River* (1948), directed by Howard Hawks, and *Sands of Iwo Jima* (1949), for which he receives an Academy Award nomination for best actor; *1952* makes *Big Jim McClain* about the FBI's search for Communist spies in Hawaii, the first film (excluding his pro-American war films) that explicitly states his conservative political views; *1951-1954* cooperates with the House Un-American Activities Committee in its investigation of alleged Communist influences in the American film industry; *1956* stars in John Ford's *The Searchers,* which depicts the Indians as brutal savages to be exterminated; *1959* stars in director Howard Hawks's *Rio Bravo,* a film designed to counteract what he considers the anti-American mindset expressed in the 1952 Gary Cooper classic, *High Noon*, by showing the importance of the community working together to overcome problems; *1960* against the recommendation of the film community, produces, directs, and stars as Davy Crockett in the epic, *The Alamo*, an event in American history which for him summarized better than any other the frontier spirit and sacrifice to a cause greater than the individual; *1964* diagnosed with lung cancer and after difficult operations and recovery beats what he calls "The Big C"; *1966* backs the concept and plays a small part in *Cast a Giant Shadow* about Mickey Marcus, an American Jew who served a significant role in the creation of the Israeli army in the 1940s, as a means of telling an important story to the American public about Israel; *1968* at the height of the Vietnam War, and the protests against it, directs and stars in *The Green Berets*, a film designed to articulate the highest principles of America's involvement and the nobility of the South Vietnamese people against a Communist aggressor; *1969* stars as over-the-hill frontier marshall Rooster Cogburn in *True Grit*, for which he receives his only Academy Award, again using the film to articulate conservative political ideals that "made America great"; *1976* stars in his last film, *The Shootist*, in which he plays an aging gunfighter dying of cancer in the turn-of-the-century West where his lifestyle and values had become obsolete; *1979* dies in Los Angeles on June 11, after a long bout with cancer.

Activities of Historical Significance

John Wayne, the most popular film star in American history, was a symbol of traditional American virtues and political conservatism. Through his films, especially later in his career, and his actions off-screen Wayne sought to pass to successive generations what he considered the ideals that had made the United States a great nation: self-reliance, willingness to take strong action when necessary, independence, democratic government, commitment to a goal beyond oneself, and a pioneering spirit. His forms of Americanism blended extreme patriotism with a certain jingoism, a conservative Republicanism, and a laissez-faire economic philosophy. Indeed he believed that his own success in rising from an unknown to a celebrity could only have taken place in such an environment.

Commitment to these ideals prompted Wayne to tailor his on-screen characters to represent them. For instance, after years of trying to gain financial backing for a film about the siege of the Alamo, he made it on his own in 1960. It was his project from start to finish; not only was he producer, director, and star but he also mortgaged many of his personal assets to finance the film. Although undoubtedly motivated by honest feelings about the subject, Wayne's film was criticized by reviewers as being much too naive and simplistic a picture of American history and too preachy in content. In the story Wayne's one hundred eighty Texans opposed a Mexican force of four thousand under Santa Anna at the Alamo in 1836 as a means of buying time for Sam Houston to rally Texans farther north to win freedom from Mexico. Although the Texans held out for twelve days they were eventually massacred. Wayne cast the defense of the Alamo as an American Thermopylae; although a military defeat, it was worth the price for it served the greater good of humanity. The number of Mexican casualties coupled with the length of time required to take the Alamo hurt Santa Anna's campaign enough to allow the Texans to reinforce their position. It expressed a patriotic sentiment advocating the ultimate sacrifice of life for freedom and democratic principles.

In another notable example, at the height of American involvement in the Vietnam War, Wayne again displayed a conservative position in making *The Green Berets*, which spoke to the positive aspects of the nation's role in the fighting. Hearkening back to some of the themes he had developed earlier in his war movies during and soon after World War II, Wayne presented the war as an epic contest between good and evil; the film depicted the United States as a good neighbor helping the outgunned but nonetheless noble South Vietnamese fight Communist aggressors who were the embodiment of evil. In the film, which was shot with poor attention to detail (near the end of the movie the sun even sets in the east), Wayne tells a young Vietnamese boy that he was the reason the United States was in the country, so that he could have the blessings of liberty and equality of opportunity. The film was butchered by critics, in part because of its hawkish statement at a time when the tenor of the nation was swinging decidedly against the war; nevertheless, it was a huge box-office success.

If Jane Fonda's visit to Hanoi made her a champion of anti-war protestors and the bane of conservatives, *The Green Berets* made Wayne a leader of conservatives, as well as a clear target for liberals. Although earlier he had been firmly in the conservative camp, for instance as a diligent supporter of Republican Barry Goldwater's 1964 presidential campaign and as a strong anti-Communist activist in California, *The Green Berets* brought Wayne and his ideals to the fore as never before. It was a position Wayne relished, genuinely feeling that the nation deserved his highest devotion. He went on the lecture circuit, in 1974 even visiting Harvard University, a hotbed of anti-war sentiment, arriving on campus in a National Guard armored-car to present his pro-American position. His 1973 best-selling phonograph album and book, *America, Why I Love Her*, especially captured his special sense of patriotism and conservatism. His films depicted a particular heroic image of America; in both his heroic screen image and his political position, Wayne made a lasting impact on the United States of his era.

Overview of Biographical Sources

There are no definitive biographies of John Wayne, but there are several popularly-written works which provide much information. By far the best of the books on Wayne's life and career is Maurice Zolotow, *Shooting Star: A Biography of John Wayne* (1974. Reprint. 1979). This is not a scholarly work, nor intends to be, but it is an insightful investigation of Wayne's place in American popular culture. Although limited to an analysis of his western movie image, Archie P. McDonald's article, "John Wayne: Hero of the Western," in *Shooting Stars: Heroes and Heroines of Western Film* (1987), presents a fine historical analysis of Wayne's impact on the image of frontier America in popular culture.

There have been several other biographies of Wayne, none of them particularly satisfying or revealing, and all of them running together in the recitations of familiar stories and handling of themes. These include: Jean Ramer, *Duke: The Real Story of John Wayne* (1973); Mike Tomkies, *Duke: The Story of John Wayne* (1971); and several books published at the time of his death in 1979: George Victor Bishop, *John Wayne, The Actor, The Man*; John Boswell and Jay Fisher, *Duke: The John Wayne Album*; and Norm Goldstein, *John Wayne: A Tribute*.

Several film biographies have also been compiled. These large-format books all emphasize photographs and contain plot synopses of Wayne movies. All are organized chronologically and are designed for fans. Some of them, however, seek to go beyond a superficial level and offer some analysis. Clearly the best is Alan Eyles, *John Wayne and the Movies* (1976. Reprint. 1979), which provides some critical analysis of Wayne's films and how they affected American popular culture.

Evaluation of Principal Biographical Sources

Barbour, Alan G. *John Wayne*. New York: Pyramid Publications, 1974. (G) A popular film biography, cataloging Wayne's movies and featuring photos and a description of plot lines.

Bishop, George Victor. *John Wayne, The Actor, The Man*. New Rochelle, NY: Arlington House, 1979. (G) A quick biography published at the time of Wayne's death. Like most others published at that time, it has little new information and no serious analysis of the man and his career in film and politics.

Boswell, John, and Jay Fisher. *Duke: The John Wayne Album*. New York: Ballantine Books, 1979. (G) A popular book, emphasizing photos and an enormous number of little-known facts about Wayne.

Carpozi, George, Jr. *The John Wayne Story.* New Rochelle, NY: Arlington House, 1972. (G) A picture book oriented toward Wayne's film career.

Eyles, Alan. *John Wayne and the Movies.* 1976. Reprint. South Brunswick: A. S. Barnes, 1979. (G) This chronological description of Wayne's films emphasizes photos and stories. It is the strongest of Wayne's film biographies, because it provides some critical analysis of the films, Wayne's role in making them, and how Wayne's character and beliefs were repeatedly stated from film to film.

Goldstein, Norm. *John Wayne: A Tribute.* New York: Holt, Rinehart and Winston, 1979. (G) Popular biography written at the time of Wayne's death.

Kieskalt, Charles J. *The Official John Wayne Reference Book.* Secaucus, NJ: Citadel Press, 1985. (G) A treasure of trivia and little-known information about Wayne, from what he liked to eat to quotations from his films.

McDonald, Archie P. "John Wayne: Hero of the Western." In *Shooting Stars: Heroes and Heroines of Western Film.* Bloomington: Indiana University Press, 1987. (A, G) A solid historical analysis of Wayne's image as an exemplar and beacon in American popular culture. As the title implies, McDonald is concerned only with Wayne's role in the western movie genre.

Ramer, Jean. *Duke: The Real Story of John Wayne.* New York: Award Books, 1973. (G) A popular biography emphasizing Wayne's on-screen persona.

Reagan, Ronald. "Unforgettable John Wayne." *Reader's Digest* 115 (October 1979): 114-119. (G) A tribute to Wayne written in commemoration of his death by a fellow actor and conservative politician. Reagan's assessment of Wayne was largely on-target: "He gave the whole world the image of what an American should be."

Ricci, Mark, Boris Zmijewsky, and Steve Zmijewsky. *The Films of John Wayne.* Secaucus, NJ: Citadel Books, 1970. (G) This is a large-sized, photograph-filled film biography of Wayne. It lacks analysis of Wayne's films and life and is useful principally for its uncritical descriptions of his films.

Shaw, Sam. *John Wayne in the Camera Eye.* London, NY: Hamlyn, 1980. (A, G) A somewhat more sophisticated analysis of Wayne's films than most works of its type.

Tomkies, Mike. *Duke: The Story of John Wayne*. Chicago: Henry Regnery, 1971. (G) Popular account sensationalizing the heroic image of Wayne developed in his successive films.

Zmijewsky, Steven. *The Complete Films of John Wayne*. Secaucus, NJ: Citadel Press, 1970. (G) A filmography of Wayne, containing capsule descriptions of each film and photos from the work.

Zolotow, Maurice. *Shooting Star: A Biography of John Wayne*. 1974. Rev. ed. New York: Simon and Schuster, 1979. (A, G) By far the most satisfying account of Wayne's life, written before his death but updated in 1979. Journalistic in style and tone but without scholarly apparatus, it is well-researched and insightful.

Overview and Evaluation of Primary Sources

Virtually all of the published primary sources relating to Wayne are in the form of memoirs by people who lived with or worked with him. For example, Chuck Roberson, Wayne's longtime friend and stunt double, published *The Fall Guy: 30 Years as the Duke's Double* (North Vancouver, BC: Hancock House, 1980; G), an interesting story of behind-the-scenes action on Wayne's movies. Donald Shepherd, Robert Slatzer, and Dave Grayson published *Duke: The Life and Times of John Wayne* (Garden City, NY: Doubleday, 1985; G), a serviceable biography of Wayne, which emphasizes the intimate side of his life. Grayson was associated with Wayne on many of his films and had a personal friendship with him, and this tie is the rationale behind the work. In the genre of "kiss-and-tell" gossip books is Pat Stacy, *Duke: A Love Story* (New York: Atheneum, 1983; G), a personal account of Wayne's last years when the author, his secretary, became his lover and constant companion. In the same category is Pilar Wayne, with Alex Thorleifson, *John Wayne: My Life with the Duke* (New York: McGraw-Hill, 1987; G), a personal account of Wayne's life written by his third wife, and although they were estranged at Wayne's death, his legal widow.

An important personal statement of Wayne's patriotism can be found in his volume, *America, Why I Love Her*, written with Billy Liebert and John Mitchum (New York: Simon and Schuster, 1973; G), and the record album by the same name. His closing paragraph summarized his basic love of his country. "Day after day in America," he wrote, "people enjoy the good life. It's solid and its real." Bessie Little edited *John Wayne: Duke's Own Story* (New York: Reliance Publications, 1979; G), which contains statements from Wayne made in various places over a lifetime of activity.

Wayne left no large collection of manuscript sources for the scholar seeking to use primary resources, but for anyone working on Wayne and the film industry there are several collections that should be reviewed, each containing some Wayne material. The Film Research Collections at Harold B. Lee Library, Brigham Young University, Provo, Utah, contains the papers of several people and organizations with which Wayne was associated: directors Cecil B. DeMille and Howard Hawks; producer Merian C. Cooper; actors James Stewart, Harry Carey, Sr., and Harry Carey, Jr.; and Argosy Productions, John Ford's company. In addition, the papers of director John Ford, with whom Wayne was closely associated throughout his career, are housed in the Lilly Library, Indiana University, Bloomington. In addition to several collections that might prove useful in a study of Wayne, the archive of Warner Brothers at the University of Southern California, and the Fox and RKO collections at UCLA, both in Los Angeles. All of the major collections have been profiled in the American Film Institute Education Newsletter.

Fiction and Adaptations

It is difficult to describe fictional works about John Wayne, especially when he made his career acting in fictional stories. Perhaps the most significant such fictional work is the series of comic books issued beginning in 1949 as "John Wayne Adventure Comics," most of which were drawn by Frank Franzetta of fantastic science fiction art fame. In 1950 Oxydol published six Wayne comics as promotional items to launch a new detergent, "Drift." Dell Publishing later put out a set of illustrated comics about Wayne's films. Perhaps most interesting, Tom Tierney released *John Wayne Paper Dolls* (1981), which has costumes from his many films.

Over the years several documentaries have been made which deal with Wayne's career. Two of the best of these are *The Duke Lives On,* produced by Home Box Office Presentations, and first aired on February 9, 1980, and *John Wayne—An American Legend,* first aired on September 5, 1979, not long after Wayne's death.

Museums, Historical Landmarks, Societies

John Wayne's Birthplace (Winterset, IA). Run by a nonprofit corporation, this site features some restored rooms from Wayne's home and a room exhibiting Wayne memorabilia.

John Wayne Cancer Clinic (Los Angeles, CA). Although not a museum, this clinic was endowed for cancer research by Wayne and has been decorated with Wayne memorabilia.

Smithsonian Institution (Washington, DC). This museum possesses some items, posters, and memorabilia on Wayne.

Other Sources

Didion, Joan. "John Wayne: A Love Song." In *Slouching Towards Bethlehem.* New York: Farrar, Straus, & Giroux, 1968. A moving and well-written portrait of Wayne and the meaning his image and films have held for the American public. Didion writes with feeling and sensitivity on such little-discussed issues as Wayne's sex appeal and charisma.

Lenihan, John. *Showdown: Confronting Modern America in Western Films.* Urbana: University of Illinois Press, 1980. An outstanding study of the role of the western as a reflection of American culture in the post-World War II era.

Mellen, Joan. *Big Bad Wolves: Masculinity in the American Film.* New York: Pantheon Books, 1977. A solid analysis of the macho image of film actors, including Wayne.

Miller, Lee O. "John Wayne: From Singin' Sandy to Just Plain Duke." In *The Great Cowboy Stars of Movies & Television.* New Rochelle, NY: Arlington House Publishers, 1979. A routine synopsis of Wayne's career.

Paige, David. *John Wayne.* Mankato, MN: Creative Education, 1971. Contains a short description of Wayne's screen career.

Suid, Lawrence. *Guts and Glory: Great American War Movies.* Reading, MA: Addison-Wesley, 1978. This useful analysis of war films, although not film criticism in the strictest sense, contains much discussion of Wayne's movies in this genre.

Tuska, Jon. *The Filming of the West.* Garden City, NY: Doubleday, 1976. This outstanding study of the western film genre includes a significant discussion of Wayne's role in its development.

Roger D. Launius
NASA Chief Historian

JOHN GREENLEAF WHITTIER
1807-1892

Chronology

Born December 17, 1807, on a farm near Haverhill, Massachusetts, to John Whittier, a farmer, and Abigail Hussey Whittier; *1826* publishes the poem "The Exile's Departure" in the *Newburyport Free Press*, edited by abolitionist William Lloyd Garrison; *1827-1828* attends Haverhill Academy for two terms; *1829* edits *American Manufacturer*; *1830* edits Haverhill's *Essex Gazette*, leaving it the same year to edit Hartford's *New England Weekly Review*; his father dies; *1831* publishes first book, *Legends of New England*; serves as delegate for Henry Clay at the Republican Convention; *1832* runs for the House of Representatives and loses; *1833* serves as delegate to the Anti-Slavery Convention in Philadelphia; *1834* elected to the Massachusetts legislature; *1836* edits the *Essex Gazette*; *1837* works for the American Anti-Slavery Society in New York; *1838* edits the *Pennsylvania Freeman*; *1844-1845* edits Lowell's *Middlesex Standard*; *1845* becomes contributing editor for Washington, D.C.'s *National Era*; *1857* his mother dies; *1866* publishes the immensely popular *Snow-Bound*; *1886* awarded doctorate of laws by Harvard University; *1892* dies September 7, of the effects of a stroke, in Hampton Falls, Massachusetts.

Activities of Historical Significance

John Greenleaf Whittier is of historical interest primarily for his accomplishments as a poet and as an opponent of slavery. He had little formal education and became interested in writing as a result of his parents, who maintained a large, eclectic library. Early in his teens, he found that he had a flare for writing simple rhymes that had broad popular appeal, and when he was older, he wrote scores of easy rhyming poems for popular magazines. He did not hold these verses in high regard, instead recognizing them as simple writings that lacked the strong imagery and depth of thought or feeling that marked good poetry. Until he reached middle age, Whittier regarded his work opposing slavery to be far more important than his poetry.

His work for abolitionism began with the publication of his poem "The Exile's Departure." One of his sisters had secretly submitted it to editor William Lloyd Garrison, signing it "W." Garrison loved the poem and wanted more of them, and he soon found out that Whittier had written it. A passionate opponent of slavery,

Garrison captured Whittier's imagination. Whittier yearned to do something great and to have a worthy cause to which he could devote himself. Garrison gave him that cause, and he quickly turned his writing talents to it. His talents were considerable, and he proved to have an able mind that could carefully think through the complex political issues of his day. Whittier argued that a slave society and a free society could not coexist; the free society of southern whites, he insisted, would inevitably be corrupted by the slave society.

During the years leading up to the Civil War, the abolitionist movement split into two rival factions: one believing that violence was the only way to root out the evil of slavery, and the other preferring peaceful solutions. Whittier belonged to this second group. He was born and raised a Quaker, and he never fully shook off the Quaker commitment to peace. It is true that on occasion, when gripped by the excitement of his cause, he did suggest that slavery should be swept away by righteous violence, but in most of his writings he maintained that slavery would eventually decline. His argument was similar to that of many other opponents of slavery, such as Abraham Lincoln. The abolitionists argued that their first task was a political one: they should work through Congress to make laws forbidding the expansion of slavery into new territories. Once the slave states were isolated in a primarily nonslave nation, economic pressures would eventually eliminate slavery. There was, in their minds, considerable evidence that wage-earning workers were far more profitable than slaves.

Whittier was disappointed by subsequent events; over much opposition, Texas was admitted to the Union as a slave state, thus making political solutions to the problem of slavery seemingly remote. Further, no amount of argument seemed to convince slave owners that they would be better off with paid employees. Despite these setbacks, Whittier never fully lost the belief that a peaceful end to slavery could be found. During the 1840s and 1850s, he helped heal the division between opponents of slavery, and he wrote many of the abolitionists' manifestos. By the Civil War, he was respected as one of abolitionism's most able spokesmen.

The Civil War left him without an important cause to which he could devote his life. During the late 1850s, he had begun to treat his poetry with more respect, devoting more of his skills to it. With the advent of the Civil War, he found solace in his verses. He still wrote poems that would lift the spirits of those who fought against slavery, and the public admired him as a patriot. However, his devotion to abolitionism had left little time for worrying about earning a good living, and in middle age he lived in genteel poverty. This changed in 1866.

By 1866 he had found a theme—America's transition from the past into the present—that seemed to draw on his best talent. This formed the basis for the blend of nostalgia and hope for a better future that made *Snow-Bound* a resounding success. Published in 1866, this poem used the example of Whittier's own family to express a love of the land; it captured the imagination of a wide audience by suggesting how the virtues of the past might still be valid in the present, even after the wrenching experience of the Civil War. From then on, Whittier's reputation as a poet grew, and he made a handsome living from his writings. To his contemporaries, he was one of America's greatest spokesmen, describing what made America and Americans special. Modern critics are divided about his literary worth, with some pointing out that most of his poetry is simplistic and shallow. Others suggest that Whittier's simple poems belong to his abolitionist years and his later poetry is of high quality and should form the basis for his claim to literary greatness.

Overview of Biographical Sources

There are two major problems with biographies of Whittier: they too often focus on his abolitionist work at the expense of the many other important aspects of his life, and they have trouble adequately accounting for his private personality. More recent biographers have noted that Whittier was an astute politician who helped political candidates win difficult elections and who was responsible for passing significant social legislation in both Massachusetts and the federal government. According to some biographers, Whittier's private life was bizarre. Whittier coined the phrase "male coquette," which some biographers have used to describe his personality. He drifted from one love affair to another, yearning for upper-class women while shunning farming or laboring women. His own explanation for never marrying was that he gave up a normal family life in order to devote himself fully to his social causes. Biographers tend to discount this as his true motivation, suggesting instead that Whittier was confused about what he really wanted in a wife and ignored realistic opportunities for marriage in order to pursue women who had little interest in him. This may be seen as an aspect of his desire to commit himself to a cause: each is a romantic pursuit of an ideal. Yet, while Whittier mastered the practical skills of politics, he did not form practical notions about love and marriage.

Evaluation of Principal Biographical Sources

Bennett, Whitman. *Whittier: Bard of Freedom.* 1941. Reprint. Port Washington, NY: Kennikat Press, 1972. (**A, G**) Declares that Whittier was "the most effective literary man in direct personal influence on our political and social system that this country has ever produced." Bennett portrays Whittier as politically astute; he sees him as a man who effectively used his talents to shape America's future. The emphasis here is on Whittier's personality, with his public and private life being directed by his need to devote himself to a cause.

Burton, Richard. *John Greenleaf Whittier*. Boston: Small Maynard, 1901. (G) Part of the Beacon Biographies Series, this short biography focuses on Whittier the man, with little discussion of his poetry. For Burton, Whittier's life is an "attractive story," exemplifying how a quiet, peaceful man could shape important events in America's history. Whittier's work against slavery receives close attention. Like most other biographers of his day, Burton is convinced of Whittier's literary greatness.

Carpenter, George Rice. *John Greenleaf Whittier*. Boston: Houghton Mifflin, 1903. (A, G) Part of the American Men of Letters Series, this scholarly work tries to pull together all the available resources on Whittier's life. The result is a pedestrian account, covering Whittier's family history, his place in the history of New England, and his influence on America's politics and literature. Carpenter devotes most of his biography to Whittier's work as an abolitionist, and consequently says very little about his life after 1860.

Fields, Annie. "Whittier: Notes of His Life and of His Friendships." In *Authors and Friends*. Boston: Houghton Mifflin, 1897. (G) This is a firsthand account of Whittier's life by someone who knew him well. Fields regards Whittier as a unique figure without historical precedence, with his personality and beliefs shaped by his Quaker faith and his experiences growing up on a New England farm. In this friendly biography, Whittier is portrayed as a man of courage and tenacity who sacrificed his hope for happiness to fight against evil.

Kennedy, W. Sloane. *John Greenleaf Whittier: His Life, Genius, and Writings*. 2d ed., rev. and enl. New York: Haskell House, 1973. (A, G) The first edition of this book infuriated Whittier; to a correspondent, possibly Elizabeth Nicholson, in a letter dated December 30, 1882, Whittier wrote: "The 'new biography' is a humbug. The author—a young man, a stranger, called on me once as a hundred others do monthly, staid about an hour, and I thought nothing of his visit, until I heard that he had been at Haverhill and other places enquiring about me, and cautioning those he spoke to, not to let me know.—Still I could not dream of his writing a book until I saw it advertised in the papers. It is very annoying and is one of the miseries of notoriety.' In spite of Whittier's assertions that this biography was poorly researched, it remains one of the principal resources for the study of Whittier's life. It is the easiest of the biographies to find; it includes firsthand accounts from people who knew Whittier; and it talks about aspects of Whittier's life that more respectful biographers of the time chose to ignore.

Lewis, Georgina King. *John Greenleaf Whittier: His Life and Work.* 1913. Reprint. Port Washington, NY: Kennikat Press, 1972. **(G)** This readable biography is appropriate for a broad general audience. It offers nothing new about Whittier's life, but it does serve as a good summary of what was known about Whittier by 1913. Students may find the opening chapter's account of Whittier's family history to be especially helpful. Lewis portrays Whittier as a literary knight errant who singlehandedly fought the injustice of slavery.

Pickard, Samuel T. *Life and Letters of John Greenleaf Whittier.* 2 vols. Boston: Houghton Mifflin, 1894. **(A, G)** This has long been treated as the standard biography of Whittier, although it has recently been supplanted by Woodwell's book. A workmanlike account of Whittier's life, these volumes provide a wealth of detail about his private and public activities. Nearly every Whittier biographer has used this book as an essential resource of factual detail, although most have found Pickard's interpretation of Whittier's personality wanting.

Wagenknecht, Edward. *John Greenleaf Whittier: A Portrait in Paradox.* New York: Oxford University Press, 1967. **(G)** Wagenknecht tries to update modern views of Whittier, arguing that the poet was more than a one-dimensional opponent of slavery, but was, instead, a man with a rich political life that included many other important social causes, including temperance. Of the relatively short biographies, this is the best one. It is engagingly written and can be enjoyed by high school students as well as adults. All the major aspects of Whittier's life are well covered, even though Wagenknecht has as much trouble making sense out of Whittier's chaotic love life as everyone else.

Woodwell, Roland H. *John Greenleaf Whittier: A Biography.* Haverhill, MA: Trustees of the John Greenleaf Whittier Homestead, 1985. **(A, G)** This outstanding biography sets a new standard for the study of Whittier's life. Woodwell makes excellent use of the vast amount of information on Whittier that has been turned up by researchers since the poet's death. Woodwell provides the most complete account of Whittier's New England ancestors that has yet been published, and clarifies how his family became part of the Quaker faith. Woodwell apologizes for Whittier's readability, perhaps responding to the general view of twentieth-century critics that Whittier sacrificed art for popularity in his writings.

Overview and Evaluation of Primary Sources

Whittier's letters have long been of interest to researchers, in part because they hope to find clues that would help explain Whittier's personality, and in part because historians hope the letters would offer insight into the abolitionist movement and other significant aspects of American society. Before the publication of John B. Pickard's edition of Whittier's letters, there were four principal sources for them: Samuel T. Pickard, ed., *Whittier as a Politician: Illustrated by His Letters to Professor Elizur Wright, Jr.* (Boston: Charles T. Goodspeed, 1900; A, G), offering insight into Whittier's politics; John Albree, ed., *Whittier Correspondence from the Oak Knoll Collection* (Salem, MA: Essex book and Print Club, 1911; A, G), a scholarly book that presents letters mostly on public matters; Marie V. Denervaud, ed., *Whittier's Unknown Romance: Letters to Elizabeth Lloyd* (Boston: Houghton Mifflin, 1922; A, G), which presents letters that reveal Whittier's bittersweet romance with Elizabeth Lloyd, a minor poet; and Thomas Franklin Currier, ed., *Elizabeth Lloyd and the Whittiers: A Budget of Letters* (Cambridge: Harvard University Press, 1939; A, G), which further develops the relationship between Whittier and Lloyd.

The standard edition of Whittier's letters is John B. Pickard, ed., *The Letters of John Greenleaf Whittier*, 3 vols. (Cambridge: Harvard University Press, 1975; A, G). Each volume includes a chronology of Whittier's life, succinct commentary by Pickard, and ample notes. Whittier was not a great letter writer, and like many other professional writers of his time, he found letter-writing to be an unpleasant chore. Nonetheless, his early letters offer descriptive passages and dramatic flair, and his later letters reveal the reflections of a thoughtful man who has been an active participant in many of the major events of his time.

Museums, Historical Landmarks, Societies

Haverhill Public Library (Haverhill, MA). Maintains the Whittier Collection, which includes photographs of the poet.

Other Sources

Hawkins, Chauncey J. *The Mind of Whittier: A Study of Whittier's Fundamental Religious Ideas*. Philadelphia: Thomas Whittaker, 1904. This book treats Whittier's profound belief in Jesus Christ and suggests the importance of religious faith in the composition of Whittier's poetry.

Kribbs, Jayne K. *Critical Essays on John Greenleaf Whittier*. Boston: G. K. Hall, 1980. This is a valuable resource for anyone researching Whittier. It includes reviews from Whittier's own day, as well as an extensive selection of critical studies from more recent times.

Mordell, Albert. *Quaker Militant: John Greenleaf Whittier.* Boston: Houghton Mifflin, 1933. A not entirely successful psychological study of Whittier.

Pickard, John B. *John Greenleaf Whittier: An Introduction and an Interpretation.* New York: Barnes and Noble, 1961. This is suited to students who need an overview of the major aspects of Whittier's life and work.

Porter, Maria S. "Recollections of John Greenleaf Whittier." In *Recollections of Louisa May Alcott, John Greenleaf Whittier, and Robert Browning, together with Several Memorial Poems: Illustrated.* Boston: New England Magazine Corporation, 1893. Porter calls Whittier "the most beloved of our poets" in this informal summary of his importance.

Warren, Robert Penn. *John Greenleaf Whittier's Poetry: An Appraisal and a Selection.* Minneapolis: University of Minnesota Press, 1971. This book's chief interest is its literary criticism; Warren comments on Whittier's poetry are valuable because they are made by a distinguished American poet. Readers should be wary of the biographical aspects of this book; not all the dates are correct, and a large section of the biographical summary is devoted to an argument that northern abolitionists were more racist than southern slave owners—a point of view that is utterly insupportable by historical evidence.

Kirk H. Beetz
National University, Sacramento

ELIE WIESEL
b. 1928

Chronology

Born Eliezer Wiesel on September 30, 1928, in Sighet, Rumania, the third of four children and the only son of Shlomo Wiesel, a grocer, and Sarah Feig Wiesel; *1934-1944* grows up in Sighet where he attends Jewish schools; *1944* Nazis come to Sighet; family sent to death camps; mother and seven-year-old younger sister die at Auschwitz; *1945* father dies at Buchenwald; *April 11* liberated from Buchenwald; sent to Normandy, France; *1946-1956* moves to Paris; teaches the Bible; studies philosophy at the Sorbonne; lives in Paris for eleven years where he adopts the French language; works as foreign correspondent for the Tel Aviv newspaper, *Yediot Aharanot*; travels to Israel; *1956* moves to the United States; *1958* publishes first novel, *Le Nuit*, in France, a work about his experiences during the Holocaust; *1960 Night* published in the U.S.; *1963* becomes a naturalized U.S. citizen; *1964* publishes *The Town Beyond the Wall* and wins the Prix Rivarol and the National Jewish Book Award; *1965* travels to the Soviet Union and begins work on *The Testament* (1981) for which he wins Le Prix Livre-Inter; *1969* marries Vienneseborn Marion Erster Rose who translates most of his work into English; *1970* publishes *A Beggar in Jerusalem* and receives the Prix Medicis; *1972* appointed distinguished professor at the City College of New York; *1976* appointed Andrew W. Mellon Professor at Boston University; *1979* appointed chairman of the President's Commission on the Holocaust (now the United States Holocaust Memorial Council); *1985* receives the Congressional Gold Medal of Achievement and pleads with President Ronald Reagan not to visit military cemetery at Bitburg, West Germany, but to visit memorials to the death camps instead; publishes *The Fifth Son*, a novel about the son of a Holocaust survivor, and wins Le Grand Prix de la Litterature de la Ville de Paris; *1986* awarded the Nobel Peace Prize; *1990* organizes conference held in Olso to study the "anatomy of hate," with principal discussion on Saddam Hussein; resides in New York City with his family; holds Andrew Mellon Chair at Boston University; continues to speak and write about the Holocaust, the Israel/Palestine conflict, and for human rights worldwide.

Activities of Historical Significance

Elie Wiesel has assumed the unofficial role of Jewish spokesman for the Holocaust, a natural position because of his life history and his skill as a writer. In

1944 the Nazis came to Sighet, Rumania, Wiesel's home, and arrested his entire family. He consequently spent time at four concentration camps: Birkenau, Auschwitz, Buna, and Buchenwald. He lost his mother and younger sister at Auschwitz and his father at Buchenwald.

For ten years after his release from Buchenwald, Wiesel was silent about his experiences. But in the mid-1950s he was encouraged by Francois Mauriac to write his story. He wrote his first novel, *Night*, in Yiddish; it was published in French (the language in which Wiesel continues to write) in 1958 and in English in 1960. The novel, which detailed his experience in the concentration camps, was well-received by critics, who compared it to *The Diary of Anne Frank.*

In his subsequent fiction Wiesel has pursued the theme of the Holocaust and the plight of its survivors. His second novel, *Dawn* (1961), the story of an eighteen-year-old Jewish soldier forced to become an executioner, explored the influence of the past on the present and established his spare, stark prose style. In *The Accident* (1962) Wiesel again dealt with the post-Holocaust world in a highly autobiographical work based on his own automobile accident. These first three fairly brief works, often classified as novellas, were later published as *Night, Dawn, The Accident; Three Tales* (1972).

The Town Beyond the Wall (1964) continued Wiesel's argument with God, begun in *Night,* about the Holocaust. The prize-winning novel tells the story of a Jew who returns to his native Hungary after the war to seek out a man who had watched the deportation of the Jews with indifference. *The Gates of the Forest* (1966) is another story about a survivor's postwar life. *The Fifth Son* (1985), a novel about the son of a Holocaust survivor, carries speculation about the post-Holocaust world further by dealing with the next generation of Jews.

The Holocaust survivor in *The Oath* (1973) copes differently than many of Wiesel's characters; he takes an oath of silence not to tell about the devastation of the camps. *Twilight* (1988), the story of a man who comes into contact with various madmen, concerns the struggle to retain sanity in a post-Holocaust world.

In 1965 Wiesel traveled to the Soviet Union and began work on *The Testament* (1981), based on Stalin's execution on August 12, 1952, of thirty Jewish poets and novelists. The book is a fictional prison diary of a Yiddish poet who espouses communism for part of his life. In 1966 and 1974, respectively, Wiesel published two other works relating to Soviet Jews: *The Jews of Silence* and *Zalmen, or The Madness of God* (a play). *The Jews of Silence,* first published in Hebrew as a series in the Tel Aviv newspaper, *Yediot Aharanot,* is a collection of articles about the plight of Soviet Jews and the lack of aid from Jews outside the Soviet Union.

In addition to his writings, Wiesel has remained a vocal spokesman for the world's need to remember the Holocaust. In 1979 he was appointed chairman of the President's Commission on the Holocaust (later named the United States Holocaust Memorial Council) and visited Babi Yar, a memorial to Jews massacred in World War II near the Soviet city of Kiev. His questioning of why Jews were not named on the Babi Yar monument later caused a scandal in the Soviet Union. In 1985 Wiesel made an emotional public plea to President Ronald Reagan not to visit the military cemetery at Bitburg, West Germany, but to visit instead memorials to those who perished in the death camps. His unflagging work for human rights and his continuing attempts to keep fresh the memory of the Holocaust earned Wiesel the Nobel Peace Prize in 1986.

Overview of Biographical Sources

Almost all of Wiesel's writings are to some extent autobiographical. His first novel, *Night* (1960), is about his experience in Nazi concentration camps. Eager to put foward his views on the Holocaust and on contemporary issues and events, Wiesel has freely consented to interviews and has given numerous lectures. In 1976 Harry James Cargas edited a book-length interview with Wiesel, *Harry James Cargas in Conversation with Elie Wiesel* (New York: Paulist Press, 1976). This dialogue between Wiesel, a Jewish survior of the Holocaust, and Cargas, a Christian teacher and writer who specializes in the Holocaust, is possibly the best overall source for information on Wiesel's life and ideas.

Irving Abrahamson's three-volume *Against Silence: The Voice and Vision of Elie Wiesel* (1985) is the most thorough compilation of all of Wiesel's supplemental statements, including interviews, essays, lectures, and articles. The only formal biography to date is Ellen Norman Stern's *Elie Wiesel: Witness for Life* (1982), a good introductory biography. Carol Greene's *Elie Wiesel: Messenger from the Holocaust* (1987) is the only biography for children, and offers a concise and illustrated description of Wiesel's life. In *From the Kingdom of Memory* (1990), Wiesel compiles articles, most previously published, and his Nobel laureate address. In *Evil and Exile* (1990) he records conversations held over one week with Phillippe Michael de Saint-Cheron, a man who converted to Judaism.

Evaluation of Principal Biographical and Critical Sources

Berenbaum, Michael. *The Vision of the Void: Theological Reflections on the Works of Elie Wiesel*. Middletown, CT: Wesleyan University Press, 1979. (A, G) Berenbaum's study examines the theological reverberations in Wiesel's work up through the mid-1970s. It offers theological interpretations that trace the author's religious consciousness over the span of the last four decades. His basic conclusion is that "Wiesel's theological vision is of the void."

Cargas, Harry James, ed. *Responses to Elie Wiesel: Critical Essays by Major Jewish and Christian Scholars.* New York: Persea Books, 1978. (**A, G**) This collection of seventeen interviews and essays by literary critics and theologians attempts to respond to Wiesel's views. It includes Josephine Knopp's well-known essay, "Wiesel and the Absurd," and Byron Sherwin's "Elie Wiesel and Jewish Theology."

Estess, Ted L. *Elie Wiesel.* New York: Ungar, 1980. (**A, G**) Estess offers general biographical information and systematically treats Wiesel's longer narratives through *The Trial of God.* This useful critical analysis traces Wiesel's themes and discusses his recurring images from literary, philosophical, and religious perspectives.

Fine, Ellen S. *Legacy of Night: The Literary Universe of Elie Wiesel.* Albany: State University of New York Press, 1982. (**A, G**) Fine's well-regarded study examines Wiesel's works in chronological order, considering them as episodes that trace Wiesel's spiritual journey.

Greene, Carol. *Elie Wiesel: Messenger from the Holocaust.* Chicago: Children's Press, 1987. (**Y**) This brief, illustrated biography focuses on Wiesel's wartime experiences and his novels.

Rittner, Carol, ed. *Elie Wiesel: Between Memory and Hope.* New York: New York University Press, 1990. (**A, G**) Rittner has collected essays especially for this project, including an essay on *Twilight* by Robert McAfee Brown. Contributors include Jewish and Christian scholars from a variety of disciplines and perspectives. Rather than highlighting biography, Rittner and others examine literary, philosophical, and theological issues in Wiesel's work.

Rosenfeld, Alvin H., and Irving Greenberg, eds. *Confronting the Holocaust: The Impact of Elie Wiesel.* Bloomington: Indiana University Press, 1978. (**A, G**) This diverse collection covers such topics as religion and ethics, the Holocaust in literature, and the moral and religious aspects of the Holocaust. The authors are well-known Wiesel scholars.

Roth, John K. *A Consuming Fire: Encounters with Elie Wiesel and the Holocaust.* Atlanta: John Knox, 1979. (**A, G**) In this dynamic study Roth explores the religious and theological implications of the Holocaust by drawing from Wiesel's work and life.

Overview and Evaluation of Primary Sources

Almost all of Wiesel's work was first written in French, and most of it has been published in English. Much of his writing can be considered as a primary source for biographical information. Dated but useful to scholars is Molly Abramowitz's *Elie Wiesel: A Bibliography* (Metuchen, NJ: Scarecrow Press, 1974; A, G), an annotated listing of all English (and many foreign language) works by and about Wiesel.

Irving Abrahamson's collection and organization of all supplemental writings by Wiesel in *Against Silence: The Voice and Vision of Elie Wiesel* (New York: Holocaust Library, 1985; A, G) includes letters, interviews, speeches, articles, book reviews, transcripts, and an early drama attempt.

Other Sources

"Elie Wiesel's Jerusalem." Transcript of Canadian Broadcasting Corp.-TV, 1979. This is an adaptation in which Wiesel describes Jerusalem.

Friedman, Maurice. *Abraham Joshua Heschel and Elie Wiesel: You Are My Witnesses*. New York: Farrar, Straus, Giroux, 1987. Friedman explores Wiesel's theology and philosophy in the second part of this highly charged and personal study.

Halpern, Irving. *Messengers from the Dead: Literature of the Holocaust*. Philadelphia: Westminster, 1970. A collection of autobiographical material from Holocaust survivors that includes a comprehensive examination of Wiesel's first five novels.

"The Itinerary of Elie Wiesel: From Sighet to Jerusalem." Transcript of National Broadcasting Co., *The Eternal Light*, NBC-TV Network (May 21, 1972). *The Eternal Light* radio series was written and narrated by Wiesel.

Langer, Lawrence L. *The Holocaust and the Literary Imagination*. New Haven: Yale University Press, 1975. Wiesel's work is prominent in this study of what Langer terms "the literature of atrocity."

Laura Gabel Hartman
Virginia Commonwealth University

JOHN WOOLMAN
1720-1772

Chronology

Born John Woolman on October 19, 1720, in Ancocas (later Rancocas) in the county of West Jersey, New Jersey, one of thirteen children of Samuel Woolman, a one-time candidate for the provincial assembly, and Elizabeth Woolman; as a child receives his only formal education at a Quaker school; serves an apprenticeship as a tailor and sets up his own shop in Mount Holly, New Jersey; *1743* is called to the Quaker ministry; *1746* visits Virginia and experiences slavery firsthand; *1749* marries Sarah Ellis; *1754* writes essay *Some Considerations of the Keeping of Negroes*; *1763* writes essay *A Plea for the Poor*; *1772* dies October 7, of smallpox while working among the poor in York, England; *1774 Journal* is published.

Activities of Historical Significance

John Woolman's contributions to American history evolve from his efforts in the Quaker ministry. Called as a young man to the Society of Friends, he journeyed throughout the American colonies and served the church in England. Like most of those involved in the Society of Friends, Woolman advocated pacifism: avoiding military service and refusing to pay taxes for military supplies. Yet his advocation of the abolition of slavery was his most significant contribution. He was an avid writer, and constantly improved his *Journal* in hopes of making it a more effective reflection of his life. His efforts achieved little attention during his lifetime, but through his *Journal* and his essay, *Some Considerations on the Keeping of Negroes*, his ideals were preserved for later generations.

Overview of Biographical Sources

Virtually all of the material available on Woolman has been written by, and largely for, members of the Quaker faith. This has its detractions and attractions; the authors are generally interested in Woolman's association with religious thought and tend to dwell on this exclusively, yet they are experts in their understanding of the nuances of the Quaker faith. Woolman's *Journal* is often the main focus and frequently the main source of information, and this work has been studied for both its religious and literary merits. It is significant that interest in

Woolman's life has peaked at times of world conflict. His *Journal* was first reprinted after the Franco-Prussian War of 1871, and again after each of the two world wars.

Evaluation of Biographical Sources

Benton, Josephine M. *John Woolman: Most Modern of Ancient Friends.* Philadelphia: Religious Education Committee of Friends General Conference, 195-. (G) A brief work describing Woolman's ideas on a variety of topics both worldly and religious. Each concise discussion of a topic is followed by useful page references to the Whitney edition of the *Journal.*

Cadbury, Henry Joel. *John Woolman in England, 1772, a Documentary Supplement.* London: Friends Historical Society, 1971. (A, G) A scholarly, readable cataloging of Woolman's final months in England. The author makes use of letters, journal entries, and travel notes to piece together Woolman's itinerary before his death. This is one of the most scholarly of the biographical works considered.

Cady, Edwin H. *John Woolman.* New York: Washington Square Press, 1965. (A, G) Part of the Great American Thinkers Series, this study portrays Woolman as an American saint. It is a studious, historical analysis of both the man and his work, geared to the undergraduate, and is an excellent source.

Gummere, Amelia M. *The John Woolman Memorial.* Mount Holly, NJ: n.p., n.d. (G) Very brief sketch of Woolman's life with notes on the property he owned in New Jersey that has been set aside as a monument. One of the houses is a simple brick cottage he had built for his daughter; the other is his own home. The book contains the records of the construction of the buildings. The garden (Woolman was an expert gardener) also receives attention.

Moorhouse, Fred. *The Significance of John Woolman for South Africa.* London: Friends Peace and International Relations Committee, 1971. (A, G) Part of the Non-Violence in Action Series, this brief pamphlet places Woolman and Quakerism in its pacifistic context. The tract discusses the role of religion in society and uses South Africa as a case study, but the material is dated.

Rosenblatt, Paul. *John Woolman.* New York: Twayne, 1969. (A, G) This biography and literary study focuses largely on the *Journal* and draws mainly from

Gummere and Whitney for its facts; the author compares Woolman to Jonathan Edwards, Ralph Waldo Emerson, Henry David Thoreau, and Walt Whitman. Part of Twayne's United States Authors Series, the book has an excellent chronology and is a very readable work.

Whitney, Janet. *John Woolman*. London: George C. Harrap, 1943. (**A, G**) This attempt to portray Woolman in the setting of his times is the most thorough of the biographies. It is well researched and scholarly, yet retains a readability that the general reader will appreciate. The author has a thorough knowledge of her subject and makes use of all available information.

Overview and Evaluation of Primary Sources

John Woolman, *The Works of John Woolman* (Philadelphia: J. Crukshank, 1774; Reprint. Miami: Mnemosyne, 1969; **A, G**), is the original source of his writings and is useful only for historiographic reasons. John Greenleaf Whittier (Boston: James R. Osgood, 1871; **A, G**) provided the basic text for a generation. It was replaced by the edition, Amelia M. Gummere, ed., *The Journal and Essays of John Woolman* (New York: Macmillan, 1922; **A, G**), which contains Woolman's *Journal* and essays as well as a very lengthy biographical sketch. Dozens of illustrations augment the text which was prepared in the context of the Versailles Peace Conference at the end of World War I. An appendix contains other significant Woolman papers of use to the historian if not the general reader. This work improved on Whittier's, but varied in many ways from the original Woolman text. Janet Whitney, *Journal of John Woolman* (Chicago: Henry Regnery, 1950; **A, G**), took advantage of the new manuscripts that came to light after 1922. Though Woolman made many changes in his *Journal*, always endeavoring to improve it, Whitney chose to use the original rather than later drafts and modernized the spelling and punctuation to make the work more palatable for general readers. Phillips P. Moulton, *The Journal and Major Essays of John Woolman* (A Library of Protestant Thought Series. New York: Oxford University Press, 1971; **A, G**), offers a scholarly edition of Woolman's writings. Many appendices clarify the difference between this edition and Whitney's. Also, a biographical note identifies the main participants in the writings. Reginald Reynolds's *The Wisdom of John Woolman with a Selection from his Writings as a Guide to the Seekers of Today* (London: George Allen and Unwin, 1948; **G**) is a brief collection of Woolman's writings arranged thematically with little modern scholarship used in editing. The introduction is useful for the beginner and the work as a whole is designed for the layman.

Museums, Historical Landmarks, Societies

The Woolman House and Gardens (Mount Holly, NJ). Operated by the John Woolman Association, this two story brick house that Woolman built for his daughter is surrounded by an eighteenth-century style garden. Many of the furnishings date back to Woolman and the home contains many of his possessions.

Other Sources

Pomfret, John E. "John Woolman." In *Dictionary of American Biography*, vol. 20, edited by Allan Johnson and Dumas Malone. New York: Charles Scribner's Sons, 1928-1936. This brief sketch is an appropriate starting point for a survey of Woolman's life and significance.

Daniel Dean Roland

FRANK LLOYD WRIGHT
1867-1959

Chronology

Born Frank Lloyd Wright on June 8, 1867, at Richland Center, Wisconsin, the son of William Russell Cary Wright, a musician and lay preacher, and Anna Lloyd-Jones, a schoolteacher; *1867* moves with family to Weymouth, Massachusetts, where he receives early schooling; *1878* returns to Wisconsin; *1885* parents divorce; *1886* enters the University of Wisconsin as a special student and takes job in Madison as a draftsman and engineer; *1887* leaves college after completing only two-thirds of his sophomore year and moves to Chicago to become an architect; secures job as draftsman in the office of architect Joseph Lyman Silsbee and designs first building, a small Unitarian chapel in Sioux City, Iowa; later in same year, joins staff of architects Dankmar Adler and Louis H. Sullivan and develops a strong working relationship with Sullivan; *1889* marries Catherine Lee Tobin; *1893* inaugurates own practice in Chicago; *1893-1910* becomes leading proponent of Prairie School of architecture and designs various residential structures in and around Chicago, including the Frederick C. Robie House (1909), incorporating the Prairie style; *1904* becomes romantically involved with Martha Borthwick "Mamah" Cheney, the wife of a client; designs Larkin Building, Buffalo, New York, his first large commercial endeavor; *1909* deserts wife and family and travels to Europe with Mamah Cheney; *1910-1911* has two-volume portfolio of his illustrations and drawings published in Germany, which influences the development of architecture in Europe well into the 1920s; *1911* settles with Mamah Cheney at Taliesin near Spring Green, Wisconsin; *1913-1914* travels to Japan and accepts commission to build the Imperial Hotel in Tokyo; *1914* Taliesin burns and Mamah Cheney and her children are killed; *1919-1922* plans and constructs the Aline Barnsdall House, Los Angeles, California; *1922* divorces Catherine; *1923* marries Maud Miriam Noel, who leaves him after six months; *1927* divorces Miriam Noel; *1928* marries Olga Iovanovna "Olgivanna" Lazovich Milanoff Hinzenberg; *1932* founds Taliesin Fellowship; *1934-1936* with Taliesin apprentices, begins Broadacre City project, near Uniontown, Pennsylvania; designs his most famous house, "Fallingwater"; designs Johnson Wax Company buildings, Racine, Wisconsin; *1938* opens winter residence at Taliesin West near Scottsdale, Arizona; *1939* lectures at London University; *1943* begins design for the Solomon R. Guggenheim Museum, New York City, which is not built until after his death; *1956* begins work on the futuristic Marin County (California) Civic Center, which is also not constructed until after his death; *1959* after an operation to remove an intestinal blockage, dies April 9 at Phoenix, Arizona.

Activities of Historical Significance

Frank Lloyd Wright received no formal schooling in architecture or environmental design, yet he became the most acclaimed American architect of the twentieth century. Wright contributed greatly to the design concept of modernism which included not only structures but city and regional planning, as well. He perceived architecture to be an organic part of human life allowing individuals greater freedom and, ultimately, he argued, leading to a more democratic society. In his career, which spanned seven decades, he designed nearly seven hundred buildings, including private residences, churches, office buildings, hotels, and museums. Four hundred of these plans were constructed and approximately three-fourths of the buildings remain extant. Not fully appreciated until the end of his life when his talents were in great demand worldwide, Wright has been both praised for pioneering modern architecture in America and criticized for not adhering to his own precepts. Nevertheless, his work challenged artistic and social convention and shaped the course of modern architecture.

Overview of Biographical Sources

In the last five decades Frank Lloyd Wright has been the subject of extensive and wide-ranging scholarship. Wright's protégé, Henry-Russell Hitchcock, wrote *In the Nature of Materials: The Buildings of Frank Lloyd Wright, 1887-1941* (1942), which is generally considered the first definitive account of Wright and his work up to 1941. This book, inspired by an exhibition of modern architecture held in 1940 at the Museum of Modern Art in New York, traces Wright's architecture building by building. In *Frank Lloyd Wright: His Life and His Architecture* (1979), Robert C. Twombly offers previously untold facts about Wright and his work. This book is more or less a revision of Twombly's first biography of Wright, *Frank Lloyd Wright, An Interpretative Biography* (1973), which the author developed from his doctoral dissertation. It provides a perceptive analysis of the psychological and historical forces that shaped the architect's thought and work. Brendan Gill's adept biography of Wright, ·*Many Masks: A Life of Frank Lloyd Wright* (1987), is perhaps the best treatment of the fascinating and brilliant architect. Gill knew Wright personally during the latter part of Wright's career, and his insights are unusually introspective. Gill does not hesitate to criticize the man and his work as he explodes some of the myths surrounding Wright's life; some of which Wright himself created in his autobiography.

Evaluation of Principal Biographical Sources

Farr, Finis. *Frank Lloyd Wright.* New York: Scribner's, 1961. (G) First full-length biography of Wright published after his death. Farr portrays the famous architect much the same as Wright himself did in his autobiography. Generally uncritical.

Gill, Brendan. *Many Masks: A Life of Frank Lloyd Wright.* New York: Putnam's, 1987. (A, G) Gill holds that Wright was a genius who did not flinch at self-promotion and self-esteem. He contends, however, that this aggrandizement was justified because of Wright's astounding abilities and achievements.

Hitchcock, Henry-Russell. *In the Nature of Materials: The Buildings of Frank Lloyd Wright, 1887-1941.* New York: Duell, Sloan and Pearce, 1942. Reprint. New York: Da Capo, 1973. (A, G) Contains more than four hundred illustrations along with commentary by Hitchcock, who had a pupil-mentor relationship with Wright.

Manson, Grant Carpenter. *Frank Lloyd Wright to 1910: The First Golden Age.* New York: Reinhold, 1958. Reprint. Van Nostrand Reinhold, n. d. (A, G) Intelligent treatment of Wright. Contains a thorough and reliable inventory of Wright's buildings up to 1910, a commentary on the influence of Louis Sullivan, and a discussion of Japanese architecture and the Froebel method.

Scully, Vincent J., Jr. *Frank Lloyd Wright.* New York: Braziller, 1960. (A, G) Brief examination of the principles of design governing Wright's work by a noted architectural historian and critic.

Smith, Norris K. *Frank Lloyd Wright: A Study in Architectural Content.* Englewood Cliffs, NJ: Prentice-Hall, 1966. Reprint. New York: Watkins Glen for the American Life Foundation, 1979. (A) Contends that in a time when the trend in architecture was toward functionalism, Wright's greatest contribution was the preservation of his craft as a romantic art form. Author's personal Christian world view affects the book's objectivity.

Twombly, Robert C. *Frank Lloyd Wright: His Life and His Architecture.* New York: Harper and Row, 1973. Rev. ed. New York: John Wiley, 1979. (A, G) Thorough, lively interpretation analyzing the motivating forces behind the man.

Willard, Charlotte. *Frank Lloyd Wright: American Architect.* New York: Macmillan, 1972. (G) Includes a chronology of the major events in Wright's life.

Evaluation of Biographies for Young People

Forsee, Aylesea. *Frank Lloyd Wright: Rebel in Concrete*. Philadelphia: Macrae Smith, 1959. Introduces teenage readers to Wright's revolutionary design concepts. Forsee shows how Wright employed these in the construction of various buildings.

Jacobs, Herbert A. *Frank Lloyd Wright: America's Greatest Architect*. New York: Harcourt, 1965. Well-illustrated survey of Wright's life by a Wisconsin journalist who lived in two Wright-designed houses. Covers the architect's struggle to gain acceptance for his new architectural concepts, his financial difficulties, and his personal life.

Naden, Corinne J. *Frank Lloyd Wright: The Rebel Architect*. New York: Franklin Watts, 1968. Encourages readers to pursue original ideas in spite of social convention.

Richards, Kenneth G. *People of Destiny: Frank Lloyd Wright*. Chicago: Childrens Press, 1968. Discusses some of Wright's basic architectural ideas and unconventional design concepts.

Salsini, Paul. *Frank Lloyd Wright: The Architectural Genius of the Twentieth Century*. New York: SamHar Press, 1971. Inspirational biography that encourages readers to pursue their talents.

Overview and Evaluation of Primary Sources

Anyone interested in doing archival research concerning Wright and his work should first consult Patrick J. Meehan's reference book, *Frank Lloyd Wright: A Research Guide to Archival Sources* (New York: Garland, 1983; A). The largest collection of Wright's drawings and correspondence is maintained at Taliesin West near Scottsdale, Arizona, by the Frank Lloyd Wright Memorial Foundation. A more accessible and diversified archive of Wright's work, however, is in the Avery Memorial Library at Columbia University, New York City.

Wright himself was almost as prolific a writer as a designer. Through essays, articles, lectures, and books, he earned the reputation of an iconoclast, propagated his ideas, and ultimately called attention to his work. His autobiography entitled simply *An Autobiography* (New York and Toronto: Longmans, Green, 1932; A, G), is generally self-serving but should be read by anyone attempting to understand Wright and his environmental ideals. It was reissued in New York in 1943 by Duell, Sloan and Pearce.

Wright wrote at least a dozen books. Those generally considered his major publications are *Modern Architecture, Being the Kahn Lectures for 1930* (Princeton: Princeton University Press, 1931; **A, G**); *The Disappearing City* (New York: William Farquhar Payson, 1932; **A, G**); *Architecture and Modern Life,* co-authored with Baker Brownell (New York: Harper and Brothers, 1937; **A, G**); *An Organic Architecture: The Architecture of Democracy* (London: Lund Humphries, 1939; **A, G**); *When Democracy Builds* (Chicago: University of Chicago Press, 1945; **A, G**); *Genius and the Mobocracy* (New York: Duell, Sloan and Pearce, 1949; **A, G**); *The Future of Architecture* (New York: Horizon Press, 1953; **A, G**); *The Natural House* (New York: Horizon Press, 1954; **A, G**); *An American Architecture* (New York: Horizon Press, 1955; **A, G**); *The Story of the Tower: The Tree That Escaped the Crowded Forest* (New York: Horizon Press, 1956; **A, G**); *A Testament* (New York: Horizon Press, 1957; **A, G**); *The Living City* (New York: Horizon Press, 1958; **A, G**); and *Drawings for a Living Architecture* (New York: Published for the Bear Run Foundation and the Edgar Kaufmann Charitable Foundation by Horizon Press, 1959; **A, G**).

In the last decade Bruce Brooks Pfeiffer, the director of the Frank Lloyd Wright Memorial Foundation at Taliesin West, has edited several volumes of Wright's correspondence. These include: *Frank Lloyd Wright: Letters to Apprentices* (Fresno: California State University Press, 1982; **A**); *Frank Lloyd Wright: Letters to Architects* (Fresno: California State University Press, 1984; **A**); *Frank Lloyd Wright: Letters to Clients* (Fresno: California State University Press, 1986; **A**); and *Frank Lloyd Wright: The Guggenheim Correspondence* (Fresno: California State University Press, 1986; **A**). Similarly, in *The Master Architect: Conversations with Frank Lloyd Wright* (New York: John Wiley, 1984; **A, G**), architect Patrick J. Meehan has compiled an interesting collection of transcribed conversations Wright had with people such as television commentator Hugh Downs and writer/poet Carl Sandburg. Meehan's second editing of Wright conversations is set more biographically. In *Truth Against the World: Frank Lloyd Wright Speaks for an Organic Architecture* (New York: John Wiley, 1987; **A, G**), Meehan has collected some of Wright's speeches and organized them under such topics as education, democracy, and improving the human condition.

Several other sources which illustrate Wright's genius for creative design deserve mention. *The Drawings of Frank Lloyd Wright* by Arthur Drexler (New York: Horizon Press for the Museum of Modern Art, 1962; **A, G**) is a catalog of original drawings by Wright between 1895 and 1959 exhibited at the Museum of Modern Art in 1962. *Treasures of Taliesin* by Bruce Brooks Pfeiffer (Fresno: California State University Press, 1985; **A, G**) is a compendium of seventy-six of Wright's unbuilt projects selected from among the thousands of drawings and renderings maintained by the Wright Memorial Foundation. *The Work of Frank Lloyd Wright* (New York: Horizon Press, 1965; **A, G**) is an over-sized volume that displays Wrights work via black-and-white photographs and scaled line drawings. It contains an introduction by Wright's third wife, Olgivanna. *Buildings, Plans, and Designs* (New York: Horizon Press, 1963; **A, G**) is the closest transla-tion/reprint of the two-volume work, *Ausgefuhrte Bauten und Entwurfe von Frank Lloyd Wright* published in 1910-1911 in Berlin by the German firm Ernst Was-muth. The German edition of Wright's designs set a standard for architecture in Europe for many years thereafter. *The Solomon Guggenheim Museum. Architect: Frank Lloyd Wright* (New York: The Solomon Guggenheim Foundation and Horizon Press, 1960; **A, G**) includes statements by Wright about the design of the museum he never saw completed.

The year of Wright's death, Olgivanna Lloyd Wright published a series of essays about her famous husband which she originally wrote for the Madison, Wisconsin, *Capital Times.* In *Our House* (New York: Horizon Press, 1959; **G**), Wright gives her impressions of living at Taliesin East and West, as well as a commentary on her husband's architectural philosophy and practice. Wright pays further tribute to her famous husband after his death in several more biographical books: *The Shining Brow: Frank Lloyd Wright* (New York: Horizon Press, 1960; **A, G**); *The Roots of Life* (New York: Horizon Press, 1963); and *Frank Lloyd Wright: His Life, His Work, His Words* (New York: Horizon Press, 1966; **A, G**). Not unlike Wright's widow, Edgar Tafel, in *Apprentice to Genius: Years with Frank Lloyd Wright* (New York: McGraw-Hill, 1979; **A, G**), gives his personal account of the nine years between 1932 and 1941 that he spent with Wright as an apprentice at Taliesin East. In his book, Tafel includes a number of personal photographs of Wright and his work. Of further interest are biographical treatments of Wright by his children. These include John Lloyd Wright, *My Father Who Is on Earth* (New York: Putnam, 1946; **A, G**), and Iovanna Lloyd Wright, *Architecture: Man in Possession of His Earth: Frank Lloyd Wright* (Garden City, NY: Double-day, 1962; **A, G**).

In *Frank Lloyd Wright's Hanna House: The Client's Report* (Cambridge: M.I.T. Press, 1981; **A, G**), Paul R. Hanna and Jean S. Hanna trace the interaction be-tween themselves and Wright in the construction of one of his first hexagonal houses. Similarly, in *Building with Frank Lloyd Wright: An Illustrated Memoir* (San Francisco: Chronicle Books, 1978; **A, G**), Herbert A. Jacobs and Katherine Jacobs document the construction of one of the two houses Wright designed for them. The Jacobs illustrate their book with a wide variety of photographs, dia-grams, and renderings.

Fiction and Adaptations

Some Flowers of the Narcissus: Frank Lloyd Wright (Radin Films, George H. Martin, producer) is a twenty-two minute documentary produced in 1967 that focuses on Wright's innovation in the design of four churches.

Museums, Historical Landmarks, Societies

Many of Wright's design creations have been preserved as historical landmarks reflective of his genius. Besides his early home and studio (1889) in Oak Park, Illinois, buildings that Wright designed which may be visited by the public include the Solomon R. Guggenheim Museum (1956) in New York City, the Johnson Wax Administration Building (1936) in Racine, Wisconsin, and the more recently completed Marin County Civic Center (1957) in San Rafael, California. Other extant buildings include: the Thomas H. Gale House (1892); the Robert W. Roloson Row House Apartments (1894), Chicago, Illinois; the Frank W. Thomas House (1901), Oak Park, Illinois; the Susan Lawrence Dana House (1903), Springfield, Illinois; the Darwin H. Martin House (1904), Buffalo, New York; the William A. Glasner House (1905), Glencoe, Illinois; the Thomas P. Hardy House (1905), Racine, Wisconsin; Unity Temple (1906), Oak Park, Illinois; the Kibben Ingalls House (1909), River Forest, Illinois; the Frederick C. Robie House (1909), Chicago, Illinois; the F. C. Bogk House (1916), Milwaukee, Wisconsin; the Aline Barnsdall House (1919) and Charles Ennis House (1924), Los Angeles, California; Taliesin East (1925), Spring Green, Wisconsin; Fallingwater (1936), the Edgar J. Kaufmann house, near Uniontown, Pennsylvania; the Paul R. Hanna House (1937), Palo Alto, California; Taliesin West (1938), Scottsdale, Arizona; the John C. Pew House (1939), Shorewood Hills, Wisconsin; the David K. Wright House (1950), Phoenix, Arizona; Price Tower (1953), Bartlesville, Oklahoma; the Annunciation Greek Orthodox Church (1956), Wauwatosa, Wisconsin; and the Beth Sholom Synagogue (1957), Elkins Park, Pennsylvania.

Other Sources

Blake, Peter. *The Master Builders: Le Corbusier, Mies van der Rohe, Frank Lloyd Wright*. New York: Alfred A. Knopf, 1960. Each architect and his work is treated separately.

Brooks, H. Allen. *The Prairie School: Frank Lloyd Wright and His Midwest Contemporaries*. Toronto: University of Toronto Press, 1972. Shows how Wright influenced other architects of his time.

————, ed. *Writings on Wright*. Cambridge: M.I.T. Press, 1981. Anthology of criticism written by people, including Lewis Mumford, who were sympathetic to Wright and his work.

Cavanaugh, Tom R., and Payne E. L. Thomas. *A Frank Lloyd Wright House: Bannerstone House, Springfield, Illinois*. Springfield, IL: Charles C. Thomas, 1970. Relates the history of the construction of the Susan Lawrence Dana House (1903).

Connors, Joseph. *The Robie House of Frank Lloyd Wright*. Chicago: The University of Chicago Press, 1984. A history of the Frederick C. Robie House, including several dozen photographs of the house and its interior during various phases of construction.

Doremus, Thomas. *Frank Lloyd Wright and Le Corbusier: The Great Dialogue*. New York: Van Nostrand Reinhold, 1985. Examines modernist thought in architectural design and Wright's role in its development.

Eaton, Leonard K. *Two Chicago Architects and Their Clients: Frank Lloyd Wright and Howard van Doren Shaw*. Cambridge: M.I.T. Press, 1969. Focuses on Wright's patrons in an historical context.

Fishman, Robert. *Urban Utopias in the Twentieth Century: Ebenezer Howard, Frank Lloyd Wright and Le Corbusier*. New York: Basic Books, 1977. Scholarly treatment of the architectural concepts that made Wright unique. A concluding chapter compares the design ideals of the three.

Futagawa, Yukio, editor and photographer, and Bruce Brooks Pfeiffer, text. *Frank Lloyd Wright: Pfeiffer Chapel, Florida Southern College, Lakeland, Florida, 1938; Beth Sholom Synagogue, Elkins Park, Pennsylvania, 1954*. Tokyo: A.D.A. Edita, 1976. Includes the original drawings and building plans of these two unique structures.

Gutheim, Frederick, ed. *Frank Lloyd Wright on Architecture*. New York: Duell, Sloan and Pearce, 1941. A collection of Wright's writings from 1894 to 1940.

————. *In the Cause of Architecture: Essays of Frank Lloyd Wright from "Architectural Record," 1908-1952*. New York: Architectural Record, 1975. Includes the ground-breaking series of articles entitled "In the Cause of Architecture" which appeared separately in *Architectural Record* 1908-1952.

Hanks, David A. *Preserving an Architectural Heritage: Decorative Designs from the Domino's Pizza Collection*. New York: E. P. Dutton, 1989. Collection of photographs (with captions) of many of the decorative items, from furniture to stained glass, that Wright designed to grace the interiors of his houses.

————. *The Decorative Designs of Frank Lloyd Wright*. New York: E. P. Dutton, 1979. Brings to light new facts concerning Wright's interest in furniture and the decorative arts.

Heinz, Thomas A. *Frank Lloyd Wright*. New York: St. Martin's, 1982. Short photographic documentary of the diversity of form and structure which was Wright's legacy. Displayed are houses which reflect both the Prairie and Usonian styles, as well as those which evidence the influence of Louis H. Sullivan.

Historic American Building Survey, J. William Rudd, comp. *Chicago and Nearby Illinois Areas: List of Measured Drawings, Photographs and Written Documentation in the Survey*. Park Forest, IL: The Prairie School Press, 1966. Includes sixteen buildings designed by Wright.

————. *The Robie House: Frank Lloyd Wright*. Palos Heights: IL: The Prairie School Press, 1968. Includes floor plans, elevations, window detail, and other structural and environmental provisions specified by Wright.

Hoag, Edwin, and Joy Hoag. *Masters of Modern Architecture: Frank Lloyd Wright, Le Corbusier, Mies van der Rohe, and Walter Gropius*. Indianapolis, IN: Bobbs-Merrill, 1977. Good sketch of Wright for juvenile readers.

Hoffmann, Donald. *Frank Lloyd Wright: Architecture and Nature*. New York: Dover, 1986. Focuses on how Wright integrated his architecture with nature. Contains 160 illustrations.

————. *Frank Lloyd Wright's Fallingwater: The House and Its History*. New York: Dover, 1978. Examines some of the technical and statistical details that went into the conceptualization of this highly unconventional structure.

————. *Frank Lloyd Wright's Robie House: An Illustrated Story of an Architectural Masterpiece*. New York: Dover, 1984. More definitive than Connors's work, this book explains the uniqueness of Wright's concept.

James, Cary. *The Imperial Hotel: Frank Lloyd Wright and the Architecture of Unity*. Rutland, VT: C. E. Tuttle, 1968. Photographic documentation of Wright's Tokyo hotel which survived an earthquake in 1923 but not the wrecking ball in 1967.

Kaufmann, Edgar J., and Ben Raeburn, eds. *Frank Lloyd Wright: Writings and Buildings*. New York: Horizon Press, 1960. Contains many of Wright's articles and lectures, including his famous "The Art and Craft of the Machine" (1901).

Kaufmann, Edgar J., Jr. *Fallingwater: A Frank Lloyd Wright Country House*. New York: Abbeville Press, 1986. Impressive "coffee-table" volume that relates the history of the design and acceptance of Wright's most famous residential building, with full-page color photographs and illustrations.

Levin, Neil. "Frank Lloyd Wright's Diagonal Planning." In *In Search of Modern Architecture: A Tribute to Henry-Russell Hitchcock*, edited by Helen Searing. Cambridge: M.I.T. Press, 1982. Traces Wright's use of diagonal shifts in axis design from the beginning of his career to his plan for Taliesin West.

Lipman, Jonathan. *Frank Lloyd Wright and the Johnson Wax Buildings*. New York: Rizzoli, 1986. The most complete account of Wright's conceptualization and design of the famous Johnson Wax complex.

Muschamp, Herbert. *Man About Town: Frank Lloyd Wright in New York City*. Cambridge: M.I.T. Press, 1983. Assessment of Wright's understanding of the role that architecture should play in humanizing large cities.

Pawley, Martin, and Yukio Futagawa. *Frank Lloyd Wright, I: Public Buildings*. New York: Simon and Schuster, 1970. Thorough survey of Wright's work in the public realm. Well-documented with illustrations.

Peisch, Mark L. *The Chicago School of Architecture: Early Followers of Sullivan and Wright*. New York: Random House, 1964. Focuses on the period between 1893 and 1914 and includes a chapter on Wright's Oak Park studio.

Pfeiffer, Bruce Brooks, ed. *Frank Lloyd Wright: The Crowning Decade, 1949-1959*. Fresno: California State University Press, 1989. Focuses on the last ten years of Wright's creative and personal life as viewed by himself, his wife, his daughter, and his Taliesin apprentices. The material, most of which has never before been published, was selected from the vast collection at the Frank Lloyd Wright Memorial Foundation.

Pfeiffer, Bruce Brooks, and Gerald Nordland. *Frank Lloyd Wright: In the Realm of Ideas.* Carbondale: Southern Illinois University Press, 1988. Profusely illustrated volume containing Wright's thoughts on such things as "The Nature of the Site," "Building for Democracy," and "Materials and Methods." Many of the color photographs that illustrate this impressive book are accompanied by sketches or renderings that Wright made of the same interior or exterior scene.

Quinan, Jack. *Frank Lloyd Wright's Larkin Building: Myth and Fact.* Cambridge: M.I.T. Press, 1987. A generously illustrated history of one of Wright's early buildings (1904) which helped earn him his singular reputation. Published in conjunction with the Architectural History Foundation of New York.

Sergeant, John. *Frank Lloyd Wright's Usonian Houses: The Case for Organic Architecture.* New York: Whitney Library of Design, 1976. Scholarly assessment of Wright during his later life. Includes a chronological listing of Wright's projects from 1929 to 1943.

Sprague, Paul E. *Frank Lloyd Wright and the Prairie School Architecture in Oak Park.* Oak Park, IL: Oak Park Bicentennial Commission of the American Revolution, 1976. 2d ed. Chicago: Follett, 1978. Annotated guide to Oak Park containing maps indicating the locations of Wright-designed houses.

Storrer, William A. *The Architecture of Frank Lloyd Wright: A Complete Catalog.* 2d ed. Cambridge: M.I.T. Press, 1974, 1978. Records the extant buildings designed by Wright and their geographical distribution throughout the U.S.

Sweeney, Robert L. *Frank Lloyd Wright: An Annotated Bibliography.* Los Angeles: Hennessey and Ingalls, 1978. Contains over two thousand bibliographic entries. Arranged chronologically by year from 1886 to 1978.

Tiltman, Hessell. *The Imperial Hotel Story.* Tokyo: The Imperial Hotel, 1970. Includes a history of Wright's design of the building as well as its use following the 1923 Tokyo earthquake and during World War II.

Howard L. Preston

APPENDIX I
HISTORICAL FIGURES GROUPED BY ERA

AGE OF EXPLORATION/COLONIAL (pre-1776)

Captain James Cook
George III
Barnard Gratz
Michael Gratz
Louis Jolliet
Jacque Marquette

George Mason
James Oglethorpe
Paul Revere
Amerigo Vespucci
John Woolman

REVOLUTIONARY/EARLY NATIONAL (1776-1827)

John James Audubon
Jim Bridger
Captain James Cook
James Forten
Barnard Gratz
Michael Gratz

Louis XVI
George Mason
Paul Revere
Elizabeth Bayley Seton
Jedediah S. Smith
Joseph Story

JACKSONIAN/ANTEBELLUM (1828-1860)

Louisa May Alcott
Richard Allen
John James Audubon
Jim Bridger
Anna Ella Carroll
Thomas Green Clemson
James Forten

James Russell Lowell
Hiram Revels
Edmund Ruffin
Joseph Story
Alexis de Tocqueville
John Greenleaf Whittier

CIVIL WAR AND RECONSTRUCTION (1861-1877)

Louisa May Alcott
John Wilkes Booth
Jim Bridger
Anna Ella Carroll
Joshua Lawrence Chamberlain

Thomas Green Clemson
Wyatt Earp
Jay Gould
Charlotte Forten Grimké
Thomas Wentworth Higginson

Oliver O. Howard   Edmund Ruffin
Julia Ward Howe   Philip H. Sheridan
James Longstreet   J. E. B. Stuart
James Russell Lowell   George Henry Thomas
Dwight L. Moody   Albion Tourgée
Frederick Law Olmsted   John Greenleaf Whittier
Hiram Revels

LATE NINETEENTH CENTURY (1878-1899)

Louisa May Alcott   Thomas Wentworth Higginson
P. T. Barnum   James Russell Lowell
Buffalo Bill   Dwight L. Moody
Saint Frances Xavier Cabrini   Frederick Law Olmsted
Jennie Jerome Churchill   Joseph Pulitzer
Thomas Green Clemson   Hiram Revels
Jacob S. Coxey   Walter Rauschenbusch
Paul Laurence Dunbar   Albion Tourgée
Wyatt Earp   John Greenleaf Whittier
Jay Gould

PROGRESSIVE ERA (1900-1916)

Buffalo Bill   Joseph Pulitzer
Saint Frances Xavier Cabrini   Walter Rauschenbusch
Jennie Jerome Churchill   Mother Teresa
Helen Keller   Frank Lloyd Wright
Robert E. Peary

WORLD WAR I - WORLD WAR II (1917-1945)

Nancy Langhorne Astor   Reinhold Niebuhr
Gwendolyn Brooks   Georgia O'Keeffe
Jennie Jerome Chruchill   William Patterson
James Michael Curley   Jackson Pollock
Walt Disney   Adam Clayton Powell, Jr.
Allen Dulles   Mother Teresa
George Gershwin   Paul Tillich
Helen Keller   John Wayne
Paul Elmer More   Frank Lloyd Wright

POST WORLD WAR II (1946-present)

Joan Baez
Gwendolyn Brooks
George Bush
Cesar Chávez
Shirley Chisholm
Eldridge Cleaver
Richard Cardinal Cushing
Walt Disney
Allen Dulles
Jimmy Hoffa
Helen Keller
Thurgood Marshall
N. Scott Momaday

Reinhold Niebuhr
Georgia O'Keeffe
William Patterson
Jackson Pollock
Adam Clayton Powell, Jr.
Elvis Presley
Alan B. Shepard Jr.
Mother Teresa
Paul Tillich
John Wayne
Elie Wiesel
Frank Lloyd Wright

APPENDIX II
SELECTED MUSEUMS AND HISTORICAL LANDMARKS

ARIZONA
Tucson
Arizona Pioneers Historical Society Museum (Wyatt Earp)

Tombstone
Tombstone Courthouse State Historical Park (Wyatt Earp)

CALIFORNIA
Los Angeles
John Wayne Cancer Center

COLORADO
Lookout Mountain
Buffalo Bill Memorial Museum

CONNECTICUT
Bridgeport
Barnum Historical Collection (P. T. Barnum)
Barnum Museum (P. T. Barnum)

Fairfield
Lindencraft (P. T. Barnum mansion)

DISTRICT OF COLUMBIA
Washington
Ford's Theatre Museum (John Wilkes Booth)
National Air and Space Museum (Alan B. Shepard)
The National Geographic Society (Robert E. Peary)
The Peterson House (John Wilkes Booth)
Sheridan Circle (Philip B. Sheridan)
Smithsonian Institution (Philip B. Sheridan)

ENGLAND
Buckinghamshire
Cliveden (Nancy Langhorne Astor)

Oxfordshire
Blenheim Palace (Jennie Jerome Churchill)

FLORIDA
Cape Canaveral
Spaceport U.S.A. (Alan B. Shepard)

Key West
Audubon House (John James Audubon)

FRANCE
St. Denis
Basilica of St. Denis (Louis XVI)

Versailles
Versailles Palace (Louis XVI)

KENTUCKY
Henderson
Audubon Museum (John James Audubon)

KANSAS
Dodge City
Boot Hill Museum (Wyatt Earp)

ILLINOIS
Chicago
Moody Bible Institute (Dwight L. Moody)

Riverside
Riverside National Historic District (Frederick Law Olmsted)

INDIANA
New Harmony (Paul Tillich)

IOWA
Winterset
John Wayne Birthplace

MAINE
Brunswick
Chamberlain House (Joshua Chamberlain)
The Peary-MacMillan Arctic Museum (Robert E. Peary)

MARYLAND
Baltimore
Paca Street House (Elizabeth Bayley Seton)

Belair
Tudor Hall (John Wilkes Booth)

Clinton
Surratt House and Tavern (John Wilkes Booth)

Emmitsburg
National Shrine of Saint Elizabeth Ann Seton

Waldorf
The Dr. Samuel Mudd Museum (John Wilkes Booth)

Westover
Kingston Hall (Anna Ella Carroll mansion)

MASSASSCHUSETTS
Boston
Boston Museum of Fine Arts (Paul Revere)
Curley Park (James M. Curley)

James M. Curley Residence
Revere House National Historic Landmark (Paul Revere)

Brookline
Frederick Law Olmsted National Historic Site

Cambridge
Elmwood (James Russell Lowell house)
Fruitlands (Louisa May Alcott house)

Concord
Louisa May Alcott House
Thoreau-Alcott House

Hanover
Portiuncula Chapel (Richard Cardinal Cushing)

Haverhill
Haverhill Public Library (John Greenleaf Whittier)

Medford
Tufts University Barnum Collection (P. T. Barnum)

Northfield
The Moody Museum (Dwight L. Moody)

MISSISSIPPI
Tupelo
Elvis Presley Birthplace

MISSOURI
St. Louis
Jefferson National Expansion Memorial (Jedediah S. Smith)

NEW JERSEY
Mount Holly
Woolman House and Gardens (John Woolman)

NEW YORK
New York
National Audubon Society
New York Historical Society (John James Audubon)
St. Frances Cabrini Chapel
Shrine of St. Elizabeth Ann Seton
Trinity Churchyard (John James Audubon)

Tarrytown
Lyndhurst (Jay Gould mansion)

NORTH CAROLINA
Ashville
Biltmore Estate (Frederick Law Olmsted)

Haw River
Charles Drew Monument

PENNSYLVANIA
Gettysburg

Gettysburg National Military Park (James Longstreet)

Mill Grove
Mill Grove (John James Audubon house)

Philadelphia
Mother Bethel African Episcopal Church (James Forten)

SOUTH CAROLINA
Clemson
Fort Hill (Thomas Green Clemson house)

Frogmore
Penn School Historical District (Charlotte Forten)

TENNESSEE
Chattanooga
Chickamauga and Chattanooga National Military Park (James Longstreet)

Memphis
Graceland (Elvis Presley mansion)

TEXAS
Houston
Johnson Space Center (Alan B. Shepard)

VIRGINIA
Danville
Astor Birthplace (Nancy Langhorne Astor)

Lorton
Gunston Hall (George Mason house)

Williamsburg
Colonial Williamsburg (George III)

WISCONSIN
Baraboo
Circus World Museum of Wisconsin (P. T. Barnum)

WYOMING
Cody
Buffalo Bill Historical Center, Buffalo Bill Museum

Fort Bridger
Fort Bridger State Museum (Jim Bridger)

CUMULATIVE INDEX FOR VOLUMES I-V
OF FIGURES AND SOURCES REVIEWED

*Manual for Use in Cases of Juvenile
  Offenders*. . . (Balch)
Miracle of Living (Balch)
Occupied Haiti (Balch)
*Origins of the Modern American Peace
  Movement* (DeBenedetti)
Our Slavic Fellow Citizens (Balch)
Papers of Emily Greene Balch (Shane, ed.)
*Pioneers for Peace: Women's Intl. League
  for Peace and Freedom* (Bussey and Tims)
Public Assistance of the Poor in France
  (Balch)
*Women at The Hague: The Intl. Congress of
  Women*. . . (Balch, Adams, and Hamilton)
*Women for all Seasons: Story of the Women's
  International League*. . . (Foster)

BANCROFT, GEORGE, 86-91
American Compromise (Vitzthum)
George Bancroft (Nye)
George Bancroft: Brahmin Rebel (Nye)
George Bancroft: The Intellectual as Democrat
  (Handlin)
History as Romantic Art (Levin)
History of the Formation of the Constitution
  (Bancroft)
History of the United States (Bancroft)
Life and Letters of George Bancroft (Howe)

BARNUM, P. T., 2357-2363
Barnum: The Legend and the Man (Saxon)
Circus, The: Wisconsin's Unique Heritage
  (Caonover)
Deceivers Generally in All Ages (Barnum)
*Humbugs of the World: An Account of
  Humbugs, Delusions, Impositions,
  Quackeries, Deceits, and Jenny and Barnum*
  (Thorp)
P. T. Barnum Bibliography (Neafie)
Pictorial History of the American Circus
  (Durant)
Selected Letters (Barnum)
*Struggles and Triumphs, or Sixty Years'
  Recollections of P. T. Barnum, Written by
  Himself* (Barnum)
The Life of P. T. Barnum, Written by Himself
  (Barnum)

BARRYMORE, ETHEL, 1815-1818
The Barrymores (Alpert)
*The Barrymores: The Royal Family in
  Hollywood* (Kotsilbas-Davis)

Ethel Barrymore (Fox)
Ethel Barrymore, Girl Actress (Newman)
Good Night, Sweet Prince (Fowler)
*Great Times, Good Times: The Odyssey of
  Maurice Barrymore* (Kotsilbas-Davis)
Memories (Barrymore)
We Barrymores (L. Barrymore and Shipp)
We Three (J. Barrymore)

BARTON, CLARA, 92-96
American Red Cross (Dulles)
Angel of the Battlefield (Ross)
Antoinette Margot and Clara Barton (Kite)
Clara Barton: A Centenary Tribute (Young)
Clara Barton: Daughter of Destiny (Williams)
*Clara Barton: Founder of the American Red
  Cross* (Boylston)
Clara Barton: Humanitarian (Foster)
Clara Barton: Professional Angel (Pryor)
Illustrious Americans (Fishwick)
Life of Clara Barton (W. E. Barton)
Life of Clara Barton (Epler)
Memorial to Clara Barton
Red Cross (Barton)
Story of the Red Cross (Barton)
Story of My Childhood (Barton)
*Under the Red Cross Flag at Home and
  Abroad* (Boardman)

BARUCH, BERNARD M., 97-102
American Industry in the War
  (Hippelheuser, ed.)
Baruch: My Own Story (Baruch)
Baruch: The Public Years (Baruch)
Bernard Baruch: Park Bench Statesman
  (Field)
Bernard M. Baruch: Portrait of a Citizen
  (White)
*Bernard M. Baruch: The Adventures of a Wall
  Street Legend* (Grant)
Cabinet Diaries of Josephus Daniels
  (Cronon, ed.)
Economic Consequences of Peace (Keynes)
Industrial America in the World War
  (Clarkson)
Journals of David E. Lilienthal (Lilienthal)
*Making of the Reparation and Economic
  Sections of the Treaty* (Baruch)
Memoirs (Krock)
Mr. Baruch (Coit)
Peace and Strength (Rosenbloom)
Philosophy for Our Time (Baruch)

Impact of American Religious Liberalism
(Cauthen)
Modernist Impulse in American Protestantism
(Hutchison)
Rauschenbusch: The Formative Years (Jaehn)
Righteousness of the Kingdom
(Stackhouse, ed.)
Rise of the Social Gospel in American
Protestantism, 1865-1915 (Handy)
Social Principles of Jesus (Rauschenbusch)
Theology for Social Gospel (Rauschenbusch)
Walter Rauschenbusch (Sharpe)
"*Walter Rauschenbusch and Labor Reform: A*
Social Gospeller's Approach" (Aiken and
McDonnell)
Walter Rauschenbusch: American Reformer
(Minus)

REAGAN, RONALD, 1275-1281
Came the Revolution: Argument in the Reagan
Era (Moynihan)
Caveat: Realism, Reagan, and Foreign Policy
(Haig)
Creative Society: Problems Facing America
(Reagan)
Early Reagan (Edwards)
For the Record: From Wall Street to
Washington (Regan)
Public Papers of Ronald Reagan
Reagan and Reality: The Two Californias
(Brown)
Reagans: A Political Portrait (Hannaford)
Report of the President's Special Review
Board
Revolution (Anderson)
Ronald Reagan: Rise to the Presidency
(Boyarsky)
Speaking Out: The Reagan Presidency
(Speakes)
Triumph of Politics: How the Revolution
Failed (Stockman)
What Makes Reagan Run: A Political Profile
(Lewis)
Where's the Rest of Me? (Reagan and Hubler)

RED CLOUD, 2093-2098
Bozeman Trail: Historical Accounts of the
Blazing of the Overland Routes (Hebard and
Brininstool)
Fighting Indian Warriors: True Tales of the
Wild Frontiers (Brininstool)

Picture Story and Biography of Red Cloud
(Garst)
Reader's Encyclopedia of the American West
(Metcalf)
Red Cloud and the Sioux Problem (Olson)
Red Cloud: Sioux War Chief (Voight)
Red Cloud: Story of an American Indian
(McGaa)
Red Cloud's Folk: History of the Oglala Sioux
Indians (Hyde)
Sioux Chronicle (Hyde)

REED, JOHN, 1282-1286
Autobiography of Lincoln Steffens (Steffens)
Day in Bohemia, or Life Among the Artists
(Reed)
Education of John Reed (Stuart)
Heroes I Have Known (Eastman)
Insurgent Mexico (Reed)
John Reed: The Making of Revolutionary
(Hicks)
Letters of Lincoln Steffens (Winter
and Hicks, eds.)
Lincoln Steffens Speaking (Steffens)
Living My Life (Goldman)
Mirrors of Moscow (Bryant)
Pancho Villa and John Reed: Romantic
Revolution (Tuck)
Romantic Revolutionary (Rosenstone)
Sisson Documents (Reed)
Six Red Months in Russia (Bryant)
So Short a Time: John Reed and Louise
Bryant (Gelb)
Ten Days that Shook the World (Reed)
War in Eastern Europe (Reed)

REVELS, HIRAM, 2723-2726
Black Americans in Congress (Christopher)
Facts of Reconstruction (Lynch)
Gentleman From Mississippi (Lawson)
Hiram R. Revels 1827-1901: A Biography
(Thompson)

REVERE, PAUL, 2727-2733
Life of Colonel Paul Revere (Goss)
Paul Revere (Taylor)
Paul Revere: The World He Lived In (Forbes)
"*Paul Revere: The Man, the Myth, and the*
Midnight Ride" (Weisberger)
Paul Revere's Three Accounts of His Famous
Ride (Morgan, ed.)